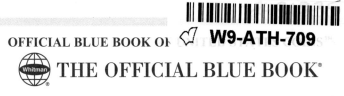

# THE OFFICIAL BLUE BOOK®

## HANDBOOK OF
# UNITED STATES
# COINS
# 2023 ~~WITHDRAWN~~

## R. S. YEOMAN

### JEFF GARRETT, SENIOR EDITOR

Q. David Bowers, Research Editor

Kenneth Bressett, Editor Emeritus

## 80th EDITION

An Illustrated Catalog of Prices Generally Paid
by Dealers for All American Coins—1616 to Date

Containing Mint records and wholesale prices for U.S. and related coins from 1616
to the present time, including colonials, regular issues, commemoratives, territorials, gold, bullion coins, Proof sets, and Mint sets. Information on collecting
coins—how coins are produced—mints and mintmarks—grading of coins—location
of mintmarks—preserving coins—starting a collection—history of mints—and
interesting descriptions of all U.S. copper, nickel, silver, and gold coins. Illustrated.

Handbook of United States Coins™
THE OFFICIAL BLUE BOOK OF UNITED STATES COINS™

THE OFFICIAL BLUE BOOK and OFFICIAL BLUE BOOK OF UNITED
STATES COINS are trademarks of Whitman Publishing, LLC.

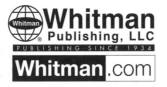

Printed in the United States of America.

© 2022 Whitman Publishing, LLC
1974 Chandalar Drive • Suite D • Pelham, AL 35124

Whitman®

# CONTRIBUTORS TO THIS EDITION

*Senior Editor: Jeff Garrett. Research Editor: Q. David Bowers.*
*Editor Emeritus: Kenneth Bressett.*
*Special Consultants: Russell Augustin, Philip Bressett,*
*Ben Garrett, Robert Rhue, Troy Thoreson.*

| | | |
|---|---|---|
| Gary Adkins | Dennis M. Gillio | Harry Miller |
| John Agre | Ronald J. Gillio | Lee S. Minshull |
| John Albanese | Rusty Goe | Scott P. Mitchell |
| Dominic Albert | Ira Goldberg | Michael Moline |
| Buddy Alleva | Lawrence Goldberg | Charles Morgan |
| Richard M. August | Kenneth M. Goldman | Alex Nocerino |
| Russell Augustin | Bob Green | Paul Nugget |
| Lee J. Bellisario | Thomas Hallenbeck | Joseph Parrella |
| Chris Berinato | James Halperin | Robert M. Paul |
| Mark Borckardt | Ash Harrison | Steve Roach |
| Larry Briggs | Stephen Hayden | Greg Rohan |
| William Bugert | Brian Hendelson | Maurice Rosen |
| H. Robert Campbell | John W. Highfill | Mark Salzberg |
| Elizabeth Coggan | Brian Hodge | Matthew Savanich |
| Gary and Alan Cohen | Jack Howes | Gerald R. Scherer Jr. |
| Stephen M. Cohen | Steve Ivy | Harry Schultz |
| Frank J. Colletti | Amandeep Jassal | Jeff Shevlin |
| Steve Contursi | Joseph Jones | Roger Siboni |
| Marc Crane | Mike Joyce | James Simek |
| Adam Crum | Donald H. Kagin | David M. Sundman |
| Raymond Czahor | Bradley S. Karoleff | Barry Sunshine |
| John Dannreuther | Jim Koenings | Anthony Terranova |
| Steven Ellsworth | John Kraljevich | Ben Todd |
| Brant Fahnestock | Richard A. Lecce | Rick Tomaska |
| Michael Fey | Julian M. Leidman | Frank Van Valen |
| Gerry Fortin | Denis W. Loring | Kevin Vinton |
| Pierre Fricke | Dwight N. Manley | Fred Weinberg |
| John Frost | David McCarthy | Douglas Winter |
| Mike Fuljenz | Jack McNamara | Mark S. Yaffe |

*Special credit is due to the following for service and data in this book:* Leonard Augsburger, Charles Davis, David Fanning, Robert W. Julian, Richard Kelly, George F. Kolbe, Christopher R. McDowell, Nancy Oliver, P. Scott Rubin, and William Spencer.

*Special credit is due to the following for service in past editions:* Mitchell Batino, Stewart Blay, Roger W. Burdette, Tom DeLorey, Bill Fivaz, Chuck Furjanic, James C. Gray, Charles Hoskins, David W. Lange, G.J. Lawson, Andy Lustig, J.P. Martin, Syd Martin, Eric P. Newman, Ken Potter, Paul Rynearson, Mary Sauvain, Richard J. Schwary, Neil Shafer, Robert W. Shippee, Craig Smith, Jerry Treglia, Mark R. Vintunic, Holland Wallace, Weimar White, John Whitney, Raymond Williams, and John Wright.

*Special photo credits are due to the following:* Al Adams, John Agre, David Akers, James Bevill, Heritage Auctions, Ira & Larry Goldberg Coins & Collectibles, Ron Karp, Massachusetts Historical Society, Christopher McDowell, Tom Mulvaney, Ken Potter, John Scanlon, Roger Siboni, the Smithsonian Institution, Stack's Bowers Galleries, Richard Stinchcomb, and the United States Mint.

Since 1942, annually revised editions of the *Official Blue Book of United States Coins™* have aided thousands of people who have coins to sell or are actively engaged in collecting United States coins. The popular coin-folder method of collecting by date has created ever-changing premium values, based on the supply and demand of each date and mint. Through its panel of contributors, the Blue Book has, over the years, reported these changing values. It also serves as a source of general numismatic information to all levels of interest in the hobby.

The values shown are representative prices paid by dealers for various United States coins. These are averages of prices assembled from many widely separated sources. On some issues slight differences in price among dealers may result from proximity to the various mints or heavily populated centers. Other factors, such as local supply and demand or dealers' stock conditions, may also cause deviations from the prices listed. While many coins bring no premium in circulated grades, they usually bring premium prices in Mint State and Proof. Extremely rare and valuable coins are usually sold at public auction, and prices vary according to current demand.

## THIS BOOK LISTS PRICES MANY COIN DEALERS WILL PAY.

*Premium prices are the average amount dealers will pay for coins (according to condition) if required for their stock. This book is not a retail price list.*

### IF YOU HAVE COINS TO SELL

Whitman Publishing, LLC, is not in the rare-coin business; however, chances are that the dealer from whom you purchased this book is engaged in the buying and selling of rare coins—contact them first. In the event that you purchased this book from a source other than a numismatic establishment, consult your local telephone directory for the names of coin dealers (they will be found sometimes under the heading of "Stamp and Coin Dealers"). If you live in a city or town that does not have any coin dealers, obtain a copy of one of the trade publications (such as *Coin World* [www.coinworld.com] or *Numismatic News* [www.numismaticnews.net]) or check the Internet in order to obtain the names and addresses of many of the country's leading dealers. Coin dealers who belong to the congressionally chartered American Numismatic Association (and who must abide by its code of ethics) are listed at www.money.org.

You will find current average *retail* valuations of American coins (the prices you can expect to pay a professional coin dealer) in the latest edition of *A Guide Book of United States Coins™* by R.S. Yeoman, edited by Jeff Garrett. Coin collectors popularly call this the "Red Book." Pricing in even greater detail is included in Mega Red—*A Guide Book of United States Coins, Deluxe Edition.*

---

### HOW TO READ THE CHARTS

A dash in a price column indicates that coins in that grade exist even though there are no current sales or auction records for them. (The dash does *not* necessarily mean that such coins are exceedingly rare.) Italicized prices indicate unsettled or speculative values. A number of listings of rare coins do not have prices or dashes in certain grades. This indicates that they are not available or not believed to exist in those grades.

Mintages of Proof coins are listed in parentheses.

Italicized mintages are estimates.

---

*Numismatics* or coin collecting is one of the world's oldest hobbies, dating back several centuries. Coin collecting in America did not develop to any extent until about 1840, as our pioneer forefathers were too busy carving a country out of wilderness to afford the luxury of a hobby. The discontinuance of the large-sized cent in 1857 encouraged many people to attempt to accumulate a complete set of the pieces while they were still in circulation. One of the first groups of collectors to band together for the study of numismatics was the American Numismatic Society, founded in 1858 and still a dynamic part of the hobby (www.numismatics.org). Lack of an economical method to house a collection held the number of devotees of coin collecting to a few thousand until Whitman Publishing and other manufacturers placed low-priced coin boards and folders on the market in the 1930s. Since that time, the number of Americans collecting coins has increased many-fold.

## THE PRODUCTION OF COINS

To collect coins intelligently it is necessary to have some knowledge of the manner in which they are produced. Coins are made in factories called "mints." The Mint of the United States was established at Philadelphia by a resolution of Congress dated April 2, 1792. The act also provided for the coinage of gold eagles ($10), half eagles, and quarter eagles; silver dollars, half dollars, quarter dollars, dimes (originally spelled "disme"), and half dismes or half dimes; and copper cents and half cents. The first coins struck were one-cent and half-cent pieces, in March of 1793 on a hand-operated press. Most numismatic authorities consider the half disme of 1792 the first United States coinage, quoting the words of George Washington as their authority. Washington, in his annual address, November 6, 1792, said, "There has been a small beginning in the coining of the half dimes, the want of small coins in circulation calling the first attention to them." Though the half disme is considered America's first coinage, it was not the first coinage produced by the Mint; these coins were produced off premises in July of 1792 before the mint was completed. In the new Philadelphia Mint are a number of implements from the original mint, and some coins discovered when the old building was wrecked. These coins included half dismes, and the placard identifying them states that Washington furnished the silver and gave some of the pieces to his friends as souvenirs.

Prior to the adoption of the Constitution, the Continental Congress arranged for the issuance of copper coins under private contract. These are known as the 1787 *Fugio coppers* from their design, which shows a sundial and the Latin word "fugio"—"I Fly" or, in connection with the sundial, "Time Flies." The ever-appropriate motto "Mind Your Business" is also on the coin.

In the manufacture of a coin, the first step is die preparation. Dies for early federal coinage were prepared by hand; generally, letters and numbers were added with punches, while portraits and other designs were engraved into the die. Eventually, eagles, Liberty heads, and the like were also added with hubs and punches. After about 1836, many dies were made from masters, which contained all elements except the date and, if applicable, the mintmark. The addition of an element to a master die ensured its consistent placement throughout the life of the die. Today, many design tasks are performed with three-dimensional computer graphics. Mint artists are either sculptor-engravers or medallic sculptors, and their work takes place mainly at the Philadelphia Mint. The dies are made of soft steel, which is hardened after the impression is received. The die is then dressed or finished to remove imperfections and make it suitable for coining. A typical die for production coinage can be used to strike hundreds of thousands of pieces. Dies for special issues such as Proofs are replaced more often.

The hand method of cutting dies accounts for the many die varieties of early United States coins. Where the amount of coinage of a given year was large enough to wear out many dies, each new die placed in the coining press created another die variety of that year. The dies being cut by hand, no two were exactly alike in every detail, even though some of the major elements such as the head or wreath, were sunk into the die by individual master punches. Of the cents dated 1794, more than sixty different die varieties have been discovered.

Thousands of dies are now used by the mints of the United States each year, but they are all made from one master die, which is produced in the following manner:

After the design is settled upon, the plaster of paris or wax model is prepared several times the actual size of the coin. When this model is finished an electrotype (an exact duplicate in metal) is made and prepared for the reducing lathe. The reducing lathe is a machine that works on the principle of the pantograph, only in this case the one point traces or follows the form of the model while another much smaller point in the form of a drill cuts away the steel and produces a reduced-size die of the model. The die is finished and details are sharpened or worked over by an engraver with chisel and graver. The master die is used to make duplicates in soft steel which are then hardened and ready for the coining press. To harden dies, they are placed in cast-iron boxes packed with carbon to exclude the air, and when heated to a bright red are cooled suddenly with water.

In the coinage operations the first step is to prepare the metal. Among the alloys that have been used are the following: silver coins, 90% silver and 10% copper; five-cent pieces, 75% copper and 25% nickel; one-cent pieces, 95% copper and 5% zinc. (The 1943 cent consists of steel coated with zinc; and the five-cent piece of 1942–1945 contains 35% silver, 56% copper, and 9% manganese.) Under the Coinage Act of 1965, the composition of dimes, quarters, and half dollars was changed to eliminate or reduce the silver content of these coins. The copper-nickel "clad" dimes, quarters, half dollars, and dollars are composed of an outer layer of copper-nickel (75% copper and 25% nickel) bonded to an inner core of pure copper. The silver clad half dollar and dollar have an outer layer of 80% silver bonded to an inner core of 21% silver, with a total content of 40% silver. Current cents are made from a core of 99.2% zinc, 0.8% copper, with a plating of pure copper. Dollars are composed of a pure copper core with outer layers of manganese-brass.

Alloys are melted in crucibles and poured into molds to form ingots. The ingots are in the form of thin bars and vary in size according to the denomination of the coin. The width is sufficient to allow three or more coins to be cut from the strips.

The ingots are next put through rolling mills to reduce the thickness to required limits. The strips are then fed into cutting presses which cut circular blanks of the approximate size of the finished coin. The blanks are run through annealing furnaces to soften them; next they move through tumbling barrels, rotating cylinders containing cleaning solutions which clean and burnish the metal; and finally into centrifugal drying machines.

The blanks are next fed into a milling machine which produces the raised or upset rim. The blank, now called a *planchet,* is now ready for the coining press.

The planchet is held firmly by a collar, as it is struck under heavy pressure varying from 40 tons for the one-cent pieces and dimes to 170 tons for silver dollars. Upper and lower dies impress the design on both sides of the coin. The pressure is sufficient to produce a raised surface level with that of the milled rim. The collar holding the blank for silver or clad coins is grooved. The pressure forces the metal into the grooves of the collar, producing the "reeding" on the edge of the finished coin.

## HOW A PROOF COIN IS MADE

Selected dies are inspected for perfection and are highly polished and cleaned. They are again wiped clean or polished after every 15 to 25 impressions and are replaced frequently to avoid imperfections from wear. Coinage blanks are polished and cleaned to assure high quality in striking. They are then hand fed into the coinage press one at a time, each blank receiving two blows from the dies to bring up sharp, high-relief details. The coinage operation is done at slow speed. Finished Proofs are individually inspected and are handled by gloves or tongs. They also receive a final inspection by packers before being sonically sealed in special plastic cases.

Certain coins, including Lincoln cents, Buffalo nickels, quarter eagles, half eagles, eagles, and double eagles, between the years 1908 and 1916, were made with Matte Proof (nickel and silver) and Sand Blast and Satin Proof (gold) finishes. These later Proofs have a dull frosted surface which was either applied to the dies, or produced by special treatment after striking.

## MINTS AND MINTMARKS

In addition to the Philadelphia Mint, the U.S. government has from time to time established branch mints in various parts of the country. At present, branch mints operate in Denver, West Point, and San Francisco. Starting in 1968, Proof sets as well as some of the regular coins were produced at the San Francisco Mint and Assay Office. The Denver Mint has operated since 1906. A mint was operated at New Orleans from 1838 to 1861 and again from 1879 to 1909. Mints were also in service at Carson City, Nevada, from 1870 to 1893; at Charlotte, North Carolina, from 1838 to 1861; at Dahlonega, Georgia, from 1838 to 1861; and at San Francisco since 1854. The U.S. government also supplied a mint in the Philippines (M mintmark) in the early 1900s.

Coins struck at Philadelphia before 1979 (except 1942 to 1945 five-cent pieces) do not bear a mintmark. Historically the mintmark was used only for branch mints. Modern exceptions include the 2017-P Lincoln cent and the Kennedy half dollar, which both use the P for Philadelphia. All circulating coins struck after 1967 have the mintmark on the obverse. The letters signifying the various mints are as follows:

    C—Charlotte, North Carolina (gold coins only; 1838–1861)
    CC—Carson City, Nevada (1870–1893)
    D—Dahlonega, Georgia (gold coins only; 1838–1861)
    D—Denver, Colorado (1906 to date)
    O—New Orleans, Louisiana (1838–1861; 1879–1909)
    P—Philadelphia, Pennsylvania (1793 to date; P not used in early years)
    S—San Francisco, California (1854 to date)
    W—West Point, New York (1984 to date)

The mintmark is of utmost importance to collectors because, historically, coinage of the branch mints has often been much smaller than quantities struck at Philadelphia. Many early coins of the branch mints are very scarce.

## SLABBED VERSUS UNSLABBED COINS

In this handbook, values from under $1 up to several hundred dollars are for "raw" coins—that is, coins that have not been graded and encapsulated by a professional third-party grading service. Coins valued near or above $500 are assumed to be third-party graded. A high-value coin that has not been professionally certified as authentic, graded, and encapsulated by an independent firm is apt to be valued lower than the prices indicated.

The general effect of third-party grading and authentication has been to increase buyers' and sellers' comfort levels with the perceived quality of rare coins in the marketplace.

Coins in high grades that have been certified (professionally graded and guaranteed authentic) and encapsulated ("slabbed") may be valued significantly higher than similar coins that have not been so treated. In today's marketplace, "raw" or non-certified coins, are usually valued at less, except for modern U.S. Mint and bullion products.

# DISTINGUISHING MARKS

The illustrations and explanations in this section will help the collector identify certain well-known varieties.

## Half Cents of 1795–1796 Showing Location of Pole to Cap

The end of the pole lies parallel with the lines of the bust, which is pointed. On some coins, the pole is missing due either to engraver error (while cutting the die) or to an error in "relapping" (when the die is ground to remove wear, clash marks, etc.).

**Pole to Cap**       **No Pole to Cap**

## Stemless Wreath Variety of Half Cents and Large Cents

For this variety, the difference is on the reverse side. Illustrations show both Stemless and Stems to Wreath types for comparison—stemless wreath found on the 1804, 1805, and 1806 half cents; and on the 1797, 1802, and 1803 large cents.

**Stemless Wreath**       **Stems to Wreath**

## 1864 Bronze Indian Head Cent With "L" on Ribbon

A small "L," the initial of the designer James B. Longacre, was added to the Indian Head design late in 1864 and was continued through 1909. For coins in less than Fine condition, this small letter will often be worn away. The point of the bust is rounded on the 1864 variety without "L"; the bust is pointed on the

variety with "L." The initial must be visible, however, for the 1864 variety to bring the higher premium. If the coin is turned slightly so that the portrait faces the observer, the highlighted details will usually appear to better advantage.

## Designer Initials, Overstrikes, Die-Doublings, and Date Varieties

*During 1909, initials appeared on the reverse of the Lincoln cent.*
*Starting in 1918, they appear below the shoulder.*

*Prior to 1990, mintmarks for all mints were usually applied directly to working dies at Philadelphia in a hand-punching operation. Occasionally, a die was accidentally marked with one letter on top of another.*

*Dies are produced by impressing the raised coin design of a hub into the end of a cylinder of steel. In early years the Mint made use of old dies by repunching the dates on their dies with new numbers. That practice was stopped prior to 1909. Since that time, all overdated coins have been the result of errors that occur when two different-dated hubs have been used in die preparation, and one is impressed over the other by accident.*

**1938-D, D Over S,
Buffalo Nickel**

**1918-S, 8 Over 7,
Standing Liberty Quarter**
*A variety of this kind is rarely found
in coinage of the 20th century.*

**1942, 2 Over 1,
Mercury Dime**

**1955, Doubled-Die Obverse
Lincoln Cent**

**Large Date Cent
(1960)**

**Small Date Cent
(1960)**

**Large Date Cent
(1982)**

**Small Date Cent
(1982)**

# COUNTERFEIT COINS

Recognizing a spurious coin can be made easier through the use of common sense and an elementary knowledge of the techniques used by counterfeiters. It is well to keep in mind that the more popular a coin is among collectors and the public, the more likely it is that counterfeits and replicas will abound. Until recently, collector coins valued at under $100 were rarely replicated because of the high cost of making such items. The same was true of counterfeits made to deceive the public. Few counterfeit coins were made because it was more profitable for the fakers to print paper money. Today, however, counterfeiters in Asia and elsewhere create fakes of a surprising variety of coins, most notably silver dollar types, but also other denominations.

Coin dealers will rarely buy coins of exceptional rarity or value without being 100% certain of authenticity. Professional authentication of rare coins for a fee is offered by commercial grading services, and by some dealers.

## Replicas

Reproductions of famous and historical coins have been distributed for decades by marketing firms and souvenir vendors. Most replicas are poorly made by the casting method, and are virtually worthless. They can sometimes be identified by a seam that runs around the edge of the piece where the two halves of the casting mold were joined together.

## Counterfeits

For many centuries, counterfeiters have produced base-metal forgeries of gold and silver coins to deceive the public in the normal course of trade. These pieces are usually crudely made and easily detected on close examination. Crudely cast counterfeit copies of older coins are the most prevalent. These can usually be detected by the casting bubbles or pimples that can be seen with low-power magnification. Pieces struck from handmade dies are more deceptive, but the engravings do not match those of genuine Mint products.

Die-struck gold coin counterfeits have been mass produced overseas since 1950. Forgeries exist of most U.S. gold coins dated between 1870 and 1933, as well as all issues of the gold dollar and three-dollar gold piece. Most of these are very well made, as they were intended to pass the close scrutiny of collectors. Many gold coins of earlier dates have been counterfeited, and all coins dated before 1930 should be carefully examined.

Silver dollars dated 1804, Lafayette dollars, several of the low-mintage commemorative half dollars, and the 1795 half dimes have been forged in quantity. Minor-coin forgeries made in recent years are the 1909-S V.D.B.; 1914-D and 1955 doubled-die Lincoln cents; 1877 Indian Head cents; 1856 Flying Eagle cents; and, on a much smaller scale, a variety of dates of half cents and large cents. Nineteenth-century copies of colonial coins are also sometimes encountered.

## Alterations

Coins are occasionally altered by the addition, removal, or change of a design feature (such as a mintmark or date digit) or by the polishing, sandblasting, acid etching, toning, or plating of the surface of a genuine piece. Among U.S. gold coins, only the 1927-D double eagle is commonly found with a spuriously added mintmark. On $2.50 and $5 gold coins, 1839 through 1856, New Orleans O mintmarks have been deceptively altered to C (for Charlotte, North Carolina) in a few instances.

Over a century ago, five-dollar gold pieces were imitated by gold plating 1883 Liberty Head five-cent coins without the word CENTS on the reverse. Other coins commonly created fraudulently through alteration include the 1799 large cent and the 1909-S; 1909-S V.D.B.; 1914-D; 1922, No D; and 1943, Copper, cents. The 1913 Liberty Head nickel has been extensively replicated by alteration of 1903 and 1912 nickels. Scarce, high-grade Denver and San Francisco Buffalo nickels of the 1920s; 1916-D and 1942, 42 Over 41, dimes; 1918-S, 8 Over 7, quarters; 1932-D and -S quarters; and 1804 silver dollars have all been made by the alteration of genuine coins of other dates or mints.

## Detection

The best way to detect counterfeit coins is to compare suspected pieces with others of the same issue. Look at the photographs in this book for comparisons. Carefully check size, color, luster, weight, edge devices, and design details. Replicas generally have less detail than their genuine counterparts when studied under magnification. Modern struck counterfeits made to deceive collectors are an exception to this rule. Any questionable gold coin should be referred to an expert for verification.

Cast forgeries are usually poorly made and of incorrect weight. Base metal is often used in place of gold or silver, and the coins are lightweight and often incorrect in color and luster. Deceptive cast pieces have been made using real metal content and modern dental techniques, but these too usually vary in quality and color. Detection of alterations sometimes involves comparative examination of the suspected areas of a coin (usually mintmarks and date digits) at magnification ranging from 10x to 40x.

# CONDITIONS OF COINS

## Essential Elements of the Official ANA Grading System

**Proof**—A specially made coin distinguished by sharpness of detail and usually with a brilliant, mirrorlike surface. *Proof* refers to the method of manufacture and is not a condition, but normally the term implies nearly perfect condition unless otherwise noted.

**Perfect Proof (PF-70)**—The perfect coin, with strike and surface of the highest quality. No contact marks are visible under magnification. There are absolutely no hairlines, scuff marks, or defects.

**Gem Proof (PF-65)**—Brilliant surfaces with no noticeable blemishes or flaws. A few scattered, barely noticeable marks or hairlines.

**Choice Proof (PF-63)**—Reflective surfaces with only a few blemishes in secondary focal places. No major flaws.

**Proof (PF-60)**—Surface may have several contact marks, hairlines, or light rubs. Luster may be dull and eye appeal lacking.

**Mint State**—The terms *Mint State (MS)* and *Uncirculated (Unc.)* are used interchangeably to describe coins showing no trace of wear. Such coins may vary to some degree because of blemishes, toning, or slight imperfections, as described in the following subdivisions:

**Perfect Uncirculated (MS-70)**—Perfect new condition, showing no trace of wear. The finest quality possible, with no evidence of scratches, handling, or contact with other coins.

**Gem Uncirculated (MS-65)**—An above average Uncirculated coin that may be brilliant or lightly toned and that has very few contact marks on the surface or rim. MS-67 through MS-62 indicate slightly higher or lower grades of preservation.

**Choice Uncirculated (MS-63)**—Has some distracting contact marks or blemishes in prime focal areas. Luster may be impaired.

**Uncirculated (MS-60)**—Has no trace of wear but may show a number of contact marks, and surface may be spotted or lack some luster.

**Choice About Uncirculated (AU-55)**—Evidence of friction on high points of design. Most of the mint luster remains.

**About Uncirculated (AU-50)**—Traces of light wear on many of the high points. At least half of the mint luster is still present.

**Choice Extremely Fine (EF-45)**—Light overall wear on highest points. All design details are very sharp. Some of the mint luster is evident.

**Extremely Fine (EF-40)**—Light wear on design throughout, but all features sharp and well defined. Traces of luster may show.

**Choice Very Fine (VF-30)**—Light, even wear on the surface and highest parts of the design. All lettering and major features are sharp.

**Very Fine (VF-20)**—Moderate wear on high points. All major details are clear.

**Fine (F-12)**—Moderate to considerable even wear. Entire design is bold with overall pleasing appearance.

**Very Good (VG-8)**—Well worn with main features clear and bold, although rather flat.

**Good (G-4)**—Heavily worn, with design visible but faint in areas. Many details are flat.

**About Good (AG-3)**—Very heavily worn with portions of lettering, date, and legend worn smooth. The date may be barely readable.

A star (or similar notation) in the grade on a slab means "exceptional quality."

*Important:* Damaged coins, such as those that are bent, corroded, scratched, holed, nicked, stained, or mutilated, are worth less than those without defects. Flawless Uncirculated coins are generally worth more than values quoted in this book. Slightly worn coins ("sliders") that have been cleaned and conditioned ("buffed") to simulate Uncirculated luster are worth considerably less than perfect pieces.

Unlike damage inflicted after striking, manufacturing defects do not always lessen values. Examples include colonial coins with planchet flaws and weakly struck designs; early silver and gold with weight-adjustment "file marks" (parallel cuts made prior to striking); and coins with "lint marks" (surface marks due to the presence of dust or other foreign matter during striking).

Brief guides to grading are placed before each major coin type. Grading standards are not scientific and often vary among collectors, dealers, and certification services. For more on grading, consult the *Official ANA Grading Standards for United States Coins*.

## PRESERVING AND CLEANING COINS

Most say, "Never clean a coin," and it is good advice! Cleaning coins almost always reduces their value. Collectors prefer coins in their original condition.

Some effort should be made to protect Uncirculated and Proof coins so they won't need cleaning. Tarnish on a coin is purely a chemical process caused by oxygen in the air acting on the metal, or by chemicals with which the coin comes in contact. One of the most common chemicals causing tarnish is sulphur; most paper, with the exception of specially manufactured "sulphur-free" kinds, contains sulphur due to the sulphuric acid that is used in paper manufacture; therefore do not wrap coins in ordinary paper. Also keep Uncirculated and Proof coins away from rubber bands (a rubber band placed on a silver coin for a few days will eventually produce a black stripe on the coin where the band touched). The utmost in protection is obtained by storing the coin in an airtight box, away from moisture and humidity, and by using holders made of inert materials.

Many coins become marred by careless handling. Always hold the coin by the edge. The accompanying illustration shows the right and wrong way to handle numismatic specimens. It is a breach of numismatic etiquette to handle another collector's coin except by the edge, even if it is not an Uncirculated or Proof piece.

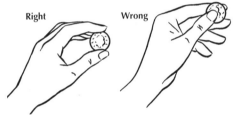

Right          Wrong

## STARTING A COLLECTION

One may start a collection of United States coins with very little expense by systematically assembling the various dates and mintmarks of all the types and denominations that are now in general circulation, using Whitman's many different coin folders and albums, especially those for quarters and dollars with various designs.

With the exception of the price paid for the coin folder, collecting coins received in everyday business transactions entails no expense whatsoever; a Jefferson nickel taken out of circulation, for example, can always be spent for five cents if the occasion arises. Filling an album or two with coins found in circulation is probably the best method of determining whether coin collecting appeals to you. Not everyone can be a successful coin collector. It requires patience, intelligence of a high order, and a certain desire to know the meaning behind a lot of things that at first glance appear meaningless. You may not be cut out to be a collector but you'll never know until you look further into the subject, and if by the time an album or two of coins are collected you have no burning desire to acquire many more different coins, you will probably never be a collector. However, chances are that you will be, because if you have read this far in this book, it shows that you are interested in the subject.

High quality is the goal of every endeavor and coin collecting is no exception. After an album has been filled with circulated specimens, the next step will be to replace them with coins in Uncirculated condition, or perhaps to start collecting an obsolete series;

in either case, it will be necessary to purchase some coins from dealers or other collectors. The most logical way to keep abreast of the market, or obtain the addresses of the country's leading dealers, is to subscribe to one or more of the trade publications. These magazines carry advertisements of various dealers listing coins for sale. Moreover, through these sources the beginner may obtain price lists and catalogs from the dealers.

There are several good reference books available at reasonable prices which will be helpful to the collector who wishes to know more about U.S. coins and paper money. R.S. Yeoman's *A Guide Book of United States Coins™* (the "Red Book") lists retail values of all regular U.S. coins and also lists all coins of the U.S. colonial period and private and territorial gold coins, plus tokens, pattern coins, errors, and other numismatic collectibles.

Most coin, book, and hobby dealers can supply the following titles:

*The Official Red Book®: A Guide Book of United States Coins™*—R.S. Yeoman, edited by Jeff Garrett

*The Official Red Book®: A Guide Book of United States Coins™, Deluxe Edition*—R.S. Yeoman, edited by Q. David Bowers

*A Guide Book of Morgan Silver Dollars*—Q. David Bowers

*The Expert's Guide to Collecting and Investing in Rare Coins*—Q. David Bowers

*Coin Collecting: A Beginner's Guide to the World of Coins*—Kenneth Bressett

*History of the United States Mint and Its Coinage*—David W. Lange

*The Official ANA Grading Standards for United States Coins*—Kenneth Bressett, et al.

*A Guide Book of United States Type Coins*—Q. David Bowers

## Join a Coin Club

Beginners should join a "coin club" if they live in a city which has one. Associating with more experienced collectors will be of great benefit. Practically all larger cities have one or more clubs and they are being rapidly organized in smaller towns. Trade publications carry information about coin clubs and events such as coin shows and conventions.

The American Numismatic Association is a national organization that collectors can join. The ANA Web site (www.money.org) has a list of member coin clubs throughout the United States. Contact the ANA by mail at 818 North Cascade Avenue, Colorado Springs, CO 80903, or by phone at 800-367-9723.

## SELLING YOUR COINS

Is it time to sell your coins? Perhaps you've inherited some of them; or maybe you've collected for years, and you want to explore a new pastime or you need to cash in on your investment. In any case, you have some decisions to make. Will you sell your collection privately, or at a public auction—or perhaps sell it yourself on the Internet? Will you sell locally or to dealers nationwide? What are the benefits of each path, and which will bring the greatest profits? To get started, ask yourself:

## What Am I Selling?

**Rolls of Modern Coins; Proof Sets; Modern Commemoratives; Bullion; Etc.**
This includes bulk investment coins, such as American Eagle bullion pieces, bags of common circulated coins, and so on. It also includes modern commemoratives and coin sets, not all of which have increased in value in the secondary market. Such accumulations are best sold privately to a coin dealer or to another collector. Auctioning

them yourself, on the Internet, is another route. Consigning them to an auction house is not likely to be your best option; this venue is typically reserved for scarcer coins.

**Coins With Sentimental—but Not Necessarily High-Dollar—Value.** You might have inherited an accumulation (as opposed to a studiously compiled collection) of coins—for example, a coffee can full of Wheat cents. Your local coin dealer can make you an offer, either buying the entire lot or searching through them to "cherrypick" the better pieces. If you have the time, you might sell them yourself, through an Internet auction site. Also, you might donate them to a local Boy Scout troop or similar organization (this may be tax-deductible).

**Rare and/or Significant Coins.** For rare, valuable, and historically significant coins, public consigned auctions are often the best way to sell—dedicated collectors know they're good sources for scarce coins. A coin consigned to a well-established auction house with numismatic experience will be carefully studied, cataloged, and presented to a serious audience. You save the time and effort of searching for potential buyers. The auction firm makes money by collecting a commission on each sale.

Another option for selling your rare and significant coins is to approach a dealer nationally recognized as an expert in the field—for example, a specialist who focuses on colonial coins. You may also receive tax benefits from donating your coins to the American Numismatic Association (ANA), the American Numismatic Society, or a museum.

## Selling to a Coin Shop

Your local coin shop has the advantage of the personal touch. Good coin-shop proprietors are happy to educate and advise their customers. An active coin dealer stays up to date on the hobby and the market, knows about tax and estate laws that might affect your sale, and can study your collection and make educated decisions. Many dealers have a wide audience for selling coins—which provides the leverage to offer you a good price.

A coin shop can be a venue for selling numismatic items of any value. The owner can often make you an offer and write you a check on the spot. Of course, very rare or specialized coins will likely fetch a higher price at public auction.

You should feel comfortable with the integrity of the shop's proprietor and staff. Talk to coin-collector friends, inquire at the local coin club, and check with the Better Business Bureau. Look at the shop's Web site, advertisements, and flyers or publications—do they project fairness and professionalism?

Coin shops can be found in a phone book or online business directory. Call to make sure the owner or a qualified assistant will be there to examine your coins. A busy dealer can schedule a convenient time to meet with you. Solicit at least two quotes before you decide to sell.

## Selling Through the Mail

You can ship your coins to a dealer for their offer; again, trust is important. Does the dealer belong to the ANA or the Professional Numismatists Guild (www.pngdealers. com)? Does he advertise in hobby newspapers such as *Coin World* and *Numismatic News?* Search the dealer's name on the Internet: do you find satisfied customers, or complaints and concerns?

Inquire by mail, email, or phone before shipping any coins. The dealer might request a list beforehand, and should be able to give you a general idea of value without seeing the coins in person. Once you're comfortable and have decided to sell, ask the dealer for advice on shipping and insurance. Keep in mind that the dealer will need to examine your coins before making a firm offer.

Even if you live near a coin shop, you can broaden the playing field if you're open to selling your coins through the mail to established, respected dealers. This is a good option if you have the time. The entire transaction (finding dealers; packing and shipping; waiting for the check) will likely take longer than getting a local offer.

## Selling to a Dealer at a Coin Show

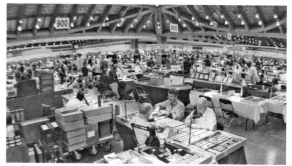

Between the national coin shows and the hundreds of coin clubs that sponsor city and regional shows, chances are a show is held somewhere near you at least once a year. With dozens or even hundreds of dealers in one venue, you can shop your coins around before you sell; and, as at a coin shop, payment is immediate.

**For best results, decide in advance which dealers would be best to appproach, especially if you'll have to travel a long way or you're interested in a narrow specialty.**

Remember, a coin show is a public venue. Be alert; use common sense. Outside the show, do not publicize the fact that you're carrying valuable coins.

Most shows list participating dealers in their programs. Decide in advance the ones you want to approach (e.g., the silver-dollar specialists, if you have Morgan dollars to sell). Or simply stroll the aisles and introduce yourself to dealers who sell items similar to those in your collection. This is all part of the fun of a coin show.

## Consigning at a Public Auction

Numismatic auction firms are often connected to larger retailers that also sell through the mail, online, etc. As always, reputation is important. Study a potential auctioneer's Web site; learn about their staff, past sales results, any media coverage they might receive. Look at their catalogs: are they professionally made? The effort and experience an auction firm brings to its work will affect how much your coins sell for.

## Selling Online

Selling your coins yourself online can be fun, but it requires time and (usually) some skill with scanning or photography. Each auction site has its own rules, policies, and rates; read them carefully. Be security-conscious (e.g., rent a Post Office box instead of using your home address, and insist on full, guaranteed payment before you ship any coins). You can also use the Internet to sell your coins at a fixed price, through a bulletin-board posting or other announcement. Any online sale to the public requires you to take on responsibilities similar to those of a coin shop or auction firm. There is work involved, but the experience can be enjoyable and profitable.

*Early American coins are rare in conditions better than those listed and consequently dealers pay much more for them.*

## BRITISH NEW WORLD ISSUES
### Sommer Islands (Bermuda)

This coinage, issued around 1616, was the first struck for England's colonies in the New World. The coins were known as "Hogge Money" or "Hoggies."

The pieces were made of copper lightly silvered, in four denominations: shilling, sixpence, threepence, and twopence, indicated by Roman numerals. The hog is the main device and appears on the obverse side of each. SOMMER ISLANDS is inscribed within beaded circles. The reverse shows a full-rigged galleon with the flag of St. George on each of four masts.

Shilling

|  | AG | G | VG | F | VF | EF |
|---|---|---|---|---|---|---|
| Twopence | $2,250 | $3,250 | $5,500 | $9,500 | $20,000 | $40,000 |
| Threepence |  |  | 20,000 |  |  |  |
| Sixpence | 1,750 | 2,500 | 4,000 | 8,500 | 17,500 | 30,000 |
| Shilling | 2,500 | 3,750 | 6,000 | 17,500 | 35,000 | 55,000 |

## Massachusetts
### *"New England" Coinage (1652)*

In 1652 the General Court of Massachusetts ordered the first metallic currency to be struck in the British Americas, the New England silver threepence, sixpence, and shilling. These coins were made from silver bullion procured principally from the West Indies. Joseph Jenks made the punches for the first coins at his Iron Works in Saugus, Massachusetts, close to Boston where the mint was located. John Hull was appointed mintmaster; his assistant was Robert Sanderson.

NE Shilling (1652)

|  | G | VG | F | VF | EF |
|---|---|---|---|---|---|
| NE Threepence *(unique)* |  |  | — |  |  |
| NE Sixpence *(8 known)* | $35,000 | $55,000 | $125,000 | $175,000 | $250,000 |
| NE Shilling | 25,000 | 45,000 | 65,000 | 95,000 | 120,000 |

### Willow Tree Coinage (1653–1660)

The simplicity of the design on the N.E. coins invited counterfeiting and clipping of the edges. Therefore, they were soon replaced by the Willow Tree, Oak Tree, and Pine Tree series. The Willow Tree coins were struck from 1653 to 1660, the Oak Trees 1660 to 1667, and the Pine Trees 1667 to 1682. All of them (with the exception of the Oak Tree twopence) bore the date 1652. Many varieties of all of these coins exist. Values shown are for the most common types.

Sixpence

| | Fair | G | VG | F | VF | EF |
|---|---|---|---|---|---|---|
| 1652 Willow Tree Threepence *(3 known)* . . . . . . | | — | — | | — | — |
| 1652 Willow Tree Sixpence *(14 known)* . . . . . . . | $6,500 | $14,000 | $20,000 | $30,000 | $75,000 | $115,000 |
| 1652 Willow Tree Shilling. . . . . . . . . . . . . . . . | 6,500 | 14,000 | 20,000 | 40,000 | 85,000 | 125,000 |

### Oak Tree Coinage (1660–1667)

Twopence          Threepence

| | G | VG | F | VF | EF | AU | Unc. |
|---|---|---|---|---|---|---|---|
| 1662 Oak Tree Twopence . . . . . . . . | $300 | $450 | $800 | $1,500 | $3,000 | $4,200 | $7,000 |
| 1652 Oak Tree Threepence . . . . . . . | 400 | 500 | 1,500 | 3,200 | 5,250 | 8,500 | 25,000 |
| 1652 Oak Tree Sixpence . . . . . . . . . | 450 | 700 | 1,600 | 3,750 | 5,500 | 8,500 | 20,000 |
| 1652 Oak Tree Shilling. . . . . . . . . . | 450 | 700 | 1,600 | 4,000 | 6,500 | 7,500 | 20,000 |

### Pine Tree Coinage (1667–1682)

The first Pine Tree coins were minted on the same size planchets as the Oak Tree pieces. Subsequent issues of the shilling were narrower and thicker, to conform to the size of English coins.

Shilling, Large Planchet (1667–1674)          Shilling, Small Planchet (1675–1682)

*See next page for chart.*

| | G | VG | F | VF | EF | AU | Unc. |
|---|---|---|---|---|---|---|---|
| 1652 Pine Tree Threepence .............. | $300 | $475 | $800 | $1,500 | $3,200 | $5,000 | $10,000 |
| 1652 Pine Tree Sixpence ............... | 350 | 500 | 1,000 | 1,950 | 3,250 | 6,000 | 11,000 |
| 1652 Pine Tree Shilling, Large Planchet.... | 450 | 725 | 1,100 | 2,500 | 4,000 | 7,000 | 16,500 |
| 1652 Pine Tree Shilling, Small Planchet.... | 375 | 575 | 1,100 | 2,000 | 3,250 | 6,250 | 15,000 |

## Maryland
### Lord Baltimore Coinage

In 1659, Cecil Calvert, Lord Baltimore and Lord Proprietor of Maryland, had coinage struck in England for use in Maryland. There were four denominations: shilling, sixpence, fourpence (groat) in silver, and copper penny (denarium). The silver coins have the bust of Lord Baltimore on the obverse, and the Baltimore family arms with the denomination in Roman numerals on the reverse.

Fourpence (groat)          Lord Baltimore Shilling

| | G | VG | F | VF | EF | AU |
|---|---|---|---|---|---|---|
| Penny copper *(9 known)* ................. | $15,000 | $30,000 | $50,000 | $85,000 | $110,000 | $150,000 |
| Fourpence .......................... | 1,600 | 3,000 | 6,500 | 12,000 | 17,500 | 30,000 |
| Sixpence ........................... | 950 | 1,300 | 2,500 | 5,000 | 8,000 | 12,500 |
| Shilling ............................ | 1,500 | 2,500 | 4,500 | 7,000 | 10,000 | 20,000 |

## New Jersey
### St. Patrick or Mark Newby Coinage

Mark Newby, who came to America from Dublin, Ireland, in November 1681, brought copper pieces believed by numismatists to have been struck in England circa 1663 to 1672. These are called St. Patrick coppers. The coin received wide circulation in the New Jersey Province, having been authorized to pass as legal tender by the General Assembly in May 1682. The smaller piece, known as a farthing, was never specifically authorized for circulation in the colonies.

St. Patrick Farthing

| | G | VG | F | VF | EF | AU |
|---|---|---|---|---|---|---|
| St. Patrick "Farthing".................. | $85 | $160 | $450 | $1,500 | $3,000 | $6,000 |
| St. Patrick "Halfpenny" ................. | 155 | 375 | 600 | 1,600 | 5,500 | 10,000 |

# COINAGE AUTHORIZED BY BRITISH ROYAL PATENT
## American Plantations Tokens

These pieces struck in nearly pure tin were the first royally authorized coinage for the British colonies in America. They were made under a franchise granted in 1688 to Richard Holt. Restrikes were made circa 1828 from original dies.

| | G | VG | F | VF | EF | AU | Unc. |
|---|---|---|---|---|---|---|---|
| (1688) James II Plantation Token Farthing . . | | | | | | | |
| 1/24 Part Real . . . . . . . . . . . . . . . . . . . . | $125 | $150 | $300 | $600 | $1,000 | $1,750 | $3,000 |
| 1/24 Part Real, Restrike . . . . . . . . . . . . . | 50 | 75 | 150 | 225 | 300 | 500 | 1000 |

## Coinage of William Wood
### *Rosa Americana Coins*

William Wood, an Englishman, obtained a patent from King George I to make coins for Ireland and the American colonies. The Rosa Americana pieces were issued in three denominations—halfpenny, penny, and twopence—and were intended for use in America.

Penny

| | VG | F | VF | EF | AU | Unc. |
|---|---|---|---|---|---|---|
| (No date) Twopence, Motto in Ribbon . . . . . . . . | $90 | $170 | $375 | $600 | $1,500 | $2,500 |
| 1722 Halfpenny, DEI GRATIA REX UTILE DULCI . . . | 55 | 125 | 210 | 400 | 725 | 1,700 |
| 1722 Penny . . . . . . . . . . . . . . . . . . . . . . . . . | 55 | 125 | 210 | 400 | 725 | 1,700 |
| 1722 Twopence . . . . . . . . . . . . . . . . . . . . . . | 75 | 140 | 250 | 500 | 800 | 2,000 |

Halfpenny

| | F | VF | EF | AU | Unc. |
|---|---|---|---|---|---|
| 1723 Halfpenny . . . . . . . . . . . . . . . . . . . . . . . . . | $35 | $100 | $150 | $325 | $700 |

*Entry continued on next page.*

Twopence

|                            | VG   | F    | VF    | EF    | AU    | Unc.    |
|----------------------------|------|------|-------|-------|-------|---------|
| 1723 Penny                 | $40  | $60  | $140  | $250  | $400  | $1,000  |
| 1723 Twopence *(illustrated)* | 75   | 110  | 175   | 400   | 700   | 1,250   |

## Wood's Hibernia Coinage

The type intended for Ireland had a seated figure with a harp on the reverse side and the word HIBERNIA. Denominations struck were the halfpenny and the farthing with dates 1722, 1723, and 1724. Although these have no association with the Americas, because of the connection with William Wood many American collectors desire to obtain them.

| 1722, Hibernia Halfpenny | First Type | Second Type |

|                                        | G    | VG    | F     | VF    | EF      | AU      | Unc.    |
|----------------------------------------|------|-------|-------|-------|---------|---------|---------|
| 1722 Farthing, first type              | $75  | $200  | $300  | $850  | $1,500  | $3,500  | $6,000  |
| 1722 Halfpenny (first or second type)  | 12   | 35    | 50    | 100   | 175     | 300     | 650     |

| 1723, Hibernia Farthing | 1724, Hibernia Halfpenny |

|                  | G    | VG    | F     | VF    | EF     | AU     | Unc.    |
|------------------|------|-------|-------|-------|--------|--------|---------|
| 1723 Farthing    | $10  | $20   | $35   | $70   | $100   | $200   | $320    |
| 1723 Halfpenny   | 10   | 20    | 30    | 65    | 90     | 175    | 300     |
| 1724 Farthing    | 15   | 40    | 95    | 250   | 450    | 750    | 1,500   |
| 1724 Halfpenny   | 12   | 35    | 60    | 170   | 325    | 500    | 950     |

## Virginia Halfpennies

In 1773, coinage of a copper halfpenny was authorized for Virginia by the British Crown. The style is similar to the regular English coinage. These pieces did not arrive in Virginia until 1775, but after then they did circulate on a limited basis. Most examples known today are Uncirculated, by virtue of a hoard of several thousand pieces that came to light in the 19th century and was distributed in numismatic channels.

| | G | VG | F | VF | EF | AU | Unc. |
|---|---|---|---|---|---|---|---|
| 1773 Halfpenny | $10 | $30 | $50 | $90 | $180 | $275 | $525 |

# EARLY AMERICAN AND RELATED TOKENS

## Elephant Tokens

### London Elephant Tokens

The London Elephant tokens were struck circa 1672 to 1694. Although they were undated, two examples are known to have been struck over 1672 British halfpennies. Most are struck in copper, but one is made of brass. The legend on this piece, GOD PRESERVE LONDON, is probably just a general plea for divine aid and not a specific reference to the outbreak of plague in 1665 or the great fire of 1666.

These pieces were not struck for the colonies, and probably did not circulate in America, although a few may have been carried there by colonists. They are associated with the 1694 Carolina and New England Elephant tokens, through a shared obverse die.

| | VG | F | VF | EF | AU | Unc. |
|---|---|---|---|---|---|---|
| (1694) Halfpenny, GOD PRESERVE LONDON, Thick or Thin Planchet | $175 | $325 | $500 | $850 | $1,500 | $2,250 |

### Carolina Elephant Tokens

Although no law is known authorizing coinage for Carolina, very interesting pieces known as Elephant tokens were made with the date 1694. These copper tokens were of halfpenny denomination. The reverse reads GOD PRESERVE CAROLINA AND THE LORDS PROPRIETERS 1694.

The Carolina pieces were probably struck in England and perhaps intended as advertising to heighten interest in the Carolina Plantation.

|  | VG | F | VF | EF | AU | Unc. |
|---|---|---|---|---|---|---|
| 1694 CAROLINA. | $2,000 | $4,000 | $6,000 | $10,000 | $15,000 | $25,000 |

### New England Elephant Tokens

Like the Carolina Tokens, the New England Elephant tokens were believed to have been struck in England as promotional pieces to increase interest in the American colonies.

|  | F | VF | EF |
|---|---|---|---|
| 1694 NEW ENGLAND. | $30,000 | $45,000 | $65,000 |

### New Yorke in America Token

Little is known about the origin of this token. The design of a heraldic eagle on a regulated staff with oak leaf finials is identical to the crest found on the arms of William Lovelace, governor of New York, 1668 to 1673. It seems likely that this piece is a token farthing struck by Lovelace for use in New York.

|  | VG | F | VF | EF |
|---|---|---|---|---|
| (Undated) Brass or Copper. | $5,000 | $10,000 | $17,500 | $25,000 |
| (Undated) Pewter. | — | — |  |  |

### Gloucester Tokens

This token appears to have been a private coinage by a merchant of Gloucester (county), Virginia. The only specimens known are struck in brass. The exact origin and use of these pieces are unknown.

| | F |
|---|---|
| 1714 Shilling, brass *(2 known)* ........................................................ | $80,000 |

## Higley or Granby Coppers

The Higley coppers were private issues. All the pieces were made of pure copper. There were seven obverse and four reverse dies. The first issue, in 1737, bore the legend THE VALUE OF THREEPENCE. After a time the quantity exceeded the local demand, and a protest arose against the stated value of the piece. The inscription was changed to VALUE ME AS YOU PLEASE.

| | AG | G | VG | F |
|---|---|---|---|---|
| 1737 THE VALVE OF THREE PENCE, CONNECTICVT, 3 Hammers.......... | $6,500 | $10,000 | $17,000 | $30,000 |
| 1737 THE VALVE OF THREE PENCE, I AM GOOD COPPER, 3 Hammers ..... | 7,500 | 15,000 | 30,000 | 45,000 |
| 1737 VALUE ME AS YOU PLEASE, I AM GOOD COPPER, 3 Hammers....... | 6,500 | 10,500 | 17,500 | 30,000 |
| (1737) VALUE ME AS YOU PLEASE, J CUT MY WAY THROUGH, Broad Axe... | 6,500 | 10,500 | 17,500 | 30,000 |
| 1739 VALUE ME AS YOU PLEASE, J CUT MY WAY THROUGH, Broad Axe.... | 7,500 | 13,500 | 24,000 | 38,000 |

## Hibernia–Voce Populi Coins

These coins, struck in the year 1760, were made in Dublin. Although these have no connection with America, they have been listed in numismatic publications in the United States for a long time and are collected by tradition.

Farthing (1760)           Halfpenny (1760)

| | G | VG | F | VF | EF | AU | Unc. |
|---|---|---|---|---|---|---|---|
| 1760 Farthing ................. | $100 | $160 | $250 | $650 | $1,000 | $1,750 | $3,500 |
| 1760 Halfpenny............... | 37 | 60 | 100 | 160 | 260 | 450 | 650 |

## Pitt Tokens

British politician William Pitt is the subject of these pieces, probably intended as commemorative medalets. He was a friend to the interests of America. The so-called halfpenny served as currency in England during a shortage of regular coinage.

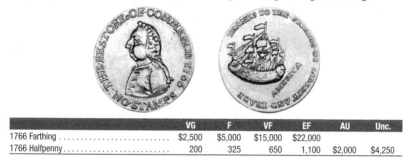

| | VG | F | VF | EF | AU | Unc. |
|---|---|---|---|---|---|---|
| 1766 Farthing . . . . . . . . . . . . . . . . . . . . . . . . . | $2,500 | $5,000 | $15,000 | $22,000 | | |
| 1766 Halfpenny . . . . . . . . . . . . . . . . . . . . . . . . | 200 | 325 | 650 | 1,100 | $2,000 | $4,250 |

## Rhode Island Ship Medals

Although this medal has a Dutch inscription, the spelling and design indicate an English or Anglo-American origin. It is believed that this token was struck in England circa 1779 for the Dutch market. Specimens are known in brass and pewter. As with many colonial issues, modern copies exist.

**1778–1779, Rhode Island Ship Medal**

*Values shown are for brass pieces. Those struck in pewter are rare and valued higher.*

| | VF | EF | AU | Unc. |
|---|---|---|---|---|
| Rhode Island Ship Medal . . . . . . . . . . . . . . . . . . . . . . . . . . . . . . . . . . . | $450 | $850 | $1,400 | $3,000 |

## John Chalmers Issues

John Chalmers, a silversmith, struck a series of silver tokens at Annapolis in 1783. Certain of the dies were by Thomas Sparrow, who also engraved bank-note plates. As most examples show wear today, these pieces seem to have served well in commerce.

| | VG | F | VF | EF | AU |
|---|---|---|---|---|---|
| 1783 Threepence . . . . . . . . . . . . . . . . . . . . . . . . . . . . | $1,000 | $2,000 | $4,000 | $7,000 | $10,000 |

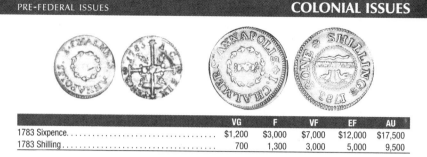

| | VG | F | VF | EF | AU |
|---|---|---|---|---|---|
| 1783 Sixpence. . . . . . . . . . . . . . . . . . . . . . . . . . . . . . . . | $1,200 | $3,000 | $7,000 | $12,000 | $17,500 |
| 1783 Shilling. . . . . . . . . . . . . . . . . . . . . . . . . . . . . . . . | 700 | 1,300 | 3,000 | 5,000 | 9,500 |

## FRENCH NEW WORLD ISSUES

None of the coins of the French regime is strictly American. They were all general issues for the French colonies of the New World. The copper of 1717 to 1722 was authorized by edicts of 1716 and 1721 for use in New France, Louisiana, and the French West Indies.

### Copper Sou or Nine Deniers

| | VG | F | VF | EF |
|---|---|---|---|---|
| 1721-B (Rouen). . . . . . . . . . . . . . . . . . . . . . . . . . . . . . . . . . . . . . . . | $250 | $500 | $1,750 | $3,500 |
| 1721-H (La Rochelle). . . . . . . . . . . . . . . . . . . . . . . . . . . . . . . . . . | 50 | 110 | 350 | 1,200 |
| 1722-H . . . . . . . . . . . . . . . . . . . . . . . . . . . . . . . . . . . . . . . . . | 50 | 110 | 350 | 1,200 |

### French Colonies in General

Coined for use in the French colonies, these circulated only unofficially in Louisiana, along with other foreign coins and tokens. Most were counterstamped RF (République Française) for use in the West Indies. The mintmark A signifies the Paris Mint.

| | VG | VF | EF | AU |
|---|---|---|---|---|
| 1767 French Colonies, Sou . . . . . . . . . . . . . . . . . . . . . . . . . . . . . . . | $45 | $125 | $350 | $700 |
| 1767 French Colonies, Sou, counterstamped RF . . . . . . . . . . . . . . . . | 40 | 90 | 150 | 275 |

## CONTINENTAL CURRENCY PIECES

The Continental Currency pieces are believed to have been made to circulate in lieu of paper dollars at their time of issue. The exact nature of their monetary role is uncertain; they might have been experimental, or they might have seen circulation. At any rate, this might have been the first dollar-sized coin proposed for the United States. They were possibly struck in Philadelphia from dies engraved by Elisha Gallaudet. As with many early pieces, numerous replicas exist.

| | G | F | VF | EF | AU | Unc. |
|---|---|---|---|---|---|---|
| 1776, CURENCY, pewter *(2 varieties)* . . . . . . . . | $4,000 | $7,000 | $14,000 | $19,000 | $27,500 | $40,000 |
| 1776, CURENCY, silver *(2 known)*. . . . . . . . . . | | 200,000 | | | | |
| 1776, CURRENCY, pewter. . . . . . . . . . . . . . . . | 4,000 | 7,000 | 14,000 | 20,000 | 30,000 | 45,000 |
| 1776, CURRENCY, EG FECIT, pewter. . . . . . . . . | 4,000 | 8,000 | 15,000 | 22,500 | 32,500 | 47,500 |

# SPECULATIVE ISSUES, TOKENS, AND PATTERNS

## Nova Constellatio Coppers

The Nova Constellatio pieces were struck supposedly by order of Gouverneur Morris. Evidence indicates that they were all struck in Birmingham, England, and imported for American circulation as a private business venture.

**1783, CONSTELLATIO,**
**Pointed Rays**

**1783, CONSTELLATIO,**
**Blunt Rays**

**1785, CONSTELLATIO,**
**Blunt Rays**

**1785, CONSTELLATIO,**
**Pointed Rays**

| | VG | F | VF | EF | AU | Unc. |
|---|---|---|---|---|---|---|
| 1783, CONSTELLATIO, Pointed Rays ......... | $55 | $110 | $210 | $450 | $750 | $1,500 |
| 1783, CONSTELATIO, Blunt Rays ............ | 55 | 110 | 225 | 700 | 1,600 | 3,000 |
| 1785, CONSTELLATIO, Pointed Rays ......... | 55 | 110 | 210 | 450 | 750 | 1,500 |
| 1785, CONSTELATIO, Blunt Rays ............ | 55 | 125 | 250 | 750 | 1,750 | 3,500 |

## Immune Columbia Pieces

Nearly all of these are very rare. Many if not most seem to be unofficial, including pieces produced at the private Machin's Mills mint in Newburgh, New York.

1785, Copper,
Star Reverse

1785, George III
Obverse

| | G | VG | F | VF | EF | AU |
|---|---|---|---|---|---|---|
| 1785 Copper, Star Reverse ............... | | | $8,500 | $14,000 | $20,000 | |
| 1785; George III Obverse ................. | $2,500 | $4,750 | 6,000 | 9,000 | | |

1787, IMMUNIS COLUMBIA, Eagle Reverse

| | G | VG | F | VF | EF | AU |
|---|---|---|---|---|---|---|
| 1785, VERMON AUCTORI Obverse, IMMUNE COLUMBIA .. | $3,200 | $5,500 | $7,500 | $20,000 | | |
| 1787, IMMUNIS COLUMBIA, Eagle Reverse ........... | 150 | 375 | 850 | 1,800 | $3,000 | $6,000 |

## Confederatio Coppers

The Confederatio and associated coppers have patriotic motifs and were made in small quantities for circulation. The die with the CONFEDERATIO legend was also combined with other designs such as a bust of George Washington, Libertas et Justitia of 1785, Immunis Columbia of 1786, the New York "Excelsiors," Inimica Tyrannis Americana, and others. In all there were 12 dies struck in 13 combinations. There are two types of the Confederatio reverse. In one instance the stars are contained in a small circle; in the other, larger stars are in a larger circle.

| Typical Obverse | Small Circle Reverse | Large Circle Reverse |

|  | VF |
| --- | --- |
| 1785, Stars in Small Circle, various obverses | $29,000 |
| 1785, Stars in Large Circle, various obverses | 35,000 |

## Speculative Patterns

| 1786, IMMUNIS COLUMBIA | Eagle Reverse | Shield Reverse |

|  | VF | EF |
| --- | --- | --- |
| 1786, IMMUNIS COLUMBIA, Eagle Reverse | $30,000 | $37,500 |
| 1786, IMMUNIS COLUMBIA, Shield Reverse | 22,500 | 30,000 |
| (No date) (1786) Washington Obverse, Shield Reverse | 40,000 | |
| 1786, Eagle Obverse, Shield Reverse | 30,000 | |
| 1786, Washington Obverse, Eagle Reverse *(2 known)* | — | |

# COINAGE OF THE STATES AND VERMONT
## Vermont

Reuben Harmon Jr. was granted permission to coin copper pieces for the Republic of Vermont beginning July 1, 1785. (Vermont would not become a state until 1791.) The franchise was extended for eight years in 1786, but in 1787 production was shifted to Machin's Mills, Newburgh, New York, in which Harmon had a proprietary interest. Although the Vermont coins were legally issued there, most other products of Machin's Mills were counterfeits, some dies for which were combined with Vermont pieces, creating several illogical pieces below, including the 1785 Immune Columbia and the 1788 Georgivs III Rex.

| 1785, IMMUNE COLUMBIA | | 1785–1786, Plow Type |

1786, Baby Head

|  | AG | G | VG | F | VF | EF |
|---|---|---|---|---|---|---|
| 1785, IMMUNE COLUMBIA............... | $1,900 | $3,200 | $5,500 | $7,500 | $17,500 | $30,000 |
| 1785, Plow Type, VERMONTS............. | 80 | 150 | 300 | 425 | 1,400 | 2,600 |
| 1786, Plow Type, VERMONTENSIUM ........ | 65 | 125 | 220 | 325 | 800 | 1,900 |
| 1786, Baby Head...................... | 85 | 170 | 325 | 600 | 1,900 | 5,000 |

1786–1787, Bust Left                    1787, BRITANNIA

1787, Bust Right

|  | AG | G | VG | F | VF | EF |
|---|---|---|---|---|---|---|
| 1786, Bust Left........................ | $30 | $75 | $180 | $400 | $1,200 | $2,000 |
| 1787, Bust Left........................ | 1,200 | 2,500 | 5,500 | 12,500 | 22,000 | — |
| 1787, BRITANNIA....................... | 20 | 55 | 85 | 115 | 225 | 700 |
| 1787, Bust Right *(several varieties)* ......... | 25 | 70 | 135 | 245 | 600 | 1,250 |

1788, Bust Right                    1788, GEORGIVS III REX

*See next page for chart.*

| | AG | G | VG | F | VF | EF |
|---|---|---|---|---|---|---|
| 1788, Bust Right *(several varieties)* . . . . . . . . . | $20 | $60 | $110 | $225 | $450 | $900 |
| 1788, GEORGIVS III REX . . . . . . . . . . . . . . . . . | 125 | 250 | 475 | 1,200 | 2,400 | 6,000 |

*Note:* This piece should not be confused with the common British halfpence with similar design and reverse legend BRITANNIA.

## New Hampshire

New Hampshire was the first of the states to consider the subject of coinage following the Declaration of Independence.

William Moulton was empowered to make a limited quantity of coins of pure copper, authorized by the State House of Representatives in 1776.

| | G | VG |
|---|---|---|
| 1776 New Hampshire Copper . . . . . . . . . . . . . . . . . . . . . . . . . . . . . . . . . . . . . . . . . . . . . . | $50,000 | $75,000 |

## Massachusetts

The coinage of Massachusetts copper cents and half cents in 1787 and 1788 was under the direction of Joshua Witherle. These were the first coins bearing the denomination *cent* as later established by Congress. Many varieties exist, the most valuable being the cent with arrows in the eagle's right talon (on the left side of the coin).

1787 Half Cent       1787 Cent

1788 Half Cent       1788 Cent

| | G | F | VF | EF | AU | Unc. |
|---|---|---|---|---|---|---|
| 1787 Half Cent . . . . . . . . . . . . . . . . . . . . . | $50 | $120 | $270 | $400 | $700 | $1,500 |
| 1787 Cent, Arrows in Right Talon . . . . . . . . . . . | 4,500 | 12,000 | 25,000 | | | |
| 1787 Cent, Arrows in Left Talon *(illustrated)* . . . . | 50 | 120 | 300 | 750 | 1,350 | 2,750 |
| 1788 Half Cent . . . . . . . . . . . . . . . . . . . . . | 50 | 130 | 300 | 500 | 900 | 1,700 |
| 1788 Cent . . . . . . . . . . . . . . . . . . . . . . . | 50 | 130 | 325 | 550 | 1,000 | 2,100 |

## Connecticut

Authority for establishing a mint near New Haven was granted by the state to Samuel Bishop, Joseph Hopkins, James Hillhouse, and John Goodrich in 1785. Today, well over 300 different die varieties are known of Connecticut coppers dated from 1785 to 1788. These pieces circulated widely and effectively; most are seen with significant evidence of circulation.

1785, Bust Facing Right

1785, Bust Facing Left

1786–1787, Mailed Bust Facing Right

1786–1787, Mailed Bust Facing Left

1787, Draped Bust Facing Left

1788, Mailed Bust Facing Right

1788, Mailed Bust Facing Left

1788, Draped Bust Facing Left

*See next page for chart.*

|  | AG | G | VG | F | VF | EF | AU |
|---|---|---|---|---|---|---|---|
| 1785, Bust Facing Left.......... | $30 | $75 | $150 | $275 | $800 | $1,500 | $3,750 |
| 1785, Bust Facing Right ......... | 12 | 30 | 40 | 80 | 275 | 750 | 1,750 |
| 1786, Mailed Bust Facing Right.... | 15 | 40 | 50 | 100 | 275 | 650 | 1,500 |
| 1786, Mailed Bust Facing Left..... | 12 | 30 | 40 | 90 | 200 | 550 | 1,400 |
| 1787, Mailed Bust Facing Right.... | 15 | 40 | 65 | 175 | 475 | 800 | 1,800 |
| 1787, Mailed Bust Facing Left..... | 10 | 25 | 35 | 75 | 200 | 500 | 1,400 |
| 1787, Draped Bust Facing Left .... | 10 | 25 | 35 | 75 | 200 | 500 | 1,200 |
| 1788, Mailed Bust Facing Right.... | 10 | 25 | 50 | 100 | 300 | 700 | 1,400 |
| 1788, Mailed Bust Facing Left..... | 10 | 25 | 32 | 80 | 210 | 550 | 1,350 |
| 1788, Draped Bust Facing Left .... | 10 | 25 | 35 | 100 | 250 | 600 | 1,900 |

## New York and Related Issues
### Brasher Doubloons

Perhaps the most famous pieces coined before the establishment of the U.S. Mint at Philadelphia were those produced by a well-known goldsmith and jeweler, Ephraim Brasher of New York.

Brasher produced a gold piece weighing about 408 grains, approximately equal in value to a Spanish doubloon (about $15.00 in New York currency).

The punch-mark EB appears in either of two positions as illustrated. This mark is found on some foreign gold coins as well, and probably was so used by Brasher as evidence of his testing of their value. Many modern forgeries exist.

|  | EF |
|---|---|
| 1787 New York gold doubloon, EB on Breast............................................. | $2,000,000 |
| 1787 New York gold doubloon, EB on Wing............................................... | 1,500,000 |

### New York Copper Coinage

No coinage was authorized by the State of New York following the Revolutionary War, although several propositions were considered. The only coinage laws passed were those regulating coins already in use. Private mints struck several unauthorized coppers.

|  | G | VG | F | VF | EF |
|---|---|---|---|---|---|
| 1786, NON VI VIRTUTE VICI ........................ | $2,500 | $4,250 | $8,500 | $18,000 | $30,000 |

| | G | VG | F | VF | EF |
|---|---|---|---|---|---|
| 1787 EXCELSIOR Copper, Eagle on Globe Facing Right .... | $1,000 | $2,000 | $4,000 | $12,500 | $25,000 |
| 1787 EXCELSIOR Copper, Eagle on Globe Facing Left ..... | 1,000 | 1,800 | 3,500 | 9,500 | 18,000 |

**1787, George Clinton and New York Arms**     **1787, Indian and New York Arms**     **1787, Indian and Eagle on Globe**

| | G | VG | F | VF | EF |
|---|---|---|---|---|---|
| 1787, George Clinton and New York Arms .............. | $4,500 | $10,000 | $23,000 | $45,000 | $110,000 |
| 1787, Indian and New York Arms.................... | 4,000 | 6,000 | 12,000 | 20,000 | 50,000 |
| 1787, Indian and Eagle on Globe..................... | 4,000 | 6,000 | 12,000 | 18,000 | 35,000 |

## Georgivs/Britannia
### *"Machin's Mills" Copper Halfpennies Made in America*

During the era of American state coinage, James F. Atlee and other coiners minted unauthorized, lightweight, imitation British halfpence. These American-made false coins have the same devices, legends, and, in some cases, dates as genuine regal halfpence, but contain less copper. Overall quality of these pieces is similar to that of British-made imitations, but details are more often poorly rendered or missing. Identification of American-made imitations has been confirmed by identifying punch marks and matching them to those of known engravers.

Dates used on these pieces were often evasive, and are as follows: 1771, 1772, and 1774 through 1776 for the first group; 1747 and 1787 for the second group; and 1776, 1778, 1787, and 1788 for the third group. Pieces generally attributed to Atlee can be identified by a single outline in the crosses (British Union) of Britannia's shield and large triangular dentils along the coin circumference. The more-valuable American-made pieces are not to be confused with the similar English-made George III counterfeits (some of which have identical dates), or with genuine British half-pence dated 1770 to 1775.

Group I coins dated 1771, 1772, and 1774 through 1776 have distinctive bold designs but lack the fine details of the original coins. Planchets are generally of high quality. Group II coins dated 1747 and 1787 are generally poorly made. The 1 in the date is not J-shaped, and the dentils are of various sizes. There are no outlines to the stripes in the shield. Group III coins dated 1776, 1778, 1787, and 1788, struck at Machin's Mills in Newberg, New York, are similar to coins of Group II, with their triangular-shaped dentils. Most have wide dates and berries in the wreath.

| | AG | G | VG | F | VF | EF | AU |
|---|---|---|---|---|---|---|---|
| 1747, GEORGIVS II. Group II . . . . . . . | $80 | $125 | $200 | $450 | $2,000 | $4,000 | — |
| 1771, GEORGIVS III. Group I . . . . . . . | 30 | 50 | 110 | 200 | 750 | 1,200 | $3,000 |
| 1772, GEORGIVS III. Group I . . . . . . . | 35 | 75 | 150 | 300 | 900 | 1,800 | 4,750 |
| 1772, GEORGIUS III. Group I . . . . . . . | 40 | 100 | 180 | 400 | 1,500 | 3,000 | — |
| 1774, GEORGIVS III. Group I . . . . . . . | 25 | 40 | 75 | 150 | 420 | 1,200 | 2,750 |
| 1774, GEORGIUS III. Group I . . . . . . . | 35 | 75 | 135 | 260 | 1,000 | 2,500 | — |
| 1775, GEORGIVS III. Group I . . . . . . . | 25 | 40 | 75 | 150 | 400 | 1,000 | 2,500 |
| 1776, GEORGIVS III. Group III . . . . . . | 90 | 150 | 250 | 500 | 1,400 | 3,500 | — |
| 1776, GEORCIVS III, Small Date . . . . | 600 | 1,200 | 2,500 | 5,000 | 10,000 | — | — |
| 1778, GEORGIVS III. Group III . . . . . . | 25 | 50 | 85 | 200 | 450 | 1,250 | 2,000 |
| 1784, GEORGIVS III . . . . . . . . . . . . . | 100 | 200 | 500 | 900 | 1,800 | 2,750 | 4,000 |
| 1787, GEORGIVS II. Group II . . . . . . . | 25 | 40 | 75 | 120 | 350 | 800 | 1,750 |
| 1787, GEORGIVS III. Group III . . . . . . | 25 | 40 | 75 | 120 | 350 | 800 | 1,750 |
| 1788, GEORGIVS III. Group III . . . . . . | 25 | 40 | 85 | 150 | 375 | 900 | 1,800 |

*Note:* Values shown are what coin dealers pay for the most common varieties in each category. Rare pieces can be worth significantly more. Also see related George III combinations under Connecticut, Vermont, and New York.

## *Nova Eborac Coinage for New York*

| 1787, NOVA EBORAC Reverse, Seated Figure Facing Right | 1787, NOVA EBORAC Reverse, Seated Figure Facing Left |

| | AG | G | F | VF | EF | AU |
|---|---|---|---|---|---|---|
| 1787, NOVA EBORAC, Seated Figure Facing Right . . . | $30 | $55 | $150 | $400 | $900 | $2,000 |
| 1787, NOVA EBORAC, Seated Figure Facing Left . . . . | 27 | 45 | 125 | 325 | 700 | 1,450 |

## New Jersey

On June 1, 1786, the New Jersey General Assembly granted to Thomas Goadsby, Albion Cox, and Walter Mould authority to coin some three million coppers no later than June 1788, on condition that they delivered to the treasurer of the state "one-tenth part of the full sum they shall strike and coin," in quarterly installments. These coppers were to pass current at 15 to the shilling. Produced in significant quantities, these coins are often seen in the market today and are widely collectible, although certain varieties can be rare and especially valuable.

Narrow Shield          Wide Shield

|  | AG | G | F | VF | EF | AU |
|---|---|---|---|---|---|---|
| 1786, Narrow Shield . . . . . . . . . . . . . . . . . . . . . | $12 | $22 | $85 | $200 | $375 | $750 |
| 1786, Wide Shield . . . . . . . . . . . . . . . . . . . . . . | 15 | 35 | 125 | 300 | 850 | 2,000 |

Small Planchet

|  | AG | G | F | VF | EF | AU |
|---|---|---|---|---|---|---|
| 1787, Horse's Head Facing Right . . . . . . . . . . . | $12 | $22 | $85 | $200 | $375 | $750 |

Fox Before Legend

|  | AG | G | F | VF | EF | AU |
|---|---|---|---|---|---|---|
| 1788, Horse's Head Facing Right . . . . . . . . . . . | $12 | $27 | $100 | $275 | $450 | $800 |
| 1788, Similar, Fox in Legend . . . . . . . . . . . . . . | 30 | 75 | 275 | 900 | 2,000 | 4,500 |
| 1788, Horse's Head Facing Left . . . . . . . . . . . . | 85 | 200 | 800 | 2,250 | 6,000 | — |

# PRIVATE TOKENS AFTER CONFEDERATION
## North American Tokens

This piece was struck in Dublin, Ireland. The obverse shows the seated figure of Hibernia facing left. Although dated 1781, it is believed to have been struck early in the next century.

| | VG | F | VF | EF |
|---|---|---|---|---|
| 1781, Copper or brass.................................... | $25 | $50 | $100 | $300 |

## Bar Coppers

The Bar copper is undated and of uncertain origin. It has 13 parallel and unconnected bars on one side. On the other side is the large roman-letter USA monogram. The design was supposedly copied from a Continental Army uniform button.

| | VG | F | VF | EF | AU |
|---|---|---|---|---|---|
| (Undated) (Circa 1785) Bar Copper ................... | $925 | $1,750 | $3,000 | $4,750 | $6,750 |

## Auctori Plebis Tokens

This token is sometimes included with the coins of Connecticut as it greatly resembles issues of that state. It was struck in England by an unknown maker.

| | G | VG | F | VF | EF | AU | Unc. |
|---|---|---|---|---|---|---|---|
| 1787, AUCTORI PLEBIS .......... | $40 | $75 | $125 | $250 | $450 | $900 | $3,750 |

## Mott Store Cards

This 19th century store card has long been considered an early token because of its date (1789). Most scholars believe it was most likely produced circa 1830 as a commemorative of the founding of the Mott Company, and probably served as a business card.

| | VG | F | VF | EF | AU | Unc. |
|---|---|---|---|---|---|---|
| "1789," Mott Token . . . . . . . . . . . . . . . . . . . . . | $45 | $90 | $175 | $250 | $320 | $600 |

## Standish Barry Threepence

Standish Barry, a Baltimore silversmith, circulated a silver threepence in 1790. The tokens were believed to have been an advertising venture at a time when small change was scarce.

| | VG | F | VF | EF |
|---|---|---|---|---|
| 1790 Threepence . . . . . . . . . . . . . . . . . . . . . . . . . . . . . . . . . . . . . . | $5,000 | $11,000 | $25,000 | $45,000 |

## Kentucky Tokens

These tokens were struck in England about 1795. Each star in the triangle represents a state, identified by its initial letter. These pieces are usually called *Kentucky cents* because the letter K (for Kentucky) happens to be at the top. In the 19th century these were often called *triangle tokens,* from the arrangement of the stars. Values are for the normal issue with plain edge; lettered-edge varieties exist and are scarcer.

| | VG | VF | EF | AU | Unc. |
|---|---|---|---|---|---|
| (1792–1794) Copper, Plain Edge . . . . . . . . . . . . . . . . . . . . | $40 | $90 | $125 | $275 | $450 |

## Franklin Press Tokens

This piece is an English tradesman's token, but, being associated with Benjamin Franklin, has accordingly been included in American collections.

| | VG | VF | EF | AU | Unc. |
|---|---|---|---|---|---|
| 1794, Franklin Press Token .......................... | $50 | $100 | $150 | $300 | $480 |

## Talbot, Allum & Lee Cents

Talbot, Allum & Lee, engaged in the India trade and located in New York, placed a large quantity of English-made coppers in circulation during 1794 and 1795. ONE CENT appears on the 1794 issue and on the edge of the 1795 issue.

1794 Cent,
With NEW YORK

1795 Cent

| | G | VG | VF | EF | AU | Unc. |
|---|---|---|---|---|---|---|
| 1794 Cent, With NEW YORK................ | $30 | $40 | $125 | $175 | $300 | $750 |
| 1794 Cent, Without NEW YORK ............. | 200 | 300 | 1,300 | 2,500 | 3,500 | 8,000 |
| 1795 Cent............................. | 25 | 35 | 120 | 150 | 250 | 450 |

# WASHINGTON PORTRAIT PIECES

An interesting series of coins and tokens dated from 1783 to 1795 bear the portrait of George Washington. The likenesses in most instances were faithfully reproduced and were designed to honor Washington. Many of these pieces were of English origin and made later than the dates indicate.

1783,
Military Bust

1783,
Draped Bust

# POST-COLONIAL ISSUES

|  | F | VF | EF | AU | Unc. |
|---|---|---|---|---|---|
| 1783, Military Bust ............................. | $40 | $90 | $180 | $375 | $950 |
| 1783, Draped Bust ............................. | 45 | 100 | 200 | 400 | 1,200 |

**1783, UNITY STATES**

|  | VG | F | VF | EF | AU | Unc. |
|---|---|---|---|---|---|---|
| 1783, UNITY STATES ...................... | $30 | $60 | $100 | $200 | $300 | $800 |

**Undated Double-Head Cent**

|  | VG | F | VF | EF | AU | Unc. |
|---|---|---|---|---|---|---|
| (Undated) Double-Head Cent ............... | $30 | $50 | $100 | $200 | $400 | $1,200 |

| Obverse | Large Eagle Reverse | Small Eagle Reverse |
|---|---|---|

|  | F | VF | EF | AU | Unc. |
|---|---|---|---|---|---|
| 1791 Cent, Large Eagle (Date on Obverse) ............. | $200 | $250 | $350 | $600 | $1,300 |
| 1791 Cent, Small Eagle (Date on Reverse). ............. | 225 | 300 | 400 | 650 | 1,500 |

|  | F | VF | EF | AU |
|---|---|---|---|---|
| 1791 Liverpool Halfpenny, Lettered Edge. ...................... | $700 | $850 | $1,600 | $2,500 |

| | | |
|---|---|---|
| 1792, Eagle With Stars, copper . . . . . . . . . . . . . . . . . . . . . . . . . . . . . . . . . . . . . . . . . . . . . . . . . . . . . . . . | | — |
| 1792, Eagle With Stars, silver . . . . . . . . . . . . . . . . . . . . . . . . . . . . . . . . . . . . . . . . . . . . . . . . . . . . . . . . . . | | — |
| 1792, Eagle With Stars, gold *(unique)* . . . . . . . . . . . . . . . . . . . . . . . . . . . . . . . . . . . . . . . . . . . . . . . . . . . . | | — |

**(1792) Undated Cent,
WASHINGTON BORN VIRGINIA**

**1792 Cent,
WASHINGTON PRESIDENT**

| | VG | F | VF |
|---|---|---|---|
| (1792) Undated Cent, WASHINGTON BORN VIRGINIA, copper . . . . . . . . . . . . . . . . . | $550 | $1,000 | $2,200 |
| 1792 Cent, WASHINGTON PRESIDENT, Plain Edge . . . . . . . . . . . . . . . . . . . . . . . . . . | 1,500 | 3,750 | 7,500 |

**1792 Getz Pattern**　　　　**1793 Ship Halfpenny**　　　　**1795 Halfpenny, Grate Token**

| | VG | F | VF | EF | AU | Unc. |
|---|---|---|---|---|---|---|
| 1792, Getz Pattern, copper . . . . . . . . . . . . . . . | $3,500 | $6,500 | $14,000 | $25,000 | | |
| 1793 Ship Halfpenny, Lettered Edge . . . . . . . . . | 35 | 100 | 200 | 300 | $450 | $1,600 |
| 1795, Grate Token, Lettered Edge . . . . . . . . . . . | 40 | 80 | 150 | 360 | 750 | 1,100 |
| 1795, Grate Token, Reeded Edge . . . . . . . . . . . . | 25 | 40 | 80 | 150 | 200 | 350 |

| | F | VF | EF | AU | Unc. |
|---|---|---|---|---|---|
| 1795, LIBERTY AND SECURITY Halfpenny, Plain Edge . . . . . | $70 | $150 | $300 | $600 | $1,500 |
| 1795, LIBERTY AND SECURITY Halfpenny, Lettered Edge . . . | 65 | 125 | 275 | 550 | 1,500 |
| (1795) Undated, LIBERTY AND SECURITY Penny . . . . . . . . . . | 150 | 250 | 400 | 750 | 1,500 |

| | G | F | VF | EF | AU |
|---|---|---|---|---|---|
| (1795) NORTH WALES Halfpenny . . . . . . . . . . . . . . . . . . . . . | $50 | $100 | $250 | $750 | $1,500 |

| | F | VF | EF | AU | Unc. |
|---|---|---|---|---|---|
| SUCCESS Medal, Large, Plain or Reeded Edge . . . . . . . . . . | $125 | $250 | $425 | $700 | $1,500 |
| SUCCESS Medal, Small, Plain or Reeded Edge . . . . . . . . . . | 100 | 200 | 350 | 650 | 1,400 |

# FUGIO CENTS

The first coins issued by authority of the United States were the 1787 "Fugio" coppers. The legends have been credited to Benjamin Franklin by many, and the coins, as a consequence, have been referred to as *Franklin cents.*

1787, With
Pointed Rays

1787, With
Club Rays

|  | G | VG | F | VF | EF | AU | Unc. |
|---|---|---|---|---|---|---|---|
| Pointed Rays, STATES UNITED at Side of Circle | | | | | | | |
| *(illustrated)* . . . . . . . . . . . . . . . . . . . . . . . . . . . . | $150 | $250 | $400 | $750 | $1,200 | $1,500 | $2,300 |
| Pointed Rays, UNITED STATES at Side of Circle . . . . . | 200 | 300 | 500 | 850 | 1,300 | 1,600 | 2,500 |
| Club Rays, Rounded Ends . . . . . . . . . . . . . . . . . . . . | 300 | 500 | 750 | 1,250 | 1,800 | 3,500 | — |

The half cent was authorized to be coined April 2, 1792. Originally the weight was to have been 132 grains, but this was changed to 104 grains by the Act of January 14, 1793, before coinage commenced. The weight was again changed to 84 grains January 26, 1796, by presidential proclamation in conformity with the Act of March 3, 1795. Coinage was discontinued by the Act of February 21, 1857. All were coined at the Philadelphia Mint.

## LIBERTY CAP (1793–1797)

**AG-3 About Good:** Clear enough to identify.
**G-4 Good:** Outline of bust of Liberty clear, no details. Date readable. Reverse lettering incomplete.
**VG-8 Very Good:** Some hair details. Reverse lettering complete.
**F-12 Fine:** Most of hair detail visible. Leaves worn, but all visible.
**VF-20 Very Fine:** Hair near ear and forehead worn, other areas distinct. Some details in leaves visible.
**EF-40 Extremely Fine:** Light wear on highest parts of head and wreath.
**AU-50 About Uncirculated:** Only a trace of wear on Liberty's face.

Head Facing Left (1793)

| | Mintage | AG-3 | G-4 | VG-8 | F-12 | VF-20 | EF-40 | AU-50 |
|---|---|---|---|---|---|---|---|---|
| 1793 . . . . . . . . . . . . . . . . . . .35,334 | | $1,750 | $2,500 | $3,500 | $5,500 | $8,000 | $13,500 | $20,000 |

Head Facing Right (1794–1797)

| Pole to Cap | Punctuated Date | No Pole to Cap |
|---|---|---|

| | Mintage | AG-3 | G-4 | VG-8 | F-12 | VF-20 | EF-40 | AU-50 |
|---|---|---|---|---|---|---|---|---|
| 1794 . . . . . . . . . . . . . . . . . . . . . .81,600 | | $275 | $425 | $700 | $1,200 | $1,500 | $4,000 | $8,000 |
| 1795, All kinds. . . . . . . . . . . . . .139,690 | | | | | | | | |
| 1795, Lettered Edge, With Pole . . . . . . | | 200 | 375 | 675 | 1,000 | 1,525 | 3,400 | 5,500 |
| 1795, Lettered Edge, Punctuated Date | | 300 | 475 | 675 | 1,000 | 1,575 | 4,450 | 7,600 |
| 1795, Plain Edge, Punctuated Date . . . | | 200 | 400 | 650 | 800 | 1,525 | 3,000 | 6,800 |
| 1795, Plain Edge, No Pole . . . . . . . . . . | | 150 | 250 | 600 | 800 | 1,275 | 3,000 | 5,100 |
| 1796, With Pole . . . . . . . . . . . . . . . .1,390 | | 8,500 | 13,500 | 18,500 | 27,500 | 37,500 | 55,000 | 70,000 |
| 1796, No Pole . . . . . . . . . . . . . . . .5,090 | | 20,000 | 25,000 | 35,000 | 80,000 | 110,000 | 150,000 | 225,000 |

* Included in number above.

| | | 1797, 1 Above 1, Plain Edge | | 1797, Plain Edge | | | |

| | Mintage | AG-3 | G-4 | VG-8 | F-12 | VF-20 | EF-40 | AU-50 |
|---|---|---|---|---|---|---|---|---|
| 1797, All kinds. . . . . . . . . .127,840 | | | | | | | | |
| 1797, 1 Above 1, Plain Edge . . . . | | $165 | $300 | $600 | $800 | $1,350 | $3,000 | $5,100 |
| 1797, Plain Edge. . . . . . . . . . . . | | 145 | 300 | 650 | 900 | 1,500 | 3,000 | 5,100 |
| 1797, Lettered Edge . . . . . . . . . | | 500 | 850 | 1,500 | 3,500 | 9,350 | 24,000 | |
| 1797, Gripped Edge. . . . . . . . . . | | 25,000 | 50,000 | 85,000 | | | | |

## DRAPED BUST (1800–1808)

**AG-3 About Good:** Clear enough to identify.
**G-4 Good:** Outline of bust of Liberty clear, few details, date readable. Reverse lettering worn and incomplete.
**VG-8 Very Good:** Some drapery visible. Date and legends complete.
**F-12 Fine:** Shoulder drapery and hair over brow worn smooth.
**VF-20 Very Fine:** Only slight wear in previously mentioned areas. Slight wear on reverse.
**EF-40 Extremely Fine:** Light wear on highest parts of head and wreath.
**AU-50 About Uncirculated:** Wear slight on hair above forehead.

| | | | 1st Reverse | | 2nd Reverse | | |

| | Mintage | AG-3 | G-4 | VG-8 | F-12 | VF-20 | EF-40 | AU-50 |
|---|---|---|---|---|---|---|---|---|
| 1800 . . . . . . . . . . . . . . . . .202,908 | | $35 | $60 | $80 | $120 | $175 | $450 | $500 |
| 1802, 2 Over 0 . . . . . . . . . . .20,266 | | 350 | 525 | 1,275 | 2,500 | 6,000 | 13,600 | |
| 1803 . . . . . . . . . . . . . . . . . .92,000 | | 35 | 60 | 80 | 115 | 225 | 550 | 1,000 |

| Plain 4 | | Crosslet 4 | | Stems to Wreath | | Stemless Wreath | |

| | Mintage | AG-3 | G-4 | VG-8 | F-12 | VF-20 | EF-40 | AU-50 |
|---|---|---|---|---|---|---|---|---|
| 1804, All kinds. . . . . . . . . . . . 1,055,312 | | | | | | | | |
| 1804, Plain 4, Stems to Wreath . . . . . . | | $60 | $95 | $180 | $275 | $325 | $800 | $1,700 |
| 1804, Plain 4, Stemless Wreath. . . . . . | | 30 | 60 | 75 | 95 | 130 | 275 | 425 |
| 1804, Crosslet 4, Stemless Wreath . . . | | 30 | 60 | 75 | 95 | 130 | 275 | 425 |
| 1804, Crosslet 4, Stems to Wreath . . . | | 30 | 60 | 75 | 95 | 130 | 275 | 425 |

| 1804, "Spiked Chin" | | Small 5 | | Large 5 | | |

| | Mintage | AG-3 | G-4 | VG-8 | F-12 | VF-20 | EF-40 | AU-50 |
|---|---|---|---|---|---|---|---|---|
| 1804, "Spiked Chin" . . . . . . . . . . . . . .* | | $30 | $60 | $95 | $135 | $170 | $275 | $650 |
| 1805, All kinds. . . . . . . . . . . . . .814,464 | | | | | | | | |
| 1805, Medium 5, Stemless Wreath . . . | | 30 | 60 | 75 | 95 | 130 | 275 | 425 |
| 1805, Small 5, Stems to Wreath . . . . . | | 300 | 600 | 1,000 | 2,400 | 5,400 | 11,000 | 23,000 |
| 1805, Large 5, Stems to Wreath . . . . . | | 30 | 60 | 75 | 105 | 175 | 300 | 500 |

\* Included in "1804, All kinds" mintage (previous page).

| Small 6 | | Large 6 | | 1808, 8 Over 7 | | Normal Date | |

| | Mintage | AG-3 | G-4 | VG-8 | F-12 | VF-20 | EF-40 | AU-50 |
|---|---|---|---|---|---|---|---|---|
| 1806, All kinds. . . . . . . . . . . . . .356,000 | | | | | | | | |
| 1806, Small 6, Stems to Wreath . . . . . | | $55 | $150 | $300 | $500 | $800 | $2,250 | $3,000 |
| 1806, Small 6, Stemless Wreath . . . . . | | 30 | 55 | 60 | 85 | 150 | 250 | 500 |
| 1806, Large 6, Stems to Wreath . . . . . | | 30 | 55 | 60 | 85 | 150 | 250 | 500 |
| 1807 . . . . . . . . . . . . . . . . . . . . .476,000 | | 30 | 55 | 60 | 85 | 150 | 300 | 550 |
| 1808, Normal Date . . . . . . . . . .400,000 | | 30 | 55 | 60 | 85 | 150 | 300 | 750 |
| 1808, 8 Over 7 . . . . . . . . . . . . . . . . .* | | 60 | 135 | 225 | 300 | 900 | 2,500 | 8,000 |

\* Included in number below.

# CLASSIC HEAD (1809–1836)

**G-4 Good:** LIBERTY only partly visible on hair band. Lettering, date, and stars worn but visible.
**VG-8 Very Good:** LIBERTY entirely visible on hair band. Lower curls worn.
**F-12 Fine:** Only partial wear on LIBERTY, and hair at top worn in spots.
**VF-20 Very Fine:** Lettering clear-cut. Hair only slightly worn.
**EF-40 Extremely Fine:** Light wear on highest points of hair and leaves.
**AU-50 About Uncirculated:** Sharp hair detail with only a trace of wear on higher points.
**MS-60 Uncirculated:** Typical brown to red surface. No trace of wear.
**MS-63 Choice Uncirculated:** Well-defined color, brown to red. No traces of wear.

1828, 13 Stars        1828, 12 Stars

*Dealers often pay more than the prices shown for brilliant or red Uncirculated coins, and less for spotted, cleaned, or discolored pieces.*

| | Mintage | AG-3 | G-4 | VG-8 | F-12 | VF-20 | EF-40 | AU-50 | MS-60 | MS-63 |
|---|---|---|---|---|---|---|---|---|---|---|
| 1809 . . . . . . . . . . . . . 1,154,572 | | $20 | $35 | $50 | $60 | $70 | $105 | $150 | $400 | $1,100 |
| 1810 . . . . . . . . . . . . . . . .215,000 | | 20 | 35 | 50 | 90 | 160 | 350 | 550 | 1,400 | 2,200 |
| 1811 . . . . . . . . . . . . . . . .63,140 | | 145 | 275 | 500 | 1,000 | 1,500 | 3,500 | 7,500 | 25,000 | 75,000 |

*Chart continued on next page.*

| | Mintage | G-4 | VG-8 | F-12 | VF-20 | EF-40 | AU-50 | MS-60 | MS-63 | PF-63 |
|---|---|---|---|---|---|---|---|---|---|---|
| 1825 . . . . . . . . . . . . . . 63,000 | | $35 | $50 | $60 | $75 | $100 | $250 | $500 | $1,500 | |
| 1826 . . . . . . . . . . . . . 234,000 | | 35 | 50 | 60 | 70 | 85 | 125 | 275 | 425 | |
| 1828, 13 Stars. . . . . . . 606,000 | | 35 | 50 | 60 | 70 | 75 | 120 | 190 | 450 | |
| 1828, 12 Stars. . . . . . . . . . .* | | 35 | 50 | 75 | 100 | 125 | 225 | 650 | 1,100 | |
| 1829 . . . . . . . . . . . . . 487,000 | | 35 | 50 | 60 | 70 | 85 | 125 | 225 | 425 | |
| 1831 . . . . . . . . . . . . . . . 2,200 | | | | | | | | | | — |
| 1832 . . . . . . . . . . . . . . 51,000 | | 35 | 50 | 60 | 70 | 80 | 115 | 175 | 300 | $10,000 |
| 1833 . . . . . . . . . . . . . 103,000 | | 35 | 50 | 60 | 70 | 80 | 115 | 175 | 300 | 4,500 |
| 1834 . . . . . . . . . . . . . 141,000 | | 35 | 50 | 60 | 70 | 80 | 115 | 175 | 300 | 3,000 |
| 1835 . . . . . . . . . . . . . 398,000 | | 35 | 50 | 60 | 70 | 80 | 115 | 175 | 300 | 3,000 |
| 1836 . . . . . . . . . . . . . . . . . . . | | | | | | | | | | 7,500 |

\* Included in number above.

## BRAIDED HAIR (1840–1857)

**VG-8 Very Good:** Beads in hair uniformly distinct. Hair lines visible in spots.
**F-12 Fine:** Hair lines above ear worn. Beads sharp.
**VF-20 Very Fine:** Lowest curl worn; hair otherwise distinct.
**EF-40 Extremely Fine:** Light wear on highest points of hair and on leaves.
**AU-50 About Uncirculated:** Very slight trace of wear on hair above Liberty's ear.
**MS-60 Uncirculated:** No trace of wear. Clear luster.
**MS-63 Choice Uncirculated:** No trace of wear.
**PF-63 Choice Proof:** Nearly perfect; only light blemishes.

*Dealers often pay more than the prices shown for brilliant or red Uncirculated coins, and less for spotted, cleaned, or discolored pieces.*

| | PF-63 | | | PF-63 |
|---|---|---|---|---|
| 1840, Original . . . . . . . . . . . . . . . . . . . . . | $6,500 | 1845, Original . . . . . . . . . . . . . . . . . . . . . | $9,500 |
| 1840, Restrike. . . . . . . . . . . . . . . . . . . . . | 4,500 | 1845, Restrike. . . . . . . . . . . . . . . . . . . . . | 5,500 |
| 1841, Original . . . . . . . . . . . . . . . . . . . . . | 6,500 | 1846, Original . . . . . . . . . . . . . . . . . . . . . | 7,500 |
| 1841, Restrike. . . . . . . . . . . . . . . . . . . . . | 4,500 | 1846, Restrike. . . . . . . . . . . . . . . . . . . . . | 5,500 |
| 1842, Original . . . . . . . . . . . . . . . . . . . . . | 6,500 | 1847, Original . . . . . . . . . . . . . . . . . . . . . | 4,500 |
| 1842, Restrike. . . . . . . . . . . . . . . . . . . . . | 4,500 | 1847, Restrike. . . . . . . . . . . . . . . . . . . . . | 4,000 |
| 1843, Original . . . . . . . . . . . . . . . . . . . . . | 6,500 | 1848, Original . . . . . . . . . . . . . . . . . . . . . | 8,500 |
| 1843, Restrike. . . . . . . . . . . . . . . . . . . . . | 4,500 | 1848, Restrike. . . . . . . . . . . . . . . . . . . . . | 4,500 |
| 1844, Original . . . . . . . . . . . . . . . . . . . . . | 6,500 | 1849, Original, Small Date. . . . . . . . . . . . . | 5,000 |
| 1844, Restrike. . . . . . . . . . . . . . . . . . . . . | 4,500 | 1849, Restrike, Small Date . . . . . . . . . . . . . | 5,000 |

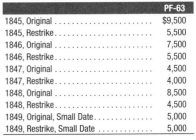

**Small Date**      **Large Date**

| | Mintage | G-4 | VG-8 | F-12 | VF-20 | EF-40 | AU-50 | MS-60 | MS-63 | PF-63 |
|---|---|---|---|---|---|---|---|---|---|---|
| 1849, Large Date. . . . . . . 39,864 | | $35 | $45 | $50 | $60 | $75 | $125 | $225 | $500 | — |
| 1850 . . . . . . . . . . . . . . . . 39,812 | | 50 | 75 | 100 | 150 | 250 | 350 | 1,000 | 1,750 | $4,500 |
| 1851 . . . . . . . . . . . . . . 147,672 | | 35 | 45 | 50 | 60 | 65 | 85 | 150 | 300 | 3,000 |
| 1852 . . . . . . . . . . . . . . . . . . . . . | | | | | | | | | | 3,500 |
| 1853 . . . . . . . . . . . . . . 129,694 | | 35 | 45 | 50 | 60 | 65 | 85 | 150 | 300 | |
| 1854 . . . . . . . . . . . . . . . . 55,358 | | 35 | 45 | 50 | 60 | 65 | 85 | 150 | 300 | 4,500 |
| 1855 . . . . . . . . . . . . . . . . 56,500 | | 35 | 45 | 50 | 60 | 65 | 85 | 150 | 300 | 3,000 |
| 1856 . . . . . . . . . . . . . . . . 40,430 | | 35 | 45 | 50 | 60 | 65 | 90 | 165 | 375 | 3,000 |
| 1857 . . . . . . . . . . . . . . . . 35,180 | | 35 | 45 | 50 | 80 | 100 | 135 | 250 | 450 | 3,000 |

Cents and half cents were the first coins struck at the United States Mint. Coinage began in 1793 with laws stating that the cent should weigh exactly twice as much as the half cent. Large cents are dated every year from 1793 to 1857 with the exception of 1815, when a lack of copper prevented production. All were coined at the Philadelphia Mint. Varieties listed are those most significant to collectors. Numerous other die varieties may be found, as each of the early dies was individually made.

## FLOWING HAIR (1793)

**AG-3 About Good:** Date and devices clear enough to identify.
**G-4 Good:** Lettering worn but readable. No detail on bust.
**VG-8 Very Good:** Date and lettering distinct, some details of head visible.
**F-12 Fine:** About half of hair and other details visible.
**VF-20 Very Fine:** Ear visible, most details visible.
**EF-40 Extremely Fine:** Wear evident on highest points of hair and back of temple.

### Chain Reverse (1793)

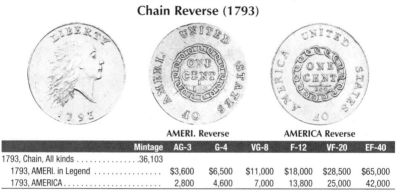

AMERI. Reverse     AMERICA Reverse

| | Mintage | AG-3 | G-4 | VG-8 | F-12 | VF-20 | EF-40 |
|---|---|---|---|---|---|---|---|
| 1793, Chain, All kinds . . . . . . . . . . . . . .36,103 | | | | | | | |
| 1793, AMERI. in Legend . . . . . . . . . . . . . . . | | $3,600 | $6,500 | $11,000 | $18,000 | $28,500 | $65,000 |
| 1793, AMERICA . . . . . . . . . . . . . . . . . . . . . . | 2,800 | 4,600 | 7,000 | 13,800 | 25,000 | 42,000 |

### Wreath Reverse (1793)

Strawberry Leaf Variety

| | Mintage | AG-3 | G-4 | VG-8 | F-12 | VF-20 | EF-40 |
|---|---|---|---|---|---|---|---|
| 1793, Wreath, All kinds . . . . . . . . . . . . . .63,353 | | | | | | | |
| 1793, Vine and Bars Edge . . . . . . . . . . . . . . | | $1,100 | $2,150 | $3,000 | $4,250 | $6,700 | $16,000 |
| 1793, Lettered Edge . . . . . . . . . . . . . . . . . . | 1,100 | 2,150 | 3,000 | 4,250 | 6,700 | 16,000 |
| 1793, Strawberry Leaf. . . . . . . . . . *(4 known)* | — | — | — | | | |

## LIBERTY CAP (1793–1796)

**1793, Vine and Bars Edge**
*Chain and Wreath types only.*

**Lettered Edge (1793–1795)**
**ONE HUNDRED FOR A DOLLAR**

*Entry continued on next page.*

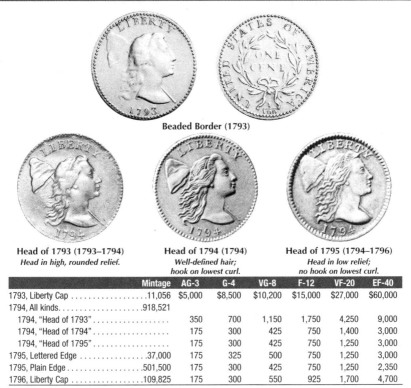

**Beaded Border (1793)**

**Head of 1793 (1793–1794)**
*Head in high, rounded relief.*

**Head of 1794 (1794)**
*Well-defined hair;*
*hook on lowest curl.*

**Head of 1795 (1794–1796)**
*Head in low relief;*
*no hook on lowest curl.*

| | Mintage | AG-3 | G-4 | VG-8 | F-12 | VF-20 | EF-40 |
|---|---|---|---|---|---|---|---|
| 1793, Liberty Cap . . . . . . . . . . . . . . . . .11,056 | $5,000 | $8,500 | $10,200 | $15,000 | $27,000 | $60,000 |
| 1794, All kinds. . . . . . . . . . . . . . . . . .918,521 | | | | | | |
|     1794, "Head of 1793" . . . . . . . . . . . . . . . . . | 350 | 700 | 1,150 | 1,750 | 4,250 | 9,000 |
|     1794, "Head of 1794" . . . . . . . . . . . . . . . . . | 175 | 300 | 425 | 750 | 1,400 | 3,000 |
|     1794, "Head of 1795" . . . . . . . . . . . . . . . . . | 175 | 300 | 425 | 750 | 1,250 | 3,000 |
| 1795, Lettered Edge . . . . . . . . . . . . . . .37,000 | 175 | 325 | 500 | 750 | 1,250 | 3,000 |
| 1795, Plain Edge . . . . . . . . . . . . . . . . .501,500 | 175 | 300 | 425 | 750 | 1,250 | 2,350 |
| 1796, Liberty Cap . . . . . . . . . . . . . . . .109,825 | 175 | 300 | 550 | 925 | 1,700 | 4,700 |

# DRAPED BUST (1796–1807)

**AG-3 About Good:** Clear enough to identify.
**G-4 Good:** Lettering worn, but clear; date clear. Bust lacking in detail.
**VG-8 Very Good:** Drapery on Liberty partly visible. Less wear in date and lettering.
**F-12 Fine:** Hair over brow smooth; some detail showing in other parts of hair.
**VF-20 Very Fine:** Hair lines slightly worn. Hair over brow better defined.
**EF-40 Extremely Fine:** Hair above forehead and left of eye outlined and detailed. Only slight wear on olive leaves.

**LIHERTY Error**

| | Mintage | AG-3 | G-4 | VG-8 | F-12 | VF-20 | EF-40 |
|---|---|---|---|---|---|---|---|
| 1796, Draped Bust . . . . . . . . . . . . . . .363,375 | $125 | $175 | $275 | $725 | $1,100 | $3,150 |
| 1796, LIHERTY Error . . . . . . . . . . . . . . . . . . . * | 375 | 1,000 | 2,000 | 2,700 | 4,500 | 10,000 |

* Included in number above.

| Gripped Edge | | With Stems | | Stemless | |
|---|---|---|---|---|---|

| | Mintage | AG-3 | G-4 | VG-8 | F-12 | VF-20 | EF-40 |
|---|---|---|---|---|---|---|---|
| 1797, All kinds. . . . . . . . . . . . . . . . . . .897,510 | | | | | | | |
| 1797, Gripped Edge, 1795-Style Reverse . . . | | $100 | $200 | $300 | $600 | $1,000 | $2,500 |
| 1797, Plain Edge, 1795-Style Reverse. . . . . . | | 240 | 440 | 800 | 1,100 | 1,850 | 3,000 |
| 1797, 1797 Reverse, With Stems. . . . . . . . . | | 65 | 125 | 200 | 450 | 850 | 1,700 |
| 1797, 1797 Reverse, Stemless . . . . . . . . . . | | 125 | 210 | 450 | 600 | 1,275 | 5,000 |

| **1798, 8 Over 7** | **1799, 9 Over 8** | **1800 Over 1798** | **1800, 80 Over 79** |
|---|---|---|---|

| | Mintage | AG-3 | G-4 | VG-8 | F-12 | VF-20 | EF-40 |
|---|---|---|---|---|---|---|---|
| 1798, All kinds. . . . . . . . . . . . . . . . . 1,841,745 | | | | | | | |
| 1798, 8 Over 7 . . . . . . . . . . . . . . . . . . . . . . | | $160 | $300 | $475 | $700 | $1,350 | $2,800 |
| 1798. . . . . . . . . . . . . . . . . . . . . . . . . . . . . | | 60 | 95 | 190 | 360 | 510 | 1,060 |
| 1799, 9 Over 8 . . . . . . . . . . . . . . . . . . . . . . | * | 3,000 | 5,100 | 9,000 | 17,000 | 32,400 | 126,000 |
| 1799, Normal Date . . . . . . . . . . . . . . . . . . . . | * | 2,400 | 3,400 | 7,200 | 10,600 | 20,700 | 90,000 |
| 1800, All kinds. . . . . . . . . . . . . . . . . 2,822,175 | | | | | | | |
| 1800, 1800 Over 1798 . . . . . . . . . . . . . . . . | | 45 | 65 | 120 | 255 | 600 | 2,975 |
| 1800, 80 Over 79 . . . . . . . . . . . . . . . . . . . | | 45 | 65 | 105 | 190 | 425 | 2,125 |
| 1800, Normal Date . . . . . . . . . . . . . . . . . . | | 45 | 65 | 105 | 190 | 425 | 1,950 |

* Included in "1798, All kinds," mintage.

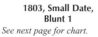

| Fraction 1/000 | Corrected Fraction | 1801 Reverse, 3 Errors |
|---|---|---|

| | Mintage | AG-3 | G-4 | VG-8 | F-12 | VF-20 | EF-40 |
|---|---|---|---|---|---|---|---|
| 1801, All kinds. . . . . . . . . . . . . . . . . 1,362,837 | | | | | | | |
| 1801, Normal Reverse. . . . . . . . . . . . . . . . . | | $45 | $65 | $115 | $235 | $360 | $1,350 |
| 1801, 3 Errors: 1/000, One Stem, and IINITED | | 90 | 250 | 500 | 1,100 | 2,500 | 5,000 |
| 1801, Fraction 1/000. . . . . . . . . . . . . . . . . | | 65 | 100 | 205 | 360 | 850 | 3,400 |
| 1801, 1/100 Over 1/000 . . . . . . . . . . . . . . | | 70 | 115 | 235 | 425 | 1,025 | 3,800 |
| 1802, All kinds. . . . . . . . . . . . . . . . . 3,435,100 | | | | | | | |
| 1802, Normal Reverse. . . . . . . . . . . . . . . . . | | 50 | 80 | 100 | 160 | 325 | 900 |
| 1802, Fraction 1/000. . . . . . . . . . . . . . . . . | | 50 | 80 | 120 | 275 | 450 | 1,500 |
| 1802, Stemless Wreath . . . . . . . . . . . . . . . | | 45 | 70 | 120 | 220 | 475 | 950 |

| **1803, Small Date, Blunt 1** | **1803, Large Date, Pointed 1** | **Small Fraction** | **Large Fraction** |
|---|---|---|---|

*See next page for chart.*

| | Mintage | AG-3 | G-4 | VG-8 | F-12 | VF-20 | EF-40 |
|---|---|---|---|---|---|---|---|
| 1803, All kinds. . . . . . . . . . . . . . . . . | 3,131,691 | | | | | | |
| 1803, Small Date, Small Fraction. . . . . . . . . | $45 | $60 | $100 | $210 | $350 | $850 |
| 1803, Small Date, Large Fraction . . . . . . . . | 45 | 60 | 100 | 210 | 350 | 850 |
| 1803, Large Date, Small Fraction . . . . . . . . | 4,250 | 6,600 | 11,000 | 13,500 | 18,000 | 40,000 |
| 1803, Large Date, Large Fraction . . . . . . . . | 125 | 210 | 340 | 750 | 1,875 | 6,375 |
| 1803, 1/100 Over 1/000 . . . . . . . . . . . . . . | 60 | 110 | 170 | 340 | 725 | 1,450 |
| 1803, Stemless Wreath . . . . . . . . . . . . . . . | 50 | 85 | 125 | 230 | 350 | 900 |

**Broken Dies**

*All genuine 1804 cents have crosslet 4 in date and a large fraction.*
*The 0 in date is in line with O in OF on reverse.*

| | Mintage | AG-3 | G-4 | VG-8 | F-12 | VF-20 | EF-40 |
|---|---|---|---|---|---|---|---|
| 1804 **(a)** . . . . . . . . . . . . . . . . . . . . . . . | 96,500 | $1,000 | $1,800 | $2,800 | $4,000 | $7,000 | $15,000 |
| 1805 . . . . . . . . . . . . . . . . . . . . . . . . | 941,116 | 45 | 60 | 80 | 170 | 340 | 775 |
| 1806 . . . . . . . . . . . . . . . . . . . . . . . . | 348,000 | 45 | 60 | 75 | 250 | 410 | 1,325 |

**a.** Values shown are for coins with normal or broken dies.

| **Small 1807, 7 Over 6** | **Large 1807, 7 Over 6** |
|---|---|
| **(Blunt 1)** | **(Pointed 1)** |

| | Mintage | AG-3 | G-4 | VG-8 | F-12 | VF-20 | EF-40 |
|---|---|---|---|---|---|---|---|
| 1807, All kinds. . . . . . . . . . . . . . . . . | 829,221 | | | | | | |
| 1807, Small 7 Over 6, Blunt 1 . . . . . . . . . . . | $1,300 | $1,900 | $4,500 | $15,000 | $20,000 | |
| 1807, Large 7 Over 6 . . . . . . . . . . . . . . . | 60 | 120 | 170 | 300 | 500 | $900 |
| 1807, Small Fraction . . . . . . . . . . . . . . . . . | 60 | 80 | 140 | 240 | 800 | 6,400 |
| 1807, Large Fraction . . . . . . . . . . . . . . . . . | 45 | 60 | 90 | 170 | 375 | 850 |

# CLASSIC HEAD (1808–1814)

**AG-3 About Good:** Details clear enough to identify.

**G-4 Good:** Legends, stars, and date worn, but plain.

**VG-8 Very Good:** LIBERTY all readable. Liberty's ear visible. Details worn but plain.

**F-12 Fine:** Hair on forehead and before ear nearly smooth. Ear and hair under ear sharp.

**VF-20 Very Fine:** Some detail in all hair lines. Slight wear on leaves on reverse.

**EF-40 Extremely Fine:** All hair lines sharp. Very slight wear on high points.

**LARGE CENTS**

|  | Mintage | AG-3 | G-4 | VG-8 | F-12 | VF-20 | EF-40 |
|---|---|---|---|---|---|---|---|
| 1808 . . . . . . . . . . . . . . . . . . . . . . . 1,007,000 | | $65 | $105 | $170 | $350 | $625 | $1,500 |
| 1809 . . . . . . . . . . . . . . . . . . . . . . . . 222,867 | | 100 | 170 | 375 | 650 | 1,100 | 2,750 |

| 1810, 10 Over 09 | 1810, Normal Date | 1811, Last 1 Over 0 | 1811, Normal Date |
|---|---|---|---|

|  | Mintage | AG-3 | G-4 | VG-8 | F-12 | VF-20 | EF-40 |
|---|---|---|---|---|---|---|---|
| 1810, All kinds . . . . . . . . . . . . . . . . 1,458,500 | | | | | | | |
| 1810, 10 Over 09 . . . . . . . . . . . . . . . . . . . . | | $65 | $105 | $170 | $410 | $765 | $1,600 |
| 1810, Normal Date . . . . . . . . . . . . . . . . . . . | | 65 | 105 | 170 | 350 | 650 | 1,500 |
| 1811, All kinds . . . . . . . . . . . . . . . . . 218,025 | | | | | | | |
| 1811, Last 1 Over 0 . . . . . . . . . . . . . . . . . . | | 125 | 210 | 340 | 550 | 1,250 | 3,500 |
| 1811, Normal Date . . . . . . . . . . . . . . . . . . . | | 85 | 140 | 250 | 400 | 850 | 1,850 |
| 1812 . . . . . . . . . . . . . . . . . . . . . . . 1,075,500 | | 65 | 105 | 175 | 325 | 600 | 1,400 |
| 1813 . . . . . . . . . . . . . . . . . . . . . . . . 418,000 | | 65 | 105 | 175 | 325 | 600 | 1,500 |
| 1814 . . . . . . . . . . . . . . . . . . . . . . . . 357,830 | | 65 | 105 | 175 | 325 | 600 | 1,400 |

# MODIFIED LIBERTY HEAD (1816–1857)

**G-4 Good:** Details on Liberty's head partly visible. Even wear in date and legends.
**VG-8 Very Good:** LIBERTY, date, stars, and legends clear. Part of hair cord visible.
**F-12 Fine:** All hair lines visible. Hair cords uniformly visible.
**VF-20 Very Fine:** Hair cords only slightly worn. Hair lines only partly worn, all well defined.
**EF-40 Extremely Fine:** Both hair cords stand out sharply. All hair lines sharp.
**AU-50 About Uncirculated:** Only traces of wear on hair and highest points on leaves and bow.
**MS-60 Uncirculated:** Typical brown surface. No trace of wear.
**MS-63 Choice Uncirculated:** Some distracting contact marks or blemishes in prime focal areas. Impaired luster possible.

## Matron Head (1816–1835)

| 1817, 13 Stars | 1817, 15 Stars |
|---|---|

*Dealers often pay more than the prices shown for brilliant or red Uncirculated coins, and less for spotted, cleaned, or discolored pieces.*

|  | Mintage | G-4 | VG-8 | F-12 | VF-20 | EF-40 | AU-50 | MS-60 | MS-63 |
|---|---|---|---|---|---|---|---|---|---|
| 1816 . . . . . . . . . . . 2,820,982 | | $20 | $25 | $35 | $70 | $205 | $300 | $550 | $750 |
| 1817, 13 Stars . . . . . 3,948,400 | | 20 | 25 | 35 | 70 | 150 | 250 | 440 | 750 |
| 1817, 15 Stars . . . . . . . . . . . * | | 27 | 34 | 55 | 130 | 510 | 850 | 2,000 | 4,200 |
| 1818 . . . . . . . . . . . 3,167,000 | | 15 | 22 | 29 | 50 | 125 | 190 | 350 | 600 |

* Included in number above.

**1819, 9 Over 8**   **1820, 20 Over 19**

| | Mintage | G-4 | VG-8 | F-12 | VF-20 | EF-40 | AU-50 | MS-60 | MS-63 |
|---|---|---|---|---|---|---|---|---|---|
| 1819 . . . . . . . . . . . 2,671,000 | | $15 | $21 | $30 | $50 | $135 | $250 | $450 | $750 |
| 1819, 9 Over 8 . . . . . . . . . . * | | 15 | 21 | 30 | 65 | 225 | 375 | 625 | 1,200 |
| 1820 . . . . . . . . . . . . 4,407,550 | | 20 | 25 | 30 | 40 | 125 | 175 | 300 | 500 |
| 1820, 20 Over 19 . . . . . . . . * | | 20 | 25 | 35 | 65 | 300 | 510 | 1,000 | 1,800 |
| 1821 **(a)** . . . . . . . . . 389,000 | | 35 | 50 | 135 | 300 | 950 | 1,500 | 6,800 | 17,000 |
| 1822 . . . . . . . . . . . . 2,072,339 | | 20 | 30 | 50 | 100 | 250 | 450 | 850 | 1,700 |

* Included in number above. **a.** Wide and closely spaced AMER varieties are valued the same.

**1823, 3 Over 2**   **1824, 4 Over 2**   **1826, 6 Over 5**

| | Mintage | G-4 | VG-8 | F-12 | VF-20 | EF-40 | AU-50 | MS-60 | MS-63 |
|---|---|---|---|---|---|---|---|---|---|
| 1823, 3 Over 2 . . . . . . . . . . * | | $85 | $185 | $350 | $700 | $1,700 | $4,700 | $15,000 | — |
| 1823, Normal Date . . . . . . . * | | 105 | 170 | 380 | 650 | 2,000 | 5,100 | 15,300 | — |
| 1824, 4 Over 2 . . . . . . . . . . * | | 85 | 105 | 150 | 300 | 650 | 2,000 | 4,500 | $15,000 |
| 1824, Normal Date . 1,262,000 | | 45 | 80 | 125 | 200 | 375 | 600 | 2,000 | 3,000 |
| 1825 . . . . . . . . . . . 1,461,100 | | 35 | 50 | 70 | 100 | 250 | 500 | 1,200 | 2,000 |
| 1826, 6 Over 5 . . . . 1,517,425 | | 85 | 105 | 170 | 300 | 700 | 1,275 | 6,500 | 13,500 |
| 1826, Normal Date . . . . . . . ** | | 35 | 50 | 70 | 95 | 175 | 325 | 750 | 1,700 |
| 1827 . . . . . . . . . . . . 2,357,732 | | 40 | 65 | 80 | 120 | 150 | 250 | 750 | 2,000 |

* Included in number below.  ** Included in number above.

**Date Size, Through 1828**   **Date Size, 1828 and Later**

| | Mintage | G-4 | VG-8 | F-12 | VF-20 | EF-40 | AU-50 | MS-60 | MS-63 |
|---|---|---|---|---|---|---|---|---|---|
| 1828, Large Narrow Date . . . . . 2,260,624 | | $25 | $35 | $50 | $65 | $225 | $300 | $750 | $1,500 |
| 1828, Small Wide Date . . . . . . . . . . . . . . . * | | 70 | 100 | 150 | 200 | 300 | 500 | 1,500 | 2,500 |
| 1829 . . . . . . . . . . . . . . . . . . . . 1,414,500 | | 40 | 65 | 70 | 80 | 90 | 110 | 500 | 1,500 |
| 1830 . . . . . . . . . . . . . . . . . . . . 1,711,500 | | 25 | 30 | 45 | 65 | 160 | 250 | 600 | 1,700 |
| 1831 . . . . . . . . . . . . . . . . . . . . 3,359,260 | | 25 | 30 | 45 | 65 | 105 | 190 | 350 | 600 |
| 1832 . . . . . . . . . . . . . . . . . . . . 2,362,000 | | 25 | 30 | 45 | 65 | 105 | 190 | 400 | 1,000 |
| 1833 . . . . . . . . . . . . . . . . . . . . 2,739,000 | | 25 | 30 | 45 | 70 | 110 | 190 | 325 | 900 |
| 1834 . . . . . . . . . . . . . . . . . . . . 1,855,100 | | 25 | 30 | 45 | 65 | 125 | 250 | 400 | 750 |
| 1835 . . . . . . . . . . . . . . . . . . . . 3,878,400 | | 25 | 30 | 50 | 60 | 120 | 180 | 600 | 900 |

* Included in number above.

# Matron Head Modified (1835–1839) and Braided Hair (1837–1857)

**G-4 Good:** Considerably worn. LIBERTY readable.

**VG-8 Very Good:** Hairlines smooth but visible; outline of ear clearly defined.

**F-12 Fine:** Hairlines at top of head and behind ear worn but visible. Braid over brow plain; ear clear.

**VF-20 Very Fine:** All details sharper than for F-12. Only slight wear on hair over brow.

**EF-40 Extremely Fine:** Hair above ear detailed, but slightly worn.

**AU-50 About Uncirculated:** Trace of wear on high points of hair above ear and eye and on highest points on leaves and bow.

**MS-60 Uncirculated:** Typical brown surface. No trace of wear.

**MS-63 Choice Uncirculated:** Some distracting contact marks or blemishes in prime focal areas. Impaired luster possible.

**1839, 1839 Over 1836**

*Dealers often pay more than the prices shown for brilliant or red Uncirculated coins, and less for spotted, cleaned, or discolored pieces.*

|  | Mintage | G-4 | VG-8 | F-12 | VF-20 | EF-40 | AU-50 | MS-60 | MS-63 |
|---|---|---|---|---|---|---|---|---|---|
| 1836 . . . . . . . . . . . . . . . . . . . . | 2,111,000 | $20 | $30 | $40 | $60 | $100 | $250 | $400 | $700 |
| 1837 . . . . . . . . . . . . . . . . . . . . | 5,558,300 | 20 | 25 | 30 | 45 | 90 | 125 | 240 | 400 |
| 1838 . . . . . . . . . . . . . . . . . . . . | 6,370,200 | 20 | 25 | 30 | 45 | 90 | 125 | 240 | 400 |
| 1839 . . . . . . . . . . . . . . . . . . . . . | 3,128,661 | 20 | 25 | 30 | 45 | 120 | 175 | 320 | 500 |
| 1839, 1839 Over 1836, Plain Cords. . . . . .* | 300 | 500 | 1,000 | 1,750 | 4,500 | 15,000 | — | — |
| 1840 . . . . . . . . . . . . . . . . . . . . | 2,462,700 | 20 | 25 | 30 | 35 | 65 | 150 | 350 | 600 |
| 1841 . . . . . . . . . . . . . . . . . . . . | 1,597,367 | 20 | 40 | 60 | 90 | 110 | 160 | 500 | 900 |
| 1842 . . . . . . . . . . . . . . . . . . . . | 2,383,390 | 20 | 25 | 30 | 35 | 65 | 160 | 350 | 850 |

* Included in number above.

**"Head of 1840"**
**Petite Head (1839–1843)**

**"Head of 1844"**
**Mature Head (1843–1857)**

**Small Letters**

**Large Letters**

|  | Mintage | G-4 | VG-8 | F-12 | VF-20 | EF-40 | AU-50 | MS-60 | MS-63 |
|---|---|---|---|---|---|---|---|---|---|
| 1843, Petite, Small Letters . . . . . | 2,425,342 | $20 | $25 | $30 | $35 | $65 | $150 | $400 | $700 |
| 1843, Petite, Large Letters. . . . . . . . . . . .* | 20 | 25 | 35 | 50 | 170 | 275 | 400 | 650 |
| 1843, Mature, Large Letters . . . . . . . . . . .* | 20 | 25 | 35 | 55 | 300 | 375 | 500 | 1,200 |
| 1844, Normal Date . . . . . . . . . | 2,398,752 | 20 | 25 | 30 | 35 | 65 | 160 | 400 | 900 |
| 1844, 44 Over 81 . . . . . . . . . . . . . . . . . .* | 55 | 85 | 100 | 150 | 300 | 600 | 1,250 | 2,600 |
| 1845 . . . . . . . . . . . . . . . . . . . . . | 3,894,804 | 20 | 25 | 30 | 35 | 40 | 95 | 200 | 350 |
| 1846 . . . . . . . . . . . . . . . . . . . . . | 4,120,800 | 20 | 25 | 30 | 35 | 45 | 95 | 150 | 300 |
| 1847 . . . . . . . . . . . . . . . . . . . . . | 6,183,669 | 20 | 25 | 30 | 35 | 60 | 120 | 250 | 350 |
| 1847, 7 Over "Small 7" . . . . . . . . . . . . . .* | 40 | 60 | 80 | 100 | 200 | 300 | 900 | 1,500 |

* Included in number above.

| | Mintage | G-4 | VG-8 | F-12 | VF-20 | EF-40 | AU-50 | MS-60 | MS-63 |
|---|---|---|---|---|---|---|---|---|---|
| 1848 | 6,415,799 | $20 | $25 | $30 | $35 | $60 | $120 | $200 | $300 |
| 1849 | 4,178,500 | 20 | 25 | 30 | 35 | 60 | 160 | 250 | 450 |
| 1850 | 4,426,844 | 20 | 25 | 30 | 35 | 40 | 90 | 125 | 200 |

| 1844, 44 Over 81 | 1851, 51 Over 81 | 1847, 7 Over "Small" 7 |
|---|---|---|

*Dealers often pay more than the prices shown for brilliant or red Uncirculated coins, and less for spotted, cleaned, or discolored pieces.*

| | Mintage | G-4 | VG-8 | F-12 | VF-20 | EF-40 | AU-50 | MS-60 | MS-63 |
|---|---|---|---|---|---|---|---|---|---|
| 1851, Normal Date | 9,889,707 | $20 | $25 | $30 | $35 | $40 | $90 | $125 | $200 |
| 1851, 51 Over 81 | * | 40 | 60 | 80 | 100 | 150 | 300 | 400 | 700 |
| 1852 | 5,063,094 | 20 | 25 | 30 | 35 | 40 | 90 | 125 | 200 |
| 1853 | 6,641,131 | 20 | 25 | 30 | 35 | 40 | 90 | 125 | 200 |
| 1854 | 4,236,156 | 20 | 25 | 30 | 35 | 40 | 90 | 125 | 200 |

* Included in number above.

| 1855, Upright 5's | 1855, Slanting 5's | 1855, Knob on Ear |
|---|---|---|

| | Mintage | G-4 | VG-8 | F-12 | VF-20 | EF-40 | AU-50 | MS-60 | MS-63 |
|---|---|---|---|---|---|---|---|---|---|
| 1855, All kinds | 1,574,829 | | | | | | | | |
|   1855, Upright 5's | | $20 | $25 | $30 | $35 | $40 | $90 | $125 | $200 |
|   1855, Slanting 5's | | 20 | 25 | 30 | 35 | 40 | 90 | 125 | 200 |
|   1855, Slanting 5's, Knob on Ear | | 35 | 40 | 60 | 80 | 100 | 190 | 300 | 600 |
| 1856, Upright 5 | 2,690,463 | 20 | 25 | 30 | 35 | 40 | 90 | 125 | 200 |
| 1856, Slanting 5 | * | 20 | 25 | 30 | 35 | 40 | 90 | 125 | 200 |

* Included in number above.

| 1857, Large Date | 1857, Small Date |
|---|---|

| | Mintage | G-4 | VG-8 | F-12 | VF-20 | EF-40 | AU-50 | MS-60 | MS-63 |
|---|---|---|---|---|---|---|---|---|---|
| 1857, Large Date | 333,546 | $40 | $80 | $110 | $125 | $160 | $190 | $300 | $400 |
| 1857, Small Date | * | 40 | 90 | 120 | 175 | 225 | 275 | 375 | 550 |

* Included in number above.

# FLYING EAGLE (1856–1858)

The Act of February 21, 1857, provided for the coinage of the new copper-nickel small cent. The 1856 Flying Eagle cent was not an authorized Mint issue, as the law governing the new-size coin was enacted after the date of issue. It is believed that nearly 1,000 original strikings and 1,500 or more restrikes were made of the 1856. They are properly referred to as *patterns*.

**G-4 Good:** All details worn, but readable.
**VG-8 Very Good:** Details in eagle's feathers and eye evident, but worn.
**F-12 Fine:** Eagle-head details and feather tips sharp.
**VF-20 Very Fine:** Considerable detail visible in feathers in right wing and tail.
**EF-40 Extremely Fine:** Slight wear, all details sharp.
**AU-50 About Uncirculated:** Slight wear on eagle's left wing and breast.
**MS-60 Uncirculated:** No trace of wear. Light blemishes.
**MS-63 Choice Uncirculated:** Some distracting contact marks or blemishes in prime focal areas. Some impairment of luster possible.
**PF-63 Choice Proof:** Nearly perfect.

| 1858, 8 Over 7 | 1856–1858, Large Letters | 1858, Small Letters |

*Dealers often pay more than the prices shown for brilliant Uncirculated and Proof coins, and less for spotted, cleaned, or discolored pieces.*

| | Mintage | G-4 | VG-8 | F-12 | VF-20 | EF-40 | AU-50 | MS-60 | MS-63 | PF-63 |
|---|---|---|---|---|---|---|---|---|---|---|
| 1856 . . . . . . . | *(1,000–1,500)* **(a)** | $5,500 | $6,000 | $7,500 | $9,000 | $9,500 | $11,500 | $12,500 | $17,500 | $13,500 |
| 1857 . . . . . . . . . . . . | 17,450,000 | 15 | 25 | 30 | 35 | 80 | 160 | 350 | 725 | |
| . . . . . . . . . . . . . . . . . | *(100)* | | | | | | | | | 5,000 |
| 1858, Large Letters . . | 24,600,000 | 15 | 25 | 30 | 35 | 80 | 160 | 350 | 725 | |
| . . . . . . . . . . . . . . . . . | *(100)* | | | | | | | | | 5,000 |
| 1858, 8 Over 7 . . . . . . . . . . . . . * | | 50 | 75 | 115 | 250 | 450 | 850 | 3,000 | 7,500 | |
| 1858, Small Letters . . . . . . . . . . * | | 15 | 25 | 30 | 35 | 80 | 160 | 400 | 775 | |
| . . . . . . . . . . . . . . . . . | *(200)* | | | | | | | | | 5,000 |

\* Included in mintage for 1858, Large Letters. **a.** Most of those seen are Proofs; a small number have been designated circulation strikes.

# INDIAN HEAD (1859–1909)

The small cent was redesigned in 1859, and a representation of Miss Liberty wearing a Native American war bonnet was adopted as the obverse device. The 1859 reverse was also changed to represent a laurel wreath. In 1860 the reverse was modified to display an oak wreath with a small shield at the top. From 1859 into 1864, cents were struck in copper-nickel. In 1864 the composition was changed to bronze, although copper-nickel cents were also struck during that year.

**G-4 Good:** No LIBERTY visible.
**VG-8 Very Good:** At least some letters of LIBERTY readable on head band.
**F-12 Fine:** LIBERTY mostly visible.
**VF-20 Very Fine:** Slight but even wear on LIBERTY.
**EF-40 Extremely Fine:** LIBERTY sharp. All other details sharp. Only slight wear on ribbon end.
**AU-50 About Uncirculated:** Very slight trace of wear above the ear and the lowest curl of hair.
**MS-60 Uncirculated:** No trace of wear. Light blemishes.
**MS-63 Choice Uncirculated:** Some distracting contact marks or blemishes in prime focal areas. Impaired luster possible.
**PF-63 Choice Proof:** Nearly perfect.

Without Shield at Top of Wreath (1859 Only)

With Shield on Reverse (1860–1909)

## Variety 1 – Copper-Nickel, Laurel Wreath Reverse (1859)

*Dealers often pay more than the prices shown for brilliant Uncirculated coins, and less for spotted, cleaned, or discolored pieces.*

| | Mintage | G-4 | VG-8 | F-12 | VF-20 | EF-40 | AU-50 | MS-60 | MS-63 | PF-63 |
|---|---|---|---|---|---|---|---|---|---|---|
| 1859 . . . . . . *(800)* . . . | 36,400,000 | $7 | $10 | $15 | $30 | $65 | $125 | $250 | $500 | $1,000 |

## Variety 2 – Copper-Nickel, Oak Wreath With Shield (1860–1864)

| | Mintage | G-4 | VG-8 | F-12 | VF-20 | EF-40 | AU-50 | MS-60 | MS-63 | PF-63 |
|---|---|---|---|---|---|---|---|---|---|---|
| 1860 . . . . . . *(1,000)* . . | 20,566,000 | $6.00 | $10 | $12 | $30 | $35 | $65 | $100 | $225 | $575 |
| 1861 . . . . . . *(1,000)* . . | 10,100,000 | 17.00 | 20 | 30 | 40 | 65 | 85 | 125 | 275 | 650 |
| 1862 *(1,500–2,000)* . . | 28,075,000 | 5.50 | 6 | 10 | 15 | 30 | 45 | 100 | 150 | 500 |
| 1863 . . *(800–1,000)* . . | 49,840,000 | 5.50 | 6 | 10 | 15 | 30 | 45 | 100 | 150 | 500 |
| 1864 . . *(800–1,000)* . . | 13,740,000 | 12.00 | 20 | 25 | 40 | 55 | 75 | 125 | 250 | 550 |

## Variety 3 – Bronze (1864–1909)

1864, Indian Head Cent
With "L"

| | Mintage | G-4 | VG-8 | F-12 | VF-20 | EF-40 | AU-50 | MS-60 | MS-63 | PF-63 |
|---|---|---|---|---|---|---|---|---|---|---|
| 1864, All kinds. . . . . . | 39,233,714 | | | | | | | | | |
| 1864, No L *(150)*. . . . . . . . . . | | $5 | $10 | $15 | $25 | $35 | $45 | $55 | $85 | $300 |
| 1864, With L *(20)*. . . . . . . . . . | | 35 | 55 | 75 | 100 | 170 | 210 | 280 | 375 | — |
| 1865 . . *(750–1,000)* . . | 35,429,286 | 10 | 12 | 15 | 20 | 25 | 35 | 50 | 100 | 200 |
| 1866 . . *(725–1,000)* . . | 9,826,500 | 35 | 40 | 55 | 75 | 125 | 175 | 200 | 300 | 220 |
| 1867 . . *(850–1,100)* . . | 9,821,000 | 35 | 40 | 55 | 75 | 125 | 175 | 200 | 300 | 220 |
| 1868 . . *(750–1,000)* . . | 10,266,500 | 30 | 40 | 55 | 75 | 125 | 175 | 200 | 300 | 200 |
| 1869 . . *(850–1,100)* . . | 6,420,000 | 55 | 55 | 90 | 150 | 225 | 275 | 300 | 600 | 250 |
| 1870 . . . . . . *(1,000)* . . | 5,275,000 | 40 | 60 | 85 | 140 | 220 | 275 | 300 | 450 | 175 |
| 1871 . . . . . . . . *(960)* . . | 3,929,500 | 50 | 70 | 125 | 180 | 225 | 300 | 365 | 550 | 175 |
| 1872 . . *(850–1,100)* . . | 4,042,000 | 75 | 100 | 180 | 250 | 300 | 450 | 550 | 700 | 250 |
| 1873 *(1,500–2,000)* . . | 11,676,500 | 15 | 20 | 30 | 40 | 80 | 125 | 160 | 275 | 175 |
| 1874 *(1,000–1,200)* . . | 14,187,500 | 15 | 20 | 25 | 30 | 50 | 75 | 110 | 175 | 175 |
| 1875 *(1,000–1,250)* . . | 13,528,000 | 15 | 20 | 25 | 35 | 55 | 85 | 115 | 175 | 200 |
| 1876 *(1,500–2,000)* . . | 7,944,000 | 20 | 25 | 35 | 60 | 100 | 145 | 185 | 275 | 225 |
| 1877 *(1,250–1,500)* . . . . | 852,500 | 325 | 425 | 650 | 850 | 1,500 | 2,000 | 3,000 | 4,000 | 2,500 |

*Dealers often pay more than the prices shown for brilliant or red Uncirculated coins, and less for spotted, cleaned, or discolored pieces.*

| | Mintage | G-4 | VG-8 | F-12 | VF-20 | EF-40 | AU-50 | MS-60 | MS-63 | PF-63 |
|---|---|---|---|---|---|---|---|---|---|---|
| 1878 .... (2,350).... 5,797,500 | | $15.00 | $20.00 | $25.00 | $65.00 | $100 | $145 | $165 | $250 | $175 |
| 1879 .... (3,200)... 16,228,000 | | 4.00 | 6.00 | 8.00 | 18.00 | 40 | 45 | 50 | 100 | 150 |
| 1880 .... (3,955)... 38,961,000 | | 1.75 | 2.00 | 3.00 | 6.00 | 15 | 25 | 40 | 70 | 150 |
| 1881 .... (3,575)... 39,208,000 | | 1.75 | 2.00 | 3.00 | 5.00 | 10 | 16 | 26 | 37 | 150 |
| 1882 .... (3,100)... 38,578,000 | | 1.75 | 2.00 | 3.00 | 5.00 | 10 | 16 | 26 | 37 | 150 |
| 1883 .... (6,609)... 45,591,500 | | 1.75 | 2.00 | 3.00 | 5.00 | 10 | 16 | 26 | 37 | 150 |
| 1884 .... (3,942)... 23,257,800 | | 2.25 | 2.50 | 3.50 | 6.00 | 14 | 20 | 30 | 60 | 150 |
| 1885 .... (3,790)... 11,761,594 | | 3.00 | 4.00 | 6.00 | 15.00 | 35 | 45 | 60 | 100 | 150 |
| 1886 .... (4,290)... 17,650,000 | | 1.75 | 3.00 | 8.00 | 25.00 | 65 | 85 | 100 | 125 | 150 |
| 1887 .... (2,960)... 45,223,523 | | 1.25 | 1.50 | 1.75 | 2.25 | 8 | 14 | 25 | 50 | 150 |
| 1888 .... (4,582)... 37,489,832 | | 0.85 | 1.10 | 1.80 | 2.75 | 8 | 14 | 25 | 60 | 150 |
| 1889 .... (3,336)... 48,866,025 | | 0.85 | 1.10 | 1.80 | 2.75 | 6 | 12 | 25 | 35 | 150 |
| 1890 .... (2,740)... 57,180,114 | | 0.85 | 1.10 | 1.80 | 2.75 | 6 | 12 | 25 | 35 | 150 |
| 1891 .... (2,350)... 47,070,000 | | 0.85 | 1.10 | 1.80 | 2.75 | 6 | 12 | 25 | 35 | 150 |
| 1892 .... (2,745)... 37,647,087 | | 0.85 | 1.10 | 1.80 | 2.75 | 6 | 12 | 25 | 35 | 150 |
| 1893 .... (2,195)... 46,640,000 | | 0.85 | 1.10 | 1.80 | 2.75 | 6 | 12 | 25 | 35 | 150 |
| 1894 .... (2,632)... 16,749,500 | | 3.00 | 4.00 | 5.00 | 8.50 | 25 | 30 | 40 | 60 | 150 |
| 1895 .... (2,062)... 38,341,574 | | 0.85 | 1.10 | 1.30 | 2.00 | 6 | 11 | 25 | 30 | 150 |
| 1896 .... (1,862)... 39,055,431 | | 0.85 | 1.10 | 1.30 | 2.00 | 6 | 11 | 25 | 30 | 150 |
| 1897 .... (1,938)... 50,464,392 | | 0.85 | 1.10 | 1.30 | 2.00 | 6 | 11 | 25 | 30 | 150 |
| 1898 .... (1,795)... 49,821,284 | | 0.85 | 1.10 | 1.30 | 2.00 | 6 | 11 | 25 | 30 | 150 |
| 1899 .... (2,031)... 53,598,000 | | 0.85 | 1.10 | 1.30 | 2.00 | 6 | 11 | 25 | 30 | 150 |
| 1900 .... (2,262)... 66,831,502 | | 0.80 | 1.00 | 1.10 | 1.50 | 5 | 10 | 20 | 30 | 150 |
| 1901 .... (1,985)... 79,609,158 | | 0.80 | 1.00 | 1.10 | 1.50 | 5 | 10 | 20 | 30 | 150 |
| 1902 .... (2,018)... 87,374,704 | | 0.80 | 1.00 | 1.10 | 1.50 | 5 | 10 | 20 | 30 | 150 |
| 1903 .... (1,790)... 85,092,703 | | 0.80 | 1.00 | 1.10 | 1.50 | 5 | 10 | 20 | 30 | 150 |
| 1904 .... (1,817)... 61,326,198 | | 0.80 | 1.00 | 1.10 | 1.50 | 5 | 10 | 20 | 30 | 150 |
| 1905 .... (2,152)... 80,717,011 | | 0.80 | 1.00 | 1.10 | 1.50 | 5 | 10 | 20 | 30 | 150 |
| 1906 .... (1,725)... 96,020,530 | | 0.80 | 1.00 | 1.10 | 1.50 | 5 | 10 | 20 | 30 | 150 |
| 1907 .... (1,475).. 108,137,143 | | 0.80 | 1.00 | 1.10 | 1.50 | 5 | 10 | 20 | 30 | 150 |

**Location of Mintmark S on Reverse of Indian Head Cent (1908 and 1909 Only)**

| | Mintage | G-4 | VG-8 | F-12 | VF-20 | EF-40 | AU-50 | MS-60 | MS-63 | PF-63 |
|---|---|---|---|---|---|---|---|---|---|---|
| 1908 .... (1,620)... 32,326,367 | | $0.80 | $1.10 | $1.25 | $1.50 | $5 | $10 | $18 | $30 | $125 |
| 1908S ............. 1,115,000 | | 60.00 | 70.00 | 100.00 | 115.00 | 150 | 175 | 200 | 300 | |
| 1909 .... (2,175)... 14,368,470 | | 4.00 | 6.00 | 8.00 | 10.00 | 12 | 16 | 25 | 45 | 150 |
| 1909S ............. 309,000 | | 200.00 | 225.00 | 300.00 | 400.00 | 450 | 550 | 750 | 950 | |

## LINCOLN, WHEAT EARS REVERSE (1909–1958)

Victor D. Brenner designed this cent, which was issued to commemorate the 100th anniversary of Abraham Lincoln's birth. The designer's initials (V.D.B.) appear on the reverse of a limited quantity of cents of 1909. Later in the year they were removed from the dies but restored in 1918 as very small incuse letters beneath the shoulder. The Lincoln type was the first cent to have the motto IN GOD WE TRUST.

**G-4 Good:** Date worn but apparent. Lines in wheat heads missing. Full rims.
**VG-8 Very Good:** Half of lines visible in upper wheat heads.
**F-12 Fine:** Wheat lines worn but visible.
**VF-20 Very Fine:** Lincoln's cheekbone and jawbone worn but separated. No worn spots on wheat heads.
**EF-40 Extremely Fine:** Slight wear. All details sharp.
**AU-50 About Uncirculated:** Slight wear on cheek and jaw and on wheat stalks.
**MS-60 Uncirculated:** No trace of wear. Light blemishes. Brown or red-brown color.
**MS-63 Choice Uncirculated:** No trace of wear. Slight blemishes. Red-brown color.
**MS-65 Gem Uncirculated:** No trace of wear. Barely noticeable blemishes. Nearly full red color.
**PF-63 Choice Proof:** Reflective surfaces with only a few blemishes in secondary focal places. No major flaws.

*Location of mintmark S or D*
*on obverse of Lincoln cent.*

**Designer's Initials**
**V.D.B. (1909 Only)**

**No V.D.B.**
**on Reverse**
**(1909–1958)**

*Dealers often pay more than the prices shown for brilliant Uncirculated coins, and less for spotted, cleaned, or discolored pieces.*

| | Mintage | G-4 | VG-8 | F-12 | VF-20 | EF-40 | AU-50 | MS-60 | MS-63 | MATTE PF-63 |
|---|---|---|---|---|---|---|---|---|---|---|
| 1909, V.D.B. . . . . . . . . . . . . . . . | | | | | | | | | | |
| . . . . (1,194). . .27,995,000 | | $3.00 | $4.00 | $5.00 | $7.00 | $9.00 | $10.00 | $13.00 | $20 | $2,000 |
| 1909S, V.D.B. . . . . . . . . 484,000 | | 450.00 | 500.00 | 575.00 | 625.00 | 700.00 | 800.00 | 900.00 | 1,200 | |
| 1909 . . . . (2,618). . .72,702,618 | | 1.00 | 1.25 | 1.60 | 2.00 | 3.00 | 6.00 | 8.50 | 15 | 300 |
| 1909S . . . . . . . . . . . . .1,825,000 | | 55.00 | 60.00 | 70.00 | 95.00 | 100.00 | 150.00 | 225.00 | 275 | |
| 1910 . . . . (4,083). .146,801,218 | | 0.10 | 0.12 | 0.15 | 0.30 | 1.00 | 2.50 | 9.00 | 15 | 270 |
| 1910S . . . . . . . . . . . .6,045,000 | | 8.00 | 10.00 | 12.00 | 14.00 | 25.00 | 40.00 | 55.00 | 70 | |
| 1911 . . . . (1,725). .101,177,787 | | 0.10 | 0.15 | 0.30 | 0.50 | 1.50 | 3.50 | 11.00 | 25 | 275 |
| 1911D . . . . . . . . . . .12,672,000 | | 2.40 | 3.00 | 4.50 | 9.00 | 21.00 | 35.00 | 50.00 | 70 | |
| 1911S . . . . . . . . . . . .4,026,000 | | 20.00 | 25.00 | 30.00 | 35.00 | 50.00 | 65.00 | 110.00 | 150 | |
| 1912 . . . . (2,172). . .68,153,060 | | 0.15 | 0.25 | 0.70 | 2.00 | 2.50 | 8.00 | 17.00 | 25 | 275 |
| 1912D . . . . . . . . . . .10,411,000 | | 2.75 | 3.50 | 4.25 | 10.00 | 25.00 | 40.00 | 75.00 | 120 | |
| 1912S . . . . . . . . . . . .4,431,000 | | 11.00 | 13.00 | 15.00 | 18.00 | 35.00 | 47.00 | 90.00 | 125 | |
| 1913 . . . . (2,983). . .76,532,352 | | 0.15 | 0.20 | 0.50 | 1.50 | 8.00 | 12.00 | 16.00 | 25 | 275 |
| 1913D . . . . . . . . . . .15,804,000 | | 0.75 | 1.00 | 1.50 | 3.50 | 20.00 | 26.00 | 50.00 | 100 | |
| 1913S . . . . . . . . . . . .6,101,000 | | 5.50 | 6.75 | 9.00 | 12.00 | 27.00 | 50.00 | 85.00 | 135 | |
| 1914 . . . . (1,365). . .75,238,432 | | 0.20 | 0.30 | 0.75 | 2.00 | 6.50 | 17.00 | 25.00 | 37 | 275 |
| 1914D **(a)** . . . . . . . . . .1,193,000 | | 100.00 | 125.00 | 150.00 | 180.00 | 450.00 | 1,000.00 | 1,750.00 | 2,500 | |
| 1914S . . . . . . . . . . . .4,137,000 | | 11.00 | 14.00 | 16.00 | 19.00 | 40.00 | 90.00 | 175.00 | 350 | |
| 1915 . . . . (1,150). . .29,092,120 | | 0.40 | 1.00 | 2.00 | 8.00 | 26.00 | 35.00 | 46.00 | 65 | 300 |
| 1915D . . . . . . . . . . .22,050,000 | | 0.50 | 1.00 | 1.50 | 2.25 | 9.00 | 22.00 | 45.00 | 60 | |
| 1915S . . . . . . . . . . . .4,833,000 | | 10.00 | 12.00 | 15.00 | 18.00 | 35.00 | 65.00 | 125.00 | 300 | |
| 1916 . . . . (1,050). .131,833,677 | | 0.10 | 0.15 | 0.25 | 0.50 | 2.00 | 5.00 | 10.00 | 15 | 1,000 |
| 1916D . . . . . . . . . . .35,956,000 | | 0.30 | 0.50 | 0.85 | 2.00 | 5.50 | 12.00 | 35.00 | 65 | |
| 1916S . . . . . . . . . . .22,510,000 | | 0.50 | 0.75 | 1.50 | 3.00 | 10.00 | 20.00 | 65.00 | 125 | |
| 1917 . . . . . . . . . . . .196,429,785 | | 0.05 | 0.07 | 0.10 | 0.25 | 0.60 | 3.00 | 10.00 | 15 | |
| 1917D . . . . . . . . . . .55,120,000 | | 0.25 | 0.40 | 0.75 | 1.50 | 15.00 | 20.00 | 45.00 | 100 | |
| 1917S . . . . . . . . . . .32,620,000 | | 0.10 | 0.15 | 0.25 | 0.50 | 2.75 | 12.00 | 50.00 | 115 | |

**a.** Beware of altered date or mintmark. No V.D.B. on shoulder of genuine 1914-D cent.

Designer's initials placed on Lincoln's shoulder next to rim, starting in 1918.

*For brilliant Unc. coins before 1934, dealers usually pay more than the prices shown. They pay less for spotted, cleaned, or discolored pieces.*

| Mintage | G-4 | VG-8 | F-12 | VF-20 | EF-40 | AU-50 | MS-60 | MS-63 |
|---|---|---|---|---|---|---|---|---|
| 1918 . . . . . 288,104,634 | $0.04 | $0.05 | $0.10 | $0.20 | $1.00 | $3.00 | $6.00 | $15.00 |
| 1918D . . . . . 47,830,000 | 0.20 | 0.25 | 0.60 | 1.25 | 6.00 | 12.00 | 45.00 | 100.00 |
| 1918S . . . . . 34,680,000 | 0.15 | 0.20 | 0.50 | 1.00 | 4.00 | 15.00 | 50.00 | 125.00 |
| 1919 . . . . . 392,021,000 | 0.04 | 0.05 | 0.07 | 0.15 | 0.75 | 1.50 | 5.00 | 14.00 |
| 1919D . . . . . 57,154,000 | 0.10 | 0.12 | 0.15 | 0.40 | 2.50 | 15.00 | 35.00 | 75.00 |
| 1919S . . . . 139,760,000 | 0.05 | 0.06 | 0.10 | 0.30 | 1.35 | 7.00 | 25.00 | 80.00 |
| 1920 . . . . . 310,165,000 | 0.03 | 0.05 | 0.07 | 0.15 | 0.50 | 1.50 | 10.00 | 15.00 |
| 1920D . . . . . 49,280,000 | 0.20 | 0.40 | 0.80 | 2.00 | 6.00 | 15.00 | 45.00 | 75.00 |
| 1920S . . . . . 46,220,000 | 0.10 | 0.20 | 0.30 | 0.70 | 3.50 | 17.00 | 65.00 | 125.00 |
| 1921 . . . . . . 39,157,000 | 0.06 | 0.08 | 0.15 | 0.35 | 1.50 | 6.00 | 25.00 | 40.00 |
| 1921S . . . . . 15,274,000 | 0.35 | 0.50 | 0.70 | 1.50 | 15.00 | 35.00 | 75.00 | 165.00 |
| 1922D . . . . . . 7,160,000 | 7.00 | 8.00 | 9.00 | 11.00 | 17.00 | 28.00 | 75.00 | 165.00 |
| 1922, No D **(b)** . . . . . . * | 325.00 | 400.00 | 500.00 | 550.00 | 1,000.00 | 2,500.00 | 7,000.00 | 12,500.00 |
| 1923 . . . . . . 74,723,000 | 0.04 | 0.05 | 0.07 | 0.15 | 1.00 | 2.50 | 7.00 | 14.00 |
| 1923S . . . . . . 8,700,000 | 1.25 | 1.50 | 2.00 | 3.00 | 15.00 | 35.00 | 150.00 | 250.00 |
| 1924 . . . . . . 75,178,000 | 0.04 | 0.05 | 0.07 | 0.15 | 1.50 | 3.50 | 15.00 | 25.00 |
| 1924D . . . . . . 2,520,000 | 18.00 | 20.00 | 25.00 | 35.00 | 65.00 | 95.00 | 200.00 | 400.00 |
| 1924S . . . . . 11,696,000 | 0.40 | 0.50 | 0.80 | 1.10 | 9.00 | 30.00 | 75.00 | 200.00 |
| 1925 . . . . . 139,949,000 | 0.03 | 0.04 | 0.05 | 0.15 | 0.50 | 2.00 | 5.00 | 10.00 |
| 1925D . . . . . 22,580,000 | 0.10 | 0.15 | 0.50 | 1.00 | 4.50 | 11.00 | 30.00 | 65.00 |
| 1925S . . . . . 26,380,000 | 0.05 | 0.06 | 0.10 | 0.25 | 3.00 | 14.00 | 45.00 | 125.00 |
| 1926 . . . . . 157,088,000 | 0.03 | 0.04 | 0.05 | 0.15 | 0.50 | 2.00 | 5.00 | 8.00 |
| 1926D . . . . . 28,020,000 | 0.25 | 0.35 | 0.70 | 1.10 | 3.00 | 10.00 | 45.00 | 75.00 |
| 1926S . . . . . . 4,550,000 | 3.00 | 3.50 | 4.50 | 6.00 | 14.00 | 32.00 | 125.00 | 300.00 |
| 1927 . . . . . 144,440,000 | 0.03 | 0.04 | 0.05 | 0.20 | 0.50 | 1.00 | 5.00 | 10.00 |
| 1927D . . . . . 27,170,000 | 0.10 | 0.15 | 0.50 | 1.00 | 2.00 | 6.00 | 35.00 | 55.00 |
| 1927S . . . . . 14,276,000 | 0.25 | 0.30 | 0.50 | 1.25 | 4.00 | 11.00 | 45.00 | 95.00 |
| 1928 . . . . . 134,116,000 | 0.03 | 0.04 | 0.05 | 0.15 | 0.50 | 1.00 | 4.50 | 10.00 |
| 1928D . . . . . 31,170,000 | 0.05 | 0.10 | 0.15 | 0.25 | 0.85 | 4.00 | 25.00 | 45.00 |
| 1928S . . . . . 17,266,000 | 0.10 | 0.12 | 0.25 | 0.50 | 1.50 | 5.00 | 50.00 | 75.00 |
| 1929 . . . . . 185,262,000 | 0.03 | 0.04 | 0.05 | 0.15 | 0.35 | 1.50 | 4.00 | 6.00 |
| 1929D . . . . . 41,730,000 | 0.04 | 0.06 | 0.10 | 0.25 | 1.00 | 2.00 | 12.00 | 25.00 |
| 1929S . . . . . 50,148,000 | 0.03 | 0.05 | 0.10 | 0.20 | 0.60 | 1.75 | 7.00 | 20.00 |
| 1930 . . . . . 157,415,000 | 0.03 | 0.04 | 0.05 | 0.15 | 0.25 | 0.75 | 2.00 | 3.50 |
| 1930D . . . . . 40,100,000 | 0.04 | 0.06 | 0.10 | 0.25 | 0.60 | 1.00 | 5.00 | 10.00 |
| 1930S . . . . . 24,286,000 | 0.03 | 0.05 | 0.10 | 0.15 | 0.40 | 2.00 | 3.50 | 5.00 |
| 1931 . . . . . 19,396,000 | 0.15 | 0.20 | 0.30 | 0.40 | 0.60 | 2.00 | 10.00 | 15.00 |
| 1931D . . . . . . 4,480,000 | 2.00 | 2.25 | 3.00 | 3.50 | 5.00 | 14.00 | 30.00 | 42.00 |
| 1931S . . . . . . . . 866,000 | 45.00 | 50.00 | 60.00 | 70.00 | 75.00 | 85.00 | 95.00 | 115.00 |
| 1932 . . . . . . . 9,062,000 | 0.40 | 0.50 | 0.60 | 1.00 | 1.25 | 3.75 | 10.00 | 13.00 |
| 1932D . . . . . 10,500,000 | 0.25 | 0.35 | 0.40 | 0.50 | 1.00 | 3.25 | 10.00 | 15.00 |
| 1933 . . . . . . 14,360,000 | 0.30 | 0.40 | 0.50 | 0.70 | 1.25 | 3.75 | 10.00 | 15.00 |
| 1933D . . . . . . 6,200,000 | 1.00 | 1.25 | 1.50 | 2.50 | 2.50 | 4.25 | 7.00 | 16.00 |

* Included in number above. **b.** 1922 cents with a weak or missing mintmark were made from extremely worn dies that originally struck normal 1922-D cents. Three different die pairs were involved; two of them produced "Weak D" coins. One die pair (no. 2, identified by a "strong reverse") is acknowledged as striking "No D" coins. Weak D cents are worth considerably less. Beware of removed mintmark.

*Chart continued on next page.*

| | Mintage | G-4 | VG-8 | F-12 | VF-20 | EF-40 | AU-50 | MS-60 | MS-63 | PF-63 |
|---|---|---|---|---|---|---|---|---|---|---|
| 1934 . . . . . . . . . . . | 219,080,000 | $0.03 | $0.03 | $0.03 | $0.03 | $0.10 | $1.00 | $3.00 | $4.50 | |
| 1934D . . . . . . . . . . | 28,446,000 | 0.04 | 0.06 | 0.08 | 0.15 | 0.50 | 2.00 | 9.00 | 15.00 | |
| 1935 . . . . . . . . . . . | 245,388,000 | 0.03 | 0.03 | 0.03 | 0.04 | 0.06 | 0.20 | 2.00 | 3.00 | |
| 1935D . . . . . . . . . . | 47,000,000 | 0.03 | 0.03 | 0.03 | 0.04 | 0.20 | 0.50 | 3.00 | 4.00 | |
| 1935S . . . . . . . . . . | 38,702,000 | 0.03 | 0.04 | 0.04 | 0.04 | 0.12 | 1.25 | 4.00 | 6.00 | |
| 1936 . . . . (5,569) . . | 309,632,000 | 0.03 | 0.03 | 0.03 | 0.04 | 0.06 | 0.25 | 1.00 | 3.00 | $100 |
| 1936D . . . . . . . . . . | 40,620,000 | 0.03 | 0.03 | 0.03 | 0.04 | 0.08 | 0.20 | 1.00 | 3.00 | |
| 1936S . . . . . . . . . . | 29,130,000 | 0.03 | 0.03 | 0.03 | 0.04 | 0.10 | 0.20 | 1.00 | 3.00 | |
| 1937 . . . . (9,320) . . | 309,170,000 | 0.02 | 0.03 | 0.03 | 0.03 | 0.05 | 0.20 | 0.50 | 3.00 | 35 |
| 1937D . . . . . . . . . . | 50,430,000 | 0.02 | 0.03 | 0.03 | 0.03 | 0.06 | 0.30 | 0.80 | 4.00 | |
| 1937S . . . . . . . . . . | 34,500,000 | 0.03 | 0.03 | 0.03 | 0.04 | 0.06 | 0.30 | 0.80 | 4.00 | |
| 1938 . . . (14,734) . . | 156,682,000 | 0.02 | 0.03 | 0.03 | 0.03 | 0.05 | 0.30 | 0.75 | 2.00 | 25 |
| 1938D . . . . . . . . . . | 20,010,000 | 0.02 | 0.03 | 0.05 | 0.06 | 0.15 | 0.50 | 1.00 | 5.00 | |
| 1938S . . . . . . . . . . | 15,180,000 | 0.06 | 0.08 | 0.10 | 0.12 | 0.15 | 0.30 | 1.00 | 4.00 | |
| 1939 . . . (13,520) . . | 316,466,000 | 0.02 | 0.03 | 0.03 | 0.03 | 0.03 | 0.20 | 0.30 | 2.50 | 23 |
| 1939D . . . . . . . . . . | 15,160,000 | 0.06 | 0.08 | 0.10 | 0.12 | 0.15 | 0.35 | 1.00 | 4.00 | |
| 1939S . . . . . . . . . . | 52,070,000 | 0.03 | 0.03 | 0.05 | 0.08 | 0.10 | 0.30 | 1.00 | 4.00 | |
| 1940 . . . (15,872) . . | 586,810,000 | 0.02 | 0.03 | 0.03 | 0.03 | 0.03 | 0.20 | 0.30 | 2.00 | 15 |
| 1940D . . . . . . . . . . | 81,390,000 | 0.02 | 0.03 | 0.03 | 0.03 | 0.03 | 0.20 | 0.40 | 2.00 | |
| 1940S . . . . . . . . . . | 112,940,000 | 0.02 | 0.03 | 0.03 | 0.03 | 0.04 | 0.20 | 0.40 | 2.75 | |
| 1941 . . . (21,100) . . | 887,018,000 | 0.02 | 0.03 | 0.03 | 0.03 | 0.03 | 0.20 | 0.30 | 2.00 | 15 |
| 1941D . . . . . . . . . . | 128,700,000 | 0.02 | 0.03 | 0.03 | 0.03 | 0.03 | 0.40 | 0.80 | 3.00 | |
| 1941S . . . . . . . . . . | 92,360,000 | 0.02 | 0.03 | 0.03 | 0.03 | 0.04 | 0.35 | 1.00 | 4.00 | |
| 1942 . . . (32,600) . . | 657,796,000 | 0.02 | 0.03 | 0.03 | 0.03 | 0.03 | 0.10 | 0.15 | 1.00 | 15 |
| 1942D . . . . . . . . . . | 206,698,000 | 0.02 | 0.03 | 0.03 | 0.03 | 0.03 | 0.10 | 0.25 | 1.50 | |
| 1942S . . . . . . . . . . | 85,590,000 | 0.02 | 0.03 | 0.03 | 0.03 | 0.10 | 1.00 | 2.25 | 6.00 | |

## Variety 2 – Zinc-Coated Steel (1943)

| | Mintage | F-12 | VF-20 | EF-40 | MS-60 | MS-63 | MS-65 |
|---|---|---|---|---|---|---|---|
| 1943 . . . . . . . . . . . . . . . . . . . . . | 684,628,670 | $0.05 | $0.10 | $0.15 | $0.70 | $1.25 | $3.25 |
| 1943D . . . . . . . . . . . . . . . . . . . . | 217,660,000 | 0.05 | 0.10 | 0.15 | 0.90 | 2.00 | 4.50 |
| 1943S . . . . . . . . . . . . . . . . . . . . | 191,550,000 | 0.06 | 0.12 | 0.20 | 1.20 | 2.75 | 9.00 |

## Variety 1 (Bronze) Resumed (1944–1958)

1944-D, D Over S

1955, Doubled-Die Obverse

| | Mintage | VF-20 | EF-40 | MS-63 | MS-65 | PF-65 |
|---|---|---|---|---|---|---|
| 1944 . . . . . . . . . . . . . . . . . . . . . . . . . . | 1,435,400,000 | $0.03 | $0.03 | $0.25 | $1.60 | |
| 1944D . . . . . . . . . . . . . . . . . . . . . . . . | 430,578,000 | 0.03 | 0.03 | 0.20 | 1.50 | |
| 1944D, D Over S . . . . . . . . . . . . . . . . . . . . . . . . | * | 65.00 | 85.00 | 200.00 | 400.00 | |
| 1944S . . . . . . . . . . . . . . . . . . . . . . . . | 282,760,000 | 0.03 | 0.03 | 0.20 | 1.50 | |

* Included in number above.

# SMALL CENTS

| | Mintage | VF-20 | EF-40 | MS-63 | MS-65 | PF-65 |
|---|---|---|---|---|---|---|
| 1945 | 1,040,515,000 | $0.03 | $0.03 | $0.20 | $0.50 | |
| 1945D | 266,268,000 | 0.03 | 0.03 | 0.15 | 0.50 | |
| 1945S | 181,770,000 | 0.03 | 0.03 | 0.10 | 1.00 | |
| 1946 | 991,655,000 | 0.03 | 0.03 | 0.10 | 0.50 | |
| 1946D | 315,690,000 | 0.03 | 0.03 | 0.15 | 1.00 | |
| 1946S | 198,100,000 | 0.03 | 0.03 | 0.15 | 1.25 | |
| 1947 | 190,555,000 | 0.03 | 0.03 | 0.25 | 0.75 | |
| 1947D | 194,750,000 | 0.03 | 0.03 | 0.12 | 0.50 | |
| 1947S | 99,000,000 | 0.03 | 0.03 | 0.15 | 1.50 | |
| 1948 | 317,570,000 | 0.03 | 0.03 | 0.15 | 0.50 | |
| 1948D | 172,637,500 | 0.03 | 0.03 | 0.12 | 0.60 | |
| 1948S | 81,735,000 | 0.03 | 0.03 | 0.20 | 1.50 | |
| 1949 | 217,775,000 | 0.03 | 0.03 | 0.30 | 0.75 | |
| 1949D | 153,132,500 | 0.03 | 0.03 | 0.20 | 0.75 | |
| 1949S | 64,290,000 | 0.04 | 0.05 | 0.50 | 2.00 | |
| 1950 (51,386) | 272,635,000 | 0.03 | 0.03 | 0.25 | 0.50 | $37 |
| 1950D | 334,950,000 | 0.03 | 0.03 | 0.10 | 0.50 | |
| 1950S | 118,505,000 | 0.03 | 0.03 | 0.25 | 0.80 | |
| 1951 (57,500) | 284,576,000 | 0.03 | 0.03 | 0.25 | 0.80 | 35 |
| 1951D | 625,355,000 | 0.03 | 0.03 | 0.10 | 0.50 | |
| 1951S | 136,010,000 | 0.03 | 0.03 | 0.25 | 0.60 | |
| 1952 (81,980) | 186,775,000 | 0.03 | 0.03 | 0.15 | 0.60 | 25 |
| 1952D | 746,130,000 | 0.03 | 0.03 | 0.15 | 0.60 | |
| 1952S | 137,800,004 | 0.03 | 0.03 | 0.50 | 1.50 | |
| 1953 (128,800) | 256,755,000 | 0.03 | 0.03 | 0.10 | 0.50 | 18 |
| 1953D | 700,515,000 | 0.03 | 0.03 | 0.10 | 0.50 | |
| 1953S | 181,835,000 | 0.03 | 0.04 | 0.12 | 0.75 | |
| 1954 (233,300) | 71,640,050 | 0.03 | 0.06 | 0.15 | 0.85 | 10 |
| 1954D | 251,552,500 | 0.03 | 0.03 | 0.05 | 0.30 | |
| 1954S | 96,190,000 | 0.03 | 0.03 | 0.05 | 0.30 | |
| 1955 (378,200) | 330,958,200 | 0.03 | 0.03 | 0.06 | 0.30 | 9 |
| 1955, Doubled-Die Obverse | * | 1,000.00 | 1,100.00 (a) | 2,000.00 | 5,500.00 | |
| 1955D | 563,257,500 | 0.03 | 0.03 | 0.05 | 0.25 | |
| 1955S | 44,610,000 | 0.10 | 0.15 | 0.15 | 0.50 | |
| 1956 (669,384) | 420,745,000 | 0.03 | 0.03 | 0.05 | 0.25 | 3 |
| 1956D | 1,098,201,100 | 0.03 | 0.03 | 0.05 | 0.30 | |
| 1957 (1,247,952) | 282,540,000 | 0.03 | 0.03 | 0.05 | 0.30 | 3 |
| 1957D | 1,051,342,000 | 0.03 | 0.03 | 0.05 | 0.30 | |
| 1958 (875,652) | 252,525,000 | 0.03 | 0.03 | 0.05 | 0.30 | 3 |
| 1958D | 800,953,300 | 0.03 | 0.03 | 0.05 | 0.30 | |

* Included in number above. **a.** For MS-60 Uncirculated coins, dealers usually pay $1,400.

## LINCOLN, MEMORIAL REVERSE (1959–2008)

Small Date          Large Date

| | Mintage | MS-63 | MS-65 | PF-65 |
|---|---|---|---|---|
| 1959 | (1,149,291) 609,715,000 | $0.02 | $0.10 | $1 |

| 1969-S, Doubled-Die Obverse | Small Date, Numbers Aligned at Top | Large Date, Low 7 in Date | Enlarged Detail of 1972 Doubled-Die Obverse |
| --- | --- | --- | --- |

| | Mintage | MS-63 | MS-65 | PF-63 |
| --- | --- | --- | --- | --- |
| 1959D | 1,279,760,000 | $0.02 | $0.10 | |
| 1960, Lg Dt | 586,405,000 | 0.02 | 0.10 | |
| | (1,691,602) | | | $0.75 |
| 1960, Sm Dt | * | 1.00 | 2.70 | |
| | * | | | 9.50 |
| 1960D, | | | | |
| Lg Dt | 1,580,884,000 | 0.02 | 0.10 | |
| 1960D, Sm Dt | * | 0.02 | 0.10 | |
| 1961 | 753,345,000 | 0.02 | 0.10 | |
| | (3,028,244) | | | 0.50 |
| 1961D | 1,753,266,700 | 0.02 | 0.10 | |
| 1962 | 606,045,000 | 0.02 | 0.10 | |
| | (3,218,019) | | | 0.50 |
| 1962D | 1,793,148,140 | 0.02 | 0.10 | |
| 1963 | 754,110,000 | 0.02 | 0.10 | |
| | (3,075,645) | | | 0.50 |
| 1963D | 1,774,020,400 | 0.02 | 0.10 | |
| 1964 | 2,648,575,000 | 0.02 | 0.10 | |
| | (3,950,762) | | | 0.50 |
| 1964D | 3,799,071,500 | 0.02 | 0.10 | |
| 1965 | 1,497,224,900 | 0.03 | 0.12 | |
| 1966 | 2,188,147,783 | 0.04 | 0.12 | |
| 1967 | 3,048,667,100 | 0.03 | 0.12 | |
| 1968 | 1,707,880,970 | 0.03 | 0.12 | |
| 1968D | 2,886,269,600 | 0.02 | 0.12 | |
| 1968S | 258,270,001 | 0.02 | 0.15 | |
| | (3,041,506) | | | 0.35 |
| 1969 | 1,136,910,000 | 0.05 | 0.20 | |
| 1969D | 4,002,832,200 | 0.03 | 0.15 | |
| 1969S | 544,375,000 | 0.03 | 0.15 | |
| | (2,934,631) | | | 0.35 |
| 1969S, DDO | * | — | — | |
| 1970 | 1,898,315,000 | 0.05 | 0.20 | |
| 1970D | 2,891,438,900 | 0.02 | 0.10 | |
| 1970S, Sm Dt | | | | |
| (High 7) | (a) | 20.00 | 30.00 | |
| | (b) | | | 20.00 |
| 1970S, Lg Dt | | | | |
| (Low 7) | 690,560,004 | 0.03 | 0.20 | |
| | (2,632,810) | | | 0.25 |

| | Mintage | MS-63 | MS-65 | PF-63 |
| --- | --- | --- | --- | --- |
| 1971 | 1,919,490,000 | $0.05 | $0.20 | |
| 1971D | 2,911,045,600 | 0.03 | 0.20 | |
| 1971S | 525,133,459 | 0.03 | 0.20 | |
| | (3,220,733) | | | $0.25 |
| 1972, DDO | ** | 250.00 | 325.00 | |
| 1972 | 2,933,255,000 | 0.02 | 0.10 | |
| 1972D | 2,665,071,400 | 0.02 | 0.10 | |
| 1972S | 376,939,108 | 0.02 | 0.10 | |
| | (3,260,996) | | | 0.25 |
| 1973 | 3,728,245,000 | 0.02 | 0.10 | |
| 1973D | 3,549,576,588 | 0.02 | 0.10 | |
| 1973S | 317,177,295 | 0.02 | 0.15 | |
| | (2,760,339) | | | 0.25 |
| 1974 | 4,232,140,523 | 0.02 | 0.10 | |
| 1974D | 4,235,098,000 | 0.02 | 0.10 | |
| 1974S | 409,426,660 | 0.03 | 0.20 | |
| | (2,612,568) | | | 0.25 |
| 1975 | 5,451,476,142 | 0.02 | 0.10 | |
| 1975D | 4,505,275,300 | 0.02 | 0.10 | |
| 1975S | (2,845,450) | | | 1.60 |
| 1976 | 4,674,292,426 | 0.02 | 0.10 | |
| 1976D | 4,221,592,455 | 0.02 | 0.10 | |
| 1976S | (4,149,730) | | | 1.25 |
| 1977 | 4,469,930,000 | 0.02 | 0.10 | |
| 1977D | 4,194,062,300 | 0.02 | 0.10 | |
| 1977S | (3,251,152) | | | 1.00 |
| 1978 | 5,558,605,000 | 0.02 | 0.10 | |
| 1978D | 4,280,233,400 | 0.02 | 0.10 | |
| 1978S | (3,127,781) | | | 1.00 |
| 1979 | 6,018,515,000 | 0.02 | 0.10 | |
| 1979D | 4,139,357,254 | 0.02 | 0.10 | |
| 1979S, Type 1 | (3,677,175) | | | 1.75 |
| 1979S, Type 2 | * | | | 2.00 |
| 1980 | 7,414,705,000 | 0.02 | 0.10 | |
| 1980D | 5,140,098,660 | 0.02 | 0.10 | |
| 1980S | (3,554,806) | | | 1.00 |
| 1981 | 7,491,750,000 | 0.02 | 0.10 | |
| 1981D | 5,373,235,677 | 0.02 | 0.10 | |
| 1981S, Type 1 | (4,063,083) | | | 1.50 |
| 1981S, Type 2 | * | | | 14.00 |

* Included in number above. ** Included in number below. **a.** Included in circulation-strike mintage for 1970-S, Large Date (Low 7). **b.** Included in Proof mintage for 1970-S, Large Date (Low 7).

**Large Date**          **Small Date**

| | Mintage | MS-63 | MS-65 | PF-63 |
|---|---|---|---|---|
| 1982, Lg Dt. | .10,712,525,000 | $0.02 | $0.10 | |
| 1982, Sm Dt | .............* | 0.03 | 0.12 | |

* Included in number above.

| | Mintage | MS-63 | MS-65 | PF-63 |
|---|---|---|---|---|
| 1982D, Lg Dt. | .6,012,979,368 | $0.02 | $0.10 | |
| 1982S, Sm Dt | . . (3,857,479) | | | $1.60 |

## Copper-Plated Zinc (1982–2008)

**Close AM**      **Wide AM**

*1995, Doubled Die showing strong doubling on word LIBERTY.*

| | Mintage | MS-63 | MS-65 | PF-63 |
|---|---|---|---|---|
| 1982, Lg Dt | .............* | $0.02 | $0.25 | |
| 1982, Sm Dt | .............* | 0.02 | 0.30 | |
| 1982D, Lg Dt. | .............* | 0.05 | 0.20 | |
| 1982D, Sm Dt | ..........* | 0.01 | 0.10 | |
| 1983 | .......7,752,355,000 | 0.01 | 0.10 | |
| 1983D | ......6,467,199,428 | 0.01 | 0.10 | |
| 1983S | ........ (3,279,126) | 0.01 | 0.05 | $1.10 |
| 1984 | .......8,151,079,000 | 0.01 | 0.05 | |
| 1984, Dbl Ear | ..........** | 50.00 | 100.00 | |
| 1984D | ......5,569,238,906 | 0.01 | 0.10 | |
| 1984S | ........ (3,065,110) | | | 1.10 |
| 1985 | .......5,648,489,887 | 0.01 | 0.05 | |
| 1985D | ......5,287,339,926 | 0.01 | 0.05 | |
| 1985S | ........ (3,362,821) | | | 1.25 |
| 1986 | .......4,491,395,493 | 0.01 | 0.06 | |
| 1986D | ......4,442,866,698 | 0.01 | 0.05 | |
| 1986S | ........ (3,010,497) | | | 2.00 |
| 1987 | .......4,682,466,931 | 0.01 | 0.05 | |
| 1987D | ......4,879,389,514 | 0.01 | 0.05 | |
| 1987S | ........ (4,227,728) | | | 1.10 |
| 1988 | .......6,092,810,000 | 0.01 | 0.05 | |
| 1988D | ......5,253,740,443 | 0.01 | 0.05 | |
| 1988S | ........ (3,262,948) | | | 2.00 |
| 1989 | .......7,261,535,000 | 0.01 | 0.05 | |
| 1989D | ......5,345,467,111 | 0.01 | 0.05 | |
| 1989S | ........ (3,220,194) | | | 2.00 |
| 1990 | .......6,851,765,000 | 0.01 | 0.05 | |
| 1990D | ......4,922,894,533 | 0.01 | 0.05 | |
| 1990S | ........ (3,299,559) | | | 2.00 |
| 1990, Pf, No S | .........** | | | — |
| 1991 | .......5,165,940,000 | 0.01 | 0.05 | |

| | Mintage | MS-63 | MS-65 | PF-63 |
|---|---|---|---|---|
| 1991D | ......4,158,446,076 | $0.01 | $0.05 | |
| 1991S | ........ (2,867,787) | | | $6.75 |
| 1992 | .......4,648,905,000 | 0.01 | 0.05 | |
| 1992, Close AM (a) | ......** | — | — | |
| 1992D | .....4,448,673,300 | 0.01 | 0.05 | |
| 1992D, Close AM (a) | .....** | — | — | |
| 1992S | ........ (4,176,560) | | | 1.10 |
| 1993 | .......5,684,705,000 | 0.01 | 0.05 | |
| 1993D | ......6,426,650,571 | 0.01 | 0.05 | |
| 1993S | ........ (3,394,792) | | | 3.00 |
| 1994 | .......6,500,850,000 | 0.01 | 0.05 | |
| 1994D | ......7,131,765,000 | 0.01 | 0.05 | |
| 1994S | ........ (3,269,923) | | | 3.00 |
| 1995 | .......6,411,440,000 | 0.01 | 0.05 | |
| 1995, DblDie Obv | .......** | 15.00 | 25.00 | |
| 1995D | ......7,128,560,000 | 0.01 | 0.05 | |
| 1995S | ........ (2,797,481) | | | 3.00 |
| 1996 | .......6,612,465,000 | 0.01 | 0.05 | |
| 1996D | ......6,510,795,000 | 0.01 | 0.05 | |
| 1996S | ........ (2,525,265) | | | 1.25 |
| 1997 | .......4,622,800,000 | 0.01 | 0.05 | |
| 1997D | ......4,576,555,000 | 0.01 | 0.05 | |
| 1997S | ........ (2,796,678) | | | 4.00 |
| 1998 | .......5,032,155,000 | 0.01 | 0.05 | |
| 1998, Wide AM (b) | .......** | 2.00 | 10.00 | |
| 1998D | ......5,225,353,500 | 0.01 | 0.05 | |
| 1998S | ........ (2,086,507) | | | 3.00 |
| 1998S, Close AM (a) | .....** | | | 150.00 |
| 1999 | .......5,237,600,000 | 0.01 | 0.05 | |
| 1999, Wide AM (b) | .......** | | | — |
| 1999D | ......6,360,065,000 | 0.01 | 0.05 | |

* Included in previous section's mintages. ** Included in number above. **a.** The circulation-strike hub adopted in 1993, with AM almost touching, was accidentally used on these cents. **b.** Varieties were made using Proof dies that have a wide space between AM in AMERICA. The letters nearly touch on other Uncirculated cents.

*Chart continued on next page.*        **65**

| Mintage | MS-63 | MS-65 | PF-63 |
|---|---|---|---|
| 1999S . . . . . . . . (3,347,966) | | | $2.00 |
| 1999S, Close AM (a) . . . . .** | | | 30.00 |
| 2000 . . . . . . .5,503,200,000 | $0.01 | $0.05 | |
| 2000, Wide AM (b). . . . . . .** | 2.00 | 5.00 | |
| 2000D . . . . . .8,774,220,000 | 0.01 | 0.05 | |
| 2000S . . . . . . . . (4,047,993) | | | 1.20 |
| 2001 . . . . . . .4,959,600,000 | 0.01 | 0.05 | |
| 2001D . . . . . .5,374,990,000 | 0.01 | 0.05 | |
| 2001S . . . . . . . . (3,184,606) | | | 1.20 |
| 2002 . . . . . . .3,260,800,000 | 0.01 | 0.05 | |
| 2002D . . . . . .4,028,055,000 | 0.01 | 0.05 | |
| 2002S . . . . . . . . (3,211,995) | | | 1.20 |
| 2003 . . . . . . .3,300,000,000 | 0.01 | 0.05 | |
| 2003D . . . . . .3,548,000,000 | 0.01 | 0.05 | |
| 2003S . . . . . . . . (3,298,439) | | | 1.20 |

| Mintage | MS-63 | MS-65 | PF-63 |
|---|---|---|---|
| 2004 . . . . . . .3,379,600,000 | $0.01 | $0.05 | |
| 2004D . . . . . .3,456,400,000 | 0.01 | 0.05 | |
| 2004S . . . . . . . . (2,965,422) | | | $1.20 |
| 2005 . . . . . . .3,935,600,000 | 0.01 | 0.05 | |
| 2005D . . . . .3,764,450,500 | 0.01 | 0.05 | |
| 2005S . . . . . . . . (3,344,679) | | | 1.20 |
| 2006 . . . . . . .4,290,000,000 | 0.01 | 0.05 | |
| 2006D . . . . . .3,944,000,000 | 0.01 | 0.05 | |
| 2006S . . . . . . . . (3,054,436) | | | 1.20 |
| 2007 . . . . . . .3,762,400,000 | 0.01 | 0.05 | |
| 2007D . . . . . .3,638,800,000 | 0.01 | 0.05 | |
| 2007S . . . . . . . . (2,577,166) | | | 1.20 |
| 2008 . . . . . . .2,558,800,000 | 0.01 | 0.05 | |
| 2008D . . . . . .2,849,600,000 | 0.01 | 0.05 | |
| 2008S . . . . . . . . (2,169,561) | | | 1.20 |

** Included in number above. **a.** The circulation-strike hub adopted in 1993, with AM almost touching, was accidentally used on these cents. **b.** Varieties were made using Proof dies that have a wide space between AM in AMERICA. The letters nearly touch on other Uncirculated cents.

## LINCOLN, BICENTENNIAL (2009)

One-cent coins issued during 2009 are a unique tribute to President Abraham Lincoln, recognizing the bicentennial of his birth and the 100th anniversary of the first issuance of the Lincoln cent. These coins use four different design themes on the reverse to represent the four major aspects of President Lincoln's life. The obverse of each of these coins carries the traditional portrait of Lincoln that has been in use since 1909.

The special reverse designs, released as quarterly issues throughout 2009, are described as: Birth and Early Childhood in Kentucky (designer, Richard Masters; sculptor, Jim Licaretz); Formative Years in Indiana (designer and sculptor, Charles Vickers); Professional Life in Illinois (designer, Joel Iskowitz; sculptor, Don Everhart); and Presidency in Washington (designer, Susan Gamble; sculptor, Joseph Menna). Those issued for commercial circulation are made of the exact same copper-plated composition used since 1982. Special versions included in collector sets are made of the same metallic composition as was used for the original 1909 cents (95% copper, 5% tin and zinc).

2009 Lincoln cent reverse designs

| | Mintage | MS-63 | MS-65 | PF-65 |
|---|---|---|---|---|
| 2009, Birth and Early Childhood. . . . . . . . . . . . . . . . . . . . . . . . . . . . . . | 284,400,000 | $0.05 | $0.10 | |
| 2009, Birth and Early Childhood, copper, Satin finish. . . . . . . . . . . . . . . | 784,614 | | 4.00 | |
| 2009D, Birth and Early Childhood . . . . . . . . . . . . . . . . . . . . . . . . . . | 350,400,000 | 0.05 | 0.10 | |
| 2009D, Birth and Early Childhood, copper, Satin finish. . . . . . . . . . . . . . | 784,614 | | 4.00 | |
| 2009S, Birth and Early Childhood . . . . . . . . . . . . . . (2,995,615) . . . . . . . . . . . . | | | | $2 |
| 2009, Formative Years. . . . . . . . . . . . . . . . . . . . . . . . . . . . . . . . . . . . | 376,000,000 | 0.05 | 0.10 | |
| 2009, Formative Years, copper, Satin finish . . . . . . . . . . . . . . . . . . . . . | 784,614 | | 4.00 | |
| 2009D, Formative Years. . . . . . . . . . . . . . . . . . . . . . . . . . . . . . . . . . . | 363,600,000 | 0.05 | 0.10 | |

| | Mintage | MS-63 | MS-65 | PF-65 |
|---|---|---|---|---|
| 2009D, Formative Years, copper, Satin finish | 784,614 | | $4.00 | |
| 2009S, Formative Years | (2,995,615) | | | $2 |
| 2009, Professional Life | 316,000,000 | $0.05 | 0.10 | |
| 2009, Professional Life, copper, Satin finish | 784,614 | | 4.00 | |
| 2009D, Professional Life | 336,000,000 | 0.05 | 0.10 | |
| 2009D, Professional Life, copper, Satin finish | 784,614 | | 4.00 | |
| 2009S, Professional Life | (2,995,615) | | | 2 |
| 2009, Presidency | 129,600,000 | 0.05 | 0.10 | |
| 2009, Presidency, copper, Satin finish | 784,614 | | 4.00 | |
| 2009D, Presidency | 198,000,000 | 0.05 | 0.10 | |
| 2009D, Presidency, copper, Satin finish | 784,614 | | 4.00 | |
| 2009S, Presidency | (2,995,615) | | | 2 |

## LINCOLN, SHIELD REVERSE (2010 TO DATE)

Since the conclusion of the 2009 Bicentennial One-Cent Program, one-cent coins feature a reverse that has "an image emblematic of President Lincoln's preservation of the United States of America as a single and united country." The Union Shield design is by Lyndall Bass, sculpted by Joseph Menna.

| | Mintage | MS-65 | PF-63 |
|---|---|---|---|
| 2010 | 1,963,630,000 | $0.01 | |
| 2010D | 2,047,200,000 | 0.01 | |
| 2010S | (1,689,216) | | $2 |
| 2011 | 2,402,400,000 | 0.01 | |
| 2011D | 2,536,140,000 | 0.01 | |
| 2011S | (1,673,010) | | 2 |
| 2012 | 3,132,000,000 | 0.01 | |
| 2012D | 2,883,200,000 | 0.01 | |
| 2012S | (1,239,148) | | 2 |
| 2013 | 3,750,400,000 | 0.01 | |
| 2013D | 3,319,600,000 | 0.01 | |
| 2013S | (1,274,505) | | 2 |
| 2014 | 3,990,800,000 | 0.01 | |
| 2014D | 4,155,600,000 | 0.01 | |
| 2014S | (1,190,369) | | 2 |
| 2015 | 4,691,300,000 | 0.01 | |
| 2015D | 4,674,000,000 | 0.01 | |
| 2015S | (1,099,182) | | 2 |
| 2016 | 4,698,000,000 | 0.01 | |
| 2016D | 4,420,400,000 | 0.01 | |
| 2016S | (978,457) | | 2 |

| | Mintage | MS-65 | PF-63 |
|---|---|---|---|
| 2017P | 4,361,220,000 | $0.01 | |
| 2017D | 4,272,800,000 | 0.01 | |
| 2017S | (979,475) | | $2 |
| 2018 | 4,066,800,000 | 0.01 | |
| 2018D | 3,736,400,000 | 0.01 | |
| 2018S | (901,072) | | 2 |
| 2019 | 3,542,800,000 | 0.01 | |
| 2019D | 3,497,600,000 | 0.01 | |
| 2019S | (1,061,558) | | 2 |
| 2019W | 346,117 | | 5 |
| 2019W, Proof | (600,423) | 0.01 | |
| 2019W, Reverse Proof | (412,508) | | |
| 2020 | 3,925,820,000 | 0.01 | |
| 2020D | 3,982,800,000 | 0.01 | |
| 2020S | (824,332) | | 2 |
| 2021 | 3,560,800,000 | 0.01 | |
| 2021D | 4,035,600,000 | 0.01 | |
| 2021S | (792,612) | | 2 |
| 2022 | | | |
| 2022D | | | |
| 2022S | | | |

## TWO-CENT PIECES (1864–1873)

The Act of April 22, 1864, which changed the copper-nickel cent to a lighter-weight bronze composition, included a provision for a new coin, the two-cent piece. Its weight was specified as 96 grains, and its bronze alloy the same as for the cent. The two-cent piece was the nation's first circulating coin to bear the motto IN GOD WE TRUST.

There are two varieties for 1864, the first year of issue: the scarcer Small Motto, and the Large Motto. The differences are illustrated in the close-ups below. On the Small Motto variety, the stem to the cluster of leaves below TRUST is plainly visible, the D in GOD is wide, the first T in TRUST is close to the ribbon crease, and the U in TRUST is squat. On the Large Motto variety there is no stem, the D is narrow, the first T is farther from the crease, and the U is tall and narrow.

1864, Small Motto

1864, Large Motto

**G-4 Good:** At least part of IN GOD visible.
**VG-8 Very Good:** WE weakly visible.
**F-12 Fine:** Complete motto visible. The word WE weak.
**VF-20 Very Fine:** WE is clear, but not strong.
**EF-40 Extremely Fine:** The word WE bold.
**AU-50 About Uncirculated:** Traces of wear visible on leaf tips, arrow points, and the word WE.
**MS-60 Uncirculated:** No trace of wear. Light blemishes.
**MS-63 Choice Uncirculated:** Some distracting contact marks or blemishes in prime focal areas. Some impairment of luster possible.
**PF-63 Choice Proof:** Reflective surfaces with only a few blemishes in secondary focal places. No major flaws.

*Dealers often pay more than the prices shown for brilliant red choice Uncirculated and Proof coins, and less for cleaned or discolored pieces.*

| | Mintage | G-4 | VG-8 | F-12 | VF-20 | EF-40 | AU-50 | MS-60 | MS-63 | PF-63 |
|---|---|---|---|---|---|---|---|---|---|---|
| 1864, Small Motto . . . . . . . . . . . . . . . * | | $150 | $185 | $275 | $375 | $500 | $750 | $1,000 | $1,250 | $17,500 |
| 1864, Large Motto *(100+)* . . | 19,822,500 | 10 | 12 | 15 | 20 | 30 | 45 | 70 | 115 | 450 |
| 1865 . . . . . . . . . .*(500+)* . . | 13,640,000 | 10 | 12 | 15 | 20 | 30 | 45 | 70 | 115 | 350 |
| 1866 . . . . . . . . . .*(725+)* . . . | 3,177,000 | 10 | 12 | 15 | 20 | 30 | 45 | 95 | 115 | 350 |
| 1867 . . . . . . . . . .*(625+)* . . . | 2,938,750 | 10 | 12 | 15 | 20 | 30 | 45 | 95 | 115 | 350 |
| 1868 . . . . . . . . . .*(600+)* . . . | 2,803,750 | 10 | 12 | 15 | 25 | 35 | 50 | 125 | 150 | 350 |
| 1869 . . . . . . . . . .*(600+)* . . . | 1,546,500 | 20 | 25 | 30 | 35 | 50 | 75 | 115 | 150 | 350 |
| 1870 . . . . . . . . .*(1,000+)* . . . . | 861,250 | 17 | 25 | 30 | 35 | 70 | 100 | 150 | 250 | 350 |
| 1871 . . . . . . . . . .*(960+)* . . . . | 721,250 | 20 | 30 | 35 | 40 | 75 | 100 | 175 | 300 | 400 |
| 1872 . . . . . . . . . .*(950+)* . . . . . . | 65,000 | 250 | 300 | 400 | 500 | 650 | 1,100 | 2,000 | 2,500 | 750 |
| 1873 . . . . . . . . . *(600)* . . . . . . . . . . . | | | | | | | | | | 2,250 |

* Included in number below.

# SILVER THREE-CENT PIECES (TRIMES) (1851–1873)

This smallest of United States silver coins was authorized by Congress March 3, 1851. The first three-cent silver pieces had no lines bordering the six-pointed star. From 1854 through 1858 there were two lines, while issues of the last 15 years show only one line. Issues from 1854 through 1873 have an olive sprig over the III and a bundle of three arrows beneath.

**G-4 Good:** Star worn smooth. Legend and date readable.
**VG-8 Very Good:** Outline of shield defined. Legend and date clear.
**F-12 Fine:** Only star points worn smooth.
**VF-20 Very Fine:** Only partial wear on star ridges.
**EF-40 Extremely Fine:** Ridges on star points visible.
**AU-50 About Uncirculated:** Trace of wear visible at each star point. Center of shield possibly weak.
**MS-60 Uncirculated:** No trace of wear. Light blemishes.
**MS-63 Choice Uncirculated:** Some distracting contact marks or blemishes in prime focal areas. Some impairment of luster possible.
**PF-63 Choice Proof:** Reflective surfaces with only a few blemishes in secondary focal places. No major flaws.

*Mintmark location.*

| No Outline Around Star (1851–1853) | Three Outlines to Star, Large Date (1854–1858) | Two Outlines to Star, Small Date (1859–1873) | 1862, 2 Over 1 |
|---|---|---|---|

*Dealers usually pay higher prices for well-struck examples.*

| | Mintage | G-4 | VG-8 | F-12 | VF-20 | EF-40 | AU-50 | MS-60 | MS-63 | PF-63 |
|---|---|---|---|---|---|---|---|---|---|---|
| 1851 . . . . . . . . . . . . . | 5,447,400 | $20 | $25 | $30 | $40 | $45 | $100 | $125 | $225 | — |
| 18510 . . . . . . . . . . . . . . | 720,000 | 30 | 40 | 50 | 65 | 125 | 250 | 525 | 800 | |
| 1852 . . . . . . . . . . . . | 18,663,500 | 20 | 25 | 30 | 40 | 45 | 100 | 125 | 225 | — |
| 1853 . . . . . . . . . . . . | 11,400,000 | 20 | 25 | 30 | 40 | 45 | 100 | 125 | 225 | |
| 1854 . . . . . . . . . . . . . . . | 671,000 | 30 | 35 | 40 | 50 | 75 | 125 | 175 | 450 | $6,000 |
| 1855 . . . . . . . . . . . . . . | 139,000 | 30 | 35 | 40 | 60 | 100 | 150 | 450 | 1,100 | 2,500 |
| 1856 . . . . . . . . . . . . | 1,458,000 | 30 | 35 | 40 | 50 | 75 | 125 | 150 | 450 | 1,800 |
| 1857 . . . . . . . . . . . . | 1,042,000 | 30 | 35 | 40 | 50 | 75 | 125 | 150 | 450 | 1,800 |
| 1858 . . . . . . . *(210)* . . | 1,603,700 | 30 | 35 | 40 | 50 | 75 | 125 | 150 | 450 | 1,200 |
| 1859 . . . . . . . (800) . . . . | 364,200 | 30 | 35 | 40 | 50 | 65 | 100 | 125 | 250 | 550 |
| 1860 . . . . . .(1,000) . . . . | 286,000 | 30 | 35 | 40 | 50 | 65 | 100 | 125 | 250 | 750 |
| 1861 . . . . . .(1,000) . . . . | 497,000 | 30 | 35 | 40 | 50 | 65 | 100 | 125 | 250 | 550 |
| 1862, 2/1 . . . . . . . . . . . . . . . .* | | 30 | 35 | 40 | 50 | 70 | 125 | 300 | 375 | |
| 1862 . . . . . . . (550) . . . . | 343,000 | 30 | 35 | 40 | 50 | 65 | 100 | 125 | 250 | 550 |
| 1863 . . . . . . . (460) . . . . . | 21,000 | | | | 450 | 550 | 650 | 800 | 1,500 | 550 |
| 1864 . . . . . . . (470) . . . . . | 12,000 | | | | 450 | 550 | 650 | 900 | 1,250 | 550 |

| | Mintage | VF-20 | EF-40 | AU-50 | MS-60 | MS-63 | PF-63 |
|---|---|---|---|---|---|---|---|
| 1865 . . . . . . . . . . . . . . . . . .(500) . . . .8,000 | | $450 | $550 | $650 | $1,000 | $1,750 | $650 |
| 1866 . . . . . . . . . . . . . . . . . .(725) . . .22,000 | | 500 | 550 | 700 | 750 | 1,250 | 650 |
| 1867 . . . . . . . . . . . . . . . . . .(625) . . . .4,000 | | 425 | 450 | 700 | 1,000 | 1,600 | 650 |
| 1868 . . . . . . . . . . . . . . . . . .(600) . . . .3,500 | | 1,000 | 1,400 | 1,500 | 3,500 | 5,000 | 650 |
| 1869 . . . . . . . . . . . . . . . . . .(600) . . . .4,500 | | 425 | 450 | 600 | 850 | 1,650 | 650 |
| 1870 . . . . . . . . . . . . . . . . (1,000) . . . .3,000 | | 425 | 450 | 550 | 800 | 1,050 | 650 |
| 1871 . . . . . . . . . . . . . . . . . .(960) . . . .3,400 | | 425 | 450 | 550 | 650 | 850 | 650 |
| 1872 . . . . . . . . . . . . . . . . . .(950) . . . .1,000 | | 1,000 | 1,250 | 1,750 | 2,500 | 3,500 | 650 |
| 1873, Proof only . . . . . . . . . . .(600) . . . . . . . | | | | | | | 1,250 |

\* Included in number below.

# NICKEL THREE-CENT PIECES (1865–1889)

Three-cent pieces struck in a nickel alloy were intended to replace the earlier silver three-cent coins, which were hoarded by the public during the Civil War. The Mint struck more than 11 million three-cent coins of the new composition (75% copper and 25% nickel) in 1865, their first year of issue, compared to only 8,000 silver pieces. The nickel coins were all made at the Philadelphia Mint. They have a plain (non-reeded) edge.

**G-4 Good:** Date and legends complete though worn. III smooth.
**VG-8 Very Good:** III half worn. Rims complete.
**VF-20 Very Fine:** Three-quarters of hair details visible.
**EF-40 Extremely Fine:** Slight, even wear.
**AU-50 About Uncirculated:** Slight wear on hair curls, above forehead, and on wreath and numeral III.
**MS-60 Uncirculated:** No trace of wear. Light blemishes.
**MS-63 Choice Uncirculated:** Some distracting contact marks or blemishes in prime focal areas. Some impairment of luster possible.
**PF-63 Choice Proof:** Reflective surfaces with only a few blemishes in secondary focal places. No major flaws.

*Dealers often pay more than the prices shown for brilliant choice Unc. and Proof coins, and less for spotted, cleaned, or discolored pieces.*

| | Mintage | G-4 | VG-8 | F-12 | VF-20 | EF-40 | AU-50 | MS-60 | MS-63 | PF-63 |
|---|---|---|---|---|---|---|---|---|---|---|
| 1865 . . . . . . *(500+)* . .11,382,000 | | $10 | $12 | $14 | $16 | $25 | $35 | $75 | $100 | $650 |
| 1866 . . . . . . *(725+)* . . 4,801,000 | | 10 | 12 | 14 | 16 | 25 | 35 | 75 | 100 | 225 |
| 1867 . . . . . . *(625+)* . . 3,915,000 | | 10 | 12 | 14 | 16 | 25 | 35 | 75 | 100 | 225 |
| 1868 . . . . . . *(600+)* . . 3,252,000 | | 10 | 12 | 14 | 16 | 25 | 35 | 85 | 100 | 225 |
| 1869 . . . . . . *(600+)* . . 1,604,000 | | 10 | 12 | 14 | 16 | 25 | 35 | 85 | 100 | 225 |
| 1870 . . . . . *(1,000+)* . . 1,335,000 | | 10 | 12 | 14 | 16 | 25 | 35 | 85 | 145 | 225 |
| 1871 . . . . . . *(960+)* . . . 604,000 | | 10 | 12 | 14 | 16 | 25 | 35 | 85 | 165 | 225 |
| 1872 . . . . . . *(950+)* . . . 862,000 | | 10 | 12 | 14 | 16 | 25 | 35 | 85 | 225 | 225 |
| 1873 . . . . . *(1,100+)* . . . 390,000 | | 10 | 12 | 14 | 16 | 25 | 35 | 85 | 200 | 225 |
| 1874 . . . . . . *(700+)* . . . 790,000 | | 10 | 12 | 14 | 16 | 25 | 35 | 85 | 150 | 225 |
| 1875 . . . . . . *(700+)* . . . 228,000 | | 10 | 12 | 14 | 16 | 25 | 35 | 100 | 150 | 225 |
| 1876 . . . . . *(1,150+)* . . . 162,000 | | 10 | 12 | 14 | 16 | 25 | 35 | 110 | 175 | 250 |
| 1877, Pf only . . (900) . . . . . . . . . | | | | | 800 | 1,000 | | | | 1,500 |
| 1878, Pf only (2,350) . . . . . . . . . | | | | | 425 | 550 | | | | 650 |
| 1879 . . . . . . (3,200) . . . . . 38,000 | | 20 | 25 | 30 | 40 | 60 | 75 | 150 | 300 | 250 |
| 1880 . . . . . . (3,955) . . . . . 21,000 | | 40 | 45 | 50 | 60 | 70 | 85 | 175 | 350 | 250 |
| 1881 . . . . . . (3,575) . . 1,077,000 | | 10 | 12 | 14 | 16 | 25 | 35 | 65 | 125 | 225 |
| 1882 . . . . . . (3,100) . . . . . 22,200 | | 50 | 55 | 65 | 75 | 85 | 125 | 225 | 450 | 225 |
| 1883 . . . . . . (6,609) . . . . . . 4,000 | | 90 | 105 | 120 | 135 | 175 | 250 | 750 | 1,750 | 235 |
| 1884 . . . . . . (3,942) . . . . . . 1,700 | | 500 | 650 | 750 | 1,000 | 1,200 | 2,500 | 3,000 | 5,500 | 300 |
| 1885 . . . . . . (3,790) . . . . . . 1,000 | | 400 | 650 | 750 | 1,000 | 1,350 | 2,000 | 2,250 | 4,500 | 275 |
| 1886, Pf only (4,290) . . . . . . . . . | | | | | 175 | 200 | | | | 250 |
| 1887 . . . . . . (2,960) . . . . . . 5,001 | | 120 | 140 | 150 | 200 | 250 | 285 | 350 | 375 | 250 |
| 1887, 7/6 . . . . . . . * . . . . . . . . . . | | | | | 225 | 250 | | | | 350 |
| 1888 . . . . . . (4,582) . . . . 36,501 | | 20 | 23 | 27 | 35 | 45 | 60 | 175 | 250 | 225 |
| 1889 . . . . . . (3,436) . . . . . 18,125 | | 35 | 45 | 60 | 75 | 100 | 125 | 175 | 275 | 225 |

* Included in number above.

# SHIELD (1866–1883)

The Shield type nickel was made possible by the Act of May 16, 1866. Its weight was set at 77-16/100 grains with the same composition as the nickel three-cent piece.

**G-4 Good:** All letters in motto readable.
**VG-8 Very Good:** Motto clear and stands out. Rims slightly worn but even. Part of shield lines visible.
**F-12 Fine:** Half of each olive leaf worn smooth.
**EF-40 Extremely Fine:** Slight wear to leaf tips and cross over shield.
**AU-50 About Uncirculated:** Traces of light wear on only the high design points. Half of mint luster present.
**MS-60 Uncirculated:** No trace of wear. Light blemishes.
**MS-63 Choice Uncirculated:** Some distracting blemishes in prime focal areas. Impaired luster possible.
**PF-63 Choice Proof:** Reflective surfaces. Only a few blemishes in secondary focal areas. No major flaws.

**With Rays (1866–1867)**          **Without Rays (1867–1883)**

1873, Close 3          1873, Open 3          **Typical Example of 1883, 3 Over 2**
*Other varieties exist.*

*Dealers often pay more than the prices shown for brilliant choice Unc. and Proof coins, and less for spotted, cleaned, or discolored pieces.*

| | Mintage | G-4 | VG-8 | F-12 | VF-20 | EF-40 | AU-50 | MS-60 | MS-63 | PF-63 |
|---|---|---|---|---|---|---|---|---|---|---|
| 1866, Rays . . . . . . *(600+)* . . | 14,742,500 | $20 | $25 | $30 | $50 | $85 | $135 | $200 | $325 | $1,200 |
| 1867, Rays . . . . . . . *(25+)* . . . | 2,019,000 | 25 | 30 | 35 | 60 | 90 | 150 | 250 | 400 | 20,000 |
| 1867, Without Rays . . . . . . . . *(600+)* . . | 28,890,500 | 20 | 22 | 25 | 30 | 40 | 50 | 100 | 150 | 275 |
| 1868 . . . . . . . . . . . *(600+)* . . | 28,817,000 | 20 | 22 | 25 | 30 | 40 | 50 | 100 | 150 | 250 |
| 1869 . . . . . . . . . . . *(600+)* . . | 16,395,000 | 20 | 22 | 25 | 30 | 40 | 50 | 100 | 150 | 250 |
| 1870 . . . . . . . . . *(1,000+)* . . | 4,806,000 | 20 | 22 | 30 | 40 | 50 | 75 | 150 | 250 | 250 |
| 1871 . . . . . . . . . . . *(960+)* . . . . | 561,000 | 45 | 55 | 85 | 125 | 185 | 245 | 325 | 600 | 250 |
| 1872 . . . . . . . . . . . *(950+)* . . . | 6,036,000 | 20 | 22 | 25 | 30 | 55 | 100 | 175 | 200 | 250 |
| 1873, Close 3 . . . *(1,100+)* . . . . | 436,050 | 20 | 30 | 40 | 65 | 100 | 150 | 275 | 500 | 250 |
| 1873, Open 3 . . . . . . . . . . | 4,113,950 | 20 | 22 | 25 | 30 | 40 | 60 | 135 | 250 | |
| 1874 . . . . . . . . . . *(700+)* . . . | 3,538,000 | 20 | 22 | 25 | 30 | 50 | 100 | 175 | 250 | 250 |
| 1875 . . . . . . . . . . *(700+)* . . . | 2,097,000 | 25 | 30 | 35 | 40 | 80 | 115 | 185 | 265 | 250 |
| 1876 . . . . . . . . . *(1,150+)* . . . | 2,530,000 | 20 | 25 | 30 | 45 | 55 | 85 | 175 | 250 | 250 |
| 1877, Pf only . . . . . *(900)* . . . . . . . . . . . . | | | 1,250 | 1,500 | 1,650 | | | | 2,000 |
| 1878, Pf only . . . *(2,350)* . . . . . . . . . . . . | | | 600 | 750 | 850 | | | | 1,000 |
| 1879 . . . . . . . . *(3,200)* . . . . . . | 25,900 | 250 | 350 | 450 | 500 | 600 | 750 | 1,250 | 1,650 | 300 |
| 1880 . . . . . . . . *(3,955)* . . . . . . . | 16,000 | 1,250 | 1,500 | 2,000 | 2,250 | 3,750 | 5,000 | 9,500 | 15,000 | 275 |
| 1881 . . . . . . . . *(3,575)* . . . . . . . | 68,800 | 175 | 225 | 300 | 325 | 400 | 550 | 850 | 1,000 | 275 |
| 1882 . . . . . . . . *(3,100)* . . . . | 11,472,900 | 15 | 20 | 22 | 25 | 35 | 55 | 100 | 150 | 250 |
| 1883 . . . . . . . . *(5,419)* . . . . . | 1,451,500 | 15 | 20 | 22 | 25 | 35 | 55 | 100 | 150 | 250 |
| 1883, 3 Over 2 . . . . . . . . . . . . . . . . . . . * | | 125 | 175 | 300 | 450 | 600 | 750 | 1,250 | 1,750 | |

* Included in number above.

## LIBERTY HEAD (1883–1913)

In 1883 the design was changed to the "Liberty head." This type first appeared without the word CENTS on the coin, merely a large letter V. These "CENTS-less" coins were goldplated by fraudsters and passed as $5 pieces. Later in that year the word CENTS was added.

**G-4 Good:** No details in head. LIBERTY obliterated.
**VG-8 Very Good:** Some letters in LIBERTY legible.
**F-12 Fine:** All letters in LIBERTY legible.
**VF-20 Very Fine:** LIBERTY bold, including letter L.
**EF-40 Extremely Fine:** LIBERTY sharp. Corn grains at bottom of wreath visible on reverse.
**AU-50 About Uncirculated:** Traces of light wear on only high points of design. Half of mint luster present.
**MS-60 Uncirculated:** No trace of wear. Contact marks possible. Surface may be spotted, or luster faded.
**MS-63 Choice Uncirculated:** No trace of wear. Light blemishes.
**PF-63 Choice Proof:** Reflective surfaces. Only a few blemishes in secondary focal areas. No major flaws.

**Variety 1, Without CENTS (1883 Only)**     **Variety 2, With CENTS (1883–1913)**     **Mintmark Location**

*Dealers often pay more than the prices shown for brilliant choice Unc. and Proof coins, and less for spotted, cleaned, or discolored pieces.*

| | Mintage | G-4 | VG-8 | F-12 | VF-20 | EF-40 | AU-50 | MS-60 | MS-63 | PF-63 |
|---|---|---|---|---|---|---|---|---|---|---|
| 1883, Without CENTS . .(5,219) . . .5,474,300 | | $2.75 | $3.25 | $3.75 | $6 | $6.50 | $9 | $20 | $35 | $200 |
| 1883, CENTS (6,783) . .16,026,200 | | 7.00 | 15.00 | 20.00 | 35 | 50.00 | 75 | 100 | 135 | 150 |
| 1884 . . . . . . .(3,942) . .11,270,000 | | 8.00 | 15.00 | 20.00 | 35 | 50.00 | 75 | 115 | 165 | 150 |
| 1885 . . . . . . .(3,790) . . .1,472,700 | | 200.00 | 375.00 | 500.00 | 750 | 900.00 | 1,150 | 1,350 | 2,500 | 800 |
| 1886 . . . . . . .(4,290) . . .3,326,000 | | 140.00 | 165.00 | 225.00 | 325 | 425.00 | 500 | 850 | 1,500 | 400 |
| 1887 . . . . . . .(2,960) . .15,260,692 | | 5.00 | 10.00 | 15.00 | 25 | 50.00 | 65 | 100 | 145 | 150 |
| 1888 . . . . . . .(4,582) . .10,167,901 | | 15.00 | 20.00 | 30.00 | 60 | 85.00 | 125 | 175 | 225 | 150 |
| 1889 . . . . . . .(3,336) . .15,878,025 | | 8.00 | 10.00 | 15.00 | 30 | 45.00 | 65 | 100 | 145 | 150 |
| 1890 . . . . . . .(2,740) . .16,256,532 | | 4.00 | 8.00 | 12.00 | 20 | 35.00 | 65 | 100 | 145 | 150 |
| 1891 . . . . . . .(2,350) . .16,832,000 | | 3.00 | 4.00 | 12.00 | 20 | 35.00 | 65 | 100 | 145 | 150 |
| 1892 . . . . . . .(2,745) . .11,696,897 | | 3.00 | 4.00 | 10.00 | 20 | 35.00 | 65 | 100 | 145 | 150 |
| 1893 . . . . . . .(2,195) . .13,368,000 | | 3.00 | 4.00 | 10.00 | 20 | 30.00 | 60 | 100 | 145 | 150 |
| 1894 . . . . . . .(2,632) . . .5,410,500 | | 10.00 | 20.00 | 55.00 | 100 | 135.00 | 200 | 250 | 325 | 165 |
| 1895 . . . . . . .(2,062) . . .9,977,822 | | 3.00 | 4.00 | 7.00 | 20 | 35.00 | 65 | 100 | 170 | 150 |
| 1896 . . . . . . .(1,862) . . .8,841,058 | | 2.00 | 5.00 | 15.00 | 25 | 50.00 | 80 | 130 | 210 | 150 |
| 1897 . . . . . . .(1,938) . .20,426,797 | | 2.00 | 5.00 | 9.00 | 12 | 22.00 | 30 | 60 | 125 | 150 |
| 1898 . . . . . . .(1,795) . .12,530,292 | | 2.00 | 5.00 | 9.00 | 12 | 25.00 | 35 | 95 | 145 | 150 |
| 1899 . . . . . . .(2,031) . .26,027,000 | | 1.00 | 1.25 | 2.50 | 6 | 15.00 | 30 | 60 | 100 | 150 |
| 1900 . . . . . . .(2,262) . .27,253,733 | | 1.00 | 1.25 | 2.50 | 6 | 15.00 | 30 | 55 | 80 | 150 |
| 1901 . . . . . . .(1,985) . .26,478,228 | | 1.00 | 1.25 | 2.50 | 6 | 15.00 | 30 | 55 | 80 | 150 |
| 1902 . . . . . . .(2,018) . .31,480,579 | | 1.00 | 1.25 | 2.50 | 6 | 15.00 | 30 | 55 | 80 | 150 |
| 1903 . . . . . . .(1,790) . .28,004,935 | | 1.00 | 1.25 | 2.50 | 6 | 15.00 | 30 | 55 | 80 | 150 |
| 1904 . . . . . . .(1,817) . .21,403,167 | | 1.00 | 1.25 | 2.50 | 6 | 15.00 | 30 | 55 | 80 | 150 |
| 1905 . . . . . . .(2,152) . .29,825,124 | | 1.00 | 1.25 | 2.50 | 6 | 15.00 | 30 | 55 | 80 | 150 |
| 1906 . . . . . . .(1,725) . .38,612,000 | | 1.00 | 1.25 | 2.50 | 6 | 15.00 | 30 | 55 | 80 | 150 |
| 1907 . . . . . . .(1,475) . .39,213,325 | | 1.00 | 1.25 | 2.50 | 6 | 15.00 | 30 | 55 | 80 | 150 |
| 1908 . . . . . . .(1,620) . .22,684,557 | | 1.00 | 1.25 | 2.50 | 6 | 15.00 | 30 | 55 | 80 | 150 |

| | Mintage | G-4 | VG-8 | F-12 | VF-20 | EF-40 | AU-50 | MS-60 | MS-63 | PF-63 |
|---|---|---|---|---|---|---|---|---|---|---|
| 1909 .... (4,763)... 11,585,763 | | $1.00 | $1.50 | $2.50 | $7.50 | $18 | $35 | $55 | $95 | $150 |
| 1910 .... (2,405)... 30,166,948 | | 1.00 | 1.25 | 2.25 | 5.00 | 15 | 30 | 45 | 80 | 150 |
| 1911 .... (1,733)... 39,557,639 | | 1.00 | 1.25 | 2.25 | 5.00 | 15 | 30 | 45 | 80 | 150 |
| 1912 .... (2,145)... 26,234,569 | | 1.00 | 1.25 | 2.25 | 5.00 | 15 | 30 | 45 | 80 | 150 |
| 1912D............. 8,474,000 | | 1.50 | 2.00 | 6.00 | 20.00 | 50 | 100 | 185 | 225 | |
| 1912S..............238,000 | | 75.00 | 100.00 | 120.00 | 250.00 | 600 | 1,000 | 1,200 | 1,400 | |
| 1913 Liberty Head *(5 known)*. ... | | | | | | | | | 2,500,000 | |

# INDIAN HEAD OR BUFFALO (1913–1938)

The Buffalo nickel was designed by James E. Fraser, whose initial F is below the date. He modeled the bison after Black Diamond in the New York Central Park Zoo.

**G-4 Good:** Legends and date readable. Buffalo's horn does not show.

**VG-8 Very Good:** Horn worn nearly flat.

**F-12 Fine:** Horn and tail smooth but partially visible. Obverse rim intact.

**VF-20 Very Fine:** Much of horn visible. Indian's cheekbone worn.

**EF-40 Extremely Fine:** Horn lightly worn. Slight wear on Indian's hair ribbon.

**AU-50 About Uncirculated:** Traces of light wear on high points of design. Half of mint luster present.

**MS-60 Uncirculated:** No trace of wear. May have several blemishes.

**MS-63 Choice Uncirculated:** No trace of wear. Light blemishes.

**Matte PF-63 Choice Proof:** Crisp surfaces. Only a few blemishes in secondary focal areas. No major flaws.

## Variety 1 – FIVE CENTS on Raised Ground (1913)

*Dealers often pay more than the prices shown for brilliant choice Unc. coins, and less for spotted, cleaned, weakly struck, or discolored pieces.*

| | Mintage | G-4 | VG-8 | F-12 | VF-20 | EF-40 | AU-50 | MS-60 | MS-63 | MATTE PF-63 |
|---|---|---|---|---|---|---|---|---|---|---|
| 1913, Variety 1 . .(1,520) . . 30,992,000 | | $5 | $8 | $10 | $12 | $15 | $18 | $22 | $35 | $1,000 |
| 1913D, Variety 1 .......... 5,337,000 | | 8 | 10 | 12 | 15 | 20 | 25 | 35 | 45 | |
| 1913S, Variety 1 .......... 2,105,000 | | 20 | 25 | 30 | 35 | 45 | 60 | 75 | 115 | |

## Variety 2 – FIVE CENTS in Recess (1913–1938)

**Mintmark Below FIVE CENTS**     **1916, Doubled-Die Obverse**     **1918-D, 8 Over 7**

| | Mintage | G-4 | VG-8 | F-12 | VF-20 | EF-40 | AU-50 | MS-60 | MS-63 | MATTE PF-63 |
|---|---|---|---|---|---|---|---|---|---|---|
| 1913, Variety 2 ..... 29,857,186 | | $5 | $7 | $8 | $10 | $12 | $15 | $22 | $32 | |
| .................(1,514) | | | | | | | | | | $750 |
| 1913D, Variety 2 ..... 4,156,000 | | 65 | 85 | 100 | 115 | 135 | 165 | 200 | 240 | |
| 1913S, Variety 2 ..... 1,209,000 | | 150 | 200 | 225 | 275 | 350 | 450 | 550 | 850 | |
| 1914............. 20,664,463 | | 10 | 11 | 12 | 14 | 16 | 22 | 35 | 50 | |
| .................(1,275) | | | | | | | | | | 750 |

*Chart continued on next page.*

*Dealers often pay more than the prices shown for brilliant choice Unc. coins, and less for spotted, cleaned, weakly struck, or discolored pieces.*

| | Mintage | G-4 | VG-8 | F-12 | VF-20 | EF-40 | AU-50 | MS-60 | MS-63 | MATTE PF-63 |
|---|---|---|---|---|---|---|---|---|---|---|
| 1914D . . . . . . . 3,912,000 | | $55.00 | $65.00 | $85.00 | $110.00 | $150 | $200 | $285 | $350 | |
| 1914S . . . . . . . 3,470,000 | | 15.00 | 20.00 | 25.00 | 35.00 | 50 | 85 | 125 | 250 | |
| 1915 . . . . . . . . 20,986,220 | | 2.50 | 3.00 | 4.00 | 7.00 | 12 | 24 | 35 | 50 | |
| . . . . . . . . . . . (1,050) | | | | | | | | | | $750 |
| 1915D . . . . . . . 7,569,000 | | 10.00 | 15.00 | 25.00 | 35.00 | 75 | 95 | 150 | 250 | |
| 1915S . . . . . . . 1,505,000 | | 20.00 | 35.00 | 40.00 | 80.00 | 200 | 300 | 500 | 850 | |
| 1916 . . . . . . . . 63,497,466 | | 2.00 | 2.50 | 3.00 | 3.50 | 5 | 10 | 28 | 45 | |
| . . . . . . . . . . . . (600) | | | | | | | | | | 850 |
| 1916, DblDie Obv . . . . . . * 3,000.00 | | 4,000.00 | 6,500.00 | 8,500.00 | 13,500 | 20,000 | 45,000 | 100,000 | | |
| 1916D . . . . . . . 13,333,000 | | 7.00 | 10.00 | 15.00 | 25.00 | 45 | 60 | 100 | 175 | |
| 1916S . . . . . . . 11,860,000 | | 5.00 | 8.00 | 12.00 | 25.00 | 45 | 65 | 135 | 200 | |
| 1917 . . . . . . . . 51,424,019 | | 2.00 | 2.50 | 3.00 | 4.00 | 7 | 16 | 30 | 85 | |
| 1917D . . . . . . . 9,910,000 | | 10.00 | 15.00 | 25.00 | 45.00 | 85 | 150 | 250 | 400 | |
| 1917S . . . . . . . 4,193,000 | | 10.00 | 20.00 | 40.00 | 55.00 | 115 | 165 | 400 | 1,150 | |
| 1918 . . . . . . . . 32,086,314 | | 1.50 | 2.00 | 2.50 | 6.00 | 16 | 22 | 85 | 175 | |

\* Included in number above.

| | Mintage | G-4 | VG-8 | F-12 | VF-20 | EF-40 | AU-50 | MS-60 | MS-63 |
|---|---|---|---|---|---|---|---|---|---|
| 1918D, 8 Over 7 . . . . . . ** | $500.00 | $750.00 | $1,600.00 | $2,500.00 | $6,000.00 | $8,500 | $27,500 | $40,000 |
| 1918D . . . . . . . 8,362,000 | | 12.00 | 20.00 | 30.00 | 70.00 | 150.00 | 200 | 300 | 750 |
| 1918S . . . . . . . 4,882,000 | | 8.00 | 15.00 | 25.00 | 55.00 | 115.00 | 250 | 450 | 1,500 |
| 1919 . . . . . . . 60,868,000 | | 0.50 | 0.55 | 0.80 | 2.00 | 7.00 | 15 | 35 | 85 |
| 1919D (a) . . . . 8,006,000 | | 10.00 | 15.00 | 45.00 | 70.00 | 140.00 | 225 | 450 | 1,000 |
| 1919S (a) . . . . 7,521,000 | | 4.00 | 10.00 | 25.00 | 60.00 | 145.00 | 225 | 400 | 1,100 |
| 1920 . . . . . . . 63,093,000 | | 0.45 | 0.60 | 1.25 | 2.50 | 6.00 | 15 | 35 | 85 |
| 1920D (a) . . . . 9,418,000 | | 4.00 | 10.00 | 20.00 | 65.00 | 175.00 | 250 | 375 | 1,000 |
| 1920S . . . . . . 9,689,000 | | 1.50 | 5.00 | 10.00 | 45.00 | 115.00 | 150 | 375 | 1,050 |
| 1921 . . . . . . . 10,663,000 | | 0.80 | 2.00 | 3.00 | 10.00 | 25.00 | 35 | 70 | 200 |
| 1921S . . . . . . 1,557,000 | | 40.00 | 60.00 | 100.00 | 200.00 | 600.00 | 850 | 1,250 | 2,000 |
| 1923 . . . . . . . 35,715,000 | | 0.45 | 0.60 | 0.80 | 4.00 | 7.50 | 18 | 35 | 80 |
| 1923S (a) . . . . 6,142,000 | | 3.00 | 5.00 | 10.00 | 55.00 | 150.00 | 200 | 350 | 650 |
| 1924 . . . . . . . 21,620,000 | | 0.40 | 0.60 | 0.80 | 4.00 | 9.00 | 25 | 40 | 125 |
| 1924D . . . . . . 5,258,000 | | 3.50 | 5.00 | 15.00 | 50.00 | 120.00 | 195 | 275 | 700 |
| 1924S . . . . . . 1,437,000 | | 10.00 | 25.00 | 55.00 | 200.00 | 650.00 | 1,200 | 1,500 | 3,000 |
| 1925 . . . . . . . 35,565,100 | | 0.75 | 1.25 | 2.00 | 4.00 | 8.00 | 16 | 25 | 55 |
| 1925D (a) . . . . 4,450,000 | | 5.00 | 12.00 | 25.00 | 45.00 | 100.00 | 200 | 300 | 650 |
| 1925S . . . . . . 6,256,000 | | 2.00 | 5.00 | 10.00 | 40.00 | 115.00 | 200 | 350 | 1,350 |
| 1926 . . . . . . . 44,693,000 | | 0.35 | 0.45 | 0.60 | 3.00 | 5.00 | 12 | 22 | 45 |
| 1926D (a) . . . . 5,638,000 | | 6.00 | 10.00 | 15.00 | 55.00 | 100.00 | 200 | 250 | 400 |
| 1926S . . . . . . 970,000 | | 15.00 | 25.00 | 50.00 | 145.00 | 450.00 | 1,650 | 2,750 | 6,000 |
| 1927 . . . . . . . 37,981,000 | | 0.50 | 0.55 | 0.60 | 1.50 | 6.00 | 10 | 25 | 50 |
| 1927D . . . . . . 5,730,000 | | 0.85 | 2.00 | 2.50 | 15.00 | 40.00 | 55 | 85 | 225 |
| 1927S . . . . . . 3,430,000 | | 0.60 | 0.90 | 1.75 | 18.00 | 45.00 | 115 | 500 | 1,650 |
| 1928 . . . . . . . 23,411,000 | | 0.40 | 0.45 | 0.60 | 2.00 | 5.00 | 10 | 22 | 45 |
| 1928D . . . . . . 6,436,000 | | 0.45 | 0.85 | 1.75 | 6.00 | 20.00 | 25 | 30 | 50 |
| 1928S . . . . . . 6,936,000 | | 0.60 | 0.75 | 1.25 | 5.00 | 15.00 | 55 | 185 | 400 |
| 1929 . . . . . . . 36,446,000 | | 0.35 | 0.40 | 0.60 | 2.00 | 5.00 | 10 | 16 | 35 |
| 1929D . . . . . . 8,370,000 | | 0.45 | 0.60 | 0.80 | 3.00 | 15.00 | 20 | 35 | 75 |
| 1929S . . . . . . 7,754,000 | | 0.40 | 0.60 | 0.75 | 0.90 | 5.50 | 12 | 25 | 45 |

\*\* Included in number below. **a.** Dealers pay considerably more for Uncirculated pieces with full, sharp details.

1937-D, "3-Legged" Variety          1938-D, D Over S

*Dealers often pay more than the prices shown for brilliant choice Unc. coins, and less for spotted, cleaned, weakly struck, or discolored pieces.*

| | Mintage | G-4 | VG-8 | F-12 | VF-20 | EF-40 | AU-50 | MS-60 | MS-63 | PF-63 |
|---|---|---|---|---|---|---|---|---|---|---|
| 1930 . . . . . . . . . . . . | 22,849,000 | $0.40 | $0.50 | $0.70 | $0.80 | $5.00 | $11.00 | $16 | $35 | |
| 1930S . . . . . . . . . . . . | 5,435,000 | 0.40 | 0.50 | 0.70 | 0.80 | 6.00 | 15.00 | 25 | 80 | |
| 1931S . . . . . . . . . . . . | 1,200,000 | 7.00 | 8.00 | 8.80 | 9.25 | 15.00 | 25.00 | 30 | 50 | |
| 1934 . . . . . . . . . . . . | 20,213,003 | 0.35 | 0.45 | 0.55 | 0.75 | 3.00 | 9.00 | 16 | 30 | |
| 1934D . . . . . . . . . . . . | 7,480,000 | 0.50 | 0.75 | 1.25 | 3.00 | 9.00 | 21.00 | 35 | 75 | |
| 1935 . . . . . . . . . . . . | 58,264,000 | 0.35 | 0.45 | 0.55 | 0.75 | 1.25 | 4.25 | 10 | 25 | |
| 1935D . . . . . . . . . . . | 12,092,000 | 0.35 | 0.50 | 1.00 | 3.00 | 6.00 | 20.00 | 30 | 40 | |
| 1935S . . . . . . . . . . . | 10,300,000 | 0.35 | 0.45 | 0.55 | 0.75 | 2.00 | 7.50 | 15 | 36 | |
| 1936 . . . . (4,420) . . | 118,997,000 | 0.35 | 0.45 | 0.55 | 0.75 | 1.25 | 4.00 | 10 | 25 | $600 |
| 1936D . . . . . . . . . . . | 24,814,000 | 0.45 | 0.60 | 0.75 | 0.95 | 1.75 | 4.50 | 15 | 20 | |
| 1936S . . . . . . . . . . . | 14,930,000 | 0.35 | 0.45 | 0.55 | 0.75 | 1.25 | 4.50 | 10 | 15 | |
| 1937 . . . . (5,769) . . . | 79,480,000 | 0.35 | 0.45 | 0.55 | 0.75 | 1.25 | 3.00 | 15 | 20 | 625 |
| 1937D . . . . . . . . . . . | 17,826,000 | 0.35 | 0.45 | 0.55 | 0.75 | 1.25 | 4.00 | 10 | 15 | |
| 1937D, 3-Legged . . . . . . . . . . * | 300.00 | 350.00 | 375.00 | 400.00 | 500.00 | 600.00 | 1,250 | 3,200 | |
| 1937S . . . . . . . . . . . . | 5,635,000 | 0.35 | 0.45 | 0.55 | 0.75 | 1.25 | 4.00 | 11 | 20 | |
| 1938D . . . . . . . . . . . . | 7,020,000 | 1.00 | 1.10 | 1.50 | 1.75 | 2.00 | 4.00 | 11 | 15 | |
| 1938D, D Over S . . . . . . . . . . . * | 1.50 | 2.00 | 4.00 | 5.00 | 8.00 | 12.00 | 25 | 36 | |

* Included in number above.

# JEFFERSON (1938–2003)

This nickel was originally designed by Felix Schlag. He won an award of $1,000 in a competition with some 390 artists. It established the definite public approval of portrait and pictorial rather than symbolic devices on our coinage. On October 8, 1942, the wartime five-cent piece composed of copper (56%), silver (35%), and manganese (9%) was introduced to eliminate nickel, a critical war material. A larger mintmark was placed above the dome. The letter P (Philadelphia) was used for the first time, indicating the change of alloy. The designer's initials FS were added below the bust starting in 1966. The mintmark position was moved to the obverse starting in 1968.

**VG-8 Very Good:** Second porch pillar from right nearly gone, other three still visible but weak.

**F-12 Fine:** Jefferson's cheekbone worn flat. Hair lines and eyebrow faint. Second pillar weak, especially at bottom.

**VF-20 Very Fine:** Second pillar plain and complete on both sides.

**EF-40 Extremely Fine:** Cheekbone, hair lines, eyebrow slightly worn but well defined. Base of triangle above pillars visible but weak.

**MS-63 Select Uncirculated:** No trace of wear. Slight blemishes.

**MS-65 Choice Uncirculated:** No trace of wear. Barely noticeable blemishes.

**PF-65 Gem Proof:** Brilliant surfaces. No noticeable blemishes or flaws. May have a few barely noticeable marks or hairlines.

Mintmark located at right of building.

Mintmark, starting in 1968.

*See next page for chart.*

*Coin dealers usually pay more than the Mint State prices shown for Uncirculated Jefferson nickels with fully struck steps visible in Monticello.*

| | Mintage | VG-8 | F-12 | VF-20 | EF-40 | MS-63 | MS-65 | PF-65 |
|---|---|---|---|---|---|---|---|---|
| 1938 . . . . . (19,365) . . . 19,496,000 | | $0.10 | $0.12 | $0.20 | $0.25 | $1.10 | $6.00 | $55 |
| 1938D . . . . . . . . . . . . . 5,376,000 | | 0.25 | 0.35 | 0.75 | 1.00 | 2.25 | 7.00 | |
| 1938S . . . . . . . . . . . . . 4,105,000 | | 0.40 | 0.60 | 0.85 | 1.50 | 2.75 | 8.00 | |
| 1939 . . . . . (12,535) . . 120,615,000 | | 0.08 | 0.10 | 0.12 | 0.25 | 1.00 | 2.00 | 55 |
| 1939D . . . . . . . . . . . . . 3,514,000 | | 1.20 | 1.60 | 3.00 | 5.00 | 30.00 | 45.00 | |
| 1939S . . . . . . . . . . . . . 6,630,000 | | 0.25 | 0.30 | 0.50 | 1.50 | 14.00 | 30.00 | |
| 1940 . . . . . (14,158) . . 176,485,000 | | 0.05 | 0.05 | 0.05 | 0.10 | 1.00 | 2.00 | 55 |
| 1940D . . . . . . . . . . . . 43,540,000 | | 0.05 | 0.05 | 0.05 | 0.10 | 1.25 | 3.50 | |
| 1940S . . . . . . . . . . . . 39,690,000 | | 0.05 | 0.05 | 0.05 | 0.10 | 1.25 | 3.50 | |
| 1941 . . . . . (18,720) . . 203,265,000 | | 0.05 | 0.05 | 0.05 | 0.10 | 0.50 | 2.00 | 45 |
| 1941D . . . . . . . . . . . . 53,432,000 | | 0.05 | 0.05 | 0.05 | 0.10 | 1.25 | 3.00 | |
| 1941S . . . . . . . . . . . . 43,445,000 | | 0.05 | 0.05 | 0.05 | 0.10 | 1.50 | 3.50 | |
| 1942 . . . . . (29,600) . . . 49,789,000 | | 0.05 | 0.05 | 0.05 | 0.10 | 1.25 | 4.00 | 45 |
| 1942D . . . . . . . . . . . . 13,938,000 | | 0.10 | 0.15 | 0.25 | 1.00 | 16.00 | 23.00 | |

## Wartime Silver Alloy (1942–1945)

Mintmark Location

1943-P, 3 Over 2

| | Mintage | VG-8 | F-12 | VF-20 | EF-40 | MS-63 | MS-65 | PF-65 |
|---|---|---|---|---|---|---|---|---|
| 1942P . . . . (27,600) . . . 57,873,000 | | $1 | $1.10 | $1.20 | $1.40 | $4 | $8 | $100 |
| 1942S . . . . . . . . . . . . 32,900,000 | | 1 | 1.10 | 1.20 | 1.40 | 4 | 9 | |
| 1943P, 3 Over 2 . . . . . . . . . . . . . * | | | 15.00 | 20.00 | 40.00 | 250 | 350 | |
| 1943P . . . . . . . . . . . 271,165,000 | | 1 | 1.10 | 1.20 | 1.40 | 3 | 8 | |
| 1943D . . . . . . . . . . . . 15,294,000 | | 1 | 1.10 | 1.20 | 1.40 | 5 | 8 | |
| 1943S . . . . . . . . . . . 104,060,000 | | 1 | 1.10 | 1.20 | 1.40 | 3 | 8 | |
| 1944P . . . . . . . . . . . 119,150,000 | | 1 | 1.10 | 1.20 | 1.40 | 5 | 9 | |
| 1944D . . . . . . . . . . . . 32,309,000 | | 1 | 1.10 | 1.20 | 1.40 | 5 | 9 | |
| 1944S . . . . . . . . . . . . 21,640,000 | | 1 | 1.10 | 1.20 | 1.40 | 4 | 8 | |
| 1945P . . . . . . . . . . . 119,408,100 | | 1 | 1.10 | 1.20 | 1.40 | 3 | 8 | |
| 1945D . . . . . . . . . . . . 37,158,000 | | 1 | 1.10 | 1.20 | 1.40 | 3 | 8 | |
| 1945S . . . . . . . . . . . . 58,939,000 | | 1 | 1.10 | 1.20 | 1.40 | 3 | 8 | |

* Included in number below.

## Prewar Composition, Mintmark Style Resumed (1946–1965)

1954-S, S Over D

1955-D, D Over S

| | Mintage | VF-20 | EF-40 | MS-63 | MS-65 | PF-65 |
|---|---|---|---|---|---|---|
| 1946 . . . . . . . . . . . . . . . . . . . . . . . . . . . . . . . 161,116,000 | | $0.05 | $0.05 | $0.60 | $5 | |
| 1946D . . . . . . . . . . . . . . . . . . . . . . . . . . . . . . 45,292,200 | | 0.05 | 0.05 | 0.60 | 4 | |
| 1946S . . . . . . . . . . . . . . . . . . . . . . . . . . . . . . 13,560,000 | | 0.05 | 0.06 | 0.35 | 4 | |

# NICKEL FIVE-CENT PIECES

| | Mintage | VF-20 | EF-40 | MS-63 | MS-65 | PF-65 |
|---|---|---|---|---|---|---|
| 1947 | 95,000,000 | $0.05 | $0.05 | $0.35 | $4.00 | |
| 1947D | 37,822,000 | 0.05 | 0.05 | 0.35 | 4.00 | |
| 1947S | 24,720,000 | 0.05 | 0.06 | 0.35 | 5.00 | |
| 1948 | 89,348,000 | 0.05 | 0.05 | 0.35 | 3.00 | |
| 1948D | 44,734,000 | 0.05 | 0.06 | 0.75 | 2.00 | |
| 1948S | 11,300,000 | 0.05 | 0.06 | 0.50 | 2.00 | |
| 1949 | 60,652,000 | 0.05 | 0.10 | 2.00 | 5.00 | |
| 1949D | 36,498,000 | 0.05 | 0.05 | 0.75 | 3.00 | |
| 1949D, D Over S | * | 18.00 | 30.00 | 125.00 | 250.00 | |
| 1949S | 9,716,000 | 0.05 | 0.10 | 0.50 | 3.00 | |
| 1950 | (51,386) 9,796,000 | 0.05 | 0.10 | 0.50 | 2.50 | $30.00 |
| 1950D | 2,630,030 | 3.00 | 3.50 | 8.50 | 12.50 | |
| 1951 | (57,500) 28,552,000 | 0.05 | 0.06 | 1.25 | 5.00 | 25.00 |
| 1951D | 20,460,000 | 0.05 | 0.06 | 1.50 | 4.00 | |
| 1951S | 7,776,000 | 0.05 | 0.10 | 1.50 | 4.00 | |
| 1952 | (81,980) 63,988,000 | 0.05 | 0.05 | 0.35 | 3.00 | 18.00 |
| 1952D | 30,638,000 | 0.05 | 0.05 | 2.00 | 5.00 | |
| 1952S | 20,572,000 | 0.05 | 0.05 | 0.55 | 4.00 | |
| 1953 | (128,800) 46,644,000 | 0.05 | 0.05 | 0.25 | 2.50 | 18.00 |
| 1953D | 59,878,600 | 0.05 | 0.05 | 0.25 | 2.75 | |
| 1953S | 19,210,900 | 0.05 | 0.05 | 0.30 | 3.00 | |
| 1954 | (233,300) 47,684,050 | 0.05 | 0.05 | 0.50 | 4.00 | 9.00 |
| 1954D | 117,183,060 | 0.05 | 0.05 | 0.40 | 10.00 | |
| 1954S | 29,384,000 | 0.05 | 0.05 | 0.50 | 5.00 | |
| 1954S, S Over D | * | 2.50 | 5.00 | 18.00 | 35.00 | |
| 1955 | (378,200) 7,888,000 | 0.06 | 0.08 | 0.40 | 5.00 | 6.00 |
| 1955D | 74,464,100 | 0.05 | 0.05 | 0.25 | 7.00 | |
| 1955D, D Over S (a) | * | 3.00 | 5.00 | 30.00 | 100.00 | |
| 1956 | (669,384) 35,216,000 | 0.05 | 0.05 | 0.25 | 7.00 | 1.00 |
| 1956D | 67,222,940 | 0.05 | 0.05 | 0.25 | 7.00 | |
| 1957 | (1,247,952) 38,408,000 | 0.05 | 0.05 | 0.25 | 5.00 | 1.00 |
| 1957D | 136,828,900 | 0.05 | 0.05 | 0.25 | 5.00 | |
| 1958 | (875,652) 17,088,000 | 0.05 | 0.05 | 0.20 | 4.00 | 1.50 |
| 1958D | 168,249,120 | 0.05 | 0.05 | 0.15 | 4.00 | |
| 1959 | (1,149,291) 27,248,000 | 0.05 | 0.05 | 0.15 | 3.00 | 0.85 |
| 1959D | 160,738,240 | 0.05 | 0.05 | 0.15 | 2.50 | |
| 1960 | (1,691,602) 55,416,000 | 0.05 | 0.05 | 0.15 | 2.50 | 0.85 |
| 1960D | 192,582,180 | 0.05 | 0.05 | 0.15 | 3.00 | |
| 1961 | (3,028,144) 73,640,100 | 0.05 | 0.05 | 0.15 | 4.00 | 0.85 |
| 1961D | 229,342,760 | 0.05 | 0.05 | 0.15 | 4.00 | |
| 1962 | (3,218,019) 97,384,000 | 0.05 | 0.05 | 0.15 | 3.00 | 0.85 |
| 1962D | 280,195,720 | 0.05 | 0.05 | 0.15 | 7.00 | |
| 1963 | (3,075,645) 175,776,000 | 0.05 | 0.05 | 0.15 | 3.00 | 0.85 |
| 1963D | 276,829,460 | 0.05 | 0.05 | 0.15 | 8.00 | |
| 1964 | (3,950,762) 1,024,672,000 | 0.05 | 0.05 | 0.15 | 2.50 | 0.85 |
| 1964D | 1,787,297,160 | 0.05 | 0.05 | 0.15 | 1.00 | |
| 1965 | 136,131,380 | 0.05 | 0.05 | 0.15 | 1.00 | |

* Included in number above. **a.** Varieties exist. Values are for the variety illustrated on previous page.

## 1966 Through 2003

| | Mintage | MS-63 | MS-65 | PF-65 | | Mintage | MS-63 | MS-65 | PF-65 |
|---|---|---|---|---|---|---|---|---|---|
| 1966 | 156,208,283 | $0.10 | $1 | | 1968D | 91,227,880 | $0.10 | $1 | |
| 1967 | 107,325,800 | 0.10 | 1 | | 1968S | 100,396,004 | 0.10 | 1 | |

*Chart continued on next page.*

| | Mintage | MS-63 | MS-65 | PF-65 |
|---|---|---|---|---|
| 1968S, Proof | (3,041,506) | | | $0.75 |
| 1969D | 202,807,500 | $0.10 | $1.00 | |
| 1969S | 120,165,000 | 0.10 | 0.80 | |
| | (2,934,631) | | | 0.75 |
| 1970D | 515,485,380 | 0.10 | 3.00 | |
| 1970S | 238,832,004 | 0.10 | 2.00 | |
| | (2,632,810) | | | 0.75 |
| 1971 | 106,884,000 | 0.25 | 0.80 | |
| 1971D | 316,144,800 | 0.10 | 0.80 | |
| 1971S | (3,220,733) | | | 0.75 |

| | Mintage | MS-63 | MS-65 | PF-65 |
|---|---|---|---|---|
| 1972 | 202,036,000 | $0.10 | $0.80 | |
| 1972D | 351,694,600 | 0.10 | 0.80 | |
| 1972S | (3,260,996) | | | $1.00 |
| 1973 | 384,396,000 | 0.10 | 0.80 | |
| 1973D | 261,405,000 | 0.10 | 0.80 | |
| 1973S | (2,760,339) | | | 0.75 |
| 1974 | 601,752,000 | 0.10 | 0.80 | |
| 1974D | 277,373,000 | 0.10 | 0.80 | |
| 1974S | (2,612,568) | | | 1.00 |

| | Mintage | MS-65 | PF-65 |
|---|---|---|---|
| 1975 | 181,772,000 | $0.75 | |
| 1975D | 401,875,300 | 0.75 | |
| 1975S | (2,845,450) | | $0.85 |
| 1976 | 367,124,000 | 0.75 | |
| 1976D | 563,964,147 | 0.75 | |
| 1976S | (4,149,730) | | 0.85 |
| 1977 | 585,376,000 | 0.75 | |
| 1977D | 297,313,422 | 0.75 | |
| 1977S | (3,251,152) | | 0.75 |
| 1978 | 391,308,000 | 0.75 | |
| 1978D | 313,092,780 | 0.75 | |
| 1978S | (3,127,781) | | 0.75 |
| 1979 | 463,188,000 | 0.75 | |
| 1979D | 325,867,672 | 1.00 | |
| 1979S, Type 1 | (3,677,175) | | 0.75 |
| 1979S, Type 2 | * | | 1.00 |
| 1980P | 593,004,000 | 0.50 | |
| 1980D | 502,323,448 | 0.50 | |
| 1980S | (3,554,806) | | 0.75 |
| 1981P | 657,504,000 | 0.50 | |
| 1981D | 364,801,843 | 0.50 | |
| 1981S, Type 1 | (4,063,083) | | 1.00 |
| 1981S, Type 2 | * | | 2.00 |
| 1982P | 292,355,000 | 3.00 | |
| 1982D | 373,726,544 | 2.00 | |
| 1982S | (3,857,479) | | 1.00 |
| 1983P | 561,615,000 | 3.00 | |
| 1983D | 536,726,276 | 1.50 | |
| 1983S | (3,279,126) | | 1.00 |
| 1984P | 746,769,000 | 1.25 | |
| 1984D | 517,675,146 | 0.75 | |
| 1984S | (3,065,110) | | 1.50 |
| 1985P | 647,114,962 | 0.50 | |
| 1985D | 459,747,446 | 0.50 | |
| 1985S | (3,362,821) | | 1.25 |
| 1986P | 536,883,483 | 0.50 | |
| 1986D | 361,819,140 | 0.50 | |
| 1986S | (3,010,497) | | 2.75 |
| 1987P | 371,499,481 | 0.70 | |
| 1987D | 410,590,604 | 0.75 | |

| | Mintage | MS-65 | PF-65 |
|---|---|---|---|
| 1987S | (4,227,728) | | $1.00 |
| 1988P | 771,360,000 | $0.60 | |
| 1988D | 663,771,652 | 0.60 | |
| 1988S | (3,262,948) | | 2.00 |
| 1989P | 898,812,000 | 0.50 | |
| 1989D | 570,842,474 | 0.50 | |
| 1989S | (3,220,194) | | 1.75 |
| 1990P | 661,636,000 | 0.50 | |
| 1990D | 663,938,503 | 0.50 | |
| 1990S | (3,299,559) | | 1.75 |
| 1991P | 614,104,000 | 0.50 | |
| 1991D | 436,496,678 | 0.50 | |
| 1991S | (2,867,787) | | 2.00 |
| 1992P | 399,552,000 | 0.75 | |
| 1992D | 450,565,113 | 0.50 | |
| 1992S | (4,176,560) | | 1.25 |
| 1993P | 412,076,000 | 0.30 | |
| 1993D | 406,084,135 | 0.30 | |
| 1993S | (3,394,792) | | 1.50 |
| 1994P | 722,160,000 | 0.50 | |
| 1994D | 715,762,110 | 0.30 | |
| 1994S | (3,269,923) | | 1.25 |
| 1995P | 774,156,000 | 0.30 | |
| 1995D | 888,112,000 | 0.30 | |
| 1995S | (2,797,481) | | 2.00 |
| 1996P | 829,332,000 | 0.30 | |
| 1996D | 817,736,000 | 0.30 | |
| 1996S | (2,525,265) | | 1.00 |
| 1997P | 470,972,000 | 0.30 | |
| 1997D | 466,640,000 | 0.50 | |
| 1997S | (2,796,678) | | 1.75 |
| 1998P | 688,272,000 | 0.30 | |
| 1998D | 635,360,000 | 0.30 | |
| 1998S | (2,086,507) | | 1.75 |
| 1999P | 1,212,000,000 | 0.30 | |
| 1999D | 1,066,720,000 | 0.30 | |
| 1999S | (3,347,966) | | 2.00 |
| 2000P | 846,240,000 | 0.30 | |
| 2000D | 1,509,520,000 | 0.30 | |
| 2000S | (4,047,993) | | 1.75 |

* Included in number above.

| | Mintage | MS-65 | PF-65 |
|---|---|---|---|
| 2001P | 675,704,000 | $0.20 | |
| 2001D | 627,680,000 | 0.20 | |
| 2001S | (3,184,606) | | $1.75 |
| 2002P | 539,280,000 | 0.20 | |
| 2002D | 691,200,000 | 0.20 | |

| | Mintage | MS-65 | PF-65 |
|---|---|---|---|
| 2002S | (3,211,995) | | $1.50 |
| 2003P | 441,840,000 | $0.20 | |
| 2003D | 383,040,000 | 0.20 | |
| 2003S | (3,298,439) | | 1.50 |

## WESTWARD JOURNEY (2004–2005)

The Westward Journey Nickel Series™ commemorates the bicentennial of the Louisiana Purchase and the journey of Meriwether Lewis and William Clark to explore that vast territory. **2004**—*Obverse:* traditional portrait of Jefferson. *Reverses:* Louisiana Purchase / Peace Medal reverse, by Mint sculptor Norman E. Nemeth. Keelboat reverse, by Mint sculptor Al Maletsky. **2005**—*Obverse:* new portrait of Jefferson, designed by Joe Fitzgerald after a 1789 marble bust by Jean-Antoine Houdon, and rendered by Mint sculptor Don Everhart. *Reverses:* American Bison reverse, designed by Jamie Franki and produced by Norman E. Nemeth. "Ocean in View" reverse, designed by Joe Fitzgerald and produced by Mint sculptor Donna Weaver.

2004 Obverse          2005 Obverse

Peace Medal          Keelboat          American Bison          Ocean in View

| | Mintage | MS-65 | PF-65 |
|---|---|---|---|
| 2004P, Peace Medal | 361,440,000 | $0.25 | |
| 2004D, Peace Medal | 372,000,000 | 0.25 | |
| 2004S, Peace Medal | (2,992,069) | | $1.25 |
| 2004P, Keelboat | 366,720,000 | 0.25 | |
| 2004D, Keelboat | 344,880,000 | 0.25 | |
| 2004S, Keelboat | (2,965,422) | | 1.25 |
| 2005P, American Bison | 448,320,000 | 0.30 | |
| 2005D, American Bison | 487,680,000 | 0.30 | |
| 2005S, American Bison | (3,344,679) | | 1.35 |
| 2005P, Ocean in View | 394,080,000 | 0.25 | |
| 2005D, Ocean in View | 411,120,000 | 0.25 | |
| 2005S, Ocean in View | (3,344,679) | | 1.25 |

## JEFFERSON MODIFIED (2006 TO DATE)

In 2006 the Monticello design of 1938 to 2003 was returned to the reverse of the nickel five-cent coin. A new obverse motif featured a facing portrait of Thomas Jefferson, designed by Jamie Franki and sculpted by Donna Weaver. These designs have continued in use to date.

*Felix Schlag's initials moved to reverse*

| | Mintage | MS-65 | PF-63 |
|---|---|---|---|
| 2006P | 693,120,000 | $0.25 | |
| 2006D | 809,280,000 | 0.25 | |
| 2006S | (3,054,436) | | $1.25 |
| 2007P | 571,680,000 | 0.20 | |
| 2007D | 626,160,000 | 0.20 | |
| 2007S | (2,577,166) | | 1.10 |
| 2008P | 279,840,000 | 0.20 | |
| 2008D | 345,600,000 | 0.20 | |
| 2008S | (2,169,561) | | 1.10 |
| 2009P | 39,840,000 | 0.50 | |
| 2009D | 46,800,000 | 0.50 | |
| 2009S | (2,179,867) | | 1.10 |
| 2010P | 260,640,000 | 0.20 | |
| 2010D | 229,920,000 | 0.20 | |
| 2010S | (1,689,216) | | 1.10 |
| 2011P | 450,000,000 | 0.20 | |
| 2011D | 540,240,000 | 0.20 | |
| 2011S | (1,673,010) | | 1.10 |
| 2012P | 464,640,000 | 0.20 | |
| 2012D | 558,960,000 | 0.20 | |
| 2012S | (1,239,148) | | 1.10 |
| 2013P | 607,440,000 | 0.20 | |
| 2013D | 615,600,000 | 0.20 | |
| 2013S | (1,274,505) | | 1.10 |
| 2014P | 635,520,000 | 0.20 | |
| 2014D | 570,720,000 | 0.20 | |
| 2014S | (1,190,369) | | 1.10 |

| | Mintage | MS-65 | PF-63 |
|---|---|---|---|
| 2015P | 752,880,000 | $0.20 | |
| 2015D | 846,720,000 | 0.20 | |
| 2015S | (1,099,182) | | $1.10 |
| 2016P | 786,960,000 | 0.20 | |
| 2016D | 759,600,000 | 0.20 | |
| 2016S | (1,011,624) | | 1.10 |
| 2017P | 710,160,000 | 0.20 | |
| 2017D | 663,120,000 | 0.20 | |
| 2017S | (979,477) | | 1.10 |
| 2018P | 629,520,000 | 0.20 | |
| 2018D | 626,880,000 | 0.20 | |
| 2018S | (901,072) | | 1.10 |
| 2019P | 567,854,400 | 0.20 | |
| 2019D | 527,040,000 | 0.20 | |
| 2019S | (1,061,558) | | 1.10 |
| 2020P | 772,780,000 | 0.20 | |
| 2020D | 798,000,000 | 0.20 | |
| 2020S | (824,332) | | 1.10 |
| 2020W | (465,080) | | 5.00 |
| 2020W, RevPf | (313,184) | | 7.50 |
| 2021P | 785,500,000 | 0.20 | |
| 2021D | 837,600,000 | 0.20 | |
| 2021S | (792,612) | | 1.10 |
| 2022P | | 0.20 | |
| 2022D | | 0.20 | |
| 2022S | | | 1.10 |

The half dime types present the same general characteristics as larger United States silver coins. Authorized by the Act of April 2, 1792, they were not coined until February 1795, although dated 1794. At first the weight was 20.8 grains, and fineness .8924. By the Act of January 18, 1837, the weight was slightly reduced to 20-5/8 grains and the fineness changed to .900. Finally, the weight was reduced to 19.2 grains by the Act of February 21, 1853.

## FLOWING HAIR (1794–1795)

**AG-3 About Good:** Details clear enough to identify.
**G-4 Good:** Eagle, wreath, bust outlined but lack details.
**VG-8 Very Good:** Some details on face. All lettering legible.
**F-12 Fine:** Hair ends visible. Hair at top smooth.
**VF-20 Very Fine:** Hair lines at top visible. Hair about ear defined.
**EF-40 Extremely Fine:** Hair above forehead and at neck well defined but shows some wear.
**AU-50 About Uncirculated:** Slight wear on high waves of hair, near ear and face, and on head and tips of eagle's wings.
**MS-60 Uncirculated:** No trace of wear. Light blemishes.
**MS-63 Choice Uncirculated:** Some distracting marks or blemishes in prime focal areas. Some impairment of luster possible.

*For Uncirculated examples, coin dealers usually pay less than the prices shown for pieces that are weakly struck.*

| | Mintage | AG-3 | G-4 | VG-8 | F-12 | VF-20 | EF-40 | AU-50 | MS-60 | MS-63 |
|---|---|---|---|---|---|---|---|---|---|---|
| 1792 . . . . . . . . . . . . . * | $25,000 | $35,000 | $45,000 | $55,000 | $65,000 | $95,000 | $115,000 | $150,000 | $250,000 |
| 1794 . . . . . . . . . . . . . * | 650 | 1,450 | 1,900 | 2,500 | 3,250 | 6,000 | 8,500 | 13,500 | 25,000 |
| 1795 . . . . . . . . . 86,416 | 500 | 1,100 | 1,250 | 1,600 | 2,250 | 4,000 | 5,000 | 7,000 | 9,000 |

* Included in number below.

## DRAPED BUST (1796–1805)

**AG-3 About Good:** Details clear enough to identify.
**G-4 Good:** Date, stars, LIBERTY readable. Bust of Liberty outlined, but no details.
**VG-8 Very Good:** Some details visible.
**F-12 Fine:** Hair and drapery lines worn, but visible.
**VF-20 Very Fine:** Only left side of drapery indistinct.
**EF-40 Extremely Fine:** Details visible in all hair lines.
**AU-50 About Uncirculated:** Slight wear on bust, shoulder, and hair; wear on eagle's head and top of wings.
**MS-60 Uncirculated:** No trace of wear. Light blemishes.
**MS-63 Choice Uncirculated:** Some distracting marks or blemishes in prime focal areas. Impaired luster possible.

### Small Eagle Reverse (1796–1797)

| | Mintage | AG-3 | G-4 | VG-8 | F-12 | VF-20 | EF-40 | AU-50 | MS-60 | MS-63 |
|---|---|---|---|---|---|---|---|---|---|---|
| 1796, 6 Over 5 . . . . . . . . 10,230 | $800 | $1,750 | $2,250 | $3,000 | $4,250 | $6,500 | $9,000 | $17,500 | $27,500 |
| 1796, LIKERTY . . . . . . . . . . . . . . * | 600 | 1,100 | 1,500 | 2,500 | 3,500 | 6,000 | 7,500 | 13,500 | 22,500 |
| 1797, 15 Stars . . . . . . . . 44,527 | 600 | 1,100 | 1,500 | 2,500 | 3,500 | 6,000 | 7,000 | 11,000 | 17,500 |
| 1797, 16 Stars . . . . . . . . . . . . . * | 600 | 1,100 | 1,500 | 2,500 | 3,500 | 5,500 | 7,500 | 11,000 | 17,500 |
| 1797, 13 Stars . . . . . . . . . . . . . * | 850 | 1,850 | 2,600 | 4,000 | 4,750 | 8,500 | 17,500 | 35,000 | 55,000 |

* Included in number above.

## Heraldic Eagle Reverse (1800–1805)

**1800 LIBEKTY**

| | Mintage | AG-3 | G-4 | VG-8 | F-12 | VF-20 | EF-40 | AU-50 | MS-60 | MS-63 |
|---|---|---|---|---|---|---|---|---|---|---|
| 1800 . . . . . . . . . . . . . . . . | 24,000 | $400 | $1,000 | $1,250 | $1,750 | $2,250 | $4,500 | $5,500 | $10,000 | $15,000 |
| 1800, LIBEKTY . . . . . . . . . | 16,000 | 400 | 1,000 | 1,500 | 1,800 | 2,750 | 4,500 | 6,000 | 11,000 | 17,500 |
| 1801 . . . . . . . . . . . . . . . . | 27,760 | 400 | 1,000 | 1,500 | 1,800 | 2,500 | 5,000 | 6,500 | 13,500 | 20,000 |
| 1802 . . . . . . . . . . . . . . . . | 3,060 | 45,000 | 75,000 | 100,000 | 125,000 | 150,000 | 175,000 | 250,000 | — | — |
| 1803 . . . . . . . . . . . . . . . . | 37,850 | 450 | 1,100 | 1,350 | 1,600 | 2,000 | 5,000 | 6,500 | 10,000 | 25,000 |
| 1805 . . . . . . . . . . . . . . . . | 15,600 | 450 | 1,350 | 1,750 | 2,200 | 3,000 | 8,500 | 18,500 | — | — |

## CAPPED BUST (1829–1837)

**G-4 Good:** Bust of Liberty outlined, no detail. Date and legend legible.
**VG-8 Very Good:** Complete legend and date plain. At least three letters
of LIBERTY on edge of cap show clearly.
**F-12 Fine:** All letters in LIBERTY visible.
**VF-20 Very Fine:** Full rims. Ear and shoulder clasp show plainly.
**EF-40 Extremely Fine:** Ear very distinct; eyebrow and hair well defined.
**AU-50 About Uncirculated:** Traces of light wear on many of the high points. At least half of mint luster
still present.
**MS-60 Uncirculated:** No trace of wear. Light blemishes.
**MS-63 Choice Uncirculated:** No trace of wear. Light blemishes. Attractive mint luster.

| | Mintage | G-4 | VG-8 | F-12 | VF-20 | EF-40 | AU-50 | MS-60 | MS-63 |
|---|---|---|---|---|---|---|---|---|---|
| 1829 . . . . . . . . . . . | 1,230,000 | $45 | $65 | $80 | $100 | $145 | $200 | $300 | $650 |
| 1830 . . . . . . . . . . . | 1,240,000 | 45 | 65 | 80 | 100 | 145 | 200 | 300 | 650 |
| 1831 . . . . . . . . . . . | 1,242,700 | 45 | 65 | 80 | 100 | 145 | 200 | 300 | 650 |
| 1832 . . . . . . . . . . . | 965,000 | 45 | 65 | 80 | 100 | 145 | 200 | 300 | 650 |
| 1833 . . . . . . . . . . . | 1,370,000 | 45 | 65 | 80 | 100 | 145 | 200 | 300 | 650 |
| 1834 . . . . . . . . . . . | 1,480,000 | 45 | 65 | 80 | 100 | 145 | 200 | 300 | 650 |
| 1835 . . . . . . . . . . . | 2,760,000 | 45 | 65 | 80 | 100 | 145 | 200 | 300 | 650 |
| 1836 . . . . . . . . . . . | 1,900,000 | 45 | 65 | 80 | 100 | 145 | 200 | 300 | 650 |
| 1837, Small 5 C. . . . . | 871,000 | 65 | 85 | 100 | 145 | 250 | 500 | 1,200 | 2,000 |
| 1837, Large 5 C. . . . . . . . . . | * | 45 | 65 | 85 | 115 | 145 | 200 | 300 | 650 |

* Included in number above.

## LIBERTY SEATED (1837–1873)

**G-4 Good:** LIBERTY on shield smooth. Date and letters legible.
**VG-8 Very Good:** At least three letters in LIBERTY visible.
**F-12 Fine:** Entire LIBERTY visible, weak spots.
**VF-20 Very Fine:** Entire LIBERTY strong and even.
**EF-40 Extremely Fine:** LIBERTY and scroll edges distinct.
**AU-50 About Uncirculated:** Traces of light wear on many of the high points. At least half of mint luster
still present.
**MS-60 Uncirculated:** No trace of wear. Light blemishes.
**MS-63 Choice Uncirculated:** No trace of wear. Light blemishes. Attractive mint luster.

## Variety 1 – No Stars on Obverse (1837–1838)

| | Mintage | G-4 | VG-8 | F-12 | VF-20 | EF-40 | AU-50 | MS-60 | MS-63 |
|---|---|---|---|---|---|---|---|---|---|
| 1837 . . . . . . . . . . . . 1,405,000 | | $25 | $35 | $65 | $100 | $175 | $275 | $475 | $750 |
| 18380, No Stars . . . . . 70,000 | | 100 | 150 | 350 | 600 | 1,750 | 3,000 | 4,500 | 8,500 |

## Variety 2 – Stars on Obverse (1838–1853)

From 1838 through 1859 the mintmark was located above the bow on the reverse. Large, medium, or small mintmark varieties occur for several dates.

| | Mintage | G-4 | VG-8 | F-12 | VF-20 | EF-40 | AU-50 | MS-60 | MS-63 |
|---|---|---|---|---|---|---|---|---|---|
| 1838 . . . . . . . . . . . . . 2,255,000 | | $20 | $30 | $32 | $40 | $65 | $125 | $200 | $350 |
| 1839 . . . . . . . . . . . . . 1,069,150 | | 20 | 25 | 32 | 40 | 65 | 125 | 200 | 350 |
| 18390 . . . . . . . . . . . . . 1,100,000 | | 20 | 25 | 30 | 50 | 100 | 225 | 650 | 1,500 |
| 1840 . . . . . . . . . . . . . 1,344,085 | | 20 | 25 | 30 | 40 | 60 | 125 | 200 | 350 |
| 18400 . . . . . . . . . . . . . . 935,000 | | 50 | 100 | 150 | 200 | 400 | 500 | 1,250 | 4,000 |
| 1841 . . . . . . . . . . . . . 1,150,000 | | 20 | 22 | 25 | 30 | 45 | 85 | 125 | 225 |
| 18410 . . . . . . . . . . . . . . 815,000 | | 45 | 65 | 100 | 145 | 200 | 275 | 750 | 1,750 |
| 1842 . . . . . . . . . . . . . . . 815,000 | | 20 | 22 | 30 | 35 | 45 | 95 | 150 | 250 |
| 18420 . . . . . . . . . . . . . . 350,000 | | 45 | 75 | 125 | 300 | 500 | 750 | 1,000 | 1,500 |
| 1843 . . . . . . . . . . . . . . . 815,000 | | 20 | 22 | 25 | 30 | 45 | 85 | 140 | 250 |
| 1844 . . . . . . . . . . . . . . . 430,000 | | 20 | 22 | 25 | 30 | 45 | 100 | 200 | 350 |
| 18440 . . . . . . . . . . . . . . 220,000 | | 65 | 150 | 225 | 550 | 1,000 | 1,750 | 5,000 | 7,500 |
| 1845 . . . . . . . . . . . . . 1,564,000 | | 20 | 22 | 25 | 30 | 45 | 100 | 150 | 250 |
| 1846 . . . . . . . . . . . . . . . . 27,000 | | 550 | 1,000 | 1,500 | 2,000 | 3,000 | 4,500 | 13,500 | 30,000 |
| 1847 . . . . . . . . . . . . . 1,274,000 | | 20 | 22 | 25 | 30 | 45 | 95 | 125 | 225 |
| 1848 . . . . . . . . . . . . . . . 668,000 | | 20 | 22 | 25 | 30 | 45 | 95 | 225 | 350 |
| 18480 . . . . . . . . . . . . . . 600,000 | | 20 | 25 | 35 | 55 | 125 | 225 | 350 | 850 |
| 1849, 9 Over 6 . . . . . . . . . . . . . * | | 20 | 25 | 40 | 65 | 85 | 150 | 375 | 750 |
| 1849, 9 Over Widely Placed 6 . . . .* | | 20 | 25 | 40 | 65 | 85 | 150 | 375 | 750 |
| 1849, Normal Date . . . 1,309,000 | | 20 | 22 | 25 | 30 | 50 | 100 | 150 | 240 |
| 18490 . . . . . . . . . . . . . . 140,000 | | 45 | 100 | 150 | 250 | 400 | 650 | 1,500 | 2,500 |
| 1850 . . . . . . . . . . . . . . . 955,000 | | 20 | 22 | 25 | 30 | 45 | 100 | 125 | 225 |
| 18500 . . . . . . . . . . . . . . 690,000 | | 20 | 22 | 25 | 50 | 85 | 200 | 500 | 1,200 |
| 1851 . . . . . . . . . . . . . . . 781,000 | | 20 | 22 | 25 | 30 | 45 | 85 | 125 | 275 |
| 18510 . . . . . . . . . . . . . . 860,000 | | 20 | 22 | 25 | 30 | 75 | 150 | 325 | 650 |
| 1852 . . . . . . . . . . . . . 1,000,500 | | 20 | 22 | 25 | 30 | 45 | 100 | 125 | 225 |
| 18520 . . . . . . . . . . . . . . 260,000 | | 25 | 35 | 65 | 100 | 200 | 350 | 650 | 2,000 |
| 1853, No Arrows . . . . . . . 135,000 | | 35 | 55 | 75 | 150 | 225 | 425 | 600 | 750 |
| 18530, No Arrows . . . . . . 160,000 | | 225 | 400 | 600 | 1,100 | 2,000 | 3,000 | 8,500 | 12,000 |

* Included in number below.

## Variety 3 – Arrows at Date (1853–1855)

As on the dimes, quarters, and halves, arrows were placed at the sides of the date for a short period starting in 1853 to denote the reduction of weight.

| | Mintage | G-4 | VG-8 | F-12 | VF-20 | EF-40 | AU-50 | MS-60 | MS-63 | PF-63 |
|---|---|---|---|---|---|---|---|---|---|---|
| 1853 . . . . . . . . . . . 13,210,020 | | $20 | $22 | $24 | $26 | $45 | $100 | $140 | $250 | — |
| 18530 . . . . . . . . . . . . 2,200,000 | | 22 | 24 | 26 | 30 | 45 | 110 | 225 | 750 | |
| 1854 . . . . . . . . . . . . . 5,740,000 | | 20 | 22 | 24 | 26 | 45 | 100 | 140 | 250 | $6,000 |

*Chart continued on next page.*

| | Mintage | G-4 | VG-8 | F-12 | VF-20 | EF-40 | AU-50 | MS-60 | MS-63 | PF-63 |
|---|---|---|---|---|---|---|---|---|---|---|
| 18540 | 1,560,000 | $22 | $24 | $26 | $30 | $55 | $125 | $225 | $650 | |
| 1855 | 1,750,000 | 20 | 22 | 24 | 26 | 45 | 100 | 140 | 225 | $6,000 |
| 18550 | 600,000 | 22 | 24 | 26 | 35 | 85 | 140 | 400 | 700 | |

## Variety 2 Resumed, with Weight Standard of 1853 (1856–1859)

1858 Over Inverted Date

| | Mintage | G-4 | VG-8 | F-12 | VF-20 | EF-40 | AU-50 | MS-60 | MS-63 | PF-63 |
|---|---|---|---|---|---|---|---|---|---|---|
| 1856 | 4,880,000 | $20 | $22 | $24 | $26 | $45 | $100 | $120 | $200 | $3,000 |
| 18560 | 1,100,000 | 20 | 22 | 24 | 26 | 65 | 165 | 350 | 650 | |
| 1857 | 7,280,000 | 20 | 22 | 24 | 26 | 45 | 100 | 120 | 200 | 1,650 |
| 18570 | 1,380,000 | 20 | 22 | 24 | 26 | 45 | 120 | 200 | 250 | |
| 1858 *(300)* | 3,500,000 | 20 | 22 | 24 | 26 | 45 | 100 | 120 | 200 | 600 |
| 1858, Over Inverted Date | * | 20 | 25 | 30 | 55 | 150 | 225 | 600 | 1,150 | |
| 18580 | 1,660,000 | 20 | 22 | 24 | 26 | 45 | 100 | 150 | 300 | |
| 1859 *(800)* | 340,000 | 20 | 22 | 24 | 26 | 45 | 100 | 150 | 250 | 600 |
| 18590 | 560,000 | 20 | 22 | 24 | 30 | 85 | 145 | 250 | 400 | |

\* Included in number above.

## Variety 4 – Legend on Obverse (1860–1873)

| | Mintage | G-4 | VG-8 | F-12 | VF-20 | EF-40 | AU-50 | MS-60 | MS-63 | PF-63 |
|---|---|---|---|---|---|---|---|---|---|---|
| 1860 *(1,000)* | 798,000 | $20 | $24 | $26 | $30 | $35 | $50 | $115 | $200 | $375 |
| 18600 | 1,060,000 | 20 | 24 | 26 | 30 | 35 | 55 | 125 | 250 | |
| 1861 *(1,000)* | 3,360,000 | 20 | 25 | 26 | 30 | 35 | 50 | 115 | 200 | 375 |
| 1862 *(550)* | 1,492,000 | 20 | 24 | 25 | 30 | 35 | 55 | 115 | 200 | 375 |
| 1863 *(460)* | 18,000 | 140 | 175 | 250 | 300 | 400 | 450 | 550 | 650 | 375 |
| 1863S | 100,000 | 25 | 40 | 75 | 100 | 150 | 275 | 550 | 750 | |
| 1864 *(470)* | 48,000 | 225 | 350 | 600 | 700 | 850 | 1,000 | 1,050 | 1,100 | 375 |
| 1864S | 90,000 | 60 | 85 | 125 | 150 | 350 | 450 | 700 | 850 | |
| 1865 *(500)* | 13,000 | 200 | 300 | 450 | 600 | 600 | 700 | 850 | 1,000 | 375 |
| 1865S | 120,000 | 30 | 50 | 85 | 120 | 200 | 400 | 850 | 1,850 | |
| 1866 *(725)* | 10,000 | 225 | 300 | 475 | 500 | 600 | 650 | 700 | 850 | 375 |
| 1866S | 120,000 | 20 | 30 | 45 | 75 | 120 | 225 | 350 | 750 | |
| 1867 *(625)* | 8,000 | 300 | 400 | 575 | 700 | 775 | 825 | 875 | 1,150 | 375 |
| 1867S | 120,000 | 30 | 45 | 65 | 100 | 125 | 200 | 425 | 750 | |
| 1868 *(600)* | 88,600 | 30 | 50 | 100 | 125 | 185 | 300 | 425 | 650 | 375 |
| 1868S | 280,000 | 20 | 24 | 28 | 32 | 45 | 85 | 250 | 350 | |
| 1869 *(600)* | 208,000 | 20 | 24 | 28 | 32 | 55 | 85 | 150 | 200 | 375 |
| 1869S | 230,000 | 20 | 24 | 28 | 32 | 60 | 95 | 225 | 650 | |
| 1870 *(1,000)* | 535,000 | 20 | 24 | 28 | 32 | 35 | 55 | 115 | 200 | 375 |
| 1870S *(unique)* | | | | | | | | 1,500,000 | | |
| 1871 *(960)* | 1,873,000 | 20 | 24 | 28 | 32 | 35 | 55 | 115 | 200 | 375 |
| 1871S | 161,000 | 20 | 25 | 30 | 45 | 60 | 100 | 165 | 250 | |
| 1872 *(950)* | 2,947,000 | 20 | 24 | 28 | 32 | 35 | 55 | 115 | 200 | 375 |
| 1872S | 837,000 | 20 | 24 | 28 | 32 | 35 | 55 | 115 | 200 | |
| 1873 *(600)* | 7,126,000 | 20 | 24 | 28 | 32 | 35 | 55 | 115 | 200 | 375 |
| 1873S | 324,000 | 20 | 24 | 28 | 32 | 35 | 55 | 115 | 200 | |

The designs of the dimes, first coined in 1796, follow closely those of the half dimes up through the Liberty Seated type. The dimes in each instance weigh twice as much as the half dimes.

# DRAPED BUST (1796–1807)
## Small Eagle Reverse (1796–1797)

**AG-3 About Good:** Details clear enough to identify.

**G-4 Good:** Date legible. Bust outlined, but no detail.

**VG-8 Very Good:** All but deepest drapery folds worn smooth. Hair lines nearly gone and curls lacking in detail.

**F-12 Fine:** All drapery lines visible. Hair partly worn.

**VF-20 Very Fine:** Only left side of drapery indistinct.

**EF-40 Extremely Fine:** Hair well outlined with details visible.

**AU-50 About Uncirculated:** Traces of light wear on many of the high points. At least half of mint luster still present.

**MS-60 Uncirculated:** No trace of wear. Light blemishes.

**MS-63 Choice Uncirculated:** Some distracting marks or blemishes in prime focal areas. Impaired luster possible.

1797, 16 Stars       1797, 13 Stars

| | Mintage | AG-3 | G-4 | VG-8 | F-12 | VF-20 | EF-40 | AU-50 | MS-60 | MS-63 |
|---|---|---|---|---|---|---|---|---|---|---|
| 1796 . . . . . . . . . . . . . . | 22,135 | $1,250 | $2,000 | $2,750 | $3,500 | $4,500 | $6,500 | $11,000 | $15,000 | $30,000 |
| 1797, All kinds. . . . . . . | 25,261 | | | | | | | | | |
|   1797, 16 Stars . . . . . . . . . . | | 1,250 | 2,000 | 2,600 | 3,500 | 5,000 | 6,500 | 10,000 | 24,000 | 35,000 |
|   1797, 13 Stars . . . . . . . . . . | | 1,250 | 2,000 | 3,000 | 4,500 | 6,500 | 10,000 | 15,500 | 40,000 | 65,000 |

## Heraldic Eagle Reverse (1798–1807)

| | Mintage | AG-3 | G-4 | VG-8 | F-12 | VF-20 | EF-40 | AU-50 | MS-60 | MS-63 |
|---|---|---|---|---|---|---|---|---|---|---|
| 1798, All kinds. . . . . . . . . | 27,550 | | | | | | | | | |
|   1798, 8 Over 7, | | | | | | | | | | |
|   16 Stars on Reverse . . . . . . | | $250 | $550 | $850 | $1,000 | $1,500 | $2,250 | $3,750 | $5,000 | $12,500 |
|   1798, 8 Over 7, | | | | | | | | | | |
|   13 Stars on Reverse . . . . . . | | 500 | 2,500 | 4,000 | 6,000 | 7,500 | 11,000 | 18,000 | | |
|   1798 . . . . . . . . . . . . . . . . . . | | 250 | 550 | 850 | 1,000 | 1,500 | 2,250 | 3,500 | 5,000 | 10,000 |
| 1800 . . . . . . . . . . . . . . . . | 21,760 | 250 | 650 | 1,000 | 1,200 | 1,650 | 2,500 | 5,000 | 14,000 | 30,000 |
| 1801 . . . . . . . . . . . . . . . . | 34,640 | 300 | 700 | 1,150 | 1,400 | 2,200 | 3,500 | 7,000 | 27,500 | 35,000 |
| 1802 . . . . . . . . . . . . . . . . | 10,975 | 450 | 1,000 | 1,500 | 2,000 | 2,500 | 4,750 | 9,000 | 25,000 | |
| 1803 . . . . . . . . . . . . . . . . | 33,040 | 200 | 850 | 1,200 | 1,500 | 1,800 | 3,000 | 6,500 | 45,000 | |
| 1804 . . . . . . . . . . . . . . . . | 8,265 | 1,500 | 3,000 | 4,500 | 8,000 | 12,000 | 25,000 | 45,000 | — | |
| 1805 . . . . . . . . . . . . . . . . | 120,780 | 225 | 450 | 750 | 1,000 | 1,350 | 2,250 | 3,000 | 5,000 | 8,000 |
| 1807 . . . . . . . . . . . . . . . . | 165,000 | 225 | 500 | 675 | 850 | 1,100 | 2,000 | 2,750 | 4,250 | 7,500 |

## CAPPED BUST (1809–1837)

**G-4 Good:** Date, letters, and stars discernible. Bust outlined, no details.
**VG-8 Very Good:** Legends and date plain. Some letters in LIBERTY visible.
**F-12 Fine:** Clear LIBERTY. Ear and shoulder clasp visible. Part of rim visible on both sides.
**VF-20 Very Fine:** LIBERTY distinct. Full rim. Ear and clasp plain and distinct.
**EF-40 Extremely Fine:** LIBERTY sharp. Ear distinct. Hair above eye well defined.
**AU-50 About Uncirculated:** Traces of light wear on only the high points of the design. Half of mint luster present.
**MS-60 Uncirculated:** No trace of wear. Light blemishes.
**MS-63 Choice Uncirculated:** Some distracting marks or blemishes in prime focal areas. Impaired luster possible.

### Variety 1 – Wide Border (1809–1828)

| 1823, 3 Over 2 | 1824, 4 Over 2 | 1828, Large Date | 1828, Small Date |

| | Mintage | G-4 | VG-8 | F-12 | VF-20 | EF-40 | AU-50 | MS-60 | MS-63 |
|---|---|---|---|---|---|---|---|---|---|
| 1809 | 51,065 | $450 | $750 | $1,000 | $1,750 | $2,500 | $3,500 | $4,500 | $7,000 |
| 1811, 11 Over 09 | 65,180 | 150 | 200 | 450 | 750 | 1,200 | 1,750 | 2,500 | 5,000 |
| 1814 | 421,500 | 50 | 75 | 100 | 175 | 400 | 500 | 1,000 | 2,000 |
| 1820 | 942,587 | 50 | 75 | 100 | 175 | 375 | 450 | 900 | 1,800 |
| 1821 | 1,186,512 | 50 | 75 | 100 | 150 | 375 | 450 | 900 | 1,800 |
| 1822 | 100,000 | 1,400 | 2,000 | 2,750 | 5,000 | 7,000 | 10,000 | 15,000 | 22,000 |
| 1823, 3 Over 2, All kinds | 440,000 | | | | | | | | |
| 1823, 3 Over 2, Small E's | | 30 | 50 | 80 | 140 | 375 | 500 | 1,000 | 1,800 |
| 1823, 3 Over 2, Large E's | | 30 | 50 | 80 | 140 | 375 | 500 | 1,000 | 1,800 |
| 1824, 4 Over 2 | 510,000 | 65 | 100 | 200 | 400 | 750 | 1,000 | 1,250 | 2,250 |
| 1825 | * | 30 | 50 | 80 | 140 | 375 | 450 | 900 | 1,800 |
| 1827 | 1,215,000 | 30 | 50 | 80 | 140 | 375 | 450 | 950 | 1,800 |
| 1828, Large Date, Curl Base 2 | 125,000 | 65 | 85 | 115 | 350 | 550 | 1,000 | 3,500 | 6,500 |

* Included in number above.

### Variety 2 – Modified Design (1828–1837)

| 1829, Small 10 C. | 1829, Large 10 C. | 1830, 30 Over 29 |

| | Mintage | G-4 | VG-8 | F-12 | VF-20 | EF-40 | AU-50 | MS-60 | MS-63 |
|---|---|---|---|---|---|---|---|---|---|
| 1828, Small Date, Square Base 2 | * | $25 | $35 | $50 | $75 | $220 | $350 | $650 | $1,500 |
| 1829, Small 10 C. | 770,000 | 20 | 30 | 40 | 65 | 200 | 300 | 650 | 1,500 |
| 1829, Medium 10 C. | * | 20 | 30 | 40 | 65 | 200 | 300 | 650 | 1,500 |
| 1829, Large 10 C. | * | 20 | 30 | 40 | 65 | 200 | 300 | 650 | 1,500 |
| 1830, 30 Over 29 | 510,000 | 20 | 30 | 50 | 90 | 225 | 375 | 675 | 1,750 |

* Included in number above.

| | Mintage | G-4 | VG-8 | F-12 | VF-20 | EF-40 | AU-50 | MS-60 | MS-63 |
|---|---|---|---|---|---|---|---|---|---|
| 1830, Large 10 C. ... * | | $20 | $30 | $40 | $65 | $200 | $275 | $600 | $1,200 |
| 1830, Small 10 C. ... * | | 20 | 30 | 40 | 65 | 200 | 275 | 600 | 1,200 |
| 1831 | 771,350 | 20 | 30 | 40 | 65 | 200 | 275 | 600 | 1,200 |
| 1832 | 522,500 | 20 | 30 | 40 | 65 | 200 | 275 | 600 | 1,200 |
| 1833 | 485,000 | 20 | 30 | 40 | 65 | 200 | 275 | 600 | 1,200 |
| 1834 | 635,000 | 20 | 30 | 40 | 65 | 200 | 275 | 600 | 1,200 |
| 1835 | 1,410,000 | 20 | 30 | 40 | 65 | 200 | 275 | 600 | 1,200 |
| 1836 | 1,190,000 | 20 | 30 | 40 | 65 | 200 | 275 | 600 | 1,200 |
| 1837 | 359,500 | 20 | 30 | 40 | 65 | 200 | 275 | 600 | 1,200 |

* Included in mintage for 1830, 30 Over 29 (previous page).

## LIBERTY SEATED (1837–1891)
### Variety 1 – No Stars on Obverse (1837–1838)

**G-4 Good:** LIBERTY on shield not readable. Date and letters legible.
**F-12 Fine:** LIBERTY visible, weak spots.
**VF-20 Very Fine:** LIBERTY strong and even.
**EF-40 Extremely Fine:** LIBERTY and scroll edges distinct.
**AU-50 About Uncirculated:** Wear on Liberty's shoulder and hair high points.
**MS-60 Uncirculated:** No trace of wear. Light blemishes.
**MS-63 Choice Uncirculated:** Some distracting marks or blemishes in focal areas. Impaired luster possible.

**No Drapery From Elbow
No Stars on Obverse**

*Mintmarks on Liberty Seated dimes on reverse, within or below the wreath. Size of mintmark varies on many dates.*

| | Mintage | G-4 | F-12 | VF-20 | EF-40 | AU-50 | MS-60 | MS-63 |
|---|---|---|---|---|---|---|---|---|
| 1837 | 682,500 | $20 | $55 | $160 | $275 | $450 | $700 | $1,200 |
| 1838O | 406,034 | 55 | 75 | 200 | 450 | 700 | 2,500 | 4,500 |

### Variety 2 – Stars on Obverse (1838–1853)

**No Drapery From Elbow, Tilted Shield
(1838–1840)**

**Drapery From Elbow, Upright Shield
(1840–1891)**

**1838, Small Stars**     **1838, Large Stars**

| | Mintage | G-4 | F-12 | VF-20 | EF-40 | AU-50 | MS-60 | MS-63 |
|---|---|---|---|---|---|---|---|---|
| 1838, All kinds. | 1,992,500 | | | | | | | |
| 1838, Small Stars | | $10 | $25 | $50 | $100 | $225 | $400 | $700 |
| 1838, Large Stars | | 10 | 12 | 25 | 80 | 175 | 275 | 550 |
| 1838, Partial Drapery | | 12 | 18 | 35 | 75 | 210 | 425 | 1,000 |
| 1839 | 1,053,115 | 10 | 15 | 25 | 80 | 175 | 275 | 550 |
| 1839O | 1,288,000 | 12 | 20 | 25 | 90 | 185 | 325 | 750 |
| 1840, No Drapery | 981,500 | 10 | 15 | 25 | 80 | 185 | 275 | 550 |
| 1840O, No Drapery | 1,175,000 | 30 | 75 | 100 | 300 | 650 | 4,500 | 8,500 |
| 1840, Drapery | 377,500 | 35 | 85 | 125 | 450 | 750 | 2,000 | 7,500 |

*Chart continued on next page.*

| | Mintage | G-4 | F-12 | VF-20 | EF-40 | AU-50 | MS-60 | MS-63 |
|---|---|---|---|---|---|---|---|---|
| 1841 . . . . . . . . . . . . . . . 1,622,500 | | $10 | $12 | $18 | $25 | $80 | $250 | $400 |
| 1841O . . . . . . . . . . . . . . 2,007,500 | | 12 | 20 | 35 | 80 | 125 | 600 | 1,000 |
| 1842 . . . . . . . . . . . . . . . 1,887,500 | | 10 | 12 | 18 | 25 | 80 | 225 | 375 |
| 1842O . . . . . . . . . . . . . . 2,020,000 | | 20 | 55 | 100 | 250 | 700 | 2,250 | 3,000 |
| 1843 . . . . . . . . . . . . . . . 1,370,000 | | 10 | 12 | 18 | 25 | 80 | 225 | 475 |
| 1843O . . . . . . . . . . . . . . .150,000 | | 125 | 400 | 850 | 1,750 | 6,500 | 45,000 | |
| 1844 . . . . . . . . . . . . . . . .72,500 | | 115 | 200 | 400 | 750 | 1,100 | 2,750 | 6,500 |
| 1845 . . . . . . . . . . . . . . . 1,755,000 | | 10 | 12 | 18 | 25 | 80 | 225 | 450 |
| 1845O . . . . . . . . . . . . . . .230,000 | | 45 | 150 | 300 | 650 | 1,500 | 7,500 | — |
| 1846 . . . . . . . . . . . . . . . .31,300 | | 250 | 375 | 950 | 1,750 | 5,000 | 15,000 | 35,000 |
| 1847 . . . . . . . . . . . . . . . .245,000 | | 10 | 16 | 35 | 100 | 200 | 1,000 | 2,000 |
| 1848 . . . . . . . . . . . . . . . .451,500 | | 10 | 12 | 30 | 45 | 85 | 450 | 550 |
| 1849 . . . . . . . . . . . . . . . .839,000 | | 10 | 12 | 20 | 40 | 100 | 350 | 600 |
| 1849O . . . . . . . . . . . . . . .300,000 | | 15 | 35 | 100 | 200 | 500 | 1,750 | 3,500 |
| 1850 . . . . . . . . . . . . . . . 1,931,500 | | 10 | 12 | 18 | 30 | 90 | 225 | 400 |
| 1850O . . . . . . . . . . . . . . .510,000 | | 15 | 30 | 75 | 150 | 350 | 1,250 | 3,000 |
| 1851 . . . . . . . . . . . . . . . 1,026,500 | | 10 | 12 | 18 | 25 | 80 | 250 | 500 |
| 1851O . . . . . . . . . . . . . . .400,000 | | 15 | 20 | 55 | 175 | 450 | 2,000 | 2,500 |
| 1852 . . . . . . . . . . . . . . . 1,535,500 | | 10 | 12 | 18 | 25 | 80 | 200 | 375 |
| 1852O . . . . . . . . . . . . . . .430,000 | | 15 | 35 | 125 | 225 | 350 | 1,250 | 2,500 |
| 1853, No Arrows . . . . . . . . . .95,000 | | 100 | 215 | 325 | 450 | 525 | 750 | 1,250 |

## Variety 3 – Arrows at Date (1853–1855)

| | Mintage | G-4 | F-12 | VF-20 | EF-40 | AU-50 | MS-60 | MS-63 | PF-63 |
|---|---|---|---|---|---|---|---|---|---|
| 1853, With Arrows . .12,173,000 | | $10 | $12 | $20 | $25 | $100 | $225 | $450 | $12,500 |
| 1853O . . . . . . . . . . . .1,100,000 | | 10 | 20 | 75 | 200 | 325 | 1,250 | 2,500 | |
| 1854 . . . . . . . . . . . .4,470,000 | | 10 | 12 | 20 | 25 | 100 | 200 | 400 | 4,500 |
| 1854O . . . . . . . . . . . .1,770,000 | | 10 | 12 | 20 | 35 | 125 | 250 | 600 | |
| 1855 . . . . . . . . . . . .2,075,000 | | 10 | 12 | 20 | 25 | 100 | 225 | 550 | 4,500 |

## Variety 2 Resumed, With Weight Standard of Variety 3 (1856–1860)

### Small Date, Arrows Removed (1856–1860)

| | Mintage | G-4 | F-12 | VF-20 | EF-40 | AU-50 | MS-60 | MS-63 | PF-63 |
|---|---|---|---|---|---|---|---|---|---|
| 1856, All kinds. . . . . .5,780,000 | | | | | | | | | |
| 1856, Large Date . . . . . . . . . | | $20 | $50 | $80 | $120 | $185 | $425 | $1,400 | |
| 1856, Small Date. . . . . . . . . | | 7 | 10 | 15 | 20 | 80 | 175 | 350 | $2,000 |
| 1856O . . . . . . . . . . . .1,180,000 | | 15 | 35 | 65 | 100 | 250 | 500 | 1,000 | |
| 1856S . . . . . . . . . . . . . 70,000 | | 200 | 400 | 650 | 1,200 | 1,500 | 5,000 | 10,000 | |

| | Mintage | G-4 | F-12 | VF-20 | EF-40 | AU-50 | MS-60 | MS-63 | PF-63 |
|---|---|---|---|---|---|---|---|---|---|
| 1857 . . . . . . . . . . . . . . | 5,580,000 | $7 | $10 | $15 | $35 | $80 | $175 | $375 | $1,800 |
| 1857O . . . . . . . . . . . . | 1,540,000 | 10 | 15 | 25 | 35 | 100 | 250 | 400 | |
| 1858 . . . . . . *(300+)*. . . | 1,540,000 | 7 | 10 | 15 | 25 | 80 | 175 | 375 | 1,000 |
| 1858O . . . . . . . . . . . . . | 200,000 | 10 | 30 | 65 | 125 | 225 | 500 | 1,250 | |
| 1858S . . . . . . . . . . . . . . | 60,000 | 150 | 275 | 550 | 950 | 1,500 | 5,000 | 10,000 | |
| 1859 . . . . . . *(800+)*. . . . . | 429,200 | 7 | 10 | 15 | 25 | 80 | 175 | 375 | 700 |
| 1859O . . . . . . . . . . . . . | 480,000 | 10 | 20 | 40 | 65 | 125 | 250 | 400 | |
| 1859S . . . . . . . . . . . . . . | 60,000 | 150 | 300 | 650 | 1,500 | 3,000 | 12,500 | 22,500 | |
| 1860S . . . . . . . . . . . . . | 140,000 | 35 | 100 | 150 | 350 | 600 | 1,500 | 5,000 | |

# Variety 4 – Legend on Obverse (1860–1873)

| | Mintage | G-4 | F-12 | VF-20 | EF-40 | AU-50 | MS-60 | MS-63 | PF-63 |
|---|---|---|---|---|---|---|---|---|---|
| 1860 . . . . . .(1,000). . . . . | 606,000 | $7 | $10 | $15 | $25 | $50 | $125 | $175 | $450 |
| 1860O . . . . . . . . . . . . . . | 40,000 | 600 | 1,100 | 2,000 | 3,500 | 6,500 | 13,500 | 25,000 | |
| 1861 . . . . . .(1,000). . . | 1,883,000 | 7 | 10 | 15 | 20 | 40 | 100 | 175 | 450 |
| 1861S . . . . . . . . . . . . . | 172,500 | 100 | 275 | 400 | 550 | 900 | 3,500 | 12,500 | |
| 1862 . . . . . . . (550). . . . . | 847,000 | 7 | 10 | 15 | 20 | 50 | 120 | 175 | 450 |
| 1862S . . . . . . . . . . . . . | 180,750 | 85 | 200 | 350 | 600 | 1,500 | 3,000 | 6,500 | |
| 1863 . . . . . . . (460). . . . . . | 14,000 | 300 | 550 | 650 | 750 | 850 | 1,000 | 1,750 | 450 |
| 1863S . . . . . . . . . . . . . | 157,500 | 75 | 200 | 300 | 550 | 750 | 2,500 | 6,500 | |
| 1864 . . . . . . . (470). . . . . . | 11,000 | 185 | 400 | 550 | 650 | 750 | 1,000 | 1,650 | 475 |
| 1864S . . . . . . . . . . . . . | 230,000 | 65 | 125 | 250 | 550 | 750 | 1,000 | 1,500 | |
| 1865 . . . . . . . (500). . . . . . | 10,000 | 250 | 500 | 650 | 750 | 850 | 2,000 | 3,000 | 450 |
| 1865S . . . . . . . . . . . . . | 175,000 | 55 | 225 | 450 | 650 | 2,000 | 4,500 | 10,000 | |
| 1866 . . . . . . . (725). . . . . . | 8,000 | 500 | 650 | 750 | 950 | 1,000 | 1,850 | 2,500 | 450 |
| 1866S . . . . . . . . . . . . . | 135,000 | 55 | 150 | 250 | 400 | 850 | 2,500 | 5,500 | |
| 1867 . . . . . . . (625). . . . . . | 6,000 | 400 | 600 | 700 | 800 | 1,000 | 1,250 | 1,500 | 350 |
| 1867S . . . . . . . . . . . . . | 140,000 | 55 | 150 | 250 | 450 | 1,000 | 2,250 | 3,500 | |
| 1868 . . . . . . . (600). . . . | 464,000 | 10 | 15 | 25 | 40 | 90 | 200 | 475 | 350 |
| 1868S . . . . . . . . . . . . . | 260,000 | 30 | 75 | 125 | 325 | 375 | 1,000 | 1,750 | |
| 1869 . . . . . . . (600). . . . | 256,000 | 10 | 15 | 55 | 125 | 150 | 350 | 600 | 350 |
| 1869S . . . . . . . . . . . . . | 450,000 | 10 | 30 | 75 | 150 | 200 | 400 | 650 | |
| 1870 . . . . . .(1,000). . . . | 470,500 | 10 | 12 | 15 | 40 | 55 | 150 | 300 | 350 |
| 1870S . . . . . . . . . . . . . | 50,000 | 150 | 400 | 500 | 600 | 800 | 1,200 | 2,000 | |
| 1871 . . . . . . . (960). . . . | 906,750 | 10 | 12 | 15 | 20 | 80 | 200 | 325 | 350 |
| 1871CC . . . . . . . . . . . . | 20,100 | 2,000 | 4,000 | 6,000 | 10,000 | 17,500 | — | — | |
| 1871S . . . . . . . . . . . . . | 320,000 | 15 | 60 | 100 | 150 | 300 | 1,000 | 2,500 | |
| 1872 . . . . . . . (950). . . | 2,395,500 | 10 | 12 | 15 | 20 | 45 | 100 | 175 | 350 |
| 1872CC . . . . . . . . . . . . | 35,480 | 750 | 2,000 | 2,500 | 7,500 | 15,000 | — | — | |
| 1872S . . . . . . . . . . . . . | 190,000 | 15 | 55 | 80 | 150 | 275 | 1,200 | 2,200 | |
| 1873, Close 3 (600). . . | *1,507,400* | 10 | 12 | 15 | 20 | 45 | 150 | 250 | 350 |
| 1873, Open 3 . . . . . . . . . | *60,000* | 10 | 30 | 45 | 80 | 110 | 325 | 750 | |
| 1873CC *(unique)* . . . . . . . . | 12,400 | | | | | | | — | |

## Variety 5 – Arrows at Date (1873–1874)

In 1873, the dime was increased in weight from 2.49 grams to 2.50 grams. Arrows at the date in 1873 and 1874 indicate this change.

| | Mintage | G-4 | F-12 | VF-20 | EF-40 | AU-50 | MS-60 | MS-63 | PF-63 |
|---|---|---|---|---|---|---|---|---|---|
| 1873 . . . . . . . (500) . . . 2,377,700 | | $10 | $18 | $30 | $100 | $175 | $275 | $575 | $600 |
| 1873CC . . . . . . . . . . . . . . 18,791 | | 2,500 | 3,000 | 6,500 | 12,500 | 27,500 | — | — | |
| 1873S . . . . . . . . . . . . . . 455,000 | | 10 | 20 | 35 | 110 | 275 | 600 | 1,100 | |
| 1874 . . . . . . . (700) . . . 2,940,000 | | 10 | 16 | 30 | 100 | 175 | 300 | 575 | 600 |
| 1874CC . . . . . . . . . . . . . . 10,817 | | 4,500 | 8,500 | 14,000 | 22,500 | 35,000 | — | — | |
| 1874S . . . . . . . . . . . . . . 240,000 | | 11 | 40 | 65 | 125 | 275 | 650 | 1,500 | |

## Variety 4 Resumed, With Weight Standard of Variety 5 (1875–1891)

| | Mintage | G-4 | F-12 | VF-20 | EF-40 | AU-50 | MS-60 | MS-63 | PF-63 |
|---|---|---|---|---|---|---|---|---|---|
| 1875 . . . . . . . (700) . . 10,350,000 | | $7 | $10 | $12 | $20 | $45 | $100 | $150 | $350 |
| 1875CC . . . . . . . . . . . 4,645,000 | | 12 | 25 | 30 | 50 | 120 | 250 | 500 | |
| 1875S . . . . . . . . . . . . . 9,070,000 | | 7 | 10 | 12 | 20 | 45 | 100 | 150 | |
| 1876 . . . . . . (1,250) . . 11,460,000 | | 7 | 10 | 12 | 20 | 45 | 100 | 150 | 350 |
| 1876CC . . . . . . . . . . . 8,270,000 | | 12 | 25 | 30 | 45 | 80 | 175 | 350 | |
| 1876S . . . . . . . . . . . 10,420,000 | | 7 | 10 | 12 | 20 | 45 | 100 | 175 | |
| 1877 . . . . . . . (510) . . . 7,310,000 | | 7 | 10 | 12 | 20 | 45 | 100 | 150 | 350 |
| 1877CC . . . . . . . . . . . 7,700,000 | | 12 | 25 | 30 | 55 | 80 | 200 | 500 | |
| 1877S . . . . . . . . . . . . . 2,340,000 | | 7 | 10 | 12 | 20 | 45 | 100 | 175 | |
| 1878 . . . . . . . (800) . . . 1,677,200 | | 7 | 10 | 12 | 20 | 45 | 100 | 175 | 350 |
| 1878CC . . . . . . . . . . . . . 200,000 | | 125 | 200 | 250 | 300 | 475 | 1,000 | 1,750 | |
| 1879 . . . . . . (1,100) . . . . . 14,000 | | 125 | 175 | 225 | 400 | 425 | 450 | 500 | 350 |
| 1880 . . . . . . (1,355) . . . . . 36,000 | | 100 | 160 | 200 | 250 | 275 | 375 | 450 | 350 |
| 1881 . . . . . . . (975) . . . . . 24,000 | | 115 | 175 | 225 | 250 | 300 | 325 | 400 | 350 |
| 1882 . . . . . . (1,100) . . . 3,910,000 | | 7 | 10 | 12 | 20 | 45 | 100 | 150 | 350 |
| 1883 . . . . . (1,039) . . . 7,674,673 | | 7 | 10 | 12 | 20 | 45 | 100 | 150 | 350 |
| 1884 . . . . . . . (875) . . . 3,365,505 | | 7 | 10 | 12 | 20 | 45 | 100 | 150 | 350 |
| 1884S . . . . . . . . . . . . . . 564,969 | | 10 | 15 | 30 | 60 | 175 | 400 | 625 | |
| 1885 . . . . . . . (930) . . . 2,532,497 | | 7 | 10 | 12 | 20 | 45 | 110 | 150 | 350 |
| 1885S . . . . . . . . . . . . . . . 43,690 | | 500 | 750 | 1,000 | 1,750 | 3,000 | 4,500 | 6,000 | |
| 1886 . . . . . . . (886) . . . 6,376,684 | | 7 | 10 | 12 | 20 | 45 | 100 | 150 | 350 |
| 1886S . . . . . . . . . . . . . . 206,524 | | 12 | 25 | 40 | 65 | 95 | 350 | 750 | |
| 1887 . . . . . . . (710) . . 11,283,229 | | 7 | 10 | 12 | 20 | 45 | 100 | 150 | 350 |
| 1887S . . . . . . . . . . . . 4,454,450 | | 7 | 10 | 12 | 20 | 45 | 100 | 150 | |
| 1888 . . . . . . . (832) . . . 5,495,655 | | 7 | 10 | 12 | 20 | 45 | 100 | 150 | 350 |
| 1888S . . . . . . . . . . . . 1,720,000 | | 7 | 10 | 12 | 25 | 45 | 125 | 450 | |
| 1889 . . . . . . . (711) . . . 7,380,000 | | 7 | 10 | 12 | 20 | 45 | 100 | 150 | 350 |
| 1889S . . . . . . . . . . . . . . 972,678 | | 10 | 15 | 25 | 40 | 75 | 225 | 500 | |
| 1890 . . . . . . . (590) . . . 9,910,951 | | 7 | 10 | 12 | 20 | 45 | 100 | 150 | 350 |
| 1890S . . . . . . . . . . . . 1,423,076 | | 7 | 12 | 20 | 40 | 75 | 180 | 400 | |
| 1891 . . . . . . . (600) . . 15,310,000 | | 7 | 10 | 12 | 20 | 45 | 100 | 150 | 350 |
| 18910 . . . . . . . . . . . . 4,540,000 | | 7 | 15 | 18 | 20 | 45 | 125 | 165 | |
| 1891S . . . . . . . . . . . . 3,196,116 | | 7 | 10 | 12 | 20 | 45 | 100 | 150 | |

**DIMES**

# BARBER OR LIBERTY HEAD (1892–1916)

This type was designed by Charles E. Barber, chief engraver of the Mint. His initial B is at the truncation of the neck. He also designed the quarters and half dollars of the same period.

**G-4 Good:** Date and letters plain. LIBERTY obliterated.
**VG-8 Very Good:** Some letters visible in LIBERTY.
**F-12 Fine:** Letters in LIBERTY visible, though some weak.
**VF-20 Very Fine:** Letters of LIBERTY evenly plain.
**EF-40 Extremely Fine:** All letters in LIBERTY sharp, distinct. Headband edges distinct.
**AU-50 About Uncirculated:** Slight traces of wear on hair cheekbone and on leaf tips in wreath.
**MS-60 Uncirculated:** No trace of wear. Light blemishes.
**MS-63 Choice Uncirculated:** Some distracting blemishes in prime focal areas. Impaired luster possible.

*Mintmark location is on reverse, below wreath.*

| | Mintage | G-4 | VG-8 | F-12 | VF-20 | EF-40 | AU-50 | MS-60 | MS-63 | PF-63 |
|---|---|---|---|---|---|---|---|---|---|---|
| 1892 . . . . (1,245) . . . | 12,120,000 | $4.00 | $4.50 | $8 | $12 | $15 | $35 | $75 | $125 | $350 |
| 1892O . . . . . . . . . . . | 3,841,700 | 4.00 | 6.00 | 15 | 25 | 35 | 45 | 125 | 250 | |
| 1892S . . . . . . . . . . . . . | 990,710 | 35.00 | 55.00 | 110 | 125 | 160 | 180 | 250 | 500 | |
| 1893, 3/2 . . . . . . . . . . . . . . . . . * | | 50.00 | 65.00 | 85 | 100 | 120 | 175 | 1,000 | 1,350 | — |
| 1893 . . . . . . (792) . . | 3,339,940 | 3.00 | 5.00 | 10 | 15 | 24 | 35 | 95 | 150 | 350 |
| 1893O . . . . . . . . . . . | 1,760,000 | 12.00 | 25.00 | 75 | 85 | 100 | 125 | 200 | 350 | |
| 1893S **(a)** . . . . . . . . . | 2,491,401 | 6.00 | 12.00 | 18 | 25 | 40 | 75 | 225 | 500 | |
| 1894 . . . . . . (970) . . . | 1,330,000 | 10.00 | 20.00 | 65 | 85 | 100 | 125 | 200 | 275 | 350 |
| 1894O . . . . . . . . . . . . | 720,000 | 30.00 | 45.00 | 110 | 160 | 250 | 400 | 1,400 | 2,250 | |
| 1894S . . . . . . . . . . . . . . . | 24 **(b)** | | | | | | | | 1,250,000 | |
| 1895 . . . . . . (880) . . . . . . | 690,000 | 35.00 | 75.00 | 180 | 275 | 325 | 400 | 500 | 700 | 350 |
| 1895O . . . . . . . . . . . . . | 440,000 | 300.00 | 400.00 | 700 | 1,000 | 1,750 | 2,500 | 4,000 | 8,000 | |
| 1895S . . . . . . . . . . . . . | 1,120,000 | 20.00 | 30.00 | 75 | 100 | 125 | 175 | 350 | 750 | |
| 1896 . . . . . . (762) . . . . | 2,000,000 | 4.50 | 10.00 | 28 | 36 | 50 | 55 | 110 | 250 | 350 |
| 1896O . . . . . . . . . . . . . | 610,000 | 50.00 | 85.00 | 175 | 225 | 280 | 400 | 950 | 2,000 | |
| 1896S . . . . . . . . . . . . . . | 576,056 | 50.00 | 70.00 | 160 | 200 | 275 | 310 | 500 | 1,000 | |
| 1897 . . . . . . (731) . . . | 10,868,533 | 2.25 | 2.50 | 3 | 6 | 12 | 35 | 75 | 125 | 350 |
| 1897O . . . . . . . . . . . . . | 666,000 | 45.00 | 65.00 | 175 | 250 | 300 | 400 | 750 | 1,000 | |
| 1897S . . . . . . . . . . . . | 1,342,844 | 8.00 | 16.00 | 50 | 75 | 90 | 140 | 250 | 625 | |
| 1898 . . . . . . (735) . . . | 16,320,000 | 2.25 | 2.50 | 3 | 5 | 12 | 35 | 75 | 125 | 350 |
| 1898O . . . . . . . . . . . | 2,130,000 | 5.00 | 10.00 | 38 | 75 | 80 | 150 | 300 | 700 | |
| 1898S . . . . . . . . . . . | 1,702,507 | 2.00 | 5.00 | 16 | 25 | 35 | 75 | 350 | 850 | |
| 1899 . . . . . . (846) . . | 19,580,000 | 2.00 | 2.50 | 3 | 5 | 12 | 35 | 75 | 125 | 350 |
| 1899O . . . . . . . . . . . | 2,650,000 | 7.00 | 9.00 | 35 | 45 | 70 | 125 | 250 | 650 | |
| 1899S . . . . . . . . . . . | 1,867,493 | 2.40 | 5.00 | 12 | 16 | 20 | 55 | 225 | 450 | |
| 1900 . . . . . . (912) . . . | 17,600,000 | 2.00 | 2.25 | 3 | 5 | 12 | 35 | 75 | 125 | 350 |

* Included in number below. **a.** Boldly doubled mintmark is valued slightly higher. **b.** Five of these were reserved for assay.

*Chart continued on next page.*

| | Mintage | G-4 | VG-8 | F-12 | VF-20 | EF-40 | AU-50 | MS-60 | MS-63 | PF-63 |
|---|---|---|---|---|---|---|---|---|---|---|
| 1900O | 2,010,000 | $10.00 | $20.00 | $65.00 | $100.00 | $150 | $200 | $350 | $650 | |
| 1900S | 5,168,270 | 2.00 | 2.25 | 5.00 | 7.00 | 14 | 35 | 115 | 250 | |
| 1901 (813) | 18,859,665 | 2.00 | 2.25 | 2.50 | 5.00 | 12 | 35 | 75 | 125 | $350 |
| 1901O | 5,620,000 | 3.00 | 3.50 | 6.00 | 10.00 | 30 | 85 | 475 | 750 | |
| 1901S | 593,022 | 50.00 | 100.00 | 250.00 | 325.00 | 400 | 500 | 1,000 | 1,500 | |
| 1902 (777) | 21,380,000 | 2.00 | 2.25 | 2.50 | 4.00 | 12 | 35 | 75 | 150 | 350 |
| 1902O | 4,500,000 | 3.00 | 3.50 | 6.00 | 12.00 | 30 | 70 | 250 | 525 | |
| 1902S | 2,070,000 | 3.00 | 8.00 | 25.00 | 40.00 | 60 | 100 | 225 | 650 | |
| 1903 (755) | 19,500,000 | 2.00 | 2.25 | 2.50 | 4.00 | 12 | 35 | 75 | 150 | 350 |
| 1903O | 8,180,000 | 3.00 | 3.50 | 7.00 | 10.00 | 20 | 40 | 150 | 350 | |
| 1903S | 613,300 | 50.00 | 85.00 | 225.00 | 350.00 | 450 | 550 | 1,000 | 1,350 | |
| 1904 (670) | 14,600,357 | 2.00 | 2.25 | 2.50 | 4.00 | 12 | 35 | 75 | 125 | 350 |
| 1904S | 800,000 | 25.00 | 45.00 | 100.00 | 150.00 | 200 | 350 | 500 | 1,250 | |
| 1905 (727) | 14,551,623 | 2.00 | 2.25 | 2.50 | 4.00 | 12 | 35 | 75 | 125 | 350 |
| 1905O | 3,400,000 | 3.00 | 4.00 | 16.00 | 25.00 | 50 | 75 | 200 | 325 | |
| 1905S | 6,855,199 | 2.00 | 2.25 | 3.00 | 7.00 | 18 | 40 | 125 | 175 | |
| 1906 (675) | 19,957,731 | 2.00 | 2.25 | 2.50 | 4.00 | 12 | 35 | 75 | 125 | 350 |
| 1906D | 4,060,000 | 2.00 | 2.25 | 2.50 | 6.00 | 15 | 35 | 100 | 225 | |
| 1906O | 2,610,000 | 4.00 | 6.00 | 22.00 | 35.00 | 47 | 65 | 150 | 300 | |
| 1906S | 3,136,640 | 2.00 | 2.25 | 5.00 | 10.00 | 18 | 55 | 150 | 250 | |
| 1907 (575) | 22,220,000 | 2.00 | 2.25 | 2.50 | 4.00 | 12 | 35 | 75 | 125 | 350 |
| 1907D | 4,080,000 | 2.00 | 2.25 | 4.00 | 6.00 | 18 | 55 | 150 | 500 | |
| 1907O | 5,058,000 | 3.00 | 3.50 | 15.00 | 22.00 | 24 | 50 | 125 | 225 | |
| 1907S | 3,178,470 | 2.00 | 2.25 | 6.00 | 10.00 | 25 | 65 | 250 | 500 | |
| 1908 (545) | 10,600,000 | 2.00 | 2.25 | 2.50 | 4.00 | 12 | 35 | 75 | 125 | 350 |
| 1908D | 7,490,000 | 2.00 | 2.25 | 2.50 | 4.00 | 14 | 35 | 75 | 150 | |
| 1908O | 1,789,000 | 3.00 | 4.00 | 22.00 | 30.00 | 45 | 65 | 200 | 425 | |
| 1908S | 3,220,000 | 2.00 | 2.25 | 4.00 | 8.00 | 18 | 75 | 200 | 450 | |
| 1909 (650) | 10,240,000 | 2.00 | 2.25 | 2.50 | 3.50 | 12 | 35 | 75 | 125 | 350 |
| 1909D | 954,000 | 3.00 | 7.00 | 35.00 | 50.00 | 75 | 125 | 325 | 625 | |
| 1909O | 2,287,000 | 1.75 | 3.00 | 5.00 | 8.00 | 25 | 85 | 200 | 475 | |
| 1909S | 1,000,000 | 3.00 | 8.00 | 40.00 | 60.00 | 90 | 175 | 300 | 675 | |
| 1910 (551) | 11,520,000 | 2.00 | 2.25 | 2.50 | 3.50 | 12 | 35 | 75 | 125 | 350 |
| 1910D | 3,490,000 | 2.00 | 2.25 | 3.00 | 6.00 | 20 | 45 | 125 | 300 | |
| 1910S | 1,240,000 | 2.00 | 2.25 | 25.00 | 35.00 | 50 | 100 | 250 | 400 | |
| 1911 (543) | 18,870,000 | 2.00 | 2.25 | 2.50 | 3.50 | 12 | 35 | 75 | 125 | 350 |
| 1911D | 11,209,000 | 2.00 | 2.25 | 2.50 | 3.50 | 12 | 35 | 75 | 125 | |
| 1911S | 3,520,000 | 2.00 | 2.25 | 3.00 | 8.50 | 16 | 45 | 125 | 225 | |
| 1912 (700) | 19,349,300 | 2.00 | 2.25 | 2.50 | 3.50 | 12 | 35 | 75 | 125 | 350 |
| 1912D | 11,760,000 | 2.00 | 2.25 | 2.50 | 3.50 | 12 | 35 | 75 | 125 | |
| 1912S | 3,420,000 | 2.00 | 2.25 | 2.50 | 3.50 | 16 | 45 | 115 | 200 | |
| 1913 (622) | 19,760,000 | 2.00 | 2.25 | 2.50 | 3.50 | 12 | 35 | 75 | 125 | 350 |
| 1913S | 510,000 | 23.00 | 35.00 | 75.00 | 100.00 | 150 | 225 | 500 | 1,000 | |
| 1914 (425) | 17,360,230 | 2.00 | 2.25 | 2.50 | 3.50 | 12 | 35 | 75 | 125 | 350 |
| 1914D | 11,908,000 | 2.00 | 2.25 | 2.50 | 3.50 | 12 | 35 | 75 | 150 | |
| 1914S | 2,100,000 | 2.00 | 2.25 | 3.00 | 7.00 | 15 | 35 | 75 | 125 | |
| 1915 (450) | 5,620,000 | 2.00 | 2.25 | 2.50 | 3.50 | 12 | 35 | 75 | 125 | 350 |
| 1915S | 960,000 | 2.25 | 4.00 | 15.00 | 20.00 | 32 | 70 | 140 | 275 | |
| 1916 | 18,490,000 | 2.00 | 2.25 | 2.75 | 3.50 | 12 | 35 | 75 | 125 | |
| 1916S | 5,820,000 | 2.00 | 2.25 | 2.75 | 3.50 | 12 | 35 | 75 | 125 | |

# WINGED LIBERTY HEAD
## OR "MERCURY" (1916–1945)

Although this coin is commonly called the *Mercury* dime, the main device is in fact a representation of Liberty. The wings crowning her cap are intended to symbolize liberty of thought. Designer Adolph Weinman's monogram, AW, is at the right of the neck. A centennial gold issue was struck in 2016.

**G-4 Good:** Letters and date clear. Lines and bands in fasces obliterated.
**VG-8 Very Good:** Half of sticks discernible in fasces.
**F-12 Fine:** All sticks in fasces defined. Diagonal bands worn nearly flat.
**VF-20 Very Fine:** Diagonal bands definitely visible.
**EF-40 Extremely Fine:** Only slight wear on diagonal bands. Braids and hair before ear clearly visible.
**AU-50 About Uncirculated:** Slight trace of wear. Most mint luster present.
**MS-63 Choice Uncirculated:** No trace of wear. Light blemishes. Attractive mint luster.
**MS-65 Gem Uncirculated:** Only light, scattered, non-distracting marks. Strong luster, good eye appeal.

Mintmark location is on reverse,
left of fasces.

*The Mint State prices shown are what coin dealers pay for average Uncirculated pieces with minimum blemishes. For coins with sharp strikes and split horizontal bands on the reverse, they usually pay much more.*

| | Mintage | G-4 | VG-8 | F-12 | VF-20 | EF-40 | MS-60 | MS-63 | MS-65 |
|---|---|---|---|---|---|---|---|---|---|
| 1916 | 22,180,080 | $2.00 | $2.50 | $3 | $4.00 | $5 | $18 | $24 | $55 |
| 1916D | 264,000 | 600.00 | 1,100.00 | 2,000 | 3,000.00 | 4,500 | 10,000 | 12,500 | 20,000 |
| 1916S | 10,450,000 | 2.00 | 2.50 | 4 | 6.00 | 10 | 20 | 50 | 125 |
| 1917 | 55,230,000 | 1.75 | 1.75 | 2 | 2.50 | 4 | 15 | 30 | 100 |
| 1917D | 9,402,000 | 2.00 | 3.00 | 5 | 10.00 | 22 | 65 | 175 | 600 |
| 1917S | 27,330,000 | 1.75 | 1.75 | 2 | 3.00 | 6 | 30 | 125 | 275 |
| 1918 | 26,680,000 | 1.75 | 1.75 | 3 | 5.00 | 13 | 40 | 75 | 225 |
| 1918D | 22,674,800 | 1.75 | 1.75 | 3 | 5.00 | 12 | 55 | 200 | 500 |
| 1918S | 19,300,000 | 1.75 | 1.75 | 2 | 4.00 | 9 | 60 | 125 | 525 |
| 1919 | 35,740,000 | 1.75 | 1.75 | 2 | 2.50 | 6 | 20 | 100 | 200 |
| 1919D | 9,939,000 | 1.75 | 1.75 | 5 | 12.00 | 22 | 105 | 350 | 1,000 |
| 1919S | 8,850,000 | 1.75 | 1.75 | 4 | 8.00 | 20 | 105 | 400 | 1,200 |
| 1920 | 59,030,000 | 1.75 | 1.75 | 2 | 2.50 | 5 | 16 | 35 | 150 |
| 1920D | 19,171,000 | 1.75 | 1.75 | 2 | 3.00 | 11 | 65 | 200 | 450 |
| 1920S | 13,820,000 | 1.75 | 1.75 | 2 | 3.00 | 10 | 65 | 225 | 850 |
| 1921 | 1,230,000 | 30.00 | 45.00 | 75 | 175.00 | 325 | 1,000 | 1,750 | 2,500 |
| 1921D | 1,080,000 | 40.00 | 80.00 | 125 | 225.00 | 475 | 1,100 | 1,800 | 2,500 |
| 1923 | 50,130,000 | 1.75 | 1.75 | 2 | 2.50 | 3 | 16 | 25 | 75 |
| 1923S | 6,440,000 | 1.75 | 1.75 | 4 | 8.00 | 32 | 90 | 300 | 850 |
| 1924 | 24,010,000 | 1.75 | 1.75 | 2 | 2.50 | 6 | 23 | 50 | 125 |
| 1924D | 6,810,000 | 1.75 | 1.75 | 3 | 9.00 | 26 | 95 | 325 | 650 |
| 1924S | 7,120,000 | 1.75 | 1.75 | 2 | 5.00 | 24 | 120 | 350 | 1,000 |
| 1925 | 25,610,000 | 1.75 | 1.75 | 2 | 2.50 | 4 | 16 | 50 | 200 |
| 1925D | 5,117,000 | 2.00 | 2.50 | 5 | 22.00 | 60 | 200 | 500 | 1,100 |
| 1925S | 5,850,000 | 1.75 | 1.75 | 3 | 7.00 | 35 | 90 | 350 | 850 |
| 1926 | 32,160,000 | 1.75 | 1.75 | 2 | 2.50 | 3 | 15 | 35 | 150 |
| 1926D | 6,828,000 | 1.75 | 1.75 | 2 | 6.00 | 16 | 60 | 200 | 350 |
| 1926S | 1,520,000 | 4.00 | 6.00 | 12 | 32.00 | 150 | 550 | 1,250 | 2,500 |
| 1927 | 28,080,000 | 1.75 | 1.75 | 2 | 2.50 | 3 | 15 | 35 | 100 |
| 1927D | 4,812,000 | 1.75 | 1.75 | 2 | 12.00 | 35 | 100 | 300 | 850 |

*Chart continued on next page.*

| | Mintage | G-4 | VG-8 | F-12 | VF-20 | EF-40 | MS-60 | MS-63 | MS-65 |
|---|---|---|---|---|---|---|---|---|---|
| 1927S | 4,770,000 | $1.75 | $1.75 | $2 | $4.00 | $15 | $175 | $450 | $850 |
| 1928 | 19,480,000 | 1.75 | 1.75 | 2 | 2.50 | 3 | 15 | 40 | 100 |
| 1928D | 4,161,000 | 1.75 | 1.75 | 4 | 10.00 | 24 | 100 | 225 | 550 |
| 1928S | 7,400,000 | 1.75 | 1.75 | 2 | 3.00 | 8 | 75 | 175 | 300 |
| 1929 | 25,970,000 | 1.75 | 1.75 | 2 | 2.50 | 3 | 13 | 20 | 40 |
| 1929D | 5,034,000 | 1.75 | 1.75 | 2 | 3.00 | 8 | 16 | 17 | 40 |
| 1929S | 4,730,000 | 1.75 | 1.75 | 2 | 2.50 | 3 | 18 | 20 | 100 |
| 1930 | 6,770,000 | 1.75 | 1.75 | 2 | 2.50 | 3 | 15 | 25 | 60 |
| 1930S | 1,843,000 | 1.75 | 1.75 | 3 | 3.50 | 8 | 35 | 75 | 125 |
| 1931 | 3,150,000 | 1.75 | 1.75 | 2 | 2.50 | 5 | 20 | 40 | 100 |
| 1931D | 1,260,000 | 3.00 | 4.00 | 6 | 8.00 | 18 | 46 | 75 | 225 |
| 1931S | 1,800,000 | 2.00 | 2.50 | 3 | 4.00 | 9 | 40 | 75 | 200 |

| | Mintage | VG-8 | F-12 | VF-20 | EF-40 | MS-60 | MS-63 | MS-65 | PF-63 |
|---|---|---|---|---|---|---|---|---|---|
| 1934 | 24,080,000 | $1.75 | $1.75 | $1.80 | $1.85 | $10.00 | $15 | $25 | |
| 1934D | 6,772,000 | 1.75 | 1.75 | 1.80 | 1.85 | 20.00 | 30 | 45 | |
| 1935 | 58,830,000 | 1.75 | 1.75 | 1.80 | 1.85 | 5.00 | 8 | 15 | |
| 1935D | 10,477,000 | 1.75 | 1.75 | 1.80 | 1.85 | 16.00 | 25 | 70 | |
| 1935S | 15,840,000 | 1.75 | 1.75 | 1.80 | 1.85 | 10.00 | 16 | 20 | |
| 1936 | (4,130) 87,500,000 | 1.75 | 1.75 | 1.80 | 1.85 | 5.00 | 8 | 15 | $500 |
| 1936D | 16,132,000 | 1.75 | 1.75 | 1.80 | 1.85 | 14.00 | 20 | 30 | |
| 1936S | 9,210,000 | 1.75 | 1.75 | 1.80 | 1.85 | 12.00 | 15 | 20 | |
| 1937 | (5,756) 56,860,000 | 1.75 | 1.75 | 1.80 | 1.85 | 4.00 | 7 | 15 | 250 |
| 1937D | 14,146,000 | 1.75 | 1.75 | 1.80 | 1.85 | 12.00 | 16 | 25 | |
| 1937S | 9,740,000 | 1.75 | 1.75 | 1.80 | 1.85 | 12.00 | 15 | 20 | |
| 1938 | (8,728) 22,190,000 | 1.75 | 1.75 | 1.80 | 1.85 | 6.00 | 7 | 15 | 125 |
| 1938D | 5,537,000 | 1.75 | 1.75 | 1.80 | 1.85 | 9.00 | 10 | 16 | |
| 1938S | 8,090,000 | 1.75 | 1.75 | 1.80 | 1.85 | 8.00 | 9 | 20 | |
| 1939 | (9,321) 67,740,000 | 1.75 | 1.75 | 1.80 | 1.85 | 4.00 | 6 | 15 | 125 |
| 1939D | 24,394,000 | 1.75 | 1.75 | 1.80 | 1.85 | 12.00 | 15 | 20 | |
| 1939S | 10,540,000 | 1.75 | 1.75 | 1.80 | 1.85 | 12.00 | 15 | 20 | |
| 1940 | (11,827) 65,350,000 | 1.75 | 1.75 | 1.80 | 1.85 | 4.00 | 6 | 15 | 100 |
| 1940D | 21,198,000 | 1.75 | 1.75 | 1.80 | 1.85 | 4.00 | 6 | 16 | |
| 1940S | 21,560,000 | 1.75 | 1.75 | 1.80 | 1.85 | 4.00 | 6 | 16 | |
| 1941 | (16,557) 175,090,000 | 1.75 | 1.75 | 1.80 | 1.85 | 4.00 | 6 | 15 | 100 |
| 1941D | 45,634,000 | 1.75 | 1.75 | 1.80 | 1.85 | 4.00 | 6 | 16 | |
| 1941S | 43,090,000 | 1.75 | 1.75 | 1.80 | 1.85 | 4.00 | 6 | 16 | |
| 1942, 42 Over 41 | * | 280.00 | 300.00 | 315.00 | 400.00 | 2,000.00 | 3,500 | 8,500 | |
| 1942 | (22,329) 205,410,000 | 1.75 | 1.75 | 1.80 | 1.85 | 4.00 | 6 | 15 | 100 |
| 1942D, 42 Over 41 | * | 225.00 | 265.00 | 290.00 | 350.00 | 1,950.00 | 3,500 | 8,500 | |
| 1942D | 60,740,000 | 1.75 | 1.75 | 1.80 | 1.85 | 5.00 | 7 | 16 | |
| 1942S | 49,300,000 | 1.75 | 1.75 | 1.80 | 1.85 | 6.00 | 7 | 16 | |
| 1943 | 191,710,000 | 1.75 | 1.75 | 1.80 | 1.85 | 4.00 | 6 | 15 | |
| 1943D | 71,949,000 | 1.75 | 1.75 | 1.80 | 1.85 | 5.00 | 7 | 16 | |
| 1943S | 60,400,000 | 1.75 | 1.75 | 1.80 | 1.85 | 5.00 | 7 | 15 | |
| 1944 | 231,410,000 | 1.75 | 1.75 | 1.80 | 1.85 | 4.00 | 6 | 15 | |
| 1944D | 62,224,000 | 1.75 | 1.75 | 1.80 | 1.85 | 5.00 | 7 | 15 | |
| 1944S | 49,490,000 | 1.75 | 1.75 | 1.80 | 1.85 | 5.00 | 7 | 15 | |
| 1945 | 159,130,000 | 1.75 | 1.75 | 1.80 | 1.85 | 4.00 | 6 | 15 | |
| 1945D | 40,245,000 | 1.75 | 1.75 | 1.80 | 1.85 | 4.00 | 6 | 16 | |
| 1945S | 41,920,000 | 1.75 | 1.75 | 1.80 | 1.85 | 5.00 | 7 | 16 | |
| 1945S, Micro S | * | 2.00 | 2.50 | 3.00 | 4.00 | 12.50 | 18 | 45 | |

* Included in number above.

# ROOSEVELT (1946 TO DATE)

John R. Sinnock (whose initials, JS, are at the truncation of the neck) designed this dime showing a portrait of Franklin D. Roosevelt. The design has heavier lettering and a more modernistic character than preceding types.

**VF-20 Very Fine:** Moderate wear on high points of design. All major details are clear.

**EF-40 Extremely Fine:** All lines of torch, flame, and hair very plain.

**MS-63 Choice Uncirculated:** Some distracting contact marks or blemishes in prime focal areas. Impaired luster possible.

**MS-65 Gem Uncirculated:** Only light, non-distracting scattered marks. Strong luster, good eye appeal.

**PF-65 Gem Proof:** Nearly perfect.

*Mintmark on reverse,*
*1946–1964.*

## Silver Coinage (1946–1964)

| | Mintage | VF-20 | EF-40 | MS-63 | MS-65 | PF-65 |
|---|---|---|---|---|---|---|
| 1946 | 255,250,000 | $1.75 | $1.75 | $2.50 | $6.00 | |
| 1946D | 61,043,500 | 1.75 | 1.75 | 2.50 | 7.00 | |
| 1946S | 27,900,000 | 1.75 | 1.75 | 4.00 | 10.00 | |
| 1947 | 121,520,000 | 1.75 | 1.75 | 2.50 | 6.00 | |
| 1947D | 46,835,000 | 1.75 | 1.75 | 2.50 | 6.00 | |
| 1947S | 34,840,000 | 1.75 | 1.75 | 2.50 | 6.00 | |
| 1948 | 74,950,000 | 1.75 | 1.75 | 2.50 | 6.00 | |
| 1948D | 52,841,000 | 1.75 | 1.75 | 2.50 | 6.00 | |
| 1948S | 35,520,000 | 1.75 | 1.75 | 2.50 | 6.00 | |
| 1949 | 30,940,000 | 1.75 | 1.75 | 14.00 | 19.00 | |
| 1949D | 26,034,000 | 1.75 | 1.75 | 5.00 | 9.00 | |
| 1949S | 13,510,000 | 1.75 | 1.75 | 22.00 | 32.50 | |
| 1950 .........(51,386) | 50,130,114 | 1.75 | 1.75 | 6.50 | 8.00 | $25 |
| 1950D | 46,803,000 | 1.75 | 1.75 | 2.50 | 6.00 | |
| 1950S | 20,440,000 | 1.75 | 1.75 | 20.00 | 30.00 | |
| 1951 .........(57,500) | 103,880,102 | 1.75 | 1.75 | 2.00 | 5.00 | 25 |
| 1951D | 56,529,000 | 1.75 | 1.75 | 2.00 | 5.00 | |
| 1951S | 31,630,000 | 1.75 | 1.75 | 7.50 | 14.00 | |
| 1952 .........(81,980) | 99,040,093 | 1.75 | 1.75 | 2.00 | 5.00 | 18 |
| 1952D | 122,100,000 | 1.75 | 1.75 | 2.00 | 4.00 | |
| 1952S | 44,419,500 | 1.75 | 1.75 | 3.75 | 6.25 | |
| 1953 .........(128,800) | 53,490,120 | 1.75 | 1.75 | 2.50 | 4.50 | 20 |
| 1953D | 136,433,000 | 1.75 | 1.75 | 2.50 | 4.50 | |
| 1953S | 39,180,000 | 1.75 | 1.75 | 2.50 | 4.50 | |
| 1954 .........(233,300) | 114,010,203 | 1.75 | 1.75 | 2.00 | 4.00 | 10 |
| 1954D | 106,397,000 | 1.75 | 1.75 | 2.00 | 4.00 | |
| 1954S | 22,860,000 | 1.75 | 1.75 | 2.00 | 4.00 | |

*Chart continued on next page.*

| | Mintage | VF-20 | EF-40 | MS-63 | MS-65 | PF-65 |
|---|---|---|---|---|---|---|
| 1955 . . . . . . . . . . . . . . . . .(378,200) . . . . . | 12,450,181 | $1.75 | $1.75 | $2 | $5.00 | $8 |
| 1955D . . . . . . . . . . . . . . . . . . . . . . . . . . . . | 13,959,000 | 1.75 | 1.75 | 2 | 4.00 | |
| 1955S . . . . . . . . . . . . . . . . . . . . . . . . . . . . | 18,510,000 | 1.75 | 1.75 | 2 | 4.00 | |
| 1956 . . . . . . . . . . . . . . . . .(669,384) . . . . | 108,640,000 | 1.75 | 1.75 | 2 | 4.00 | 4 |
| 1956D . . . . . . . . . . . . . . . . . . . . . . . . . . . . | 108,015,100 | 1.75 | 1.75 | 2 | 3.50 | |
| 1957 . . . . . . . . . . . . . . . . (1,247,952) . . . . | 160,160,000 | 1.75 | 1.75 | 2 | 3.50 | 3 |
| 1957D . . . . . . . . . . . . . . . . . . . . . . . . . . . . | 113,354,330 | 1.75 | 1.75 | 2 | 3.25 | |
| 1958 . . . . . . . . . . . . . . . . .(875,652) . . . . . | 31,910,000 | 1.75 | 1.75 | 2 | 4.00 | 3 |
| 1958D . . . . . . . . . . . . . . . . . . . . . . . . . . . . | 136,564,600 | 1.75 | 1.75 | 2 | 4.00 | |
| 1959 . . . . . . . . . . . . . . . . (1,149,291) . . . . . | 85,780,000 | 1.75 | 1.75 | 2 | 3.50 | 3 |
| 1959D . . . . . . . . . . . . . . . . . . . . . . . . . . . . | 164,919,790 | 1.75 | 1.75 | 2 | 3.50 | |
| 1960 . . . . . . . . . . . . . . . . (1,691,602) . . . . . | 70,390,000 | 1.75 | 1.75 | 2 | 3.50 | 3 |
| 1960D . . . . . . . . . . . . . . . . . . . . . . . . . . . . | 200,160,400 | 1.75 | 1.75 | 2 | 3.00 | |
| 1961 . . . . . . . . . . . . . . . . (3,028,244) . . . . . | 93,730,000 | 1.75 | 1.75 | 2 | 3.00 | 3 |
| 1961D . . . . . . . . . . . . . . . . . . . . . . . . . . . . | 209,146,550 | 1.75 | 1.75 | 2 | 3.00 | |
| 1962 . . . . . . . . . . . . . . . . (3,218,019) . . . . | 72,450,000 | 1.75 | 1.75 | 2 | 3.00 | 3 |
| 1962D . . . . . . . . . . . . . . . . . . . . . . . . . . . . | 334,948,380 | 1.75 | 1.75 | 2 | 3.00 | |
| 1963 . . . . . . . . . . . . . . . . (3,075,645) . . . . | 123,650,000 | 1.75 | 1.75 | 2 | 3.00 | 3 |
| 1963D . . . . . . . . . . . . . . . . . . . . . . . . . . . . | 421,476,530 | 1.75 | 1.75 | 2 | 3.00 | |
| 1964 . . . . . . . . . . . . . . . . (3,950,762) . . . . | 929,360,000 | 1.75 | 1.75 | 2 | 3.00 | 3 |
| 1964D . . . . . . . . . . . . . . . . . . . . . . . . . . . . | 1,357,517,180 | 1.75 | 1.75 | 2 | 3.00 | |

## Clad Coinage and Silver Proofs (1965 to Date)

Mintmark on obverse,
starting in 1968.

| | Mintage | MS-63 | MS-65 | PF-65 |
|---|---|---|---|---|
| 1965 . . . . . . . | 1,652,140,570 | $0.15 | $1.00 | |
| 1966 . . . . . . . | 1,382,734,540 | 0.15 | 0.90 | |
| 1967 . . . . . . . | 2,244,007,320 | 0.15 | 0.80 | |
| 1968 . . . . . . . | 424,470,400 | 0.15 | 0.80 | |
| 1968D . . . . . | 480,748,280 | 0.15 | 0.80 | |
| 1968S . . . . . . . | (3,041,506) | | | $0.80 |
| 1969 . . . . . . . | 145,790,000 | 0.25 | 1.00 | |
| 1969D . . . . . . | 563,323,870 | 0.15 | 0.75 | |
| 1969S . . . . . . | (2,394,631) | | | 0.80 |
| 1970 . . . . . . . | 345,570,000 | 0.15 | 0.50 | |
| 1970D . . . . . . | 754,942,100 | 0.15 | 0.50 | |
| 1970S . . . . . . | (2,632,810) | | | 0.80 |
| 1971 . . . . . . . | 162,690,000 | 0.18 | 0.75 | |
| 1971D . . . . . . | 377,914,240 | 0.16 | 0.65 | |
| 1971S . . . . . . | (3,220,733) | | | 0.80 |
| 1972 . . . . . . . | 431,540,000 | 0.15 | 0.50 | |
| 1972D . . . . . . | 330,290,000 | 0.15 | 0.50 | |
| 1972S . . . . . . | (3,260,996) | | | 0.80 |
| 1973 . . . . . . . | 315,670,000 | 0.15 | 0.50 | |
| 1973D . . . . . . | 455,032,426 | 0.15 | 0.50 | |

| | Mintage | MS-63 | MS-65 | PF-65 |
|---|---|---|---|---|
| 1973S . . . . . . . | (2,760,339) | | | $0.80 |
| 1974 . . . . . . . | 470,248,000 | $0.15 | $0.50 | |
| 1974D . . . . . . | 571,083,000 | 0.15 | 0.50 | |
| 1974S . . . . . . | (2,612,568) | | | 0.80 |
| 1975 . . . . . . . | 585,673,900 | 0.15 | 0.50 | |
| 1975D . . . . . . | 313,705,300 | 0.15 | 0.50 | |
| 1975S . . . . . . | (2,845,450) | | | 1.00 |
| 1976 . . . . . . . | 568,760,000 | 0.15 | 0.50 | |
| 1976D . . . . . . | 695,222,774 | 0.15 | 0.50 | |
| 1976S . . . . . . | (4,149,730) | | | 1.00 |
| 1977 . . . . . . . | 796,930,000 | 0.15 | 0.50 | |
| 1977D . . . . . . | 376,607,228 | 0.15 | 0.50 | |
| 1977S . . . . . . | (3,251,152) | | | 0.80 |
| 1978 . . . . . . . | 663,980,000 | 0.15 | 0.50 | |
| 1978D . . . . . . | 282,847,540 | 0.15 | 0.50 | |
| 1978S . . . . . . | (3,127,781) | | | 0.80 |
| 1979 . . . . . . . | 315,440,000 | 0.15 | 0.50 | |
| 1979D . . . . . . | 390,921,184 | 0.15 | 0.50 | |
| 1979S, Type 1 . . | (3,677,175) | | | 2.75 |
| 1979S, Type 2 . . . . . . . . . .* | | | | 4.00 |

* Included in number above.

| | Mintage | MS-63 | MS-65 | PF-65 |
|---|---|---|---|---|
| 1980P | 735,170,000 | $0.15 | $0.50 | |
| 1980D | 719,354,321 | 0.15 | 0.50 | |
| 1980S | (3,554,806) | | | $0.80 |
| 1981P | 676,650,000 | 0.15 | 0.50 | |
| 1981D | 712,284,143 | 0.15 | 0.50 | |
| 1981S, Type 1 | (4,063,083) | | | 2.75 |
| 1981S, Type 2 | .........* | | | 14.00 |
| 1982, No Mmk. | .......... | 30.00 | 50.00 | |
| 1982P | 519,475,000 | 1.50 | 2.75 | |
| 1982D | 542,713,584 | 0.60 | 1.50 | |
| 1982S | (3,857,479) | | | 1.50 |
| 1983P | 647,025,000 | 1.25 | 2.75 | |
| 1983D | 730,129,224 | 0.50 | 1.75 | |
| 1983S | (3,279,126) | | | 1.00 |
| 1984P | 856,669,000 | 0.15 | 0.60 | |
| 1984D | 704,803,976 | 0.20 | 0.75 | |
| 1984S | (3,065,110) | | | 1.00 |
| 1985P | 705,200,962 | 0.15 | 0.60 | |
| 1985D | 587,979,970 | 0.15 | 0.60 | |
| 1985S | (3,362,821) | | | 1.00 |
| 1986P | 682,649,693 | 0.25 | 0.75 | |
| 1986D | 473,326,970 | 0.25 | 0.75 | |
| 1986S | (3,010,497) | | | 1.75 |
| 1987P | 762,709,481 | 0.15 | 0.60 | |
| 1987D | 653,203,402 | 0.15 | 0.60 | |
| 1987S | (4,227,728) | | | 1.25 |
| 1988P | 1,030,550,000 | 0.12 | 0.50 | |
| 1988D | 962,385,489 | 0.12 | 0.50 | |
| 1988S | (3,262,948) | | | 1.75 |
| 1989P | 1,298,400,000 | 0.10 | 0.50 | |
| 1989D | 896,535,597 | 0.10 | 0.50 | |
| 1989S | (3,220,194) | | | 1.75 |
| 1990P | 1,034,340,000 | 0.10 | 0.50 | |
| 1990D | 839,995,824 | 0.10 | 0.50 | |
| 1990S | (3,299,559) | | | 1.00 |
| 1991P | 927,220,000 | 0.10 | 0.50 | |
| 1991D | 601,241,114 | 0.12 | 0.50 | |
| 1991S | (2,867,787) | | | 1.70 |
| 1992P | 593,500,000 | 0.10 | 0.50 | |
| 1992D | 616,273,932 | 0.10 | 0.50 | |
| 1992S | (2,858,981) | | | 1.50 |
| 1992S, Silver | (1,317,579) | | | 3.00 |
| 1993P | 766,180,000 | 0.10 | 0.50 | |
| 1993D | 750,110,166 | 0.10 | 0.50 | |
| 1993S | (2,633,439) | | | 2.25 |
| 1993S, Silver | (761,353) | | | 3.50 |
| 1994P | 1,189,000,000 | 0.10 | 0.50 | |
| 1994D | 1,303,268,110 | 0.10 | 0.50 | |
| 1994S | (2,484,594) | | | 2.25 |
| 1994S, Silver | (785,329) | | | 3.75 |

| | Mintage | MS-63 | MS-65 | PF-65 |
|---|---|---|---|---|
| 1995P | 1,125,500,000 | $0.10 | $0.50 | |
| 1995D | 1,274,890,000 | 0.15 | 0.50 | |
| 1995S | (2,117,496) | | | $5.50 |
| 1995S, Silver | (679,985) | | | 7.50 |
| 1996P | 1,421,163,000 | 0.10 | 0.50 | |
| 1996D | 1,400,300,000 | 0.10 | 0.50 | |
| 1996W | 1,457,000 | 6.00 | 11.00 | |
| 1996S | (1,750,244) | | | 1.25 |
| 1996S, Silver | (775,021) | | | 3.50 |
| 1997P | 991,640,000 | 0.10 | 0.50 | |
| 1997D | 979,810,000 | 0.10 | 0.50 | |
| 1997S | (2,055,000) | | | 3.50 |
| 1997S, Silver | (741,678) | | | 7.00 |
| 1998P | 1,163,000,000 | 0.10 | 0.50 | |
| 1998D | 1,172,250,000 | 0.10 | 0.50 | |
| 1998S | (2,086,507) | | | 1.75 |
| 1998S, Silver | (878,792) | | | 3.00 |
| 1999P | 2,164,000,000 | 0.10 | 0.50 | |
| 1999D | 1,397,750,000 | 0.10 | 0.50 | |
| 1999S | (2,543,401) | | | 1.75 |
| 1999S, Silver | (804,565) | | | 3.50 |
| 2000P | 1,842,500,000 | 0.10 | 0.50 | |
| 2000D | 1,818,700,000 | 0.10 | 0.50 | |
| 2000S | (3,082,572) | | | 1.00 |
| 2000S, Silver | (965,421) | | | 3.00 |
| 2001P | 1,369,590,000 | 0.10 | 0.50 | |
| 2001D | 1,412,800,000 | 0.10 | 0.50 | |
| 2001S | (2,294,909) | | | 0.75 |
| 2001S, Silver | (889,697) | | | 3.00 |
| 2002P | 1,187,500,000 | 0.10 | 0.50 | |
| 2002D | 1,379,500,000 | 0.10 | 0.50 | |
| 2002S | (2,319,766) | | | 0.75 |
| 2002S, Silver | (892,229) | | | 3.00 |
| 2003P | 1,085,500,000 | 0.10 | 0.50 | |
| 2003D | 986,500,000 | 0.10 | 0.50 | |
| 2003S | (2,172,684) | | | 0.75 |
| 2003S, Silver | (1,125,755) | | | 3.00 |
| 2004P | 1,328,000,000 | 0.10 | 0.50 | |
| 2004D | 1,159,500,000 | 0.10 | 0.50 | |
| 2004S | (1,789,488) | | | 0.75 |
| 2004S, Silver | (1,175,934) | | | 3.00 |
| 2005P | 1,412,000,000 | 0.10 | 0.50 | |
| 2005D | 1,423,500,000 | 0.10 | 0.50 | |
| 2005S | (2,275,000) | | | 0.75 |
| 2005S, Silver | (1,069,679) | | | 3.00 |
| 2006P | 1,381,000,000 | 0.10 | 0.50 | |
| 2006D | 1,447,000,000 | 0.10 | 0.50 | |
| 2006S | (2,000,428) | | | 0.75 |
| 2006S, Silver | (1,054,008) | | | 3.00 |
| 2007P | 1,047,500,000 | 0.10 | 0.50 | |

* Included in number above.

*Chart continued on next page.*

| | Mintage | MS-63 | MS-65 | PF-65 |
|---|---|---|---|---|
| 2007D | 1,042,000,000 | $0.10 | $0.50 | |
| 2007S | (1,702,116) | | | $0.75 |
| 2007S, Silver | (875,050) | | | 3.00 |
| 2008P | 391,000,000 | 0.10 | 0.50 | |
| 2008D | 624,500,000 | 0.10 | 0.50 | |
| 2008S | (1,405,674) | | | 0.75 |
| 2008S, Silver | (763,887) | | | 3.00 |
| 2009P | 96,500,000 | 0.20 | 0.50 | |
| 2009D | 49,500,000 | 0.20 | 0.50 | |
| 2009S | (1,482,502) | | | 0.75 |
| 2009S, Silver | (697,365) | | | 3.00 |
| 2010P | 557,000,000 | 0.10 | 0.50 | |
| 2010D | 562,000,000 | 0.10 | 0.50 | |
| 2010S | (1,103,815) | | | 0.75 |
| 2010S, Silver | (585,401) | | | 3.00 |
| 2011P | 748,000,000 | 0.10 | 0.50 | |
| 2011D | 754,000,000 | 0.10 | 0.50 | |
| 2011S | (1,098,835) | | | 0.75 |
| 2011S, Silver | (574,175) | | | 3.00 |
| 2012P | 808,000,000 | 0.10 | 0.50 | |
| 2012D | 868,000,000 | 0.10 | 0.50 | |
| 2012S | (843,705) | | | $0.75 |
| 2012S, Silver | (445,612) | | | 12.00 |
| 2013P | 1,086,500,000 | $0.10 | $0.50 | |
| 2013D | 1,025,500,000 | 0.10 | 0.50 | |
| 2013S | (856,953) | | | 0.75 |
| 2013S, Silver | (467,691) | | | 3.00 |
| 2014P | 1,125,500,000 | 0.10 | 0.50 | |
| 2014D | 1,177,000,000 | 0.10 | 0.50 | |
| 2014S | (764,206) | | | 0.75 |
| 2014S, Silver | (472,107) | | | 3.00 |
| 2015P | 1,497,510,000 | 0.10 | 0.50 | |
| 2015D | 1,543,500,000 | 0.10 | 0.50 | |
| 2015P, Rev Pf, Silver (a) | (74,430) | | | 20.00 |
| 2015S | (711,872) | | | 0.75 |
| 2015S, Silver | (387,310) | | | 3.00 |
| 2015W, Silver (a) | (74,430) | | | 5.00 |
| 2016P | 1,517,000,000 | 0.10 | 0.50 | |
| 2016D | 1,437,000,000 | 0.10 | 0.50 | |
| 2016S | (641,775) | | | 0.75 |
| 2016S, Silver | (419,496) | | | 3.00 |

a. Included in March of Dimes commemorative Proof set.

| | Mintage | SP-67 | SP-70 |
|---|---|---|---|
| 2016W, Gold (a) | 124,885 | $200 | $225 |

a. In 2016 the Mint issued a centennial version of the Winged Liberty Head ("Mercury") dime in gold.

| | Mintage | MS-63 | MS-65 | PF-65 |
|---|---|---|---|---|
| 2017P | 1,437,500,000 | $0.10 | $0.50 | |
| 2017D | 1,290,500,000 | 0.10 | 0.50 | |
| 2017S | (621,390) | | | $0.75 |
| 2017S, Silver | (406,986) | | | 3.00 |
| 2018P | 1,193,000,000 | 0.10 | 0.50 | |
| 2018D | 1,006,000,000 | 0.10 | 0.50 | |
| 2018S | (568,804) | | | 0.75 |
| 2018S, Silver | (381,748) | | | 3.00 |
| 2019P | 1,147,500,000 | 0.10 | 0.50 | |
| 2019D | 1,001,500,000 | 0.10 | 0.50 | |
| 2019S | (649,050) | | | 0.75 |
| 2019S, Silver | (460,925) | | | 3.00 |
| 2020P | 1,349,250,000 | $0.10 | $0.50 | |
| 2020D | 1,481,000,000 | 0.10 | 0.50 | |
| 2020S | (511,148) | | | $0.75 |
| 2020S, Silver (a) | (363,179) | | | 3.00 |
| 2021P | 1,333,500,000 | 0.10 | 0.50 | |
| 2021D | 1,445,000,000 | 0.10 | 0.50 | |
| 2021S | (521,826) | | | 0.75 |
| 2021S, Silver (a) | (319,317) | | | 3.00 |
| 2022P | | 0.10 | 0.50 | |
| 2022D | | 0.10 | 0.50 | |
| 2022S | | | | 0.75 |
| 2022S, Silver (a) | | | | 3.00 |

a. In 2019, the fineness of all silver Proofs was changed from .900 to .999.

## LIBERTY SEATED (1875–1878)

The twenty-cent piece was a short-lived coin authorized by the Act of March 3, 1875. The edge of the coin is plain. Most of the 1876-CC coins were melted at the Mint and never released. The mintmark is on the reverse below the eagle.

**G-4 Good:** LIBERTY on shield obliterated. Letters and date legible.

**VG-8 Very Good:** One or two letters in LIBERTY barely visible. Other details bold.

**F-12 Fine:** Some letters of LIBERTY possibly visible.

**VF-20 Very Fine:** LIBERTY readable, but partly weak.

**EF-40 Extremely Fine:** LIBERTY mostly sharp. Only slight wear on high points of coin.

**AU-50 About Uncirculated:** Slight trace of wear on breast, head, and knees.

**MS-60 Uncirculated:** No trace of wear. Light blemishes.

**MS-63 Choice Uncirculated:** Some distracting blemishes in prime focal areas. Some impairment of luster possible.

**PF-63 Choice Proof:** Reflective surfaces with only a few blemishes in secondary focal places. No major flaws.

| | Mintage | G-4 | VG-8 | F-12 | VF-20 | EF-40 | AU-50 | MS-60 | MS-63 | PF-63 |
|---|---|---|---|---|---|---|---|---|---|---|
| 1875 .... (1,200) ....... 38,500 | | $150 | $175 | $200 | $225 | $300 | $400 | $650 | $1,100 | $1,850 |
| 1875CC ............. 133,290 | | 160 | 200 | 275 | 325 | 525 | 750 | 1,350 | 1,850 | |
| 1875S ............. 1,155,000 | | 85 | 95 | 105 | 140 | 175 | 225 | 525 | 750 | |
| 1876 .... (1,150) ....... 14,750 | | 165 | 200 | 250 | 350 | 425 | 500 | 700 | 1,250 | 1,850 |
| 1876CC ............... 10,000 | | | | | | | 125,000 | 175,000 | 250,000 | |
| 1877 ...... (510) ............ | | | | | 2,500 | 3,500 | | | | 6,000 |
| 1878 ...... (600) ............ | | | | | 1,750 | 2,250 | | | | 3,500 |

Authorized in 1792, this denomination was not issued until four years later. The first type weighed 104 grains, the standard until modified to 103-1/8 grains by the Act of January 18, 1837. As with the dime and half dime, the weight was reduced and arrows placed at the date in 1853. Rays were placed in the field of the reverse during that year only.

## DRAPED BUST (1796–1807)

**AG-3 About Good:** Details clear enough to identify.
**G-4 Good:** Date readable. Bust outlined, but no detail.
**VG-8 Very Good:** All but deepest drapery folds worn smooth. Hairlines nearly gone and curls lacking in detail.
**F-12 Fine:** All drapery lines visible. Hair partly worn.
**VF-20 Very Fine:** Only left side of drapery indistinct.
**EF-40 Extremely Fine:** Hair well outlined and detailed.
**AU-50 About Uncirculated:** Slight trace of wear on shoulder and highest waves of hair.
**MS-60 Uncirculated:** No trace of wear. Light blemishes.
**MS-63 Choice Uncirculated:** Some distracting marks or blemishes in focal areas. Impaired luster possible.

### Small Eagle Reverse (1796)

| | Mintage | AG-3 | G-4 | VG-8 | F-12 | VF-20 | EF-40 | AU-50 | MS-60 | MS-63 |
|---|---|---|---|---|---|---|---|---|---|---|
| 1796 . . . . . . . . . . 6,146 | | $4,750 | $8,250 | $13,500 | $20,000 | $25,000 | $38,500 | $43,500 | $60,000 | $105,000 |

### Heraldic Eagle Reverse (1804–1807)

| | Mintage | AG-3 | G-4 | VG-8 | F-12 | VF-20 | EF-40 | AU-50 | MS-60 | MS-63 |
|---|---|---|---|---|---|---|---|---|---|---|
| 1804 . . . . . . . . . . 6,738 | | $1,350 | $2,750 | $4,500 | $6,500 | $10,000 | $27,500 | $42,500 | $75,000 | $140,000 |
| 1805 . . . . . . . . 121,394 | | 140 | 300 | 400 | 575 | 1,100 | 2,350 | 3,500 | 9,000 | 15,000 |
| 1806, 6 Over 5 . . . . . .* | | 140 | 300 | 400 | 775 | 1,150 | 2,750 | 4,500 | 9,000 | 18,000 |
| 1806 . . . . . . . . 206,124 | | 140 | 300 | 400 | 575 | 1,100 | 2,250 | 3,500 | 9,000 | 15,000 |
| 1807 . . . . . . . . 220,643 | | 140 | 300 | 400 | 575 | 1,000 | 2,250 | 3,500 | 9,000 | 15,000 |

* Included in number below.

## CAPPED BUST (1815–1838)
### Variety 1 – Large Diameter (1815–1828)

**AG-3 About Good:** Details clear enough to identify.
**G-4 Good:** Date, letters, stars legible. Hair under Liberty's headband smooth. Cap lines worn smooth.
**VG-8 Very Good:** Rim well defined. Main details visible. Full LIBERTY on cap. Hair above eye nearly smooth.
**F-12 Fine:** All hair lines visible, but only partial detail visible in drapery. Shoulder clasp distinct.
**VF-20 Very Fine:** All details visible, but some wear evident. Clasp and ear sharp.
**EF-40 Extremely Fine:** All details distinct. Hair well outlined.
**AU-50 About Uncirculated:** Slight trace of wear on tips of curls and above the eye, and on the wing and claw tips.
**MS-60 Uncirculated:** No trace of wear. Light blemishes.
**MS-63 Choice Uncirculated:** Some distracting marks or blemishes in focal areas. Impaired luster possible.

| | Mintage | AG-3 | G-4 | VG-8 | F-12 | VF-20 | EF-40 | AU-50 | MS-60 | MS-63 |
|---|---|---|---|---|---|---|---|---|---|---|
| 1815 | 89,235 | $85 | $175 | $250 | $375 | $550 | $1,750 | $2,000 | $3,500 | $5,500 |
| 1818, 8 Over 5 | * | 45 | 90 | 125 | 225 | 400 | 1,000 | 1,350 | 2,500 | 5,500 |
| 1818, Normal Date | 361,174 | 45 | 85 | 110 | 190 | 325 | 1,000 | 1,350 | 2,500 | 5,500 |
| 1819 | 144,000 | 45 | 85 | 110 | 190 | 325 | 1,000 | 1,450 | 3,000 | 6,500 |
| 1820 | 127,444 | 45 | 85 | 110 | 175 | 325 | 1,000 | 1,500 | 2,750 | 5,000 |
| 1821 | 216,851 | 45 | 85 | 110 | 175 | 325 | 1,000 | 1,350 | 2,500 | 5,000 |
| 1822 | 64,080 | 80 | 160 | 250 | 350 | 600 | 1,250 | 1,750 | 2,750 | 6,500 |
| 1822, 25 Over 50 C. | * | 2,250 | 4,500 | 8,500 | 15,000 | 20,000 | 30,000 | 37,500 | 45,000 | |
| 1823, 3 Over 2 | 17,800 | 18,000 | 35,000 | 45,000 | 55,000 | 65,000 | 75,000 | 125,000 | — | |
| 1824, 4 Over 2 | ** | 225 | 400 | 700 | 1,200 | 1,400 | 3,000 | 5,000 | 17,500 | |
| 1825 | 168,000 | 60 | 125 | 175 | 325 | 475 | 1,000 | 1,500 | 2,850 | 4,500 |
| 1827, Original (Curl Base 2 in 25 C.) (a) | 4,000 | | | | | | | | | 175,000 |
| 1827, Restrike (Square Base 2 in 25 C.) (a) | * | | | | | | | | | 45,000 |
| 1828 | 102,000 | 45 | 90 | 125 | 190 | 325 | 800 | 1,500 | 2,750 | 4,500 |
| 1828, 25 Over 50 C. | * | 400 | 800 | 1,250 | 1,800 | 2,250 | 5,250 | 8,500 | 11,500 | 75,000 |

* Included in regular mintage. ** Included in 1825 mintage. **a.** The 7 is punched over a 3, which is punched over an earlier 2.

## Variety 2 – Reduced Diameter (1831–1838), Motto Removed

**G-4 Good:** Bust of Liberty well defined. Hair under
headband smooth. Date, letters, stars legible. Scant rims.
**VG-8 Very Good:** Details apparent but worn on high
spots. Rims strong. Full LIBERTY.
**F-12 Fine:** All hair lines visible. Drapery partly worn.
Shoulder clasp distinct.
**VF-20 Very Fine:** Only top spots worn. Clasp sharp.
Ear distinct.
**EF-40 Extremely Fine:** Hair details and clasp bold
and clear.

**AU-50 About Uncirculated:** Slight trace of wear on hair around forehead, on cheek, and at top and bottom
tips of eagle's wings and left claw.
**MS-60 Uncirculated:** No trace of wear. Light blemishes.
**MS-63 Choice Uncirculated:** Some distracting contact marks or blemishes in prime focal areas. Impaired
luster possible.

| | Mintage | G-4 | VG-8 | F-12 | VF-20 | EF-40 | AU-50 | MS-60 | MS-63 |
|---|---|---|---|---|---|---|---|---|---|
| 1831 | 398,000 | $70 | $80 | $100 | $120 | $275 | $500 | $1,400 | $2,500 |
| 1832 | 320,000 | 70 | 80 | 100 | 120 | 275 | 500 | 1,400 | 2,500 |
| 1833 | 156,000 | 70 | 80 | 100 | 120 | 275 | 500 | 1,400 | 2,500 |
| 1834 | 286,000 | 70 | 80 | 100 | 120 | 275 | 500 | 1,400 | 2,500 |
| 1835 | 1,952,000 | 70 | 80 | 100 | 120 | 275 | 500 | 1,400 | 2,500 |
| 1836 | 472,000 | 70 | 80 | 100 | 120 | 275 | 500 | 1,400 | 2,500 |
| 1837 | 252,400 | 70 | 80 | 100 | 120 | 275 | 500 | 1,400 | 2,500 |
| 1838 | 366,000 | 70 | 80 | 100 | 120 | 275 | 500 | 1,400 | 2,500 |

## LIBERTY SEATED (1838–1891)

**G-4 Good:** Scant rim. LIBERTY on shield worn off. Date and letters legible.
**VG-8 Very Good:** Rim fairly defined, at least three letters in LIBERTY evident.
**F-12 Fine:** LIBERTY complete, but partly weak.
**VF-20 Very Fine:** LIBERTY strong.
**EF-40 Extremely Fine:** Complete LIBERTY and edges of scroll. Shoulder clasp clear on Liberty's gown.
**AU-50 About Uncirculated:** Slight wear on Liberty's knees and breast and on eagle's neck, wing tips, and claws.
**MS-60 Uncirculated:** No trace of wear. Light blemishes.
**MS-63 Choice Uncirculated:** Some distracting marks or blemishes in focal areas. Impaired luster possible.

### Variety 1 – No Motto Above Eagle (1838–1853)

Small Date

Large Date

*Mintmark location is on reverse, below eagle.*

| | Mintage | G-4 | VG-8 | F-12 | VF-20 | EF-40 | AU-50 | MS-60 | MS-63 |
|---|---|---|---|---|---|---|---|---|---|
| 1838 | 466,000 | $20 | $25 | $35 | $130 | $325 | $700 | $1,200 | $2,750 |
| 1839 | 491,146 | 20 | 25 | 35 | 130 | 325 | 700 | 1,200 | 2,750 |
| 1840 | 188,127 | 18 | 22 | 45 | 115 | 240 | 400 | 1,250 | 3,500 |
| 18400 | 425,200 | 30 | 35 | 65 | 110 | 260 | 450 | 1,000 | 2,500 |
| 1841 | 120,000 | 40 | 65 | 90 | 185 | 350 | 550 | 900 | 1,250 |
| 18410 | 452,000 | 25 | 30 | 40 | 85 | 225 | 280 | 625 | 1,200 |
| 1842, Small Date (Proof only) | | | | | | | | | 40,000 |
| 1842, Large Date | 88,000 | 45 | 60 | 95 | 180 | 300 | 525 | 1,050 | 3,250 |
| 18420, Small Date | * | 450 | 900 | 1,200 | 2,250 | 5,500 | 9,000 | 27,500 | |
| 18420, Large Date | 769,000 | 35 | 35 | 48 | 85 | 200 | 400 | 1,200 | 3,250 |
| 1843 | 645,600 | 20 | 22 | 25 | 50 | 150 | 180 | 500 | 1,000 |
| 18430 | 968,000 | 32 | 50 | 110 | 250 | 650 | 875 | 1,850 | 4,000 |
| 1844 | 421,200 | 20 | 22 | 25 | 30 | 50 | 120 | 500 | 1,250 |
| 18440 | 740,000 | 35 | 40 | 50 | 80 | 100 | 240 | 1,000 | 1,150 |
| 1845 | 922,000 | 20 | 22 | 25 | 42 | 60 | 125 | 400 | 725 |
| 1846 | 510,000 | 32 | 50 | 70 | 85 | 185 | 300 | 650 | 1,400 |
| 1847 | 734,000 | 20 | 22 | 25 | 30 | 60 | 180 | 500 | 1,250 |
| 18470 | 368,000 | 75 | 110 | 220 | 375 | 650 | 1,200 | 5,000 | 10,000 |
| 1848 | 146,000 | 32 | 50 | 75 | 105 | 125 | 260 | 850 | 3,500 |
| 1849 | 340,000 | 20 | 22 | 25 | 50 | 80 | 220 | 700 | 1,000 |
| 18490 | (a) 1,050 | 1,500 | 2,000 | 2,500 | 5,000 | 6,000 | 13,500 | 16,500 |
| 1850 | 190,800 | 22 | 36 | 65 | 85 | 180 | 425 | 1,200 | 2,000 |
| 18500 | 412,000 | 35 | 80 | 110 | 160 | 400 | 575 | 1,250 | 3,500 |
| 1851 | 160,000 | 65 | 110 | 160 | 250 | 400 | 700 | 1,000 | 1,600 |
| 18510 | 88,000 | 325 | 500 | 775 | 850 | 2,000 | 2,600 | 6,750 | |
| 1852 | 177,060 | 45 | 65 | 95 | 190 | 350 | 525 | 850 | 1,350 |
| 18520 | 96,000 | 225 | 350 | 525 | 1,050 | 1,600 | 4,500 | 7,500 | 22,500 |
| 1853, Recut Date, No Arrows or Rays | 44,200 | 900 | 1,300 | 2,000 | 2,500 | 3,250 | 4,350 | 4,500 | 5,500 |

\* Included in number below. **a.** Mintage for 1849-O included with 1850-O.

### Variety 2 – Arrows at Date, Rays Around Eagle (1853)

1853, 3 Over 4

# QUARTER DOLLARS

| | Mintage | G-4 | VG-8 | F-12 | VF-20 | EF-40 | AU-50 | MS-60 | MS-63 |
|---|---|---|---|---|---|---|---|---|---|
| 1853 . . . . . . | 15,210,020 | $18 | $20 | $26 | $30 | $130 | $200 | $700 | $1,150 |
| 1853, 3 Over 4 . . . . . . | * | 42 | 65 | 125 | 200 | 375 | 600 | 1,100 | 2,750 |
| 1853O . . . . . . | 1,332,000 | 32 | 42 | 65 | 110 | 290 | 700 | 3,000 | 6,750 |

* Included in number above.

## Variety 3 – Arrows at Date, No Rays (1854–1855)

| | Mintage | G-4 | VG-8 | F-12 | VF-20 | EF-40 | AU-50 | MS-60 | MS-63 |
|---|---|---|---|---|---|---|---|---|---|
| 1854 . . . . . . | 12,380,000 | $18 | $22 | $27 | $30 | $65 | $165 | $450 | $800 |
| 1854O . . . . . . | 1,484,000 | 32 | 38 | 45 | 60 | 85 | 225 | 725 | 1,250 |
| 1855 . . . . . . . | 2,857,000 | 18 | 22 | 27 | 30 | 65 | 165 | 450 | 750 |
| 1855O . . . . . . . | 176,000 | 85 | 135 | 225 | 400 | 800 | 1,500 | 3,500 | 10,500 |
| 1855S . . . . . . . | 396,400 | 85 | 135 | 225 | 325 | 775 | 950 | 1,750 | 5,750 |

## Variety 1 Resumed, With Weight Standard of Variety 2 (1856–1865)

| | Mintage | G-4 | VG-8 | F-12 | VF-20 | EF-40 | AU-50 | MS-60 | MS-63 | PF-63 |
|---|---|---|---|---|---|---|---|---|---|---|
| 1856 . . . . . . . . . . . . . | 7,264,000 | $18 | $22 | $26 | $32 | $60 | $130 | $250 | $400 | $3,250 |
| 1856O . . . . . . . . . . . . . | 968,000 | 34 | 40 | 55 | 90 | 185 | 400 | 900 | 1,450 | |
| 1856S . . . . . . . . . . . . . | 286,000 | 250 | 360 | 450 | 550 | 1,200 | 2,250 | 5,750 | 9,250 | |
| 1857 . . . . . . . . . . . . . | 9,644,000 | 18 | 22 | 26 | 32 | 60 | 130 | 250 | 400 | 2,000 |
| 1857O . . . . . . . . . . . . . | 1,180,000 | 34 | 42 | 65 | 110 | 200 | 350 | 900 | 1,850 | |
| 1857S . . . . . . . . . . . . . | 82,000 | 150 | 250 | 300 | 525 | 700 | 1,300 | 2,750 | 4,500 | |
| 1858 . . . . . . (300+) . . . | 7,368,000 | 18 | 22 | 26 | 32 | 60 | 135 | 250 | 400 | 1,150 |
| 1858O . . . . . . . . . . . . . | 520,000 | 34 | 40 | 55 | 90 | 200 | 450 | 3,000 | 7,000 | |
| 1858S . . . . . . . . . . . . . | 121,000 | 180 | 290 | 400 | 675 | 1,800 | 3,250 | 16,500 | — | |
| 1859 . . . . . . (800) . . . . | 1,343,200 | 18 | 22 | 26 | 32 | 60 | 130 | 300 | 650 | 750 |
| 1859O . . . . . . . . . . . . . | 260,000 | 40 | 55 | 75 | 120 | 225 | 800 | 1,850 | 5,000 | |
| 1859S . . . . . . . . . . . . . | 80,000 | 300 | 425 | 675 | 1,000 | 3,250 | 8,000 | — | — | |
| 1860 . . . . (1,000) . . . . . | 804,400 | 18 | 22 | 26 | 32 | 60 | 130 | 350 | 700 | 725 |
| 1860O . . . . . . . . . . . . . | 388,000 | 34 | 40 | 55 | 75 | 185 | 325 | 800 | 1,450 | |
| 1860S . . . . . . . . . . . . . | 56,000 | 750 | 1,150 | 2,250 | 4,000 | 6,500 | 11,500 | — | — | |
| 1861 . . . . (1,000) . . . . | 4,853,600 | 18 | 22 | 26 | 32 | 60 | 140 | 260 | 500 | 700 |
| 1861S . . . . . . . . . . . . . | 96,000 | 475 | 675 | 925 | 1,800 | 3,350 | 7,250 | 32,500 | — | |
| 1862 . . . . . . (550) . . . . . | 932,000 | 18 | 22 | 26 | 32 | 75 | 130 | 275 | 550 | 700 |
| 1862S . . . . . . . . . . . . . | 67,000 | 130 | 220 | 300 | 450 | 975 | 1,800 | 3,000 | 5,750 | |
| 1863 . . . . . . (460) . . . . . | 191,600 | 25 | 36 | 45 | 85 | 200 | 300 | 575 | 900 | 700 |
| 1864 . . . . . . (470) . . . . . | 93,600 | 130 | 185 | 200 | 300 | 450 | 600 | 1,050 | 1,800 | 700 |
| 1864S . . . . . . . . . . . . . | 20,000 | 750 | 875 | 1,050 | 1,600 | 3,850 | 5,250 | 10,500 | 1,600 | |
| 1865 . . . . . . (500) . . . . . | 58,800 | 65 | 90 | 160 | 290 | 350 | 575 | 1,000 | 1,350 | 700 |
| 1865S . . . . . . . . . . . . . | 41,000 | 185 | 220 | 300 | 450 | 775 | 875 | 3,000 | 4,750 | |

## Variety 4 – Motto Above Eagle (1866–1873)

| | Mintage | G-4 | VG-8 | F-12 | VF-20 | EF-40 | AU-50 | MS-60 | MS-63 | PF-63 |
|---|---|---|---|---|---|---|---|---|---|---|
| 1866 . . . . . . (725) . . . . . . . | 16,800 | $525 | $775 | $900 | $1,050 | $1,200 | $1,400 | $1,850 | $2,000 | $550 |
| 1866S . . . . . . . . . . . . . . . | 28,000 | 400 | 675 | 1,000 | 1,200 | 1,850 | 2,250 | 4,500 | 11,500 | |

*Chart continued on next page.*

| | Mintage | G-4 | VG-8 | F-12 | VF-20 | EF-40 | AU-50 | MS-60 | MS-63 | PF-63 |
|---|---|---|---|---|---|---|---|---|---|---|
| 1867 . . . . . . . . (625) . . . . 20,000 | | $300 | $450 | $575 | $775 | $1,050 | $1,350 | $1,800 | $3,000 | $550 |
| 1867S . . . . . . . . . . . . . . 48,000 | | 425 | 700 | 900 | 1,150 | 2,250 | 6,000 | 8,000 | — | |
| 1868 . . . . . . . . (600) . . . 29,400 | | 180 | 250 | 300 | 350 | 550 | 775 | 1,350 | 2,750 | 550 |
| 1868S . . . . . . . . . . . . . . 96,000 | | 90 | 135 | 225 | 525 | 625 | 1,350 | 3,750 | 6,750 | |
| 1869 . . . . . . . . (600) . . . 16,000 | | 350 | 450 | 550 | 650 | 825 | 1,050 | 1,500 | 3,500 | 550 |
| 1869S . . . . . . . . . . . . . . 76,000 | | 120 | 185 | 300 | 475 | 850 | 1,250 | 3,500 | 5,250 | |
| 1870 . . . . . . . (1,000) . . . 86,400 | | 45 | 65 | 110 | 185 | 300 | 500 | 750 | 1,850 | 550 |
| 1870CC . . . . . . . . . . . . . . 8,340 | | 6,000 | 9,000 | 13,000 | 17,000 | 32,500 | 110,000 | — | | |
| 1871 . . . . . . . . (960) . . 118,200 | | 35 | 50 | 75 | 110 | 225 | 325 | 525 | 1,200 | 550 |
| 1871CC . . . . . . . . . . . . . 10,890 | | 5,000 | 9,000 | 12,000 | 16,500 | 28,500 | 52,500 | — | — | |
| 1871S . . . . . . . . . . . . . . 30,900 | | 625 | 950 | 1,450 | 1,850 | 3,000 | 3,500 | 5,750 | 8,500 | |
| 1872 . . . . . . . . (950) . . 182,000 | | 45 | 65 | 120 | 160 | 300 | 400 | 1,050 | 1,850 | 550 |
| 1872CC . . . . . . . . . . . . . 22,850 | | 1,700 | 2,000 | 3,500 | 5,250 | 10,000 | 15,000 | 45,000 | | |
| 1872S . . . . . . . . . . . . . . 83,000 | | 1,850 | 2,000 | 2,500 | 3,000 | 3,750 | 4,500 | 6,750 | | |
| 1873 . . . . . . . . (600) . . 212,000 | | 65 | 90 | 130 | 200 | 280 | 400 | 900 | 1,750 | 550 |
| 1873CC . . . . . . . . . . . . . . 4,000 | | | | | — | 65,000 | — | — | | |

## Variety 5 – Arrows at Date (1873–1874)

| | Mintage | G-4 | VG-8 | F-12 | VF-20 | EF-40 | AU-50 | MS-60 | MS-63 | PF-63 |
|---|---|---|---|---|---|---|---|---|---|---|
| 1873 . . . . . . . . (500) . . 1,271,200 | | $20 | $22 | $32 | $65 | $130 | $300 | $600 | $850 | $1,000 |
| 1873CC . . . . . . . . . . . . . 12,462 | | 4,000 | 7,500 | 9,500 | 14,000 | 17,500 | 37,500 | 72,500 | 100,000 | |
| 1873S . . . . . . . . . . . . . 156,000 | | 65 | 90 | 125 | 185 | 325 | 475 | 1,350 | 3,000 | |
| 1874 . . . . . . . . (700) . . . 471,200 | | 20 | 22 | 30 | 65 | 130 | 300 | 575 | 850 | 1,000 |
| 1874S . . . . . . . . . . . . . 392,000 | | 22 | 25 | 38 | 70 | 185 | 350 | 600 | 875 | |

## Variety 4 Resumed, With Weight Standard of Variety 5 (1875–1891)

1877-S, S Over Horizontal S

| | Mintage | G-4 | VG-8 | F-12 | VF-20 | EF-40 | AU-50 | MS-60 | MS-63 | PF-63 |
|---|---|---|---|---|---|---|---|---|---|---|
| 1875 . . . . . . (700) . . . . 4,292,800 | | $20 | $22 | $25 | $30 | $50 | $110 | $210 | $375 | $525 |
| 1875CC . . . . . . . . . . . . 140,000 | | 185 | 275 | 400 | 650 | 1,000 | 1,600 | 4,000 | 6,750 | |
| 1875S . . . . . . . . . . . . . 680,000 | | 22 | 30 | 45 | 75 | 135 | 200 | 475 | 600 | |
| 1876 . . . . (1,150) . . . 17,816,000 | | 20 | 22 | 25 | 30 | 50 | 110 | 210 | 375 | 525 |
| 1876CC . . . . . . . . . . . 4,944,000 | | 40 | 60 | 80 | 100 | 145 | 220 | 475 | 875 | |
| 1876S . . . . . . . . . . . . 8,596,000 | | 20 | 22 | 26 | 30 | 50 | 110 | 210 | 375 | |
| 1877 . . . . . . (510) . . 10,911,200 | | 20 | 22 | 25 | 30 | 50 | 110 | 210 | 375 | 525 |
| 1877CC . . . . . . . . . . . 4,192,000 | | 40 | 60 | 80 | 100 | 135 | 240 | 400 | 800 | |
| 1877S . . . . . . . . . . . . 8,996,000 | | 20 | 22 | 25 | 30 | 50 | 110 | 210 | 375 | |

| | Mintage | G-4 | VG-8 | F-12 | VF-20 | EF-40 | AU-50 | MS-60 | MS-63 | PF-63 |
|---|---|---|---|---|---|---|---|---|---|---|
| 1877S, S Over Horizontal S . . . . .* | | $22 | $32 | $55 | $140 | $225 | $400 | $825 | $1,200 | |
| 1878 . . . . . . . .(800). . 2,260,000 | | 20 | 22 | 25 | 30 | 50 | 110 | 200 | 375 | $525 |
| 1878CC . . . . . . . . . . . . .996,000 | | 40 | 50 | 60 | 90 | 190 | 275 | 600 | 1,050 | |
| 1878S . . . . . . . . . . . . . .140,000 | | 225 | 325 | 425 | 600 | 850 | 1,200 | 1,850 | 3,750 | |
| 1879 . . . . . . (1,100). . . . .13,600 | | 110 | 145 | 210 | 280 | 350 | 400 | 475 | 625 | 525 |
| 1880 . . . . . . (1,355). . . . .13,600 | | 110 | 145 | 210 | 280 | 375 | 425 | 525 | 625 | 525 |
| 1881 . . . . . . . .(975). . . . .12,000 | | 110 | 145 | 210 | 275 | 400 | 450 | 550 | 700 | 525 |
| 1882 . . . . . . (1,100). . . . .15,200 | | 110 | 145 | 210 | 275 | 375 | 400 | 525 | 625 | 525 |
| 1883 . . . . . . (1,039). . . . .14,400 | | 110 | 145 | 210 | 275 | 375 | 400 | 525 | 625 | 525 |
| 1884 . . . . . . . .(875). . . . . .8,000 | | 160 | 185 | 250 | 275 | 375 | 400 | 525 | 625 | 525 |
| 1885 . . . . . . . .(930). . . . .13,600 | | 110 | 145 | 185 | 275 | 375 | 400 | 525 | 625 | 525 |
| 1886 . . . . . . . .(886). . . . . .5,000 | | 200 | 250 | 350 | 425 | 550 | 650 | 800 | 875 | 525 |
| 1887 . . . . . . . .(710). . . . .10,000 | | 135 | 185 | 225 | 300 | 425 | 500 | 675 | 875 | 525 |
| 1888 . . . . . . . .(832). . . . .10,001 | | 135 | 185 | 210 | 275 | 375 | 425 | 550 | 650 | 525 |
| 1888S . . . . . . . . . . . . . 1,216,000 | | 20 | 22 | 25 | 30 | 50 | 145 | 275 | 550 | |
| 1889 . . . . . . . .(711). . . . .12,000 | | 110 | 145 | 210 | 250 | 300 | 350 | 550 | 850 | 525 |
| 1890 . . . . . . . .(590). . . . .80,000 | | 90 | 110 | 135 | 185 | 210 | 250 | 210 | 575 | 525 |
| 1891 . . . . . . . .(600). . 3,920,000 | | 20 | 22 | 25 | 30 | 50 | 110 | 200 | 375 | 525 |
| 18910 . . . . . . . . . . . . . . .68,000 | | 275 | 400 | 750 | 1,050 | 1,850 | 2,750 | 5,750 | 10,000 | |
| 1891S . . . . . . . . . . . . . 2,216,000 | | 20 | 22 | 25 | 30 | 50 | 110 | 210 | 375 | |

* Included in 1877-S regular mintage (previous page).

## BARBER OR LIBERTY HEAD (1892–1916)

Like other silver coins of this type, the quarter dollars minted from 1892 to 1916 were designed by U.S. Mint chief engraver Charles E. Barber. His initial B is found at the truncation of the neck of Miss Liberty.

**G-4 Good:** Date and legends legible. LIBERTY worn off headband.
**VG-8 Very Good:** Some letters in LIBERTY legible.
**F-12 Fine:** LIBERTY completely legible but not sharp.
**VF-20 Very Fine:** All letters in LIBERTY evenly plain.
**EF-40 Extremely Fine:** LIBERTY bold, its ribbon distinct.
**AU-50 About Uncirculated:** Slight trace of wear above forehead, on cheek, and on eagle's head, wings, and tail.
**MS-60 Uncirculated:** No trace of wear. Light blemishes.
**MS-63 Choice Uncirculated:** Some distracting marks or blemishes in focal areas. Impaired luster possible.

**PF-63 Choice Proof:** Reflective surfaces with only a few blemishes in secondary focal places. No major flaws.

| | Mintage | G-4 | VG-8 | F-12 | VF-20 | EF-40 | AU-50 | MS-60 | MS-63 | PF-63 |
|---|---|---|---|---|---|---|---|---|---|---|
| 1892 . . . . . . (1,245). . 8,236,000 | | $6.50 | $7 | $12 | $20 | $30 | $75 | $150 | $250 | $500 |
| 18920 . . . . . . . . . . . . 2,460,000 | | 8.00 | 9 | 15 | 25 | 40 | 85 | 200 | 300 | |
| 1892S . . . . . . . . . . . . . .964,079 | | 25.00 | 35 | 50 | 85 | 125 | 225 | 450 | 750 | |
| 1893 . . . . . . . .(792). . 5,444,023 | | 6.50 | 7 | 12 | 15 | 30 | 75 | 175 | 300 | 500 |
| 18930 . . . . . . . . . . . . 3,396,000 | | 8.00 | 9 | 12 | 25 | 45 | 85 | 225 | 350 | |
| 1893S . . . . . . . . . . . . 1,454,535 | | 9.00 | 12 | 30 | 60 | 80 | 150 | 300 | 750 | |
| 1894 . . . . . . . .(972). . 3,432,000 | | 6.50 | 7 | 12 | 15 | 35 | 75 | 175 | 300 | 500 |
| 18940 . . . . . . . . . . . . 2,852,000 | | 6.50 | 7 | 15 | 30 | 60 | 125 | 200 | 450 | |
| 1894S . . . . . . . . . . . . 2,648,821 | | 6.50 | 7 | 12 | 25 | 55 | 100 | 200 | 425 | |
| 1895 . . . . . . . .(880). . 4,440,000 | | 6.50 | 7 | 12 | 15 | 30 | 75 | 175 | 300 | 500 |
| 18950 . . . . . . . . . . . . 2,816,000 | | 6.50 | 8 | 15 | 30 | 60 | 125 | 300 | 675 | |
| 1895S . . . . . . . . . . . . 1,764,681 | | 9.00 | 13 | 35 | 60 | 75 | 175 | 300 | 750 | |
| 1896 . . . . . . . .(762). . 3,874,000 | | 6.50 | 7 | 10 | 15 | 35 | 75 | 150 | 250 | 500 |
| 18960 . . . . . . . . . . . . 1,484,000 | | 30.00 | 40 | 100 | 160 | 275 | 450 | 800 | 1,500 | |

*Chart continued on next page.*

| | Mintage | G-4 | VG-8 | F-12 | VF-20 | EF-40 | AU-50 | MS-60 | MS-63 | PF-63 |
|---|---|---|---|---|---|---|---|---|---|---|
| 1896S | 188,039 | $450.00 | $1,000.00 | $1,450 | $2,250 | $3,750 | $4,500 | $10,000 | $16,500 | |
| 1897 | (731) 8,140,000 | 6.50 | 7.00 | 8 | 15 | 30 | 75 | 150 | 250 | $500 |
| 1897O | 1,414,800 | 12.00 | 30.00 | 100 | 160 | 200 | 275 | 650 | 1,200 | |
| 1897S | 542,229 | 65.00 | 75.00 | 175 | 325 | 600 | 850 | 1,200 | 2,250 | |
| 1898 | (735) 11,100,000 | 6.50 | 7.00 | 8 | 15 | 30 | 75 | 150 | 250 | 500 |
| 1898O | 1,868,000 | 8.00 | 12.00 | 35 | 65 | 125 | 250 | 650 | 1,200 | |
| 1898S | 1,020,592 | 15.00 | 20.00 | 40 | 100 | 125 | 200 | 500 | 1,500 | |
| 1899 | (846) 12,624,000 | 6.50 | 7.00 | 8 | 15 | 30 | 75 | 150 | 250 | 500 |
| 1899O | 2,644,000 | 7.00 | 8.00 | 15 | 30 | 60 | 150 | 350 | 550 | |
| 1899S | 708,000 | 15.00 | 25.00 | 65 | 85 | 115 | 250 | 850 | 1,200 | |
| 1900 | (912) 10,016,000 | 6.50 | 7.00 | 8 | 15 | 30 | 75 | 150 | 250 | 500 |
| 1900O | 3,416,000 | 10.00 | 15.00 | 30 | 50 | 70 | 200 | 500 | 700 | |
| 1900S | 1,858,585 | 6.50 | 7.00 | 12 | 20 | 30 | 75 | 300 | 750 | |
| 1901 | (813) 8,892,000 | 6.50 | 8.00 | 15 | 30 | 35 | 75 | 150 | 250 | 500 |
| 1901O | 1,612,000 | 30.00 | 50.00 | 140 | 250 | 450 | 650 | 1,250 | 2,000 | |
| 1901S | 72,664 | 3,000.00 | 6,800.00 | 11,000 | 15,000 | 23,000 | 27,500 | 32,500 | 40,000 | |
| 1902 | (777) 12,196,967 | 6.00 | 6.50 | 8 | 15 | 30 | 75 | 150 | 250 | 500 |
| 1902O | 4,748,000 | 6.50 | 7.00 | 20 | 30 | 60 | 125 | 325 | 750 | |
| 1902S | 1,524,612 | 7.00 | 9.00 | 20 | 35 | 70 | 125 | 350 | 700 | |
| 1903 | (755) 9,759,309 | 6.00 | 6.50 | 8 | 15 | 30 | 75 | 150 | 300 | 500 |
| 1903O | 3,500,000 | 6.50 | 7.00 | 15 | 25 | 50 | 125 | 300 | 675 | |
| 1903S | 1,036,000 | 10.00 | 15.00 | 20 | 35 | 65 | 150 | 350 | 750 | |
| 1904 | (670) 9,588,143 | 6.00 | 6.50 | 8 | 15 | 30 | 75 | 175 | 300 | 500 |
| 1904O | 2,456,000 | 10.00 | 16.00 | 35 | 75 | 125 | 250 | 650 | 850 | |
| 1905 | (727) 4,967,523 | 6.00 | 12.00 | 20 | 30 | 40 | 75 | 150 | 300 | 500 |
| 1905O | 1,230,000 | 20.00 | 25.00 | 55 | 100 | 125 | 200 | 400 | 1,100 | |
| 1905S | 1,884,000 | 12.00 | 18.00 | 30 | 45 | 55 | 110 | 350 | 750 | |
| 1906 | (675) 3,655,760 | 6.00 | 6.50 | 8 | 15 | 30 | 75 | 150 | 250 | 500 |
| 1906D | 3,280,000 | 6.00 | 6.50 | 8 | 15 | 30 | 75 | 150 | 275 | |
| 1906O | 2,056,000 | 6.00 | 7.00 | 12 | 20 | 45 | 100 | 175 | 350 | |
| 1907 | (575) 7,132,000 | 6.00 | 6.50 | 8 | 15 | 30 | 75 | 150 | 250 | 500 |
| 1907D | 2,484,000 | 6.00 | 6.50 | 10 | 15 | 30 | 80 | 250 | 450 | |
| 1907O | 4,560,000 | 6.00 | 7.00 | 8 | 15 | 30 | 75 | 175 | 300 | |
| 1907S | 1,360,000 | 6.00 | 6.50 | 15 | 30 | 55 | 150 | 350 | 1,100 | |
| 1908 | (545) 4,232,000 | 6.00 | 6.50 | 8 | 15 | 30 | 75 | 150 | 250 | 500 |
| 1908D | 5,788,000 | 6.00 | 6.50 | 8 | 15 | 30 | 75 | 150 | 250 | |
| 1908O | 6,244,000 | 6.00 | 7.00 | 8 | 15 | 30 | 75 | 150 | 250 | |
| 1908S | 784,000 | 20.00 | 35.00 | 85 | 100 | 150 | 275 | 650 | 950 | |
| 1909 | (650) 9,268,000 | 6.00 | 6.50 | 8 | 15 | 30 | 75 | 150 | 250 | 500 |
| 1909D | 5,114,000 | 6.00 | 6.50 | 8 | 15 | 30 | 85 | 150 | 250 | |
| 1909O | 712,000 | 50.00 | 125.00 | 350 | 650 | 1,500 | 2,250 | 3,250 | 4,000 | |
| 1909S | 1,348,000 | 6.00 | 6.50 | 12 | 20 | 40 | 100 | 250 | 600 | |
| 1910 | (551) 2,244,000 | 6.00 | 6.50 | 10 | 15 | 30 | 75 | 150 | 250 | 500 |
| 1910D | 1,500,000 | 6.00 | 6.50 | 15 | 30 | 50 | 125 | 250 | 500 | |
| 1911 | (543) 3,720,000 | 6.00 | 6.50 | 8 | 15 | 30 | 75 | 150 | 250 | 500 |
| 1911D | 933,600 | 15.00 | 35.00 | 100 | 200 | 300 | 400 | 600 | 750 | |
| 1911S | 988,000 | 6.00 | 6.50 | 20 | 35 | 70 | 125 | 225 | 425 | |
| 1912 | (700) 4,400,000 | 6.00 | 6.50 | 8 | 15 | 30 | 75 | 150 | 250 | 500 |
| 1912S | 708,000 | 8.00 | 12.00 | 25 | 40 | 55 | 125 | 300 | 650 | |
| 1913 | (613) 484,000 | 10.00 | 14.00 | 40 | 75 | 185 | 300 | 500 | 600 | 500 |
| 1913D | 1,450,800 | 6.00 | 6.50 | 12 | 20 | 35 | 90 | 150 | 250 | |
| 1913S | 40,000 | 1,000.00 | 1,750.00 | 3,000 | 5,500 | 7,500 | 9,500 | 12,500 | 15,000 | |

| | Mintage | G-4 | VG-8 | F-12 | VF-20 | EF-40 | AU-50 | MS-60 | MS-63 | PF-63 |
|---|---|---|---|---|---|---|---|---|---|---|
| 1914 . . . . . . (380) . . . . | 6,244,230 | $6.00 | $6.50 | $7.00 | $15 | $30 | $75 | $150 | $250 | $500 |
| 1914D . . . . . . . . . . . . | 3,046,000 | 6.00 | 6.50 | 7.00 | 15 | 30 | 75 | 150 | 250 | |
| 1914S . . . . . . . . . . . . . | 264,000 | 65.00 | 115.00 | 300.00 | 400 | 600 | 800 | 1,200 | 2,000 | |
| 1915 . . . . . . (450) . . . | 3,480,000 | 6.00 | 6.50 | 7.00 | 15 | 30 | 75 | 150 | 250 | 500 |
| 1915D . . . . . . . . . . . . | 3,694,000 | 6.00 | 6.50 | 7.00 | 15 | 30 | 75 | 150 | 250 | |
| 1915S . . . . . . . . . . . . . | 704,000 | 10.00 | 20.00 | 30.00 | 45 | 50 | 125 | 175 | 325 | |
| 1916 . . . . . . . . . . . . | 1,788,000 | 6.50 | 7.00 | 7.50 | 15 | 30 | 75 | 150 | 250 | |
| 1916D . . . . . . . . . . . . | 6,540,800 | 6.00 | 6.50 | 7.00 | 15 | 30 | 75 | 150 | 250 | |

## STANDING LIBERTY (1916–1930)

This design is by Hermon A. MacNeil, whose initial M is above and to the right of the date. Liberty bears a shield of protection in her left arm, while the right hand holds the olive branch of peace. There was a modification in 1917. The reverse had a new arrangement of stars and the eagle was higher. After 1924 the date was "recessed," thereby giving it greater protection from the effects of circulation. A centennial gold issue was struck in 2016.

**G-4 Good:** Date and lettering legible. Top of date worn. Liberty's right leg and toes worn off. Much wear evident on left leg and drapery lines.

**VG-8 Very Good:** Distinct date. Toes faintly visible. Drapery lines visible above Liberty's left leg.

**F-12 Fine:** High curve of right leg flat from thigh to ankle. Only slight wear evident on left leg. Drapery lines over right thigh seen only at sides of leg.

**VF-20 Very Fine:** Garment line across right leg worn, but visible at sides.

**EF-40 Extremely Fine:** Flattened only at high spots. Liberty's toes are sharp. Drapery lines across right leg evident.

**AU-50 About Uncirculated:** Slight trace of wear on head, kneecap, shield's center, and highest point on eagle's body.

**MS-60 Uncirculated:** No trace of wear, but contact marks, surface spots, or faded luster possible.

**MS-63 Choice Uncirculated:** No trace of wear. Light blemishes. Attractive mint luster.

### Variety 1 – No Stars Below Eagle (1916–1917)

*Mintmark location is on obverse, to left of date.*

| | Mintage | G-4 | VG-8 | F-12 | VF-20 | EF-40 | AU-50 | MS-60 | MS-63 |
|---|---|---|---|---|---|---|---|---|---|
| 1916 . . . . . . . . . . . . . | 52,000 | $2,750 | $3,750 | $4,500 | $5,000 | $6,750 | $8,000 | $10,500 | $12,500 |
| 1917, Variety 1 . . . . | 8,740,000 | 16 | 35 | 45 | 70 | 100 | 125 | 185 | 250 |
| 1917D, Variety 1 . . . | 1,509,200 | 18 | 50 | 65 | 80 | 110 | 175 | 225 | 300 |
| 1917S, Variety 1 . . . | 1,952,000 | 22 | 55 | 75 | 110 | 135 | 200 | 250 | 300 |

### Variety 2 – Stars Below Eagle (1917–1930)
#### *Pedestal Date (1917–1924)*

**1918-S, 8 Over 7**

*See next page for chart.*

| | Mintage | G-4 | VG-8 | F-12 | VF-20 | EF-40 | AU-50 | MS-60 | MS-63 |
|---|---|---|---|---|---|---|---|---|---|
| 1917, Variety 2 . . . . . . .13,880,000 | | $15 | $30 | $38 | $45 | $75 | $95 | $145 | $210 |
| 1917D, Variety 2 . . . . . . .6,224,400 | | 30 | 48 | 75 | 100 | 110 | 150 | 195 | 275 |
| 1917S, Variety 2 . . . . . . .5,552,000 | | 28 | 48 | 70 | 90 | 110 | 145 | 190 | 250 |
| 1918 . . . . . . . . . . . . . .14,240,000 | | 11 | 16 | 20 | 25 | 35 | 60 | 110 | 200 |
| 1918D . . . . . . . . . . . . . .7,380,000 | | 16 | 30 | 52 | 70 | 100 | 135 | 200 | 290 |
| 1918S, Normal Date . . .11,072,000 | | 11 | 13 | 20 | 26 | 40 | 65 | 115 | 200 |
| 1918S, 8 Over 7 . . . . . . . . . . . . .* | | 1,150 | 1,800 | 2,500 | 3,000 | 5,000 | 8,500 | 14,500 | 19,500 |
| 1919 . . . . . . . . . . . . . .11,324,000 | | 24 | 35 | 45 | 50 | 60 | 85 | 125 | 200 |
| 1919D . . . . . . . . . . . . . .1,944,000 | | 60 | 100 | 160 | 320 | 475 | 675 | 1,000 | 1,650 |
| 1919S . . . . . . . . . . . . . .1,836,000 | | 55 | 90 | 150 | 300 | 500 | 725 | 1,750 | 2,450 |
| 1920 . . . . . . . . . . . . . .27,860,000 | | 11 | 13 | 16 | 25 | 35 | 70 | 125 | 210 |
| 1920D . . . . . . . . . . . . . .3,586,400 | | 80 | 90 | 110 | 135 | 175 | 240 | 475 | 850 |
| 1920S . . . . . . . . . . . . . .6,380,000 | | 11 | 16 | 20 | 25 | 55 | 130 | 275 | 725 |
| 1921 . . . . . . . . . . . . . .1,916,000 | | 120 | 135 | 240 | 375 | 525 | 750 | 1,150 | 1,450 |
| 1923 . . . . . . . . . . . . . .9,716,000 | | 10 | 13 | 22 | 26 | 40 | 70 | 130 | 220 |
| 1923S . . . . . . . . . . . . . .1,360,000 | | 200 | 300 | 450 | 575 | 1,000 | 1,500 | 2,000 | 2,750 |
| 1924 . . . . . . . . . . . . . .10,920,000 | | 11 | 13 | 16 | 25 | 35 | 75 | 125 | 210 |
| 1924D . . . . . . . . . . . . . .3,112,000 | | 35 | 45 | 75 | 100 | 140 | 170 | 200 | 275 |
| 1924S . . . . . . . . . . . . . .2,860,000 | | 18 | 22 | 30 | 45 | 85 | 160 | 225 | 675 |

* Included in number above.

## Recessed Date (1925–1930)

| | Mintage | G-4 | VG-8 | F-12 | VF-20 | EF-40 | AU-50 | MS-60 | MS-63 |
|---|---|---|---|---|---|---|---|---|---|
| 1925 . . . . . . . . . . . . . .12,280,000 | | $6 | $6.50 | $9 | $11 | $26 | $60 | $110 | $190 |
| 1926 . . . . . . . . . . . . . .11,316,000 | | 6 | 6.50 | 9 | 11 | 26 | 60 | 110 | 190 |
| 1926D . . . . . . . . . . . . . .1,716,000 | | 8 | 11.00 | 18 | 34 | 70 | 95 | 125 | 190 |
| 1926S . . . . . . . . . . . . . .2,700,000 | | 6 | 6.50 | 11 | 30 | 80 | 150 | 360 | 900 |
| 1927 . . . . . . . . . . . . . .11,912,000 | | 6 | 6.50 | 9 | 11 | 26 | 60 | 110 | 190 |
| 1927D . . . . . . . . . . . . . . 976,000 | | 11 | 15.00 | 22 | 55 | 110 | 150 | 180 | 225 |
| 1927S . . . . . . . . . . . . . . 396,000 | | 38 | 55.00 | 78 | 200 | 550 | 1,450 | 4,000 | 5,250 |
| 1928 . . . . . . . . . . . . . .6,336,000 | | 6 | 6.50 | 9 | 11 | 26 | 60 | 110 | 190 |
| 1928D . . . . . . . . . . . . . .1,627,600 | | 6 | 6.50 | 9 | 11 | 26 | 60 | 110 | 190 |
| 1928S . . . . . . . . . . . . . .2,644,000 | | 6 | 6.50 | 9 | 11 | 26 | 60 | 110 | 190 |
| 1929 . . . . . . . . . . . . . .11,140,000 | | 6 | 6.50 | 9 | 11 | 26 | 60 | 110 | 190 |
| 1929D . . . . . . . . . . . . . .1,358,000 | | 6 | 6.50 | 9 | 11 | 26 | 60 | 110 | 190 |
| 1929S . . . . . . . . . . . . . .1,764,000 | | 6 | 6.50 | 9 | 11 | 26 | 60 | 110 | 190 |
| 1930 . . . . . . . . . . . . . .5,632,000 | | 6 | 6.50 | 9 | 11 | 26 | 60 | 110 | 190 |
| 1930S . . . . . . . . . . . . . .1,556,000 | | 6 | 6.50 | 9 | 11 | 26 | 60 | 110 | 190 |

# WASHINGTON (1932 TO DATE)

This type was intended to be a commemorative issue marking the 200th anniversary of President Washington's birth. John Flanagan, a New York sculptor, was the designer. The initials JF are found at the base of the neck. The mintmark is on the reverse below the wreath for coins from 1932 to 1964. Starting in 1968, the mintmark was moved to the obverse at the right of the ribbon.

**F-12 Fine:** Hair lines about Washington's ear visible. Tiny feathers on eagle's breast faintly visible.
**VF-20 Very Fine:** Most hair details visible. Wing feathers clear.
**EF-40 Extremely Fine:** Hair lines sharp. Wear spots confined to top of eagle's legs and center of breast.
**MS-60 Uncirculated:** No trace of wear, but many contact marks, surface spotting, or faded luster possible.
**MS-63 Choice Uncirculated:** No trace of wear. Light blemishes. Attractive mint luster.
**MS-64 Uncirculated:** A few scattered contact marks. Good eye appeal and attractive luster.
**MS-65 Gem Uncirculated:** Only light, scattered, non-distracting marks. Strong luster, good eye appeal.
**PF-65 Gem Proof:** Hardly any blemishes, and no flaws.

# QUARTER DOLLARS

## Silver Coinage (1932–1964)

| | Mintage | VG-8 | F-12 | VF-20 | EF-40 | MS-60 | MS-63 | MS-65 | PF-63 |
|---|---|---|---|---|---|---|---|---|---|
| 1932 | 5,404,000 | $4.50 | $6.00 | $7.00 | $8.00 | $20.00 | $32.50 | $200 | |
| 1932D | 436,800 | 65.00 | 75.00 | 95.00 | 135.00 | 725.00 | 1,100.00 | 7,000 | |
| 1932S | 408,000 | 60.00 | 70.00 | 75.00 | 90.00 | 275.00 | 375.00 | 1,800 | |
| 1934 | 31,912,052 | 4.50 | 6.00 | 7.00 | 8.00 | 18.00 | 25.00 | 70 | |
| 1934D | 3,527,200 | 4.50 | 5.00 | 7.00 | 12.50 | 45.00 | 165.00 | 300 | |
| 1935 | 32,484,000 | 4.50 | 4.75 | 7.00 | 8.00 | 12.50 | 22.00 | 50 | |
| 1935D | 5,780,000 | 4.50 | 7.00 | 11.00 | 25.00 | 150.00 | 190.00 | 275 | |
| 1935S | 5,660,000 | 5.50 | 6.00 | 8.00 | 12.50 | 67.50 | 75.00 | 140 | |
| 1936 (3,837) | 41,300,000 | 4.50 | 4.75 | 6.50 | 8.50 | 18.00 | 22.00 | 55 | $650 |
| 1936D | 5,374,000 | 4.50 | 7.00 | 20.00 | 45.00 | 425.00 | 475.00 | 650 | |
| 1936S | 3,828,000 | 4.50 | 4.75 | 8.00 | 12.50 | 75.00 | 90.00 | 180 | |
| 1937 (5,542) | 19,696,000 | 4.50 | 4.75 | 7.00 | 5.50 | 25.00 | 30.00 | 70 | 225 |
| 1937D | 7,189,600 | 5.50 | 6.00 | 8.00 | 15.00 | 50.00 | 60.00 | 90 | |
| 1937S | 1,652,000 | 4.50 | 7.00 | 12.00 | 22.50 | 110.00 | 175.00 | 235 | |
| 1938 (8,045) | 9,472,000 | 4.50 | 4.75 | 7.00 | 16.00 | 75.00 | 90.00 | 120 | 125 |
| 1938S | 2,832,000 | 4.50 | 4.75 | 7.00 | 18.50 | 55.00 | 90.00 | 125 | |
| 1939 (8,795) | 33,540,000 | 4.50 | 4.75 | 6.50 | 7.00 | 16.00 | 18.00 | 45 | 105 |
| 1939D | 7,092,000 | 5.50 | 6.00 | 7.00 | 9.00 | 30.00 | 37.50 | 65 | |
| 1939S | 2,628,000 | 4.50 | 4.75 | 8.00 | 18.00 | 55.00 | 90.00 | 165 | |

| | Mintage | F-12 | VF-20 | EF-40 | MS-60 | MS-63 | MS-65 | PF-65 |
|---|---|---|---|---|---|---|---|---|
| 1940 (11,246) | 35,704,000 | $4.75 | $7.00 | $8.00 | $22.00 | $23.00 | $25 | $80 |
| 1940D | 2,797,600 | 5.50 | 6.00 | 27.50 | 100.00 | 125.00 | 150 | |
| 1940S | 8,244,000 | 5.50 | 6.00 | 9.00 | 25.00 | 32.50 | 40 | |
| 1941 (15,287) | 79,032,000 | 4.50 | 4.75 | 5.00 | 7.00 | 11.00 | 18 | 75 |
| 1941D | 16,714,800 | 4.50 | 4.75 | 6.00 | 32.50 | 40.00 | 50 | |
| 1941S | 16,080,000 | 4.50 | 4.75 | 5.00 | 27.50 | 35.00 | 55 | |
| 1942 (21,123) | 102,096,000 | 4.50 | 4.75 | 5.00 | 7.00 | 7.50 | 10 | 75 |
| 1942D | 17,487,200 | 4.50 | 4.75 | 5.00 | 14.00 | 15.00 | 35 | |
| 1942S | 19,384,000 | 4.50 | 4.75 | 8.00 | 55.00 | 65.00 | 70 | |
| 1943 | 99,700,000 | 4.50 | 4.75 | 5.00 | 6.00 | 7.50 | 18 | |
| 1943D | 16,095,600 | 4.50 | 4.75 | 7.00 | 20.00 | 30.00 | 45 | |
| 1943S | 21,700,000 | 4.50 | 4.75 | 6.00 | 27.50 | 32.50 | 45 | |
| 1944 | 104,956,000 | 4.50 | 4.75 | 5.00 | 6.00 | 7.50 | 13 | |
| 1944D | 14,600,800 | 4.50 | 4.75 | 5.00 | 9.00 | 12.50 | 15 | |
| 1944S | 12,560,000 | 4.50 | 4.75 | 5.00 | 9.00 | 12.50 | 15 | |
| 1945 | 74,372,000 | 4.50 | 4.75 | 5.00 | 6.50 | 7.50 | 17 | |
| 1945D | 12,341,600 | 4.50 | 4.75 | 5.00 | 6.50 | 18.00 | 24 | |
| 1945S | 17,004,001 | 4.50 | 4.75 | 5.00 | 6.50 | 9.00 | 12 | |
| 1946 | 53,436,000 | 4.50 | 4.75 | 5.00 | 6.50 | 7.50 | 15 | |
| 1946D | 9,072,800 | 4.50 | 4.75 | 5.00 | 6.50 | 9.00 | 12 | |
| 1946S | 4,204,000 | 4.50 | 4.75 | 5.00 | 6.50 | 7.50 | 12 | |
| 1947 | 22,556,000 | 4.50 | 4.75 | 5.00 | 6.50 | 12.50 | 15 | |

*Chart continued on next page.*

| | Mintage | F-12 | VF-20 | EF-40 | MS-60 | MS-63 | MS-65 | PF-65 |
|---|---|---|---|---|---|---|---|---|
| 1947D | 15,338,400 | $4.50 | $4.75 | $5 | $6.50 | $12.00 | $14.00 | |
| 1947S | 5,532,000 | 4.50 | 4.75 | 5 | 6.50 | 11.00 | 15.00 | |
| 1948 | 35,196,000 | 4.50 | 4.75 | 5 | 6.50 | 7.50 | 10.00 | |
| 1948D | 16,766,800 | 4.50 | 4.75 | 5 | 6.50 | 12.50 | 20.00 | |
| 1948S | 15,960,000 | 4.50 | 4.75 | 5 | 6.50 | 8.00 | 15.00 | |
| 1949 | 9,312,000 | 4.50 | 4.75 | 7 | 25.00 | 30.00 | 45.00 | |
| 1949D | 10,068,400 | 4.50 | 4.75 | 7 | 12.50 | 22.50 | 35.00 | |
| 1950 (51,386) | 24,920,126 | 4.50 | 4.75 | 5 | 6.00 | 11.00 | 20.00 | $42.50 |
| 1950D | 21,075,600 | 4.50 | 4.75 | 5 | 6.00 | 12.50 | 15.00 | |
| 1950D, D Over S * | | 40.00 | 60.00 | 85 | 175.00 | 500.00 | 2,750.00 | |
| 1950S | 10,284,004 | 4.50 | 4.75 | 5 | 6.50 | 10.00 | 25.00 | |
| 1950S, S Over D * | | 45.00 | 80.00 | 150 | 275.00 | 350.00 | 950.00 | |
| 1951 (57,500) | 43,448,102 | 4.50 | 4.75 | 5 | 6.00 | 7.50 | 22.00 | 35.00 |
| 1951D | 35,354,800 | 4.50 | 4.75 | 5 | 6.00 | 8.00 | 22.00 | |
| 1951S | 9,048,000 | 4.50 | 4.75 | 5 | 6.00 | 15.00 | 26.00 | |
| 1952 (81,980) | 38,780,093 | 4.50 | 4.75 | 5 | 6.00 | 9.00 | 22.00 | 32.50 |
| 1952D | 49,795,200 | 4.50 | 4.75 | 5 | 6.00 | 8.00 | 20.00 | |
| 1952S | 13,707,800 | 4.50 | 4.75 | 5 | 7.00 | 12.50 | 26.00 | |
| 1953 (128,800) | 18,536,120 | 4.50 | 4.75 | 5 | 6.00 | 8.00 | 16.50 | 30.00 |
| 1953D | 56,112,400 | 4.50 | 4.75 | 5 | 6.00 | 9.00 | 22.00 | |
| 1953S | 14,016,000 | 4.50 | 4.75 | 5 | 7.00 | 7.50 | 18.00 | |
| 1954 (233,300) | 54,412,203 | 4.50 | 4.75 | 5 | 5.25 | 5.50 | 11.00 | 12.50 |
| 1954D | 42,305,500 | 4.50 | 4.75 | 5 | 5.25 | 5.50 | 16.50 | |
| 1954S | 11,834,722 | 4.50 | 4.75 | 5 | 5.25 | 5.50 | 13.50 | |
| 1955 (378,200) | 18,180,181 | 4.50 | 4.75 | 5 | 5.25 | 5.50 | 20.00 | 12.50 |
| 1955D | 3,182,400 | 4.50 | 4.75 | 5 | 6.00 | 6.50 | 22.50 | |
| 1956 (669,384) | 44,144,000 | 4.50 | 4.75 | 5 | 5.25 | 5.50 | 11.00 | 9.00 |
| 1956D | 32,334,500 | 4.50 | 4.75 | 5 | 5.25 | 5.50 | 13.50 | |
| 1957 (1,247,952) | 46,532,000 | 4.50 | 4.75 | 5 | 5.25 | 5.50 | 11.00 | 9.00 |
| 1957D | 77,924,160 | 4.50 | 4.75 | 5 | 5.25 | 5.50 | 18.50 | |
| 1958 (875,652) | 6,360,000 | 4.50 | 4.75 | 5 | 5.25 | 5.50 | 11.00 | 9.00 |
| 1958D | 78,124,900 | 4.50 | 4.75 | 5 | 5.25 | 5.50 | 20.00 | |
| 1959 (1,149,291) | 24,384,000 | 4.50 | 4.75 | 5 | 5.25 | 5.50 | 11.00 | 9.00 |
| 1959D | 62,054,232 | 4.50 | 4.75 | 5 | 5.25 | 5.50 | 11.00 | |
| 1960 (1,691,602) | 29,164,000 | 4.50 | 4.75 | 5 | 5.25 | 5.50 | 11.00 | 7.00 |
| 1960D | 63,000,324 | 4.50 | 4.75 | 5 | 5.25 | 5.50 | 14.50 | |
| 1961 (3,028,244) | 37,036,000 | 4.50 | 4.75 | 5 | 5.25 | 5.50 | 16.50 | 7.00 |
| 1961D | 83,656,928 | 4.50 | 4.75 | 5 | 5.25 | 5.50 | 20.00 | |
| 1962 (3,218,019) | 36,156,000 | 4.50 | 4.75 | 5 | 5.25 | 5.50 | 20.00 | 7.00 |
| 1962D | 127,554,756 | 4.50 | 4.75 | 5 | 5.25 | 5.50 | 18.00 | |
| 1963 (3,075,645) | 74,316,000 | 4.50 | 4.75 | 5 | 5.25 | 5.50 | 18.00 | 7.00 |
| 1963D | 135,288,184 | 4.50 | 4.75 | 5 | 5.25 | 5.50 | 18.00 | |
| 1964 (3,950,762) | 560,390,585 | 4.50 | 4.75 | 5 | 5.25 | 5.50 | 18.00 | 7.00 |
| 1964D | 704,135,528 | 4.50 | 4.75 | 5 | 5.25 | 5.50 | 16.50 | |

* Included in number above.

## Clad Coinage and Silver Proofs (1965 to Date)

| | Mintage | MS-63 | MS-65 | PF-65 | | Mintage | MS-63 | MS-65 | PF-65 |
|---|---|---|---|---|---|---|---|---|---|
| 1965 | 1,819,717,540 | $0.30 | $4.00 | | 1968D | 101,534,000 | $0.30 | $3.00 | |
| 1966 | 821,101,500 | 0.30 | 3.00 | | 1968S | (3,041,506) | | | $1 |
| 1967 | 1,524,031,848 | 0.30 | 3.00 | | 1969 | 176,212,000 | 0.75 | 3.50 | |
| 1968 | 220,731,500 | 0.50 | 3.50 | | 1969D | 114,372,000 | 0.50 | 4.00 | |

| | Mintage | MS-63 | MS-65 | PF-65 |
|---|---|---|---|---|
| 1969S | (2,934,631) | | | $1 |
| 1970 | 136,420,000 | $0.25 | $3 | |
| 1970D | 417,341,364 | 0.25 | 2 | |
| 1970S | (2,632,810) | | | 1 |
| 1971 | 109,284,000 | 0.30 | 2 | |
| 1971D | 258,634,428 | 0.30 | 2 | |
| 1971S | (3,220,733) | | | 1 |
| 1972 | 215,048,000 | 0.30 | 2 | |

| | Mintage | MS-63 | MS-65 | PF-65 |
|---|---|---|---|---|
| 1972D | 311,067,732 | $0.30 | $2 | |
| 1972S | (3,260,996) | | | $1 |
| 1973 | 346,924,000 | 0.30 | 2 | |
| 1973D | 232,977,400 | 0.30 | 2 | |
| 1973S | (2,760,339) | | | 1 |
| 1974 | 801,456,000 | 0.30 | 2 | |
| 1974D | 353,160,300 | 0.30 | 3 | |
| 1974S | (2,612,568) | | | 1 |

## Bicentennial (1776–1976)

| | Mintage | MS-63 | MS-65 | PF-65 |
|---|---|---|---|---|
| 1776–1976, Copper-Nickel Clad | 809,784,016 | $0.30 | $2 | |
| 1776–1976D, Copper-Nickel Clad | 860,118,839 | 0.30 | 2 | |
| 1776–1976S, Copper-Nickel Clad | (7,059,099) | | | $1 |
| 1776–1976S, Silver Clad | 11,000,000 | 2.50 | 3 | |
| 1776–1976S, Silver Clad | (4,000,000) | | | 3 |

Note: Mintage figures for 1976-S silver clad coins are approximate; many were melted in 1982.

## Eagle Reverse Resumed (1977–1998)
### (Dies Slightly Modified to Lower Relief)

| | Mintage | MS-63 | MS-65 | PF-65 |
|---|---|---|---|---|
| 1977 | 468,556,000 | $0.27 | | |
| 1977D | 256,524,978 | 0.27 | $1.00 | |
| 1977S | (3,251,152) | | | $1 |
| 1978 | 521,452,000 | 0.27 | 1.50 | |
| 1978D | 287,373,152 | 0.27 | 1.50 | |
| 1978S | (3,127,781) | | | 1 |
| 1979 | 515,708,000 | 0.28 | 1.50 | |
| 1979D | 489,789,780 | 0.27 | 1.25 | |
| 1979S | (3,677,175) | | | |
| Type 1 | | | | 1 |
| Type 2 | | | | 2 |
| 1980P | 635,832,000 | 0.27 | 1.50 | |
| 1980D | 518,327,487 | 0.27 | 1.25 | |
| 1980S | (3,554,806) | | | 1 |
| 1981P | 601,716,000 | 0.27 | 1.50 | |
| 1981D | 575,722,833 | 0.27 | 1.00 | |
| 1981S | (4,063,083) | | | |
| Type 1 | | | | 3 |
| Type 2 | | | | 6 |
| 1982P | 500,931,000 | 1.00 | 10.00 | |
| 1982D | 480,042,788 | 1.00 | 8.00 | |
| 1982S | (3,857,479) | | | 1 |
| 1983P | 673,535,000 | 8.00 | 25.00 | |

| | Mintage | MS-63 | MS-65 | PF-65 |
|---|---|---|---|---|
| 1983D | 617,806,446 | $3.00 | $20 | |
| 1983S | (3,279,126) | | | $1 |
| 1984P | 676,545,000 | 0.30 | 3 | |
| 1984D | 546,483,064 | 0.30 | 3 | |
| 1984S | (3,065,110) | | | 1 |
| 1985P | 775,818,962 | 0.50 | 5 | |
| 1985D | 519,962,888 | 0.35 | 3 | |
| 1985S | (3,362,821) | | | 1 |
| 1986P | 551,199,333 | 1.00 | 4 | |
| 1986D | 504,298,660 | 2.00 | 9 | |
| 1986S | (3,010,497) | | | 1 |
| 1987P | 582,499,481 | 0.27 | 3 | |
| 1987D | 655,594,696 | 0.27 | 1 | |
| 1987S | (4,227,728) | | | 1 |
| 1988P | 562,052,000 | 0.50 | 5 | |
| 1988D | 596,810,688 | 0.50 | 4 | |
| 1988S | (3,262,948) | | | 1 |
| 1989P | 512,868,000 | 0.30 | 5 | |
| 1989D | 896,535,597 | 0.27 | 1 | |
| 1989S | (3,220,194) | | | 1 |
| 1990P | 613,792,000 | 0.27 | 4 | |
| 1990D | 927,638,181 | 0.28 | 4 | |
| 1990S | (3,299,559) | | | 1 |

*Chart continued on next page.*

| | Mintage | MS-63 | MS-65 | PF-65 |
|---|---|---|---|---|
| 1991P . . . . . . 570,968,000 | $0.30 | $4 | | |
| 1991D . . . . . . 630,966,693 | 0.30 | 4 | | |
| 1991S . . . . . . . (2,867,787) | | | | $1.25 |
| 1992P . . . . . . 384,764,000 | 0.35 | 5 | | |
| 1992D . . . . . . 389,777,107 | 0.35 | 5 | | |
| 1992S . . . . . . . (2,858,981) | | | | 1.25 |
| 1992S, Silver. . . (1,317,579) | | | | 5.00 |
| 1993P . . . . . . 639,276,000 | 0.30 | 2 | | |
| 1993D . . . . . . 645,476,128 | 0.30 | 2 | | |
| 1993S . . . . . . . (2,633,439) | | | | 1.25 |
| 1993S, Silver. . . . . (761,353) | | | | 5.00 |
| 1994P . . . . . . 825,600,000 | 0.30 | 4 | | |
| 1994D . . . . . . 880,034,110 | 0.30 | 4 | | |
| 1994S . . . . . . . (2,484,594) | | | | 1.25 |
| 1994S, Silver. . . . . (785,329) | | | | 5.00 |
| 1995P . . . . . . 1,004,336,000 | 0.30 | 4 | | |

| | Mintage | MS-63 | MS-65 | PF-65 |
|---|---|---|---|---|
| 1995D . . . . . . 1,103,216,000 | $0.30 | $3 | | |
| 1995S . . . . . . . . (2,117,496) | | | | $3.00 |
| 1995S, Silver. . . . . (679,985) | | | | 5.00 |
| 1996P . . . . . . 925,040,000 | 0.25 | 3 | | |
| 1996D . . . . . . 906,868,000 | 0.25 | 3 | | |
| 1996S . . . . . . . (1,750,244) | | | | 2.00 |
| 1996S, Silver. . . . . (775,021) | | | | 5.00 |
| 1997P . . . . . . 595,740,000 | 0.25 | 3 | | |
| 1997D . . . . . . 599,680,000 | 0.25 | 3 | | |
| 1997S . . . . . . . (2,055,000) | | | | 2.00 |
| 1997S, Silver. . . . . (741,678) | | | | 5.00 |
| 1998P . . . . . . 896,268,000 | 0.25 | 2 | | |
| 1998D . . . . . . 821,000,000 | 0.25 | 2 | | |
| 1998S . . . . . . . (2,086,507) | | | | 2.50 |
| 1998S, Silver. . . . . (878,792) | | | | 5.00 |

## State Quarters (1999–2008)

The United States Mint 50 State Quarters® Program, which began in 1999, produced a series of 50 quarter dollar coins with special designs honoring each state. Five different designs were issued each year during the period 1999 through 2008. States were commemorated in the order of their entrance into statehood.

These are all legal-tender coins of standard weight and composition. The obverse side depicting President George Washington was modified to include some of the wording previously used on the reverse. The modification was authorized by special legislation, and carried out by Mint sculptor-engraver William Cousins, whose initials were added to the truncation of Washington's neck adjacent to those of the original designer, John Flanagan.

Each state theme was proposed, and the design approved, by the governor of the state. Final designs were created by Mint personnel.

Circulation coins were made at the Philadelphia and Denver mints. Proof coins were made in San Francisco. Both copper-nickel and silver Proof coins were made each year.

| | Mintage | AU-50 | MS-63 | PF-65 |
|---|---|---|---|---|
| Delaware | | | | |
| 1999P . . . . . 373,400,000 | $0.25 | $0.50 | | |
| 1999D . . . . . 401,424,000 | 0.25 | 0.50 | | |
| 1999S . . . . . . (3,713,359) | | | | $1.75 |
| 1999S, Silver. . . (804,565) | | | | 14.00 |
| Pennsylvania | | | | |
| 1999P . . . . . 349,000,000 | 0.25 | 0.50 | | |
| 1999D . . . . . 358,332,000 | 0.25 | 0.50 | | |
| 1999S . . . . . . (3,713,359) | | | | 1.75 |
| 1999S, Silver. . . (804,565) | | | | 14.00 |

| | Mintage | AU-50 | MS-63 | PF-65 |
|---|---|---|---|---|
| New Jersey | | | | |
| 1999P . . . . . 363,200,000 | $0.25 | $0.30 | | |
| 1999D . . . . . 299,028,000 | 0.25 | 0.35 | | |
| 1999S . . . . . . (3,713,359) | | | | $1.75 |
| 1999S, Silver. . . (804,565) | | | | 14.00 |
| Georgia | | | | |
| 1999P . . . . . 451,188,000 | 0.25 | 0.30 | | |
| 1999D . . . . . 488,744,000 | 0.25 | 0.30 | | |
| 1999S . . . . . . (3,713,359) | | | | 1.75 |
| 1999S, Silver. . . (804,565) | | | | 14.00 |

# QUARTER DOLLARS

| | Mintage | AU-50 | MS-63 | PF-65 |
|---|---|---|---|---|
| Connecticut | | | | |
| 1999P | 688,744,000 | $0.25 | $0.30 | |
| 1999D | 657,880,000 | 0.25 | 0.30 | |

| | Mintage | AU-50 | MS-63 | PF-65 |
|---|---|---|---|---|
| Connecticut | | | | |
| 1999S | (3,713,359) | | | $1.75 |
| 1999S, Silver | (804,565) | | | 14.00 |

| | Mintage | AU-50 | MS-63 | PF-65 |
|---|---|---|---|---|
| Massachusetts | | | | |
| 2000P | 628,600,000 | $0.25 | $0.30 | |
| 2000D | 535,184,000 | 0.25 | 0.30 | |
| 2000S | (4,020,172) | | | $1.50 |
| 2000S, Silver | (965,421) | | | 6.00 |
| Maryland | | | | |
| 2000P | 678,200,000 | 0.25 | 0.30 | |
| 2000D | 556,532,000 | 0.25 | 0.30 | |
| 2000S | (4,020,172) | | | 1.50 |
| 2000S, Silver | (965,421) | | | 6.00 |
| South Carolina | | | | |
| 2000P | 742,576,000 | 0.25 | 0.32 | |
| 2000D | 566,208,000 | 0.25 | 0.32 | |

| | Mintage | AU-50 | MS-63 | PF-65 |
|---|---|---|---|---|
| South Carolina | | | | |
| 2000S | (4,020,172) | | | $1.50 |
| 2000S, Silver | (965,421) | | | 6.00 |
| New Hampshire | | | | |
| 2000P | 673,040,000 | $0.25 | $0.30 | |
| 2000D | 495,976,000 | 0.25 | 0.30 | |
| 2000S | (4,020,172) | | | 1.50 |
| 2000S, Silver | (965,421) | | | 6.00 |
| Virginia | | | | |
| 2000P | 943,000,000 | 0.25 | 0.30 | |
| 2000D | 651,616,000 | 0.25 | 0.30 | |
| 2000S | (4,020,172) | | | 1.50 |
| 2000S, Silver | (965,421) | | | 6.00 |

| | Mintage | AU-50 | MS-63 | PF-65 |
|---|---|---|---|---|
| New York | | | | |
| 2001P | 655,400,000 | $0.25 | $0.30 | |
| 2001D | 619,640,000 | 0.25 | 0.30 | |
| 2001S | (3,094,140) | | | $1.50 |
| 2001S, Silver | (889,697) | | | 8.00 |
| North Carolina | | | | |
| 2001P | 627,600,000 | 0.25 | 0.30 | |
| 2001D | 427,876,000 | 0.25 | 0.30 | |
| 2001S | (3,094,140) | | | 1.50 |
| 2001S, Silver | (889,697) | | | 8.00 |
| Rhode Island | | | | |
| 2001P | 423,400,000 | 0.25 | 0.30 | |
| 2001D | 447,100,000 | 0.25 | 0.30 | |

| | Mintage | AU-50 | MS-63 | PF-65 |
|---|---|---|---|---|
| Rhode Island | | | | |
| 2001S | (3,094,140) | | | $1.50 |
| 2001S, Silver | (889,697) | | | 8.00 |
| Vermont | | | | |
| 2001P | 423,400,000 | $0.25 | $0.30 | |
| 2001D | 459,404,000 | 0.25 | 0.30 | |
| 2001S | (3,094,140) | | | 1.50 |
| 2001S, Silver | (889,697) | | | 8.00 |
| Kentucky | | | | |
| 2001P | 353,000,000 | 0.25 | 0.30 | |
| 2001D | 370,564,000 | 0.25 | 0.30 | |
| 2001S | (3,094,140) | | | 1.50 |
| 2001S, Silver | (889,697) | | | 8.00 |

| | Mintage | AU-50 | MS-63 | PF-65 |
|---|---|---|---|---|
| Tennessee | | | | |
| 2002P..... | 361,600,000 | $0.30 | $0.40 | |
| 2002D..... | 286,468,000 | 0.25 | 0.40 | |

| | Mintage | AU-50 | MS-63 | PF-65 |
|---|---|---|---|---|
| Tennessee | | | | |
| 2002S...... | (3,084,245) | | | $1.50 |
| 2002S, Silver... | (892,229) | | | 8.00 |

| | AU-50 | MS-63 |
|---|---|---|
| Any P-Mint (except TN), 2002–2008* | $0.25 | $0.30 |
| Any D-Mint (except TN), 2002–2008* | 0.25 | 0.30 |

| | PF-65 |
|---|---|
| Any S-Mint (except TN and HI), 2002–2008* | $1.50 |
| Any S-Mint (except TN), Silver, 2002–2008* | 6.00 |

* See above for Tennessee values; 2008-S, Hawaii, clad Proof, is valued at $3 in PF-65.

| | Mintage | | Mintage | | Mintage | | Mintage |
|---|---|---|---|---|---|---|---|
| **Ohio** | | **Arkansas** | | **Kansas** | | **Washington** | |
| 2002P | 217,200,000 | 2003S | (3,408,516) | 2005P | 263,400,000 | 2007S | (2,374,778) |
| 2002D | 414,832,000 | 2003S, Silver | (1,125,755) | 2005D | 300,000,000 | 2007S, Silver | (1,313,481) |
| 2002S | (3,084,245) | **Michigan** | | 2005S | (3,262,960) | **Idaho** | |
| 2002S, Silver | (892,229) | 2004P | 233,800,000 | 2005S, Silver | (1,678,649) | 2007P | 294,600,000 |
| **Louisiana** | | 2004D | 225,800,000 | **West Virginia** | | 2007D | 286,800,000 |
| 2002P | 362,000,000 | 2004S | (2,740,684) | 2005P | 365,400,000 | 2007S | (2,374,778) |
| 2002D | 402,204,000 | 2004S, Silver | (1,769,786) | 2005D | 356,200,000 | 2007S, Silver | (1,313,481) |
| 2002S | (3,084,245) | **Florida** | | 2005S | (3,262,960) | **Wyoming** | |
| 2002S, Silver | (892,229) | 2004P | 240,200,000 | 2005S, Silver | (1,678,649) | 2007P | 243,600,000 |
| **Indiana** | | 2004D | 241,600,000 | **Nevada** | | 2007D | 320,800,000 |
| 2002P | 362,600,000 | 2004S | (2,740,684) | 2006P | 277,000,000 | 2007S | (2,374,778) |
| 2002D | 327,200,000 | 2004S, Silver | (1,769,786) | 2006D | 312,800,000 | 2007S, Silver | (1,313,481) |
| 2002S | (3,084,245) | **Texas** | | 2006S | (2,882,428) | **Utah** | |
| 2002S, Silver | (892,229) | 2004P | 278,800,000 | 2006S, Silver | (1,585,008) | 2007P | 255,000,000 |
| **Mississippi** | | 2004D | 263,000,000 | **Nebraska** | | 2007D | 253,200,000 |
| 2002P | 290,000,000 | 2004S | (2,740,684) | 2006P | 318,000,000 | 2007S | (2,374,778) |
| 2002D | 289,600,000 | 2004S, Silver | (1,769,786) | 2006D | 273,000,000 | 2007S, Silver | (1,313,481) |
| 2002S | (3,084,245) | **Iowa** | | 2006S | (2,882,428) | **Oklahoma** | |
| 2002S, Silver | (892,229) | 2004P | 213,800,000 | 2006S, Silver | (1,585,008) | 2008P | 222,000,000 |
| **Illinois** | | 2004D | 251,400,000 | **Colorado** | | 2008D | 194,600,000 |
| 2003P | 225,800,000 | 2004S | (2,740,684) | 2006P | 274,800,000 | 2008S | (2,078,112) |
| 2003D | 237,400,000 | 2004S, Silver | (1,769,786) | 2006D | 294,200,000 | 2008S, Silver | (1,192,908) |
| 2003S | (3,408,516) | **Wisconsin** | | 2006S | (2,882,428) | **New Mexico** | |
| 2003S, Silver | (1,125,755) | 2004P | 226,400,000 | 2006S, Silver | (1,585,008) | 2008P | 244,200,000 |
| **Alabama** | | 2004D | 226,800,000 | **North Dakota** | | 2008D | 244,400,000 |
| 2003P | 225,000,000 | 2004S | (2,740,684) | 2006P | 305,800,000 | 2008S | (2,078,112) |
| 2003D | 232,400,000 | 2004S, Silver | (1,769,786) | 2006D | 359,000,000 | 2008S, Silver | (1,192,908) |
| 2003S | (3,408,516) | **California** | | 2006S | (2,882,428) | **Arizona** | |
| 2003S, Silver | (1,125,755) | 2005P | 257,200,000 | 2006S, Silver | (1,585,008) | 2008P | 244,600,000 |
| **Maine** | | 2005D | 263,200,000 | **South Dakota** | | 2008D | 265,000,000 |
| 2003P | 217,400,000 | 2005S | (3,262,960) | 2006P | 245,000,000 | 2008S | (2,078,112) |
| 2003D | 231,400,000 | 2005S, Silver | (1,678,649) | 2006D | 265,800,000 | 2008S, Silver | (1,192,908) |
| 2003S | (3,408,516) | **Minnesota** | | 2006S | (2,882,428) | **Alaska** | |
| 2003S, Silver | (1,125,755) | 2005P | 239,600,000 | 2006S, Silver | (1,585,008) | 2008P | 251,800,000 |
| **Missouri** | | 2005D | 248,400,000 | **Montana** | | 2008D | 254,000,000 |
| 2003P | 225,000,000 | 2005S | (3,262,960) | 2007P | 257,000,000 | 2008S | (2,078,112) |
| 2003D | 228,200,000 | 2005S, Silver | (1,678,649) | 2007D | 256,240,000 | 2008S, Silver | (1,192,908) |
| 2003S | (3,408,516) | **Oregon** | | 2007S | (2,374,778) | **Hawaii** | |
| 2003S, Silver | (1,125,755) | 2005P | 316,200,000 | 2007S, Silver | (1,313,481) | 2008P | 254,000,000 |
| **Arkansas** | | 2005D | 404,000,000 | **Washington** | | 2008D | 263,600,000 |
| 2003P | 228,000,000 | 2005S | (3,262,960) | 2007P | 265,200,000 | 2008S | (2,078,112) |
| 2003D | 229,800,000 | 2005S, Silver | (1,678,649) | 2007D | 280,000,000 | 2008S, Silver | (1,192,908) |

Some State quarters were accidentally made with misaligned dies and are valued higher than ordinary pieces. Normal United States coins have dies oriented in "coin alignment," such that the reverse appears upside down when the coin is rotated from right to left. Values for the rotated-die quarters vary according to the amount of shifting. The most valuable are those that are shifted 180 degrees, so that both sides appear upright when the coin is turned over (called *medal alignment*).

Manufacturing varieties showing die doubling or other minor, unintentional characteristics are of interest to collectors and are often worth premium prices.

### District of Columbia and U.S. Territories Quarters (2009)

At the ending of the U.S. Mint 50 State Quarters® Program a new series of quarter-dollar reverse designs was authorized to recognize the District of Columbia and the five U.S. territories: the Commonwealth of Puerto Rico, Guam, American Samoa, the U.S. Virgin Islands, and the Commonwealth of the Northern Mariana Islands. Each of these coins, issued sequentially during 2009, has the portrait  of George Washington, as in the past, and is made of the same weight and composition. Each coin commemorates the history, geography, or traditions of the place it represents.

| | Mintage | AU-50 | MS-63 | PF-65 |
|---|---|---|---|---|
| District of Columbia | | | | |
| 2009P . . . . . . | 83,600,000 | $0.25 | $0.30 | |
| 2009D . . . . . . | 88,800,000 | 0.25 | 0.30 | |
| 2009S . . . . . . | (2,113,478) | | | $1.50 |
| 2009S, Silver . . . | (996,548) | | | 6.00 |
| Puerto Rico | | | | |
| 2009P . . . . . . | 53,200,000 | 0.25 | 0.30 | |
| 2009D . . . . . . | 86,000,000 | 0.25 | 0.30 | |
| 2009S . . . . . . | (2,113,478) | | | 1.50 |
| 2009S, Silver . . . | (996,548) | | | 6.00 |
| Guam | | | | |
| 2009P . . . . . . | 45,000,000 | 0.25 | 0.30 | |
| 2009D . . . . . . | 42,600,000 | 0.25 | 0.30 | |
| 2009S . . . . . . | (2,113,478) | | | 1.50 |
| 2009S, Silver . . . | (996,548) | | | 6.00 |

| | Mintage | AU-50 | MS-63 | PF-65 |
|---|---|---|---|---|
| American Samoa | | | | |
| 2009P . . . . . . | 42,600,000 | $0.25 | $0.30 | |
| 2009D . . . . . . | 39,600,000 | 0.25 | 0.30 | |
| 2009S . . . . . . | (2,113,478) | | | $1.50 |
| 2009S, Silver . . . | (996,548) | | | 6.00 |
| U.S. Virgin Islands | | | | |
| 2009P . . . . . . | 41,000,000 | 0.25 | 0.40 | |
| 2009D . . . . . . | 41,000,000 | 0.25 | 0.40 | |
| 2009S . . . . . . | (2,113,478) | | | 1.50 |
| 2009S, Silver . . . | (996,548) | | | 6.00 |
| Northern Mariana Islands | | | | |
| 2009P . . . . . . | 35,200,000 | 0.25 | 0.30 | |
| 2009D . . . . . . | 37,600,000 | 0.25 | 0.30 | |
| 2009S . . . . . . | (2,113,478) | | | 1.50 |
| 2009S, Silver . . . | (996,548) | | | 6.00 |

### America the Beautiful™ Quarters Program (2010–2021)

Following up on the popularity of the 50 State Quarters® Program, Congress authorized the production of new circulating commemorative quarters from 2010 to 2021. The coins honor a site of "natural or historic significance" from each of the 50 states, five U.S. territories, and the District of Columbia. They continue to bear George Washington's portrait on the obverse.

Five designs were released each year from 2010 through 2020, in the order the coins' featured locations were designated national parks or national sites. The 56th and final coin of the series was issued in early 2021.

In addition to the circulating quarters, a series of five-ounce silver bullion pieces were coined each year with designs nearly identical to those of the America the Beautiful™ quarters, with two main exceptions: the size, which is three inches in diameter; and the edge, which is marked .999 FINE SILVER 5.0 OUNCE, rather than reeded as on the standard quarters.

| | AU-50 | MS-63 | PF-65 |
|---|---|---|---|
| Any P-Mint, 2010–2021 | $0.25 | $0.30 | |
| Any D-Mint, 2010–2021 | 0.25 | 0.30 | |
| Any S-Mint, 2010–2021 (a) | | 0.50 | $1.50 |

| | MS-63 | PF-65 |
|---|---|---|
| Any S-Mint, Silver, 2010–2018 | | $6.00 |
| Any S-Mint, Silver, 2019–2021 (b) | | 6.50 |
| Any W-Mint, 2020 | | 6.00 |

**a.** Uncirculated strikes were made at the San Francisco Mint starting in 2012. Not intended for circulation, they were sold to collectors in rolls and bags at a premium above face value. **b.** In 2019, the fineness of all silver Proofs was changed from .900 to .999.

**Mintage**

**Hot Springs Nat'l Park (AR)**
2010P . . . . . . 35,600,000
2010D . . . . . . 34,000,000
2010S . . . . . . (1,402,889)
2010S, Silver. . . . (859,417)

**Yellowstone National Park (WY)**
2010P . . . . . . 33,600,000
2010D . . . . . . 34,800,000
2010S . . . . . . (1,404,259)
2010S, Silver. . . . (859,417)

**Yosemite Nat'l Park (CA)**
2010P . . . . . . 35,200,000
2010D . . . . . . 34,800,000
2010S . . . . . . (1,401,522)
2010S, Silver. . . . (859,417)

**Grand Canyon National Park (AZ)**
2010P . . . . . . 34,800,000
2010D . . . . . . 35,400,000
2010S . . . . . . (1,401,462)
2010S, Silver. . . . (859,417)

**Mount Hood National Forest (OR)**
2010P . . . . . . 34,400,000
2010D . . . . . . 34,400,000
2010S . . . . . . (1,398,106)
2010S, Silver. . . . (859,417)

**Gettysburg National Military Park (PA)**
2011P . . . . . . 30,800,000
2011D . . . . . . 30,400,000
2011S . . . . . . (1,273,068)
2011S, Silver. . . . (722,076)

**Glacier Nat'l Park (MT)**
2011P . . . . . . 30,400,000
2011D . . . . . . 31,200,000
2011S . . . . . . (1,269,422)

**Mintage**

**Glacier Nat'l Park (MT)**
2011S, Silver. . . . (722,076)

**Olympic Nat'l Park (WA)**
2011P . . . . . . 30,400,000
2011D . . . . . . 30,600,000
2011S . . . . . . (1,268,231)
2011S, Silver. . . . (722,076)

**Vicksburg National Military Park (MS)**
2011P . . . . . . 30,800,000
2011D . . . . . . 33,400,000
2011S . . . . . . (1,268,623)
2011S, Silver. . . . (722,076)

**Chickasaw National Recreation Area (OK)**
2011P . . . . . . 73,800,000
2011D . . . . . . 69,400,000
2011S . . . . . . (1,266,825)
2011S, Silver. . . . (722,076)

**El Yunque Nat'l Forest (PR)**
2012P . . . . . . 25,800,000
2012D . . . . . . 25,000,000
2012S . . . . . . 1,680,140
2012S . . . . . . (1,012,094)
2012S, Silver. . . . (608,060)

**Chaco Culture National Historical Park (NM)**
2012P . . . . . . 22,000,000
2012D . . . . . . 22,000,000
2012S . . . . . . 1,389,020
2012S . . . . . . (961,464)
2012S, Silver. . . . (608,060)

**Acadia National Park (ME)**
2012P . . . . . . 24,800,000
2012D . . . . . . 21,606,000
2012S . . . . . . 1,409,120
2012S . . . . . . (962,038)
2012S, Silver. . . . (608,060)

**Mintage**

**Hawai'i Volcanoes National Park (HI)**
2012P . . . . . . 46,200,000
2012D . . . . . . 78,600,000
2012S . . . . . . 1,409,120
2012S . . . . . . (962,447)
2012S, Silver. . . . (608,060)

**Denali National Park and Preserve (AK)**
2012P . . . . . . 135,400,000
2012D . . . . . . 166,600,000
2012S . . . . . . 1,409,220
2012S . . . . . . (959,602)
2012S, Silver. . . . (608,060)

**White Mountain National Forest (NH)**
2013P . . . . . . 68,800,000
2013D . . . . . 107,600,000
2013S . . . . . . 1,606,900
2013S . . . . . . (989,803)
2013S, Silver. . . . (467,691)

**Perry's Victory and Int'l Peace Memorial (OH)**
2013P . . . . . . 107,800,000
2013D . . . . . . 131,600,000
2013S . . . . . . 1,425,860
2013S . . . . . . (947,815)
2013S, Silver. . . . (467,691)

**Great Basin Nat'l Park (NV)**
2013P . . . . . . 122,400,000
2013D . . . . . . 141,400,000
2013S . . . . . . 1,316,500
2013S . . . . . . (945,777)
2013S, Silver. . . . (467,691)

**Ft. McHenry Nat'l Mon. and Historic Shrine (MD)**
2013P . . . . . . 120,000,000
2013D . . . . . . 151,400,000

**Mintage**

**Ft. McHenry Nat'l Mon. and Historic Shrine (MD)**
2013S . . . . . . . 1,313,680
2013S . . . . . . . .(946,380)
2013S, Silver. . . .(467,691)

**Mount Rushmore National Memorial (SD)**
2013P . . . . . . 231,800,000
2013D . . . . . . 272,400,000
2013S . . . . . . . 1,373,260
2013S . . . . . . . .(958,853)
2013S, Silver. . . .(467,691)

**Great Smoky Mountains National Park (TN)**
2014P . . . . . . 73,200,000
2014D . . . . . . . 99,400,000
2014S . . . . . . . 1,360,780
2014S . . . . . . . .(881,896)
2014S, Silver. . . .(472,107)

**Shenandoah Nat'l Park (VA)**
2014P . . . . . . 112,800,000
2014D . . . . . . 197,800,000
2014S . . . . . . . 1,266,720
2014S . . . . . . . .(846,441)
2014S, Silver. . . .(472,107)

**Arches National Park (UT)**
2014P . . . . . . 214,200,000
2014D . . . . . . 251,400,000
2014S . . . . . . . 1,235,940
2014S . . . . . . . .(844,775)
2014S, Silver. . . .(472,107)

**Great Sand Dunes National Park (CO)**
2014P . . . . . . 159,600,000
2014D . . . . . . 171,800,000
2014S . . . . . . . 1,176,760
2014S . . . . . . . .(843,238)
2014S, Silver. . . .(472,107)

| Mintage |
|---|
| **Everglades Nat'l Park (FL)** |
| 2014P . . . . . .157,601,200 |
| 2014D . . . . . .142,400,000 |
| 2014S . . . . . . . .1,180,900 |
| 2014S . . . . . . . . (856,139) |
| 2014S, Silver. . . (472,107) |
| **Homestead National** |
| **Mon. of America (NE)** |
| 2015P . . . . . .214,400,000 |
| 2015D . . . . . .248,600,000 |
| 2015S . . . . . . . .1,153,840 |
| 2015S . . . . . . . . (831,503) |
| 2015S, Silver. . . (490,829) |
| **Kisatchie Nat'l Forest (LA)** |
| 2015P . . . . . .397,200,000 |
| 2015D . . . . . .379,600,000 |
| 2015S . . . . . . . .1,099,380 |
| 2015S . . . . . . . . (762,407) |
| 2015S, Silver. . . (490,829) |

| Mintage |
|---|
| **Blue Ridge Parkway (NC)** |
| 2015P . . . . . .325,616,000 |
| 2015D . . . . . .505,200,000 |
| 2015S . . . . . . . .1,096,620 |
| 2015S . . . . . . . . (762,407) |
| 2015S, Silver. . . (490,829) |
| **Bombay Hook National** |
| **Wildlife Refuge (DE)** |
| 2015P . . . . . .275,000,000 |
| 2015D . . . . . .206,400,000 |
| 2015S . . . . . . . .1,013,920 |
| 2015S . . . . . . . . (762,407) |
| 2015S, Silver. . . (490,829) |
| **Saratoga National** |
| **Historical Park (NY)** |
| 2015P . . . . . .223,000,000 |
| 2015D . . . . . .215,800,000 |
| 2015S . . . . . . . .1,045,500 |
| 2015S . . . . . . . . (791,347) |

| Mintage |
|---|
| **Saratoga National** |
| **Historical Park (NY)** |
| 2015S, Silver. . . (490,829) |
| **Shawnee Nat'l Forest (IL)** |
| 2016P . . . . . .155,600,000 |
| 2016D . . . . . .151,800,000 |
| 2016S . . . . . . .(1,081,914) |
| 2016S . . . . . . . . (696,564) |
| 2016S, Silver. . . (502,039) |
| **Cumberland Gap National** |
| **Historical Park (KY)** |
| 2016P . . . . . .215,400,000 |
| 2016D . . . . . .223,200,000 |
| 2016S . . . . . . .(1,036,093) |
| 2016S . . . . . . . . 666,857 |
| 2016S, Silver. . . (502,039) |
| **Harpers Ferry National** |
| **Historical Park (WV)** |
| 2016P . . . . . .434,630,000 |

| Mintage |
|---|
| **Harpers Ferry National** |
| **Historical Park (WV)** |
| 2016D . . . . . .424,000,000 |
| 2016S . . . . . . .(1,050,185) |
| 2016S . . . . . . . . 666,857 |
| 2016S, Silver. . . (502,039) |
| **Theodore Roosevelt** |
| **National Park (ND)** |
| 2016P . . . . . .231,600,000 |
| 2016D . . . . . .223,200,000 |
| 2016S . . . . . . .(1,073,092) |
| 2016S . . . . . . . . (666,857) |
| 2016S, Silver. . . (502,039) |
| **Ft. Moultrie at Ft. Sumter** |
| **Nat'l Monument (SC)** |
| 2016P . . . . . .154,400,000 |
| 2016D . . . . . .142,200,000 |
| 2016S . . . . . . . . (979,566) |
| 2016S . . . . . . . . (683,741) |
| 2016S, Silver. . . (502,039) |

| | Mintage | SP-67 | SP-70 |
|---|---|---|---|
| 2016W, Gold **(a)** . . . . . . . . . . . . . . . . . . . . . . . . . . . . . . . . . . . . . . . . . . . . . | *91,752* | $450 | $500 |

**a.** In 2016 the Mint issued a centennial version of the Standing Liberty quarter in gold.

| | Mintage | | Mintage | | Mintage | | Mintage |
|---|---|---|---|---|---|---|---|
| **Effigy Mounds National Monument (IA)** | | **Pictured Rocks National Lakeshore (MI)** | | **American Memorial Park (N. Mariana Islands)** | | **Weir Farm National Historic Site (CT)** | |
| 2017P | 271,200,000 | 2018P | 186,714,000 | 2019P | 142,800,000 | 2020P | 125,600,000 |
| 2017D | 210,800,000 | 2018D | 182,600,000 | 2019D | 182,600,000 | 2020D | 155,000,000 |
| 2017S | 945,853 | 2018S | 931,220 | 2019S | 904,880 | 2020S | 945,820 |
| 2017S | (692,129) | 2018S | (653,176) | 2019S | (712,674) | 2020S | (544,660) |
| 2017S, Silver | (496,618) | 2018S, Silver | (461,048) | 2019S, Silver (a) | (539,510) | 2020S, Silver (a) | (427,191) |
| **Frederick Douglass National Historic Site (DC)** | | **Apostle Islands National Lakeshore (WI)** | | 2019W | 2,000,000 | 2020W (b) | 2,000,000 |
| 2017P | 184,800,000 | 2018P | 223,200,000 | **War in the Pacific Nat'l Historical Park (Guam)** | | **Salt River Bay National Historical Park and Ecological Preserve (USVI)** | |
| 2017D | 185,800,000 | 2018D | 216,600,000 | 2019P | 116,600,000 | |
| 2017S | 950,503 | 2018S | 889,080 | 2019D | 114,400,000 | 2020P | 580,200,000 |
| 2017S | (657,587) | 2018S | (618,988) | 2019S | 924,380 | 2020D | 515,000,000 |
| 2017S, Silver | (496,618) | 2018S, Silver | (461,048) | 2019S | (712,768) | 2020S | 930,960 |
| **Ozark National Scenic Riverways (MO)** | | **Voyageurs Nat'l Park (MN)** | | 2019S, Silver (a) | (539,510) | 2020S | (544,515) |
| 2018P | 237,400,000 | 2019W | 2,000,000 | 2020S, Silver (a) | (427,191) |
| 2017P | 203,000,000 | 2018D | 197,800,000 | **San Antonio Missions Nat'l Historical Park (TX)** | | 2020W (b) | 2,000,000 |
| 2017D | 200,000,000 | 2018S | 867,400 | **Marsh-Billings-Rockefeller Nat'l Historical Park (VT)** | |
| 2017S | 921,747 | 2018S | (619,013) | 2019P | 142,800,000 | |
| 2017S | (657,587) | 2018S, Silver | (461,048) | 2019D | 129,400,000 | 2020P | 304,600,000 |
| 2017S, Silver | (496,618) | **Cumberland Island National Seashore (GA)** | | 2019S | 931,580 | 2020D | 345,800,000 |
| **Ellis Island (Statue of Liberty National Monument, NJ)** | | 2019S | (712,743) | 2020S | 928,940 |
| 2018P | 138,000,000 | 2019S, Silver (a) | (539,510) | 2020S | (544,589) |
| 2018D | 151,600,000 | 2019W | 2,000,000 | 2020S, Silver (a) | (427,191) |
| 2017P | 234,000,000 | 2018S | 880,940 | **Franch Church River of No Return Wilderness (ID)** | | 2020W (b) | 2,000,000 |
| 2017D | 254,000,000 | 2018S | (618,725) | **Tallgrass Prairie National Preserve (KS)** | |
| 2017S | 973,147 | 2018S, Silver | (461,048) | 2019P | 223,400,000 | |
| 2017S | (657,587) | **Block Island National Wildlife Refuge (RI)** | | 2019D | 251,600,000 | 2020P | 101,200,000 |
| 2017S, Silver | (496,618) | 2019S | 901,920 | 2020D | 142,400,000 |
| **George Rogers Clark Nat'l Historical Park (IN)** | | 2018P | 159,600,000 | 2019S | (730,874) | 2020S | 931,060 |
| 2018D | 159,600,000 | 2019S, Silver (a) | (539,510) | 2020S | (561,452) |
| 2017P | 191,600,000 | 2018S | 854,940 | 2019W | 2,000,000 | 2020S, Silver (a) | (427,191) |
| 2017D | 180,800,000 | 2018S | (636,372) | **Nat'l Park of American Samoa (American Samoa)** | | 2020W (b) | 2,000,000 |
| 2017S | 933,150 | 2018S, Silver | (461,048) | **Tuskegee Airmen National Historic Site (AL)** | |
| 2017S | (675,757) | **Lowell National Historical Park (MA)** | | 2020P | 286,000,000 | |
| 2017S, Silver | (496,618) | 2020D | 212,200,000 | 2021P | 160,400,000 |
| | | 2019P | 165,800,000 | 2020S | 939,760 | 2021D | 304,000,000 |
| | | 2019D | 182,200,000 | 2020S | (574,037) | 2021S | |
| | | 2019S | 909,080 | 2020S, Silver (a) | (427,191) | 2021S | |
| | | 2019S | (539,510) | 2020W (b) | 2,000,000 | 2021S, Silver (a) | |
| | | 2019S, Silver (a) | (780,732) | | | | |
| | | 2019W | 2,000,000 | | | | |

**a.** In 2019, the fineness of all silver Proofs was changed from .900 to .999. **b.** The 2020-W quarters have a "V75" privy mark on the obverse commemorating the 75th anniversary of the end of World War II.

## Crossing the Delaware (2021)

The America's Beautiful National Parks Quarter Dollar Coin Act of 2008 specified what would happen to the coin after that program ended in 2021: "The reverse of the quarter dollar shall contain an image of General Washington crossing the Delaware River prior to the Battle of Trenton," and the obverse would "revert to the same design containing an image of President Washington" that was used before the State quarters program started in 1999.

| | Mintage | AU-50 | MS-63 | | PF-65 |
|---|---|---|---|---|---|
| 2021P | | $0.25 | $0.30 | 2021S | $1.50 |
| 2021D | | 0.25 | 0.30 | 2021S, Silver (a) | 6.50 |

a. In 2019, the fineness of U.S. Mint silver coins was changed from .900 to .999.

## American Women (2022–2025)

The Circulating Collectible Coin Redesign Act of 2020, signed into law January 13, 2021, brought wide-ranging changes involving all of America's circulating coins. In particular, it scheduled the quarter dollar as the venue for several new educational coin programs, including the American Women Quarters program.

From 2022 to 2025, the quarter commemorates prominent American women and the ratification of the Nineteenth Amendment granting women the right to vote. Five coins are being issued per year, each featuring a new reverse design honoring a woman selected from fields and accomplishments such as "suffrage, civil rights, abolition, government, humanities, science, space, and arts."

Common obverse design by Laura Gardin Fraser.

Scan to learn more about the program honorees.

| | AU-50 | MS-63 | PF-65 |
|---|---|---|---|
| 2022P, M. Angelou | $0.25 | $0.30 | |
| 2022D, M. Angelou | 0.25 | 0.30 | |
| 2022S, M. Angelou | | 0.50 | $1.50 |
| 2022S, M. Angelou, Silver (a) | | | 6.50 |
| 2022P, S. Ride | 0.25 | 0.30 | |
| 2022D, S. Ride | 0.25 | 0.30 | |
| 2022S, S. Ride | | 0.50 | 1.50 |
| 2022S, S. Ride, Silver (a) | | | 6.50 |
| 2022P, W. Mankiller | 0.25 | 0.30 | |
| 2022D, W. Mankiller | 0.25 | 0.30 | |

| | AU-50 | MS-63 | PF-65 |
|---|---|---|---|
| 2022S, W. Mankiller | | $0.50 | $1.50 |
| 2022S, W. Mankiller, Silver (a) | | | 6.50 |
| 2022P, N. Otero-Warren | $0.25 | 0.30 | |
| 2022D, N. Otero-Warren | 0.25 | 0.30 | |
| 2022S, N. Otero-Warren | | 0.50 | 1.50 |
| 2022S, N. Otero-Warren, Silver (a) | | | 6.50 |
| 2022P, A.M. Wong | 0.25 | 0.30 | |
| 2022D, A.M. Wong | 0.25 | 0.30 | |
| 2022S, A.M. Wong | | 0.50 | 1.50 |
| 2022S, A.M. Wong, Silver (a) | | | 6.50 |

a. In 2019, the fineness of all silver Proofs was changed from .900 to .999.

## THE NEAR FUTURE OF THE
## QUARTER DOLLAR (2022–2025)

The American Women quarters are significant for many reasons. The 2022 honorees introduce many "firsts" to American coinage. Dr. Sally Ride was the first American woman in space. Wilma Mankiller was the first female principal chief of the Cherokee Nation. Anna May Wong—the first Chinese American film star in Hollywood. Before Nina Otero-Warren no Hispanic woman had run for U.S. Congress. And Maya Angelou was the first African American woman to write and present a poem at a presidential inauguration.

The choice of Laura Gardin Fraser's George Washington portrait is noteworthy. The artist originally submitted it as a candidate for the new Washington quarter of 1932. Now, ninety years after "what might have been," Fraser's artistry takes its place on its intended denomination.

Significantly, the Circulating Collectible Coin Redesign Act of 2020 directs the Federal Reserve System and the Treasury Department to "take steps to ensure that an adequate supply of coins" is available for commerce and for collectors.

It also authorizes a marketing and educational campaign to help promote the coins (and collecting in general) and to develop related non-numismatic products.

The design selection for these coins involves recommendations from the public, consultation with the U.S. Commission of Fine Arts, and review by the Citizens Coinage Advisory Committee. Other input comes from the Smithsonian Institution and the Bipartisan Women's Caucus.

The Circulating Collectible Coin Redesign Act is one of the most significant pieces of coinage legislation in United States history. It will provide generations of Americans dozens of historically and culturally important coins to collect directly from our pocket change.

The half dollar, authorized by the Act of April 2, 1792, was not minted until December 1794. The weight of the half dollar was 208 grains and its fineness .8924 when first issued. This standard was not changed until 1837 when the Act of January 18, 1837, specified 206-1/4 grains, .900 fine. This fineness continued in use until 1965.

Arrows at the date in 1853 indicate the reduction of weight to 192 grains. During that year only, rays were added to the reverse. Arrows remained in 1854 and 1855. In 1873 the weight was raised by .9 grains and arrows were again placed at the date.

## FLOWING HAIR (1794–1795)

**AG-3 About Good:** Clear enough to identify.

**G-4 Good:** Date and letters sufficient to be legible. Main devices outlined, but lacking in detail.

**VG-8 Very Good:** Major details discernible. Letters well formed but worn.

**F-12 Fine:** Hair ends distinguishable. Top hair lines visible, but otherwise worn smooth.

**VF-20 Very Fine:** Some detail visible in hair in center; other details more bold.

**EF-40 Extremely Fine:** Hair above head and down neck detailed, with slight wear.

**AU-50 About Uncirculated:** All hair visible; slight wear on bust of Liberty and on top edges of eagle's wings, head, and breast.

1795, 2 Leaves Under Each Wing

1795, 3 Leaves Under Each Wing

| | Mintage | AG-3 | G-4 | VG-8 | F-12 | VF-20 | EF-40 | AU-50 |
|---|---|---|---|---|---|---|---|---|
| 1794 . . . . . . . . . . . . . . . . . . . . . . . . 23,464 | | $1,250 | $2,250 | $3,250 | $4,500 | $8,000 | $22,500 | $47,500 |
| 1795 . . . . . . . . . . . . . . . . . . . . . . 299,680 | | 350 | 800 | 950 | 1,350 | 2,000 | 4,500 | 10,000 |
| 1795, Recut Date. . . . . . . . . . . . . . . . .* | | 350 | 800 | 1,000 | 1,350 | 3,500 | 7,000 | 15,000 |
| 1795, 3 Leaves Under Each Wing . . . . . .* | | 800 | 1,500 | 2,000 | 3,500 | 5,000 | 12,000 | 25,000 |

* Included in number above.

## DRAPED BUST (1796–1807)

**AG-3 About Good:** Clear enough to identify.

**G-4 Good:** Date and letters sufficiently clear to be legible. Main devices outlined, but lacking in detail.

**VG-8 Very Good:** Major details discernible. Letters well formed but worn.

**F-12 Fine:** Hair ends distinguishable. Top hair lines visible, but otherwise worn smooth.

**VF-20 Very Fine:** Right side of drapery slightly worn. Left side to curls smooth.

**EF-40 Extremely Fine:** All lines in drapery on bust distinctly visible around to hair curls.

**AU-50 About Uncirculated:** Slight trace of wear on cheek, hair, and shoulder.

### Small Eagle Reverse (1796–1797)

1796, 16 Stars

1797, 15 Stars

*See next page for chart.*

| | Mintage | AG-3 | G-4 | VG-8 | F-12 | VF-20 | EF-40 | AU-50 |
|---|---|---|---|---|---|---|---|---|
| 1796, All kinds. . . . . . . . . . . . . . . .3,918 | | | | | | | | |
| 1796, 15 Stars . . . . . . . . . . . . . . . . | | $12,500 | $25,000 | $32,500 | $35,000 | $50,000 | $90,000 | $125,000 |
| 1796, 16 Stars . . . . . . . . . . . . . . . | | 12,500 | 25,000 | 32,500 | 35,000 | 50,000 | 90,000 | 125,000 |
| 1797, 15 Stars . . . . . . . . . . . . . . . | | 12,500 | 25,000 | 32,500 | 35,000 | 50,000 | 90,000 | 125,000 |

## Heraldic Eagle Reverse (1801–1807)

1805, 5 Over 4

1806, 6 Over 5

| | Mintage | G-4 | VG-8 | F-12 | VF-20 | EF-40 | AU-50 | MS-60 |
|---|---|---|---|---|---|---|---|---|
| 1801 . . . . . . . . . . . . . . . . . . . . . .30,289 | | $600 | $1,150 | $1,700 | $2,000 | $4,000 | $11,000 | $62,500 |
| 1802 . . . . . . . . . . . . . . . . . . . . . .29,890 | | 1,000 | 1,200 | 1,750 | 2,000 | 4,000 | 12,500 | 50,000 |
| 1803 . . . . . . . . . . . . . . . . . . . . . .188,234 | | 240 | 300 | 350 | 525 | 1,350 | 2,250 | 18,000 |
| 1805, All kinds. . . . . . . . . . . . . .211,722 | | | | | | | | |
| 1805, 5 Over 4 . . . . . . . . . . . . . . . | | 350 | 625 | 900 | 1,250 | 2,350 | 5,750 | 25,000 |
| 1805, Normal Date . . . . . . . . . . . . . | | 180 | 275 | 350 | 475 | 1,350 | 3,000 | 18,500 |
| 1806, All kinds. . . . . . . . . . . . . .839,576 | | | | | | | | |
| 1806, Normal Date . . . . . . . . . . . . . | | 160 | 200 | 260 | 475 | 1,150 | 1,750 | 11,000 |
| 1806, 6 Over 5 . . . . . . . . . . . . . . . | | 225 | 300 | 400 | 550 | 1,800 | 2,750 | 9,500 |
| 1806, 6 Over Inverted 6. . . . . . . . . . | | 250 | 325 | 700 | 1,050 | 3,000 | 5,500 | 20,000 |
| 1807 . . . . . . . . . . . . . . . . . . . . . .301,076 | | 160 | 200 | 260 | 475 | 1,100 | 1,750 | 5,500 |

## CAPPED BUST, LETTERED EDGE (1807–1836)

John Reich designed this capped-head concept of Liberty. Reich's design of Liberty facing left was used on all U.S. silver denominations for the next 30 years.

**G-4 Good:** Date and letters legible. Bust worn smooth with outline distinct.

**VG-8 Very Good:** LIBERTY faint. Legends distinguishable. Clasp at shoulder visible; curl above it nearly smooth.

**F-12 Fine:** Clasp and adjacent curl clearly outlined with slight details.

**VF-20 Very Fine:** Clasp at shoulder clear. Wear visible on highest point of curl. Hair over brow distinguishable.

**EF-40 Extremely Fine:** Clasp and adjacent curl fairly sharp. Brow and hair above distinct. Curls well defined.

**AU-50 About Uncirculated:** Trace of wear on hair over eye and over ear.

**MS-60 Uncirculated:** No trace of wear. Light blemishes. Possible slide marks from storage handling.

**MS-63 Choice Uncirculated:** Some distracting contact marks or blemishes in prime focal areas. Impaired luster possible.

## First Style (1807–1808)

**HALF DOLLARS**

| | Mintage | G-4 | VG-8 | F-12 | VF-20 | EF-40 | AU-50 | MS-60 | MS-63 |
|---|---|---|---|---|---|---|---|---|---|
| 1807 | 750,500 | $100 | $145 | $350 | $475 | $750 | $1,800 | $5,250 | $8,000 |
| 1808, 8 Over 7 | * | 80 | 120 | 190 | 260 | 500 | 1,000 | 3,750 | 7,000 |
| 1808 | 1,368,600 | 55 | 65 | 85 | 115 | 250 | 750 | 2,500 | 4,750 |

* Included in number below.

## Remodeled Portrait and Eagle (1809–1836)

| | Mintage | G-4 | VG-8 | F-12 | VF-20 | EF-40 | AU-50 | MS-60 | MS-63 |
|---|---|---|---|---|---|---|---|---|---|
| 1809 | 1,405,810 | $65 | $90 | $125 | $180 | $400 | $700 | $1,850 | $4,500 |
| 1810 | 1,276,276 | 55 | 75 | 95 | 150 | 325 | 500 | 1,800 | 3,750 |
| 1811 | 1,203,644 | 55 | 75 | 95 | 150 | 325 | 600 | 1,500 | 2,250 |

1812, 2 Over 1

1813, 50 C. Over UNI

1814, 4 Over 3

| | Mintage | G-4 | VG-8 | F-12 | VF-20 | EF-40 | AU-50 | MS-60 | MS-63 |
|---|---|---|---|---|---|---|---|---|---|
| 1812, All kinds | 1,628,059 | | | | | | | | |
| 1812, 2 Over 1 | | $90 | $110 | $150 | $225 | $500 | $900 | $2,500 | $6,500 |
| 1812 | | 55 | 75 | 95 | 125 | 325 | 550 | 1,350 | 2,250 |
| 1813 | 1,241,903 | 50 | 70 | 90 | 125 | 325 | 575 | 2,000 | 3,250 |
| 1813, 50 C. Over UNI | * | 90 | 125 | 200 | 325 | 600 | 1,100 | 2,250 | 5,750 |
| 1814, All kinds | 1,039,075 | | | | | | | | |
| 1814, 4 Over 3 | | 120 | 170 | 250 | 350 | 775 | 1,300 | 3,250 | 8,000 |
| 1814 | | 70 | 90 | 110 | 170 | 425 | 625 | 1,450 | 3,250 |

* Included in number above.

1817, 7 Over 3

1817, 7 Over 4

1817, "Punctuated" Date

| | Mintage | G-4 | VG-8 | F-12 | VF-20 | EF-40 | AU-50 | MS-60 | MS-63 |
|---|---|---|---|---|---|---|---|---|---|
| 1815, 5 Over 2 | 47,150 | $1,200 | $2,000 | $2,750 | $3,000 | $4,500 | $7,000 | $15,000 | $37,500 |
| 1817, All kinds | 1,215,567 | | | | | | | | |
| 1817, 7 Over 3 | | 125 | 200 | 350 | 475 | 900 | 2,000 | 5,500 | 18,000 |
| 1817, 7 Over 4 (8 known) | | | | 125,000 | 175,000 | 250,000 | | | |
| 1817, Dated 181.7 | | 90 | 135 | 180 | 225 | 600 | 2,000 | 8,000 | |
| 1817 | | 75 | 100 | 115 | 180 | 300 | 750 | 1,750 | 4,250 |

1818, 2nd 8 Over 7

1819, 9 Over 8

1820, 20 Over 19

| | Mintage | G-4 | VG-8 | F-12 | VF-20 | EF-40 | AU-50 | MS-60 | MS-63 |
|---|---|---|---|---|---|---|---|---|---|
| 1818, 2nd 8 Over 7 . . . . . . . * | | $60 | $70 | $110 | $160 | $450 | $950 | $2,500 | $5,500 |
| 1818 . . . . . . . . . . . 1,960,322 | | 45 | 55 | 70 | 115 | 250 | 475 | 1,450 | 3,000 |
| 1819, 9 Over 8 . . . . . . . . . . * | | 55 | 60 | 75 | 120 | 300 | 425 | 1,700 | 6,000 |
| 1819 . . . . . . . . . . . 2,208,000 | | 45 | 55 | 75 | 130 | 225 | 425 | 1,500 | 3,250 |
| 1820, 20 Over 19 . . . . . . . . * | | 65 | 90 | 110 | 180 | 600 | 850 | 4,000 | 8,500 |
| 1820 . . . . . . . . . . . 751,122 | | 55 | 80 | 110 | 160 | 375 | 675 | 2,500 | 5,250 |
| 1821 . . . . . . . . . . . 1,305,797 | | 55 | 60 | 70 | 110 | 250 | 400 | 1,250 | 2,500 |
| 1822 . . . . . . . . . . . 1,559,573 | | 45 | 55 | 70 | 110 | 250 | 350 | 1,100 | 1,550 |
| 1823 . . . . . . . . . . . 1,694,200 | | 45 | 55 | 70 | 100 | 200 | 400 | 1,000 | 2,000 |

\* Included in number below.

"Various Dates"
*Probably 4 Over
2 Over 0.*

1824, 4 Over 1

1828, Curl Base,
Knob 2

1828, Square
Base 2

| | Mintage | G-4 | VG-8 | F-12 | VF-20 | EF-40 | AU-50 | MS-60 | MS-63 |
|---|---|---|---|---|---|---|---|---|---|
| 1824, All kinds. . . . . . . . . . . 3,504,954 | | | | | | | | | |
| 1824, 4 Over Various Dates . . . . . . . . | | $55 | $65 | $90 | $115 | $325 | $850 | $2,400 | $4,250 |
| 1824, 4 Over 1 . . . . . . . . . . . . . . . . | | 65 | 90 | 110 | 125 | 250 | 425 | 1,750 | 5,000 |
| 1824 . . . . . . . . . . . . . . . . . . . . . . | | 45 | 50 | 60 | 65 | 125 | 240 | 900 | 1,600 |
| 1825 . . . . . . . . . . . . . . . . . . . 2,943,166 | | 45 | 50 | 60 | 65 | 125 | 240 | 675 | 1,250 |
| 1826 . . . . . . . . . . . . . . . . . . . 4,004,180 | | 45 | 50 | 60 | 65 | 125 | 240 | 675 | 1,450 |
| 1827, All kinds. . . . . . . . . . . . 5,493,400 | | | | | | | | | |
| 1827, 7 Over 6 . . . . . . . . . . . . . . . . | | 70 | 90 | 110 | 140 | 300 | 500 | 1,450 | 3,000 |
| 1827 . . . . . . . . . . . . . . . . . . . . . . | | 45 | 50 | 60 | 70 | 140 | 250 | 675 | 1,500 |
| 1828, All kinds. . . . . . . . . . . . 3,075,200 | | | | | | | | | |
| 1828, Curl Base No Knob 2 . . . . . . . . | | 45 | 50 | 60 | 70 | 125 | 250 | 900 | 1,800 |
| 1828, Curl Base Knob 2. . . . . . . . . . | | 50 | 60 | 85 | 115 | 180 | 450 | 1,650 | 3,000 |
| 1828, Square Base 2. . . . . . . . . . . . | | 45 | 50 | 60 | 70 | 140 | 250 | 825 | 1,600 |
| 1829, 9 Over 7 . . . . . . . . . . . . . . . . . * | | 50 | 60 | 90 | 125 | 250 | 500 | 1,100 | 2,500 |
| 1829 . . . . . . . . . . . . . . . . . . . 3,712,156 | | 45 | 50 | 60 | 70 | 125 | 225 | 650 | 1,200 |
| 1830 . . . . . . . . . . . . . . . . . . . 4,764,800 | | 45 | 50 | 60 | 70 | 125 | 225 | 650 | 1,200 |
| 1831 . . . . . . . . . . . . . . . . . . . 5,873,660 | | 45 | 50 | 60 | 70 | 125 | 225 | 650 | 1,200 |
| 1832 . . . . . . . . . . . . . . . . . . . 4,797,000 | | 45 | 50 | 60 | 70 | 125 | 225 | 650 | 1,200 |
| 1833 . . . . . . . . . . . . . . . . . . . 5,206,000 | | 45 | 50 | 60 | 70 | 125 | 225 | 650 | 1,200 |
| 1834 . . . . . . . . . . . . . . . . . . . 6,412,004 | | 45 | 50 | 60 | 70 | 125 | 225 | 650 | 1,200 |
| 1835 . . . . . . . . . . . . . . . . . . . 5,352,006 | | 45 | 50 | 60 | 70 | 125 | 225 | 650 | 1,200 |
| 1836 . . . . . . . . . . . . . . . . . . . 6,545,000 | | 45 | 50 | 60 | 70 | 125 | 225 | 650 | 1,200 |
| 1836, 50 Over 00 . . . . . . . . . . . . . . ** | | 90 | 110 | 150 | 240 | 325 | 550 | 2,000 | 3,500 |

\* Included in number below.    \*\* Included in number above.

# CAPPED BUST, REEDED EDGE (1836–1839)

**G-4 Good:** LIBERTY barely discernible on headband.
**VG-8 Very Good:** Some letters in LIBERTY clear.
**F-12 Fine:** LIBERTY complete but faint.
**VF-20 Very Fine:** LIBERTY sharp. Shoulder clasp clear.
**EF-40 Extremely Fine:** LIBERTY sharp and strong. Hair details visible.
**AU-50 About Uncirculated:** Slight trace of wear on cap, cheek, and hair above forehead, and on eagle's claws, wing tops, and head.
**MS-60 Uncirculated:** No trace of wear. Light blemishes.
**MS-63 Choice Uncirculated:** Some distracting marks or blemishes in focal areas. Impaired luster possible.

## Reverse 50 CENTS (1836–1837)

| | Mintage | G-4 | VG-8 | F-12 | VF-20 | EF-40 | AU-50 | MS-60 | MS-63 |
|---|---|---|---|---|---|---|---|---|---|
| 1836 . . . . . . . . . . . . . | *1,200+* | $800 | $1,000 | $1,450 | $1,800 | $2,750 | $4,000 | $7,000 | $15,000 |
| 1837 . . . . . . . . . . | 3,629,820 | 50 | 55 | 65 | 90 | 150 | 325 | 825 | 2,000 |

## Reverse HALF DOL. (1838–1839)

On half dollars of 1838 and 1839, the mintmark appears on the obverse; on those thereafter, through 1915, it is on the reverse.

| | Mintage | G-4 | VG-8 | F-12 | VF-20 | EF-40 | AU-50 | MS-60 | MS-63 |
|---|---|---|---|---|---|---|---|---|---|
| 1838 . . . . . . . . . . . | 3,546,000 | $50 | $55 | $65 | $90 | $150 | $325 | $825 | $2,000 |
| 1838O . . . . . . . . . . . . . . . | *20* | | | | | 250,000 | 300,000 | 350,000 | |
| 1839 . . . . . . . . . . | 1,392,976 | 50 | 55 | 65 | 95 | 190 | 375 | 1,050 | 2,500 |
| 1839O . . . . . . . . . . | 116,000 | 300 | 500 | 725 | 950 | 1,250 | 1,850 | 5,500 | 10,500 |

# LIBERTY SEATED (1839–1891)

**G-4 Good:** Scant rim. LIBERTY on shield worn off. Date and letters legible.
**VG-8 Very Good:** Rim fairly defined. Some letters in LIBERTY evident.
**F-12 Fine:** LIBERTY complete, but weak.
**VF-20 Very Fine:** LIBERTY mostly sharp.
**EF-40 Extremely Fine:** LIBERTY entirely sharp. Scroll edges and clasp distinct.
**AU-50 About Uncirculated:** Slight wear on Liberty's breast and knees; eagle's head, claws, and wing tops.
**MS-60 Uncirculated:** No trace of wear. Light blemishes.
**MS-63 Choice Uncirculated:** Some distracting blemishes in prime focal areas. Impaired luster possible.
**PF-63 Choice Proof:** Reflective surfaces with only a few blemishes in secondary focal places. No major flaws.

127

## Variety 1 – No Motto Above Eagle (1839–1853)

1842, Small Date

1842, Medium Date

No Drapery
From Elbow

Drapery
From Elbow
(Starting 1839)

| | Mintage | G-4 | VG-8 | F-12 | VF-20 | EF-40 | AU-50 | MS-60 | MS-63 |
|---|---|---|---|---|---|---|---|---|---|
| 1839, No Drapery From Elbow.....* | | $90 | $180 | $300 | $500 | $1,000 | $2,000 | $5,250 | $20,000 |
| 1839, Drapery .........1,972,400 | | 32 | 50 | 60 | 85 | 175 | 375 | 1,000 | 1,800 |
| 1840 ................1,435,008 | | 50 | 75 | 90 | 110 | 200 | 300 | 675 | 1,250 |
| 18400 ................ 855,100 | | 40 | 50 | 70 | 125 | 225 | 325 | 1,600 | 4,000 |
| 1841 ................ 310,000 | | 50 | 65 | 85 | 125 | 275 | 500 | 1,050 | 2,000 |
| 18410 ................ 401,000 | | 50 | 65 | 85 | 110 | 250 | 500 | 950 | 2,500 |
| 1842, Small Date.......2,012,764 | | 50 | 60 | 75 | 95 | 175 | 350 | 1,100 | 2,500 |
| 1842, Medium Date............** | | 40 | 55 | 65 | 90 | 150 | 325 | 800 | 1,650 |
| 18420, Small Date ....... 957,000 | | 600 | 850 | 1,150 | 1,500 | 2,500 | 5,000 | 11,500 | 22,500 |
| 18420, Medium Date...........** | | 40 | 50 | 65 | 90 | 150 | 325 | 850 | 1,650 |
| 1843 ................3,844,000 | | 35 | 40 | 50 | 65 | 125 | 200 | 675 | 1,500 |
| 18430 ................2,268,000 | | 45 | 55 | 65 | 75 | 160 | 325 | 1,050 | 2,500 |
| 1844 ................1,766,000 | | 35 | 40 | 50 | 80 | 125 | 225 | 525 | 1,150 |
| 18440 ................2,005,000 | | 35 | 40 | 60 | 90 | 190 | 300 | 1,000 | 2,250 |
| 1845 ................ 589,000 | | 35 | 50 | 60 | 100 | 160 | 450 | 900 | 2,750 |
| 18450 ................2,094,000 | | 35 | 50 | 60 | 90 | 140 | 325 | 725 | 2,500 |
| 1846 ................2,210,000 | | 35 | 40 | 50 | 65 | 130 | 325 | 725 | 1,200 |
| 1846, 6 Over Horizontal 6 .......** | | 180 | 260 | 400 | 750 | 1,350 | 2,000 | 3,500 | 6,500 |
| 18460 ................2,304,000 | | 35 | 45 | 70 | 110 | 180 | 325 | 1,150 | 3,500 |
| 1847 ................1,156,000 | | 35 | 40 | 50 | 80 | 110 | 150 | 500 | 1,450 |
| 18470 ................2,584,000 | | 35 | 40 | 50 | 70 | 125 | 350 | 800 | 2,000 |
| 1848 ................ 580,000 | | 35 | 40 | 90 | 140 | 240 | 500 | 900 | 2,000 |
| 18480 ................3,180,000 | | 35 | 40 | 50 | 90 | 175 | 350 | 1,050 | 1,500 |
| 1849 ................1,252,000 | | 35 | 55 | 60 | 90 | 125 | 275 | 700 | 1,650 |
| 18490 ................2,310,000 | | 35 | 50 | 55 | 70 | 250 | 500 | 925 | 2,000 |
| 1850 ................ 227,000 | | 300 | 400 | 500 | 600 | 725 | 950 | 1,500 | 2,850 |
| 18500 ................2,456,000 | | 35 | 40 | 50 | 80 | 150 | 250 | 725 | 1,450 |
| 1851 ................ 200,750 | | 600 | 675 | 800 | 1,000 | 1,500 | 1,850 | 2,650 | 3,500 |
| 18510 ................ 402,000 | | 50 | 75 | 110 | 125 | 375 | 650 | 1,050 | 2,500 |
| 1852 ................ 77,130 | | 350 | 450 | 525 | 750 | 1,150 | 1,650 | 2,500 | 3,250 |
| 18520 ................ 144,000 | | 250 | 375 | 450 | 600 | 850 | 1,300 | 2,850 | 8,000 |
| 18530 *(4 known)*. ............... | | | 140,000 | 225,000 | 300,000 | | | | |

* Included in number below.  **Included in number above.

## Variety 2 – Arrows at Date, Rays Around Eagle (1853)

| | Mintage | G-4 | VG-8 | F-12 | VF-20 | EF-40 | AU-50 | MS-60 | MS-63 |
|---|---|---|---|---|---|---|---|---|---|
| 1853 . . . . . . . . . . . | 3,532,708 | $40 | $60 | $70 | $100 | $180 | $375 | $1,000 | $2,000 |
| 1853O . . . . . . . . . . | 1,328,000 | 40 | 60 | 70 | 100 | 225 | 600 | 2,000 | 4,000 |

## Variety 3 – Arrows at Date, No Rays (1854–1855)

| | Mintage | G-4 | VG-8 | F-12 | VF-20 | EF-40 | AU-50 | MS-60 | MS-63 |
|---|---|---|---|---|---|---|---|---|---|
| 1854 . . . . . . . . . . . | 2,982,000 | $35 | $40 | $50 | $60 | $110 | $200 | $400 | $900 |
| 1854O . . . . . . . . . . | 5,240,000 | 35 | 40 | 50 | 60 | 110 | 200 | 400 | 900 |
| 1855, Over 1854 . . . . . . . . | * | 65 | 110 | 150 | 250 | 375 | 725 | 1,500 | 2,850 |
| 1855 . . . . . . . . . . . | 759,500 | 35 | 40 | 50 | 60 | 125 | 275 | 700 | 1,250 |
| 1855O . . . . . . . . . . | 3,688,000 | 35 | 40 | 50 | 60 | 115 | 200 | 400 | 900 |
| 1855S . . . . . . . . . . | 129,950 | 375 | 850 | 1,000 | 1,250 | 2,500 | 4,500 | 25,000 | 42,500 |

* Included in number below.

## Variety 1 Resumed, With Weight Standard of Variety 2 (1856–1866)

| | Mintage | G-4 | VG-8 | F-12 | VF-20 | EF-40 | AU-50 | MS-60 | MS-63 | PF-63 |
|---|---|---|---|---|---|---|---|---|---|---|
| 1856 . . . . . . . . . . . . . | 938,000 | $35 | $40 | $50 | $65 | $100 | $180 | $450 | $1,000 | |
| 1856O . . . . . . . . . . . | 2,658,000 | 35 | 40 | 50 | 65 | 100 | 210 | 375 | 775 | |
| 1856S . . . . . . . . . . . | 211,000 | 110 | 140 | 250 | 400 | 850 | 1,500 | 4,000 | 10,000 | |
| 1857 . . . . . . . . . . . . | 1,988,000 | 35 | 40 | 50 | 65 | 100 | 180 | 350 | 775 | |
| 1857O . . . . . . . . . . . . | 818,000 | 35 | 40 | 50 | 65 | 140 | 300 | 1,100 | 2,500 | |
| 1857S . . . . . . . . . . . | 158,000 | 140 | 180 | 250 | 350 | 900 | 1,450 | 2,750 | 7,000 | |
| 1858 . . . . . . (300+). . | 4,225,700 | 35 | 40 | 50 | 65 | 100 | 180 | 350 | 750 | $1,350 |
| 1858O . . . . . . . . . . . | 7,294,000 | 35 | 40 | 50 | 65 | 110 | 185 | 350 | 1,000 | |
| 1858S . . . . . . . . . . . | 476,000 | 40 | 60 | 90 | 160 | 250 | 450 | 1,500 | 3,250 | |
| 1859 . . . . . . (800). . . . | 747,200 | 35 | 40 | 50 | 65 | 100 | 180 | 325 | 750 | 1,350 |
| 1859O . . . . . . . . . . . | 2,834,000 | 35 | 50 | 55 | 70 | 110 | 210 | 500 | 1,450 | |
| 1859S . . . . . . . . . . . | 566,000 | 45 | 60 | 70 | 125 | 200 | 450 | 1,000 | 2,750 | |
| 1860 . . . . (1,000). . . . . | 302,700 | 35 | 40 | 50 | 65 | 125 | 250 | 450 | 750 | 1,000 |
| 1860O . . . . . . . . . . . | 1,290,000 | 35 | 40 | 50 | 75 | 130 | 210 | 500 | 800 | |
| 1860S . . . . . . . . . . . | 472,000 | 45 | 65 | 90 | 100 | 225 | 350 | 1,250 | 3,750 | |
| 1861 . . . . . (1,000). . . . | 2,887,400 | 35 | 40 | 50 | 65 | 100 | 225 | 400 | 775 | 1,000 |
| 1861O . . . . . . . . . . . | 2,532,633 | 50 | 70 | 90 | 125 | 225 | 350 | 700 | 1,850 | |
| 1861S . . . . . . . . . . . | 939,500 | 40 | 50 | 70 | 90 | 300 | 525 | 900 | 2,500 | |
| 1862 . . . . . . (550). . . . | 253,000 | 55 | 75 | 100 | 150 | 250 | 550 | 850 | 1,350 | 1,000 |
| 1862S . . . . . . . . . . . | 1,352,000 | 45 | 60 | 65 | 110 | 180 | 325 | 950 | 1,950 | |
| 1863 . . . . . (460). . . . . | 503,200 | 50 | 80 | 110 | 180 | 275 | 500 | 675 | 1,050 | 1,000 |
| 1863S . . . . . . . . . . . | 916,000 | 45 | 60 | 85 | 120 | 225 | 350 | 1,000 | 1,500 | |
| 1864 . . . . . (470). . . . . | 379,100 | 50 | 80 | 110 | 250 | 375 | 600 | 1,200 | 1,750 | 1,000 |
| 1864S . . . . . . . . . . . | 658,000 | 65 | 100 | 140 | 180 | 350 | 550 | 1,500 | 3,750 | |
| 1865 . . . . . (500). . . . . | 511,400 | 80 | 90 | 120 | 200 | 500 | 900 | 1,750 | 2,000 | 1,000 |
| 1865S . . . . . . . . . . . | 675,000 | 90 | 110 | 140 | 190 | 425 | 600 | 1,800 | 3,000 | |
| 1866S, No Motto . . . . . . . | 60,000 | 500 | 600 | 700 | 850 | 1,600 | 2,000 | 7,000 | 11,500 | |

## Variety 4 – Motto Above Eagle (1866–1873)

| | Mintage | G-4 | VG-8 | F-12 | VF-20 | EF-40 | AU-50 | MS-60 | MS-63 | PF-63 |
|---|---|---|---|---|---|---|---|---|---|---|
| 1866 . . . . . . (725) . . . . . . 744,900 | | $45 | $55 | $60 | $80 | $140 | $225 | $550 | $1,500 | $900 |
| 1866S . . . . . . . . . . . . . . 994,000 | | 50 | 60 | 75 | 125 | 190 | 325 | 950 | 2,200 | |
| 1867 . . . . . . (625) . . . . . . 449,300 | | 55 | 75 | 110 | 175 | 250 | 400 | 750 | 1,100 | 900 |
| 1867S . . . . . . . . . . . . . 1,196,000 | | 45 | 55 | 75 | 100 | 180 | 400 | 1,350 | 2,500 | |
| 1868 . . . . . . (600) . . . . . . 417,600 | | 60 | 75 | 90 | 140 | 225 | 400 | 700 | 1,450 | 900 |
| 1868S . . . . . . . . . . . . . 1,160,000 | | 40 | 45 | 60 | 100 | 180 | 275 | 950 | 2,250 | |
| 1869 . . . . . . (600) . . . . . . 795,300 | | 45 | 55 | 65 | 75 | 150 | 250 | 525 | 1,000 | 900 |
| 1869S . . . . . . . . . . . . . . 656,000 | | 50 | 60 | 70 | 80 | 180 | 350 | 900 | 2,250 | |
| 1870 . . . . (1,000) . . . . . . 633,900 | | 35 | 45 | 55 | 70 | 140 | 275 | 525 | 1,150 | 900 |
| 1870CC . . . . . . . . . . . . . . 54,617 | | 1,100 | 2,200 | 3,500 | 4,500 | 7,000 | 22,500 | — | — | |
| 1870S . . . . . . . . . . . . . 1,004,000 | | 50 | 70 | 90 | 125 | 325 | 500 | 1,800 | 3,000 | |
| 1871 . . . . . . (960) . . . . 1,203,600 | | 35 | 40 | 50 | 65 | 110 | 200 | 525 | 1,000 | 900 |
| 1871CC . . . . . . . . . . . . . 153,950 | | 400 | 625 | 800 | 1,350 | 2,250 | 3,750 | 22,500 | 37,500 | |
| 1871S . . . . . . . . . . . . . 2,178,000 | | 35 | 40 | 50 | 60 | 130 | 200 | 700 | 1,650 | |
| 1872 . . . . . . (950) . . . . . . 880,600 | | 35 | 40 | 50 | 60 | 125 | 200 | 575 | 1,000 | 900 |
| 1872CC . . . . . . . . . . . . . 257,000 | | 200 | 350 | 550 | 800 | 1,500 | 2,750 | 18,000 | 50,000 | |
| 1872S . . . . . . . . . . . . . . 580,000 | | 35 | 45 | 75 | 130 | 225 | 450 | 1,450 | 2,750 | |
| 1873 . . . . . . (600) . . . . . . 801,200 | | 35 | 45 | 55 | 90 | 125 | 225 | 675 | 1,150 | 825 |
| 1873CC . . . . . . . . . . . . . 122,500 | | 275 | 450 | 800 | 1,450 | 2,500 | 4,500 | 9,500 | 25,000 | |

## Variety 5 – Arrows at Date (1873–1874)

| | Mintage | G-4 | VG-8 | F-12 | VF-20 | EF-40 | AU-50 | MS-60 | MS-63 | PF-63 |
|---|---|---|---|---|---|---|---|---|---|---|
| 1873 . . . . . . (800) . . . . 1,815,200 | | $35 | $40 | $50 | $70 | $160 | $300 | $650 | $1,250 | $1,500 |
| 1873CC . . . . . . . . . . . . . 214,560 | | 190 | 350 | 450 | 750 | 1,500 | 2,500 | 6,500 | 12,000 | |
| 1873S . . . . . . . . . . . . . . 228,000 | | 55 | 110 | 150 | 180 | 450 | 550 | 2,250 | 6,000 | |
| 1874 . . . . . . (700) . . . . 2,359,600 | | 35 | 40 | 55 | 70 | 160 | 300 | 650 | 1,250 | 1,500 |
| 1874CC . . . . . . . . . . . . . . 59,000 | | 850 | 1,200 | 1,800 | 2,500 | 4,000 | 6,000 | 11,500 | 27,500 | |
| 1874S . . . . . . . . . . . . . . 394,000 | | 65 | 130 | 150 | 175 | 275 | 500 | 1,200 | 2,000 | |

## Variety 4 Resumed, With Weight Standard of Variety 5 (1875–1891)

| | Mintage | G-4 | VG-8 | F-12 | VF-20 | EF-40 | AU-50 | MS-60 | MS-63 | PF-63 |
|---|---|---|---|---|---|---|---|---|---|---|
| 1875 . . . . . . (700) . . . . | 6,026,800 | $35 | $40 | $50 | $65 | $90 | $150 | $300 | $600 | $800 |
| 1875CC . . . . . . . . . . . . | 1,008,000 | 55 | 90 | 150 | 225 | 400 | 700 | 1,350 | 2,250 | |
| 1875S . . . . . . . . . . . . . | 3,200,000 | 35 | 40 | 50 | 60 | 90 | 150 | 300 | 600 | |
| 1876 . . . . (1,150) . . . . | 8,418,000 | 35 | 40 | 50 | 60 | 90 | 150 | 300 | 600 | 800 |
| 1876CC . . . . . . . . . . . | 1,956,000 | 60 | 70 | 110 | 180 | 350 | 600 | 900 | 1,800 | |
| 1876S . . . . . . . . . . . . | 4,528,000 | 35 | 40 | 50 | 60 | 90 | 150 | 300 | 600 | |
| 1877 . . . . . . (510) . . . . | 8,304,000 | 35 | 40 | 50 | 60 | 90 | 150 | 300 | 600 | 800 |
| 1877CC . . . . . . . . . . . | 1,420,000 | 60 | 70 | 95 | 160 | 275 | 350 | 1,000 | 1,850 | |
| 1877S . . . . . . . . . . . . | 5,356,000 | 35 | 40 | 50 | 60 | 90 | 150 | 300 | 600 | |
| 1878 . . . . . . (800) . . . . | 1,377,600 | 45 | 70 | 85 | 95 | 140 | 200 | 350 | 900 | 800 |
| 1878CC . . . . . . . . . . . . . | 62,000 | 900 | 1,250 | 1,750 | 2,000 | 2,850 | 3,250 | 9,000 | 16,000 | |
| 1878S . . . . . . . . . . . . . . . | 12,000 | 22,500 | 30,000 | 35,000 | 42,500 | 57,500 | 62,500 | 75,000 | 110,000 | |
| 1879 . . . . (1,100) . . . . . . . . | 4,800 | 200 | 250 | 300 | 375 | 575 | 675 | 850 | 1,000 | 800 |
| 1880 . . . . (1,355) . . . . . . . . | 8,400 | 225 | 350 | 425 | 500 | 650 | 725 | 850 | 1,150 | 800 |
| 1881 . . . . . . (975) . . . . . . . | 10,000 | 225 | 250 | 325 | 400 | 600 | 700 | 850 | 1,250 | 800 |
| 1882 . . . . (1,100) . . . . . . . . | 4,400 | 225 | 250 | 325 | 400 | 600 | 700 | 850 | 1,100 | 800 |
| 1883 . . . . (1,039) . . . . . . . . | 8,000 | 225 | 250 | 325 | 400 | 600 | 700 | 850 | 1,250 | 800 |
| 1884 . . . . . . (875) . . . . . . . . | 4,400 | 240 | 275 | 325 | 400 | 600 | 700 | 850 | 1,200 | 800 |
| 1885 . . . . . . (930) . . . . . . . . | 5,200 | 250 | 275 | 325 | 400 | 600 | 700 | 850 | 1,450 | 800 |
| 1886 . . . . . . (886) . . . . . . . . | 5,000 | 275 | 350 | 350 | 400 | 600 | 725 | 850 | 1,100 | 800 |
| 1887 . . . . . . (710) . . . . . . . . | 5,000 | 350 | 400 | 425 | 475 | 600 | 700 | 850 | 1,450 | 800 |
| 1888 . . . . . . (832) . . . . . . . | 12,001 | 200 | 250 | 325 | 375 | 600 | 700 | 850 | 1,000 | 800 |
| 1889 . . . . . . (711) . . . . . . . | 12,000 | 180 | 250 | 325 | 375 | 625 | 725 | 900 | 1,750 | 900 |
| 1890 . . . . . . (590) . . . . . . . | 12,000 | 180 | 250 | 325 | 375 | 500 | 700 | 850 | 1,000 | 800 |
| 1891 . . . . . . (600) . . . . . . | 200,000 | 40 | 60 | 100 | 110 | 160 | 250 | 350 | 900 | 800 |

## BARBER OR LIBERTY HEAD (1892–1915)

Like the dime and quarter dollar, this type was designed by U.S. Mint chief engraver Charles E. Barber, whose initial B is on the truncation of the neck.

**G-4 Good:** Date and legends legible. LIBERTY worn off headband.

**VG-8 Very Good:** Some letters legible in LIBERTY.

**F-12 Fine:** LIBERTY nearly completely legible, but worn.

**VF-20 Very Fine:** All letters in LIBERTY evenly plain.

**EF-40 Extremely Fine:** LIBERTY bold, and its ribbon distinct.

**AU-50 About Uncirculated:** Slight trace of wear above forehead, leaf tips, and cheek, and on eagle's head, tail, and wing tips.

**MS-60 Uncirculated:** No trace of wear. Light blemishes.

**MS-63 Choice Uncirculated:** Some distracting contact marks or blemishes in prime focal areas. Impaired luster possible.

**PF-63 Choice Proof:** Reflective surfaces with only a few blemishes in secondary focal places. No major flaws.

*Mintmark location on reverse, below eagle.*

| | Mintage | G-4 | VG-8 | F-12 | VF-20 | EF-40 | AU-50 | MS-60 | MS-63 | PF-63 |
|---|---|---|---|---|---|---|---|---|---|---|
| 1892 . . . . (1,245) . . . . . . | 934,000 | $15 | $20 | $40 | $75 | $125 | $225 | $400 | $600 | $750 |
| 1892O . . . . . . . . . . . . . . | 390,000 | 200 | 300 | 400 | 450 | 500 | 600 | 750 | 1,250 | |

*Chart continued on next page.*

| | Mintage | G-4 | VG-8 | F-12 | VF-20 | EF-40 | AU-50 | MS-60 | MS-63 | PF-63 |
|---|---|---|---|---|---|---|---|---|---|---|
| 1892S . . . . . . . . . . . . | 1,029,028 | $175 | $225 | $250 | $400 | $500 | $650 | $850 | $1,350 | |
| 1893 . . . . . . (792) . . . . | 1,826,000 | 15 | 20 | 55 | 100 | 150 | 225 | 400 | 750 | $750 |
| 1893O . . . . . . . . . . . . | 1,389,000 | 25 | 45 | 85 | 150 | 250 | 300 | 600 | 800 | |
| 1893S . . . . . . . . . . . . . | 740,000 | 100 | 165 | 350 | 500 | 850 | 1,100 | 1,500 | 3,000 | |
| 1894 . . . . . . (972) . . . . | 1,148,000 | 15 | 25 | 60 | 120 | 160 | 225 | 400 | 650 | 750 |
| 1894O . . . . . . . . . . . . | 2,138,000 | 13 | 20 | 50 | 125 | 225 | 275 | 400 | 750 | |
| 1894S . . . . . . . . . . . . | 4,048,690 | 13 | 20 | 40 | 75 | 135 | 225 | 450 | 1,000 | |
| 1895 . . . . . . (880) . . . . | 1,834,338 | 13 | 15 | 40 | 75 | 125 | 225 | 400 | 650 | 750 |
| 1895O . . . . . . . . . . . . | 1,766,000 | 20 | 35 | 70 | 125 | 175 | 250 | 500 | 1,100 | |
| 1895S . . . . . . . . . . . . | 1,108,086 | 20 | 45 | 100 | 150 | 200 | 275 | 425 | 850 | |
| 1896 . . . . . . (762) . . . . . . | 950,000 | 20 | 25 | 55 | 100 | 150 | 225 | 450 | 700 | 750 |
| 1896O . . . . . . . . . . . . . | 924,000 | 20 | 25 | 125 | 300 | 1,250 | 2,250 | 4,000 | 8,000 | |
| 1896S . . . . . . . . . . . . | 1,140,948 | 45 | 60 | 115 | 350 | 750 | 1,000 | 1,650 | 2,500 | |
| 1897 . . . . . . (731) . . . | 2,480,000 | 13 | 15 | 30 | 70 | 125 | 225 | 400 | 650 | 750 |
| 1897O . . . . . . . . . . . . . | 632,000 | 85 | 110 | 300 | 500 | 700 | 850 | 1,500 | 3,000 | |
| 1897S . . . . . . . . . . . . . | 933,900 | 90 | 145 | 250 | 400 | 750 | 1,000 | 2,000 | 2,750 | |
| 1898 . . . . . . (735) . . . | 2,956,000 | 13 | 15 | 30 | 70 | 125 | 225 | 400 | 600 | 750 |
| 1898O . . . . . . . . . . . . . | 874,000 | 20 | 65 | 145 | 250 | 400 | 550 | 1,000 | 1,850 | |
| 1898S . . . . . . . . . . . . | 2,358,550 | 15 | 20 | 55 | 100 | 225 | 350 | 1,000 | 1,750 | |
| 1899 . . . . . . (846) . . . | 5,538,000 | 13 | 15 | 30 | 70 | 140 | 225 | 400 | 600 | 750 |
| 1899O . . . . . . . . . . . . | 1,724,000 | 13 | 20 | 40 | 115 | 200 | 300 | 650 | 1,100 | |
| 1899S . . . . . . . . . . . . | 1,686,411 | 13 | 20 | 50 | 100 | 135 | 275 | 550 | 1,500 | |
| 1900 . . . . . . (912) . . . | 4,762,000 | 9 | 11 | 30 | 70 | 125 | 225 | 400 | 650 | 750 |
| 1900O . . . . . . . . . . . . | 2,744,000 | 9 | 11 | 45 | 125 | 225 | 325 | 900 | 2,000 | |
| 1900S . . . . . . . . . . . . | 2,560,322 | 9 | 11 | 35 | 75 | 175 | 225 | 550 | 1,500 | |
| 1901 . . . . . . (813) . . . | 4,268,000 | 9 | 11 | 30 | 70 | 125 | 225 | 400 | 600 | 750 |
| 1901O . . . . . . . . . . . . | 1,124,000 | 9 | 15 | 40 | 150 | 850 | 1,100 | 1,650 | 3,000 | |
| 1901S . . . . . . . . . . . . . | 847,044 | 9 | 30 | 100 | 250 | 950 | 1,350 | 2,500 | 5,000 | |
| 1902 . . . . . . (777) . . . | 4,922,000 | 9 | 11 | 30 | 70 | 125 | 225 | 400 | 600 | 750 |
| 1902O . . . . . . . . . . . . | 2,526,000 | 9 | 11 | 30 | 70 | 125 | 325 | 600 | 1,500 | |
| 1902S . . . . . . . . . . . . | 1,460,670 | 9 | 11 | 30 | 90 | 175 | 225 | 1,000 | 2,000 | |
| 1903 . . . . . . (755) . . . | 2,278,000 | 9 | 11 | 30 | 70 | 125 | 225 | 400 | 850 | 750 |
| 1903O . . . . . . . . . . . . | 2,100,000 | 9 | 11 | 30 | 70 | 125 | 225 | 500 | 1,100 | |
| 1903S . . . . . . . . . . . . | 1,920,772 | 9 | 11 | 30 | 75 | 150 | 300 | 650 | 1,250 | |
| 1904 . . . . . . (670) . . . | 2,992,000 | 9 | 11 | 30 | 70 | 125 | 225 | 400 | 600 | 750 |
| 1904O . . . . . . . . . . . . | 1,117,600 | 10 | 12 | 45 | 125 | 325 | 550 | 1,100 | 2,500 | |
| 1904S . . . . . . . . . . . . . | 553,038 | 40 | 100 | 275 | 650 | 1,650 | 4,500 | 9,500 | 13,500 | |
| 1905 . . . . . . (727) . . . . . . | 662,000 | 10 | 12 | 50 | 110 | 150 | 225 | 500 | 900 | 750 |
| 1905O . . . . . . . . . . . . . | 505,000 | 10 | 20 | 60 | 125 | 200 | 225 | 650 | 1,250 | |
| 1905S . . . . . . . . . . . . | 2,494,000 | 9 | 11 | 30 | 75 | 125 | 225 | 500 | 1,100 | |
| 1906 . . . . . . (675) . . . | 2,638,000 | 9 | 11 | 30 | 70 | 125 | 225 | 400 | 600 | 750 |
| 1906D . . . . . . . . . . . . | 4,028,000 | 9 | 11 | 30 | 70 | 125 | 225 | 400 | 600 | |
| 1906O . . . . . . . . . . . . | 2,446,000 | 9 | 11 | 30 | 70 | 125 | 225 | 600 | 1,000 | |
| 1906S . . . . . . . . . . . . | 1,740,154 | 9 | 11 | 30 | 70 | 125 | 225 | 500 | 1,000 | |
| 1907 . . . . . . (575) . . . | 2,598,000 | 9 | 11 | 30 | 70 | 125 | 225 | 400 | 600 | 750 |
| 1907D . . . . . . . . . . . . | 3,856,000 | 9 | 11 | 30 | 70 | 125 | 225 | 400 | 600 | |
| 1907O . . . . .* . . . . . . . | 3,946,600 | 9 | 11 | 30 | 70 | 125 | 225 | 400 | 600 | |
| 1907S . . . . . . . . . . . . | 1,250,000 | 9 | 20 | 40 | 100 | 225 | 425 | 1,500 | 3,750 | |
| 1908 . . . . . . (545) . . . | 1,354,000 | 9 | 11 | 30 | 70 | 125 | 225 | 400 | 600 | 750 |
| 1908D . . . . . . . . . . . . | 3,280,000 | 9 | 11 | 30 | 70 | 125 | 225 | 400 | 600 | |
| 1908O . . . . . . . . . . . . | 5,360,000 | 9 | 11 | 30 | 70 | 125 | 225 | 400 | 600 | |
| 1908S . . . . . . . . . . . . | 1,644,828 | 9 | 11 | 40 | 100 | 175 | 225 | 500 | 1,450 | |

| | Mintage | G-4 | VG-8 | F-12 | VF-20 | EF-40 | AU-50 | MS-60 | MS-63 | PF-63 |
|---|---|---|---|---|---|---|---|---|---|---|
| 1909 . . . . . (650). . . . | 2,368,000 | $9 | $11 | $30 | $70 | $125 | $225 | $400 | $600 | $750 |
| 19090 . . . . . . . . . . . . . | 925,400 | 9 | 11 | 40 | 110 | 250 | 475 | 900 | 1,100 | |
| 1909S . . . . . . . . . . . . | 1,764,000 | 9 | 11 | 35 | 70 | 125 | 225 | 400 | 950 | |
| 1910 . . . . . . (551). . . . . . | 418,000 | 10 | 15 | 45 | 110 | 200 | 225 | 500 | 900 | 750 |
| 1910S . . . . . . . . . . . . | 1,948,000 | 9 | 12 | 30 | 70 | 125 | 225 | 650 | 1,000 | |
| 1911 . . . . . . (543). . . . | 1,406,000 | 9 | 11 | 30 | 70 | 125 | 225 | 400 | 600 | 750 |
| 1911D . . . . . . . . . . . . . | 695,080 | 9 | 11 | 30 | 70 | 125 | 225 | 400 | 600 | |
| 1911S . . . . . . . . . . . . | 1,272,000 | 9 | 11 | 30 | 70 | 125 | 225 | 650 | 1,000 | |
| 1912 . . . . . . (700). . . . | 1,550,000 | 9 | 11 | 30 | 70 | 125 | 225 | 400 | 600 | 750 |
| 1912D . . . . . . . . . . . . | 2,300,800 | 9 | 11 | 30 | 70 | 125 | 225 | 400 | 600 | |
| 1912S . . . . . . . . . . . . | 1,370,000 | 9 | 11 | 30 | 70 | 125 | 225 | 400 | 750 | |
| 1913 . . . . . . (627). . . . . . | 188,000 | 40 | 50 | 125 | 275 | 400 | 525 | 1,250 | 1,650 | 750 |
| 1913D . . . . . . . . . . . . | 534,000 | 9 | 15 | 30 | 70 | 125 | 225 | 400 | 600 | |
| 1913S . . . . . . . . . . . . | 604,000 | 9 | 15 | 30 | 70 | 125 | 225 | 650 | 1,100 | |
| 1914 . . . . . . (380). . . . . . | 124,230 | 65 | 100 | 200 | 325 | 475 | 650 | 1,350 | 1,650 | 750 |
| 1914S . . . . . . . . . . . . | 992,000 | 9 | 11 | 30 | 70 | 125 | 225 | 500 | 800 | |
| 1915 . . . . . . (450). . . . . . | 138,000 | 50 | 75 | 185 | 225 | 350 | 550 | 1,000 | 2,000 | 750 |
| 1915D . . . . . . . . . . . . | 1,170,400 | 9 | 11 | 30 | 70 | 125 | 225 | 400 | 600 | |
| 1915S . . . . . . . . . . . . | 1,604,000 | 9 | 11 | 30 | 70 | 125 | 225 | 400 | 600 | |

# LIBERTY WALKING (1916–1947)

This type was designed by American sculptor Adolph A. Weinman, whose monogram, AW, appears under the tip of the tail feathers. On the 1916 coins and some of the 1917 coins, the mintmark is located on the obverse below the motto. A centennial gold issue was struck in 2016.

**G-4 Good:** Rims defined. Motto IN GOD WE TRUST legible.

**VG-8 Very Good:** Motto distinct. About half of skirt lines at left clear.

**F-12 Fine:** All skirt lines evident, but worn in spots. Clear details in sandal below motto.

**VF-20 Very Fine:** Skirt lines sharp, including leg area. Little wear on breast and right arm.

**EF-40 Extremely Fine:** All skirt lines bold.

**AU-50 About Uncirculated:** Slight trace of wear on Liberty's head, knee, and breast tips and on eagle's claws and head.

**MS-60 Uncirculated:** No trace of wear. Light blemishes.

**MS-63 Choice Uncirculated:** Some distracting contact marks or blemishes in prime focal areas. Impaired luster possible.

**PF-63 Choice Proof:** Reflective surfaces with only a few blemishes in secondary focal places. No major flaws.

**PF-65 Gem Proof:** Brilliant surfaces with no noticeable blemishes or flaws. A few scattered, barely noticeable marks or hairlines possible.

Mintmark
Locations

*1916–1917*          *1917–1947*

*Coin dealers often pay more than the Mint State prices shown for choice Uncirculated examples that are well struck.*

| | Mintage | G-4 | VG-8 | F-12 | VF-20 | EF-40 | AU-50 | MS-60 | MS-63 |
|---|---|---|---|---|---|---|---|---|---|
| 1916 . . . . . . . . . . . . . . . . . . . . . | 608,000 | $35.00 | $40 | $65 | $120 | $175 | $240 | $500 | $825 |
| 1916D, Obverse Mintmark. . . . | 1,014,400 | 32.00 | 45 | 65 | 100 | 175 | 200 | 500 | 700 |
| 1916S, Obverse Mintmark. . . . . . | 508,000 | 60.00 | 100 | 175 | 300 | 425 | 775 | 1,250 | 2,250 |
| 1917 . . . . . . . . . . . . . . . . . . | 12,292,000 | 9.50 | 10 | 14 | 16 | 28 | 50 | 110 | 180 |
| 1917D, Obverse Mintmark. . . . . . | 765,400 | 20.00 | 32 | 70 | 110 | 225 | 275 | 550 | 1,000 |

*Chart continued on next page.*

| | Mintage | G-4 | VG-8 | F-12 | VF-20 | EF-40 | AU-50 | MS-60 | MS-63 |
|---|---|---|---|---|---|---|---|---|---|
| 1917D, Reverse Mintmark.... | 1,940,000 | $13 | $18.00 | $35.00 | $90 | $210 | $375 | $875 | $1,250 |
| 1917S, Obverse Mintmark...... | 952,000 | 22 | 40.00 | 120.00 | 240 | 600 | 950 | 2,850 | 4,000 |
| 1917S, Reverse Mintmark.... | 5,554,000 | 9 | 10.00 | 16.00 | 30 | 85 | 180 | 600 | 1,000 |
| 1918................... | 6,634,000 | 9 | 10.00 | 18.00 | 50 | 80 | 200 | 450 | 950 |
| 1918D................. | 3,853,040 | 13 | 18.00 | 32.00 | 70 | 170 | 350 | 1,050 | 1,650 |
| 1918S................. | 10,282,000 | 9 | 14.00 | 18.00 | 26 | 65 | 150 | 450 | 975 |
| 1919................... | 962,000 | 22 | 27.00 | 60.00 | 190 | 425 | 800 | 2,250 | 2,750 |
| 1919D................. | 1,165,000 | 22 | 55.00 | 140.00 | 250 | 700 | 1,500 | 3,500 | 6,000 |
| 1919S................. | 1,552,000 | 14 | 27.00 | 55.00 | 240 | 650 | 1,450 | 3,250 | 6,000 |
| 1920.................. | 6,372,000 | 9 | 10.00 | 16.00 | 28 | 55 | 125 | 350 | 550 |
| 1920D................. | 1,551,000 | 13 | 18.00 | 45.00 | 200 | 525 | 1,050 | 2,250 | 4,250 |
| 1920S................. | 4,624,000 | 9 | 10.00 | 18.00 | 65 | 165 | 450 | 950 | 2,250 |
| 1921.................. | 246,000 | 80 | 135.00 | 250.00 | 475 | 1,500 | 2,650 | 4,500 | 5,500 |
| 1921D................. | 208,000 | 140 | 240.00 | 400.00 | 675 | 2,350 | 4,000 | 6,250 | 10,000 |
| 1921S................. | 548,000 | 60 | 90.00 | 160.00 | 550 | 2,750 | 6,000 | 15,000 | 27,500 |
| 1923S................. | 2,178,000 | 14 | 18.00 | 35.00 | 140 | 525 | 1,250 | 2,500 | 4,000 |
| 1927S................. | 2,392,000 | 9 | 10.00 | 13.00 | 45 | 200 | 525 | 1,100 | 1,900 |
| 1928S................. | 1,940,000 | 9 | 10.00 | 13.00 | 55 | 175 | 625 | 1,250 | 2,650 |
| 1929D................. | 1,001,200 | 9 | 10.00 | 13.00 | 30 | 65 | 130 | 400 | 800 |
| 1929S................. | 1,902,000 | 9 | 10.00 | 13.00 | 22 | 90 | 180 | 350 | 725 |
| 1933S................. | 1,786,000 | 10 | 10.50 | 14.00 | 25 | 55 | 175 | 525 | 900 |
| 1934.................. | 6,964,000 | 9 | 9.50 | 9.50 | 10 | 13 | 16 | 55 | 70 |
| 1934D................. | 2,361,000 | 9 | 9.50 | 10.00 | 14 | 22 | 55 | 100 | 210 |
| 1934S................. | 3,652,000 | 9 | 9.50 | 9.50 | 10 | 32 | 65 | 250 | 600 |
| 1935.................. | 9,162,000 | 9 | 9.50 | 9.50 | 10 | 22 | 30 | 40 | 60 |
| 1935D................. | 3,003,800 | 9 | 9.50 | 9.50 | 13 | 22 | 45 | 100 | 190 |
| 1935S................. | 3,854,000 | 9 | 9.50 | 9.50 | 10 | 26 | 70 | 240 | 400 |

| | Mintage | G-4 | VG-8 | F-12 | VF-20 | EF-40 | AU-50 | MS-60 | MS-63 | PF-63 | PF-65 |
|---|---|---|---|---|---|---|---|---|---|---|---|
| 1936... (3,901).. | 12,614,000 | $8.50 | $8.75 | $9 | $9.50 | $14 | $17 | $25 | $48 | $1,200 | $2,350 |
| 1936D.......... | 4,252,400 | 8.50 | 8.75 | 9 | 9.50 | 16 | 30 | 65 | 95 | | |
| 1936S.......... | 3,884,000 | 8.50 | 8.75 | 9 | 9.50 | 22 | 45 | 100 | 160 | | |
| 1937... (5,728).. | 9,522,000 | 8.50 | 8.75 | 9 | 9.50 | 14 | 17 | 30 | 45 | 375 | 600 |
| 1937D.......... | 1,676,000 | 8.50 | 8.75 | 9 | 14.00 | 32 | 70 | 160 | 200 | | |
| 1937S.......... | 2,090,000 | 8.50 | 8.75 | 9 | 9.50 | 18 | 45 | 115 | 145 | | |
| 1938... (8,152).. | 4,110,000 | 8.50 | 8.75 | 9 | 12.00 | 14 | 25 | 50 | 115 | 350 | 550 |
| 1938D.......... | 491,600 | 32.00 | 36.00 | 55 | 70.00 | 100 | 160 | 340 | 500 | | |
| 1939... (8,808).. | 6,812,000 | 8.50 | 8.75 | 9 | 9.50 | 12 | 22 | 40 | 55 | 325 | 500 |
| 1939D.......... | 4,267,800 | 8.50 | 8.75 | 9 | 9.50 | 13 | 17 | 34 | 55 | | |
| 1939S.......... | 2,552,000 | 8.50 | 8.75 | 9 | 9.50 | 18 | 55 | 100 | 120 | | |

| | Mintage | VG-8 | F-12 | VF-20 | EF-40 | AU-50 | MS-60 | MS-63 | PF-63 | PF-65 |
|---|---|---|---|---|---|---|---|---|---|---|
| 1940... (11,279).... | 9,156,000 | $8.75 | $9 | $9.50 | $10 | $18 | $25 | $40 | $325 | $450 |
| 1940S............ | 4,550,000 | 8.75 | 9 | 9.50 | 13 | 25 | 35 | 50 | | |
| 1941... (15,412)... | 24,192,000 | 8.75 | 9 | 9.50 | 10 | 12 | 25 | 40 | 280 | 360 |
| 1941D........... | 11,248,400 | 8.75 | 9 | 9.50 | 10 | 12 | 28 | 50 | | |
| 1941S............ | 8,098,000 | 8.75 | 9 | 9.50 | 11 | 20 | 55 | 75 | | |
| 1942... (21,120)... | 47,818,000 | 8.75 | 9 | 9.50 | 10 | 12 | 25 | 40 | 280 | 350 |

| | Mintage | VG-8 | F-12 | VF-20 | EF-40 | AU-50 | MS-60 | MS-63 |
|---|---|---|---|---|---|---|---|---|
| 1942D.............. | 10,973,800 | $8.75 | $9 | $9.50 | $10 | $12 | $28 | $60 |
| 1942S.............. | 12,708,000 | 8.75 | 9 | 9.50 | 10 | 18 | 28 | 55 |
| 1943............... | 53,190,000 | 8.75 | 9 | 9.50 | 10 | 13 | 30 | 55 |
| 1943D.............. | 11,346,000 | 8.75 | 9 | 9.50 | 10 | 16 | 30 | 55 |
| 1943S.............. | 13,450,000 | 8.75 | 9 | 9.50 | 10 | 18 | 30 | 45 |
| 1944............... | 28,206,000 | 8.75 | 9 | 9.50 | 10 | 12 | 25 | 40 |

| | Mintage | VG-8 | F-12 | VF-20 | EF-40 | AU-50 | MS-60 | MS-63 |
|---|---|---|---|---|---|---|---|---|
| 1944D | 9,769,000 | $8.75 | $9 | $9.50 | $10 | $16 | $28 | $45 |
| 1944S | 8,904,000 | 8.75 | 9 | 9.50 | 10 | 20 | 34 | 45 |
| 1945 | 31,502,000 | 8.75 | 9 | 9.50 | 10 | 12 | 25 | 40 |
| 1945D | 9,966,800 | 8.75 | 9 | 9.50 | 10 | 12 | 25 | 40 |
| 1945S | 10,156,000 | 8.75 | 9 | 9.50 | 10 | 20 | 25 | 45 |
| 1946 | 12,118,000 | 8.75 | 9 | 9.50 | 10 | 12 | 25 | 40 |
| 1946D | 2,151,000 | 8.75 | 9 | 9.50 | 14 | 23 | 25 | 40 |
| 1946S | 3,724,000 | 8.75 | 9 | 9.50 | 13 | 27 | 40 | 45 |
| 1947 | 4,094,000 | 8.75 | 9 | 9.50 | 13 | 16 | 35 | 40 |
| 1947D | 3,900,600 | 8.75 | 9 | 9.50 | 13 | 22 | 35 | 40 |

## FRANKLIN (1948–1963)

The Benjamin Franklin half dollar and the Roosevelt dime were both designed by U.S. Mint chief engraver John R. Sinnock. His initials appear below the shoulder.

**VF-20 Very Fine:** At least half of the lower and upper incused lines on rim of Liberty Bell on reverse visible.

**EF-40 Extremely Fine:** Wear spots at top of end of Franklin's curls and hair at back of ears. Wear evident at top and on lettering of Liberty Bell.

**MS-60 Uncirculated:** No trace of wear. Light blemishes.

**MS-63 Choice Uncirculated:** Some distracting contact marks or blemishes in prime focal areas. Impaired luster possible.

**MS-65 Gem Uncirculated:** Only light, scattered contact marks that are not distracting. Strong luster, good eye appeal.

**PF-63 Choice Proof:** Reflective surfaces with only a few blemishes in secondary focal places. No major flaws.

**PF-65 Gem Proof:** Brilliant surfaces with no noticeable blemishes or flaws. A few scattered, barely noticeable marks or hairlines possible.

**Mintmark Location**

*Coin dealers usually pay more than the Mint State prices shown for well-struck Uncirculated halves with full bell lines.*

| | Mintage | VF-20 | EF-40 | MS-60 | MS-63 | MS-65 | PF-63 | PF-65 |
|---|---|---|---|---|---|---|---|---|
| 1948 | 3,006,814 | $8.75 | $9 | $14.00 | $16.00 | $50 | | |
| 1948D | 4,028,600 | 8.75 | 9 | 13.00 | 15.00 | 65 | | |
| 1949 | 5,614,000 | 8.75 | 9 | 22.00 | 26.00 | 90 | | |
| 1949D | 4,120,600 | 8.75 | 9 | 34.00 | 35.00 | 180 | | |
| 1949S | 3,744,000 | 8.75 | 9 | 55.00 | 60.00 | 90 | | |
| 1950 (51,386) | 7,742,123 | 8.75 | 9 | 14.00 | 16.00 | 60 | $300 | $450 |
| 1950D | 8,031,600 | 8.75 | 9 | 18.00 | 22.00 | 125 | | |
| 1951 (57,500) | 16,802,102 | 8.75 | 9 | 10.00 | 11.00 | 35 | 225 | 290 |
| 1951D | 9,475,200 | 8.75 | 9 | 22.00 | 25.00 | 100 | | |
| 1951S | 13,696,000 | 8.75 | 9 | 15.00 | 18.00 | 40 | | |
| 1952 (81,980) | 21,192,093 | 8.75 | 9 | 10.00 | 11.00 | 35 | 130 | 180 |
| 1952D | 25,395,600 | 8.75 | 9 | 10.00 | 11.00 | 80 | | |
| 1952S | 5,526,000 | 8.75 | 9 | 37.50 | 42.50 | 75 | | |
| 1953 (128,800) | 2,668,120 | 8.75 | 9 | 10.00 | 16 | 50 | 95 | 135 |
| 1953D | 20,900,400 | 8.75 | 9 | 10.00 | 11 | 60 | | |
| 1953S | 4,148,000 | 8.75 | 9 | 20.00 | 22 | 34 | | |
| 1954 (233,300) | 13,188,202 | 8.75 | 9 | 10.00 | 11 | 28 | 45 | 65 |
| 1954D | 25,445,580 | 8.75 | 9 | 10.00 | 11 | 55 | | |
| 1954S | 4,993,400 | 8.75 | 9 | 12.00 | 14 | 22 | | |

*Chart continued on next page.*

| | Mintage | VF-20 | EF-40 | MS-60 | MS-63 | MS-65 | PF-63 | PF-65 |
|---|---|---|---|---|---|---|---|---|
| 1955 .... (378,200).... | 2,498,181 | $8.75 | $9 | $12 | $14 | $30 | $45 | $60 |
| 1956 .... (669,384).... | 4,032,000 | 8.75 | 9 | 10 | 11 | 22 | 22 | 25 |
| 1957 ...(1,247,952).... | 5,114,000 | 8.75 | 9 | 10 | 12 | 15 | 16 | 22 |
| 1957D ............. | 19,966,850 | 8.75 | 9 | 10 | 12 | 20 | | |
| 1958 .... (875,652).... | 4,042,000 | 8.75 | 9 | 10 | 12 | 15 | 20 | 24 |
| 1958D ............. | 23,962,412 | 8.75 | 9 | 10 | 12 | 15 | | |
| 1959 ...(1,149,291).... | 6,200,000 | 8.75 | 9 | 10 | 12 | 25 | 16 | 18 |
| 1959D ............. | 13,053,750 | 8.75 | 9 | 10 | 12 | 40 | | |
| 1960 ...(1,691,602).... | 6,024,000 | 8.75 | 9 | 10 | 12 | 45 | 16 | 18 |
| 1960D ............. | 18,215,812 | 8.75 | 9 | 10 | 12 | 100 | | |
| 1961 ...(3,028,244).... | 8,290,000 | 8.75 | 9 | 10 | 12 | 20 | 16 | 18 |
| 1961D ............. | 20,276,442 | 8.75 | 9 | 10 | 12 | 60 | | |
| 1962 ...(3,218,019).... | 9,714,000 | 8.75 | 9 | 10 | 12 | 40 | 16 | 18 |
| 1962D ............. | 35,473,281 | 8.75 | 9 | 10 | 12 | 35 | | |
| 1963 ...(3,075,645)... | 22,164,000 | 8.75 | 9 | 10 | 12 | 15 | 16 | 18 |
| 1963D ............. | 67,069,292 | 8.75 | 9 | 10 | 12 | 15 | | |

## KENNEDY (1964 TO DATE)

Gilroy Roberts, chief engraver of the U.S. Mint from 1948 to 1964, designed the obverse of this coin, a tribute to President John F. Kennedy, who was assassinated in November 1963. Roberts's stylized initials are on the truncation of the forceful bust of Kennedy. The reverse, which uses as its motif the eagle from the Seal of the President of the United States, is the work of assistant engraver Frank Gasparro. The Kennedy half dollar was minted in 90% silver in its first year of issue, 1964. From 1965 to 1970 its fineness was reduced to 40% silver. Since 1971 the coin has been struck in copper-nickel (except for certain silver Proofs, 1992 to date). Dates after 2001 have not been released into general circulation, instead being made available in 20-coin rolls, 200-coin bags, and coin sets sold by the Mint. In 2014 a .999 fine gold version was made for collectors, dual-dated 1964–2014 to mark the coin's 50th anniversary.

In the early 1970s an open contest was held to select a new reverse design for the Kennedy half dollar, to celebrate the nation's bicentennial. Seth G. Huntington's winning entry featured a view of Independence Hall in Philadelphia. The Bicentennial half dollars bear the dual date 1776–1976.

Mintmark Location (1964)

Mintmark Location (1968 to Date)

### Silver Coinage (1964)

| | Mintage | MS-63 | PF-63 | PF-65 |
|---|---|---|---|---|
| 1964 ................................... (3,950,762)..... | 273,304,004 | $9 | $10 | $13 |
| 1964D ................................................ | 156,205,446 | 9 | | |

## Silver Clad Coinage (1965–1970)

| | Mintage | MS-63 | PF-63 | PF-65 | | Mintage | MS-63 | PF-63 | PF-65 |
|---|---|---|---|---|---|---|---|---|---|
| 1965 | 65,879,366 | $4.75 | | | 1969D | 129,881,800 | $4.75 | | |
| 1966 | 108,984,932 | 4.75 | | | 1969S | (2,934,631) | | $3.50 | $4.50 |
| 1967 | 295,046,978 | 4.75 | | | 1970D | 2,150,000 | 12.00 | | |
| 1968D | 246,951,930 | 4.75 | | | 1970S | (2,632,810) | | 3.50 | 4.50 |
| 1968S | (3,041,506) | | $3 | $3.25 | | | | | |

## Clad Coinage and Silver Proofs (1971 to Date)

| | Mintage | MS-63 | PF-63 | PF-65 | | Mintage | MS-63 | PF-63 | PF-65 |
|---|---|---|---|---|---|---|---|---|---|
| 1971 | 155,164,000 | $0.75 | | | 1973 | 64,964,000 | $0.75 | | |
| 1971D | 302,097,424 | 0.75 | | | 1973D | 83,171,400 | 0.75 | | |
| 1971S | (3,220,733) | | $1.25 | $1.75 | 1973S | (2,760,339) | | $1.25 | $1.75 |
| 1972 | 153,180,000 | 0.75 | | | 1974 | 201,596,000 | 0.75 | | |
| 1972D | 141,890,000 | 0.75 | | | 1974D | 79,066,300 | 0.75 | | |
| 1972S | (3,260,996) | | 1.25 | 1.75 | 1974S | (2,612,568) | | 1.00 | 1.50 |

## Bicentennial (1776–1976)

| | Mintage | MS-63 | PF-63 | PF-65 |
|---|---|---|---|---|
| 1776–1976, Clad | 234,308,000 | $0.75 | | |
| 1776–1976D, Clad | 287,565,248 | 0.75 | | |
| 1776–1976S, Clad | (7,059,099) | | $1.25 | $1.75 |
| 1776–1976S, Silver | *11,000,000* | 4.00 | | |
| 1776–1976S, Silver | *(4,000,000)* | | 4.50 | 8.00 |

*Note:* Mintage figures for 1976-S silver coins are approximate; many were melted in 1982.

## Eagle Reverse Resumed (1977 to Date)

| | Mintage | MS-63 | PF-63 | PF-65 | | Mintage | MS-63 | PF-63 | PF-65 |
|---|---|---|---|---|---|---|---|---|---|
| 1977 | 43,598,000 | $0.75 | | | 1981P | 29,544,000 | $0.75 | | |
| 1977D | 31,449,106 | 0.75 | | | 1981D | 27,839,533 | 0.75 | | |
| 1977S | (3,251,152) | | $2.00 | $3.50 | 1981S | (4,063,083) | | | |
| 1978 | 14,350,000 | 0.75 | | | Type 1 | | | $1.00 | $1.25 |
| 1978D | 13,765,799 | 0.75 | | | Type 2 | | | 7.50 | 12.00 |
| 1978S | (3,127,781) | | 1.25 | 1.50 | 1982P | 10,819,000 | 0.75 | | |
| 1979 | 68,312,000 | 0.75 | | | 1982D | 13,140,102 | 4.50 | | |
| 1979D | 15,815,422 | 0.75 | | | 1982S | (3,857,479) | | 1.00 | 1.50 |
| 1979S | (3,677,175) | | | | 1983P | 34,139,000 | 4.00 | | |
| Type 1 | | | 1.00 | 1.75 | 1983D | 32,472,244 | 0.75 | | |
| Type 2 | | | 5.00 | 7.50 | 1983S | (3,279,126) | | 1.00 | 2.75 |
| 1980P | 44,134,000 | 0.75 | | | 1984P | 26,029,000 | 0.75 | | |
| 1980D | 33,456,449 | 0.75 | | | 1984D | 26,262,158 | 0.75 | | |
| 1980S | (3,554,806) | | 2.00 | 3.50 | 1984S | (3,065,110) | | 1.00 | 1.25 |

*Chart continued on next page.*

| | Mintage | MS-63 | PF-63 | PF-65 |
|---|---|---|---|---|
| 1985P | 18,706,962 | $0.75 | | |
| 1985D | 19,814,034 | 0.75 | | |
| 1985S | (3,362,821) | | $1.00 | $1.25 |
| 1986P | 13,107,633 | 1.00 | | |
| 1986D | 15,336,145 | 0.75 | | |
| 1986S | (3,010,497) | | 1.00 | 1.75 |
| 1987P (a) | 2,890,758 | 2.00 | | |
| 1987D (a) | 2,890,758 | 2.00 | | |
| 1987S | (4,227,728) | | 1.00 | 1.75 |
| 1988P | 13,626,000 | 0.75 | | |
| 1988D | 12,000,096 | 0.75 | | |
| 1988S | (3,262,948) | | 1.00 | 1.50 |
| 1989P | 24,542,000 | 0.75 | | |
| 1989D | 23,000,216 | 0.75 | | |
| 1989S | (3,220,194) | | 1.25 | 1.75 |
| 1990P | 22,278,000 | 0.75 | | |
| 1990D | 20,096,242 | 0.75 | | |
| 1990S | (3,299,559) | | 1.25 | 1.75 |
| 1991P | 14,874,000 | 0.75 | | |
| 1991D | 15,054,678 | 0.75 | | |
| 1991S | (2,867,787) | | 1.25 | 1.75 |
| 1992P | 17,628,000 | 0.75 | | |
| 1992D | 17,000,106 | 0.75 | | |
| 1992S | (2,858,981) | | 1.25 | 1.75 |
| 1992S, Silver | (1,317,579) | | 7.00 | 9.50 |
| 1993P | 15,510,000 | 0.75 | | |
| 1993D | 15,000,006 | 0.75 | | |
| 1993S | (2,633,439) | | 1.25 | 1.75 |
| 1993S, Silver | (761,353) | | 7.00 | 9.50 |
| 1994P | 23,718,000 | 0.75 | | |
| 1994D | 23,828,110 | 0.75 | | |
| 1994S | (2,484,594) | | 3.00 | 4.00 |
| 1994S, Silver | (785,329) | | 7.00 | 9.50 |
| 1995P | 26,496,000 | 0.75 | | |
| 1995D | 26,288,000 | 0.75 | | |
| 1995S | (2,117,496) | | 6.00 | 8.00 |
| 1995S, Silver | (679,985) | | 7.50 | 10.50 |
| 1996P | 24,442,000 | 0.75 | | |
| 1996D | 24,744,000 | 0.75 | | |
| 1996S | (1,750,244) | | 1.50 | 2.75 |
| 1996S, Silver | (775,021) | | 8.00 | 11.50 |
| 1997P | 20,882,000 | 0.75 | | |
| 1997D | 19,876,000 | 0.75 | | |
| 1997S | (2,055,000) | | 2.00 | 3.75 |
| 1997S, Silver | (741,678) | | 8.00 | 11.50 |
| 1998P | 15,646,000 | 0.75 | | |
| 1998D | 15,064,000 | 0.75 | | |
| 1998S | (2,086,507) | | 2.00 | 3.75 |
| 1998S, Silver | (878,792) | | 8.00 | 11.50 |
| 1998S, Silver, Matte Finish | (62,000) | | 75.00 | 100.00 |

| | Mintage | MS-63 | PF-63 | PF-65 |
|---|---|---|---|---|
| 1999P | 8,900,000 | $0.75 | | |
| 1999D | 10,682,000 | 0.75 | | |
| 1999S | (2,543,401) | | $2.00 | $3.75 |
| 1999S, Silver | (804,565) | | 10.00 | 14.50 |
| 2000P | 22,600,000 | 0.75 | | |
| 2000D | 19,466,000 | 0.75 | | |
| 2000S | (3,082,483) | | 2.00 | 3.75 |
| 2000S, Silver | (965,421) | | 8.00 | 11.50 |
| 2001P | 21,200,000 | 0.75 | | |
| 2001D | 19,504,000 | 0.75 | | |
| 2001S | (2,294,909) | | 2.00 | 3.75 |
| 2001S, Silver | (889,697) | | 8.00 | 11.50 |
| 2002P (a) | 3,100,000 | 0.75 | | |
| 2002D (a) | 2,500,000 | 0.75 | | |
| 2002S | (2,319,766) | | 2.00 | 3.75 |
| 2002S, Silver | (892,229) | | 7.00 | 9.50 |
| 2003P (a) | 2,500,000 | 0.75 | | |
| 2003D (a) | 2,500,000 | 0.75 | | |
| 2003S | (2,172,684) | | 1.75 | 2.75 |
| 2003S, Silver | (1,125,755) | | 7.00 | 9.50 |
| 2004P (a) | 2,900,000 | 0.75 | | |
| 2004D (a) | 2,900,000 | 0.75 | | |
| 2004S | (1,789,488) | | 2.00 | 3.75 |
| 2004S, Silver | (1,175,934) | | 7.00 | 9.50 |
| 2005P (a) | 3,800,000 | 0.75 | | |
| 2005D (a) | 3,500,000 | 0.75 | | |
| 2005S | (2,275,000) | | 1.00 | 1.50 |
| 2005S, Silver | (1,069,679) | | 7.00 | 9.50 |
| 2006P (a) | 2,400,000 | 0.75 | | |
| 2006D (a) | 2,000,000 | 0.75 | | |
| 2006S | (2,000,428) | | 2.00 | 3.75 |
| 2006S, Silver | (1,054,008) | | 7.00 | 9.50 |
| 2007P (a) | 2,400,000 | 0.75 | | |
| 2007D (a) | 2,400,000 | 0.75 | | |
| 2007S | (1,702,116) | | 2.00 | 3.75 |
| 2007S, Silver | (875,050) | | 8.00 | 10.00 |
| 2008P (a) | 1,700,000 | 0.75 | | |
| 2008D (a) | 1,700,000 | 0.75 | | |
| 2008S | (1,405,674) | | 3.50 | 5.50 |
| 2008S, Silver | (763,887) | | 7.00 | 9.50 |
| 2009P (a) | 1,900,000 | 0.75 | | |
| 2009D (a) | 1,900,000 | 0.75 | | |
| 2009S | (1,482,502) | | 1.00 | 1.50 |
| 2009S, Silver | (697,365) | | 7.00 | 9.50 |
| 2010P (a) | 1,800,000 | 0.75 | | |
| 2010D (a) | 1,700,000 | 0.75 | | |
| 2010S | (1,103,815) | | 6.00 | 10.00 |
| 2010S, Silver | (585,401) | | 10.00 | 12.00 |
| 2011P (a) | 1,750,000 | 0.75 | | |
| 2011D (a) | 1,700,000 | 0.75 | | |
| 2011S | (1,098,835) | | 3.50 | 4.75 |

a. Not issued for circulation.

| | Mintage | MS-63 | PF-63 | PF-65 |
|---|---|---|---|---|
| 2011S, Silver | (574,175) | | $7 | $9.50 |
| 2012P (a) | 1,800,000 | $0.75 | | |
| 2012D (a) | 1,700,000 | 0.75 | | |
| 2012S | (843,705) | | 5 | 7.50 |
| 2012S, Silver | (445,612) | | 45 | 55.00 |
| 2013P (a) | 5,000,000 | 0.75 | | |
| 2013D (a) | 4,600,000 | 0.75 | | |
| 2013S | (854,785) | | 3 | 3.75 |
| 2013S, Silver | (467,691) | | 7 | 9.50 |
| 2014P (a) | 2,500,000 | 1.00 | | |
| 2014P, High Relief (b) | 197,608 | 1.00 | | |
| 2014P, Silver (c) | (219,173) | | 7 | 9.50 |
| 2014D (a) | 2,100,000 | 1.00 | | |
| 2014D, High Relief (b) | 197,608 | 1.00 | | |
| 2014D, Silver (c) | 219,173 | 18.00 | | |

| | Mintage | MS-63 | PF-63 | PF-65 |
|---|---|---|---|---|
| 2014S, Silver Enh. Unc. (c) | 219,173 | $20.00 | | |
| 2014S | (767,977) | | $3 | $4.50 |
| 2014S, Silver | (472,107) | | 7 | 9.50 |
| 2014W, Reverse Proof, Silver (c) | (219,173) | | 20 | 25.00 |
| 2014W, 50th Anniversary, Gold (d) | (73,722) | | 1,350 | 1,500.00 |
| 2015P (a) | 2,300,000 | 0.75 | | |
| 2015D (a) | 2,300,000 | 0.75 | | |
| 2015S | (711,872) | | 7 | 10.00 |
| 2015S, Silver | (387,310) | | 10 | 13.00 |
| 2016P (a) | 2,100,000 | 0.75 | | |
| 2016D (a) | 2,100,000 | 0.75 | | |
| 2016S | (621,774) | | 9 | 12.50 |
| 2016S, Silver | (406,330) | | 7 | 9.50 |

**a.** Not issued for circulation. **b.** To celebrate the 50th anniversary of the Kennedy half dollar, the U.S. Mint issued an Uncirculated two-coin set featuring a Kennedy half dollar from Philadelphia and one from Denver. **c.** Featured in the 2014 half dollar silver-coin collection released by the U.S. Mint to commemorate the 50th anniversary of the Kennedy half dollar. **d.** First gold half dollar offered by the U.S. Mint. It commemorates the 50th anniversary of the first release of the Kennedy half dollar in 1964.

| | Mintage | SP-67 | SP-70 |
|---|---|---|---|
| 2016W, Gold (a) | 65,509 | $950 | $1,050 |

**a.** In 2016 the Mint issued a centennial version of the Liberty Walking half dollar in gold.

| | Mintage | MS-63 | PF-63 | PF-65 |
|---|---|---|---|---|
| 2017P (a) | 1,800,000 | $0.75 | | |
| 2017D (a) | 2,900,000 | 0.75 | | |
| 2017S | (621,390) | | $10 | $14.00 |
| 2017S, Silver | (406,986) | | 11 | 15.00 |
| 2018P (a) | 4,800,000 | 0.75 | | |
| 2018D (a) | 6,100,000 | 0.75 | | |
| 2018S | (568,804) | | 7 | 9.50 |
| 2018S, Silver | (381,748) | | 10 | 13.50 |
| 2019P (a) | 1,700,000 | 0.75 | | |
| 2019D (a) | 1,700,000 | 0.75 | | |
| 2019S | (687,480) | | 4 | 5.50 |
| 2019S, Silver (b,c) | (460,925) | | 7 | 10.00 |
| 2019S, Enh. RevPf. | (99,998) | | 7 | 10.00 |

| | Mintage | MS-63 | PF-63 | PF-65 |
|---|---|---|---|---|
| 2020P (a) | 5,400,000 | $0.75 | | |
| 2020D (a) | 7,700,000 | 0.75 | | |
| 2020S | (511,148) | | $4 | $5.50 |
| 2020S, Silver (c) | (363,179) | | 7 | 10.00 |
| 2021P | 2,300,000 | 0.75 | | |
| 2021D | 3,400,000 | 0.75 | | |
| 2021S | (521,826) | | 4 | 7.00 |
| 2021S, Silver (c) | (319,317) | | 7 | 10.00 |
| 2022P | | 0.75 | | |
| 2022D | | 0.75 | | |
| 2022S | | | 4 | 7.00 |
| 2022S, Silver (c) | | | 7 | 10.00 |

**a.** Not issued for circulation. **b.** In 2019, an Enhanced Reverse Proof half dollar from the San Francisco Mint was included in the Apollo 11 50th Anniversary Half Dollar Set. **c.** In 2019, the fineness of all silver Proofs was changed from .900 to .999.

The silver dollar was authorized by Congress April 2, 1792. Its weight was specified at 416 grains and its fineness at .8924. The first issues appeared in 1794, and until 1804 all silver dollars had the value stamped on the edge: HUNDRED CENTS, ONE DOLLAR OR UNIT. After a lapse in coinage of the silver dollar during the period 1804 to 1835, coins were made with either plain (1836 only) or reeded edges and the value was placed on the reverse side.

Mintages shown here are as reported by the Mint for calendar years and do not necessarily refer to the dates on the coins.

The weight was changed by the law of January 18, 1837, to 412-1/2 grains, fineness .900. The coinage was discontinued by the Act of February 12, 1873, and reauthorized by the Act of February 28, 1878. The silver dollar was again discontinued after 1935, and since then copper-nickel and other base-metal pieces have been coined for circulation. (See also "$1 American Silver Eagle Coins" on page 242.)

## FLOWING HAIR (1794–1795)

**AG-3 About Good:** Clear enough to identify.
**G-4 Good:** Date and letters legible. Main devices outlined, but lacking in detail.
**VG-8 Very Good:** Major details discernible. Letters well formed but worn.
**F-12 Fine:** Hair ends distinguishable. Top hair lines visible, but otherwise worn smooth.
**VF-20 Very Fine:** Some detail visible in hair in center. Other details more bold.
**EF-40 Extremely Fine:** Hair well defined but with some wear.
**AU-50 About Uncirculated:** Slight trace of wear on tips of highest curls; breast feathers usually weak.
**MS-60 Uncirculated:** No trace of wear. Light blemishes.

| | Mintage | AG-3 | G-4 | VG-8 | F-12 | VF-20 | EF-40 | AU-50 | MS-60 |
|---|---|---|---|---|---|---|---|---|---|
| 1794 | 1,758 | $32,500 | $55,000 | $85,000 | $105,000 | $135,000 | $275,000 | $450,000 | — |
| 1795 | 160,295 | 900 | 1,650 | 2,000 | 2,800 | 4,250 | 9,000 | 12,500 | $50,000 |

## DRAPED BUST (1795–1804)
### Small Eagle Reverse (1795–1798)

**AG-3 About Good:** Clear enough to identify.
**G-4 Good:** Bust outlined, no detail. Date legible, some leaves evident.
**VG-8 Very Good:** Drapery worn except deepest folds. Hair lines smooth.
**F-12 Fine:** All drapery lines distinguishable. Some detail visible in hair lines near cheek and neck.
**VF-20 Very Fine:** Left side of drapery worn smooth.
**EF-40 Extremely Fine:** Drapery distinctly visible. Hair well outlined and detailed.
**AU-50 About Uncirculated:** Slight trace of wear on the bust shoulder and hair to left of forehead, as well as on eagle's breast and top edges of wings.
**MS-60 Uncirculated:** No trace of wear. Light blemishes.

| | Mintage | AG-3 | G-4 | VG-8 | F-12 | VF-20 | EF-40 | AU-50 | MS-60 |
|---|---|---|---|---|---|---|---|---|---|
| 1795, Bust Type. . *42,738* | $700 | $1,550 | $1,750 | $2,850 | $3,750 | $7,000 | $12,500 | $37,500 |
| 1796 . . . . . . . . .79,920 | 700 | 1,600 | 1,750 | 2,850 | 3,750 | 7,000 | 12,500 | 37,500 |
| 1797 . . . . . . . . . .7,776 | 700 | 1,600 | 1,750 | 2,850 | 3,750 | 7,000 | 12,500 | 42,000 |
| 1798 . . . . . . . . . .*40,000* | 850 | 1,650 | 1,850 | 3,000 | 4,250 | 8,000 | 15,000 | 85,000 |

## Heraldic Eagle Reverse (1798–1804)

**G-4 Good:** Letters and date legible.
E PLURIBUS UNUM illegible.
**VG-8 Very Good:** Motto
partially legible. Only
deepest drapery details
visible. All other lines
smooth.
**F-12 Fine:** All drapery
lines distinguishable.
Some detail visible in
hair lines near cheek
and neck.
**VF-20 Very Fine:** Left
side of drapery worn smooth.
**EF-40 Extremely Fine:** Drapery distinct. Hair well detailed.
**AU-50 About Uncirculated:** Slight trace of wear on the bust shoulder and hair to left of forehead, as well as on eagle's breast and top edges of wings.
**MS-60 Uncirculated:** No trace of wear. Light blemishes.

| | Mintage | G-4 | VG-8 | F-12 | VF-20 | EF-40 | AU-50 | MS-60 |
|---|---|---|---|---|---|---|---|---|
| 1798, Heraldic Eagle . . . . . . . . . . . . . . .* | $750 | $900 | $1,250 | $1,800 | $3,000 | $5,000 | $17,500 |
| 1799 . . . . . . . . . . . . . . . . . . . . 423,515 | 750 | 900 | 1,250 | 1,800 | 3,000 | 5,000 | 17,500 |
| 1800 . . . . . . . . . . . . . . . . . . . . 220,920 | 750 | 900 | 1,250 | 1,800 | 3,000 | 5,000 | 17,500 |
| 1801 . . . . . . . . . . . . . . . . . . . . . 54,454 | 750 | 950 | 1,350 | 2,050 | 3,250 | 5,500 | 18,500 |
| 1802 . . . . . . . . . . . . . . . . . . . . . 41,650 | 750 | 900 | 1,300 | 1,800 | 3,000 | 5,000 | 17,500 |
| 1803 . . . . . . . . . . . . . . . . . . . . . 85,634 | 850 | 1,100 | 1,450 | 2,100 | 3,250 | 6,500 | 20,000 |
| 1804, Class I, First Rev (0 Above Cloud) **(a)** *(8 known)* . . . . . . . . . . | | | | Proof: $3,500,000 | | | | |
| 1804, Class II, Second Rev (0 Above Space Between Clouds) **(b)** . . . | | | | *(unique, in Smithsonian collection)* | | | | |
| 1804, Class III, Second Rev (0 Above Space Between Clouds) **(a)** *(6 known)* . . . . . . . . . . . . . . . . . . . | | | | Proof: $3,500,000 | | | | |

\* Included in number above. **a.** Numerous counterfeits exist. **b.** Electrotype copies exist, made at the Mint from their specimen.

## GOBRECHT (1836–1839)

Silver dollars of 1836, 1838, and 1839 were mostly made as patterns and restrikes, but some dated 1836 were made for general circulation.

| | VF-20 | EF-40 | AU-50 | PF-60 |
|---|---|---|---|---|
| 1836, C. GOBRECHT F. on base. Reverse eagle flying upward amid stars. Plain edge. Although scarce, this is the most common variety and was issued for circulation as regular coinage................... | $8,000 | $11,000 | $13,500 | $20,000 |
| 1838, Similar obverse, designer's name omitted, stars added around border. Reverse eagle flying left in plain field. Reeded edge............... | 10,000 | 15,000 | 16,500 | 22,500 |
| 1839, Obverse as above. Reverse eagle in plain field. Reeded edge. Issued for circulation as regular coinage........................... | 9,500 | 12,500 | 12,500 | 21,000 |

## LIBERTY SEATED (1840–1873)

Starting again in 1840, silver dollars were issued for general circulation, continuing to about 1850, after which their main use was in the export trade to China. The seated figure of Liberty was adopted for the obverse, and a heraldic eagle for the reverse.

**VG-8 Very Good:** Any three letters of LIBERTY at least two-thirds complete.
**F-12 Fine:** All seven letters of LIBERTY visible, though weak.
**VF-20 Very Fine:** LIBERTY strong, but slight wear visible on its ribbon.
**EF-40 Extremely Fine:** Horizontal lines of shield complete. Eagle's eye plain.
**AU-50 About Uncirculated:** Traces of light wear on only the high points of the design. Half of mint luster present.
**MS-60 Uncirculated:** No trace of wear. Light marks or blemishes.
**PF-60 Proof:** Several contact marks, hairlines, or light rubs possible on surface. Luster possibly dull and eye appeal lacking.
**PF-63 Choice Proof:** Reflective surfaces with only a few blemishes in secondary focal places. No major flaws.

### No Motto (1840–1865)

*Location of mintmark, when present, is on reverse, below eagle.*

| | Mintage | VG-8 | F-12 | VF-20 | EF-40 | AU-50 | MS-60 | PF-60 | PF-63 |
|---|---|---|---|---|---|---|---|---|---|
| 1840 . . . . . . . . . . . . . . . .61,005 | | $300 | $350 | $450 | $650 | $1,100 | $4,000 | $9,500 | $20,000 |
| 1841 . . . . . . . . . . . . . .173,000 | | 300 | 350 | 400 | 550 | 900 | 2,500 | 18,500 | 35,000 |
| 1842 . . . . . . . . . . . . . .184,618 | | 300 | 350 | 400 | 550 | 750 | 2,250 | 11,000 | 25,000 |
| 1843 . . . . . . . . . . . . . .165,100 | | 300 | 350 | 400 | 550 | 850 | 1,850 | 9,000 | 20,000 |
| 1844 . . . . . . . . . . . . . . .20,000 | | 300 | 350 | 450 | 700 | 1,200 | 3,250 | 13,500 | 25,000 |
| 1845 . . . . . . . . . . . . . . .24,500 | | 350 | 450 | 550 | 750 | 1,250 | 4,250 | 9,000 | 19,000 |
| 1846 . . . . . . . . . . . . . .110,600 | | 300 | 350 | 400 | 500 | 800 | 1,600 | 7,500 | 18,000 |
| 1846O . . . . . . . . . . . . . .59,000 | | 300 | 350 | 400 | 600 | 1,000 | 5,000 | | |
| 1847 . . . . . . . . . . . . . .140,750 | | 300 | 350 | 400 | 500 | 650 | 2,250 | 9,000 | 17,500 |
| 1848 . . . . . . . . . . . . . . .15,000 | | 350 | 500 | 600 | 1,200 | 1,650 | 5,000 | 9,000 | 20,000 |
| 1849 . . . . . . . . . . . . . . .62,600 | | 300 | 350 | 400 | 500 | 750 | 2,250 | 10,000 | 25,000 |
| 1850 . . . . . . . . . . . . . . . .7,500 | | 500 | 650 | 800 | 1,500 | 2,500 | 4,500 | 9,000 | 17,500 |
| 1850O . . . . . . . . . . . . . .40,000 | | 300 | 450 | 650 | 1,250 | 2,500 | 7,500 | | |
| 1851 . . . . . . . . . . . . . . . .1,300 | | 9,000 | 9,500 | 11,500 | 16,000 | 25,000 | 27,500 | 17,500 | 25,000 |
| 1852 . . . . . . . . . . . . . . . .1,100 | | 4,500 | 7,500 | 10,000 | 15,000 | 25,000 | 30,000 | 18,500 | 25,000 |
| 1853 . . . . . . . . . . . . . . .46,110 | | 450 | 550 | 650 | 1,000 | 1,200 | 3,000 | 18,500 | 25,000 |
| 1854 . . . . . . . . . . . . . . .33,140 | | 1,500 | 2,000 | 3,000 | 4,000 | 5,000 | 8,000 | 9,500 | 12,500 |
| 1855 . . . . . . . . . . . . . . .26,000 | | 1,350 | 1,850 | 3,000 | 3,500 | 5,500 | 7,500 | 8,500 | 12,500 |
| 1856 . . . . . . . . . . . . . . .63,500 | | 600 | 800 | 1,000 | 1,500 | 2,500 | 4,500 | 4,000 | 10,000 |
| 1857 . . . . . . . . . . . . . . .94,000 | | 700 | 900 | 1,250 | 2,000 | 2,500 | 4,500 | 3,500 | 9,500 |
| 1858 . . . . . . .(210) . . . . . . . . | | 2,500 | 3,000 | 3,500 | 4,500 | 6,000 | | 6,500 | 8,500 |
| 1859 . . . . . . .(800) . . . .255,700 | | 350 | 400 | 500 | 600 | 1,000 | 2,500 | 1,650 | 3,500 |
| 1859O . . . . . . . . . . . . .360,000 | | 300 | 350 | 400 | 500 | 600 | 1,350 | | |
| 1859S . . . . . . . . . . . . . .20,000 | | 500 | 750 | 1,100 | 1,300 | 3,000 | 5,500 | | |
| 1860 . . . . .(1,330) . . . .217,600 | | 300 | 350 | 400 | 500 | 750 | 1,800 | 1,650 | 3,500 |
| 1860O . . . . . . . . . . . . .515,000 | | 300 | 350 | 400 | 500 | 650 | 1,500 | | |
| 1861 . . . . . .(1,000) . . . .77,500 | | 1,000 | 1,500 | 2,000 | 2,750 | 3,500 | 5,000 | 1,650 | 3,500 |
| 1862 . . . . . . .(550) . . . .11,540 | | 550 | 900 | 1,500 | 2,250 | 3,500 | 5,000 | 1,650 | 3,500 |
| 1863 . . . . . . .(460) . . . .27,200 | | 800 | 1,000 | 1,500 | 2,000 | 2,750 | 3,750 | 1,650 | 3,500 |
| 1864 . . . . . . .(470) . . . .30,700 | | 450 | 600 | 1,000 | 1,500 | 2,750 | 3,250 | 1,650 | 3,500 |
| 1865 . . . . . . .(500) . . . .46,500 | | 550 | 650 | 1,000 | 1,850 | 2,000 | 3,750 | 1,650 | 3,500 |

## With Motto IN GOD WE TRUST (1866–1873)

**Motto IN GOD WE TRUST on Reverse (1866–1873)**

| | Mintage | VG-8 | F-12 | VF-20 | EF-40 | AU-50 | MS-60 | PF-60 | PF-63 |
|---|---|---|---|---|---|---|---|---|---|
| 1866 . . . . . . .(725) . . . .48,900 | | $300 | $350 | $450 | $700 | $1,000 | $2,000 | $1,650 | $3,250 |
| 1867 . . . . . . .(625) . . . .46,900 | | 300 | 350 | 500 | 600 | 1,000 | 2,000 | 1,650 | 3,250 |
| 1868 . . . . . . .(600) . . . .162,100 | | 300 | 350 | 500 | 600 | 850 | 2,000 | 1,650 | 3,250 |
| 1869 . . . . . . .(600) . . . .423,700 | | 300 | 350 | 500 | 600 | 900 | 1,850 | 1,650 | 3,250 |

*Chart continued on next page.*

| | Mintage | VG-8 | F-12 | VF-20 | EF-40 | AU-50 | MS-60 | PF-60 | PF-63 |
|---|---|---|---|---|---|---|---|---|---|
| 1870 ... (1,000)... 415,000 | | $300 | $350 | $375 | $600 | $650 | $1,350 | $1,650 | $3,250 |
| 1870CC .......... 11,758 | | 1,000 | 1,500 | 2,000 | 3,500 | 4,500 | 20,000 | | |
| 1870S ................. 175,000 | | 250,000 | 350,000 | 450,000 | 800,000 | 1,250,000 | | | |
| 1871 ..... (960)..1,073,800 | | 300 | 350 | 375 | 450 | 600 | 1,350 | 1,650 | 3,250 |
| 1871CC ............ 1,376 | | 3,500 | 4,500 | 6,500 | 8,500 | 17,500 | 65,000 | | |
| 1872 ..... (950)..1,105,500 | | 300 | 350 | 375 | 450 | 600 | 1,350 | 1,650 | 3,250 |
| 1872CC ............ 3,150 | | 1,850 | 2,500 | 3,000 | 4,250 | 7,500 | 17,500 | | |
| 1872S ............. 9,000 | | 500 | 700 | 1,000 | 1,500 | 2,500 | 9,000 | | |
| 1873 ..... (600)... 293,000 | | 300 | 350 | 375 | 450 | 650 | 1,750 | 1,650 | 3,250 |
| 1873CC ............ 2,300 | | 10,000 | 13,500 | 16,500 | 25,000 | 42,500 | 100,000 | | |

# TRADE DOLLARS (1873–1885)

This trade dollar was issued for circulation in Asia to compete with dollar-size coins of other countries. It weighed 420 grains compared to 412-1/2 grains, the weight of the regular silver dollar.

**VG-8 Very Good:** About half of mottoes IN GOD WE TRUST (on Liberty's pedestal) and E PLURIBUS UNUM (on obverse ribbon) visible. Rim on both sides well defined.

**F-12 Fine:** Mottoes and LIBERTY legible but worn.

**EF-40 Extremely Fine:** Mottoes and LIBERTY sharp. Only slight wear on rims.

**AU-50 About Uncirculated:** Slight trace of wear on Liberty's left breast and left knee and on hair above ear, as well as on eagle's head, knee, and wing tips.

**MS-60 Uncirculated:** No trace of wear. Light blemishes.

**MS-63 Choice Uncirculated:** Some distracting contact marks or blemishes in prime focal areas. Impaired luster possible.

**PF-63 Choice Proof:** Reflective surfaces with only a few blemishes in secondary focal places. No major flaws.

1875-S, S Over CC

| | Mintage | VG-8 | F-12 | EF-40 | AU-50 | MS-60 | MS-63 | PF-63 |
|---|---|---|---|---|---|---|---|---|
| 1873 ....... (600)..... 396,900 | | $145 | $165 | $350 | $450 | $950 | $2,250 | $2,500 |
| 1873CC ............... 124,500 | | 250 | 450 | 1,250 | 2,000 | 6,000 | 20,000 | |
| 1873S ............... 703,000 | | 145 | 175 | 350 | 500 | 1,000 | 2,750 | |
| 1874 ....... (700)..... 987,100 | | 145 | 155 | 350 | 450 | 900 | 2,000 | 2,500 |
| 1874CC ............. 1,373,200 | | 225 | 325 | 700 | 950 | 2,150 | 4,000 | |
| 1874S ............. 2,549,000 | | 145 | 155 | 250 | 325 | 750 | 1,500 | |
| 1875 ....... (700)..... 218,200 | | 225 | 350 | 850 | 1,000 | 2,000 | 3,250 | 2,500 |
| 1875CC ............. 1,573,700 | | 250 | 325 | 500 | 650 | 1,750 | 3,500 | |
| 1875S ............. 4,487,000 | | 125 | 150 | 250 | 325 | 750 | 1,100 | |
| 1875S, S Over CC ............. * | | 250 | 450 | 1,100 | 1,250 | 4,500 | 15,000 | |
| 1876 ..... (1,150)..... 455,000 | | 125 | 150 | 300 | 400 | 750 | 1,250 | 2,500 |
| 1876CC ............... 509,000 | | 300 | 500 | 950 | 1,350 | 5,500 | 15,000 | |

* Included in number above.

| | Mintage | VG-8 | F-12 | EF-40 | AU-50 | MS-60 | MS-63 | PF-63 |
|---|---|---|---|---|---|---|---|---|
| 1876S . . . . . . . . . . . . . . 5,227,000 | | $125 | $150 | $250 | $350 | $700 | $1,200 | |
| 1877 . . . . . . . (510) . . . . 3,039,200 | | 125 | 175 | 250 | 400 | 750 | 1,300 | $2,500 |
| 1877CC . . . . . . . . . . . . . .534,000 | | 325 | 500 | 1,000 | 1,350 | 3,250 | 7,500 | |
| 1877S . . . . . . . . . . . . . . 9,519,000 | | 125 | 155 | 250 | 350 | 750 | 1,100 | |
| 1878 . . . . . . . . (900). . . . . . . . . . | | | | 850 | | | | 2,500 |
| 1878CC (a) . . . . . . . . . . . . .97,000 | | 550 | 1,000 | 3,500 | 5,500 | 12,500 | 25,000 | |
| 1878S . . . . . . . . . . . . . 4,162,000 | | 125 | 150 | 250 | 350 | 750 | 1,100 | |
| 1879 . . . . . . (1,541). . . . . . . . . . . | | | | 850 | | | | 2,500 |
| 1880 . . . . . . (1,987). . . . . . . . . . . | | | | 900 | | | | 2,500 |
| 1881 . . . . . . . . (960). . . . . . . . . . | | | | 900 | | | | 2,500 |
| 1882 . . . . . . (1,097). . . . . . . . . . . | | | | 900 | | | | 2,500 |
| 1883 . . . . . . . . (979). . . . . . . . . . | | | | 900 | | | | 2,500 |
| 1884 (b) . . . . . . (10). . . . . . . . . . | | | | | | | | 400,000 |
| 1885 (b) . . . . . . .(5). . . . . . . . . . | | | | | | | | 1,500,000 |

**a.** 44,148 trade dollars were melted on July 19, 1878. Many of these may have been 1878-CC. **b.** The trade dollars of 1884 and 1885 were unknown to collectors until 1908. None are listed in the Mint director's report, and numismatists believe that they are not a part of the regular Mint issue.

# MORGAN (1878–1921)

George T. Morgan, formerly a pupil of William Wyon at the Royal Mint in London, designed the new dollar. His initial M is found at the truncation of the neck, at the last tress. It also appears on the reverse on the left-hand loop of the ribbon.

Sharply struck prooflike coins have a highly reflective surface and usually command substantial premiums.

The 1921 Silver Dollar Coin Anniversary Act authorized the Mint to produce coins celebrating the 2021 centennial of the last Morgan dollar.

**VF-20 Very Fine:** Two thirds of hair lines from top of forehead to ear visible. Ear well defined. Feathers on eagle's breast worn.

**EF-40 Extremely Fine:** All hair lines strong and ear bold. Eagle's feathers all plain but with slight wear on breast and wing tips.

**AU-50 About Uncirculated:** Slight trace of wear on the bust shoulder and hair left of forehead, and on eagle's breast and top edges of wings.

**MS-60 Uncirculated:** No trace of wear. Full mint luster present, but may be noticeably marred by scuff marks or bag abrasions.

**MS-63 Choice Uncirculated:** No trace of wear; full mint luster; few noticeable surface marks.

**MS-64 Uncirculated:** A few scattered contact marks. Good eye appeal and attractive luster.

**MS-65 Gem Uncirculated:** Only light, scattered contact marks that are not distracting. Strong luster, good eye appeal.

**8 Tail Feathers, 1878, Philadelphia Only**
*Mintmark location on reverse, below wreath.*

Most Proof Morgan dollars, where indicated in mintage records (quantity shown in parentheses), are valued by coin dealers approximately as follows:
Proof-60 – $600; Proof-63 – $1,400; Proof-65 – $3,000.

*Most Uncirculated silver dollars have scratches or nicks because of handling of mint bags in shipping and storage. Coin dealers usually pay more than the listed prices for choice sharply struck pieces with full brilliance and without blemishes.*

| | Mintage | VF-20 | EF-40 | AU-50 | MS-60 | MS-63 | MS-65 |
|---|---|---|---|---|---|---|---|
| 1878, 8 Feathers . . . . . . . . (500) . . . . . *749,500* | | $65 | $75 | $100 | $250 | $350 | $1,500 |
| 1878, 7 Feathers . . . . . . . . (250) . . . *9,759,300* | | 40 | 45 | 60 | 100 | 165 | 600 |
| 1878, 7/8 Clear Doubled Feathers . . . . . . . . . * | | 40 | 45 | 85 | 200 | 375 | 1,500 |
| 1878CC . . . . . . . . . . . . . . . . . . . . . . 2,212,000 | | 125 | 160 | 215 | 375 | 475 | 1,350 |
| 1878S . . . . . . . . . . . . . . . . . . . . . . 9,774,000 | | 35 | 40 | 40 | 65 | 85 | 300 |
| 1879 . . . . . . . . . . . . . (1,100) . . 14,806,000 | | 35 | 37 | 40 | 55 | 80 | 400 |
| 1879CC, CC Over CC . . . . . . . . . . . . . .756,000 | | 350 | 1,100 | 2,150 | 4,250 | 6,500 | 18,500 |
| 1879O . . . . . . . . . . . . . . . . . . . . . . 2,887,000 | | 35 | 37 | 45 | 85 | 285 | 2,000 |
| 1879S . . . . . . . . . . . . . . . . . . . . . . 9,110,000 | | 35 | 37 | 40 | 55 | 75 | 175 |
| 1880 . . . . . . . . . . . . . . (1,355) . . 12,600,000 | | 35 | 37 | 40 | 45 | 65 | 350 |
| 1880CC . . . . . . . . . . . . . . . . . . . . . . *591,000* | | 185 | 225 | 275 | 525 | 650 | 1,000 |
| 1880O . . . . . . . . . . . . . . . . . . . . . . 5,305,000 | | 35 | 37 | 40 | 115 | 425 | 10,000 |
| 1880S . . . . . . . . . . . . . . . . . . . . . . 8,900,000 | | 35 | 37 | 40 | 50 | 65 | 175 |
| 1881 . . . . . . . . . . . . . . . . (984) . . . 9,163,000 | | 35 | 37 | 40 | 45 | 65 | 350 |
| 1881CC . . . . . . . . . . . . . . . . . . . . . . .296,000 | | 300 | 350 | 375 | 500 | 625 | 850 |
| 1881O . . . . . . . . . . . . . . . . . . . . . . 5,708,000 | | 35 | 37 | 40 | 45 | 65 | 675 |
| 1881S . . . . . . . . . . . . . . . . . . . . . . 12,760,000 | | 35 | 37 | 40 | 50 | 65 | 175 |
| 1882 . . . . . . . . . . . . . . . (1,100) . . 11,100,000 | | 35 | 37 | 40 | 45 | 65 | 250 |
| 1882CC . . . . . . . . . . . . . . . . . . . . . . 1,133,000 | | 125 | 155 | 250 | 325 | 350 | 500 |
| 1882O . . . . . . . . . . . . . . . . . . . . . . 6,090,000 | | 35 | 37 | 40 | 45 | 65 | 450 |
| 1882S . . . . . . . . . . . . . . . . . . . . . . 9,250,000 | | 35 | 37 | 40 | 50 | 65 | 175 |
| 1883 . . . . . . . . . . . . . . . (1,039) . . 12,290,000 | | 35 | 37 | 40 | 45 | 65 | 175 |
| 1883CC . . . . . . . . . . . . . . . . . . . . . . 1,204,000 | | 125 | 155 | 250 | 325 | 350 | 500 |
| 1883O . . . . . . . . . . . . . . . . . . . . . . 8,725,000 | | 35 | 37 | 40 | 45 | 60 | 165 |
| 1883S . . . . . . . . . . . . . . . . . . . . . . 6,250,000 | | 35 | 60 | 145 | 900 | 2,000 | 22,500 |
| 1884 . . . . . . . . . . . . . . . . (875) . . 14,070,000 | | 35 | 37 | 40 | 45 | 60 | 200 |
| 1884CC . . . . . . . . . . . . . . . . . . . . . . 1,136,000 | | 125 | 155 | 250 | 325 | 350 | 500 |
| 1884O . . . . . . . . . . . . . . . . . . . . . . 9,730,000 | | 35 | 37 | 40 | 45 | 60 | 165 |
| 1884S . . . . . . . . . . . . . . . . . . . . . . 3,200,000 | | 40 | 65 | 250 | 8,000 | 25,000 | 175,000 |
| 1885 . . . . . . . . . . . . . . . . (930) . . 17,787,000 | | 35 | 37 | 40 | 45 | 60 | 165 |
| 1885CC . . . . . . . . . . . . . . . . . . . . . . .228,000 | | 475 | 500 | 525 | 550 | 650 | 1,000 |
| 1885O . . . . . . . . . . . . . . . . . . . . . . 9,185,000 | | 35 | 37 | 40 | 45 | 60 | 165 |
| 1885S . . . . . . . . . . . . . . . . . . . . . . 1,497,000 | | 35 | 45 | 85 | 285 | 400 | 1,250 |
| 1886 . . . . . . . . . . . . . . . . (886) . . 19,963,000 | | 35 | 37 | 40 | 45 | 60 | 165 |
| 1886O . . . . . . . . . . . . . . . . . . . . . . 10,710,000 | | 35 | 37 | 125 | 950 | 2,500 | 125,000 |
| 1886S . . . . . . . . . . . . . . . . . . . . . . .750,000 | | 60 | 90 | 115 | 350 | 450 | 1,250 |
| 1887 . . . . . . . . . . . . . . . . (710) . . 20,290,000 | | 35 | 37 | 40 | 45 | 60 | 165 |
| 1887O . . . . . . . . . . . . . . . . . . . . . . 11,550,000 | | 35 | 37 | 40 | 50 | 155 | 1,500 |
| 1887S . . . . . . . . . . . . . . . . . . . . . . 1,771,000 | | 35 | 37 | 45 | 130 | 250 | 1,250 |
| 1888 . . . . . . . . . . . . . . . . (833) . . 19,183,000 | | 35 | 37 | 40 | 45 | 60 | 165 |
| 1888O . . . . . . . . . . . . . . . . . . . . . . 12,150,000 | | 35 | 37 | 40 | 50 | 75 | 250 |
| 1888S . . . . . . . . . . . . . . . . . . . . . . .657,000 | | 110 | 120 | 150 | 325 | 500 | 1,750 |
| 1889 . . . . . . . . . . . . . . . . (811) . . 21,726,000 | | 35 | 37 | 40 | 45 | 60 | 175 |
| 1889CC . . . . . . . . . . . . . . . . . . . . . . .350,000 | | 1,250 | 3,000 | 6,500 | 19,000 | 35,000 | 225,000 |
| 1889O . . . . . . . . . . . . . . . . . . . . . . 11,875,000 | | 35 | 37 | 65 | 325 | 425 | 2,000 |

* Included in number above.

| | Mintage | VF-20 | EF-40 | AU-50 | MS-60 | MS-63 | MS-65 |
|---|---|---|---|---|---|---|---|
| 1889S . . . . . . . . . . . . . . | .700,000 | $50 | $55 | $85 | $225 | $325 | $1,050 |
| 1890 . . . . . . . (590) . . . | 16,802,000 | 35 | 37 | 40 | 50 | 70 | 600 |
| 1890CC . . . . . . . . . . . . | 2,309,041 | 125 | 200 | 285 | 600 | 1,000 | 2,450 |
| 1890O . . . . . . . . . . . . | 10,701,000 | 35 | 37 | 40 | 80 | 150 | 800 |
| 1890S . . . . . . . . . . . . . | 8,230,373 | 35 | 37 | 40 | 70 | 125 | 700 |
| 1891 . . . . . . . (650) . . . . | 8,693,556 | 35 | 37 | 40 | 70 | 155 | 1,750 |
| 1891CC . . . . . . . . . . . . | 1,618,000 | 125 | 200 | 275 | 600 | 800 | 2,500 |
| 1891O . . . . . . . . . . . . . | 7,954,529 | 45 | 65 | 85 | 200 | 450 | 3,250 |
| 1891S . . . . . . . . . . . . . | 5,296,000 | 35 | 37 | 40 | 125 | 225 | 1,000 |
| 1892 . . . . . . (1,245) . . . . | 1,036,000 | 35 | 60 | 95 | 425 | 575 | 2,000 |
| 1892CC . . . . . . . . . . . . | 1,352,000 | 275 | 500 | 750 | 1,350 | 2,000 | 5,000 |
| 1892O . . . . . . . . . . . . | 2,744,000 | 35 | 55 | 85 | 350 | 450 | 2,250 |
| 1892S . . . . . . . . . . . . . | 1,200,000 | 115 | 375 | 1,500 | 40,000 | 75,000 | 175,000 |
| 1893 . . . . . . . (792) . . . . | .378,000 | 185 | 325 | 500 | 1,250 | 1,750 | 4,000 |
| 1893CC . . . . . . . . . . . . | .677,000 | 650 | 1,850 | 2,500 | 4,250 | 6,750 | 65,000 |
| 1893O . . . . . . . . . . . . . | .300,000 | 300 | 450 | 850 | 3,750 | 6,000 | 135,000 |
| 1893S . . . . . . . . . . . . . | .100,000 | 4,250 | 7,500 | 17,500 | 155,000 | 300,000 | 500,000 |
| 1894 . . . . . . . (972) . . . . | .110,000 | 675 | 850 | 1,100 | 2,750 | 4,000 | 27,500 |
| 1894O . . . . . . . . . . . . | 1,723,000 | 35 | 100 | 225 | 1,650 | 4,000 | 37,500 |
| 1894S . . . . . . . . . . . . . | 1,260,000 | 85 | 150 | 450 | 850 | 1,500 | 4,000 |
| 1895 . . . . . . . (880) . . . . . . . . . . . | | 32,500 (a) | 35,000 (a) | 42,500 (a) | 45,000 (a) | 60,000 (a) |
| 1895O . . . . . . . . . . . . | .450,000 | 275 | 450 | 1,100 | 12,000 | 42,500 | 165,000 |
| 1895S . . . . . . . . . . . . . | .400,000 | 550 | 850 | 1,500 | 4,000 | 6,000 | 12,500 |
| 1896 . . . . . . . (762) . . . . | 9,976,000 | 35 | 37 | 40 | 45 | 60 | 175 |
| 1896O . . . . . . . . . . . . | 4,900,000 | 35 | 37 | 100 | 1,600 | 3,250 | 125,000 |
| 1896S . . . . . . . . . . . . . | 5,000,000 | 65 | 250 | 850 | 2,500 | 3,000 | 9,000 |
| 1897 . . . . . . . (731) . . . . | 2,822,000 | 35 | 37 | 40 | 45 | 60 | 215 |
| 1897O . . . . . . . . . . . . | 4,004,000 | 35 | 45 | 100 | 950 | 3,000 | 45,000 |
| 1897S . . . . . . . . . . . . . | 5,825,000 | 35 | 37 | 40 | 70 | 150 | 450 |
| 1898 . . . . . . . (735) . . . . | 5,884,000 | 35 | 37 | 40 | 45 | 60 | 175 |
| 1898O . . . . . . . . . . . . | 4,440,000 | 35 | 37 | 40 | 45 | 60 | 165 |
| 1898S . . . . . . . . . . . . . | 4,102,000 | 35 | 50 | 100 | 425 | 650 | 1,600 |
| 1899 . . . . . . . (846) . . . . . | .330,000 | 125 | 135 | 140 | 250 | 300 | 650 |
| 1899O . . . . . . . . . . . . | 12,290,000 | 35 | 37 | 40 | 45 | 60 | 165 |
| 1899S . . . . . . . . . . . . . | 2,562,000 | 40 | 80 | 185 | 500 | 750 | 1,600 |
| 1900 . . . . . . . (912) . . . . | 8,830,000 | 35 | 37 | 40 | 45 | 60 | 165 |
| 1900O . . . . . . . . . . . . | 12,590,000 | 35 | 37 | 40 | 45 | 60 | 165 |
| 1900S . . . . . . . . . . . . . | 3,540,000 | 35 | 40 | 100 | 425 | 550 | 1,000 |
| 1901 . . . . . . . (813) . . . | 6,962,000 | 35 | 125 | 300 | 3,500 | 7,000 | 40,000 |
| 1901O . . . . . . . . . . . . | 13,320,000 | 35 | 37 | 40 | 45 | 60 | 165 |
| 1901S . . . . . . . . . . . . . | 2,284,000 | 40 | 100 | 200 | 500 | 900 | 2,250 |
| 1902 . . . . . . . (777) . . . . | 7,994,000 | 35 | 37 | 40 | 120 | 185 | 350 |
| 1902O . . . . . . . . . . . . | 8,636,000 | 35 | 37 | 40 | 45 | 60 | 165 |
| 1902S . . . . . . . . . . . . . | 1,530,000 | 115 | 185 | 215 | 450 | 700 | 1,750 |
| 1903 . . . . . . . (755) . . . . | 4,652,000 | 35 | 37 | 40 | 45 | 100 | 225 |
| 1903O . . . . . . . . . . . . | 4,450,000 | 350 | 400 | 420 | 485 | 550 | 750 |
| 1903S . . . . . . . . . . . . . | 1,241,000 | 185 | 450 | 1,500 | 5,000 | 7,500 | 10,000 |
| 1904 . . . . . . . (650) . . . . | 2,788,000 | 35 | 37 | 40 | 100 | 325 | 1,350 |
| 1904O . . . . . . . . . . . . | 3,720,000 | 35 | 37 | 40 | 45 | 60 | 165 |
| 1904S . . . . . . . . . . . . . | 2,304,000 | 65 | 250 | 850 | 2,500 | 4,000 | 6,500 |
| 1921 . . . . . . . . . . . . . . | 44,690,000 | 35 | 37 | 40 | 42 | 50 | 150 |
| 1921D . . . . . . . . . . . . | 20,345,000 | 35 | 37 | 40 | 55 | 105 | 400 |
| 1921S . . . . . . . . . . . . . | 21,695,000 | 35 | 37 | 40 | 65 | 100 | 550 |

**a.** Values are for Proofs.

# PEACE (1921–1935)

Anthony de Francisci, a medalist, designed this dollar. His monogram is located in the field of the coin under the neck of Liberty.

The 1921 Silver Dollar Coin Anniversary Act authorized the Mint to produce coins celebrating the 2021 centennial of the first Peace dollar.

**VF-20 Very Fine:** Hair over eye well worn. Some strands over ear well defined. Some eagle feathers on top and outside edge of right wing visible.

**EF-40 Extremely Fine:** Hair lines over brow and ear are strong, though slightly worn. Outside wing feathers at right and those at top visible but faint.

**AU-50 About Uncirculated:** Slight trace of wear. Most luster present, although marred by contact marks.

**MS-60 Uncirculated:** No trace of wear. Full mint luster, but possibly noticeably marred by stains, surface marks, or bag abrasions.

**MS-63 Choice Uncirculated:** Some distracting contact marks or blemishes in prime focal areas. Impaired luster possible.

**MS-64 Uncirculated:** A few scattered contact marks. Good eye appeal and attractive luster.

**MS-65 Gem Uncirculated:** Only light, scattered, non-distracting contact marks. Strong luster, good eye appeal.

**PF-65 Choice Proof:** Satin surfaces, no noticeable blemishes or flaws.

*Most Uncirculated silver dollars have scratches or nicks because of handling of mint bags in shipping and storage. Coin dealers usually pay more than the listed prices for choice sharply struck pieces with full brilliance and without blemishes.*

*Mintmark location on reverse, below ONE.*

|  | Mintage | VF-20 | EF-40 | AU-50 | MS-60 | MS-63 | MS-65 | PF-65 |
|---|---|---|---|---|---|---|---|---|
| 1921 . . . . . . . . . . . . . . . | 1,006,473 | $165 | $215 | $250 | $450 | $875 | $2,350 | $125,000 |
| 1922 . . . . . . . . . . . . . . | 51,737,000 | 26 | 28 | 30 | 32 | 45 | 105 | 185,000 |
| 1922D . . . . . . . . . . . . | 15,063,000 | 26 | 28 | 30 | 40 | 75 | 425 | |
| 1922S . . . . . . . . . . . . | 17,475,000 | 26 | 28 | 30 | 40 | 75 | 900 | |
| 1923 . . . . . . . . . . . . . . | 30,800,000 | 26 | 28 | 30 | 32 | 45 | 110 | |
| 1923D . . . . . . . . . . . . | 6,811,000 | 26 | 28 | 40 | 75 | 185 | 850 | |
| 1923S . . . . . . . . . . . . | 19,020,000 | 26 | 28 | 30 | 50 | 85 | 1,500 | |
| 1924 . . . . . . . . . . . . . . | 11,811,000 | 26 | 28 | 30 | 32 | 45 | 105 | |
| 1924S . . . . . . . . . . . . | 1,728,000 | 26 | 40 | 55 | 200 | 450 | 4,250 | |
| 1925 . . . . . . . . . . . . . . | 10,198,000 | 26 | 28 | 30 | 32 | 45 | 105 | |
| 1925S . . . . . . . . . . . . | 1,610,000 | 26 | 40 | 45 | 100 | 225 | 17,500 | |
| 1926 . . . . . . . . . . . . . . | 1,939,000 | 26 | 28 | 35 | 55 | 85 | 325 | |
| 1926D . . . . . . . . . . . . | 2,348,700 | 26 | 28 | 45 | 85 | 185 | 650 | |
| 1926S . . . . . . . . . . . . | 6,980,000 | 26 | 28 | 35 | 45 | 75 | 500 | |
| 1927 . . . . . . . . . . . . . . | 848,000 | 30 | 35 | 45 | 65 | 185 | 1,100 | |
| 1927D . . . . . . . . . . . . | 1,268,900 | 35 | 45 | 75 | 155 | 350 | 2,650 | |
| 1927S . . . . . . . . . . . . | 866,000 | 35 | 45 | 75 | 150 | 475 | 5,000 | |
| 1928 . . . . . . . . . . . . . . | 360,649 | 200 | 225 | 250 | 350 | 600 | 2,750 | |
| 1928S . . . . . . . . . . . . | 1,632,000 | 35 | 40 | 65 | 125 | 400 | 10,000 | |
| 1934 . . . . . . . . . . . . . . | 954,057 | 30 | 35 | 60 | 100 | 175 | 500 | |
| 1934D . . . . . . . . . . . . | 1,569,500 | 30 | 50 | 65 | 115 | 275 | 1,000 | |
| 1934S . . . . . . . . . . . . | 1,011,000 | 55 | 100 | 300 | 2,250 | 4,500 | 9,000 | |
| 1935 . . . . . . . . . . . . . . | 1,576,000 | 35 | 40 | 55 | 65 | 150 | 475 | |
| 1935S . . . . . . . . . . . . | 1,964,000 | 35 | 45 | 70 | 225 | 375 | 900 | |

## EISENHOWER (1971–1978)
### Eagle Reverse (1971–1974)

Honoring both President Dwight D. Eisenhower and the first landing of man on the moon, this design is the work of Chief Engraver Frank Gasparro, whose initials are on the truncation of the President's neck and below the eagle. The reverse is an adaptation of the official *Apollo 11* insignia.

*Mintmark location is above date.*

| | Mintage | EF-40 | MS-63 | PF-63 | PF-65 |
|---|---|---|---|---|---|
| 1971, Copper-Nickel Clad | 47,799,000 | $1.20 | $2.00 | | |
| 1971D, Copper-Nickel Clad | 68,587,424 | 1.20 | 1.75 | | |
| 1971S, Silver Clad | (4,265,234) . . . 6,868,530 | | 9.00 | $9.50 | $12.00 |
| 1972, Copper-Nickel Clad | 75,890,000 | 1.20 | 1.75 | | |
| 1972D, Copper-Nickel Clad | 92,548,511 | 1.20 | 1.75 | | |
| 1972S, Silver Clad | (1,811,631) . . . 2,193,056 | | 9.00 | 9.50 | 12.00 |
| 1973, Copper-Nickel Clad **(a)** | 2,000,056 | 1.20 | 3.50 | | |
| 1973D, Copper-Nickel Clad **(a)** | 2,000,000 | 1.20 | 3.50 | | |
| 1973S, Copper-Nickel Clad | (2,760,339) | | | 2.50 | 7.00 |
| 1973S, Silver Clad | (1,013,646) . . . 1,883,140 | | 10.00 | 22.00 | 27.00 |
| 1974, Copper-Nickel Clad | 27,366,000 | 1.20 | 1.75 | | |
| 1974D, Copper-Nickel Clad | 45,517,000 | 1.20 | 1.75 | | |
| 1974S, Copper-Nickel Clad | (2,612,568) | | | 2.50 | 3.75 |
| 1974S, Silver Clad | (1,306,579) . . . 1,900,156 | | 9.00 | 12.00 | 14.00 |

**a.** 1,769,258 of each sold only in sets and not released for circulation. Unissued coins destroyed at mint.

### Bicentennial (1776–1976)

Obverse        Reverse Variety 2        Reverse Variety 1

*Variety 1: Design in low relief, bold lettering on reverse.*
*Variety 2: Sharp design, delicate lettering on reverse.*

*See next page for chart.*     

| | Mintage | EF-40 | MS-63 | PF-63 | PF-65 |
|---|---|---|---|---|---|
| 1776–1976, Copper-Nickel Clad, Variety 1 . . . . . . . . . . . . . . 4,019,000 | | $1.20 | $3.00 | | |
| 1776–1976, Copper-Nickel Clad, Variety 2 . . . . . . . . . . . 113,318,000 | | 1.20 | 1.75 | | |
| 1776–1976D, Copper-Nickel Clad, Variety 1 . . . . . . . . . . . 21,048,710 | | 1.20 | 1.75 | | |
| 1776–1976D, Copper-Nickel Clad, Variety 2 . . . . . . . . . . . 82,179,564 | | 1.20 | 1.75 | | |
| 1776–1976S, Copper-Nickel Clad, Variety 1 . . (2,845,450) . . . . . . . . . | | | | $3 | $5.50 |
| 1776–1976S, Copper-Nickel Clad, Variety 2 . . (4,149,730) . . . . . . . . . | | | | 3 | 4.00 |
| 1776–1976S, Silver Clad, Variety 1 . . . . . . . . . . . . . . . . . . 11,000,000 | | | 9.00 | | |
| 1776–1976S, Silver Clad, Variety 1 . . . . . . . . (4,000,000) . . . . . . . . . | | | | 12 | 13.00 |

### Eagle Reverse Resumed (1977–1978)

| | Mintage | EF-40 | MS-63 | PF-63 | PF-65 |
|---|---|---|---|---|---|
| 1977, Copper-Nickel Clad . . . . . . . . . . . . . . . . . . . . . . . . . . 12,596,000 | | $1.20 | $1.75 | | |
| 1977D, Copper-Nickel Clad . . . . . . . . . . . . . . . . . . . . . . . . . 32,983,006 | | 1.20 | 1.75 | | |
| 1977S, Copper-Nickel Clad . . . . . . . . . (3,251,152). . . . . . . . . . . . . | | | | $3 | $5.00 |
| 1978, Copper-Nickel Clad . . . . . . . . . . . . . . . . . . . . . . . . . . 25,702,000 | | 1.20 | 1.75 | | |
| 1978D, Copper-Nickel Clad . . . . . . . . . . . . . . . . . . . . . . . . . 33,012,890 | | 1.20 | 1.75 | | |
| 1978S, Copper-Nickel Clad . . . . . . . . . (3,127,781). . . . . . . . . . . . . | | | | 3 | 5.00 |

### SUSAN B. ANTHONY (1979–1999)

Filled S            Clear S

| | Mintage | MS-63 |
|---|---|---|
| 1979P, Narrow Rim. . . . . . . . . . . . . . . . . . . . . . . . . . . . . . . . . . . . . . . . . . . 360,222,000 | | $1.10 |
| 1979P, Wide Rim. . . . . . . . . . . . . . . . . . . . . . . . . . . . . . . . . . . . . . . . . . . . . . . . . * | | 27.00 |
| 1979D. . . . . . . . . . . . . . . . . . . . . . . . . . . . . . . . . . . . . . . . . . . . . . . . . 288,015,744 | | 1.10 |
| 1979S. . . . . . . . . . . . . . . . . . . . . . . . . . . . . . . . . . . . . . . . . . . . . . . . . 109,576,000 | | 1.10 |

* Included in number above.

| | Mintage | MS-65 | PF-63 | PF-65 |
|---|---|---|---|---|
| 1979S, Proof, | | | | |
| Type 1. . . . (3,677,175) | | $2.50 | | $4 |
| 1979S, Proof, | | | | |
| Type 2. . . . . . . . . . . .* | | 20.00 | | 40 |
| 1980P . . . . . . . . 27,610,000 | | $1.10 | | |
| 1980D . . . . . . . . 41,628,708 | | 1.10 | | |
| 1980S . . . . . . . . 20,422,000 | | 1.10 | | |
| 1980S, Proof . . . (3,554,806) | | | 2.50 | 3 |
| 1981P . . . . . . . . . 3,000,000 | | 2.00 | | |

| | Mintage | MS-65 | PF-63 | PF-65 |
|---|---|---|---|---|
| 1981D . . . . . . . . 3,250,000 | | $2.00 | | |
| 1981S . . . . . . . . 3,492,000 | | 2.00 | | |
| 1981S, Proof, | | | | |
| Type 1. . . . (4,063,083) | | | $2.50 | $4 |
| 1981S, Proof, | | | | |
| Type 2. . . . . . . . . . . .* | | | 35.00 | 75 |
| 1999P . . . . . . . . 29,592,000 | | 2.50 | | |
| 1999P, Proof . . . . . (750,000) | | | 13.00 | 16 |
| 1999D . . . . . . . . 11,776,000 | | 2.50 | | |

* Included in number above.

### SACAGAWEA (2000–2008)

The design of this coin was selected in national competition from among 120 submissions that were considered by a panel appointed by Treasury Secretary Robert Rubin. The adopted motif depicts Sacagawea, a young Native American Shoshone, as rendered by artist Glenna Goodacre. On her back she carries Jean Baptiste, her infant son. The reverse shows an eagle in flight, designed by Mint engraver Thomas D. Rogers Sr.

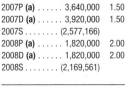

The composition exemplifies the spirit of Liberty, Peace, and Freedom shown by Sacagawea in her conduct as interpreter and guide to explorers Meriwether Lewis and William Clark during their famed journey westward from St. Louis to the Pacific.

These coins have a distinctive golden color and a plain edge to distinguish them from other denominations or coins of a similar size. The change in composition and appearance was mandated under the United States Dollar Coin Act of 1997.

Several distinctive finishes can be identified on the Sacagawea dollars as a result of the Mint attempting to adjust the dies, blanks, strikes, or finishing to produce coins with minimal spotting and a better surface color. One group of 5,000 pieces dated 2000 with a special finish were presented to sculptor Glenna Goodacre in payment for the obverse design. Unexplained error coins made from mismatched dies (a State quarter obverse combined with a Sacagawea dollar reverse) are extremely rare.

| | Mintage | MS-65 | PF-63 | PF-65 |
|---|---|---|---|---|
| 2000P | 767,140,000 | $1.10 | | |
| 2000D | 518,916,000 | 1.10 | | |
| 2000S | (4,097,904) | | $3 | $5 |
| 2001P | 62,468,000 | 1.10 | | |
| 2001D | 70,939,500 | 1.10 | | |
| 2001S | (3,183,740) | | 7 | 9 |
| 2002P (a) | 3,865,610 | 1.25 | | |
| 2002D (a) | 3,732,000 | 1.25 | | |
| 2002S | (3,211,995) | | 3 | 5 |
| 2003P (a) | 3,080,000 | 1.50 | | |
| 2003D (a) | 3,080,000 | 1.50 | | |
| 2003S | (3,298,439) | | 3 | 5 |
| 2004P (a) | 2,660,000 | 1.50 | | |
| 2004D (a) | 2,660,000 | 1.50 | | |

| | Mintage | MS-65 | PF-63 | PF-65 |
|---|---|---|---|---|
| 2004S | (2,965,422) | | $3 | $5 |
| 2005P (a) | 2,520,000 | $1.50 | | |
| 2005D (a) | 2,520,000 | 1.50 | | |
| 2005S | (3,344,679) | | 3 | 5 |
| 2006P (a) | 4,900,000 | 1.50 | | |
| 2006D (a) | 2,800,000 | 1.50 | | |
| 2006S | (3,054,436) | | 3 | 5 |
| 2007P (a) | 3,640,000 | 1.50 | | |
| 2007D (a) | 3,920,000 | 1.50 | | |
| 2007S | (2,577,166) | | 3 | 5 |
| 2008P (a) | 1,820,000 | 2.00 | | |
| 2008D (a) | 1,820,000 | 2.00 | | |
| 2008S | (2,169,561) | | 6 | 8 |

a. Not issued for circulation.

## PRESIDENTIAL (2007–2016, 2020)

Four different coins, each bearing the image of a former U.S. president, were issued each year in the order that the presidents served. The size and composition of these coins is the same as that of the Native American dollars that are also made each year. A companion series of ten-dollar gold bullion coins (listed in the Bullion section) honors the spouse of each president.

Presidential Dollars Reverse

Date, Mintmark, and Motto Incused on Edge (Motto Moved to Obverse in 2009)

The 2016 Ronald Reagan issues brought the regular production of Presidential dollars to a close. In 2020, the Mint produced a new coin to honor President George H.W. Bush (d. November 30, 2018), along with a gold bullion coin honoring Barbara Bush, his late wife.

| | Mintage | MS-65 | PF-65 |
|---|---|---|---|
| 2007P, Washington .... | 176,680,000 | $1.10 | |
| 2007D, Washington .... | 163,680,000 | 1.10 | |
| 2007S, Washington ..... | (3,965,989) | | $1.50 |
| 2007P, J. Adams ....... | 112,420,000 | 1.10 | |
| 2007D, J. Adams ...... | 112,140,000 | 1.10 | |
| 2007S, J. Adams ....... | (3,965,989) | | 2.00 |

| | Mintage | MS-65 | PF-65 |
|---|---|---|---|
| 2007P, Jefferson ...... | 100,800,000 | $1.10 | |
| 2007D, Jefferson ...... | 102,810,000 | 1.10 | |
| 2007S, Jefferson ....... | (3,965,989) | | $2 |
| 2007P, Madison ....... | 84,560,000 | 1.10 | |
| 2007D, Madison ...... | 87,780,000 | 1.10 | |
| 2007S, Madison ....... | (3,965,989) | | 2 |

| | Mintage | MS-65 | PF-65 |
|---|---|---|---|
| 2008P, Monroe ........ | 64,260,000 | $1.10 | |
| 2008D, Monroe ........ | 60,230,000 | 1.10 | |
| 2008S, Monroe ........ | (3,083,940) | | $2 |
| 2008P, J.Q. Adams ..... | 57,540,000 | 1.10 | |
| 2008D, J.Q. Adams ..... | 57,720,000 | 1.10 | |
| 2008S, J.Q. Adams ..... | (3,083,940) | | 2 |

| | Mintage | MS-65 | PF-65 |
|---|---|---|---|
| 2008P, Jackson ........ | 61,180,000 | $1.10 | |
| 2008D, Jackson ....... | 61,070,000 | 1.10 | |
| 2008S, Jackson ........ | (3,083,940) | | $2 |
| 2008P, Van Buren ...... | 51,520,000 | 1.10 | |
| 2008D, Van Buren ...... | 50,960,000 | 1.10 | |
| 2008S, Van Buren ...... | (3,083,940) | | 2 |

| | Mintage | MS-65 | PF-65 |
|---|---|---|---|
| 2009P, Harrison ........ | 43,260,000 | $1.10 | |
| 2009D, Harrison ....... | 55,160,000 | 1.10 | |
| 2009S, Harrison ....... | (2,809,452) | | $2 |
| 2009P, Tyler .......... | 43,540,000 | 1.10 | |
| 2009D, Tyler .......... | 43,540,000 | 1.10 | |
| 2009S, Tyler .......... | (2,809,452) | | 2 |

| | Mintage | MS-65 | PF-65 |
|---|---|---|---|
| 2009P, Polk ........... | 46,620,000 | $1.10 | |
| 2009D, Polk ........... | 41,720,000 | 1.10 | |
| 2009S, Polk ........... | (2,809,452) | | $2 |
| 2009P, Taylor ......... | 41,580,000 | 1.10 | |
| 2009D, Taylor ......... | 36,680,000 | 1.10 | |
| 2009S, Taylor ......... | (2,809,452) | | 2 |

*Note: Errors have been reported in the Presidential dollar series, including coins minted without edge lettering. Depending on their rarity, dealers may pay a premium for such errors.*

| | Mintage | MS-65 | PF-65 |
|---|---|---|---|
| 2010P, Fillmore | 37,520,000 | $1.10 | |
| 2010D, Fillmore | 36,960,000 | 1.10 | |
| 2010S, Fillmore | (2,224,613) | | $2 |
| 2010P, Pierce | 38,220,000 | 1.10 | |
| 2010D, Pierce | 38,360,000 | 1.10 | |
| 2010S, Pierce | (2,224,613) | | 2 |

| | Mintage | MS-65 | PF-65 |
|---|---|---|---|
| 2010P, Buchanan | 36,820,000 | $1.10 | |
| 2010D, Buchanan | 36,540,000 | 1.10 | |
| 2010S, Buchanan | (2,224,613) | | $2 |
| 2010P, Lincoln | 49,000,000 | 1.10 | |
| 2010D, Lincoln | 48,020,000 | 1.10 | |
| 2010S, Lincoln | (2,224,613) | | 3 |

| | Mintage | MS-65 | PF-65 |
|---|---|---|---|
| 2011P, A. Johnson | 35,560,000 | $1.10 | |
| 2011D, A. Johnson | 37,100,000 | 1.10 | |
| 2011S, A. Johnson | (1,972,863) | | $2 |
| 2011P, Grant | 38,080,000 | 1.10 | |
| 2011D, Grant | 37,940,000 | 1.10 | |
| 2011S, Grant | (1,972,863) | | 2 |

| | Mintage | MS-65 | PF-65 |
|---|---|---|---|
| 2011P, Hayes | 37,660,000 | $1.10 | |
| 2011D, Hayes | 36,820,000 | 1.10 | |
| 2011S, Hayes | (1,972,863) | | $2 |
| 2011P, Garfield | 37,100,000 | 1.10 | |
| 2011D, Garfield | 37,100,000 | 1.10 | |
| 2011S, Garfield | (1,972,863) | | 2 |

| | Mintage | MS-65 | PF-65 |
|---|---|---|---|
| 2012P, Arthur **(a)** | 6,020,000 | $1.10 | |
| 2012D, Arthur **(a)** | 4,060,000 | 1.10 | |
| 2012S, Arthur | (1,438,743) | | $3 |
| 2012P, Cleveland, Variety 1 **(a)** | 5,460,000 | 1.10 | |
| 2012D, Cleveland, Variety 1 **(a)** | 4,060,000 | 1.10 | |
| 2012S, Cleveland, Variety 1 | (1,438,743) | | 3 |

| | Mintage | MS-65 | PF-65 |
|---|---|---|---|
| 2012P, Harrison **(a)** | 5,640,000 | $1.10 | |
| 2012D, Harrison **(a)** | 4,200,000 | 1.10 | |
| 2012S, Harrison | (1,438,743) | | $3 |
| 2012P, Cleveland, Variety 2 **(a)** | 10,680,000 | 1.10 | |
| 2012D, Cleveland, Variety 2 **(a)** | 3,920,000 | 1.10 | |
| 2012S, Cleveland, Variety 2 | (1,438,743) | | 3 |

**a.** Not issued for circulation.

| | Mintage | MS-65 | PF-65 |
|---|---|---|---|
| 2013P, McKinley **(a)** | 4,760,000 | $1.10 | |
| 2013D, McKinley **(a)** | 3,365,100 | 1.10 | |
| 2013S, McKinley | (1,488,798) | | $2 |
| 2013P, T. Roosevelt **(a)** | 5,310,700 | 1.10 | |
| 2013D, T. Roosevelt **(a)** | 3,920,000 | 1.10 | |
| 2013S, T. Roosevelt | (1,503,943) | | 2 |

| | Mintage | MS-65 | PF-65 |
|---|---|---|---|
| 2013P, Taft **(a)** | 4,760,000 | $1.10 | |
| 2013D, Taft **(a)** | 3,360,000 | 1.10 | |
| 2013S, Taft | (1,488,798) | | $2 |
| 2013P, Wilson **(a)** | 4,620,000 | 1.10 | |
| 2013D, Wilson **(a)** | 3,360,000 | 1.10 | |
| 2013S, Wilson | (1,488,798) | | 2 |

a. Not issued for circulation.

| | Mintage | MS-65 | PF-65 |
|---|---|---|---|
| 2014P, Harding **(a)** | 6,160,000 | $1.10 | |
| 2014D, Harding **(a)** | 3,780,000 | 1.10 | |
| 2014S, Harding | (1,373,569) | | $3 |
| 2014P, Coolidge **(a)** | 4,480,000 | 1.10 | |
| 2014D, Coolidge **(a)** | 3,780,000 | 1.10 | |
| 2014S, Coolidge | (1,373,569) | | 3 |

| | Mintage | MS-65 | PF-65 |
|---|---|---|---|
| 2014P, Hoover **(a)** | 4,480,000 | $1.10 | |
| 2014D, Hoover **(a)** | 3,780,000 | 1.10 | |
| 2014S, Hoover | (1,373,569) | | $3 |
| 2014P, F.D. Roosevelt **(a)** | 4,760,000 | 1.10 | |
| 2014D, F.D. Roosevelt **(a)** | 3,920,000 | 1.10 | |
| 2014S, F.D. Roosevelt | (1,392,619) | | 3 |

a. Not issued for circulation.

| | Mintage | MS-65 | PF-65 |
|---|---|---|---|
| 2015P, Truman **(a)** | 4,900,000 | $1.10 | |
| 2015P, Truman, RevPf | (16,812) | | $18 |
| 2015D, Truman **(a)** | 3,500,000 | 1.10 | |
| 2015S, Truman | (1,272,232) | | 3 |
| 2015P, Eisenhower **(a)** | 4,900,000 | 1.10 | |
| 2015P, Eisenhower, Ref Pf | (16,744) | | 18 |
| 2015D, Eisenhower **(a)** | 3,645,998 | 1.10 | |
| 2015S, Eisenhower | (1,272,232) | | 3 |

| | Mintage | MS-65 | PF-65 |
|---|---|---|---|
| 2015P, Kennedy **(a)** | 6,160,000 | $1.10 | |
| 2015P, Kennedy, RevPf | (49,051) | | $18 |
| 2015D, Kennedy **(a)** | 5,180,000 | 1.10 | |
| 2015S, Kennedy | (1,272,232) | | 3 |
| 2015P, L. Johnson **(a)** | 7,840,000 | 1.10 | |
| 2015P, L. Johnson, RevPf | (23,905) | | 18 |
| 2015D, L. Johnson **(a)** | 4,200,000 | 1.10 | |
| 2015S, L.B. Johnson | (1,272,232) | | 3 |

a. Not issued for circulation.

| | Mintage | MS-65 | PF-65 |
|---|---|---|---|
| 2016P, Nixon **(a)** ........ | 5,460,000 | $1.10 | |
| 2016D, Nixon **(a)** ........ | 4,340,000 | 1.10 | |
| 2016S, Nixon .......... | (1,196,582) | | $3 |
| 2016P, Ford **(a)** ......... | 5,460,000 | 1.10 | |
| 2016P, Ford **(a)** ......... | 5,040,000 | 1.10 | |
| 2016S, Ford ........... | (1,196,582) | | 3 |
| 2016P, Reagan **(a)** ....... | 7,140,000 | 1.10 | |

| | Mintage | MS-65 | PF-65 |
|---|---|---|---|
| 2016D, Reagan **(a)** ...... | 5,880,000 | $1.10 | |
| 2016S, Reagan ........ | (1,196,582) | | $3 |
| 2016S, Reagan, RevPf ..... | (47,447) | | 18 |
| 2020P, G.H.W. Bush **(a)** ... | *1,242,275* | 1.10 | |
| 2020D, G.H.W. Bush **(a)** ... | *1,502,425* | 1.10 | |
| 2020S, G.H.W. Bush .............. | | | 3 |
| 2020S, G.H.W. Bush, RevPf ........ | | | 18 |

**a.** Not issued for circulation.

# NATIVE AMERICAN (2009 TO DATE)

| Obverse | Three Sisters (2009) | Great Law of Peace (2010) | Wampanoag Treaty (2011) |
|---|---|---|---|
| **Trade Routes in the 17th Century (2012)** | **Treaty With the Delawares (2013)** | **Native Hospitality (2014)** | **Mohawk Ironworkers (2015)** |
| **Code Talkers (2016)** | **Sequoyah (2017)** | **Jim Thorpe (2018)** | **American Indians in Space (2019)** |

*Entry continued on next page.*

Elizabeth Peratrovich and Alaska's Anti-Discrimination Law (2020) — American Indians in the U.S. Military (2021) — Ely S. Parker (2022)

| | Mintage | MS-65 | PF-65 | | Mintage | MS-65 | PF-65 |
|---|---|---|---|---|---|---|---|
| 2009P, Three Sisters | 39,200,000 | $1.25 | | 2016S, Code Talkers | (931,866) | | $3 |
| 2009D, Three Sisters | 35,700,000 | 1.25 | | 2017P, Sequoyah (a) | 1,820,000 | $1.50 | |
| 2009S, Three Sisters | (2,179,867) | | $3 | 2017D, Sequoyah (a) | 1,540,000 | 1.50 | |
| 2010P, Great Law | 32,060,000 | 1.75 | | 2017S, Sequoyah, Enh. Unc. | 210,419 | 8.75 | |
| 2010D, Great Law | 48,720,000 | 1.75 | | 2017S, Sequoyah | (926,763) | | 3 |
| 2010S, Great Law | (1,689,216) | | 3 | 2018P, Jim Thorpe (a) | 1,400,000 | 1.50 | |
| 2011P, Wampanoag | 29,400,000 | 2.00 | | 2018D, Jim Thorpe (a) | 1,400,000 | 1.50 | |
| 2011D, Wampanoag | 48,160,000 | 2.00 | | 2018S, Jim Thorpe | (849,321) | | 3 |
| 2011S, Wampanoag | (1,673,010) | | 3 | 2019P, Am. Indians / Space (a) | 1,400,000 | 1.50 | |
| 2012P, Trade Routes (a) | 2,800,000 | 1.75 | | 2019P, Am. Indians / Space, | | | |
| 2012D, Trade Routes (a) | 2,080,000 | 1.75 | | Enhanced Uncirculated | 46,964 | 8.75 | |
| 2012S, Trade Routes | (1,189,445) | | 7 | 2019D, Am. Indians /Space (a) | 1,540,000 | 1.50 | |
| 2013P, Treaty, Delawares (a) | 1,820,000 | 1.50 | | 2019S, Am. Indians in Space | (1,101,282) | | 3 |
| 2013D, Treaty, Delawares (a) | 1,820,000 | 1.50 | | 2020P, E. Peratrovich / Alaska's | | | |
| 2013S, Treaty, Delawares | (1,222,180) | | 3 | Anti-Discrimination Law (a) | 1,260,000 | 1.50 | |
| 2014P, Native Hospitality (a) | 3,080,000 | 1.50 | | 2020D, E. Peratrovich / Alaska's | | | |
| 2014D, Native Hospitality (a) | 2,800,000 | 1.50 | | Anti-Discrimination Law (a) | 1,260,000 | 1.50 | |
| 2014D, Native Hospitality, | | | | 2020S, E. Peratrovich / Alaska's | | | |
| Enhanced Uncirculated | 50,000 | 8.75 | | Anti-Discrimination Law | (778,264) | | 3 |
| 2014S, Native Hospitality | (1,144,154) | | 3 | 2021P, American Indians | | | |
| 2015P, Mohawk Ironworkers (a) | 2,800,000 | 1.50 | | in the U.S. Military (a) | 1,400,000 | 1.50 | |
| 2015D, Mohawk Ironworkers (a) | 2,240,000 | 1.50 | | 2021D, American Indians | | | |
| 2015S, Mohawk Ironworkers | (1,050,164) | | 3 | in the U.S. Military (a) | 1,260,000 | 1.50 | |
| 2015W, Mohawk Ironworkers, | | | | 2021S, American Indians | | | |
| Enhanced Uncirculated | 88,805 | 8.75 | | in the U.S. Military | (745,815) | | 3 |
| 2016P, Code Talkers (a) | 2,800,000 | 1.50 | | 2022P, Ely S. Parker (a) | | | |
| 2016D, Code Talkers (a) | 2,100,000 | 1.50 | | 2022D, Ely S. Parker (a) | | | |
| 2016S, Code Talkers, Enh. Unc. | 50,737 | 8.75 | | 2022S, Ely S. Parker | | | |

a. Not issued for circulation.

# AMERICAN INNOVATION (2018–2032)

In 2018, the U.S. Mint inaugurated a new, 15-year coin series: the American Innovation $1 Coin Program. Each of the golden dollars in the program features a reverse design that "symbolizes quintessentially American traits—the willingness to explore, to discover, and to create one's own destiny." Four new designs, in Uncirculated and Proof finishes, are issued each year from 2019 through 2032—one for each state, in the order in which the states ratified the Constitution or were admitted to the Union, and then for the District of Columbia and each of the five U.S. territories (Puerto Rico, Guam, American Samoa, the U.S. Virgin Islands, and the Northern Mariana Islands). Like all dollar coins minted after 2011, they are issued for numismatic sales only; none are distributed for circulation.

**Privy Marks**

2019    2020

Obverse    American Innovators
(2018)

2021

Delaware: Classifying
the Stars (2019)

Pennsylvania: Polio
Vaccine (2019)

New Jersey:
Light Bulb (2019)

Georgia: Trustees'
Garden (2019)

Connecticut: Gerber
Variable Scale (2020)

Massachusetts:
Telephone (2020)

Maryland: The Hubble
Space Telescope (2020)

South Carolina:
Septima Clark (2020)

New Hampshire:
Ralph Baer (2021)

Virginia: Chesapeake Bay
Bridge-Tunnel (2021)

New York:
Erie Canal (2021)

North Carolina:
Higher Learning (2021)

| | Mintage | MS-65 | PF-65 |
|---|---|---|---|
| 2018P, Innovators | 502,150 | $1.50 | |
| 2018D, Innovators | 582,825 | 1.50 | |
| 2018S, Innovators | (243,567) | | $3 |
| 2018S, Innovators, RevPf. | (74,720) | | 5 |
| 2019P, Delaware | 472,750 | 1.50 | |
| 2019D, Delaware | 479,975 | 1.50 | |
| 2019S, Delaware | (137,696) | | 3 |
| 2019S, Delaware, RevPf | (66,517) | | 5 |
| 2019P, Pennsylvania | 490,200 | 1.50 | |

| | Mintage | MS-65 | PF-65 |
|---|---|---|---|
| 2019D, Pennsylvania | 443,800 | $1.50 | |
| 2019S, Pennsylvania | (137,696) | | $3 |
| 2019S, Pennsylvania, RevPf. | (50,866) | | 5 |
| 2019P, New Jersey | 521,175 | 1.50 | |
| 2019D, New Jersey | 476,275 | 1.50 | |
| 2019S, New Jersey | (137,696) | | 3 |
| 2019S, New Jersey, RevPf. | (46,785) | | 5 |
| 2019P, Georgia | 474,550 | 1.50 | |
| 2019D, Georgia | 455,800 | 1.50 | |

*Chart continued on next page.*     

| | Mintage | MS-65 | PF-65 | | Mintage | MS-65 | PF-65 |
|---|---|---|---|---|---|---|---|
| 2019S, Georgia . . . . . . . . . . | (137,696) | | $3 | 2021S, Virginia, RevPf . . . . . . . | (43,204) | | $5 |
| 2019S, Georgia, RevPf. . . . . . . | (43,420) | | 5 | 2021P, New York (a) . . . . . . . . | 451,750 | $1.50 | |
| 2020P, Connecticut . . . . . . . . | 436,000 | $1.50 | | 2021D, New York (a). . . . . . . . | 451,175 | 1.50 | |
| 2020D, Connecticut. . . . . . . . | 435,325 | 1.50 | | 2021S, New York. . . . . . . . . . | (69,489) | | 3 |
| 2020S, Connecticut. . . . . . . . | (101,593) | | 3 | 2021S, New York, RevPf . . . . . | (43,204) | | 5 |
| 2020S, Connecticut, RevPf. . . | (43,653) | | 5 | 2021P, North Carolina . . . . . . . | 405,950 | 1.50 | |
| 2020P, Massachusetts. . . . . . . | 436,750 | 1.50 | | 2021D, North Carolina. . . . . . . | 389,725 | 1.50 | |
| 2020D, Massachusetts . . . . . . | 436,425 | 1.50 | | 2021S, North Carolina . . . . . . . | (69,489) | | 3 |
| 2020S, Massachusetts . . . . . | (101,593) | | 3 | 2021S, North Carolina, RevPf . | (43,204) | | 5 |
| 2020S, Massachusetts, RevPf . | (43,258) | | 5 | 2022P, Rhode Island . . . . . . . . . . . . | | 1.50 | |
| 2020P, Maryland . . . . . . . . . . | 434,825 | 1.50 | | 2022D, Rhode Island . . . . . . . . . . . . | | 1.50 | |
| 2020D, Maryland. . . . . . . . . . | 435,475 | 1.50 | | 2022S, Rhode Island . . . . . . . . . . . . | | | 3 |
| 2020S, Maryland. . . . . . . . . | (101,593) | | 3 | 2022S, Rhode Island, RevPf. . . . . . . . | | | 5 |
| 2020S, Maryland, RevPf . . . . . | (43,926) | | 5 | 2022P, Vermont. . . . . . . . . . . . . . . . | | 1.50 | |
| 2020P, South Carolina. . . . . . . | 432,850 | 1.50 | | 2022D, Vermont. . . . . . . . . . . . . . . . | | 1.50 | |
| 2020D, South Carolina. . . . . . | 397,775 | 1.50 | | 2022S, Vermont. . . . . . . . . . . . . . . . | | | 3 |
| 2020S, South Carolina. . . . . . | (101,593) | | 3 | 2022S, Vermont, RevPf . . . . . . . . . . . | | | 5 |
| 2020S, South Carolina, RevPf . | (36,409) | | 5 | 2022P, Kentucky . . . . . . . . . . . . . . . | | 1.50 | |
| 2021P, New Hampshire . . . . . . | 453,825 | 1.50 | | 2022D, Kentucky. . . . . . . . . . . . . . . | | 1.50 | |
| 2021D, New Hampshire. . . . . . | 450,725 | 1.50 | | 2022S, Kentucky. . . . . . . . . . . . . . . | | | 3 |
| 2021S, New Hampshire. . . . . . | (69,489) | | 3 | 2022S, Kentucky, RevPf . . . . . . . . . . | | | 5 |
| 2021S, New Hampshire, RevPf | (43,204) | | 5 | 2022P, Tennessee . . . . . . . . . . . . . . | | 1.50 | |
| 2021P, Virginia (a) . . . . . . . . . | 423,600 | 1.50 | | 2022D, Tennessee. . . . . . . . . . . . . . | | 1.50 | |
| 2021D, Virginia (a) . . . . . . . . | 422,875 | 1.50 | | 2022S, Tennessee. . . . . . . . . . . . . . | | | 3 |
| 2021S, Virginia . . . . . . . . . . . | (69,489) | | 3 | 2022S, Tennessee, RevPf . . . . . . . . . | | | 5 |

## 1921 SILVER DOLLAR ANNIVERSARY COINS (2021 TO DATE)

Congress passed the 1921 Silver Dollar Coin Anniversary Act "to mint and issue $1 coins in recognition of the 100th anniversary of completion of coinage of the Morgan dollar and the 100th anniversary of commencement of coinage of the Peace dollar." The resulting products, first minted in 2021, are not precise copies of the older coins, but, in the words of the legislation, "honor" the originals with "renditions" of the designs used on the original Morgan and Peace silver dollars.

The Mint's artists used modern technology and historical Mint assets to create the modern designs.

For the Morgan anniversary coins, some were minted in Philadelphia with "CC" and "O" privy marks to represent the historical mintages of Carson City and New Orleans.

In November 2021 the Mint announced plans to produce the coins as recurring annual products, in various finishes and using multiple Mint facilities.

"CC" privy mark

"O" privy mark

| | Mintage | Unc. | MS-69 | MS-70 |
|---|---|---|---|---|
| 2021(P), Morgan, No Privy Mark | 173,875 | $120 | $135 | $225 |
| 2021(P), Morgan, CC Privy Mark | 173,444 | 150 | 170 | 300 |
| 2021(P), Morgan, O Privy Mark | 173,102 | 120 | 135 | 225 |
| 2021S, Morgan | 174,093 | 125 | 140 | 230 |
| 2021D, Morgan | 173,730 | 120 | 135 | 300 |
| 2021(P), Peace | 198,772 | 145 | 160 | 250 |
| 2022S, Morgan, Proof | | | | |
| 2022S, Peace, Proof | | | | |

The Coinage Act of 1792 established the independent monetary system of the United States, with the dollar as its basic monetary unit. Silver dollar coins were made starting in 1794. Coinage of a gold dollar coin, however, was not authorized until the Act of March 3, 1849. Its weight was set at 25.8 grains, fineness .900.

The first type, struck until 1854, is known as the Liberty Head. In 1854 the gold dollar was made larger in diameter and thinner, while keeping the same weight. Along with that modification, the design was changed to a female wearing a feather headdress, generally referred to as the Indian Princess Head type. In 1856 this was changed slightly by enlarging the size of the head.

## LIBERTY HEAD (1849–1854)

**VF-20 Very Fine:** LIBERTY on headband complete and legible. Knobs on coronet defined.
**EF-40 Extremely Fine:** Slight wear on Liberty's hair. Knobs on coronet sharp.
**AU-50 About Uncirculated:** Trace of wear on headband. Nearly full luster.
**AU-55 Choice About Uncirculated:** Evidence of friction on design high points.
**MS-60 Uncirculated:** No trace of wear. Light marks and blemishes.
**MS-63 Choice Uncirculated:** Some distracting contact marks or blemishes in prime focal areas. Impaired luster possible.

| | Mintage | VF-20 | EF-40 | AU-50 | AU-55 | MS-60 | MS-63 |
|---|---|---|---|---|---|---|---|
| 1849, Open Wreath, | | | | | | | |
| No L on Truncation ........ 688,567 | | $205 | $250 | $300 | $325 | $600 | $1,200 |
| 1849, Close Wreath................ * | | 200 | 235 | 250 | 260 | 375 | 850 |
| 1849C, Open Wreath .......... 11,634 | | 155,000 | 200,000 | 250,000 | 300,000 | | |
| 1849C, Close Wreath............... * | | 1,100 | 1,600 | 2,200 | 2,850 | 6,500 | 12,500 |
| 1849D..................... 21,588 | | 1,350 | 1,750 | 2,100 | 2,600 | 4,000 | 13,500 |
| 1849O................... 215,000 | | 225 | 240 | 275 | 425 | 775 | 2,250 |
| 1850..................... 481,953 | | 200 | 235 | 250 | 265 | 300 | 600 |
| 1850C..................... 6,966 | | 1,100 | 1,600 | 2,750 | 3,200 | 4,750 | 20,000 |
| 1850D..................... 8,382 | | 1,350 | 2,000 | 3,000 | 3,700 | 7,500 | 30,000 |
| 1850O................... 14,000 | | 250 | 500 | 750 | 800 | 2,000 | 5,000 |
| 1851...................3,317,671 | | 200 | 235 | 250 | 260 | 300 | 500 |
| 1851C..................... 41,267 | | 1,050 | 1,300 | 1,500 | 1,750 | 2,500 | 4,750 |
| 1851D..................... 9,882 | | 1,350 | 1,750 | 2,500 | 2,750 | 4,000 | 13,500 |
| 1851O................... 290,000 | | 200 | 235 | 275 | 285 | 550 | 1,350 |
| 1852...................2,045,351 | | 200 | 235 | 250 | 260 | 300 | 500 |
| 1852C..................... 9,434 | | 1,100 | 1,200 | 1,600 | 2,100 | 3,250 | 8,000 |
| 1852D..................... 6,360 | | 1,300 | 1,600 | 2,500 | 3,000 | 6,500 | 25,000 |
| 1852O................... 140,000 | | 200 | 235 | 275 | 500 | 850 | 2,750 |
| 1853...................4,076,051 | | 200 | 235 | 250 | 260 | 300 | 500 |
| 1853C..................... 11,515 | | 1,200 | 1,450 | 1,750 | 2,450 | 3,500 | 12,000 |
| 1853D..................... 6,583 | | 1,350 | 1,750 | 2,600 | 3,000 | 6,000 | 17,500 |
| 1853O................... 290,000 | | 200 | 235 | 275 | 285 | 450 | 1,400 |
| 1854..................... 855,502 | | 200 | 235 | 250 | 260 | 300 | 500 |
| 1854D..................... 2,935 | | 2,000 | 3,250 | 5,000 | 5,500 | 7,500 | 30,000 |
| 1854S................... 14,632 | | 300 | 600 | 850 | 950 | 2,400 | 5,500 |

* Included in number above.

## INDIAN PRINCESS HEAD, SMALL HEAD (1854–1856)

**VF-20 Very Fine:** Feather-curl tips on headdress outlined but details worn.
**EF-40 Extremely Fine:** Slight wear on tips of feather curls on headdress.
**AU-50 About Uncirculated:** Trace of wear on feathers, nearly full luster.
**AU-55 Choice About Uncirculated:** Evidence of friction on design high points. Most of original mint luster present.
**MS-60 Uncirculated:** No trace of wear. Light marks and blemishes.
**MS-63 Choice Uncirculated:** Some distracting contact marks or blemishes in prime focal areas. Impaired luster possible.
**PF-63 Choice Proof:** Reflective surfaces with only a few blemishes in secondary focal areas. No major flaws.

| | Mintage | VF-20 | EF-40 | AU-50 | AU-55 | MS-60 | MS-63 | PF-63 |
|---|---|---|---|---|---|---|---|---|
| 1854 | 783,943 | $265 | $325 | $400 | $525 | $1,000 | $3,250 | $125,000 |
| 1855 | 758,269 | 265 | 325 | 400 | 525 | 1,000 | 3,250 | 110,000 |
| 1855C | 9,803 | 2,500 | 4,000 | 4,500 | 6,500 | 16,500 | | |
| 1855D | 1,811 | 15,000 | 21,000 | 32,500 | 35,000 | 50,000 | 80,000 | |
| 1855O | 55,000 | 550 | 900 | 1,500 | 1,850 | 6,000 | 22,000 | |
| 1856S | 24,600 | 600 | 1,200 | 1,750 | 2,500 | 6,000 | 17,500 | |

## INDIAN PRINCESS HEAD, LARGE HEAD (1856–1889)

**VF-20 Very Fine:** Slight detail in curled feathers in headdress. Details worn smooth at eyebrow, hair below headdress, and behind ear and bottom curl.
**EF-40 Extremely Fine:** Slight wear above and to right of eye and on top of curled feathers.
**AU-50 About Uncirculated:** Trace of wear on feathers, nearly full luster.
**AU-55 Choice About Uncirculated:** Evidence of friction on design high points. Most of original mint luster present.
**MS-60 Uncirculated:** No trace of wear. Light marks and blemishes.
**MS-63 Choice Uncirculated:** Some distracting contact marks or blemishes in prime focal areas. Impaired luster possible.
**PF-63 Choice Proof:** Reflective surfaces with only a few blemishes in secondary focal places. No major flaws.

| | Mintage | VF-20 | EF-40 | AU-50 | AU-55 | MS-60 | MS-63 | PF-63 |
|---|---|---|---|---|---|---|---|---|
| 1856 | 1,762,936 | $250 | $265 | $260 | $265 | $325 | $550 | $22,500 |
| 1856D | 1,460 | 4,000 | 6,000 | 7,500 | 8,750 | 24,000 | 55,000 | |
| 1857 | 774,789 | 250 | 265 | 260 | 265 | 325 | 550 | 9,500 |
| 1857C | 13,280 | 1,200 | 1,450 | 2,750 | 3,000 | 7,000 | | |
| 1857D | 3,533 | 1,350 | 1,650 | 3,100 | 4,250 | 8,500 | | |
| 1857S | 10,000 | 425 | 500 | 950 | 1,150 | 3,500 | 15,500 | |
| 1858 | 117,995 | 250 | 265 | 260 | 265 | 325 | 800 | 7,500 |
| 1858D | 3,477 | 1,300 | 1,750 | 2,500 | 3,200 | 6,000 | 17,000 | |

*See next page for chart.*

**1873, Close 3**          **1873, Open 3**

| | Mintage | VF-20 | EF-40 | AU-50 | AU-55 | MS-60 | MS-63 | PF-63 |
|---|---|---|---|---|---|---|---|---|
| 1858S | 10,000 | $300 | $600 | $900 | $1,350 | $4,250 | $12,500 | |
| 1859 | (80) ....168,244 | 250 | 255 | 260 | 265 | 325 | 600 | $7,500 |
| 1859C | 5,235 | 1,650 | 2,450 | 3,000 | 3,600 | 5,500 | 22,500 | |
| 1859D | 4,952 | 1,350 | 1,750 | 2,500 | 2,600 | 6,750 | 16,500 | |
| 1859S | 15,000 | 275 | 375 | 875 | 1,200 | 3,500 | 12,000 | |
| 1860 | (154) .....36,514 | 250 | 255 | 260 | 265 | 325 | 800 | 7,000 |
| 1860D | 1,566 | 3,000 | 4,500 | 7,000 | 8,250 | 15,500 | 40,000 | |
| 1860S | 13,000 | 300 | 400 | 600 | 800 | 2,000 | 4,500 | |
| 1861 | (349) ....527,150 | 250 | 255 | 260 | 265 | 375 | 550 | 5,000 |
| 1861D | 1,250 | 25,000 | 30,000 | 45,000 | 50,000 | 75,000 | 125,000 | |
| 1862 | (35) .. 1,361,355 | 250 | 255 | 260 | 265 | 325 | 550 | 5,500 |
| 1863 | (50) .....6,200 | 1,000 | 1,350 | 2,350 | 2,850 | 4,750 | 7,500 | 8,500 |
| 1864 | (50) .....5,900 | 500 | 700 | 900 | 1,100 | 1,600 | 3,250 | 8,500 |
| 1865 | (25) .....3,700 | 450 | 650 | 850 | 1,000 | 1,300 | 3,250 | 8,500 |
| 1866 | (30) .....7,100 | 350 | 500 | 600 | 750 | 850 | 2,000 | 8,500 |
| 1867 | (50) .....5,200 | 350 | 500 | 550 | 650 | 1,000 | 1,850 | 8,500 |
| 1868 | (25) .....10,500 | 325 | 475 | 525 | 550 | 850 | 1,500 | 8,500 |
| 1869 | (25) .....5,900 | 325 | 475 | 525 | 600 | 825 | 1,350 | 8,500 |
| 1870 | (35) .....6,300 | 325 | 475 | 525 | 575 | 700 | 1,450 | 8,500 |
| 1870S | 3,000 | 600 | 850 | 1,200 | 1,450 | 2,500 | 6,500 | |
| 1871 | (30) .....3,900 | 275 | 350 | 375 | 500 | 625 | 1,150 | 8,000 |
| 1872 | (30) .....3,500 | 275 | 350 | 375 | 475 | 700 | 1,500 | 8,500 |
| 1873, Close 3 ... (25) ...1,800 | | 350 | 550 | 675 | 775 | 1,200 | 2,750 | 11,000 |
| 1873, Open 3 | 123,300 | 250 | 255 | 260 | 265 | 325 | 550 | |
| 1874 | (20) ....198,800 | 250 | 255 | 260 | 265 | 325 | 550 | 8,500 |
| 1875 | (20) .......400 | 3,000 | 3,850 | 4,750 | 5,750 | 8,750 | 13,000 | 22,500 |
| 1876 | (45) .....3,200 | 300 | 325 | 425 | 450 | 650 | 1,000 | 6,500 |
| 1877 | (20) .....3,900 | 300 | 325 | 425 | 450 | 650 | 1,100 | 5,500 |
| 1878 | (20) .....3,000 | 300 | 325 | 400 | 450 | 600 | 950 | 5,500 |
| 1879 | (30) .....3,000 | 275 | 285 | 300 | 325 | 450 | 850 | 5,000 |
| 1880 | (36) .....1,600 | 275 | 285 | 300 | 325 | 400 | 750 | 4,500 |
| 1881 | (87) .....7,620 | 265 | 275 | 285 | 300 | 400 | 650 | 4,500 |
| 1882 | (125) .....5,000 | 265 | 275 | 285 | 310 | 400 | 600 | 5,000 |
| 1883 | (207) .....10,800 | 265 | 275 | 285 | 310 | 400 | 600 | 4,500 |
| 1884 | (1,006) .....5,230 | 265 | 275 | 285 | 310 | 400 | 600 | 4,500 |
| 1885 | (1,105) .....11,156 | 265 | 275 | 285 | 310 | 375 | 600 | 4,000 |
| 1886 | (1,016) .....5,000 | 265 | 275 | 285 | 310 | 375 | 600 | 4,000 |
| 1887 | (1,043) .....7,500 | 265 | 275 | 285 | 310 | 375 | 575 | 4,000 |
| 1888 | (1,079) .....15,501 | 265 | 275 | 285 | 310 | 375 | 575 | 4,000 |
| 1889 | (1,779) .....28,950 | 250 | 255 | 260 | 265 | 325 | 550 | 4,000 |

Although authorized by the Act of April 2, 1792, coinage of quarter eagles ($2.50) gold coins) was not begun until 1796.

## CAPPED BUST TO RIGHT (1796–1807)

**F-12 Fine:** Hair worn smooth on high spots. E PLURIBUS UNUM on ribbon weak but legible.
**VF-20 Very Fine:** Some wear on high spots.
**EF-40 Extremely Fine:** Only slight wear on Liberty's hair and cheek.
**AU-50 About Uncirculated:** Trace of wear on cap, hair, cheek, and drapery.
**AU-55 Choice About Uncirculated:** Evidence of friction on design high points. Some original mint luster.
**MS-60 Uncirculated:** No trace of wear. Light blemishes.

No Stars on Obverse (1796)          Stars on Obverse (1796–1807)

| | Mintage | F-12 | VF-20 | EF-40 | AU-50 | AU-55 | MS-60 |
|---|---|---|---|---|---|---|---|
| 1796, No Stars on Obverse . . . . . . . . . . . . 963 | $50,000 | $70,000 | $100,000 | $125,000 | $135,000 | $225,000 |
| 1796, Stars on Obverse . . . . . . . . . . . . . . 432 | 47,500 | 60,000 | 75,000 | 95,000 | 125,000 | 165,000 |
| 1797 . . . . . . . . . . . . . . . . . . . . . . . . . . . . 427 | 11,000 | 17,500 | 27,500 | 145,000 | 100,000 | 185,000 |
| 1798 . . . . . . . . . . . . . . . . . . . . . . . . . . .1,094 | 4,000 | 7,000 | 12,500 | 22,500 | 30,000 | 95,000 |
| 1802, 2 Over 1 . . . . . . . . . . . . . . . . . . . .3,035 | 4,000 | 5,000 | 12,000 | 14,500 | 16,500 | 27,500 |
| 1804, 13-Star Reverse . . . . . . . . . . . . . . . . * | 42,500 | 70,000 | 115,000 | 150,000 | 300,000 | |
| 1804, 14-Star Reverse . . . . . . . . . . . . . .3,327 | 5,500 | 7,250 | 10,500 | 13,000 | 15,500 | 27,500 |
| 1805 . . . . . . . . . . . . . . . . . . . . . . . . . . .1,781 | 4,000 | 5,500 | 10,500 | 13,000 | 15,500 | 27,500 |
| 1806, 6/4, 8 Stars Left, 5 Right . . . . . . . .1,136 | 4,000 | 6,000 | 10,500 | 13,000 | 15,500 | 30,000 |
| 1806, 6/5, 7 Stars Left, 6 Right . . . . . . . . . 480 | 5,000 | 7,000 | 12,500 | 16,500 | 35,000 | 75,000 |
| 1807 . . . . . . . . . . . . . . . . . . . . . . . . . . .6,812 | 4,000 | 5,500 | 10,500 | 13,000 | 15,500 | 27,500 |

* Included in number below.

## DRAPED BUST TO LEFT, LARGE SIZE (1808)

**F-12 Fine:** E PLURIBUS UNUM on reverse, and LIBERTY on headband, legible but weak.
**VF-20 Very Fine:** Motto and LIBERTY clear.
**EF-40 Extremely Fine:** All details of hair plain.
**AU-50 About Uncirculated:** Trace of wear above eye, on top of cap, and on cheek and hair.
**AU-55 Choice About Uncirculated:** Evidence of friction on design high points. Some original mint luster present.
**MS-60 Uncirculated:** No trace of wear. Light blemishes.

| | Mintage | F-12 | VF-20 | EF-40 | AU-50 | AU-55 | MS-60 |
|---|---|---|---|---|---|---|---|
| 1808 . . . . . . . . . . . . . . . . . . . . . . . . . . .2,710 | $35,000 | $45,000 | $65,000 | $100,000 | $115,000 | $165,000 |

## CAPPED HEAD TO LEFT (1821–1834)

Those dated 1829 to 1834 are smaller in diameter than the 1821 to 1827 pieces.

Large Diameter          Reduced Diameter

*See next page for chart.*

| | Mintage | F-12 | VF-20 | EF-40 | AU-50 | AU-55 | MS-60 |
|---|---|---|---|---|---|---|---|
| 1821 | 6,448 | $5,500 | $7,500 | $10,500 | $12,500 | $15,000 | $26,500 |
| 1824, 4 Over 1 | 2,600 | 5,500 | 7,000 | 10,000 | 12,500 | 15,000 | 27,500 |
| 1825 | 4,434 | 6,000 | 7,000 | 10,000 | 12,500 | 15,000 | 28,500 |
| 1826, 6 Over 6 | 760 | 7,000 | 8,500 | 13,000 | 20,000 | 27,500 | 55,000 |
| 1827 | 2,800 | 5,500 | 7,000 | 9,500 | 11,000 | 15,000 | 23,500 |
| 1829 | 3,403 | 4,750 | 6,000 | 8,000 | 11,000 | 13,500 | 18,500 |
| 1830 | 4,540 | 4,750 | 6,000 | 8,000 | 11,000 | 13,500 | 18,500 |
| 1831 | 4,520 | 4,750 | 6,000 | 8,000 | 11,000 | 13,500 | 18,500 |
| 1832 | 4,400 | 4,750 | 6,000 | 8,000 | 11,000 | 13,500 | 18,500 |
| 1833 | 4,160 | 4,750 | 6,000 | 8,000 | 11,000 | 13,500 | 18,500 |
| 1834, With Motto | 4,000 | 25,000 | 30,000 | 55,000 | 95,000 | 120,000 | 125,000 |

## CLASSIC HEAD, NO MOTTO ON REVERSE (1834–1839)

In 1834, the quarter eagle was redesigned. A ribbon binding the hair, bearing the word LIBERTY, replaced the Liberty cap. The motto was omitted from the reverse.

**F-12 Fine:** LIBERTY on headband legible and complete. Curl under ear outlined but no detail.
**VF-20 Very Fine:** LIBERTY plain; detail in hair curl.
**EF-40 Extremely Fine:** Small amount of wear on top of hair and below L in LIBERTY. Wear evident on wing.
**AU-50 About Uncirculated:** Trace of wear on coronet and hair above ear.
**AU-55 Choice About Uncirculated:** Evidence of friction on design high points. Some of original mint luster present.
**MS-60 Uncirculated:** No trace of wear. Light blemishes.
**MS-63 Choice Uncirculated:** Some distracting contact marks or blemishes in prime focal areas. Impaired luster possible.

*Mintmark location.*

| | Mintage | F-12 | VF-20 | EF-40 | AU-50 | AU-55 | MS-60 | MS-63 |
|---|---|---|---|---|---|---|---|---|
| 1834, No Motto | 112,234 | $285 | $400 | $650 | $850 | $1,150 | $2,500 | $5,750 |
| 1835 | 131,402 | 285 | 400 | 650 | 850 | 1,150 | 2,500 | 8,500 |
| 1836 | 547,986 | 285 | 400 | 650 | 850 | 1,150 | 2,500 | 5,750 |
| 1837 | 45,080 | 400 | 600 | 800 | 1,200 | 1,750 | 3,500 | 11,000 |
| 1838 | 47,030 | 325 | 550 | 700 | 1,150 | 1,500 | 2,500 | 7,000 |
| 1838C | 7,880 | 3,200 | 4,250 | 6,000 | 8,000 | 10,000 | 20,000 | 45,000 |
| 1839 | 27,021 | 550 | 850 | 1,350 | 2,500 | 3,250 | 5,500 | 30,000 |
| 1839C | 18,140 | 2,000 | 3,500 | 4,500 | 7,500 | 8,500 | 20,000 | 55,000 |
| 1839D | 13,674 | 2,750 | 3,750 | 5,500 | 7,500 | 11,000 | 25,000 | 60,000 |
| 1839O | 17,781 | 800 | 1,500 | 2,500 | 3,250 | 5,000 | 8,500 | 27,500 |

## LIBERTY HEAD (1840–1907)

**4** Plain 4

**4** Crosslet 4

*Mintmark location.*

| | Mintage | VF-20 | EF-40 | AU-50 | AU-55 | MS-60 | MS-63 |
|---|---|---|---|---|---|---|---|
| 1840 | 18,859 | $700 | $800 | $1,500 | $2,750 | $5,750 | $12,000 |
| 1840C | 12,822 | 1,350 | 2,750 | 2,850 | 4,000 | 8,000 | 22,500 |
| 1840D | 3,532 | 2,650 | 7,000 | 8,500 | 15,000 | 30,000 | |
| 1840O | 33,580 | 550 | 1,350 | 2,000 | 2,850 | 7,500 | 22,500 |

| | Mintage | VF-20 | EF-40 | AU-50 | AU-55 | MS-60 | MS-63 |
|---|---|---|---|---|---|---|---|
| 1841 . . . . . . . . . . . . . . . . . . . . . . . (unknown) | | $50,000 | $85,000 | $110,000 | $130,000 | | |
| 1841C . . . . . . . . . . . . . . . . . . . . . . .10,281 | | 1,500 | 2,350 | 3,600 | 4,250 | $13,500 | |
| 1841D . . . . . . . . . . . . . . . . . . . . . . .4,164 | | 3,000 | 5,000 | 7,000 | 10,000 | 25,000 | $40,000 |
| 1842 . . . . . . . . . . . . . . . . . . . . . . . .2,823 | | 1,800 | 3,750 | 5,500 | 9,000 | 15,500 | 45,000 |
| 1842C . . . . . . . . . . . . . . . . . . . . . . .6,729 | | 1,700 | 3,000 | 6,000 | 8,000 | 17,500 | 40,000 |
| 1842D . . . . . . . . . . . . . . . . . . . . . . .4,643 | | 2,250 | 4,250 | 7,000 | 8,250 | 30,000 | |
| 1842O . . . . . . . . . . . . . . . . . . . . . . .19,800 | | 550 | 950 | 1,650 | 3,250 | 7,500 | 18,500 |
| 1843 . . . . . . . . . . . . . . . . . . . . . . . .100,546 | | 450 | 500 | 550 | 800 | 1,800 | 5,000 |
| 1843C, Large Date. . . . . . . . . . . . . . .23,076 | | 1,500 | 2,250 | 2,750 | 3,000 | 6,000 | 17,000 |
| 1843C, Small Date. . . . . . . . . . . . . . .2,988 | | 2,250 | 4,500 | 5,750 | 6,750 | 18,000 | |
| 1843D . . . . . . . . . . . . . . . . . . . . . . .36,209 | | 1,600 | 2,000 | 2,800 | 3,250 | 5,000 | 22,500 |
| 1843O . . . . . . . . . . . . . . . . . . . . . . .364,002 | | 450 | 500 | 525 | 600 | 1,250 | 4,500 |
| 1844 . . . . . . . . . . . . . . . . . . . . . . . .6,784 | | 650 | 950 | 1,850 | 3,000 | 7,000 | 22,500 |
| 1844C . . . . . . . . . . . . . . . . . . . . . . .11,622 | | 1,500 | 2,500 | 3,750 | 4,500 | 12,000 | 35,000 |
| 1844D . . . . . . . . . . . . . . . . . . . . . . .17,332 | | 1,500 | 1,950 | 3,000 | 4,000 | 7,000 | 20,000 |
| 1845 . . . . . . . . . . . . . . . . . . . . . . . .91,051 | | 450 | 500 | 525 | 550 | 1,000 | 4,000 |
| 1845D . . . . . . . . . . . . . . . . . . . . . . .19,460 | | 1,600 | 2,150 | 2,500 | 3,500 | 7,500 | 35,000 |
| 1845O . . . . . . . . . . . . . . . . . . . . . . .4,000 | | 1,650 | 3,200 | 5,500 | 8,000 | 25,000 | 75,000 |
| 1846 . . . . . . . . . . . . . . . . . . . . . . . .21,598 | | 550 | 600 | 750 | 1,000 | 3,500 | 17,500 |
| 1846C . . . . . . . . . . . . . . . . . . . . . . .4,808 | | 1,600 | 2,650 | 4,500 | 7,500 | 16,000 | 35,000 |
| 1846D . . . . . . . . . . . . . . . . . . . . . . .19,303 | | 1,650 | 2,250 | 2,750 | 3,250 | 7,500 | 26,500 |
| 1846O . . . . . . . . . . . . . . . . . . . . . . .62,000 | | 500 | 550 | 850 | 1,500 | 4,500 | 15,000 |
| 1847 . . . . . . . . . . . . . . . . . . . . . . . .29,814 | | 450 | 500 | 700 | 750 | 2,750 | 10,000 |
| 1847C . . . . . . . . . . . . . . . . . . . . . . .23,226 | | 1,500 | 1,850 | 2,500 | 3,000 | 4,500 | 12,000 |
| 1847D . . . . . . . . . . . . . . . . . . . . . . .15,784 | | 1,600 | 1,850 | 2,500 | 3,750 | 7,000 | 20,000 |
| 1847O . . . . . . . . . . . . . . . . . . . . . . .124,000 | | 500 | 525 | 750 | 1,250 | 3,500 | 15,000 |
| 1848 . . . . . . . . . . . . . . . . . . . . . . . .6,500 | | 750 | 1,100 | 2,150 | 3,500 | 5,000 | 12,500 |

## CAL. Gold Quarter Eagle (1848)

In 1848, about 230 ounces of gold were sent to Secretary of War William L. Marcy by Colonel R.B. Mason, military governor of California. The gold was turned over to the Mint and made into quarter eagles. The distinguishing mark CAL. was punched above the eagle on the reverse side while the coins were in the die.

CAL. Above Eagle on Reverse (1848)

| | Mintage | VF-20 | EF-40 | AU-50 | AU-55 | MS-60 | MS-63 |
|---|---|---|---|---|---|---|---|
| 1848, CAL. Above Eagle. . . . . . . . . . . . . .1,389 | | $30,000 | $45,000 | $55,000 | $65,000 | $75,000 | $115,000 |
| 1848C . . . . . . . . . . . . . . . . . . . . . . .16,788 | | 1,250 | 2,250 | 2,750 | 3,500 | 8,500 | 35,000 |
| 1848D . . . . . . . . . . . . . . . . . . . . . . .13,771 | | 1,550 | 2,150 | 2,850 | 3,500 | 7,000 | 23,500 |
| 1849 . . . . . . . . . . . . . . . . . . . . . . . .23,294 | | 500 | 650 | 700 | 1,000 | 2,250 | 6,000 |
| 1849C . . . . . . . . . . . . . . . . . . . . . . .10,220 | | 1,500 | 2,350 | 4,250 | 5,000 | 11,000 | 30,000 |
| 1849D . . . . . . . . . . . . . . . . . . . . . . .10,945 | | 1,750 | 2,500 | 2,750 | 4,000 | 12,000 | 26,000 |
| 1850 . . . . . . . . . . . . . . . . . . . . . . . .252,923 | | 450 | 500 | 525 | 550 | 700 | 3,500 |
| 1850C . . . . . . . . . . . . . . . . . . . . . . .9,148 | | 1,350 | 2,250 | 2,850 | 4,250 | 9,000 | 30,000 |
| 1850D . . . . . . . . . . . . . . . . . . . . . . .12,148 | | 1,500 | 2,000 | 3,250 | 4,000 | 9,500 | 32,000 |

*Chart continued on next page.*

| | Mintage | VF-20 | EF-40 | AU-50 | AU-55 | MS-60 | MS-63 | PF-63 |
|---|---|---|---|---|---|---|---|---|
| 1850O . . . . . . . . . . . . . . .84,000 | | $500 | $525 | $750 | $900 | $3,500 | $18,500 | |
| 1851 . . . . . . . . . . . . . 1,372,748 | | 400 | 450 | 475 | 500 | 525 | 850 | |
| 1851C . . . . . . . . . . . . . . .14,923 | | 1,200 | 1,800 | 2,750 | 3,500 | 6,750 | 27,500 | |
| 1851D . . . . . . . . . . . . . . .11,264 | | 1,350 | 2,150 | 3,250 | 4,000 | 10,500 | 25,000 | |
| 1851O . . . . . . . . . . . . . . .148,000 | | 400 | 425 | 600 | 1,000 | 3,000 | 9,500 | |
| 1852 . . . . . . . . . . . . . 1,159,681 | | 400 | 425 | 450 | 475 | 500 | 750 | |
| 1852C . . . . . . . . . . . . . . .9,772 | | 1,250 | 1,850 | 3,000 | 4,000 | 7,500 | 27,500 | |
| 1852D . . . . . . . . . . . . . . .4,078 | | 1,500 | 2,750 | 5,500 | 6,250 | 14,500 | 40,000 | |
| 1852O . . . . . . . . . . . . . . .140,000 | | 400 | 425 | 650 | 800 | 3,500 | 9,000 | |
| 1853 . . . . . . . . . . . . . 1,404,668 | | 400 | 425 | 450 | 500 | 525 | 750 | |
| 1853D . . . . . . . . . . . . . . .3,178 | | 1,900 | 3,000 | 5,000 | 6,000 | 12,000 | 45,000 | |
| 1854 . . . . . . . . . . . . . .596,258 | | 400 | 425 | 450 | 465 | 500 | 950 | |
| 1854C . . . . . . . . . . . . . . .7,295 | | 1,750 | 2,500 | 3,500 | 4,500 | 9,000 | 50,000 | |
| 1854D . . . . . . . . . . . . . . .1,760 | | 3,000 | 5,500 | 8,500 | 14,500 | 25,000 | 60,000 | |
| 1854O . . . . . . . . . . . . . . .153,000 | | 400 | 425 | 450 | 550 | 1,250 | 7,500 | |
| 1854S . . . . . . . . . . . . . . 246 | | 225,000 | 280,000 | 375,000 | | | | |
| 1855 . . . . . . . . . . . . . . .235,480 | | 400 | 425 | 450 | 465 | 500 | 1,500 | |
| 1855C . . . . . . . . . . . . . . .3,677 | | 2,000 | 3,000 | 4,500 | 5,500 | 16,500 | 40,000 | |
| 1855D . . . . . . . . . . . . . . .1,123 | | 3,750 | 6,750 | 15,000 | 17,500 | 40,000 | 75,000 | |
| 1856 . . . . . . . . . . . . . . .384,240 | | 400 | 425 | 450 | 465 | 500 | 950 | $50,000 |
| 1856C . . . . . . . . . . . . . . .7,913 | | 1,500 | 2,500 | 3,250 | 4,650 | 9,000 | 22,500 | |
| 1856D . . . . . . . . . . . . . . 874 | | 11,500 | 18,500 | 27,500 | 35,000 | 70,000 | | |
| 1856O . . . . . . . . . . . . . . .21,100 | | 500 | 750 | 1,250 | 2,250 | 7,000 | | |
| 1856S . . . . . . . . . . . . . . .72,120 | | 425 | 475 | 650 | 1,000 | 3,000 | 8,000 | |
| 1857 . . . . . . . . . . . . . . .214,130 | | 400 | 425 | 450 | 465 | 500 | 1,100 | 45,000 |
| 1857D . . . . . . . . . . . . . . .2,364 | | 1,500 | 2,250 | 4,000 | 6,000 | 10,000 | 25,000 | |
| 1857O . . . . . . . . . . . . . . .34,000 | | 425 | 450 | 850 | 1,200 | 3,750 | 10,000 | |
| 1857S . . . . . . . . . . . . . . .69,200 | | 425 | 450 | 800 | 1,300 | 3,500 | 10,000 | |
| 1858 . . . . . . . . . . . . . . .47,377 | | 400 | 425 | 450 | 465 | 900 | 3,000 | 30,000 |
| 1858C . . . . . . . . . . . . . . .9,056 | | 1,500 | 2,000 | 3,000 | 3,500 | 6,000 | 20,000 | |
| 1859 . . . . . . . . (80) . . . . . .39,364 | | 400 | 450 | 500 | 600 | 1,000 | 3,000 | 20,000 |
| 1859D . . . . . . . . . . . . . . .2,244 | | 1,650 | 2,500 | 3,500 | 4,250 | 15,000 | 45,000 | |
| 1859S . . . . . . . . . . . . . . .15,200 | | 400 | 850 | 1,500 | 2,150 | 4,000 | 13,500 | |
| 1860 . . . . . . . (112) . . . .22,563 | | 400 | 425 | 450 | 465 | 1,100 | 3,000 | 16,500 |
| 1860C . . . . . . . . . . . . . . .7,469 | | 1,550 | 2,500 | 3,000 | 5,500 | 12,500 | 27,500 | |
| 1860S . . . . . . . . . . . . . . .35,600 | | 425 | 500 | 1,100 | 1,350 | 3,000 | 12,500 | |
| 1861 . . . . . . . . (90) . . . 1,283,788 | | 400 | 425 | 450 | 465 | 600 | 1,000 | 16,000 |
| 1861S . . . . . . . . . . . . . . .24,000 | | 500 | 950 | 3,000 | 3,750 | 11,000 | | |
| 1862, 2 Over 1 . . . . . . . . . . . . . . * | | 700 | 1,500 | 2,750 | 3,750 | 7,500 | 22,500 | |
| 1862 . . . . . . . . (35) . . . .98,508 | | 400 | 475 | 1,250 | 1,750 | 3,500 | 8,000 | 16,000 |
| 1862S . . . . . . . . . . . . . . .8,000 | | 1,650 | 2,250 | 3,500 | 5,000 | 15,000 | 25,000 | |
| 1863, Proof only (30) . . . . . . . . . . . | | | | | | | | 60,000 |
| 1863S . . . . . . . . . . . . . . .10,800 | | 1,000 | 2,250 | 3,500 | 5,250 | 12,500 | 25,000 | |
| 1864 . . . . . . . . (50) . . . .2,774 | | 17,500 | 30,000 | 50,000 | 65,000 | 85,000 | | 16,000 |
| 1865 . . . . . . . . (25) . . . .1,520 | | 3,750 | 8,000 | 15,000 | 27,500 | 50,000 | | 16,000 |
| 1865S . . . . . . . . . . . . . . .23,376 | | 600 | 1,000 | 1,750 | 2,000 | 3,500 | 15,000 | |
| 1866 . . . . . . . . (30) . . . .3,080 | | 850 | 2,750 | 4,500 | 6,500 | 11,500 | 25,000 | 16,000 |
| 1866S . . . . . . . . . . . . . . .38,960 | | 400 | 500 | 900 | 1,500 | 6,500 | 20,000 | |
| 1867 . . . . . . . . (50) . . . .3,200 | | 450 | 850 | 1,250 | 2,000 | 5,500 | 15,000 | 16,000 |
| 1867S . . . . . . . . . . . . . . .28,000 | | 400 | 450 | 1,000 | 1,000 | 4,000 | 12,000 | |
| 1868 . . . . . . . . (25) . . . .3,600 | | 400 | 425 | 650 | 675 | 2,000 | 9,500 | 16,000 |

* Included in number below.

# QUARTER EAGLES ($2.50)

| | Mintage | VF-20 | EF-40 | AU-50 | AU-55 | MS-60 | MS-63 | PF-63 |
|---|---|---|---|---|---|---|---|---|
| 1868S | 34,000 | $400 | $425 | $750 | $950 | $2,500 | $7,500 | |
| 1869 | (25)....4,320 | 400 | 425 | 650 | 900 | 2,500 | 8,500 | $16,000 |
| 1869S | 29,500 | 400 | 450 | 550 | 775 | 2,250 | 7,000 | |
| 1870 | (35)....4,520 | 400 | 425 | 700 | 1,150 | 3,000 | 9,500 | 16,000 |
| 1870S | 16,000 | 400 | 425 | 600 | 1,000 | 3,000 | 12,500 | |
| 1871 | (30)....5,320 | 400 | 450 | 600 | 750 | 1,500 | 4,000 | 16,000 |
| 1871S | 22,000 | 400 | 425 | 450 | 600 | 1,500 | 3,500 | |
| 1872 | (30)....3,000 | 450 | 700 | 1,250 | 2,000 | 3,500 | 13,500 | 16,000 |
| 1872S | 18,000 | 400 | 425 | 600 | 1,000 | 3,500 | 8,500 | |
| 1873 | (25)....178,000 | 400 | 425 | 435 | 445 | 465 | 600 | 16,000 |
| 1873S | 27,000 | 400 | 425 | 500 | 750 | 1,500 | 5,000 | |
| 1874 | (20)....3,920 | 400 | 425 | 550 | 700 | 1,700 | 4,500 | 22,500 |
| 1875 | (20)....400 | 6,000 | 9,500 | 11,000 | 15,000 | 25,000 | 100,000 | 27,500 |
| 1875S | 11,600 | 400 | 425 | 450 | 850 | 2,750 | 5,000 | |
| 1876 | (45)....4,176 | 500 | 600 | 750 | 1,100 | 2,500 | 7,500 | 11,000 |
| 1876S | 5,000 | 400 | 425 | 750 | 1,100 | 2,000 | 7,000 | |
| 1877 | (20)....1,632 | 450 | 800 | 1,100 | 1,500 | 2,500 | 10,000 | 11,000 |
| 1877S | 35,400 | 400 | 425 | 435 | 445 | 465 | 1,750 | |
| 1878 | (20)....286,240 | 400 | 415 | 425 | 430 | 450 | 500 | 11,000 |
| 1878S | 178,000 | 400 | 415 | 425 | 430 | 450 | 850 | |
| 1879 | (30)....88,960 | 400 | 415 | 425 | 430 | 450 | 550 | 11,000 |
| 1879S | 43,500 | 400 | 415 | 425 | 430 | 1,250 | 4,000 | |
| 1880 | (36)....2,960 | 400 | 450 | 550 | 650 | 1,000 | 2,650 | 8,500 |
| 1881 | (51)....640 | 2,000 | 2,750 | 5,000 | 5,500 | 7,500 | 22,500 | 7,500 |
| 1882 | (67)....4,000 | 400 | 450 | 475 | 500 | 900 | 2,250 | 6,000 |
| 1883 | (82)....1,920 | 550 | 1,150 | 2,250 | 3,700 | 5,000 | 8,500 | 6,000 |
| 1884 | (73)....1,950 | 400 | 475 | 500 | 700 | 1,500 | 2,750 | 6,000 |
| 1885 | (87)....800 | 800 | 1,500 | 3,000 | 3,500 | 5,000 | 10,000 | 6,000 |
| 1886 | (88)....4,000 | 400 | 450 | 465 | 475 | 950 | 3,000 | 6,000 |
| 1887 | (122)....6,160 | 400 | 415 | 425 | 435 | 700 | 1,100 | 5,500 |
| 1888 | (97)....16,001 | 400 | 415 | 425 | 435 | 450 | 650 | 5,500 |
| 1889 | (48)....17,600 | 400 | 415 | 425 | 435 | 450 | 650 | 5,500 |
| 1890 | (93)....8,720 | 400 | 415 | 425 | 435 | 450 | 1,200 | 5,500 |
| 1891 | (80)....10,960 | 400 | 415 | 425 | 435 | 450 | 950 | 5,500 |
| 1892 | (105)....2,440 | 400 | 415 | 425 | 435 | 650 | 1,750 | 5,500 |
| 1893 | (106)....30,000 | 400 | 415 | 425 | 435 | 450 | 550 | 5,500 |
| 1894 | (122)....4,000 | 400 | 415 | 425 | 435 | 500 | 1,500 | 5,500 |
| 1895 | (119)....6,000 | 400 | 415 | 425 | 435 | 450 | 1,000 | 5,500 |
| 1896 | (132)....19,070 | 400 | 415 | 425 | 435 | 450 | 550 | 5,500 |
| 1897 | (136)....29,768 | 400 | 415 | 425 | 435 | 450 | 550 | 5,500 |
| 1898 | (165)....24,000 | 400 | 415 | 425 | 435 | 450 | 550 | 5,500 |
| 1899 | (150)....27,200 | 400 | 415 | 425 | 435 | 450 | 550 | 5,500 |
| 1900 | (205)....67,000 | 400 | 415 | 425 | 435 | 450 | 550 | 4,750 |
| 1901 | (223)....91,100 | 400 | 415 | 425 | 435 | 450 | 550 | 4,750 |
| 1902 | (193)....133,540 | 400 | 415 | 425 | 435 | 450 | 550 | 4,750 |
| 1903 | (197)....201,060 | 400 | 415 | 425 | 435 | 450 | 550 | 4,750 |
| 1904 | (170)....160,790 | 400 | 415 | 425 | 435 | 450 | 550 | 4,750 |
| 1905S | (144)....217,800 | 400 | 415 | 425 | 435 | 450 | 550 | 4,750 |
| 1906 | (160)....176,330 | 400 | 415 | 425 | 435 | 450 | 550 | 4,750 |
| 1907 | (154)....336,294 | 400 | 415 | 425 | 435 | 450 | 550 | 4,750 |

# INDIAN HEAD (1908–1929)

American sculptor Bela Lyon Pratt, a former student of Augustus Saint-Gaudens, designed this coin and the similar five-dollar gold piece. It features no raised rim, and the main devices and legends are in sunken relief below the surface of the coin. President Theodore Roosevelt, who sought to improve the overall aesthetic quality of American coinage, was enthusiastic about the innovative new design. Collectors and the public were not as pleased. Some feared that the recessed design would collect dirt and germs—an unfounded concern. Over time the design has been recognized as a classic, and part of the early 20th-century renaissance of American coinage.

**VF-20 Very Fine:** Hair-cord knot distinct. Feathers at top of head clear. Cheekbone worn.
**EF-40 Extremely Fine:** Cheekbone, war bonnet, and headband feathers slightly worn.
**AU-50 About Uncirculated:** Trace of wear on cheekbone and headdress.
**MS-60 Uncirculated:** No trace of wear. Light blemishes.
**MS-63 Choice Uncirculated:** Some distracting contact marks or blemishes in prime focal areas. Impaired luster possible.
**MS-64 Uncirculated:** A few scattered contact marks visible. Good eye appeal and attractive luster.
**Matte PF-63 Choice Proof:** Few blemishes in secondary focal areas. No major flaws. Matte surfaces.

*Mintmark location is on reverse, to left of arrows.*

| | Mintage | VF-20 | EF-40 | AU-50 | MS-60 | MS-63 | MS-64 | MATTE PF-63 |
|---|---|---|---|---|---|---|---|---|
| 1908 . . . . . . . .(236). . . . . .564,821 | | $370 | $375 | $380 | $425 | $900 | $1,350 | $10,000 |
| 1909 . . . . . . . .(139). . . . . .441,760 | | 370 | 375 | 380 | 425 | 1,300 | 2,000 | 10,000 |
| 1910 . . . . . . . .(682). . . . . .492,000 | | 370 | 375 | 380 | 425 | 1,000 | 1,350 | 10,000 |
| 1911 . . . . . . . .(191). . . . . .704,000 | | 370 | 375 | 380 | 425 | 750 | 1,250 | 10,000 |
| 1911D . . . . . . . . . . . . . . . .55,680 | | 2,000 | 2,250 | 2,500 | 3,750 | 9,000 | 12,500 | |
| 1912 . . . . . . . .(197). . . . . .616,000 | | 370 | 375 | 380 | 425 | 1,350 | 2,400 | 10,000 |
| 1913 . . . . . . . .(165). . . . . .722,000 | | 370 | 375 | 380 | 425 | 800 | 1,250 | 10,000 |
| 1914 . . . . . . . .(117). . . . . .240,000 | | 370 | 375 | 380 | 500 | 2,000 | 3,500 | 10,000 |
| 1914D . . . . . . . . . . . . . . . .448,000 | | 370 | 375 | 380 | 425 | 1,200 | 2,250 | |
| 1915 . . . . . . . .(100). . . . . .606,000 | | 370 | 375 | 380 | 425 | 850 | 1,250 | 10,000 |
| 1925D . . . . . . . . . . . . . . . .578,000 | | 370 | 375 | 380 | 425 | 550 | 675 | |
| 1926 . . . . . . . . . . . . . . . .446,000 | | 370 | 375 | 380 | 425 | 550 | 675 | |
| 1927 . . . . . . . . . . . . . . . .388,000 | | 370 | 375 | 380 | 425 | 550 | 675 | |
| 1928 . . . . . . . . . . . . . . . .416,000 | | 370 | 375 | 380 | 425 | 550 | 675 | |
| 1929 . . . . . . . . . . . . . . . .532,000 | | 370 | 375 | 380 | 425 | 550 | 675 | |

The three-dollar gold piece was authorized by the Act of February 21, 1853. Coinage was struck beginning in 1854. It was never popular and saw very little circulation.

**VF-20 Very Fine:** Eyebrow, hair about forehead and ear, and bottom curl all worn smooth. Faint details visible on curled feather-ends of headdress.

**EF-40 Extremely Fine:** Light wear above and to right of eye, and on top of curled feathers.

**AU-50 About Uncirculated:** Trace of wear on top of curled feathers and in hair above and to right of eye.

**AU-55 Choice About Uncirculated:** Evidence of friction on design high points. Much of original mint luster present.

**MS-60 Uncirculated:** No trace of wear. Light blemishes.

**MS-63 Choice Uncirculated:** Some distracting contact marks or blemishes in prime focal areas. Impaired luster possible.

*Mintmark location is on reverse, below wreath.*

**PF-63 Choice Proof:** Reflective surfaces with only a few blemishes in secondary focal places. No major flaws.

| | Mintage | VF-20 | EF-40 | AU-50 | AU-55 | MS-60 | MS-63 | PF-63 |
|---|---|---|---|---|---|---|---|---|
| 1854 | 138,618 | $625 | $750 | $800 | $1,250 | $1,600 | $4,000 | $60,000 |
| 1854D | 1,120 | 17,500 | 32,500 | 37,500 | 47,500 | 70,000 | | |
| 1854O | 24,000 | 1,350 | 1,900 | 3,000 | 3,600 | 32,500 | | |
| 1855 | 50,555 | 700 | 725 | 800 | 1,300 | 1,750 | 4,500 | 35,000 |
| 1855S | 6,600 | 1,000 | 2,000 | 4,250 | 7,500 | 30,000 | 70,000 | |
| 1856 | 26,010 | 725 | 750 | 850 | 1,300 | 2,500 | 5,500 | 30,000 |
| 1856S | 34,500 | 800 | 1,100 | 1,850 | 4,250 | 9,500 | 26,500 | |
| 1857 | 20,891 | 700 | 750 | 850 | 1,600 | 2,500 | 4,750 | 30,000 |
| 1857S | 14,000 | 800 | 1,550 | 3,500 | 6,500 | 17,500 | 50,000 | |
| 1858 | 2,133 | 1,000 | 1,750 | 3,000 | 3,500 | 8,000 | 18,500 | 20,000 |
| 1859 | (80)...15,558 | 750 | 900 | 950 | 1,500 | 2,500 | 5,500 | 16,500 |
| 1860 | (119)....7,036 | 750 | 1,100 | 1,500 | 1,700 | 3,500 | 6,000 | 11,000 |
| 1860S | 7,000 | 900 | 2,800 | 5,000 | 8,000 | 20,000 | | |
| 1861 | (113)....5,959 | 1,350 | 2,250 | 3,000 | 3,750 | 6,500 | 10,000 | 13,000 |
| 1862 | (35)....5,750 | 1,350 | 2,000 | 3,250 | 4,000 | 6,500 | 13,500 | 13,000 |
| 1863 | (39)....5,000 | 1,100 | 2,000 | 3,000 | 4,000 | 6,500 | 10,000 | 13,000 |
| 1864 | (50)....2,630 | 1,200 | 3,000 | 4,250 | 5,000 | 7,000 | 12,000 | 13,000 |
| 1865 | (25)....1,140 | 2,200 | 3,750 | 7,000 | 8,000 | 11,500 | 20,000 | 16,000 |
| 1866 | (30)....4,000 | 900 | 1,100 | 1,500 | 1,800 | 3,500 | 7,500 | 13,000 |
| 1867 | (50)....2,600 | 1,050 | 1,500 | 2,250 | 2,650 | 5,000 | 12,000 | 13,000 |
| 1868 | (25)....4,850 | 900 | 1,000 | 1,350 | 1,850 | 3,000 | 7,000 | 13,000 |
| 1869 | (25)....2,500 | 900 | 1,300 | 2,000 | 2,350 | 4,000 | 10,000 | 13,000 |
| 1870 | (35)....3,500 | 950 | 1,250 | 1,750 | 1,850 | 4,000 | 10,000 | 13,000 |
| 1870S (unique) | | | — | | | | | |
| 1871 | (30)....1,300 | 950 | 1,350 | 1,850 | 1,950 | 4,000 | 10,000 | 15,000 |
| 1872 | (30)....2,000 | 950 | 1,350 | 2,000 | 2,500 | 4,000 | 10,000 | 13,000 |
| 1873, Open 3 (Original) | (25) | | 10,000 | 13,500 | | | | 45,000 |
| 1873, Close 3 | | 3,650 | 7,500 | 9,000 | 12,500 | 25,000 | 40,000 | 45,000 |
| 1874 | (20)...41,800 | 700 | 750 | 800 | 900 | 1,600 | 4,000 | 24,000 |
| 1875, Proof only | (20) | | | 40,000 | 50,000 | | | 110,000 |
| 1876, Proof only | (45) | | | 15,000 | 20,000 | | | 45,000 |
| 1877 | (20)....1,468 | 3,250 | 6,000 | 7,000 | 10,000 | 18,500 | 35,000 | 17,500 |
| 1878 | (20)...82,304 | 650 | 750 | 800 | 850 | 1,600 | 3,750 | 17,500 |
| 1879 | (30)....3,000 | 800 | 1,000 | 1,300 | 1,850 | 2,250 | 5,000 | 13,000 |
| 1880 | (36)....1,000 | 1,100 | 1,650 | 3,000 | 3,250 | 5,000 | 6,500 | 13,000 |
| 1881 | (54).....500 | 1,900 | 3,500 | 6,500 | 7,000 | 10,000 | 14,000 | 13,000 |
| 1882 | (76).....1,500 | 1,100 | 1,400 | 2,000 | 2,200 | 3,500 | 7,000 | 11,000 |
| 1883 | (89).....900 | 1,300 | 1,850 | 2,200 | 2,500 | 4,000 | 7,000 | 11,000 |
| 1884 | (106)....1,000 | 1,300 | 2,000 | 2,750 | 3,000 | 4,000 | 9,500 | 11,000 |
| 1885 | (110).....800 | 1,300 | 2,000 | 2,800 | 3,000 | 5,000 | 9,000 | 11,000 |
| 1886 | (142)....1,000 | 1,100 | 1,600 | 2,250 | 2,500 | 3,750 | 10,000 | 11,000 |
| 1887 | (160)....6,000 | 750 | 1,350 | 1,650 | 1,750 | 3,000 | 5,000 | 11,000 |
| 1888 | (291)....5,000 | 750 | 1,100 | 1,500 | 1,650 | 3,000 | 4,500 | 11,000 |
| 1889 | (129)....2,300 | 750 | 1,100 | 1,500 | 1,650 | 3,000 | 4,500 | 11,000 |

## STELLA (1879–1880)

These pattern coins were first suggested by the Hon. John A. Kasson, then U.S. envoy extraordinary and minister plenipotentiary to Austria-Hungary. It was through the efforts of Dr. W.W. Hubbell, who patented the alloy goloid (used in making another pattern piece, the goloid metric dollar) that we have these beautiful and interesting coins.

The four-dollar Stella—so called because of the five-pointed star on the reverse—was envisioned by Kasson as America's answer to various foreign gold coins popular in the international market. The British sovereign, Italy's 20 lire, and the 20 pesetas of Spain were three such coins: each smaller than a U.S. five-dollar gold piece, they were used widely in international trade.

The Stella was one of many proposals made to Congress for an international trade coin, and one of only several that made it to pattern coin form (others include the 1868 five dollar and 1874 Bickford ten dollar).

Odds were stacked against the Stella from the start. The denomination of four U.S. dollars didn't match any of the coin's European counterparts, and at any rate the U.S. double eagle (twenty-dollar coin)—already used in international commerce—was a more convenient medium of exchange. The Stella was never minted in quantities for circulation.

There are two distinct types in both years of issue. Charles E. Barber is thought to have designed the Flowing Hair type, and George T. Morgan the Coiled Hair. They were struck as patterns in gold, aluminum, copper, and white metal. Only those struck in gold are listed.

**Flowing Hair**                                    **Coiled Hair**

| | Mintage | EF-40 | AU-50 | PF-60 | PF-63 | PF-65 |
|---|---|---|---|---|---|---|
| 1879, Flowing Hair | (425+) | $75,000 | $85,000 | $100,000 | $135,000 | $175,000 |
| 1879, Coiled Hair *(12 known)* | | | | 200,000 | 400,000 | 800,000 |
| 1880, Flowing Hair *(17 known)* | 100,000 | 115,000 | 125,000 | 165,000 | 350,000 |
| 1880, Coiled Hair *(8 known)* | | | | 500,000 | 700,000 | 1,250,000 |

While the 1856 Flying Eagle cent, the 1879 and 1880 four-dollar Stellas, and a few other patterns are listed in this book, there are more than 1,800 other trial pieces that were minted from 1792 to the present. These are listed in Whitman's *United States Pattern Coins* book and are a fascinating numismatic specialty. Most patterns are rare, and most were made in Proof formats.

The half eagle (five-dollar gold coin) was the first gold coin struck for the United States. It was authorized to be coined by the Act of April 2, 1792. The first type weighed 135 grains, of .91667 fineness. The weight was changed by the Act of June 28, 1834, to 129 grains, of .899225 fineness. Fineness became .900 by the Act of January 18, 1837.

# CAPPED BUST TO RIGHT (1795–1807)

**F-12 Fine:** Liberty's hair worn smooth but with distinct outline. For heraldic type, E PLURIBUS UNUM faint but legible.
**VF-20 Very Fine:** Slight to noticeable wear on high spots such as hair, turban, and eagle's head and wings.
**EF-40 Extremely Fine:** Slight wear on hair and highest part of cheek.
**AU-50 About Uncirculated:** Trace of wear on cap, hair, cheek, and drapery.
**MS-60 Uncirculated:** No trace of wear. Light blemishes.
**MS-63 Choice Uncirculated:** Some distracting marks or blemishes in focal areas. Impaired luster possible.

## Small Eagle Reverse (1795–1798)

1795
Obverse

1795
Reverse

1796, 6 Over 5     1797, 15 Stars     1797, 16 Stars

| | Mintage | F-12 | VF-20 | EF-40 | AU-50 | AU-55 | MS-60 | MS-63 |
|---|---|---|---|---|---|---|---|---|
| 1795, Small Eagle . . . . . . . . . .8,707 | | $17,000 | $22,500 | $30,000 | $40,000 | $50,000 | $70,000 | $145,000 |
| 1796, 6 Over 5 . . . . . . . . . . . .6,196 | | 17,000 | 25,000 | 35,000 | 50,000 | 60,000 | 90,000 | 175,000 |
| 1797, 15 Stars. . . . . . . . . . . .3,609 | | 25,000 | 32,500 | 60,000 | 100,000 | 145,000 | 200,000 | |
| 1797, 16 Stars. . . . . . . . . . . . . . . * | | 25,000 | 32,500 | 60,000 | 100,000 | 135,000 | 250,000 | |
| 1798, Small Eagle *(6 known)*. . . . . . | | | 175,000 | 350,000 | 750,000 | 1,000,000 | — | |

\* Included in number above.

## Heraldic Eagle Reverse (1795–1807)

| | Mintage | F-12 | VF-20 | EF-40 | AU-50 | AU-55 | MS-60 | MS-63 |
|---|---|---|---|---|---|---|---|---|
| 1795, Heraldic Eagle . . . . . . . . . . . . . . * | | $8,000 | $17,500 | $25,000 | $50,000 | $60,000 | $75,000 | $165,000 |
| 1797, 7 Over 5 . . . . . . . . . . . . . . . . . . * | | 27,500 | 30,000 | 37,500 | 55,000 | 100,000 | 150,000 | |
| 1798, Large 8, 13-Star Reverse. . 24,867 | | 3,500 | 4,000 | 8,500 | 10,000 | 13,500 | 20,000 | |
| 1798, Large 8, 14-Star Reverse. . . . . . ** | | 4,000 | 4,500 | 8,500 | 15,000 | 27,500 | 85,000 | |
| 1799 . . . . . . . . . . . . . . . . . . . . . . 7,451 | | 3,000 | 3,750 | 6,500 | 10,000 | 12,500 | 20,000 | 55,000 |
| 1800 . . . . . . . . . . . . . . . . . . . . . 37,628 | | 3,000 | 3,750 | 6,500 | 7,500 | 8,500 | 10,000 | 30,000 |

\* Included in number below. \*\* Included in number above.

*Chart continued on next page.*     **171**

| | Mintage | F-12 | VF-20 | EF-40 | AU-50 | AU-55 | MS-60 | MS-63 |
|---|---|---|---|---|---|---|---|---|
| 1802, 2 Over 1 | 53,176 | $3,000 | $3,500 | $5,500 | $7,500 | $8,500 | $10,000 | $22,500 |
| 1803, 3 Over 2 | 33,506 | 3,000 | 3,500 | 5,500 | 7,500 | 8,500 | 10,000 | 25,000 |
| 1804 | 30,475 | 3,000 | 3,500 | 5,500 | 7,500 | 8,500 | 10,000 | 27,500 |
| 1805 | 33,183 | 3,000 | 3,500 | 5,500 | 7,500 | 8,500 | 10,000 | 16,000 |
| 1806 | 64,093 | 3,000 | 3,500 | 5,500 | 7,500 | 8,500 | 10,000 | 16,000 |
| 1807 | 32,488 | 3,000 | 3,500 | 5,500 | 7,500 | 8,500 | 10,000 | 16,000 |

## DRAPED BUST TO LEFT (1807–1812)

**F-12 Fine:** LIBERTY on cap legible but partly weak.
**VF-20 Very Fine:** Headband edges slightly worn. LIBERTY bold.
**EF-40 Extremely Fine:** Slight wear on highest portions of hair; 80% of major curls plain.
**AU-50 About Uncirculated:** Trace of wear above eye and on top of cap, cheek, and hair.
**AU-55 Choice About Uncirculated:** Evidence of friction on design high points. Some mint luster present.
**MS-60 Uncirculated:** No trace of wear. Light blemishes.

**MS-63 Choice Uncirculated:** Some distracting contact marks or blemishes in prime focal areas. Impaired luster possible.

| | Mintage | F-12 | VF-20 | EF-40 | AU-50 | AU-55 | MS-60 | MS-63 |
|---|---|---|---|---|---|---|---|---|
| 1807 | 51,605 | $2,750 | $3,250 | $5,000 | $7,000 | $8,000 | $9,500 | $16,500 |
| 1808, All kinds | 55,578 | | | | | | | |
| 1808, 8 Over 7 | | 2,750 | 4,000 | 5,500 | 7,500 | 9,000 | 12,000 | 25,000 |
| 1808 | | 2,750 | 3,250 | 5,000 | 7,000 | 8,000 | 9,500 | 20,000 |
| 1809, 9 Over 8 | 33,875 | 2,750 | 3,250 | 5,000 | 7,000 | 8,000 | 9,500 | 18,500 |
| 1810 | 100,287 | 2,750 | 3,250 | 5,000 | 7,000 | 8,000 | 9,500 | 18,000 |
| 1811 | 99,581 | 2,750 | 3,250 | 5,000 | 7,000 | 8,000 | 9,500 | 18,000 |
| 1812 | 58,087 | 2,750 | 3,250 | 5,000 | 7,000 | 8,000 | 9,500 | 18,000 |

## CAPPED HEAD TO LEFT (1813–1834)

Large Diameter                    Reduced Diameter

### Large Diameter (1813–1829)

| | Mintage | F-12 | VF-20 | EF-40 | AU-50 | AU-55 | MS-60 | MS-63 |
|---|---|---|---|---|---|---|---|---|
| 1813 | 95,428 | $3,000 | $4,000 | $6,000 | $7,500 | $8,000 | $9,000 | $20,000 |
| 1814, 4 Over 3 | 15,454 | 4,000 | 5,500 | 7,500 | 9,500 | 12,000 | 15,000 | 35,000 |
| 1815 | 635 | 30,000 | 75,000 | 150,000 | 175,000 | 200,000 | 225,000 | 300,000 |
| 1818 | 48,588 | 4,000 | 5,000 | 10,000 | 12,500 | 13,500 | 16,000 | 37,500 |
| 1819 | 51,723 | 20,000 | 30,000 | 40,000 | 55,000 | 55,000 | 60,000 | 90,000 |
| 1820 | 263,806 | 4,000 | 5,500 | 10,000 | 11,500 | 14,000 | 17,500 | 32,500 |
| 1821 | 34,641 | 25,000 | 35,000 | 55,000 | 95,000 | 125,000 | 165,000 | 250,000 |
| 1822 *(3 known)* | 17,796 | | | 6,500,000 | | | | |
| 1823 | 14,485 | 4,500 | 5,500 | 10,000 | 13,000 | 16,000 | 22,500 | 45,000 |

| | Mintage | F-12 | VF-20 | EF-40 | AU-50 | AU-55 | MS-60 | MS-63 |
|---|---|---|---|---|---|---|---|---|
| 1824 . . . . . . . . . . . . . . . . . .17,340 | | $7,500 | $10,000 | $27,500 | $30,000 | $35,000 | $50,000 | $70,000 |
| 1825, 5 Over Partial 4 . . . . . .29,060 | | 6,500 | 10,000 | 25,000 | 30,000 | 40,000 | 45,000 | 65,000 |
| 1825, 5 Over 4 *(2 known)* . . . . . . . * | | | | 300,000 | | | | |
| 1826 . . . . . . . . . . . . . . . . . .18,069 | | 5,500 | 8,500 | 20,000 | 25,000 | 32,500 | 55,000 | 90,000 |
| 1827 . . . . . . . . . . . . . . . . . .24,913 | | 7,500 | 12,500 | 22,000 | 30,000 | 35,000 | 45,000 | 90,000 |
| 1828, 8 Over 7 *(5 known)* . . . . . . .** | | 15,000 | 25,000 | 50,000 | 65,000 | 80,000 | 150,000 | 250,000 |
| 1828 . . . . . . . . . . . . . . . . . .28,029 | | 12,000 | 20,000 | 30,000 | 45,000 | 50,000 | 90,000 | 200,000 |
| 1829, Large Date . . . . . . . . .57,442 | | 12,500 | 25,000 | 50,000 | 65,000 | 75,000 | 120,000 | 275,000 |

\* Included in number above. \*\* Included in number below.

## Reduced Diameter (1829–1834)

| | Mintage | F-12 | VF-20 | EF-40 | AU-50 | AU-55 | MS-60 | MS-63 |
|---|---|---|---|---|---|---|---|---|
| 1829, Small Date . . . . . . . . . . . . . . .* | | $25,000 | $45,000 | $60,000 | $95,000 | $125,000 | $250,000 | $300,000 |
| 1830 . . . . . . . . . . . . . . . . . . . . . 126,351 | | 12,500 | 27,500 | 37,500 | 42,500 | 50,000 | 55,000 | 80,000 |
| 1831 . . . . . . . . . . . . . . . . . . . . . 140,594 | | 12,500 | 27,500 | 37,500 | 42,500 | 50,000 | 55,000 | 100,000 |
| 1832, Curved-Base 2, <br> 12 Stars *(5 known)* . . . . . 157,487 | | 75,000 | 125,000 | 175,000 | 250,000 | | | |
| 1832, Square-Base 2, 13 Stars . . . . . ** | | 12,500 | 27,500 | 37,500 | 42,500 | 50,000 | 60,000 | 75,000 |
| 1833 . . . . . . . . . . . . . . . . . . . . . 193,630 | | 12,500 | 27,500 | 37,500 | 42,500 | 50,000 | 55,000 | 75,000 |
| 1834 . . . . . . . . . . . . . . . . . . . . 50,141 | | 12,500 | 27,500 | 37,500 | 42,500 | 50,000 | 60,000 | 85,000 |

\* Included in mintage for 1829, Large Date (previous chart). \*\* Included in number above.

## CLASSIC HEAD, NO MOTTO (1834–1838)

| | Mintage | F-12 | VF-20 | EF-40 | AU-50 | AU-55 | MS-60 | MS-63 |
|---|---|---|---|---|---|---|---|---|
| 1834 . . . . . . . . . . . . . . . . . .657,460 | | $525 | $600 | $800 | $1,000 | $1,350 | $2,750 | $8,000 |
| 1835 . . . . . . . . . . . . . . . . . .371,534 | | 525 | 600 | 800 | 1,000 | 1,350 | 2,750 | 8,000 |
| 1836 . . . . . . . . . . . . . . . . . .553,147 | | 525 | 600 | 800 | 1,050 | 1,350 | 2,750 | 9,500 |
| 1837 . . . . . . . . . . . . . . . . . .207,121 | | 525 | 600 | 850 | 1,300 | 1,650 | 4,500 | 17,500 |
| 1838 . . . . . . . . . . . . . . . . . .286,588 | | 525 | 600 | 800 | 1,250 | 1,550 | 3,250 | 9,000 |
| 1838C . . . . . . . . . . . . . . . . . .17,179 | | 2,750 | 4,250 | 9,000 | 12,500 | 17,500 | 60,000 | 200,000 |
| 1838D . . . . . . . . . . . . . . . . . .20,583 | | 2,800 | 4,250 | 7,000 | 11,000 | 18,000 | 27,500 | 75,000 |

## LIBERTY HEAD (1839–1908)
### Variety 1 – No Motto Above Eagle (1839–1866)

**VF-20 Very Fine:** LIBERTY on coronet bold. Major lines show in curls on neck.

**EF-40 Extremely Fine:** Details clear in curls on neck. Slight wear on top and lower part of coronet and on hair.

**AU-50 About Uncirculated:** Trace of wear on coronet and hair above eye.

**AU-55 Choice About Uncirculated:** Evidence of friction on design high points. Some original mint luster.

**MS-60 Uncirculated:** No trace of wear. Light blemishes.

*Mintmark: 1839, above date; 1840–1908, below eagle.*

**MS-63 Choice Uncirculated:** Some distracting contact marks or blemishes in prime focal areas. Impaired luster possible.

**PF-63 Choice Proof:** Attractive reflective surfaces with only a few blemishes in secondary focal places. No major flaws.

| 1842, Large Date | | Small Letters | | | Large Letters | | |
|---|---|---|---|---|---|---|---|

| | Mintage | VF-20 | EF-40 | AU-50 | AU-55 | MS-60 | MS-63 | PF-63 |
|---|---|---|---|---|---|---|---|---|
| 1839 . . . . . . . . . . . . . . . .118,143 | | $550 | $900 | $1,500 | $2,000 | $6,000 | $22,500 | |
| 1839C . . . . . . . . . . . . . . .17,205 | | 3,000 | 4,500 | 9,500 | 15,000 | 25,000 | 50,000 | |
| 1839D . . . . . . . . . . . . . . .18,939 | | 3,000 | 6,000 | 8,000 | 15,000 | 22,500 | | |
| 1840 . . . . . . . . . . . . . . . .137,382 | | 525 | 600 | 800 | 950 | 3,000 | 7,500 | |
| 1840C . . . . . . . . . . . . . . .18,992 | | 1,700 | 3,250 | 5,000 | 6,000 | 17,500 | 45,000 | |
| 1840D . . . . . . . . . . . . . . .22,896 | | 1,850 | 3,000 | 4,500 | 5,500 | 10,000 | 32,500 | |
| 1840O . . . . . . . . . . . . . . .40,120 | | 550 | 900 | 1,750 | 2,500 | 8,000 | 30,000 | |
| 1841 . . . . . . . . . . . . . . . . .15,833 | | 525 | 700 | 1,250 | 1,600 | 3,250 | 10,000 | |
| 1841C . . . . . . . . . . . . . . .21,467 | | 1,500 | 2,000 | 4,000 | 5,000 | 12,500 | 30,000 | |
| 1841D . . . . . . . . . . . . . . .29,392 | | 1,500 | 2,500 | 4,000 | 5,000 | 10,000 | 20,000 | |
| 1842, Small Letters . . . . . . .27,578 | | 550 | 900 | 2,250 | 3,000 | 10,000 | 15,000 | |
| 1842, Large Letters . . . . . . . . . . . * | | 600 | 1,250 | 2,500 | 3,000 | 8,000 | 16,000 | |
| 1842C, Small Date. . . . . . . .27,432 | | 7,000 | 15,000 | 22,500 | 30,000 | 70,000 | | |
| 1842C, Large Date. . . . . . . . . . . * | | 1,500 | 2,000 | 3,250 | 4,000 | 9,500 | 25,000 | |
| 1842D, Small Date . . . . . . .59,608 | | 1,600 | 2,250 | 4,000 | 4,500 | 12,500 | 25,000 | |
| 1842D, Large Date . . . . . . . . . . . * | | 3,000 | 6,500 | 10,000 | 14,500 | 37,500 | | |
| 1842O . . . . . . . . . . . . . . .16,400 | | 1,850 | 3,000 | 8,000 | 9,000 | 17,500 | 35,000 | |
| 1843 . . . . . . . . . . . . . . . .611,205 | | 500 | 515 | 525 | 550 | 1,200 | 8,000 | |
| 1843C . . . . . . . . . . . . . . .44,277 | | 1,500 | 2,200 | 3,000 | 3,750 | 8,000 | 25,000 | |
| 1843D . . . . . . . . . . . . . . .98,452 | | 1,750 | 2,000 | 2,750 | 3,500 | 8,000 | 20,000 | |
| 1843O, Small Letters . . . . . .19,075 | | 525 | 1,300 | 2,500 | 3,500 | 15,000 | 30,000 | |
| 1843O, Large Letters . . . . . .82,000 | | 550 | 600 | 2,000 | 4,000 | 10,000 | 22,500 | |
| 1844 . . . . . . . . . . . . . . . .340,330 | | 500 | 515 | 525 | 600 | 1,500 | 7,500 | |
| 1844C . . . . . . . . . . . . . . .23,631 | | 1,850 | 2,750 | 4,500 | 5,000 | 12,000 | 26,000 | |
| 1844D . . . . . . . . . . . . . . .88,982 | | 1,600 | 2,000 | 3,000 | 3,750 | 7,500 | 24,000 | |
| 1844O . . . . . . . . . . . . . . .364,600 | | 500 | 650 | 750 | 1,100 | 3,750 | 17,500 | |
| 1845 . . . . . . . . . . . . . . . .417,099 | | 500 | 515 | 525 | 550 | 1,500 | 7,000 | |
| 1845D . . . . . . . . . . . . . . .90,629 | | 1,600 | 2,000 | 2,750 | 3,750 | 6,750 | 20,000 | |
| 1845O . . . . . . . . . . . . . . .41,000 | | 575 | 1,100 | 3,000 | 4,000 | 8,750 | 40,000 | |
| 1846, Large Date. . . . . . . .395,942 | | 500 | 515 | 575 | 750 | 1,750 | 10,000 | |
| 1846, Small Date. . . . . . . . . . . . * | | 500 | 515 | 600 | 850 | 2,500 | 10,000 | |
| 1846C . . . . . . . . . . . . . . .12,995 | | 1,650 | 3,000 | 4,500 | 6,000 | 12,500 | 50,000 | |
| 1846D . . . . . . . . . . . . . . .80,294 | | 1,650 | 1,950 | 2,750 | 4,000 | 10,000 | 35,000 | |
| 1846O . . . . . . . . . . . . . . .58,000 | | 650 | 1,200 | 3,000 | 4,000 | 10,000 | 40,000 | |
| 1847 . . . . . . . . . . . . . . . .915,981 | | 500 | 515 | 550 | 650 | 1,100 | 4,000 | |
| 1847C . . . . . . . . . . . . . . .84,151 | | 1,400 | 1,950 | 2,750 | 3,500 | 7,500 | 25,000 | |
| 1847D . . . . . . . . . . . . . . .64,405 | | 1,400 | 2,000 | 3,000 | 3,750 | 7,000 | 15,000 | |
| 1847O . . . . . . . . . . . . . . .12,000 | | 2,250 | 7,000 | 9,500 | 12,000 | 18,000 | | |
| 1848 . . . . . . . . . . . . . . . .260,775 | | 500 | 515 | 550 | 650 | 1,450 | 8,500 | |
| 1848C . . . . . . . . . . . . . . .64,472 | | 1,600 | 2,000 | 2,750 | 3,750 | 12,500 | 32,500 | |
| 1848D . . . . . . . . . . . . . . .47,465 | | 1,600 | 2,250 | 3,250 | 4,000 | 10,000 | 22,500 | |
| 1849 . . . . . . . . . . . . . . . .133,070 | | 500 | 515 | 550 | 1,200 | 2,000 | 10,000 | |
| 1849C . . . . . . . . . . . . . . .64,823 | | 1,500 | 1,750 | 2,750 | 3,500 | 7,500 | 20,000 | |
| 1849D . . . . . . . . . . . . . . .39,036 | | 1,550 | 2,100 | 2,750 | 3,750 | 10,000 | 25,000 | |
| 1850 . . . . . . . . . . . . . . . .64,491 | | 500 | 515 | 700 | 1,000 | 2,500 | 15,000 | |

* Included in number above.

| | Mintage | VF-20 | EF-40 | AU-50 | AU-55 | MS-60 | MS-63 | PF-63 |
|---|---|---|---|---|---|---|---|---|
| 1850C | 63,591 | $1,500 | $1,650 | $2,500 | $3,250 | $8,500 | $16,500 | |
| 1850D | 43,984 | 1,600 | 2,000 | 3,250 | 4,000 | 20,000 | | |
| 1851 | 377,505 | 500 | 515 | 550 | 600 | 1,500 | 7,500 | |
| 1851C | 49,176 | 1,500 | 1,900 | 2,500 | 3,500 | 9,500 | 30,000 | |
| 1851D | 62,710 | 1,500 | 2,000 | 2,500 | 3,250 | 9,000 | 20,000 | |
| 1851O | 41,000 | 700 | 1,250 | 3,000 | 5,000 | 8,500 | 20,000 | |
| 1852 | 573,901 | 500 | 515 | 550 | 650 | 1,200 | 4,000 | |
| 1852C | 72,574 | 1,750 | 2,000 | 2,500 | 3,000 | 5,000 | 17,500 | |
| 1852D | 91,584 | 1,500 | 2,000 | 2,500 | 3,500 | 7,000 | 22,500 | |
| 1853 | 305,770 | 500 | 515 | 550 | 600 | 1,050 | 5,000 | |
| 1853C | 65,571 | 1,550 | 2,200 | 2,750 | 3,250 | 5,500 | 18,000 | |
| 1853D | 89,678 | 1,500 | 2,250 | 2,750 | 3,750 | 5,750 | 15,000 | |
| 1854 | 160,675 | 500 | 515 | 550 | 600 | 1,500 | 6,500 | |
| 1854C | 39,283 | 1,500 | 2,000 | 3,250 | 3,750 | 10,000 | 32,500 | |
| 1854D | 56,413 | 1,500 | 2,000 | 3,250 | 4,000 | 6,500 | 22,500 | |
| 1854O | 46,000 | 600 | 650 | 1,100 | 1,750 | 6,000 | 20,000 | |
| 1854S (2 known) | 268 | | 2,000,000 | | | | | |
| 1855 | 117,098 | 500 | 515 | 550 | 600 | 1,500 | 5,500 | |
| 1855C | 39,788 | 1,500 | 2,000 | 2,750 | 4,000 | 10,000 | 37,500 | |
| 1855D | 22,432 | 1,500 | 2,250 | 3,250 | 4,000 | 11,500 | 32,500 | |
| 1855O | 11,100 | 1,100 | 2,750 | 4,000 | 6,000 | 17,500 | | |
| 1855S | 61,000 | 650 | 900 | 1,550 | 2,750 | 10,000 | | |
| 1856 | 197,990 | 500 | 515 | 550 | 600 | 1,250 | 6,000 | — |
| 1856C | 28,457 | 1,500 | 1,850 | 2,750 | 3,500 | 12,000 | 40,000 | |
| 1856D | 19,786 | 1,500 | 2,000 | 2,750 | 3,750 | 7,500 | 25,000 | |
| 1856O | 10,000 | 750 | 1,500 | 3,500 | 5,250 | 10,000 | | |
| 1856S | 105,100 | 550 | 625 | 900 | 1,650 | 5,500 | 20,000 | |
| 1857 | 98,188 | 500 | 515 | 550 | 600 | 1,600 | 5,500 | — |
| 1857C | 31,360 | 1,400 | 1,900 | 2,500 | 3,000 | 5,500 | 22,500 | |
| 1857D | 17,046 | 1,900 | 2,450 | 3,250 | 4,250 | 12,000 | 37,500 | |
| 1857O | 13,000 | 725 | 1,500 | 3,250 | 4,000 | 11,000 | 40,000 | |
| 1857S | 87,000 | 550 | 600 | 800 | 1,500 | 7,500 | 25,000 | |
| 1858 | 15,136 | 650 | 850 | 1,250 | 1,650 | 3,000 | 7,500 | — |
| 1858C | 38,856 | 1,550 | 2,000 | 2,750 | 3,500 | 7,000 | 25,000 | |
| 1858D | 15,362 | 1,600 | 2,200 | 2,800 | 3,500 | 8,500 | 25,000 | |
| 1858S | 18,600 | 1,250 | 2,650 | 3,600 | 6,500 | 25,000 | | |
| 1859 (80) | 16,734 | 750 | 1,000 | 1,500 | 2,200 | 5,000 | 17,500 | $65,000 |
| 1859C | 31,847 | 1,450 | 1,750 | 2,600 | 3,800 | 8,500 | 32,500 | |
| 1859D | 10,366 | 1,650 | 2,200 | 2,800 | 3,750 | 7,500 | 30,000 | |
| 1859S | 13,220 | 1,350 | 2,850 | 4,250 | 5,000 | 20,000 | | |
| 1860 (62) | 19,763 | 600 | 900 | 1,350 | 1,850 | 5,000 | 16,500 | 35,000 |
| 1860C | 14,813 | 1,850 | 2,500 | 3,500 | 5,750 | 8,500 | 20,000 | |
| 1860D | 14,635 | 1,750 | 2,250 | 3,250 | 4,250 | 9,500 | 40,000 | |
| 1860S | 21,200 | 1,800 | 2,850 | 5,000 | 8,500 | 22,500 | | |
| 1861 (66) | 688,084 | 500 | 515 | 550 | 600 | 1,300 | 4,500 | 35,000 |
| 1861C | 6,879 | 5,000 | 8,750 | 12,000 | 15,000 | 27,500 | 75,000 | |
| 1861D | 1,597 | 21,500 | 32,500 | 40,000 | 50,000 | 75,000 | 150,000 | |
| 1861S | 18,000 | 2,250 | 5,000 | 7,500 | 10,000 | | | |
| 1862 (35) | 4,430 | 1,800 | 4,000 | 7,000 | 12,500 | 25,000 | 30,000 | 35,000 |
| 1862S | 9,500 | 3,500 | 7,000 | 12,000 | 15,500 | 35,000 | | |
| 1863 (30) | 2,442 | 3,250 | 7,000 | 15,000 | 25,000 | 45,000 | | 30,000 |
| 1863S | 17,000 | 2,800 | 4,250 | 12,000 | 20,000 | 32,500 | | |
| 1864 (50) | 4,170 | 4,650 | 7,000 | 8,500 | 14,500 | 20,000 | | 30,000 |
| 1864S | 3,888 | 17,500 | 37,500 | 60,000 | 100,000 | 150,000 | | |
| 1865 (25) | 1,270 | 6,000 | 10,000 | 17,500 | 20,000 | 30,000 | | 30,000 |
| 1865S | 27,612 | 2,000 | 3,000 | 5,500 | 7,500 | 13,500 | 30,000 | |
| 1866S | 9,000 | 1,750 | 3,500 | 8,250 | 10,500 | 27,500 | | |

## Variety 2 – Motto Above Eagle (1866–1908)

**VF-20 Very Fine:** Half of hair lines above coronet missing. Hair curls under ear evident, but worn. Motto and its ribbon sharp.

**EF-40 Extremely Fine:** Small amount of wear on top of hair and below L in LIBERTY. Wear evident on wing tips and neck of eagle.

**AU-50 About Uncirculated:** Trace of wear on tip of coronet and hair above eye.

**AU-55 Choice About Uncirculated:** Evidence of friction on design high points. Some original mint luster present.

**MS-60 Uncirculated:** No trace of wear. Light blemishes.

**MS-63 Choice Uncirculated:** Some distracting contact marks or blemishes in prime focal areas. Impaired luster possible.

**PF-63 Choice Proof:** Reflective surfaces with only a few blemishes in secondary focal places. No major flaws.

| | Mintage | VF-20 | EF-40 | AU-50 | AU-55 | MS-60 | MS-63 | PF-63 |
|---|---|---|---|---|---|---|---|---|
| 1866 . . . . . . . . (30) . . . . . . . 6,700 | | $800 | $1,750 | $2,000 | $3,500 | $10,000 | $35,000 | $20,000 |
| 1866S . . . . . . . . . . . . . . . . 34,920 | | 1,000 | 2,500 | 6,000 | 7,500 | 17,500 | | |
| 1867 . . . . . . . . (50) . . . . . . . 6,870 | | 800 | 1,750 | 2,750 | 4,000 | 8,500 | | 20,000 |
| 1867S . . . . . . . . . . . . . . . . 29,000 | | 900 | 2,000 | 5,500 | 7,500 | 25,000 | | |
| 1868 . . . . . . . . (25) . . . . . . . 5,700 | | 550 | 650 | 2,000 | 3,250 | 9,500 | | 20,000 |
| 1868S . . . . . . . . . . . . . . . . 52,000 | | 550 | 1,000 | 2,450 | 3,250 | 17,500 | | |
| 1869 . . . . . . . . (25) . . . . . . . 1,760 | | 900 | 2,250 | 4,000 | 7,000 | 10,000 | 25,000 | 20,000 |
| 1869S . . . . . . . . . . . . . . . . 31,000 | | 550 | 1,250 | 2,400 | 4,000 | 15,000 | | |
| 1870 . . . . . . . . (35) . . . . . . . 4,000 | | 700 | 1,450 | 2,250 | 4,000 | 12,500 | | 20,000 |
| 1870CC . . . . . . . . . . . . . . . . 7,675 | | 20,000 | 35,000 | 55,000 | 85,000 | 125,000 | | |
| 1870S . . . . . . . . . . . . . . . . 17,000 | | 860 | 1,850 | 4,000 | 7,000 | 20,000 | | |
| 1871 . . . . . . . . (30) . . . . . . . 3,200 | | 1,000 | 1,250 | 2,500 | 3,500 | 7,500 | | 20,000 |
| 1871CC . . . . . . . . . . . . . . . . 20,770 | | 3,750 | 10,000 | 12,500 | 20,000 | 45,000 | 75,000 | |
| 1871S . . . . . . . . . . . . . . . . 25,000 | | 525 | 850 | 2,000 | 2,750 | 12,500 | 25,000 | |
| 1872 . . . . . . . . (30) . . . . . . . 1,660 | | 800 | 1,650 | 3,500 | 4,750 | 10,000 | 15,000 | 20,000 |
| 1872CC . . . . . . . . . . . . . . . . 16,980 | | 3,250 | 7,500 | 14,500 | 20,000 | 45,000 | | |
| 1872S . . . . . . . . . . . . . . . . 36,400 | | 700 | 800 | 2,000 | 3,000 | 8,000 | | |
| 1873 . . . . . . . . (25) . . . . . 112,505 | | 500 | 510 | 515 | 520 | 700 | 2,500 | 20,000 |
| 1873CC . . . . . . . . . . . . . . . . 7,416 | | 6,500 | 12,500 | 25,000 | 30,000 | 70,000 | | |
| 1873S . . . . . . . . . . . . . . . . 31,000 | | 500 | 800 | 1,500 | 2,750 | 15,000 | | |
| 1874 . . . . . . . . (20) . . . . . . . 3,488 | | 650 | 1,200 | 1,750 | 2,500 | 8,500 | 20,000 | 25,000 |
| 1874CC . . . . . . . . . . . . . . . . 21,198 | | 2,500 | 5,000 | 10,000 | 15,000 | 32,500 | | |
| 1874S . . . . . . . . . . . . . . . . 16,000 | | 650 | 1,250 | 2,250 | 4,000 | 13,500 | | |
| 1875 . . . . . . . . (20) . . . . . . . . 200 | | 60,000 | 75,000 | 120,000 | 165,000 | | | 80,000 |
| 1875CC . . . . . . . . . . . . . . . . 11,828 | | 3,000 | 7,000 | 12,500 | 20,000 | 40,000 | | |
| 1875S . . . . . . . . . . . . . . . . 9,000 | | 900 | 2,000 | 3,500 | 5,000 | 15,000 | | |
| 1876 . . . . . . . . (45) . . . . . . . 1,432 | | 1,500 | 3,250 | 4,750 | 5,500 | 11,500 | 17,500 | 15,000 |
| 1876CC . . . . . . . . . . . . . . . . 6,887 | | 3,750 | 6,500 | 15,000 | 20,000 | 47,500 | | |
| 1876S . . . . . . . . . . . . . . . . 4,000 | | 2,750 | 5,000 | 9,500 | 13,000 | 40,000 | | |
| 1877 . . . . . . . . (20) . . . . . . . 1,132 | | 1,650 | 2,750 | 4,500 | 5,000 | 9,000 | 15,000 | 15,000 |
| 1877CC . . . . . . . . . . . . . . . . 8,680 | | 2,750 | 5,000 | 9,000 | 17,500 | 40,000 | | |
| 1877S . . . . . . . . . . . . . . . . 26,700 | | 500 | 575 | 1,200 | 2,000 | 6,500 | 17,500 | |
| 1878 . . . . . . . . (20) . . . . . 131,720 | | 500 | 510 | 515 | 520 | 550 | 1,500 | 22,500 |
| 1878CC . . . . . . . . . . . . . . . . 9,054 | | 4,500 | 10,000 | 18,000 | 30,000 | 55,000 | | |
| 1878S . . . . . . . . . . . . . . . . 144,700 | | 500 | 510 | 515 | 520 | 550 | 2,250 | |
| 1879 . . . . . . . . (30) . . . . . 301,920 | | 500 | 510 | 515 | 520 | 550 | 1,000 | 15,000 |
| 1879CC . . . . . . . . . . . . . . . . 17,281 | | 2,500 | 4,000 | 5,000 | 6,750 | 22,500 | | |
| 1879S . . . . . . . . . . . . . . . . 426,200 | | 500 | 510 | 515 | 520 | 550 | 1,250 | |
| 1880 . . . . . . . . (36) . . . . 3,166,400 | | 500 | 510 | 515 | 520 | 550 | 600 | 15,000 |
| 1880CC . . . . . . . . . . . . . . . . 51,017 | | 1,000 | 1,500 | 1,750 | 5,000 | 12,000 | 40,000 | |
| 1880S . . . . . . . . . . . . . 1,348,900 | | 500 | 510 | 515 | 520 | 550 | 600 | |

| | Mintage | VF-20 | EF-40 | AU-50 | AU-55 | MS-60 | MS-63 | PF-63 |
|---|---|---|---|---|---|---|---|---|
| 1881 . . . . . . . . (42) . . . . | 5,708,760 | $500 | $510 | $515 | $520 | $550 | $600 | $15,000 |
| 1881CC . . . . . . . . . . . . . . | 13,886 | 1,500 | 4,000 | 6,000 | 9,500 | 19,500 | 40,000 | |
| 1881S . . . . . . . . . . . . . . | 969,000 | 500 | 510 | 515 | 520 | 550 | 600 | |
| 1882 . . . . . . . . (48) . . . . | 2,514,520 | 500 | 510 | 515 | 520 | 550 | 600 | 13,000 |
| 1882CC . . . . . . . . . . . . . . | 82,817 | 850 | 1,750 | 2,250 | 4,500 | 10,000 | 35,000 | |
| 1882S . . . . . . . . . . . . . . | 969,000 | 500 | 510 | 515 | 520 | 550 | 600 | |
| 1883 . . . . . . . . (61) . . . . . | 233,400 | 500 | 510 | 515 | 520 | 550 | 1,000 | 13,000 |
| 1883CC . . . . . . . . . . . . . . | 12,598 | 1,500 | 3,000 | 4,500 | 6,500 | 15,000 | 45,000 | |
| 1883S . . . . . . . . . . . . . . | 83,200 | 500 | 510 | 515 | 520 | 550 | 1,250 | |
| 1884 . . . . . . . . (48) . . . . . | 191,030 | 500 | 510 | 515 | 520 | 550 | 1,200 | 13,000 |
| 1884CC . . . . . . . . . . . . . . | 16,402 | 850 | 2,250 | 4,000 | 6,500 | 18,500 | | |
| 1884S . . . . . . . . . . . . . . | 177,000 | 500 | 510 | 515 | 520 | 550 | 800 | |
| 1885 . . . . . . . . (66) . . . . . | 601,440 | 500 | 510 | 515 | 520 | 550 | 600 | 12,000 |
| 1885S . . . . . . . . . . . . . | 1,211,500 | 500 | 510 | 515 | 520 | 550 | 600 | |
| 1886 . . . . . . . . (72) . . . . . | 388,360 | 500 | 510 | 515 | 520 | 550 | 600 | 12,000 |
| 1886S . . . . . . . . . . . . . | 3,268,000 | 500 | 510 | 515 | 520 | 550 | 600 | |
| 1887, Proof only (87) . . . . . . . . . . . | | | | | | | | 37,500 |
| 1887S . . . . . . . . . . . . . | 1,912,000 | 500 | 510 | 515 | 520 | 550 | 675 | |
| 1888 . . . . . . . . (95) . . . . . . | 18,201 | 500 | 510 | 515 | 520 | 550 | 1,250 | 12,000 |
| 1888S . . . . . . . . . . . . . . | 293,900 | 500 | 510 | 515 | 520 | 650 | 2,750 | |
| 1889 . . . . . . . . (45) . . . . . . . | 7,520 | 500 | 510 | 515 | 600 | 1,200 | 3,750 | 12,000 |
| 1890 . . . . . . . . (88) . . . . . . . | 4,240 | 500 | 510 | 550 | 1,000 | 2,000 | 4,500 | 12,000 |
| 1890CC . . . . . . . . . . . . . . | 53,800 | 650 | 750 | 1,000 | 1,500 | 1,850 | 6,500 | |
| 1891 . . . . . . . . (53) . . . . . . | 61,360 | 500 | 510 | 515 | 520 | 550 | 1,000 | 11,000 |
| 1891CC . . . . . . . . . . . . . . | 208,000 | 650 | 700 | 950 | 1,250 | 1,750 | 3,250 | |
| 1892 . . . . . . . . (92) . . . . . | 753,480 | 500 | 510 | 515 | 520 | 550 | 600 | 11,000 |
| 1892CC . . . . . . . . . . . . . . | 82,968 | 650 | 750 | 1,000 | 1,500 | 2,250 | 7,000 | |
| 1892O . . . . . . . . . . . . . . | 10,000 | 1,500 | 1,800 | 2,250 | 3,000 | 5,000 | 17,500 | |
| 1892S . . . . . . . . . . . . . . | 298,400 | 500 | 510 | 515 | 520 | 550 | 1,500 | |
| 1893 . . . . . . . . (77) . . . . | 1,528,120 | 500 | 510 | 515 | 520 | 550 | 600 | 11,000 |
| 1893CC . . . . . . . . . . . . . . | 60,000 | 650 | 750 | 1,100 | 1,750 | 3,250 | 7,500 | |
| 1893O . . . . . . . . . . . . . . | 110,000 | 500 | 525 | 550 | 600 | 800 | 4,500 | |
| 1893S . . . . . . . . . . . . . . | 224,000 | 500 | 510 | 515 | 520 | 550 | 650 | |
| 1894 . . . . . . . . (75) . . . . . | 957,880 | 500 | 510 | 515 | 520 | 550 | 600 | 11,000 |
| 1894O . . . . . . . . . . . . . . | 16,600 | 550 | 575 | 600 | 750 | 1,500 | 8,500 | |
| 1894S . . . . . . . . . . . . . . | 55,900 | 500 | 510 | 515 | 600 | 1,650 | 7,500 | |
| 1895 . . . . . . . . (81) . . . . | 1,345,855 | 500 | 510 | 515 | 520 | 550 | 600 | 11,000 |
| 1895S . . . . . . . . . . . . . . | 112,000 | 500 | 510 | 515 | 520 | 700 | 3,750 | |
| 1896 . . . . . . . (103) . . . . . . | 58,960 | 500 | 510 | 515 | 520 | 550 | 600 | 10,000 |
| 1896S . . . . . . . . . . . . . . | 155,400 | 500 | 510 | 515 | 520 | 600 | 3,500 | |
| 1897 . . . . . . . . (83) . . . . . | 867,800 | 500 | 510 | 515 | 520 | 550 | 600 | 10,000 |
| 1897S . . . . . . . . . . . . . . | 354,000 | 500 | 510 | 515 | 520 | 600 | 2,750 | |
| 1898 . . . . . . . . (75) . . . . . | 633,420 | 500 | 510 | 515 | 520 | 550 | 600 | 10,000 |
| 1898S . . . . . . . . . . . . . | 1,397,400 | 500 | 510 | 515 | 520 | 550 | 800 | |
| 1899 . . . . . . . . (99) . . . . | 1,710,630 | 500 | 510 | 515 | 520 | 550 | 600 | 10,000 |
| 1899S . . . . . . . . . . . . . | 1,545,000 | 500 | 510 | 515 | 520 | 550 | 600 | |
| 1900 . . . . . . . (230) . . . . | 1,405,500 | 500 | 510 | 515 | 520 | 550 | 600 | 10,000 |
| 1900S . . . . . . . . . . . . . . | 329,000 | 500 | 510 | 515 | 520 | 550 | 650 | |
| 1901 . . . . . . . (140) . . . . . | 615,900 | 500 | 510 | 515 | 520 | 550 | 600 | 9,000 |
| 1901S, 1 Over 0 . . . . . . . | 3,648,000 | 500 | 510 | 515 | 520 | 550 | 650 | |
| 1901S . . . . . . . . . . . . . . . . . | * | 500 | 510 | 515 | 520 | 550 | 600 | |
| 1902 . . . . . . . (162) . . . . . | 172,400 | 500 | 510 | 515 | 520 | 550 | 600 | 9,000 |
| 1902S . . . . . . . . . . . . . . | 939,000 | 500 | 510 | 515 | 520 | 550 | 600 | |
| 1903 . . . . . . . (154) . . . . . | 226,870 | 500 | 510 | 515 | 520 | 550 | 600 | 9,000 |
| 1903S . . . . . . . . . . . . . | 1,855,000 | 500 | 510 | 515 | 520 | 550 | 600 | |

* Included in number above.

*Chart continued on next page.*     

| | Mintage | VF-20 | EF-40 | AU-50 | AU-55 | MS-60 | MS-63 | PF-63 |
|---|---|---|---|---|---|---|---|---|
| 1904 . . . . . . . . (136) . . . . .392,000 | | $500 | $510 | $515 | $520 | $550 | $600 | $9,000 |
| 1904S . . . . . . . . . . . . . . .97,000 | | 500 | 510 | 515 | 520 | 550 | 2,000 | |
| 1905 . . . . . . . (108) . . . . .302,200 | | 500 | 510 | 515 | 520 | 550 | 600 | 9,000 |
| 1905S . . . . . . . . . . . . . .880,700 | | 500 | 510 | 515 | 520 | 550 | 900 | |
| 1906 . . . . . . . (85) . . . . .348,735 | | 500 | 510 | 515 | 520 | 550 | 600 | 9,000 |
| 1906D . . . . . . . . . . . . . .320,000 | | 500 | 510 | 515 | 520 | 550 | 600 | |
| 1906S . . . . . . . . . . . . . .598,000 | | 500 | 510 | 515 | 520 | 550 | 650 | |
| 1907 . . . . . . . . (92) . . . . .626,100 | | 500 | 510 | 515 | 520 | 550 | 600 | 9,000 |
| 1907D . . . . . . . . . . . . . .888,000 | | 500 | 510 | 515 | 520 | 550 | 600 | |
| 1908 . . . . . . . . . . . . . . .421,874 | | 500 | 510 | 515 | 520 | 550 | 600 | |

## INDIAN HEAD (1908–1929)

This type conforms in design to the quarter eagle of the same date. The sunken-relief designs and lettering make the Indian Head a unique series, along with the quarter eagle, in United States coinage.

**VF-20 Very Fine:** Noticeable wear on large middle feathers and tip of eagle's wing.
**EF-40 Extremely Fine:** Cheekbone, war bonnet, and headband feathers slightly worn. Feathers on eagle's upper wing show considerable wear.
**AU-50 About Uncirculated:** Trace of wear on cheekbone and headdress.
**AU-55 Choice About Uncirculated:** Evidence of friction on design high points. Much of original mint luster present.
**MS-60 Uncirculated:** No trace of wear. Light blemishes.
**MS-63 Choice Uncirculated:** Some distracting contact marks or blemishes in prime focal areas. Impaired luster possible.

Mintmark Location

**Matte PF-63 Choice Proof:** Matte surfaces with few blemishes in secondary focal places. No major flaws.

*Coin dealers usually pay higher prices than those listed for scarcer coins with well-struck mintmarks.*

| | Mintage | VF-20 | EF-40 | AU-50 | AU-55 | MS-60 | MS-63 | MATTE PF-63 |
|---|---|---|---|---|---|---|---|---|
| 1908 . . . . . . . (167) . . . . .577,845 | | $575 | $600 | $625 | $650 | $700 | $1,200 | $16,000 |
| 1908D . . . . . . . . . . . . . .148,000 | | 575 | 600 | 625 | 650 | 700 | 1,250 | |
| 1908S . . . . . . . . . . . . . . .82,000 | | 575 | 650 | 1,100 | 1,500 | 4,500 | 9,000 | |
| 1909 . . . . . . . . (78) . . . . .627,060 | | 575 | 600 | 625 | 650 | 700 | 1,250 | 16,000 |
| 1909D . . . . . . . . . . . . 3,423,560 | | 575 | 600 | 625 | 650 | 700 | 1,000 | |
| 1909O . . . . . . . . . . . . . . .34,200 | | 3,750 | 5,500 | 8,500 | 11,000 | 18,500 | 70,000 | |
| 1909S . . . . . . . . . . . . . .297,200 | | 600 | 615 | 625 | 650 | 1,500 | 8,500 | |
| 1910 . . . . . . . (250) . . . . .604,000 | | 575 | 600 | 625 | 650 | 700 | 1,250 | 16,000 |
| 1910D . . . . . . . . . . . . . .193,600 | | 575 | 600 | 625 | 650 | 700 | 2,500 | |
| 1910S . . . . . . . . . . . . . .770,200 | | 575 | 600 | 625 | 650 | 800 | 8,000 | |
| 1911 . . . . . . . (139) . . . . .915,000 | | 575 | 600 | 625 | 650 | 700 | 1,200 | 16,000 |
| 1911D . . . . . . . . . . . . . . .72,500 | | 600 | 900 | 1,450 | 1,500 | 5,000 | 20,000 | |
| 1911S . . . . . . . . . . . . 1,416,000 | | 575 | 600 | 625 | 650 | 750 | 3,500 | |
| 1912 . . . . . . . (144) . . . . .790,000 | | 575 | 600 | 625 | 650 | 700 | 1,250 | 16,000 |
| 1912S . . . . . . . . . . . . . .392,000 | | 575 | 600 | 625 | 650 | 1,250 | 12,000 | |
| 1913 . . . . . . . . (99) . . . . .915,901 | | 575 | 600 | 625 | 650 | 700 | 1,250 | 16,000 |
| 1913S . . . . . . . . . . . . . .408,000 | | 575 | 600 | 625 | 700 | 1,650 | 8,750 | |
| 1914 . . . . . . . (125) . . . . .247,000 | | 575 | 600 | 625 | 650 | 700 | 1,300 | 16,000 |
| 1914D . . . . . . . . . . . . . .247,000 | | 575 | 600 | 625 | 650 | 700 | 2,000 | |
| 1914S . . . . . . . . . . . . . .263,000 | | 575 | 600 | 625 | 700 | 1,500 | 6,500 | |
| 1915 . . . . . . . . (75) . . . . .588,000 | | 575 | 600 | 625 | 650 | 700 | 1,250 | 17,500 |
| 1915S . . . . . . . . . . . . . .164,000 | | 575 | 600 | 625 | 750 | 2,000 | 9,500 | |
| 1916S . . . . . . . . . . . . . .240,000 | | 575 | 600 | 625 | 650 | 750 | 4,000 | |
| 1929 . . . . . . . . . . . . . . .662,000 | | 11,500 | 15,000 | 17,000 | 18,500 | 25,000 | 28,500 | |

Coinage authorization, specified weights, and fineness of the eagle coins conform to those of the half eagle. The Small Eagle reverse was used until 1797, when the large, Heraldic Eagle replaced it.

## CAPPED BUST TO RIGHT (1795–1804)

**F-12 Fine:** Details on turban and head obliterated.

**VF-20 Very Fine:** Hair lines in curls on neck and details under turban and over forehead worn but distinguishable.

**EF-40 Extremely Fine:** Definite wear on hair to left of eye and strand of hair across and around turban, as well as on eagle's wing tips.

**AU-50 About Uncirculated:** Trace of wear on cap, hair, cheek, and drapery.

**AU-55 Choice About Uncirculated:** Evidence of friction on design high points. Most of original mint luster present.

**MS-60 Uncirculated:** No trace of wear. Light blemishes.

**MS-63 Choice Uncirculated:** Some distracting contact marks or blemishes in prime focal areas. Impaired luster possible.

### Small Eagle Reverse (1795–1797)

|  | Mintage | F-12 | VF-20 | EF-40 | AU-50 | AU-55 | MS-60 | MS-63 |
|---|---|---|---|---|---|---|---|---|
| 1795 | 5,583 | $25,000 | $30,000 | $45,000 | $55,000 | $65,000 | $90,000 | $225,000 |
| 1796 | 4,146 | 26,000 | 32,500 | 47,500 | 60,000 | 70,000 | 95,000 | 350,000 |
| 1797, Small Eagle | 3,615 | 32,500 | 45,000 | 75,000 | 90,000 | 115,000 | 185,000 | |

### Heraldic Eagle Reverse (1797–1804)

|  | Mintage | F-12 | VF-20 | EF-40 | AU-50 | AU-55 | MS-60 | MS-63 |
|---|---|---|---|---|---|---|---|---|
| 1797, Large Eagle | 10,940 | $9,000 | $13,500 | $18,500 | $25,000 | $30,000 | $45,000 | $125,000 |
| 1798, 8 Over 7, 9 Stars Left, 4 Right | 900 | 12,000 | 15,000 | 30,000 | 40,000 | 70,000 | 125,000 | 250,000 |
| 1798, 8 Over 7, 7 Stars Left, 6 Right | 842 | 37,500 | 55,000 | 85,000 | 150,000 | 175,000 | 350,000 | |
| 1799 | 37,449 | 8,000 | 9,000 | 12,000 | 15,000 | 16,500 | 22,500 | 50,000 |
| 1800 | 5,999 | 8,000 | 9,000 | 12,000 | 15,000 | 16,500 | 22,500 | 65,000 |
| 1801 | 44,344 | 8,000 | 9,000 | 12,000 | 15,000 | 16,500 | 22,500 | 50,000 |
| 1803 | 15,017 | 8,000 | 9,000 | 12,000 | 15,000 | 16,500 | 22,500 | 50,000 |
| 1804 | 3,757 | 15,000 | 22,500 | 27,500 | 40,000 | 55,000 | 75,000 | 225,000 |

*Chart continued on next page.*         **179**

## LIBERTY HEAD, NO MOTTO ABOVE EAGLE (1838–1866)

In 1838 the weight and diameter of the eagle were reduced and the obverse and reverse were redesigned. Liberty now faced left and the word LIBERTY was placed on the coronet.

**VF-20 Very Fine:** Hair lines above coronet partly worn. Curls under ear worn but defined.

**EF-40 Extremely Fine:** Small amount of wear on top of hair and below L in LIBERTY. Wear evident on wing tips and neck of eagle.

**AU-50 About Uncirculated:** Trace of wear on tip of coronet and hair above eye.

**AU-55 Choice About Uncirculated:** Evidence of friction on design high points. Some of original mint luster present.

**MS-60 Uncirculated:** No trace of wear. Light blemishes.

*Mintmark is on reverse, below eagle.*

**MS-63 Choice Uncirculated:** Some distracting contact marks or blemishes in prime focal areas. Impaired luster possible.

**PF-63 Choice Proof:** Attractive reflective surfaces with only a few blemishes in secondary focal places. No major flaws.

| | Mintage | VF-20 | EF-40 | AU-50 | AU-55 | MS-60 | MS-63 | PF-63 |
|---|---|---|---|---|---|---|---|---|
| 1838 | 7,200 | $2,750 | $7,000 | $12,500 | $25,000 | $55,000 | $85,000 | |
| 1839, Large Letters | 25,801 | 1,500 | 3,850 | 4,500 | 7,500 | 22,500 | 70,000 | |
| 1839, Small Letters | 12,447 | 3,000 | 8,500 | 12,000 | 16,500 | 40,000 | 100,000 | |
| 1840 | 47,338 | 900 | 1,350 | 1,500 | 2,250 | 7,500 | | |
| 1841 | 63,131 | 900 | 910 | 1,100 | 2,000 | 9,000 | 35,000 | |
| 1841O | 2,500 | 6,000 | 10,000 | 22,500 | 50,000 | | | |
| 1842 | 81,507 | 900 | 910 | 1,250 | 2,000 | 11,500 | 22,500 | |
| 1842O | 27,400 | 950 | 1,500 | 3,000 | 6,000 | 45,000 | 200,000 | |
| 1843 | 75,462 | 900 | 910 | 1,500 | 3,250 | 12,500 | | |
| 1843O | 175,162 | 950 | 1,000 | 1,500 | 3,500 | 12,500 | 75,000 | |
| 1844 | 6,361 | 2,000 | 3,750 | 5,000 | 12,500 | 20,000 | 60,000 | |
| 1844O | 118,700 | 925 | 1,150 | 1,500 | 3,000 | 10,000 | 60,000 | |
| 1845 | 26,153 | 900 | 1,400 | 2,000 | 3,000 | 12,000 | | |
| 1845O | 47,500 | 925 | 1,450 | 2,500 | 5,500 | 15,000 | 55,000 | |
| 1846 | 20,095 | 1,000 | 1,500 | 3,750 | 6,500 | 27,500 | | |
| 1846O | 81,780 | 950 | 1,750 | 2,750 | 4,500 | 12,500 | 25,000 | |
| 1847 | 862,258 | 900 | 910 | 925 | 950 | 2,500 | 17,500 | |
| 1847O | 571,500 | 925 | 950 | 1,000 | 1,500 | 4,500 | 27,500 | |
| 1848 | 145,484 | 900 | 910 | 925 | 950 | 5,000 | 25,000 | |
| 1848O | 35,850 | 1,150 | 3,250 | 3,500 | 5,000 | 12,500 | 25,000 | |
| 1849 | 653,618 | 900 | 910 | 925 | 950 | 2,750 | 15,000 | |
| 1849O | 23,900 | 1,400 | 2,650 | 4,500 | 8,000 | 20,000 | | |
| 1850 | 291,451 | 900 | 910 | 925 | 1,000 | 4,000 | 25,000 | |
| 1850O | 57,500 | 950 | 1,100 | 2,500 | 4,750 | 17,500 | 40,000 | |
| 1851 | 176,328 | 900 | 910 | 925 | 1,000 | 3,500 | 25,000 | |
| 1851O | 263,000 | 925 | 1,000 | 1,200 | 2,000 | 8,500 | 30,000 | |
| 1852 | 263,106 | 900 | 910 | 925 | 1,000 | 2,500 | 20,000 | |
| 1852O | 18,000 | 1,250 | 2,750 | 4,500 | 8,500 | 75,000 | | |
| 1853, 3 Over 2 | 201,253 | 1,000 | 1,200 | 1,500 | 2,250 | 12,500 | | |
| 1853 | * | 900 | 910 | 925 | 1,000 | 2,500 | 15,000 | |
| 1853O | 51,000 | 1,000 | 1,250 | 1,600 | 3,500 | 15,000 | | |
| 1854 | 54,250 | 900 | 910 | 925 | 1,000 | 5,000 | | |
| 1854O | 52,500 | 950 | 1,250 | 1,650 | 2,500 | 10,000 | 35,000 | |
| 1854S | 123,826 | 950 | 1,100 | 1,500 | 2,500 | 12,500 | 25,000 | |
| 1855 | 121,701 | 900 | 910 | 925 | 1,000 | 3,000 | 15,000 | |
| 1855O | 18,000 | 1,250 | 3,250 | 5,500 | 8,000 | 20,000 | | |

* Included in number above.

# EAGLES ($10)

| | Mintage | VF-20 | EF-40 | AU-50 | AU-55 | MS-60 | MS-63 | PF-63 |
|---|---|---|---|---|---|---|---|---|
| 1855S . . . . . . . . . . . . . . . .9,000 | | $2,750 | $3,000 | $5,500 | $9,500 | | | |
| 1856 . . . . . . . . . . . . . . . .60,490 | | 900 | 910 | 925 | 1,100 | $3,000 | $15,000 | |
| 1856O . . . . . . . . . . . . . . .14,500 | | 1,000 | 2,250 | 3,500 | 7,500 | 25,000 | | |
| 1856S . . . . . . . . . . . . . . .68,000 | | 900 | 910 | 1,500 | 2,250 | 10,000 | | |
| 1857 . . . . . . . . . . . . . . . .16,606 | | 900 | 950 | 1,350 | 2,000 | 10,000 | | |
| 1857O . . . . . . . . . . . . . . . .5,500 | | 2,250 | 5,500 | 7,000 | 10,000 | 20,000 | | |
| 1857S . . . . . . . . . . . . . . .26,000 | | 1,250 | 1,500 | 2,000 | 3,250 | 8,000 | 25,000 | |
| 1858 . . . . . . . . . . . . . . . . .2,521 | | 4,000 | 6,000 | 9,000 | 14,500 | 25,000 | 150,000 | $85,000 |
| 1858O . . . . . . . . . . . . . . .20,000 | | 1,000 | 1,500 | 2,250 | 2,750 | 10,000 | 35,000 | |
| 1858S . . . . . . . . . . . . . . .11,800 | | 1,200 | 3,000 | 6,000 | 8,500 | | | |
| 1859 . . . . . . . . (80) . . . . . .16,013 | | 900 | 950 | 1,250 | 2,250 | 15,000 | 55,000 | 50,000 |
| 1859O . . . . . . . . . . . . . . . .2,300 | | 5,500 | 11,000 | 20,000 | 30,000 | 50,000 | | |
| 1859S . . . . . . . . . . . . . . . .7,000 | | 2,500 | 4,250 | 17,500 | 25,000 | 35,000 | | |
| 1860 . . . . . . . . (50) . . . . . .15,055 | | 900 | 910 | 1,250 | 1,850 | 6,500 | 30,000 | 40,000 |
| 1860O . . . . . . . . . . . . . . .11,100 | | 1,500 | 2,500 | 3,750 | 5,750 | 15,000 | | |
| 1860S . . . . . . . . . . . . . . . .5,000 | | 4,500 | 11,000 | 14,500 | 22,500 | 35,000 | | |
| 1861 . . . . . . . . (69) . . . . .113,164 | | 900 | 925 | 1,250 | 2,000 | 4,500 | 20,000 | 40,000 |
| 1861S . . . . . . . . . . . . . . .15,500 | | 3,500 | 8,000 | 12,500 | 15,000 | 37,500 | | |
| 1862 . . . . . . . . (35) . . . . . .10,960 | | 2,750 | 3,500 | 5,500 | 6,500 | 15,000 | | 40,000 |
| 1862S . . . . . . . . . . . . . . .12,500 | | 3,500 | 6,500 | 9,500 | 20,000 | | | |
| 1863 . . . . . . . . (30) . . . . . . .1,218 | | 12,500 | 27,500 | 40,000 | 50,000 | 65,000 | 100,000 | 40,000 |
| 1863S . . . . . . . . . . . . . . .10,000 | | 5,500 | 10,000 | 15,000 | 22,500 | 95,000 | | |
| 1864 . . . . . . . . (50) . . . . . . .3,530 | | 5,500 | 8,500 | 20,000 | 30,000 | 55,000 | | 40,000 |
| 1864S . . . . . . . . . . . . . . . .2,500 | | 40,000 | 85,000 | 135,000 | | | | |
| 1865 . . . . . . . . (25) . . . . . . .3,980 | | 3,250 | 4,500 | 15,000 | 20,000 | 32,500 | | 40,000 |
| 1865S . . . . . . . . . . . . . . .16,700 | | 4,500 | 10,000 | 16,000 | 27,500 | 70,000 | | |
| 1866S . . . . . . . . . . . . . . . .8,500 | | 5,000 | 12,000 | 15,000 | 20,000 | 37,500 | | |

## LIBERTY HEAD, MOTTO ABOVE EAGLE (1866–1907)

**VF-20 Very Fine:** Half of hair lines over coronet visible. Curls under ear worn but defined. IN GOD WE TRUST and its ribbon sharp.

**EF-40 Extremely Fine:** Small amount of wear on top of hair and below L in LIBERTY. Wear evident on wing tips and neck of eagle.

**AU-50 About Uncirculated:** Trace of wear on hair above eye and on coronet.

**AU-55 Choice About Uncirculated:** Evidence of friction on design high points. Some of original mint luster present.

*Mintmark is on reverse, below eagle.*

**MS-60 Uncirculated:** No trace of wear. Light blemishes.

**MS-63 Choice Uncirculated:** Some distracting marks or blemishes in focal areas. Impaired luster possible.

**PF-63 Choice Proof:** Reflective surfaces with only a few blemishes in secondary focal areas. No major flaws.

| | Mintage | VF-20 | EF-40 | AU-50 | AU-55 | MS-60 | MS-63 | PF-63 |
|---|---|---|---|---|---|---|---|---|
| 1866 . . . . . . . . (30) . . . . . . .3,750 | | $1,200 | $2,500 | $3,750 | $9,000 | $32,500 | | $30,000 |
| 1866S . . . . . . . . . . . . . . .11,500 | | 1,850 | 4,000 | 6,000 | 8,000 | 20,000 | | |
| 1867 . . . . . . . . (50) . . . . . . .3,090 | | 2,250 | 3,000 | 6,000 | 10,000 | 30,000 | | 30,000 |
| 1867S . . . . . . . . . . . . . . . .9,000 | | 4,000 | 5,500 | 8,500 | 13,500 | 25,000 | | |
| 1868 . . . . . . . . (25) . . . . . .10,630 | | 1,100 | 1,250 | 2,000 | 2,750 | 12,000 | | 30,000 |
| 1868S . . . . . . . . . . . . . . .13,500 | | 1,500 | 2,000 | 3,000 | 5,000 | 15,000 | | |
| 1869 . . . . . . . . (25) . . . . . . .1,830 | | 1,350 | 3,500 | 5,000 | 10,000 | 30,000 | | 30,000 |
| 1869S . . . . . . . . . . . . . . . .6,430 | | 1,750 | 3,000 | 5,000 | 9,500 | 25,000 | | |
| 1870 . . . . . . . . (35) . . . . . . .3,990 | | 1,500 | 1,750 | 3,000 | 6,500 | 25,000 | | 27,500 |
| 1870CC . . . . . . . . . . . . . . .5,908 | | 50,000 | 60,000 | 85,000 | 125,000 | | | |
| 1870S . . . . . . . . . . . . . . . .8,000 | | 1,350 | 3,500 | 4,500 | 10,000 | 30,000 | | |
| 1871 . . . . . . . . (30) . . . . . . .1,790 | | 1,100 | 2,500 | 4,000 | 6,500 | 40,000 | | 27,500 |
| 1871CC . . . . . . . . . . . . . . .8,085 | | 5,000 | 15,000 | 20,000 | 25,000 | 55,000 | | |

*Chart continued on next page.*

| | Mintage | VF-20 | EF-40 | AU-50 | AU-55 | MS-60 | MS-63 | PF-63 |
|---|---|---|---|---|---|---|---|---|
| 1871S | 16,500 | $1,250 | $1,500 | $3,500 | $5,500 | | | |
| 1872 (30) | 1,620 | 2,750 | 4,750 | 7,500 | 15,000 | $35,000 | $45,000 | $27,500 |
| 1872CC | 4,600 | 7,500 | 12,500 | 25,000 | 35,000 | 50,000 | | |
| 1872S | 17,300 | 900 | 1,250 | 2,000 | 4,000 | 20,000 | | |
| 1873 (25) | 800 | 7,500 | 15,000 | 30,000 | 45,000 | 55,000 | | 30,000 |
| 1873CC | 4,543 | 12,500 | 25,000 | 45,000 | 70,000 | 100,000 | | |
| 1873S | 12,000 | 1,000 | 2,500 | 3,750 | 5,500 | 25,000 | | |
| 1874 (20) | 53,140 | 900 | 910 | 920 | 925 | 1,000 | 10,000 | 30,000 |
| 1874CC | 16,767 | 2,750 | 5,000 | 9,000 | 22,500 | 70,000 | 150,000 | |
| 1874S | 10,000 | 1,000 | 1,600 | 3,500 | 8,000 | 25,000 | | |
| 1875 (20) | 100 | 75,000 | 125,000 | 300,000 | 350,000 | | | 125,000 |
| 1875CC | 7,715 | 4,000 | 9,000 | 15,000 | 45,000 | 95,000 | 150,000 | |
| 1876 (45) | 687 | 4,000 | 7,000 | 20,000 | 27,500 | 55,000 | | 25,000 |
| 1876CC | 4,696 | 5,500 | 12,500 | 18,500 | 27,500 | 50,000 | | |
| 1876S | 5,000 | 1,750 | 4,000 | 6,500 | 17,500 | 22,000 | | |
| 1877 (20) | 797 | 3,500 | 5,750 | 9,500 | 15,000 | 37,500 | | 25,000 |
| 1877CC | 3,332 | 7,500 | 10,000 | 22,500 | 70,000 | | | |
| 1877S | 17,000 | 900 | 1,100 | 1,750 | 4,000 | 25,000 | | |
| 1878 (20) | 73,780 | 900 | 910 | 920 | 925 | 950 | 3,000 | 25,000 |
| 1878CC | 3,244 | 7,000 | 15,000 | 30,000 | 55,000 | | | |
| 1878S | 26,100 | 900 | 910 | 920 | 1,750 | 12,500 | 25,000 | |
| 1879 (30) | 384,740 | 900 | 910 | 920 | 925 | 950 | 2,000 | 22,500 |
| 1879CC | 1,762 | 10,000 | 20,000 | 37,500 | 50,000 | | | |
| 1879O | 1,500 | 9,000 | 13,500 | 22,500 | 30,000 | 70,000 | | |
| 1879S | 224,000 | 900 | 910 | 920 | 925 | 950 | 3,500 | |
| 1880 (36) | 1,644,840 | 900 | 910 | 920 | 925 | 950 | 1,000 | 22,500 |
| 1880CC | 11,190 | 1,750 | 2,500 | 3,500 | 5,500 | 27,500 | | |
| 1880O | 9,200 | 1,200 | 2,000 | 3,500 | 4,000 | 15,000 | 30,000 | |
| 1880S | 506,250 | 900 | 910 | 920 | 925 | 950 | 1,000 | |
| 1881 (40) | 3,877,220 | 900 | 910 | 920 | 925 | 950 | 1,050 | 22,500 |
| 1881CC | 24,015 | 1,500 | 2,000 | 3,250 | 4,500 | 7,500 | 35,000 | |
| 1881O | 8,350 | 1,000 | 1,450 | 2,500 | 3,500 | 15,000 | | |
| 1881S | 970,000 | 900 | 910 | 920 | 925 | 950 | 1,200 | |
| 1882 (40) | 2,324,440 | 900 | 910 | 920 | 925 | 950 | 1,050 | 20,000 |
| 1882CC | 6,764 | 1,650 | 3,000 | 5,500 | 10,000 | 27,500 | 65,000 | |
| 1882O | 10,820 | 950 | 1,250 | 1,500 | 2,750 | 8,500 | 30,000 | |
| 1882S | 132,000 | 900 | 910 | 920 | 925 | 950 | 1,500 | |
| 1883 (40) | 208,700 | 900 | 910 | 920 | 925 | 950 | 1,050 | 18,500 |
| 1883CC | 12,000 | 1,500 | 3,000 | 4,500 | 7,500 | 30,000 | | |
| 1883O | 800 | 17,500 | 32,500 | 57,500 | 75,000 | 125,000 | | |
| 1883S | 38,000 | 900 | 910 | 920 | 925 | 1,000 | 7,000 | |
| 1884 (45) | 76,860 | 900 | 910 | 920 | 925 | 950 | 2,000 | 18,500 |
| 1884CC | 9,925 | 1,500 | 3,000 | 5,000 | 6,000 | 15,000 | 80,000 | |
| 1884S | 124,250 | 900 | 910 | 920 | 950 | 1,000 | 3,000 | |
| 1885 (65) | 253,462 | 900 | 910 | 920 | 925 | 950 | 1,100 | 18,500 |
| 1885S | 228,000 | 900 | 910 | 920 | 925 | 950 | 1,050 | |
| 1886 (60) | 236,100 | 900 | 910 | 920 | 925 | 950 | 1,500 | 18,500 |
| 1886S | 826,000 | 900 | 910 | 920 | 925 | 950 | 1,050 | |
| 1887 (80) | 53,600 | 900 | 910 | 920 | 950 | 1,000 | 4,000 | 18,500 |
| 1887S | 817,000 | 900 | 910 | 920 | 925 | 950 | 1,000 | |
| 1888 (75) | 132,921 | 900 | 910 | 920 | 925 | 950 | 4,500 | 18,500 |
| 1888O | 21,335 | 900 | 910 | 925 | 950 | 1,000 | 5,000 | |
| 1888S | 648,700 | 900 | 910 | 920 | 925 | 950 | 1,050 | |
| 1889 (45) | 4,440 | 1,000 | 1,200 | 1,250 | 1,500 | 3,000 | 8,500 | 18,500 |
| 1889S | 425,400 | 900 | 910 | 920 | 925 | 950 | 1,050 | |
| 1890 (63) | 57,980 | 900 | 910 | 920 | 950 | 1,050 | 2,500 | 15,000 |
| 1890CC | 17,500 | 1,000 | 1,250 | 1,750 | 2,500 | 4,000 | 15,000 | |
| 1891 (48) | 91,820 | 900 | 910 | 920 | 925 | 950 | 1,250 | 15,000 |

| | Mintage | VF-20 | EF-40 | AU-50 | AU-55 | MS-60 | MS-63 | PF-63 |
|---|---|---|---|---|---|---|---|---|
| 1891CC | 103,732 | $1,000 | $1,100 | $1,350 | $1,750 | $2,250 | $6,500 | |
| 1892 | (72) 797,480 | 900 | 910 | 920 | 925 | 950 | 1,050 | $12,500 |
| 1892CC | 40,000 | 1,000 | 1,100 | 1,650 | 2,250 | 4,500 | 25,000 | |
| 1892O | 28,688 | 900 | 910 | 920 | 950 | 1,100 | 6,500 | |
| 1892S | 115,500 | 900 | 910 | 920 | 925 | 950 | 1,500 | |
| 1893 | (55) 1,840,840 | 900 | 910 | 920 | 925 | 950 | 1,050 | 12,500 |
| 1893CC | 14,000 | 1,250 | 2,000 | 3,500 | 5,500 | 25,000 | | |
| 1893O | 17,000 | 900 | 910 | 925 | 950 | 1,000 | 4,500 | |
| 1893S | 141,350 | 900 | 910 | 920 | 925 | 950 | 1,200 | |
| 1894 | (43) 2,470,735 | 900 | 910 | 920 | 925 | 950 | 1,050 | 12,500 |
| 1894O | 107,500 | 900 | 910 | 925 | 935 | 1,000 | 4,000 | |
| 1894S | 25,000 | 900 | 925 | 950 | 1,100 | 3,500 | | |
| 1895 | (56) 567,770 | 900 | 910 | 920 | 925 | 950 | 1,050 | 12,500 |
| 1895O | 98,000 | 900 | 910 | 925 | 935 | 1,000 | 4,250 | |
| 1895S | 49,000 | 900 | 910 | 950 | 1,000 | 1,500 | 6,000 | |
| 1896 | (78) 76,270 | 900 | 910 | 920 | 925 | 950 | 1,050 | 12,500 |
| 1896S | 123,750 | 900 | 910 | 950 | 1,000 | 1,500 | 6,000 | |
| 1897 | (69) 1,000,090 | 900 | 910 | 920 | 925 | 950 | 1,050 | 12,500 |
| 1897O | 42,500 | 900 | 910 | 925 | 950 | 1,000 | 4,500 | |
| 1897S | 234,750 | 900 | 910 | 920 | 925 | 1,000 | 3,500 | |
| 1898 | (67) 812,130 | 900 | 910 | 920 | 925 | 950 | 1,050 | 12,500 |
| 1898S | 473,600 | 900 | 910 | 920 | 925 | 950 | 1,250 | |
| 1899 | (86) 1,262,219 | 900 | 910 | 920 | 925 | 950 | 1,050 | 12,500 |
| 1899O | 37,047 | 900 | 910 | 925 | 950 | 1,000 | 6,500 | |
| 1899S | 841,000 | 900 | 910 | 920 | 925 | 950 | 1,200 | |
| 1900 | (120) 293,840 | 900 | 910 | 920 | 925 | 950 | 1,050 | 12,500 |
| 1900S | 81,000 | 900 | 910 | 920 | 925 | 950 | 3,500 | |
| 1901 | (85) 1,718,740 | 900 | 910 | 920 | 925 | 950 | 1,050 | 12,500 |
| 1901O | 72,041 | 900 | 910 | 920 | 925 | 950 | 2,250 | |
| 1901S | 2,812,750 | 900 | 910 | 920 | 925 | 950 | 1,050 | |
| 1902 | (113) 82,400 | 900 | 910 | 920 | 925 | 950 | 1,050 | 12,500 |
| 1902S | 469,500 | 900 | 910 | 920 | 925 | 950 | 1,050 | |
| 1903 | (96) 125,830 | 900 | 910 | 920 | 925 | 950 | 1,050 | 12,500 |
| 1903O | 112,771 | 900 | 910 | 920 | 925 | 950 | 1,500 | |
| 1903S | 538,000 | 900 | 910 | 920 | 925 | 950 | 1,050 | |
| 1904 | (108) 161,930 | 900 | 910 | 920 | 925 | 950 | 1,050 | 12,500 |
| 1904O | 108,950 | 900 | 910 | 920 | 925 | 950 | 1,500 | |
| 1905 | (86) 200,992 | 900 | 910 | 920 | 925 | 950 | 1,050 | 12,500 |
| 1905S | 369,250 | 900 | 910 | 920 | 925 | 950 | 2,500 | |
| 1906 | (77) 165,420 | 900 | 910 | 920 | 925 | 950 | 1,050 | 12,500 |
| 1906D | 981,000 | 900 | 910 | 920 | 925 | 950 | 1,050 | |
| 1906O | 86,895 | 900 | 910 | 920 | 925 | 950 | 3,500 | |
| 1906S | 457,000 | 900 | 910 | 920 | 925 | 950 | 1,250 | |
| 1907 | (74) 1,203,899 | 900 | 910 | 920 | 925 | 950 | 1,050 | 12,500 |
| 1907D | 1,030,000 | 900 | 910 | 920 | 925 | 950 | 1,200 | |
| 1907S | 210,500 | 900 | 910 | 920 | 925 | 950 | 2,500 | |

# INDIAN HEAD (1907–1933)

**VF-20 Very Fine:** Bonnet feathers worn near band. Wear visible on high points of hair.

**EF-40 Extremely Fine:** Slight wear on cheekbone and headdress feathers. Slight wear visible on eagle's eye and left wing.

**AU-50 About Uncirculated:** Trace of wear on hair above eye and on forehead.

**AU-55 Choice About Uncirculated:** Evidence of friction on design high points. Much of original mint luster present.

**MS-60 Uncirculated:** No trace of wear. Light blemishes.

**MS-63 Choice Uncirculated:** Some distracting contact marks or blemishes in prime focal areas. Impaired luster possible.

**Matte PF-63 Choice Proof:** Matte surfaces with few blemishes in secondary focal places. No major flaws.

*Chart continued on next page.*

**No Motto**
*Mintmark is above
left tip of branch on
1908-D No Motto.*

**With Motto
IN GOD WE TRUST**
*Mintmark is at left
of arrow points.*

*Gem Uncirculated (MS-65) coins are rare, and dealers usually pay substantial premiums for them.*

| | Mintage | VF-20 | EF-40 | AU-50 | AU-55 | MS-60 | MS-63 |
|---|---|---|---|---|---|---|---|
| 1907, Wire Rim, Periods | 500 | $14,000 | $17,500 | $20,000 | $25,000 | $30,000 | $40,000 |
| 1907, Rounded Rim, Periods Before and After •E•PLURIBUS•UNUM• | 50 | 35,000 | 40,000 | 47,500 | 50,000 | 85,000 | 125,000 |
| 1907, No Periods | 239,406 | 1,050 | 1,100 | 1,125 | 1,150 | 1,250 | 1,500 |
| 1908, No Motto | 33,500 | 1,050 | 1,100 | 1,125 | 1,150 | 1,300 | 3,500 |
| 1908D, No Motto | 210,000 | 1,050 | 1,100 | 1,125 | 1,150 | 1,300 | 5,000 |

## Variety 2 – Motto on Reverse (1908–1933)

| | Mintage | VF-20 | EF-40 | AU-50 | AU-55 | MS-60 | MS-63 | MATTE PF-63 |
|---|---|---|---|---|---|---|---|---|
| 1908 . . . . . . . . (116) | 341,370 | $1,050 | $1,100 | $1,125 | $1,150 | $1,200 | $1,500 | $17,500 |
| 1908D | 836,500 | 1,050 | 1,100 | 1,125 | 1,150 | 1,200 | 3,500 | |
| 1908S | 59,850 | 1,050 | 1,200 | 1,250 | 1,400 | 3,500 | 9,000 | |
| 1909 . . . . . . . . (74) | 184,789 | 1,050 | 1,100 | 1,125 | 1,150 | 1,200 | 1,500 | 18,500 |
| 1909D | 121,540 | 1,050 | 1,100 | 1,125 | 1,150 | 1,200 | 3,000 | |
| 1909S | 292,350 | 1,050 | 1,100 | 1,125 | 1,150 | 1,250 | 3,500 | |
| 1910 . . . . . . . . (204) | 318,500 | 1,050 | 1,100 | 1,125 | 1,150 | 1,200 | 1,400 | 17,500 |
| 1910D | 2,356,640 | 1,050 | 1,100 | 1,125 | 1,150 | 1,200 | 1,300 | |
| 1910S | 811,000 | 1,050 | 1,100 | 1,125 | 1,150 | 1,300 | 4,500 | |
| 1911 . . . . . . . . (95) | 505,500 | 1,050 | 1,100 | 1,125 | 1,150 | 1,200 | 1,300 | 17,500 |
| 1911D | 30,100 | 1,200 | 1,650 | 1,850 | 2,700 | 6,000 | 14,000 | |
| 1911S | 51,000 | 1,050 | 1,100 | 1,125 | 1,150 | 2,750 | 10,000 | |
| 1912 . . . . . . . . (83) | 405,000 | 1,050 | 1,100 | 1,125 | 1,150 | 1,200 | 1,300 | 17,500 |
| 1912S | 300,000 | 1,050 | 1,100 | 1,125 | 1,150 | 1,250 | 5,000 | |
| 1913 . . . . . . . . (71) | 442,000 | 1,050 | 1,100 | 1,125 | 1,150 | 1,200 | 1,400 | 17,500 |
| 1913S | 66,000 | 1,050 | 1,100 | 1,125 | 1,250 | 3,500 | 17,500 | |
| 1914 . . . . . . . . (50) | 151,000 | 1,050 | 1,100 | 1,125 | 1,150 | 1,200 | 1,500 | 17,500 |
| 1914D | 343,500 | 1,050 | 1,100 | 1,125 | 1,150 | 1,200 | 1,250 | |
| 1914S | 208,000 | 1,050 | 1,100 | 1,125 | 1,150 | 1,400 | 4,000 | |
| 1915 . . . . . . . . (75) | 351,000 | 1,050 | 1,100 | 1,125 | 1,150 | 1,200 | 1,500 | 18,500 |
| 1915S | 59,000 | 1,050 | 1,150 | 1,350 | 1,500 | 5,000 | 14,000 | |
| 1916S | 138,500 | 1,050 | 1,100 | 1,125 | 1,150 | 1,200 | 4,500 | |
| 1920S | 126,500 | 20,000 | 26,000 | 32,500 | 35,000 | 50,000 | 85,000 | |
| 1926 | 1,014,000 | 1,050 | 1,100 | 1,125 | 1,150 | 1,200 | 1,250 | |
| 1930S | 96,000 | 16,000 | 20,000 | 25,000 | 27,500 | 35,000 | 40,000 | |
| 1932 | 4,463,000 | 1,050 | 1,100 | 1,125 | 1,150 | 1,200 | 1,250 | |
| 1933 | 312,500 | | | 150,000 | 165,000 | 175,000 | 225,000 | |

This largest denomination of all regular United States issues was authorized to be coined by the Act of March 3, 1849. The coin's weight was set at 516 grains, and its fineness at .900. A single twenty-dollar gold specimen of 1849 resides in the Smithsonian.

## LIBERTY HEAD (1850–1907)

**VF-20 Very Fine:** LIBERTY on crown bold; prongs on crown defined; lower half worn flat. Hair worn about ear.

**EF-40 Extremely Fine:** Trace of wear on rounded prongs of crown and down hair curls. Minor bagmarks.

**AU-50 About Uncirculated:** Trace of wear on hair over eye and on coronet.

**AU-55 Choice About Uncirculated:** Evidence of friction on design high points. Some of original mint luster present.

**MS-60 Uncirculated:** No trace of wear. Light blemishes.

**MS-63 Choice Uncirculated:** Some distracting marks or blemishes in focal areas. Impaired luster possible.

**PF-63 Choice Proof:** Reflective surfaces with only a few blemishes in secondary focal areas. No major flaws.

### Without Motto on Reverse (1850–1866)

Mintmark is below eagle.

| | Mintage | VF-20 | EF-40 | AU-50 | AU-55 | MS-60 | MS-63 | PF-63 |
|---|---|---|---|---|---|---|---|---|
| 1850 | 1,170,261 | $2,000 | $2,750 | $3,500 | $5,000 | $9,500 | $60,000 | |
| 1850O | 141,000 | 3,500 | 5,500 | 10,000 | 20,000 | 47,500 | | |
| 1851 | 2,087,155 | 1,850 | 1,875 | 1,900 | 2,000 | 4,000 | 17,000 | |
| 1851O | 315,000 | 2,250 | 3,250 | 4,500 | 6,750 | 25,000 | 100,000 | |
| 1852 | 2,053,026 | 1,850 | 1,875 | 1,900 | 2,100 | 3,500 | 18,500 | |
| 1852O | 190,000 | 2,250 | 3,000 | 4,500 | 6,500 | 27,500 | 100,000 | |
| 1853 | 1,261,326 | 1,850 | 1,875 | 1,900 | 2,400 | 4,250 | 30,000 | |
| 1853O | 71,000 | 2,500 | 5,000 | 7,000 | 12,000 | 30,000 | | |
| 1854 | 757,899 | 1,850 | 1,875 | 1,900 | 2,000 | 4,750 | 27,500 | |
| 1854O | 3,250 | 110,000 | 175,000 | 275,000 | 325,000 | | | |
| 1854S | 141,468 | 3,000 | 6,000 | 10,000 | 15,000 | 20,000 | 45,000 | |
| 1855 | 364,666 | 1,850 | 1,875 | 2,000 | 2,500 | 7,500 | 40,000 | |
| 1855O | 8,000 | 12,500 | 32,500 | 38,000 | 50,000 | 95,000 | | |
| 1855S | 879,675 | 1,850 | 1,875 | 1,900 | 2,400 | 5,000 | 20,000 | |
| 1856 | 329,878 | 1,850 | 1,875 | 2,000 | 2,600 | 5,000 | 27,500 | |
| 1856O | 2,250 | 145,000 | 200,000 | 300,000 | 350,000 | | | |
| 1856S | 1,189,750 | 1,850 | 1,875 | 1,900 | 2,000 | 3,250 | 15,000 | |
| 1857 | 439,375 | 1,850 | 1,875 | 1,900 | 2,100 | 6,000 | 35,000 | |
| 1857O | 30,000 | 4,500 | 7,000 | 11,000 | 15,000 | 70,000 | 200,000 | |
| 1857S **(a)** | 970,500 | 1,850 | 1,875 | 1,900 | 2,100 | 3,000 | 6,000 | |
| 1858 | 211,714 | 1,850 | 2,000 | 2,250 | 3,750 | 5,500 | 30,000 | |
| 1858O | 35,250 | 4,000 | 7,500 | 15,000 | 25,000 | 47,500 | 150,000 | |
| 1858S | 846,710 | 1,850 | 1,875 | 1,900 | 2,100 | 6,000 | 35,000 | |
| 1859 (80) | 43,597 | 2,750 | 5,500 | 7,500 | 13,500 | 25,000 | | $100,000 |
| 1859O | 9,100 | 12,000 | 22,500 | 40,000 | 55,000 | 135,000 | | |
| 1859S | 636,445 | 1,850 | 1,875 | 1,900 | 4,000 | 8,000 | 45,000 | |
| 1860 (59) | 577,611 | 1,850 | 1,875 | 1,900 | 2,100 | 3,500 | 15,000 | 75,000 |
| 1860O | 6,600 | 12,000 | 30,000 | 45,000 | 55,000 | 125,000 | | |
| 1860S | 544,950 | 1,850 | 1,875 | 1,900 | 2,750 | 5,500 | 30,000 | |

**a.** Different size mintmarks exists; the Large S variety is rarest.

*Chart continued on next page.*

| | Mintage | VF-20 | EF-40 | AU-50 | AU-55 | MS-60 | MS-63 | PF-63 |
|---|---|---|---|---|---|---|---|---|
| 1861 . . . . . . . . (66) . . . . | 2,976,387 | $1,850 | $1,875 | $1,900 | $2,200 | $3,000 | $14,500 | $75,000 |
| 1861O . . . . . . . . . . . . . . . . | 17,741 | 15,000 | 30,000 | 45,000 | 55,000 | 225,000 | | |
| 1861S . . . . . . . . . . . . . . . | 768,000 | 1,850 | 1,875 | 2,000 | 3,000 | 12,500 | 45,000 | |
| 1862 . . . . . . . . (35) . . . . . | 92,098 | 4,500 | 8,500 | 14,000 | 17,500 | 32,500 | 75,000 | 50,000 |
| 1862S . . . . . . . . . . . . . . . | 854,173 | 1,850 | 1,875 | 2,000 | 3,000 | 7,000 | 35,000 | |
| 1863 . . . . . . . . (30) . . . . . | 142,760 | 2,500 | 5,500 | 10,000 | 13,500 | 25,000 | 60,000 | 50,000 |
| 1863S . . . . . . . . . . . . . . . | 966,570 | 1,850 | 1,875 | 1,900 | 2,750 | 5,500 | 30,000 | |
| 1864 . . . . . . . . (50) . . . . . | 204,235 | 2,500 | 4,000 | 6,000 | 8,750 | 20,000 | 75,000 | 47,500 |
| 1864S . . . . . . . . . . . . . . . | 793,660 | 1,850 | 1,875 | 1,900 | 2,500 | 5,500 | 35,000 | |
| 1865 . . . . . . . . (25) . . . . . | 351,175 | 1,850 | 2,000 | 2,500 | 3,200 | 6,000 | 15,000 | 47,500 |
| 1865S . . . . . . . . . . . . . | 1,042,500 | 1,850 | 1,875 | 1,900 | 2,500 | 5,000 | 12,500 | |
| 1866S . . . . . . . . . . . . . . . | 120,000 | 8,500 | 15,000 | 25,000 | 45,000 | 125,000 | | |

## Motto Above Eagle (1866–1907)
### *Value TWENTY D. (1866–1876)*

| | Mintage | VF-20 | EF-40 | AU-50 | AU-55 | MS-60 | MS-63 | PF-63 |
|---|---|---|---|---|---|---|---|---|
| 1866 . . . . . . . . (30) . . . . . | 698,745 | $1,850 | $1,900 | $3,000 | $4,000 | $7,000 | $45,000 | $45,000 |
| 1866S . . . . . . . . . . . . . . . | 842,250 | 1,850 | 1,860 | 2,400 | 5,000 | 10,000 | | |
| 1867 . . . . . . . . (50) . . . . . | 251,015 | 1,850 | 1,860 | 1,900 | 3,000 | 4,000 | 20,000 | 45,000 |
| 1867S . . . . . . . . . . . . . . . | 920,750 | 1,850 | 1,860 | 1,900 | 3,000 | 7,000 | | |
| 1868 . . . . . . . . (25) . . . . . | 98,575 | 1,850 | 1,860 | 3,250 | 9,000 | 15,000 | 50,000 | 45,000 |
| 1868S . . . . . . . . . . . . . . . | 837,500 | 1,850 | 1,860 | 1,900 | 2,400 | 4,500 | 35,000 | |
| 1869 . . . . . . . . (25) . . . . . | 175,130 | 1,850 | 1,860 | 2,400 | 4,000 | 8,500 | 30,000 | 45,000 |
| 1869S . . . . . . . . . . . . . . . | 686,750 | 1,850 | 1,860 | 1,900 | 2,000 | 3,500 | 30,000 | |
| 1870 . . . . . . . . (35) . . . . . | 155,150 | 1,850 | 1,860 | 2,250 | 4,500 | 10,000 | 40,000 | 45,000 |
| 1870CC . . . . . . . . . . . . . . . | 3,789 | 175,000 | 325,000 | 450,000 | 750,000 | | | |
| 1870S . . . . . . . . . . . . . . . | 982,000 | 1,850 | 1,860 | 1,900 | 1,950 | 3,500 | 35,000 | |
| 1871 . . . . . . . . (30) . . . . . | 80,120 | 1,850 | 1,860 | 2,500 | 5,000 | 7,000 | 35,000 | 45,000 |
| 1871CC . . . . . . . . . . . . . . . | 17,387 | 25,000 | 35,000 | 55,000 | 75,000 | 100,000 | | |
| 1871S . . . . . . . . . . . . . . . | 928,000 | 1,850 | 1,860 | 1,900 | 1,925 | 3,500 | 16,000 | |
| 1872 . . . . . . . . (30) . . . . . | 251,850 | 1,850 | 1,860 | 1,900 | 1,925 | 3,000 | 20,000 | 45,000 |
| 1872CC . . . . . . . . . . . . . . . | 26,900 | 4,000 | 8,000 | 13,500 | 20,000 | 65,000 | | |
| 1872S . . . . . . . . . . . . . . . | 780,000 | 1,850 | 1,860 | 1,900 | 1,925 | 2,750 | 20,000 | |
| 1873 . . . . . . . . (25) . . . . | 1,709,800 | 1,850 | 1,860 | 1,875 | 1,900 | 1,925 | 3,500 | 45,000 |
| 1873CC . . . . . . . . . . . . . . . | 22,410 | 3,250 | 8,500 | 17,500 | 20,000 | 45,000 | | |
| 1873S . . . . . . . . . . . . . | 1,040,600 | 1,850 | 1,860 | 1,875 | 1,900 | 2,200 | 15,000 | |
| 1874 . . . . . . . . (20) . . . . . | 366,780 | 1,850 | 1,860 | 1,875 | 1,900 | 2,400 | 15,000 | 45,000 |
| 1874CC . . . . . . . . . . . . . . . | 115,085 | 2,250 | 3,000 | 3,500 | 7,500 | 17,500 | 55,000 | |
| 1874S . . . . . . . . . . . . . | 1,214,000 | 1,850 | 1,860 | 1,875 | 1,900 | 2,400 | 20,000 | |
| 1875 . . . . . . . . (20) . . . . . | 295,720 | 1,850 | 1,860 | 1,875 | 1,900 | 1,925 | 6,000 | 67,500 |
| 1875CC . . . . . . . . . . . . . . . | 111,151 | 2,250 | 3,000 | 3,250 | 4,250 | 9,000 | 30,000 | |
| 1875S . . . . . . . . . . . . . | 1,230,000 | 1,850 | 1,860 | 1,875 | 1,900 | 1,925 | 6,000 | |
| 1876 . . . . . . . . (45) . . . . . | 583,860 | 1,850 | 1,860 | 1,875 | 1,900 | 2,500 | 5,500 | 42,500 |
| 1876CC . . . . . . . . . . . . . . . | 138,441 | 2,500 | 3,250 | 3,750 | 4,000 | 8,500 | 35,000 | |
| 1876S . . . . . . . . . . . . . | 1,597,000 | 1,850 | 1,860 | 1,875 | 1,900 | 1,925 | 4,000 | |

## Value TWENTY DOLLARS (1877–1907)

| | Mintage | VF-20 | EF-40 | AU-50 | AU-55 | MS-60 | MS-63 | PF-63 |
|---|---|---|---|---|---|---|---|---|
| 1877 . . . . . . . . . . (20) . .397,650 | | $1,850 | $1,860 | $1,875 | $1,900 | $1,925 | $10,000 | $35,000 |
| 1877CC . . . . . . . . . . . . . .42,565 | | 2,500 | 3,500 | 7,500 | 10,000 | 25,000 | | |
| 1877S . . . . . . . . . . . . . 1,735,000 | | 1,850 | 1,860 | 1,875 | 1,900 | 1,925 | 10,000 | |
| 1878 . . . . . . . . . . (20) . .543,625 | | 1,850 | 1,860 | 1,875 | 1,900 | 1,925 | 7,500 | 35,000 |
| 1878CC . . . . . . . . . . . . . .13,180 | | 5,500 | 8,000 | 15,000 | 25,000 | 40,000 | | |
| 1878S . . . . . . . . . . . . . 1,739,000 | | 1,850 | 1,860 | 1,875 | 1,900 | 1,925 | 10,000 | |
| 1879 . . . . . . . . . . (30) . .207,600 | | 1,850 | 1,860 | 1,875 | 1,900 | 1,925 | 12,500 | 35,000 |
| 1879CC . . . . . . . . . . . . . .10,708 | | 6,500 | 9,500 | 15,000 | 25,000 | 45,000 | | |
| 18790 . . . . . . . . . . . . . . . .2,325 | | 25,000 | 45,000 | 55,000 | 70,000 | 125,000 | 225,000 | |
| 1879S . . . . . . . . . . . . . 1,223,800 | | 1,850 | 1,860 | 1,875 | 1,900 | 1,925 | 25,000 | |
| 1880 . . . . . . . . . . (36) . .51,420 | | 1,850 | 1,860 | 1,875 | 1,900 | 6,500 | 27,500 | 35,000 |
| 1880S . . . . . . . . . . . . . . .836,000 | | 1,850 | 1,860 | 1,875 | 1,900 | 2,250 | 13,500 | |
| 1881 . . . . . . . . . . (61) . . . .2,199 | | 15,000 | 27,500 | 35,000 | 55,000 | 95,000 | | 35,000 |
| 1881S . . . . . . . . . . . . . . .727,000 | | 1,850 | 1,860 | 1,875 | 1,900 | 1,925 | 15,000 | |
| 1882 . . . . . . . . . . (59) . . . . . 571 | | 25,000 | 47,500 | 85,000 | 95,000 | 115,000 | 175,000 | 35,000 |
| 1882CC . . . . . . . . . . . . . .39,140 | | 2,450 | 3,500 | 5,000 | 5,500 | 8,500 | 100,000 | |
| 1882S . . . . . . . . . . . . . 1,125,000 | | 1,850 | 1,860 | 1,875 | 1,900 | 1,925 | 8,000 | |
| 1883, Proof only . . . (92) . . . . . . . . | | | | | | | | 60,000 |
| 1883CC . . . . . . . . . . . . . .59,962 | | 2,650 | 3,500 | 4,500 | 6,000 | 8,750 | 45,000 | |
| 1883S . . . . . . . . . . . . . 1,189,000 | | 1,850 | 1,860 | 1,875 | 1,900 | 1,925 | 4,500 | |
| 1884, Proof only . . . (71) . . . . . . . . | | | | | | | | 55,000 |
| 1884CC . . . . . . . . . . . . . .81,139 | | 2,500 | 3,000 | 3,500 | 4,500 | 8,000 | 35,000 | |
| 1884S . . . . . . . . . . . . . . .916,000 | | 1,850 | 1,860 | 1,875 | 1,900 | 1,925 | 3,500 | |
| 1885 . . . . . . . . . . (77) . . . . . 751 | | 17,500 | 25,000 | 42,500 | 50,000 | 65,000 | 95,000 | 45,000 |
| 1885CC . . . . . . . . . . . . . .9,450 | | 5,500 | 10,000 | 15,000 | 25,000 | 32,500 | 100,000 | |
| 1885S . . . . . . . . . . . . . . .683,500 | | 1,850 | 1,860 | 1,875 | 1,900 | 1,925 | 3,500 | |
| 1886 . . . . . . . . . . (106) . . . .1,000 | | 35,000 | 65,000 | 75,000 | 100,000 | 125,000 | 135,000 | 35,000 |
| 1887, Proof only . . (121) . . . . . . . . | | | | | | | | 50,000 |
| 1887S . . . . . . . . . . . . . . .283,000 | | 1,850 | 1,860 | 1,875 | 1,900 | 1,925 | 6,000 | |
| 1888 . . . . . . . . . . (105) . .226,161 | | 1,850 | 1,860 | 1,875 | 1,900 | 1,925 | 8,500 | 32,500 |
| 1888S . . . . . . . . . . . . . . .859,600 | | 1,850 | 1,860 | 1,875 | 1,900 | 1,925 | 3,500 | |
| 1889 . . . . . . . . . . (41) . . .44,070 | | 1,850 | 1,860 | 1,875 | 1,900 | 1,925 | 11,500 | 32,500 |
| 1889CC . . . . . . . . . . . . . .30,945 | | 2,650 | 4,000 | 5,500 | 6,500 | 10,000 | 60,000 | |
| 1889S . . . . . . . . . . . . . . .774,700 | | 1,850 | 1,860 | 1,875 | 1,900 | 1,925 | 3,000 | |
| 1890 . . . . . . . . . . (55) . .75,940 | | 1,850 | 1,860 | 1,875 | 1,900 | 1,925 | 6,000 | 32,500 |
| 1890CC . . . . . . . . . . . . . .91,209 | | 2,250 | 2,750 | 3,000 | 4,500 | 7,250 | 35,000 | |
| 1890S . . . . . . . . . . . . . . .802,750 | | 1,850 | 1,860 | 1,875 | 1,900 | 1,925 | 3,500 | |
| 1891 . . . . . . . . . . (52) . . . .1,390 | | 12,500 | 18,500 | 35,000 | 45,000 | 72,500 | 125,000 | 32,500 |
| 1891CC . . . . . . . . . . . . . .5,000 | | 9,500 | 15,000 | 20,000 | 30,000 | 40,000 | 80,000 | |
| 1891S . . . . . . . . . . . . . 1,288,125 | | 1,850 | 1,860 | 1,875 | 1,900 | 1,925 | 3,250 | |
| 1892 . . . . . . . . . . (93) . . . .4,430 | | 3,500 | 6,500 | 8,000 | 12,000 | 20,000 | 30,000 | 32,500 |

*Chart continued on next page.*

| | Mintage | VF-20 | EF-40 | AU-50 | AU-55 | MS-60 | MS-63 | PF-63 |
|---|---|---|---|---|---|---|---|---|
| 1892CC | 27,265 | $2,350 | $3,000 | $4,000 | $5,500 | $10,500 | $47,500 | |
| 1892S | 930,150 | 1,850 | 1,860 | 1,875 | 1,900 | 1,925 | 3,000 | |
| 1893 (59) | 344,280 | 1,850 | 1,860 | 1,875 | 1,900 | 1,925 | 3,000 | $32,500 |
| 1893CC | 18,402 | 3,000 | 4,500 | 5,500 | 6,500 | 9,500 | 45,000 | |
| 1893S | 996,175 | 1,850 | 1,860 | 1,875 | 1,900 | 1,925 | 2,500 | |
| 1894 (50) | 1,368,940 | 1,850 | 1,860 | 1,875 | 1,900 | 1,925 | 3,000 | 32,500 |
| 1894S | 1,048,550 | 1,850 | 1,860 | 1,875 | 1,900 | 1,925 | 3,000 | |
| 1895 (51) | 1,114,605 | 1,850 | 1,860 | 1,875 | 1,900 | 1,925 | 2,100 | 32,500 |
| 1895S | 1,143,500 | 1,850 | 1,860 | 1,875 | 1,900 | 1,925 | 3,000 | |
| 1896 (128) | 792,535 | 1,850 | 1,860 | 1,875 | 1,900 | 1,925 | 2,750 | 32,500 |
| 1896S | 1,403,925 | 1,850 | 1,860 | 1,875 | 1,900 | 1,925 | 3,000 | |
| 1897 (86) | 1,383,175 | 1,850 | 1,860 | 1,875 | 1,900 | 1,925 | 2,100 | 32,500 |
| 1897S | 1,470,250 | 1,850 | 1,860 | 1,875 | 1,900 | 1,925 | 2,100 | |
| 1898 (75) | 170,395 | 1,850 | 1,860 | 1,875 | 1,900 | 1,925 | 3,000 | 32,500 |
| 1898S | 2,575,175 | 1,850 | 1,860 | 1,875 | 1,900 | 1,925 | 2,100 | |
| 1899 (84) | 1,669,300 | 1,850 | 1,860 | 1,875 | 1,900 | 1,925 | 2,100 | 32,500 |
| 1899S | 2,010,300 | 1,850 | 1,860 | 1,875 | 1,900 | 1,925 | 3,000 | |
| 1900 (124) | 1,874,460 | 1,850 | 1,860 | 1,875 | 1,900 | 1,925 | 2,100 | 32,500 |
| 1900S | 2,459,500 | 1,850 | 1,860 | 1,875 | 1,900 | 1,925 | 2,400 | |
| 1901 (96) | 111,430 | 1,850 | 1,860 | 1,875 | 1,900 | 1,925 | 2,100 | 32,500 |
| 1901S | 1,596,000 | 1,850 | 1,860 | 1,875 | 1,900 | 1,925 | 2,500 | |
| 1902 (114) | 31,140 | 1,850 | 1,860 | 1,875 | 1,900 | 1,925 | 7,500 | 32,500 |
| 1902S | 1,753,625 | 1,850 | 1,860 | 1,875 | 1,900 | 1,925 | 2,750 | |
| 1903 (158) | 287,270 | 1,850 | 1,860 | 1,875 | 1,900 | 1,925 | 2,100 | 32,500 |
| 1903S | 954,000 | 1,850 | 1,860 | 1,875 | 1,900 | 1,925 | 2,750 | |
| 1904 (98) | 6,256,699 | 1,850 | 1,860 | 1,875 | 1,900 | 1,925 | 2,100 | 32,500 |
| 1904S | 5,134,175 | 1,850 | 1,860 | 1,875 | 1,900 | 1,925 | 2,100 | |
| 1905 (92) | 58,919 | 1,850 | 1,860 | 1,875 | 1,900 | 1,925 | 6,500 | 32,500 |
| 1905S | 1,813,000 | 1,850 | 1,860 | 1,875 | 1,900 | 1,925 | 2,300 | |
| 1906 (94) | 69,596 | 1,850 | 1,860 | 1,875 | 1,900 | 1,925 | 6,000 | 32,500 |
| 1906D | 620,250 | 1,850 | 1,860 | 1,875 | 1,900 | 1,925 | 2,750 | |
| 1906S | 2,065,750 | 1,850 | 1,860 | 1,875 | 1,900 | 1,925 | 3,000 | |
| 1907 (78) | 1,451,786 | 1,850 | 1,860 | 1,875 | 1,900 | 1,925 | 2,100 | 32,500 |
| 1907D | 842,250 | 1,850 | 1,860 | 1,875 | 1,900 | 1,925 | 2,750 | |
| 1907S | 2,165,800 | 1,850 | 1,860 | 1,875 | 1,900 | 1,925 | 2,100 | |

## SAINT-GAUDENS (1907–1933)

The twenty-dollar gold piece designed by Augustus Saint-Gaudens is considered by many to be the most beautiful United States coin. The first coins issued were slightly more than 12,000 high-relief pieces struck for general circulation. The relief is much higher than that of later issues and the date 1907 is in Roman numerals. A few of the Proof coins were made using the lettered-edge collar from the Ultra High Relief version. These can be distinguished by a pronounced bottom left serif on the N in UNUM, and other minor differences. Flat-relief double eagles were issued later in 1907 with Arabic numerals, and continued through 1933.

The field of the rare, Ultra High Relief experimental pieces is extremely concave and connects directly with the edge without any border, giving it a sharp knifelike appearance. Liberty's skirt shows two folds on the side of her right leg; the Capitol building in the background at left is very small; the sun, on the reverse side, has 14 rays, as opposed to the regular high-relief coins, which have only 13 rays extending from the sun. High-relief Proofs are trial or experimental pieces.

**VF-20 Very Fine:** Minor wear on Liberty's legs and toes. Eagle's left wing and breast feathers worn.

**EF-40 Extremely Fine:** Drapery lines on chest visible. Wear on left breast, knee, and below. Eagle's feathers on breast and right wing bold.

**AU-50 About Uncirculated:** Trace of wear on nose, breast, and knee. Wear visible on eagle's wings.

**AU-55 Choice About Uncirculated:** Evidence of friction on design high points. Most of mint luster remains.

**MS-60 Uncirculated:** No trace of wear. Light marks or blemishes.

**MS-63 Select Uncirculated:** Some distracting contact marks or blemishes in prime focal areas. Impaired luster possible.

**Matte PF-63 Choice Proof:** Matte surfaces with only a few blemishes in secondary focal places. No major flaws.

## Ultra High Relief Pattern, MCMVII (1907)

| | PF-67 |
|---|---|
| 1907, Ultra High Relief, Plain Edge *(unique)*. | — |
| 1907, Ultra High Relief, Lettered Edge. | — |

# No Motto IN GOD WE TRUST (1907–1908) and With Motto IN GOD WE TRUST (1908–1933)

High Relief, MCMVII (1907)

| | Mintage | VF-20 | EF-40 | AU-50 | AU-55 | MS-60 | MS-63 | PF |
|---|---|---|---|---|---|---|---|---|
| 1907, High Relief, Roman Numerals (MCMVII), Wire Rim | 12,367 | $6,500 | $7,500 | $8,500 | $9,000 | $10,000 | $15,000 | — |

Arabic Numerals (1907–1933)   No Motto (1907–1908)   With Motto IN GOD WE TRUST (1908–1933)

Mintmark is on obverse, above date.

1909, 9 Over 8

*See next page for chart.*                                                                 **189**

| | Mintage | VF-20 | EF-40 | AU-50 | AU-55 | MS-60 | MS-63 | MATTE PF-63 |
|---|---|---|---|---|---|---|---|---|
| 1907 | 361,667 | $1,850 | $1,860 | $1,875 | $1,900 | $1,915 | $2,250 | |
| 1908 | 4,271,551 | 1,850 | 1,860 | 1,875 | 1,900 | 1,915 | 1,950 | |
| 1908D | 663,750 | 1,850 | 1,860 | 1,875 | 1,900 | 1,915 | 1,950 | |
| 1908, With Motto.. (101) | 156,258 | 1,850 | 1,860 | 1,875 | 1,900 | 1,950 | 2,100 | $30,000 |
| 1908D, With Motto | 349,500 | 1,850 | 1,860 | 1,875 | 1,900 | 1,915 | 1,950 | |
| 1908S, With Motto | 22,000 | 2,000 | 2,750 | 4,000 | 4,500 | 9,500 | 17,500 | |
| 1909, 9 Over 8 | * | 1,850 | 1,860 | 1,875 | 1,900 | 1,950 | 2,500 | |
| 1909 (67) | 161,282 | 1,850 | 1,860 | 1,875 | 1,900 | 1,915 | 2,000 | 30,000 |
| 1909D | 52,500 | 1,850 | 1,860 | 1,875 | 1,900 | 2,500 | 5,000 | |
| 1909S | 2,774,925 | 1,850 | 1,860 | 1,875 | 1,900 | 1,915 | 1,950 | |
| 1910 (167) | 482,000 | 1,850 | 1,860 | 1,875 | 1,900 | 1,915 | 1,950 | 30,000 |
| 1910D | 429,000 | 1,850 | 1,860 | 1,875 | 1,900 | 1,915 | 1,950 | |
| 1910S | 2,128,250 | 1,850 | 1,860 | 1,875 | 1,900 | 1,915 | 2,000 | |
| 1911 (100) | 197,250 | 1,850 | 1,860 | 1,875 | 1,900 | 1,915 | 2,250 | 30,000 |
| 1911D | 846,500 | 1,850 | 1,860 | 1,875 | 1,900 | 1,915 | 2,000 | |
| 1911S | 775,750 | 1,850 | 1,860 | 1,875 | 1,900 | 1,915 | 1,950 | |
| 1912 (74) | 149,750 | 1,850 | 1,860 | 1,875 | 1,900 | 1,915 | 2,000 | 30,000 |
| 1913 (58) | 168,780 | 1,850 | 1,860 | 1,875 | 1,900 | 1,915 | 1,950 | 30,000 |
| 1913D | 393,500 | 1,850 | 1,860 | 1,875 | 1,900 | 1,915 | 1,950 | |
| 1913S | 34,000 | 1,850 | 1,860 | 1,875 | 2,000 | 2,500 | 4,000 | |
| 1914 (70) | 95,250 | 1,850 | 1,860 | 1,875 | 1,900 | 1,915 | 2,250 | 30,000 |
| 1914D | 453,000 | 1,850 | 1,860 | 1,875 | 1,900 | 1,915 | 1,950 | |
| 1914S | 1,498,000 | 1,850 | 1,860 | 1,875 | 1,900 | 1,915 | 1,950 | |
| 1915 (50) | 152,000 | 1,850 | 1,860 | 1,875 | 1,900 | 1,915 | 2,250 | 32,500 |
| 1915S | 567,500 | 1,850 | 1,860 | 1,875 | 1,900 | 1,915 | 1,950 | |
| 1916S | 796,000 | 1,850 | 1,860 | 1,875 | 1,900 | 1,915 | 1,950 | |
| 1920 | 228,250 | 1,850 | 1,860 | 1,875 | 1,900 | 1,915 | 2,000 | |
| 1920S | 558,000 | 16,000 | 20,000 | 25,000 | 27,500 | 40,000 | 75,000 | |
| 1921 | 528,500 | 28,500 | 35,000 | 45,000 | 50,000 | 70,000 | 150,000 | |
| 1922 | 1,375,500 | 1,850 | 1,860 | 1,875 | 1,900 | 1,915 | 1,950 | |
| 1922S | 2,658,000 | 2,000 | 2,100 | 2,200 | 2,250 | 2,500 | 3,500 | |
| 1923 | 566,000 | 1,850 | 1,860 | 1,875 | 1,900 | 1,915 | 1,950 | |
| 1923D | 1,702,250 | 1,850 | 1,860 | 1,875 | 1,900 | 1,915 | 1,950 | |
| 1924 | 4,323,500 | 1,850 | 1,860 | 1,875 | 1,900 | 1,915 | 1,950 | |
| 1924D | 3,049,500 | 2,250 | 2,450 | 2,650 | 2,850 | 4,000 | 6,000 | |
| 1924S | 2,927,500 | 2,250 | 2,450 | 2,650 | 2,850 | 4,000 | 8,000 | |
| 1925 | 2,831,750 | 1,850 | 1,860 | 1,875 | 1,900 | 1,915 | 1,950 | |
| 1925D | 2,938,500 | 2,500 | 2,600 | 2,750 | 3,000 | 5,500 | 7,500 | |
| 1925S | 3,776,500 | 2,500 | 2,850 | 4,000 | 4,500 | 7,500 | 12,500 | |
| 1926 | 816,750 | 1,850 | 1,860 | 1,875 | 1,900 | 1,915 | 1,950 | |
| 1926D | 481,000 | 7,000 | 9,500 | 10,500 | 11,000 | 12,500 | 20,000 | |
| 1926S | 2,041,500 | 2,500 | 2,750 | 2,850 | 3,000 | 3,250 | 5,000 | |
| 1927 | 2,946,750 | 1,850 | 1,860 | 1,875 | 1,900 | 1,915 | 1,950 | |
| 1927D | 180,000 | | | | | 750,000 | 1,000,000 | |
| 1927S | 3,107,000 | 5,000 | 9,500 | 12,500 | 13,500 | 20,000 | 40,000 | |
| 1928 | 8,816,000 | 1,850 | 1,860 | 1,875 | 1,900 | 1,915 | 1,950 | |
| 1929 | 1,779,750 | 12,500 | 13,500 | 15,000 | 16,000 | 20,000 | 37,500 | |
| 1930S | 74,000 | 22,500 | 35,000 | 40,000 | 42,500 | 55,000 | 75,000 | |
| 1931 | 2,938,250 | 15,000 | 17,500 | 20,000 | 22,500 | 30,000 | 50,000 | |
| 1931D | 106,500 | 15,000 | 25,000 | 30,000 | 32,500 | 45,000 | 65,000 | |
| 1932 | 1,101,750 | 15,000 | 20,000 | 22,500 | 25,000 | 27,500 | 60,000 | |
| 1933 | 445,500 | | | *None placed in circulation.* | | | | |

* Included in number below.

Collecting United States commemorative coins is like gathering snapshots for an album of important events, places, and people in the nation's history. Because they represent so many different aspects of America—from wars and Olympic games to presidents and historical landmarks, every collector can assemble a set with its own special significance.

All U.S. commemorative coins are issued as legal tender, though in all cases the precious metal of the coins surpasses their face values. The weight and fineness for commemoratives follow those of standard-issue gold, silver, and clad coins.

## CLASSIC COMMEMORATIVE SILVER AND GOLD

(1892–1893) World's Columbian Exposition Half Dollar

| | Distribution | AU-50 | MS-60 | MS-63 | MS-65 |
|---|---|---|---|---|---|
| 1892, World's Columbian Exposition half dollar . . . . . . . . . . . 950,000 | | $12 | $20 | $45 | $250 |
| 1893, Same type. . . . . . . . . . . . . . . . . . . . . . . . . . . . . . . . 1,550,405 | | 12 | 20 | 45 | 250 |

(1893) World's Columbian Exposition, Isabella Quarter Dollar

| | Distribution | AU-50 | MS-60 | MS-63 | MS-65 |
|---|---|---|---|---|---|
| 1893, World's Columbian Exposition, Chicago, quarter dollar . . 24,214 | | $200 | $260 | $300 | $1,100 |

(1900) Lafayette Dollar

| | Distribution | AU-50 | MS-60 | MS-63 | MS-65 |
|---|---|---|---|---|---|
| 1900, Lafayette silver dollar . . . . . . . . . . . . . . . . . . . . . . . . 36,026 | | $275 | $550 | $1,100 | $4,500 |

### (1903) Louisiana Purchase Exposition

| | Distribution | AU-50 | MS-60 | MS-63 | MS-65 |
|---|---|---|---|---|---|
| 1903, Louisiana Purchase / Thomas Jefferson gold dollar . . . . . 17,500 | | $360 | $425 | $575 | $950 |
| 1903, Louisiana Purchase / William McKinley gold dollar . . . . . 17,500 | | 350 | 425 | 475 | 950 |

### (1904–1905) Lewis and Clark Exposition

| | Distribution | AU-50 | MS-60 | MS-63 | MS-65 |
|---|---|---|---|---|---|
| 1904, Lewis and Clark Exposition gold dollar. . . . . . . . . . . . . . 10,025 | | $550 | $600 | $800 | $3,000 |
| 1905, Lewis and Clark Exposition gold dollar. . . . . . . . . . . . . . 10,041 | | 550 | 700 | 900 | 5,500 |

### (1915) Panama-Pacific Exposition

| | Distribution | AU-50 | MS-60 | MS-63 | MS-65 |
|---|---|---|---|---|---|
| 1915S, Panama-Pacific Exposition half dollar . . . . . . . . . . . . . . 27,134 | | $250 | $325 | $525 | $675 |
| 1915S, Panama-Pacific Exposition gold dollar. . . . . . . . . . . . . 15,000 | | 375 | 425 | 500 | 950 |
| 1915S, Panama-Pacific Exposition gold $2.50. . . . . . . . . . . . . . 6,749 | | 1,000 | 1,500 | 3,000 | 4,000 |
| 1915S, Panama-Pacific Exposition gold $50 Round. . . . . . . . . . . 483 | | 35,000 | 45,000 | 63,000 | 120,000 |

## (1915) Panama-Pacific Exposition

| | Distribution | AU-50 | MS-60 | MS-63 | MS-65 |
|---|---|---|---|---|---|
| 1915S, Panama-Pacific Exposition gold $50 Octagonal . . . . . . . . . . | 645 | $35,000 | $44,000 | $60,000 | $120,000 |

## (1916–1917) McKinley Memorial

| | Distribution | AU-50 | MS-60 | MS-63 | MS-65 |
|---|---|---|---|---|---|
| 1916, McKinley Memorial gold dollar. . . . . . . . . . . . . . . . . . . | 15,000 | $325 | $375 | $400 | $850 |
| 1917, McKinley Memorial gold dollar. . . . . . . . . . . . . . . . . . . | 5,000 | 340 | 475 | 600 | 1,100 |

## (1918) Illinois Centennial

| | Distribution | AU-50 | MS-60 | MS-63 | MS-65 |
|---|---|---|---|---|---|
| 1918, Illinois Centennial half dollar . . . . . . . . . . . . . . . . . . . | 100,058 | $100 | $110 | $125 | $225 |

## (1920) Maine Centennial

| | Distribution | AU-50 | MS-60 | MS-63 | MS-65 |
|---|---|---|---|---|---|
| 1920, Maine Centennial half dollar . . . . . . . . . . . . . . . . . . . | 50,028 | $75 | $90 | $100 | $240 |

(1920–1921) Pilgrim Tercentenary

With 1921 in Field
on Obverse

|  | Distribution | AU-50 | MS-60 | MS-63 | MS-65 |
|---|---|---|---|---|---|
| 1920, Pilgrim Tercentenary half dollar................... 152,112 | | $55 | $65 | $70 | $130 |
| 1921, Same, With Date Added in Field .................... 20,053 | | 100 | 115 | 130 | 185 |

(1921) Missouri Centennial

With 2★4 in Field

|  | Distribution | AU-50 | MS-60 | MS-63 | MS-65 |
|---|---|---|---|---|---|
| 1921, Missouri Centennial half dollar, "2★4" in Field ......... 9,400 | | $410 | $460 | $700 | $1,200 |
| 1921, Missouri Centennial half dollar, Plain................. 11,400 | | 260 | 340 | 550 | 1,500 |

(1921) Alabama Centennial

Without 2X2 in Field

|  | Distribution | AU-50 | MS-60 | MS-63 | MS-65 |
|---|---|---|---|---|---|
| 1921, Alabama Centennial half dollar, With "2X2" in Field of Obverse.....6,006 | | $200 | $215 | $290 | $975 |
| 1921, Alabama Centennial half dollar, Plain.........................16,014 | | 100 | 135 | 275 | 800 |

# COMMEMORATIVES

Star in Field

(1922) Grant Memorial

| | Distribution | AU-50 | MS-60 | MS-63 | MS-65 |
|---|---|---|---|---|---|
| 1922, Grant Memorial, With Star* half dollar . . . . . . . . . . . . . . . 4,256 | | $610 | $825 | $1,125 | $4,000 |
| 1922, Same type, No Star in Obverse Field . . . . . . . . . . . . . . . 67,405 | | 70 | 80 | 100 | 375 |
| 1922, Grant Memorial, With Star* gold dollar. . . . . . . . . . . . . . 5,016 | | 1,050 | 1,100 | 1,200 | 1,600 |
| 1922, Grant Memorial, No Star in Obverse Field . . . . . . . . . . . 5,016 | | 960 | 1,000 | 1,200 | 1,600 |

* Fake stars usually have a flattened spot on the reverse.

(1923) Monroe Doctrine Centennial

| | Distribution | AU-50 | MS-60 | MS-63 | MS-65 |
|---|---|---|---|---|---|
| 1923S, Monroe Doctrine Centennial half dollar . . . . . . . . . . . . 274,077 | | $33 | $45 | $85 | $650 |

(1924) Huguenot-Walloon Tercentenary

| | Distribution | AU-50 | MS-60 | MS-63 | MS-65 |
|---|---|---|---|---|---|
| 1924, Huguenot-Walloon Tercentenary half dollar . . . . . . . . . . 142,080 | | $85 | $90 | $95 | $170 |

(1925) Lexington-Concord Sesquicentennial

| | Distribution | AU-50 | MS-60 | MS-63 | MS-65 |
|---|---|---|---|---|---|
| 1925, Lexington-Concord Sesquicentennial half dollar. . . . . . . | 162,013 | $50 | $65 | $67 | $250 |

(1925) Stone Mountain Memorial

| | Distribution | AU-50 | MS-60 | MS-63 | MS-65 |
|---|---|---|---|---|---|
| 1925, Stone Mountain Memorial half dollar . . . . . . . . . . . . . | 1,314,709 | $38 | $45 | $55 | $125 |

(1925) California Diamond Jubilee

| | Distribution | AU-50 | MS-60 | MS-63 | MS-65 |
|---|---|---|---|---|---|
| 1925S, California Diamond Jubilee half dollar . . . . . . . . . . . . | 86,594 | $110 | $130 | $140 | $400 |

(1925) Fort Vancouver Centennial

| | Distribution | AU-50 | MS-60 | MS-63 | MS-65 |
|---|---|---|---|---|---|
| 1925, Fort Vancouver Centennial half dollar . . . . . . . . . . . . . | 14,994 | $200 | $225 | $250 | $400 |

(1926) Sesquicentennial
of American Independence

| | Distribution | AU-50 | MS-60 | MS-63 | MS-65 |
|---|---|---|---|---|---|
| 1926, Sesquicentennial of American Independence half dollar .... | 141,120 | $50 | $70 | $85 | $1,450 |
| 1926, Sesquicentennial of American Independence gold $2.50..... | 46,019 | 325 | 350 | 400 | 1,650 |

(1926–1939) Oregon Trail Memorial

| | Distribution | AU-50 | MS-60 | MS-63 | MS-65 |
|---|---|---|---|---|---|
| 1926, Oregon Trail Memorial half dollar................... | 47,955 | $95 | $110 | $125 | $160 |
| 1926S, Same type, S Mint............................ | 83,055 | 95 | 110 | 125 | 160 |
| 1928, Oregon Trail Memorial half dollar (same as 1926)....... | 6,028 | 100 | 110 | 125 | 180 |
| 1933D, Oregon Trail Memorial half dollar................. | 5,008 | 240 | 250 | 275 | 325 |
| 1934D, Oregon Trail Memorial half dollar ................. | 7,006 | 120 | 130 | 135 | 210 |
| 1936, Oregon Trail Memorial half dollar.................. | 10,006 | 105 | 115 | 125 | 170 |
| 1936S, Same type, S Mint............................ | 5,006 | 110 | 120 | 125 | 170 |
| 1937D, Oregon Trail Memorial half dollar ................. | 12,008 | 110 | 125 | 135 | 170 |
| 1938, Oregon Trail Memorial half dollar (same as 1926)....... | 6,006 | | | | |
| 1938D, Same type, D Mint ........................... | 6,005 | *Set:* | 375 | 400 | 600 |
| 1938S, Same type, S Mint............................ | 6,006 | | | | |
| 1939, Oregon Trail Memorial half dollar (same as 1926)....... | 3,004 | | | | |
| 1939D, Same type, D Mint ........................... | 3,004 | *Set:* | 950 | 1,025 | 1,200 |
| 1939S, Same type, S Mint............................ | 3,005 | | | | |
| Oregon Trail Memorial half dollar, single type coin ............... | | 95 | 110 | 130 | 160 |

(1927) Vermont Sesquicentennial

| | Distribution | AU-50 | MS-60 | MS-63 | MS-65 |
|---|---|---|---|---|---|
| 1927, Vermont Sesquicentennial (Battle of Bennington) half dollar .. | 28,142 | $185 | $190 | $200 | $325 |

(1928) Hawaiian Sesquicentennial

| | Distribution | AU-50 | MS-60 | MS-63 | MS-65 |
|---|---|---|---|---|---|
| 1928, Hawaiian Sesquicentennial half dollar . . . . . . . . . . . . . . . . . . . . . . .10,008 | | $1,250 | $1,550 | $1,700 | $2,750 |
| 1928, Hawaiian Sesquicentennial, Sandblast Proof Presentation Piece . . . . . (50) | | | | 8,000 | 15,000 |

(1934) Maryland Tercentenary

| | Distribution | AU-50 | MS-60 | MS-63 | MS-65 |
|---|---|---|---|---|---|
| 1934, Maryland Tercentenary half dollar . . . . . . . . . . . . . . . . . | 25,015 | $90 | $105 | $110 | $135 |

(1934–1938) Texas Independence Centennial

| | Distribution | AU-50 | MS-60 | MS-63 | MS-65 |
|---|---|---|---|---|---|
| 1934, Texas Independence Centennial half dollar . . . . . . . . . . . . . . . . | 61,463 | $88 | $90 | $100 | $135 |
| 1935, Texas Independence Centennial half dollar (same as 1934). . . . . | 9,996 | | | | |
| 1935D, Same type, D Mint . . . . . . . . . . . . . . . . . . . . . . . . . . . . . . . | 10,007 | Set: | 265 | 275 | 425 |
| 1935S, Same type, S Mint. . . . . . . . . . . . . . . . . . . . . . . . . . . . . . . . | 10,008 | | | | |
| 1936, Texas Independence Centennial half dollar (same as 1934). . . . . | 8,911 | | | | |
| 1936D, Same type, D Mint . . . . . . . . . . . . . . . . . . . . . . . . . . . . . . . | 9,039 | Set: | 265 | 275 | 425 |
| 1936S, Same type, S Mint. . . . . . . . . . . . . . . . . . . . . . . . . . . . . . . . | 9,055 | | | | |
| 1937, Texas Independence Centennial half dollar (same as 1934). . . . . | 6,571 | | | | |
| 1937D, Same type, D Mint . . . . . . . . . . . . . . . . . . . . . . . . . . . . . . . | 6,605 | Set: | 265 | 275 | 425 |
| 1937S, Same type, S Mint. . . . . . . . . . . . . . . . . . . . . . . . . . . . . . . . | 6,637 | | | | |

| | Distribution | AU-50 | MS-60 | MS-63 | MS-65 |
|---|---|---|---|---|---|
| 1938, Texas Independence Centennial half dollar (same as 1934) | 3,780 | | | | |
| 1938D, Same type, D Mint | 3,775 | *Set:* | $460 | $480 | $850 |
| 1938S, Same type, S Mint | 3,814 | | | | |
| Texas Independence Centennial half dollar, single type coin | | $88 | 90 | 100 | 140 |

**(1934–1938) Daniel Boone Bicentennial**      **1934 Added on Reverse**

| | Distribution | AU-50 | MS-60 | MS-63 | MS-65 |
|---|---|---|---|---|---|
| 1934, Daniel Boone Bicentennial half dollar | 10,007 | $88 | $95 | $100 | $120 |
| 1935, Daniel Boone Bicentennial half dollar | 10,010 | | | | |
| 1935D, Same type, D Mint | 5,005 | *Set:* | 285 | 300 | 375 |
| 1935S, Same type, S Mint | 5,005 | | | | |
| 1935, Same as 1934 but Small 1934 on reverse | 10,008 | | | | |
| 1935D, Same type, D Mint | 2,003 | *Set:* | 500 | 550 | 1,100 |
| 1935S, Same type, S Mint | 2,004 | | | | |
| 1936, Daniel Boone Bicentennial half dollar (same as preceding) | 12,012 | | | | |
| 1936D, Same type, D Mint | 5,005 | *Set:* | 300 | 350 | 500 |
| 1936S, Same type, S Mint | 5,006 | | | | |
| 1937, Daniel Boone Bicentennial half dollar (same as preceding) | 9,810 | | | | |
| 1937D, Same type, D Mint | 2,506 | *Set:* | 425 | 500 | 650 |
| 1937S, Same type, S Mint | 2,506 | | | | |
| 1938, Daniel Boone Bicentennial half dollar (same as preceding) | 2,100 | | | | |
| 1938D, Same type, D Mint | 2,100 | *Set:* | 650 | 750 | 1,000 |
| 1938S, Same type, S Mint | 2,100 | | | | |
| Daniel Boone Bicentennial half dollar, single type coin | | 85 | 95 | 100 | 115 |

**(1935) Connecticut Tercentenary**

| | Distribution | AU-50 | MS-60 | MS-63 | MS-65 |
|---|---|---|---|---|---|
| 1935, Connecticut Tercentenary half dollar | 25,018 | $140 | $145 | $150 | $250 |

**(1935–1939)
Arkansas Centennial**

| | Distribution | AU-50 | MS-60 | MS-63 | MS-65 |
|---|---|---|---|---|---|
| 1935, Arkansas Centennial half dollar . . . . . . . . . . . . . . . . . . . . . . . . 13,012 | | | | | |
| 1935D, Same type, D Mint . . . . . . . . . . . . . . . . . . . . . . . . . . . . . . . . 5,505 | *Set:* | $200 | $205 | $330 | |
| 1935S, Same type, S Mint. . . . . . . . . . . . . . . . . . . . . . . . . . . . . . . . 5,506 | | | | | |
| 1936, Arkansas Centennial half dollar (same as 1935 but 1936 on rev) 9,660 | | | | | |
| 1936D, Same type, D Mint . . . . . . . . . . . . . . . . . . . . . . . . . . . . . . . . 9,660 | *Set:* | 200 | 205 | 350 | |
| 1936S, Same type, S Mint. . . . . . . . . . . . . . . . . . . . . . . . . . . . . . . . 9,662 | | | | | |
| 1937, Arkansas Centennial half dollar (same as 1935) . . . . . . . . . . . . 5,505 | | | | | |
| 1937D, Same type, D mint . . . . . . . . . . . . . . . . . . . . . . . . . . . . . . . . 5,505 | *Set:* | 215 | 225 | 450 | |
| 1937S, Same type, S mint. . . . . . . . . . . . . . . . . . . . . . . . . . . . . . . . 5,506 | | | | | |
| 1938, Arkansas Centennial half dollar (same as 1935) . . . . . . . . . . . . 3,156 | | | | | |
| 1938D, Same type, D Mint . . . . . . . . . . . . . . . . . . . . . . . . . . . . . . . . 3,155 | *Set:* | 275 | 310 | 750 | |
| 1938S, Same type, S Mint. . . . . . . . . . . . . . . . . . . . . . . . . . . . . . . . 3,156 | | | | | |
| 1939, Arkansas Centennial half dollar (same as 1935) . . . . . . . . . . . . 2,104 | | | | | |
| 1939D, Same type, D Mint . . . . . . . . . . . . . . . . . . . . . . . . . . . . . . . . 2,104 | *Set:* | 475 | 550 | 1,600 | |
| 1939S, Same type, S Mint. . . . . . . . . . . . . . . . . . . . . . . . . . . . . . . . 2,105 | | | | | |
| Arkansas Centennial half dollar, single type coin . . . . . . . . . . . . . . . . . . | $65 | 68 | 70 | 100 | |

**(1936) Arkansas
Centennial – Robinson**

| | Distribution | AU-50 | MS-60 | MS-63 | MS-65 |
|---|---|---|---|---|---|
| 1936, Arkansas Centennial (Robinson) half dollar . . . . . . . . . . . 25,265 | $75 | $80 | $90 | $140 |

**(1935) Hudson, New
York, Sesquicentennial**

| | Distribution | AU-50 | MS-60 | MS-63 | MS-65 |
|---|---|---|---|---|---|
| 1935, Hudson, New York, Sesquicentennial half dollar . . . . . . . 10,008 | $500 | $550 | $600 | $750 |

(1935–1936) California-Pacific International Exposition

| | Distribution | AU-50 | MS-60 | MS-63 | MS-65 |
|---|---|---|---|---|---|
| 1935S, California-Pacific International Exposition half dollar . . . | 70,132 | $64 | $68 | $72 | $85 |
| 1936D, California-Pacific International Exposition half dollar . . . | 30,092 | 65 | 68 | 72 | 90 |

(1935) Old Spanish Trail

| | Distribution | AU-50 | MS-60 | MS-63 | MS-65 |
|---|---|---|---|---|---|
| 1935, Old Spanish Trail half dollar. . . . . . . . . . . . . . . . . . . . . | 10,008 | $725 | $750 | $775 | $850 |

(1936) Providence, Rhode Island, Tercentenary

| | Distribution | AU-50 | MS-60 | MS-63 | MS-65 |
|---|---|---|---|---|---|
| 1936, Providence, Rhode Island, Tercentenary half dollar . . . . . | 20,013 | | | | |
| 1936D, Same type, D Mint . . . . . . . . . . . . . . . . . . . . . . . . . . . | 15,010 | *Set:* | $200 | $225 | $300 |
| 1936S, Same type, S Mint. . . . . . . . . . . . . . . . . . . . . . . . . . . | 15,011 | | | | |
| Providence, Rhode Island, Tercentenary half dollar, single type coin . . . | | $65 | 68 | 72 | 90 |

### (1936) Cleveland Centennial / Great Lakes Exposition

| | Distribution | AU-50 | MS-60 | MS-63 | MS-65 |
|---|---|---|---|---|---|
| 1936, Cleveland Centennial / Great Lakes Exposition half dollar | 50,030 | $64 | $72 | $80 | $100 |

### (1936) Wisconsin Territorial Centennial

| | Distribution | AU-50 | MS-60 | MS-63 | MS-65 |
|---|---|---|---|---|---|
| 1936, Wisconsin Territorial Centennial half dollar . . . . . . . . . . | 25,015 | $115 | $120 | $130 | $160 |

### (1936) Cincinnati Music Center

| | Distribution | AU-50 | MS-60 | MS-63 | MS-65 |
|---|---|---|---|---|---|
| 1936, Cincinnati Music Center half dollar . . . . . . . . . . . . . . . . . | 5,005 | | | | |
| 1936D, Same type, D Mint . . . . . . . . . . . . . . . . . . . . . . . . . . . | 5,005 | *Set:* | $550 | $700 | $950 |
| 1936S, Same type, S Mint. . . . . . . . . . . . . . . . . . . . . . . . . . . | 5,006 | | | | |
| Cincinnati Music Center half dollar, single type coin . . . . . . . . . . . . . . . | | $190 | 200 | 240 | 300 |

### (1936) Long Island Tercentenary

| | Distribution | AU-50 | MS-60 | MS-63 | MS-65 |
|---|---|---|---|---|---|
| 1936, Long Island Tercentenary half dollar . . . . . . . . . . . . . . . . 81,826 | $50 | $60 | $65 | $130 |

### (1936) York County, Maine, Tercentenary

| | Distribution | AU-50 | MS-60 | MS-63 | MS-65 |
|---|---|---|---|---|---|
| 1936, York County, Maine, Tercentenary half dollar. . . . . . . . . . 25,015 | $100 | $110 | $120 | $140 |

### (1936) Bridgeport, Connecticut, Centennial

| | Distribution | AU-50 | MS-60 | MS-63 | MS-65 |
|---|---|---|---|---|---|
| 1936, Bridgeport, Connecticut, Centennial half dollar . . . . . . . . 25,015 | $90 | $95 | $100 | $125 |

### (1936) Lynchburg, Virginia, Sesquicentennial

| | Distribution | AU-50 | MS-60 | MS-63 | MS-65 |
|---|---|---|---|---|---|
| 1936, Lynchburg, Virginia, Sesquicentennial half dollar. . . . . . . 20,013 | $150 | $155 | $175 | $200 |

(1936) Elgin, Illinois, Centennial

| | Distribution | AU-50 | MS-60 | MS-63 | MS-65 |
|---|---|---|---|---|---|
| 1936, Elgin, Illinois, Centennial half dollar . . . . . . . . . . . . . . . . . | 20,015 | $115 | $120 | $130 | $155 |

(1936) Albany, New York, Charter

| | Distribution | AU-50 | MS-60 | MS-63 | MS-65 |
|---|---|---|---|---|---|
| 1936, Albany, New York, Charter half dollar . . . . . . . . . . . . . . . | 17,671 | $145 | $150 | $160 | $200 |

(1936) San Francisco – Oakland Bay Bridge Opening

| | Distribution | AU-50 | MS-60 | MS-63 | MS-65 |
|---|---|---|---|---|---|
| 1936S, San Francisco–Oakland Bay Bridge Opening half dollar . . | 71,424 | $130 | $135 | $140 | $150 |

(1936) Delaware Tercentenary

| | Distribution | AU-50 | MS-60 | MS-63 | MS-65 |
|---|---|---|---|---|---|
| 1936, Delaware Tercentenary half dollar . . . . . . . . . . . . . . . . . . | 20,993 | $145 | $150 | $160 | $185 |

(1936) Columbia, South Carolina, Sesquicentennial

| | Distribution | AU-50 | MS-60 | MS-63 | MS-65 |
|---|---|---|---|---|---|
| 1936, Columbia, South Carolina, Sesquicentennial half dollar . . . . . . . 9,007 | | | | | |
| 1936D, Same type, D Mint . . . . . . . . . . . . . . . . . . . . . . . . . . . . . . . . 8,009 | *Set:* | $425 | $435 | $500 | |
| 1936S, Same type, S Mint. . . . . . . . . . . . . . . . . . . . . . . . . . . . . . . 8,007 | | | | | |
| Columbia, South Carolina, Sesquicentennial half dollar, single type coin . . . . . | $120 | 140 | 145 | 165 | |

(1936) Battle of Gettysburg Anniversary

| | Distribution | AU-50 | MS-60 | MS-63 | MS-65 |
|---|---|---|---|---|---|
| 1936, Battle of Gettysburg Anniversary half dollar . . . . . . . . . . 26,928 | $340 | $350 | $375 | $500 |

(1936) Norfolk, Virginia, Bicentennial

| | Distribution | AU-50 | MS-60 | MS-63 | MS-65 |
|---|---|---|---|---|---|
| 1936, Norfolk, Virginia, Bicentennial half dollar . . . . . . . . . . . . . 16,936 | $210 | $212 | $216 | $225 |

(1937) Roanoke Island, North Carolina, 350th Anniversary

| | Distribution | AU-50 | MS-60 | MS-63 | MS-65 |
|---|---|---|---|---|---|
| 1937, Roanoke Island, North Carolina, 350th Anniversary half dollar. . | 29,030 | $120 | $125 | $130 | $160 |

(1937) Battle of Antietam Anniversary

| | Distribution | AU-50 | MS-60 | MS-63 | MS-65 |
|---|---|---|---|---|---|
| 1937, Battle of Antietam Anniversary half dollar . . . . . . . . . . . . | 18,028 | $410 | $425 | $450 | $475 |

(1938) New Rochelle, New York, 250th Anniversary

| | Distribution | AU-50 | MS-60 | MS-63 | MS-65 |
|---|---|---|---|---|---|
| 1938, New Rochelle, New York, 250th Anniversary half dollar. . | 15,266 | $200 | $210 | $220 | $260 |

(1946) Iowa Centennial

| | Distribution | AU-50 | MS-60 | MS-63 | MS-65 |
|---|---|---|---|---|---|
| 1946, Iowa Centennial half dollar . . . . . . . . . . . . . . . . . . . . . . | 100,057 | $45 | $50 | $60 | $80 |

(1946–1951) Booker T. Washington Memorial

| | Distribution | AU-50 | MS-60 | MS-63 | MS-65 |
|---|---|---|---|---|---|
| 1946, Booker T. Washington Memorial half dollar **(a)** . . . . . . . . . . . . | 700,546 | | | | |
| 1946D, Same type, D Mint . . . . . . . . . . . . . . . . . . . . . . . . . . . . . . . . | 50,000 | Set: | $40 | $48 | $110 |
| 1946S, Same type, S Mint. . . . . . . . . . . . . . . . . . . . . . . . . . . . . . . . | 500,279 | | | | |
| 1947, Booker T. Washington Memorial half dollar (same as 1946) . . . . | 6,000 | | | | |
| 1947D, Same type, D Mint . . . . . . . . . . . . . . . . . . . . . . . . . . . . . . . . | 6,000 | Set: | 55 | 110 | 140 |
| 1947S, Same type, S Mint. . . . . . . . . . . . . . . . . . . . . . . . . . . . . . . . | 6,000 | | | | |
| 1948, Booker T. Washington Memorial half dollar (same as 1946) . . . . | 8,005 | | | | |
| 1948D, Same type, D Mint . . . . . . . . . . . . . . . . . . . . . . . . . . . . . . . . | 8,005 | Set: | 55 | 120 | 155 |
| 1948S, Same type, S Mint. . . . . . . . . . . . . . . . . . . . . . . . . . . . . . . . | 8,005 | | | | |
| 1949, Booker T. Washington Memorial half dollar (same as 1946) . . . . | 6,004 | | | | |
| 1949D, Same type, D Mint . . . . . . . . . . . . . . . . . . . . . . . . . . . . . . . . | 6,004 | Set: | 90 | 120 | 300 |
| 1949S, Same type, S Mint. . . . . . . . . . . . . . . . . . . . . . . . . . . . . . . . | 6,004 | | | | |
| 1950, Booker T. Washington Memorial half dollar (same as 1946) . . . . | 6,004 | | | | |
| 1950D, Same type, D Mint . . . . . . . . . . . . . . . . . . . . . . . . . . . . . . . . | 6,004 | Set: | 55 | 105 | 185 |
| 1950S, Same type, S Mint. . . . . . . . . . . . . . . . . . . . . . . . . . . . . . . . | 62,091 | | | | |
| 1951, Booker T. Washington Memorial half dollar (same as 1946) . . | 210,082 | | | | |
| 1951D, Same type, D Mint . . . . . . . . . . . . . . . . . . . . . . . . . . . . . . . . | 7,004 | Set: | 60 | 105 | 165 |
| 1951S, Same type, S Mint. . . . . . . . . . . . . . . . . . . . . . . . . . . . . . . . | 7,004 | | | | |
| Booker T. Washington Memorial, single type coin . . . . . . . . . . . . . . . . . . . . . . | | $11 | 13 | 15 | 35 |

a. Minted; quantity melted unknown.

(1951–1954) Carver/Washington Commemorative

| | Distribution | AU-50 | MS-60 | MS-63 | MS-65 |
|---|---|---|---|---|---|
| 1951, Carver/Washington half dollar . . . . . . . . . . . . . . . . . . . . | 20,018 | | | | |
| 1951D, Same type, D Mint . . . . . . . . . . . . . . . . . . . . . . . . . . . . | 10,004 | Set: | $45 | $70 | $225 |
| 1951S, Same type, S Mint. . . . . . . . . . . . . . . . . . . . . . . . . . . . . | 10,004 | | | | |
| 1952, Carver/Washington half dollar (same as 1951) . . . . . . | 1,106,292 | | | | |
| 1952D, Same type, D Mint . . . . . . . . . . . . . . . . . . . . . . . . . . . . | 8,006 | Set: | 55 | 70 | 190 |
| 1952S, Same type, S Mint. . . . . . . . . . . . . . . . . . . . . . . . . . . . . | 8,006 | | | | |

*Chart continued on next page.*

| | Distribution | AU-50 | MS-60 | MS-63 | MS-65 |
|---|---|---|---|---|---|
| 1953, Carver/Washington half dollar (same as 1951) ........ 8,003 | | | | | |
| 1953D, Same type, D Mint ............................ 8,003 | | *Set:* | $60 | $75 | $170 |
| 1953S, Same type, S Mint............................. 88,020 | | | | | |
| 1954, Carver/Washington half dollar (same as 1951) ........ 12,006 | | | | | |
| 1954D, Same type, D Mint ............................ 12,006 | | *Set:* | 50 | 60 | 130 |
| 1954S, Same type, S Mint............................. 42,024 | | | | | |
| Carver/Washington half dollar, single type coin ................... | | $11 | 13 | 15 | 40 |

# MODERN COMMEMORATIVES

(1982) George Washington 250th Anniversary of Birth

| | Distribution | Mint Pkg |
|---|---|---|
| 1982D, George Washington 250th Anniversary silver half dollar, Uncirculated ............. 2,210,458 | | $9 |
| 1982S, George Washington 250th Anniversary silver half dollar, Proof ................. (4,894,044) | | 10 |

(1983–1984) Los Angeles Olympiad

| | Distribution | Mint Pkg |
|---|---|---|
| 1983P, Discus Thrower silver dollar, Uncirculated | 294,543 | $15 |
| 1983D, Discus Thrower silver dollar, Uncirculated | 174,014 | 15 |
| 1983S, Discus Thrower silver dollar, Uncirculated | 174,014 | 15 |
| 1983S, Discus Thrower silver dollar, Proof | (1,577,025) | 16 |
| 1984P, Olympic Coliseum silver dollar, Uncirculated | 217,954 | 15 |
| 1984D, Olympic Coliseum silver dollar, Uncirculated | 116,675 | 15 |
| 1984S, Olympic Coliseum silver dollar, Uncirculated | 116,675 | 15 |
| 1984S, Olympic Coliseum silver dollar, Proof | (1,801,210) | 16 |
| 1984P, Olympic Torch Bearers gold $10, Uncirculated | (33,309) | 900 |
| 1984D, Olympic Torch Bearers gold $10, Uncirculated | (34,533) | 900 |
| 1984S, Olympic Torch Bearers gold $10, Uncirculated | (48,551) | 900 |
| 1984W, Olympic Torch Bearers gold $10, Uncirculated | 75,886 | 900 |
| 1984W, Olympic Torch Bearers gold $10, Proof | (381,085) | 900 |
| 1983–1984 2-coin set. Both Proof silver dollars | | 32 |
| 1983–1984 6-coin set. One each of Proof and Uncirculated silver dollars, Proof and Uncirculated gold $10 **(a)** | | 1,850 |
| 1983 3-piece Collector set. P, D, and S Uncirculated silver dollars | | 48 |
| 1984 3-piece Collector set. P, D, and S Uncirculated silver dollars | | 48 |
| 1983–1984 Gold and Silver set. Uncirculated 1983 and 1984 silver dollars and Uncirculated gold $10 | | 932 |
| 1983–1984 Gold and Silver set. Proof 1983 and 1984 silver dollars and Proof gold $10 | | 932 |

*Note:* Proof Los Angeles Olympiad silver dollars for 1983 and 1984 were also included in Prestige Sets; see page 235.
**a.** Packaged in a cherrywood box.

### (1986) Statue of Liberty Centennial

| | Distribution | Mint Pkg |
|---|---|---|
| 1986D, Statue of Liberty Centennial clad half dollar, Uncirculated | 928,008 | $1 |
| 1986S, Statue of Liberty Centennial clad half dollar, Proof | (6,925,627) | 1 |
| 1986P, Statue of Liberty Centennial silver dollar, Uncirculated | 723,635 | 15 |
| 1986S, Statue of Liberty Centennial silver dollar, Proof | (6,414,638) | 16 |
| 1986W, Statue of Liberty Centennial gold $5, Uncirculated | 95,248 | 450 |
| 1986W, Statue of Liberty Centennial gold $5, Proof | (404,013) | 450 |
| 2-coin set. Uncirculated silver dollar and clad half dollar | | 20 |
| 2-coin set. Uncirculated and Proof gold $5 | | 900 |

*Note:* Proof Statue of Liberty Centennial clad half dollars and silver dollars were also included in Prestige Sets; see page 235.

*Chart continued on next page.*

| | Distribution | Mint Pkg |
|---|---|---|
| 2-coin set. Proof silver dollar and clad half dollar . . . . . . . . . . . . . . . . . . . . . . . . . . . . . . . . . . . . | | $16 |
| 3-coin set. Uncirculated silver dollar, clad half dollar, and gold $5. . . . . . . . . . . . . . . . . . . . . . . . . | | 468 |
| 3-coin set. Proof silver dollar, clad half dollar, and gold $5. . . . . . . . . . . . . . . . . . . . . . . . . . . . . . | | 465 |
| 6-coin set. One each of Proof and Uncirculated clad half dollar, silver dollar, and gold $5 **(a)** . . . . . . . . | | 940 |

*Note:* Proof Statue of Liberty Centennial clad half dollars and silver dollars were also included in Prestige Sets; see page 235. **a.** Packaged in a cherrywood box.

(1987) U.S. Constitution Bicentennial

| | Distribution | Mint Pkg |
|---|---|---|
| 1987P, U.S. Constitution Bicentennial silver dollar, Uncirculated. . . . . . . . . . . . . . . . . . . . . . . . | 451,629 | $15 |
| 1987S, U.S. Constitution Bicentennial silver dollar, Proof. . . . . . . . . . . . . . . . . . . . . . . . . . . . . | (2,747,116) | 16 |
| 1987W, U.S. Constitution Bicentennial gold $5, Uncirculated. . . . . . . . . . . . . . . . . . . . . . . . . . . | 214,225 | 450 |
| 1987W, U.S. Constitution Bicentennial gold $5, Proof. . . . . . . . . . . . . . . . . . . . . . . . . . . . . . . . | (651,659) | 450 |
| 2-coin set. Uncirculated silver dollar and gold $5 . . . . . . . . . . . . . . . . . . . . . . . . . . . . . . . . . . | | 465 |
| 2-coin set. Proof silver dollar and gold $5 . . . . . . . . . . . . . . . . . . . . . . . . . . . . . . . . . . . . . . . | | 465 |
| 4-coin set. One each of Proof and Uncirculated silver dollar and gold $5 **(a)**. . . . . . . . . . . . . . . . . . . | | 960 |

*Note:* Proof U.S. Constitution Bicentennial silver dollars were also included in Prestige Sets; see page 235. **a.** Packaged in a cherrywood box.

(1988) Seoul Olympiad

| | Distribution | Mint Pkg |
|---|---|---|
| 1988D, Seoul Olympiad silver dollar, Uncirculated . . . . . . . . . . . . . . . . . . . . . . . . . . . . . . . . . . | 191,368 | $15 |
| 1988S, Seoul Olympiad silver dollar, Proof. . . . . . . . . . . . . . . . . . . . . . . . . . . . . . . . . . . . . . . | (1,359,366) | 15 |
| 1988W, Seoul Olympiad gold $5, Uncirculated. . . . . . . . . . . . . . . . . . . . . . . . . . . . . . . . . . . . . | 62,913 | 450 |
| 1988W, Seoul Olympiad gold $5, Proof . . . . . . . . . . . . . . . . . . . . . . . . . . . . . . . . . . . . . . . . . | (281,465) | 450 |
| 2-coin set. Uncirculated silver dollar and gold $5 . . . . . . . . . . . . . . . . . . . . . . . . . . . . . . . . . . | | 465 |
| 2-coin set. Proof silver dollar and gold $5 . . . . . . . . . . . . . . . . . . . . . . . . . . . . . . . . . . . . . . . | | 465 |
| 4-coin set. One each of Proof and Uncirculated silver dollar and gold $5 **(a)**. . . . . . . . . . . . . . . . . . . | | 930 |

*Note:* Proof Seoul Olympiad silver dollars were also included in Prestige Sets; see page 235. **a.** Packaged in a cherrywood box.

**(1989) Congress Bicentennial**

| | Distribution | Mint Pkg |
|---|---|---|
| 1989D, Congress Bicentennial clad half dollar, Uncirculated . . . . . . . . . . . . . . . . . . . . . . . . . . . . . 163,753 | | $3 |
| 1989S, Congress Bicentennial clad half dollar, Proof . . . . . . . . . . . . . . . . . . . . . . . . . . . . . . . | (767,897) | 4 |
| 1989D, Congress Bicentennial silver dollar, Uncirculated . . . . . . . . . . . . . . . . . . . . . . . . . . . . . 135,203 | | 15 |
| 1989S, Congress Bicentennial silver dollar, Proof. . . . . . . . . . . . . . . . . . . . . . . . . . . . . . . . . | (762,198) | 16 |
| 1989W, Congress Bicentennial gold $5, Uncirculated. . . . . . . . . . . . . . . . . . . . . . . . . . . . . . . 46,899 | | 450 |
| 1989W, Congress Bicentennial gold $5, Proof . . . . . . . . . . . . . . . . . . . . . . . . . . . . . . . . . . | (164,690) | 450 |
| 2-coin set. Proof clad half dollar and silver dollar . . . . . . . . . . . . . . . . . . . . . . . . . . . . . . . . | | 19 |
| 3-coin set. Proof clad half dollar, silver dollar, and gold $5. . . . . . . . . . . . . . . . . . . . . . . . . . . | | 20 |
| 2-coin set. Uncirculated clad half dollar and silver dollar . . . . . . . . . . . . . . . . . . . . . . . . . . . . | | 470 |
| 3-coin set. Uncirculated clad half dollar, silver dollar, and gold $5 . . . . . . . . . . . . . . . . . . . . . . | | 470 |
| 6-coin set. One each of Proof and Uncirculated clad half dollar, silver dollar, and gold $5 **(a)** . . . . . . . . | | 940 |

*Note:* Proof Congress Bicentennial clad half dollars and silver dollars were also included in Prestige Sets; see page 235.
**a.** Packaged in a cherrywood box.

**(1990) Eisenhower Centennial**

| | Distribution | Mint Pkg |
|---|---|---|
| 1990W, Eisenhower Centennial silver dollar, Uncirculated . . . . . . . . . . . . . . . . . . . . . . . . . . . . 241,669 | | $19 |
| 1990P, Eisenhower Centennial silver dollar, Proof . . . . . . . . . . . . . . . . . . . . . . . . . . . . . . . . | (1,144,461) | 16 |

*Note:* Proof Eisenhower Centennial silver dollars were also included in Prestige Sets; see page 235.

(1991) Mount Rushmore Golden Anniversary

| | Distribution | Mint Pkg |
|---|---|---|
| 1991D, Mount Rushmore Golden Anniversary clad half dollar, Uncirculated . . . . . . . . . . . . . . . | 172,754 | $7 |
| 1991S, Mount Rushmore Golden Anniversary clad half dollar, Proof. . . . . . . . . . . . . . . . . . . . | (753,257) | 5 |
| 1991P, Mount Rushmore Golden Anniversary silver dollar, Uncirculated. . . . . . . . . . . . . . . . . | 133,139 | 25 |
| 1991S, Mount Rushmore Golden Anniversary silver dollar, Proof . . . . . . . . . . . . . . . . . . . . . . | (738,419) | 17 |
| 1991W, Mount Rushmore Golden Anniversary gold $5, Uncirculated . . . . . . . . . . . . . . . . . . . | 31,959 | 450 |
| 1991W, Mount Rushmore Golden Anniversary gold $5, Proof. . . . . . . . . . . . . . . . . . . . . . . . . | (111,991) | 450 |
| 2-coin set. Uncirculated clad half dollar and silver dollar . . . . . . . . . . . . . . . . . . . . . . . . . . . . . | | 29 |
| 2-coin set. Proof clad half dollar and silver dollar . . . . . . . . . . . . . . . . . . . . . . . . . . . . . . . . . . | | 22 |
| 3-coin set. Uncirculated clad half dollar, silver dollar, and gold $5 . . . . . . . . . . . . . . . . . . . . . . . | | 480 |
| 3-coin set. Proof clad half dollar, silver dollar, and gold $5. . . . . . . . . . . . . . . . . . . . . . . . . . . . | | 475 |
| 6-coin set. One each of Proof and Uncirculated clad half dollar, silver dollar, and gold $5 **(a)** . . . . . . . . . | | 965 |

*Note:* Proof Mount Rushmore Golden Anniversary clad half dollars and silver dollars were also included in Prestige Sets; see page 235. **a.** Packaged in a cherrywood box.

(1991) Korean War Memorial

| | Distribution | Mint Pkg |
|---|---|---|
| 1991D, Korean War Memorial silver dollar, Uncirculated . . . . . . . . . . . . . . . . . . . . . . . . . . . . | 213,049 | $20 |
| 1991P, Korean War Memorial silver dollar, Proof . . . . . . . . . . . . . . . . . . . . . . . . . . . . . . . . . | (618,488) | 16 |

### (1991) United Service Organizations

| | Distribution | Mint Pkg |
|---|---|---|
| 1991D, United Service Organizations silver dollar, Uncirculated | 124,958 | $20 |
| 1991S, United Service Organizations silver dollar, Proof | (321,275) | 16 |

### (1992) XXV Olympiad

| | Distribution | Mint Pkg |
|---|---|---|
| 1992P, XXV Olympiad clad half dollar, Uncirculated | 161,607 | $3 |
| 1992S, XXV Olympiad clad half dollar, Proof | (519,645) | 4 |
| 1992D, XXV Olympiad silver dollar, Uncirculated | 187,552 | 17 |
| 1992S, XXV Olympiad silver dollar, Proof | (504,505) | 16 |
| 1992W, XXV Olympiad gold $5, Uncirculated | 27,732 | 450 |
| 1992W, XXV Olympiad gold $5, Proof | (77,313) | 450 |
| 2-coin set. Uncirculated clad half dollar and silver dollar | | 20 |
| 2-coin set. Proof clad half dollar and silver dollar | | 21 |
| 3-coin set. Uncirculated clad half dollar, silver dollar, and gold $5 | | 471 |
| 3-coin set. Proof clad half dollar, silver dollar, and gold $5 | | 470 |
| 6-coin set. One each of Proof and Uncirculated clad half dollar, silver dollar, and gold $5 **(a)** | | 943 |

*Note:* Proof XXV Olympiad half dollars and silver dollars were also included in Prestige Sets; see page 235. **a.** Packaged in a cherrywood box.

### (1992) White House 200th Anniversary

| | Distribution | Mint Pkg |
|---|---|---|
| 1992D, White House 200th Anniversary silver dollar, Uncirculated | 123,803 | $25 |
| 1992W, White House 200th Anniversary silver dollar, Proof | (375,851) | 16 |

### (1992) Christopher Columbus Quincentenary

| | Distribution | Mint Pkg |
|---|---|---|
| 1992D, Christopher Columbus Quincentenary clad half dollar, Uncirculated | 135,702 | $6 |
| 1992S, Christopher Columbus Quincentenary clad half dollar, Proof | (390,154) | 6 |
| 1992D, Christopher Columbus Quincentenary silver dollar, Uncirculated | 106,949 | 23 |
| 1992P, Christopher Columbus Quincentenary silver dollar, Proof | (385,241) | 16 |
| 1992W, Christopher Columbus Quincentenary gold $5, Uncirculated | 24,329 | 450 |
| 1992W, Christopher Columbus Quincentenary gold $5, Proof | (79,730) | 450 |
| 2-coin set. Uncirculated clad half dollar and silver dollar | | 30 |
| 2-coin set. Proof clad half dollar and silver dollar | | 25 |
| 3-coin set. Uncirculated clad half dollar, silver dollar, and gold $5 | | 480 |
| 3-coin set. Proof clad half dollar, silver dollar, and gold $5 | | 475 |
| 6-coin set. One each of Proof and Uncirculated clad half dollar, silver dollar, and gold $5 **(a)** | | 955 |

a. Packaged in a cherrywood box.

# COMMEMORATIVES

### (1993) Bill of Rights

| | Distribution | Mint Pkg |
|---|---|---|
| 1993W, Bill of Rights silver half dollar, Uncirculated | 193,346 | $12 |
| 1993S, Bill of Rights silver half dollar, Proof | (586,315) | 9 |
| 1993D, Bill of Rights silver dollar, Uncirculated | 98,383 | 20 |
| 1993S, Bill of Rights silver dollar, Proof | (534,001) | 16 |
| 1993W, Bill of Rights gold $5, Uncirculated | 23,266 | 450 |
| 1993W, Bill of Rights gold $5, Proof | (78,651) | 450 |
| 2-coin set. Uncirculated silver half dollar and silver dollar | | 32 |
| 2-coin set. Proof silver half dollar and silver dollar | | 25 |
| 3-coin set. Uncirculated silver half dollar, silver dollar, and gold $5 | | 482 |
| 3-coin set. Proof silver half dollar, silver dollar, and gold $5 | | 475 |
| 6-coin set. One each of Proof and Uncirculated silver half dollar, silver dollar, and gold $5 **(a)** | | 960 |
| Young Collector set. Uncirculated silver half dollar | | 9 |
| Coin and Medal set. Silver half dollar and bronze James Madison Peace medal replica | | 9 |
| Coin and Stamp set. Proof silver half dollar and themed 25¢ postage stamp | | 9 |

*Note:* Proof Bill of Rights half dollars and silver dollars were also included in Prestige Sets; see page 235. **a.** Packaged in a cherrywood box.

### (1993) 50th Anniversary of World War II, 1991–1995

| | Distribution | Mint Pkg |
|---|---|---|
| (1993P) 1991–1995 World War II clad half dollar, Uncirculated | 197,072 | $10 |
| (1993P) 1991–1995 World War II clad half dollar, Proof | (317,396) | 8 |

*Entry continued on next page.*

(1993) 50th Anniversary of World War II, 1991–1995

| | Distribution | Mint Pkg |
|---|---|---|
| (1993D) 1991–1995 World War II silver dollar, Uncirculated . . . . . . . . . . . . . . . . . . . . . . . . . . . 107,240 | | $24 |
| (1993W) 1991–1995 World War II silver dollar, Proof. . . . . . . . . . . . . . . . . . . . . . . . . . . . . . . . (342,041) | | 24 |
| (1993W) 1991–1995 World War II gold $5, Uncirculated . . . . . . . . . . . . . . . . . . . . . . . . . . . . . . 23,672 | | 450 |
| (1993W) 1991–1995 World War II gold $5, Proof. . . . . . . . . . . . . . . . . . . . . . . . . . . . . . . . . . . . . . (67,026) | | 450 |
| 2-coin set. Uncirculated clad half dollar and silver dollar. . . . . . . . . . . . . . . . . . . . . . . . . . . . . . . . . | | 32 |
| 2-coin set. Proof clad half dollar and silver dollar . . . . . . . . . . . . . . . . . . . . . . . . . . . . . . . . . . . . . . | | 34 |
| 3-coin set. Uncirculated clad half dollar, silver dollar, and gold $5. . . . . . . . . . . . . . . . . . . . . . . . . | | 482 |
| 3-coin set. Proof clad half dollar, silver dollar, and gold $5. . . . . . . . . . . . . . . . . . . . . . . . . . . . . . . | | 485 |
| 6-coin set. One each of Proof and Uncirculated clad half dollar, silver dollar, and gold $5 **(a)** . . . . . . . . | | 970 |
| Young Collector's set. Uncirculated clad half dollar . . . . . . . . . . . . . . . . . . . . . . . . . . . . . . . . . . . . . | | 9 |
| Victory Medal set. Uncirculated clad half dollar and bronze Victory medal replica . . . . . . . . . . . . . . . . . | | 9 |

**a.** Packaged in a cherrywood box.

(1994) Thomas Jefferson 250th Anniversary of Birth, 1993

| | Distribution | Mint Pkg |
|---|---|---|
| 1993P (1994) Thomas Jefferson 250th Anniversary of Birth, 1993 silver dollar, Uncirculated . . 266,927 | | $17 |
| 1993P (1994) Thomas Jefferson 250th Anniversary of Birth, 1993 silver dollar, Proof . . . . . . (332,891) | | 16 |
| Coinage and Currency set (issued in 1994). Uncirculated silver dollar, Matte Finish 1994P Jefferson nickel, and $2 Federal Reserve Note. . . . . . . . . . . . . . . . . . . . . . . . | | 25 |

(1994) World Cup Tournament

| | Distribution | Mint Pkg |
|---|---|---|
| 1994D, World Cup Tournament clad half dollar, Uncirculated . . . . . . . . . . . . . . . . . . . . . . . . . . . . | 168,208 | $5 |
| 1994P, World Cup Tournament clad half dollar, Proof . . . . . . . . . . . . . . . . . . . . . . . . . . . . . . . . | (609,354) | 5 |
| 1994D, World Cup Tournament silver dollar, Uncirculated . . . . . . . . . . . . . . . . . . . . . . . . . . . . | 81,524 | 16 |
| 1994S, World Cup Tournament silver dollar, Proof . . . . . . . . . . . . . . . . . . . . . . . . . . . . . . . . . | (577,090) | 16 |
| 1994W, World Cup Tournament gold $5, Uncirculated . . . . . . . . . . . . . . . . . . . . . . . . . . . . . . . | 22,447 | 450 |
| 1994W, World Cup Tournament gold $5, Proof . . . . . . . . . . . . . . . . . . . . . . . . . . . . . . . . . . . . | (89,614) | 450 |
| 2-coin set. Uncirculated clad half dollar and silver dollar . . . . . . . . . . . . . . . . . . . . . . . . . . . . | | 21 |
| 2-coin set. Proof clad half dollar and silver dollar . . . . . . . . . . . . . . . . . . . . . . . . . . . . . . . . | | 21 |
| 3-coin set. Uncirculated clad half dollar, silver dollar, and gold $5 . . . . . . . . . . . . . . . . . . . . . | | 471 |
| 3-coin set. Proof clad half dollar, silver dollar, and gold $5. . . . . . . . . . . . . . . . . . . . . . . . . . . | | 471 |
| 6-coin set. One each of Proof and Uncirculated clad half dollar, silver dollar, and gold $5 **(a)** . . . . . . . . | | 942 |
| Young Collector set. Uncirculated clad half dollar. . . . . . . . . . . . . . . . . . . . . . . . . . . . . . . . . | | 5 |
| Special Edition set. Proof clad half dollar and silver dollar . . . . . . . . . . . . . . . . . . . . . . . . . . . | | 25 |

*Note:* Proof World Cup Tournament half dollars and silver dollars were also included in Prestige Sets; see page 236. The Mint also issued other minor sets under this program; they are not listed here. **a.** Packaged in a cherrywood box.

(1994) Vietnam Veterans Memorial

| | Distribution | Mint Pkg |
|---|---|---|
| 1994W, Vietnam Veterans Memorial silver dollar, Uncirculated. . . . . . . . . . . . . . . . . . . . . . . . . | 57,290 | $32 |
| 1994P, Vietnam Veterans Memorial silver dollar, Proof . . . . . . . . . . . . . . . . . . . . . . . . . . . . . | (227,671) | 33 |

*Chart continued on next page.*

| | Distribution | Mint Pkg |
|---|---|---|
| U.S. Veterans set. Uncirculated Vietnam, POW, and Women in Military Service silver dollars (a). . . . . . . | | $75 |
| U.S. Veterans set. Proof Vietnam, POW, and Women in Military Service silver dollars (a) . . . . . . . . . . . . | | 72 |

**a.** Same set as listed under U.S. Prisoner of War Museum and Women in Military Service Memorial.

(1994) U.S. Prisoner of War Museum

| | Distribution | Mint Pkg |
|---|---|---|
| 1994W, U.S. Prisoner of War Museum silver dollar, Uncirculated . . . . . . . . . . . . . . . . . . . . . . . . 54,893 | | $32 |
| 1994P, U.S. Prisoner of War Museum silver dollar, Proof . . . . . . . . . . . . . . . . . . . . . . . . . . . . (224,449) | | 24 |
| U.S. Veterans set. Uncirculated POW, Vietnam, and Women in Military Service silver dollars (a). . . . . . . | | 75 |
| U.S. Veterans set. Proof POW, Vietnam, and Women in Military Service silver dollars (a) . . . . . . . . . . . . | | 72 |

**a.** Same set as listed under Vietnam Veterans Memorial and Women in Military Service Memorial.

(1994) Women in Military Service Memorial

| | Distribution | Mint Pkg |
|---|---|---|
| 1994W, Women in Military Service Memorial silver dollar, Uncirculated . . . . . . . . . . . . . . . . . . 69,860 | | $21 |
| 1994P, Women in Military Service Memorial silver dollar, Proof . . . . . . . . . . . . . . . . . . . . . . . (241,278) | | 23 |
| U.S. Veterans set. Uncirculated Women in Military Service, POW, and Vietnam silver dollars (a). . . . . . . | | 75 |
| U.S. Veterans set. Proof Women in Military Service, POW, and Vietnam silver dollars (a) . . . . . . . . . . . . | | 72 |

**a.** Same set as listed under Vietnam Veterans Memorial and U.S. Prisoner of War Museum.

### (1994) U.S. Capitol Bicentennial

| | Distribution | Mint Pkg |
|---|---|---|
| 1994D, U.S. Capitol Bicentennial silver dollar, Uncirculated . . . . . . . . . . . . . . . . . . . . . . . . . . . . . | 68,332 | $16 |
| 1994S, U.S. Capitol Bicentennial silver dollar, Proof. . . . . . . . . . . . . . . . . . . . . . . . . . . . . . . | (279,579) | 18 |

### (1995) Civil War Battlefield Preservation

| | Distribution | Mint Pkg |
|---|---|---|
| 1995S, Civil War Battlefield Preservation clad half dollar, Uncirculated . . . . . . . . . . . . . . . . . . | 119,520 | $20 |
| 1995S, Civil War Battlefield Preservation clad half dollar, Proof . . . . . . . . . . . . . . . . . . . . . . . | (330,002) | 20 |
| 1995P, Civil War Battlefield Preservation silver dollar, Uncirculated . . . . . . . . . . . . . . . . . . . . | 45,866 | 34 |
| 1995S, Civil War Battlefield Preservation silver dollar, Proof. . . . . . . . . . . . . . . . . . . . . . . . . | (437,114) | 24 |
| 1995W, Civil War Battlefield Preservation gold $5, Uncirculated. . . . . . . . . . . . . . . . . . . . . . . | 12,735 | 450 |
| 1995W, Civil War Battlefield Preservation gold $5, Proof . . . . . . . . . . . . . . . . . . . . . . . . . . . | (55,246) | 450 |
| 2 coin set. Uncirculated clad half dollar and silver dollar. . . . . . . . . . . . . . . . . . . . . . . . . . . . . . | | 54 |
| 2-coin set. Proof clad half dollar and silver dollar . . . . . . . . . . . . . . . . . . . . . . . . . . . . . . . . . | | 44 |
| 3-coin set. Uncirculated clad half dollar, silver dollar, and gold $5. . . . . . . . . . . . . . . . . . . . . | | 505 |
| 3-coin set. Proof clad half dollar, silver dollar, and gold $5. . . . . . . . . . . . . . . . . . . . . . . . . . | | 490 |
| 6-coin set. One each of Proof and Uncirculated clad half dollar, silver dollar, and gold $5 **(a)** . . . . . . . . | | 1,000 |
| Young Collector set. Uncirculated clad half dollar. . . . . . . . . . . . . . . . . . . . . . . . . . . . . . . . . . | | 20 |
| 2-coin Union set. Proof clad half dollar and silver dollar in photo case. . . . . . . . . . . . . . . . . . . | | 50 |
| 3-coin Union set. Proof clad half dollar, silver dollar, and gold $5 in photo case. . . . . . . . . . . . . | | 500 |

*Note:* Proof Civil War Battlefield Preservation half dollars and silver dollars were also included in Prestige Sets; see page 236. **a.** Packaged in a cherrywood box.

(1995–1996) Atlanta Centennial Olympic Games

| | Distribution | Mint Pkg |
|---|---|---|
| 1995S, Basketball clad half dollar, Uncirculated | 171,001 | $10.00 |
| 1995S, Basketball clad half dollar, Proof | (169,655) | 10.50 |
| 1995S, Baseball clad half dollar, Uncirculated | 164,605 | 11.00 |
| 1995S, Baseball clad half dollar, Proof | (118,087) | 11.00 |
| 1996S, Swimming clad half dollar, Uncirculated | 49,533 | 40.00 |
| 1996S, Swimming clad half dollar, Proof | (114,315) | 13.00 |
| 1996S, Soccer clad half dollar, Uncirculated | 52,836 | 27.00 |
| 1996S, Soccer clad half dollar, Proof | (112,412) | 27.00 |
| 1995D, Gymnastics silver dollar, Uncirculated | 42,497 | 28.00 |
| 1995P, Gymnastics silver dollar, Proof | (182,676) | 17.00 |
| 1995D, Paralympics silver dollar, Uncirculated | 28,649 | 60.00 |
| 1995P, Paralympics silver dollar, Proof | (138,337) | 23.00 |
| 1995D, Track and Field silver dollar, Uncirculated | 24,976 | 37.00 |
| 1995P, Track and Field silver dollar, Proof | (136,935) | 22.00 |
| 1995D, Cycling silver dollar, Uncirculated | 19,662 | 60.00 |
| 1995P, Cycling silver dollar, Proof | (118,795) | 24.00 |
| 1996D, Tennis silver dollar, Uncirculated | 15,983 | 60.00 |
| 1996P, Tennis silver dollar, Proof | (92,016) | 37.00 |
| 1996D, Paralympics silver dollar, Uncirculated | 14,497 | 65.00 |
| 1996P, Paralympics silver dollar, Proof | (84,280) | 23.00 |
| 1996D, Rowing silver dollar, Uncirculated | 16,258 | 85.00 |
| 1996P, Rowing silver dollar, Proof | (151,890) | 33.00 |
| 1996D, High Jump silver dollar, Uncirculated | 15,697 | 100.00 |
| 1996P, High Jump silver dollar, Proof | (124,502) | 24.00 |
| 1995W, Torch Runner gold $5, Uncirculated | 14,675 | 450.00 |
| 1995W, Torch Runner gold $5, Proof | (57,442) | 450.00 |
| 1995W, Stadium gold $5, Uncirculated | 10,579 | 450.00 |
| 1995W, Stadium gold $5, Proof | (43,124) | 450.00 |
| 1996W, Flag Bearer gold $5, Uncirculated | 9,174 | 450.00 |
| 1996W, Flag Bearer gold $5, Proof | (32,886) | 450.00 |

*Note: Proof Atlanta Centennial Olympic Games half dollars and silver dollars were also included in Prestige Sets; see page 236.*

| | Distribution | Mint Pkg |
|---|---|---|
| 1996W, Cauldron gold $5, Uncirculated | 9,210 | $450 |
| 1996W, Cauldron gold $5, Proof | (38,555) | 450 |
| 2-coin set #1. Proof silver dollars (Gymnastics, Paralympics) | | 50 |
| 4-coin set #1. Uncirculated clad half dollar (Basketball), silver dollars (Gymnastics, Paralympics), and gold $5 (Torch Bearer) | | 550 |
| 4-coin set #2. Proof clad half dollar (Basketball), silver dollars (Gymnastics, Paralympics), and gold ($5 Torch Bearer) | | 490 |
| 4-coin set #3. Proof clad half dollar (Baseball), silver dollars (Cyclist, Track Runner), and gold $5 (Olympic Stadium) | | 515 |
| Young Collector's set #1. Uncirculated Basketball clad half dollar | | 15 |
| Young Collector's set #2. Uncirculated Baseball clad half dollar | | 15 |
| Young Collector's set #3. Uncirculated Swimming clad half dollar | | 65 |
| Young Collector's set #4. Uncirculated Soccer clad half dollar | | 35 |
| 1995–1996 16-coin set. One each of all Uncirculated coins **(a)** | | 2,450 |
| 1995–1996 16-coin set. One each of all Proof coins **(a)** | | 2,350 |
| 1995–1996 8-coin set. One each of all Proof silver dollars | | 230 |
| 1995–1996 32-coin set. One each of all Uncirculated and Proof coins **(a)** | | 4,800 |

*Note:* Proof Atlanta Centennial Olympic Games half dollars and silver dollars were also included in Prestige Sets; see page 236. **a.** Packaged in a cherrywood box.

**(1995) Special Olympics World Games**

| | Distribution | Mint Pkg |
|---|---|---|
| 1995W, Special Olympics World Games silver dollar, Uncirculated | 89,301 | $25 |
| 1995P, Special Olympics World Games silver dollar, Proof | (351,764) | 16 |
| 2-coin set. Proof silver dollar and 1995S Kennedy half dollar | | 35 |

**(1996) National Community Service**

*See next page for chart.*

| | Distribution | Mint Pkg |
|---|---|---|
| 1996S, National Community Service silver dollar, Uncirculated . . . . . . . . . . . . . . . . . . . . . . . . 23,500 | | $45 |
| 1996S, National Community Service silver dollar, Proof . . . . . . . . . . . . . . . . . . . . . . . . . . . . (101,543) | | 16 |
| Coin and Stamp set. Proof silver dollar and 3¢ Saint-Gaudens postage stamp . . . . . . . . . . . . . . . . . . . | | 30 |

### (1996) Smithsonian Institution 150th Anniversary

| | Distribution | Mint Pkg |
|---|---|---|
| 1996D, Smithsonian Institution 150th Anniversary silver dollar, Uncirculated . . . . . . . . . . . . . . . 31,320 | | $24 |
| 1996P, Smithsonian Institution 150th Anniversary silver dollar, Proof . . . . . . . . . . . . . . . . . . . (129,152) | | 34 |
| 1996W, Smithsonian Institution 150th Anniversary gold $5, Uncirculated . . . . . . . . . . . . . . . . . 9,068 | | 450 |
| 1996W, Smithsonian Institution 150th Anniversary gold $5, Proof . . . . . . . . . . . . . . . . . . . . . (21,772) | | 450 |
| 2-coin set. Proof silver dollar and gold $5 . . . . . . . . . . . . . . . . . . . . . . . . . . . . . . . . . . . . . | | 480 |
| 4-coin set. One each of Proof and Uncirculated silver dollars and gold $5 **(a)** . . . . . . . . . . . . . . . . . . . | | 950 |
| Young Collector's set. Proof silver dollar . . . . . . . . . . . . . . . . . . . . . . . . . . . . . . . . . . . . . . . | | 30 |

**a.** Packaged in a cherrywood box.

### (1997) U.S. Botanic Garden

| | Distribution | Mint Pkg |
|---|---|---|
| 1997P, U.S. Botanic Garden silver dollar, Uncirculated . . . . . . . . . . . . . . . . . . . . . . . . . . . . . 58,505 | | $16 |
| 1997P, U.S. Botanic Garden silver dollar, Proof . . . . . . . . . . . . . . . . . . . . . . . . . . . . . . . (189,671) | | 27 |
| Coinage and Currency set. Uncirculated silver dollar, Matte Finish 1997P Jefferson nickel, and $1 Federal Reserve Note . . . . . . . . . . . . . . . . . . . . . . . . . . . . . . . . . . . . . . . . . . . . . | | 40 |

*Note:* Proof U.S. Botanic Garden silver dollars were also included in Prestige Sets; see page 236.

(1997) Jackie Robinson

| | Distribution | Mint Pkg |
|---|---|---|
| 1997S, Jackie Robinson silver dollar, Uncirculated .................................... 30,180 | | $35 |
| 1997S, Jackie Robinson silver dollar, Proof...................................... (110,002) | | 38 |
| 1997W, Jackie Robinson gold $5, Uncirculated ...................................... 5,174 | | 450 |
| 1997W, Jackie Robinson gold $5, Proof............................................ (24,072) | | 450 |
| 2-coin set. Proof silver dollar and gold $5............................................. | | 490 |
| 4-coin set. One each of Proof and Uncirculated silver dollars and gold $5 **(a)** ..................... | | 970 |
| Legacy set. Proof gold $5, baseball card, and pin **(a)**......................................... | | 450 |

**a.** Packaged in a cherrywood box.

(1997) Franklin D. Roosevelt

| | Distribution | Mint Pkg |
|---|---|---|
| 1997W, Franklin D. Roosevelt gold $5, Uncirculated .................................... 11,894 | | $450 |
| 1997W, Franklin D. Roosevelt gold $5, Proof...................................... (29,474) | | 450 |
| 2-coin set. One each of Proof and Uncirculated gold $5 ...................................... | | 900 |

(1997) National Law Enforcement Officers Memorial

| | Distribution | Mint Pkg |
|---|---|---|
| 1997P, National Law Enforcement Officers Memorial silver dollar, Uncirculated.............. 28,575 | | $65 |
| 1997P, National Law Enforcement Officers Memorial silver dollar, Proof ................ (110,428) | | 32 |
| Insignia set. Proof silver dollar, lapel pin, and patch......................................... | | 35 |

223

**(1998) Robert F. Kennedy**

| | Distribution | Mint Pkg |
|---|---|---|
| 1998S, Robert F. Kennedy silver dollar, Uncirculated . . . . . . . . . . . . . . . . . . . . . . . . . . . . . . . . . | 106,422 | $20 |
| 1998S, Robert F. Kennedy silver dollar, Proof. . . . . . . . . . . . . . . . . . . . . . . . . . . . . . . . . . . . . . . | (99,020) | 34 |
| 2-coin Collector's set. Uncirculated RFK silver dollar and Matte Finish 1998S JFK silver half dollar. . . . . | | 85 |
| 2-coin set. Proof and Uncirculated RFK silver dollars. . . . . . . . . . . . . . . . . . . . . . . . . . . . . . . . . . | | 53 |

**(1998) Black Revolutionary War Patriots**

| | Distribution | Mint Pkg |
|---|---|---|
| 1998S, Black Revolutionary War Patriots silver dollar, Uncirculated . . . . . . . . . . . . . . . . . . . . . | 37,210 | $40 |
| 1998S, Black Revolutionary War Patriots silver dollar, Proof. . . . . . . . . . . . . . . . . . . . . . . . . . . | (75,070) | 34 |
| 2-coin set. Proof and Uncirculated silver dollars . . . . . . . . . . . . . . . . . . . . . . . . . . . . . . . . . . . . | | 74 |
| Young Collector set. Uncirculated silver dollar . . . . . . . . . . . . . . . . . . . . . . . . . . . . . . . . . . . . . . | | 30 |
| Coin and Stamp set. Proof silver dollar and four themed postage stamps (10¢, 13¢, 15¢, and 25¢) . . . . | | 30 |

**(1999) Dolley Madison**

| | Distribution | Mint Pkg |
|---|---|---|
| 1999P, Dolley Madison silver dollar, Uncirculated | 89,104 | $20 |
| 1999P, Dolley Madison silver dollar, Proof | (224,403) | 20 |
| 2-coin set. Proof and Uncirculated silver dollars | | 40 |

**(1999) George Washington Death Bicentennial**

| | Distribution | Mint Pkg |
|---|---|---|
| 1999W, George Washington Death Bicentennial gold $5, Uncirculated | 22,511 | $450 |
| 1999W, George Washington Death Bicentennial gold $5, Proof | (41,693) | 450 |
| 2-coin set. One each of Proof and Uncirculated gold $5 | | 900 |

**(1999) Yellowstone National Park**

| | Distribution | Mint Pkg |
|---|---|---|
| 1999P, Yellowstone National Park silver dollar, Uncirculated | 82,563 | $24 |
| 1999P, Yellowstone National Park silver dollar, Proof | (187,595) | 24 |
| 2-coin set. One each of Proof and Uncirculated gold $5 | | 48 |

**(2000) Library of Congress Bicentennial**

*See next page for chart.*

| | Distribution | Mint Pkg |
|---|---|---|
| 2000P, Library of Congress Bicentennial silver dollar, Uncirculated . . . . . . . . . . . . . . . . . . . . . 53,264 | | $16 |
| 2000P, Library of Congress Bicentennial silver dollar, Proof . . . . . . . . . . . . . . . . . . . . . . . . . (198,503) | | 18 |
| 2000W, Library of Congress Bicentennial bimetallic (gold/platinum) $10, Uncirculated . . . . . . . . 7,261 | | 800 |
| 2000W, Library of Congress Bicentennial bimetallic (gold/platinum) $10, Proof . . . . . . . . . . . . (27,445) | | 750 |

### (2000) Leif Ericson Millennium

| | Distribution | Mint Pkg |
|---|---|---|
| 2000P, Leif Ericson Millennium silver dollar, Uncirculated . . . . . . . . . . . . . . . . . . . . . . . . . . . . 28,150 | | $42 |
| 2000P, Leif Ericson Millennium silver dollar, Proof . . . . . . . . . . . . . . . . . . . . . . . . . . . . . . . . (144,748) | | 32 |
| 2-coin set. Proof silver dollar and Icelandic 1,000 krónur . . . . . . . . . . . . . . . . . . . . . . . . . . . . . . | | 50 |

### (2001) American Buffalo Commemorative

| | Distribution | Mint Pkg |
|---|---|---|
| 2001D, American Buffalo silver dollar, Uncirculated . . . . . . . . . . . . . . . . . . . . . . . . . . . . . . . . 227,131 | | $65 |
| 2001P, American Buffalo silver dollar, Proof . . . . . . . . . . . . . . . . . . . . . . . . . . . . . . . . . . . . . (272,869) | | 75 |
| 2-coin set. One each of Proof and Uncirculated silver dollars . . . . . . . . . . . . . . . . . . . . . . . . . . . | | 140 |
| Coinage and Currency set. Uncirculated silver dollar, face reprint of 1899 $5 Indian Chief Silver Certificate, 1987 Chief Red Cloud 10¢ stamp, and 2001 Bison 21¢ stamp . . . . . . . . . . . . . . . . . . | | 85 |

## (2001) Capitol Visitor Center

| | Distribution | Mint Pkg |
|---|---|---|
| 2001P, U.S. Capitol Visitor Center clad half dollar, Uncirculated . . . . . . . . . . . . . . . . . . . . . . . . . . . . . . . 99,157 | | $12 |
| 2001P, U.S. Capitol Visitor Center clad half dollar, Proof. . . . . . . . . . . . . . . . . . . . . . . . . . . . . . . . (77,962) | | 14 |
| 2001P, U.S. Capitol Visitor Center silver dollar, Uncirculated. . . . . . . . . . . . . . . . . . . . . . . . . . . . . 35,380 | | 16 |
| 2001P, U.S. Capitol Visitor Center silver dollar, Proof . . . . . . . . . . . . . . . . . . . . . . . . . . . . . . . . (143,793) | | 24 |
| 2001W, U.S. Capitol Visitor Center gold $5, Uncirculated . . . . . . . . . . . . . . . . . . . . . . . . . . . . . . . . 6,761 | | 450 |
| 2001W, U.S. Capitol Visitor Center gold $5, Proof . . . . . . . . . . . . . . . . . . . . . . . . . . . . . . . . . . . (27,652) | | 450 |
| 3-coin set. Proof clad half dollar, silver dollar, and gold $5. . . . . . . . . . . . . . . . . . . . . . . . . . . . . . . . . . . | | 490 |

## (2002) Salt Lake Olympic Games

| | Distribution | Mint Pkg |
|---|---|---|
| 2002P, Salt Lake Olympic Games silver dollar, Uncirculated. . . . . . . . . . . . . . . . . . . . . . . . . . . . . . . 40,257 | | $21 |
| 2002P, Salt Lake Olympic Games silver dollar, Proof . . . . . . . . . . . . . . . . . . . . . . . . . . . . . . . . . (166,864) | | 16 |
| 2002W, Salt Lake Olympic Games gold $5, Uncirculated . . . . . . . . . . . . . . . . . . . . . . . . . . . . . . . 10,585 | | 450 |
| 2002W, Salt Lake Olympic Games gold $5, Proof. . . . . . . . . . . . . . . . . . . . . . . . . . . . . . . . . . . . (32,877) | | 450 |
| 2-coin set. Proof silver dollar and gold $5 . . . . . . . . . . . . . . . . . . . . . . . . . . . . . . . . . . . . . . . . . . | | 470 |
| 4-coin set. One each of Proof and Uncirculated silver dollar and gold $5. . . . . . . . . . . . . . . . . . . . . . | | 940 |

(2002) West Point Bicentennial

| | Distribution | Mint Pkg |
|---|---|---|
| 2002W, West Point Bicentennial silver dollar, Uncirculated............................. | 103,201 | $16 |
| 2002W, West Point Bicentennial silver dollar, Proof ................................. | (288,293) | 26 |

(2003) First Flight Centennial

| | Distribution | Mint Pkg |
|---|---|---|
| 2003P, First Flight Centennial clad half dollar, Uncirculated ............................ | 57,122 | $12 |
| 2003P, First Flight Centennial clad half dollar, Proof.................................. | (109,710) | 13 |
| 2003P, First Flight Centennial silver dollar, Uncirculated................................ | 53,533 | 24 |
| 2003P, First Flight Centennial silver dollar, Proof .................................. | (190,240) | 26 |
| 2003W, First Flight Centennial gold $10, Uncirculated................................ | 10,009 | 900 |
| 2003W, First Flight Centennial gold $10, Proof.................................... | (21,676) | 900 |
| 3-coin set. Proof clad half dollar, silver dollar, and gold $10..................................... | | 940 |

## (2004) Thomas Alva Edison

| | Distribution | Mint Pkg |
|---|---|---|
| 2004P, Thomas Alva Edison silver dollar, Uncirculated . . . . . . . . . . . . . . . . . . . . . . . . . . . . . . . . . . | 92,510 | $16 |
| 2004P, Thomas Alva Edison silver dollar, Proof. . . . . . . . . . . . . . . . . . . . . . . . . . . . . . . . . . . . . . . | (211,055) | 16 |
| Collector's set. Uncirculated silver dollar in case with functioning light bulb . . . . . . . . . . . . . . . . . . . . . | | 16 |

## (2004) Lewis and Clark Bicentennial

| | Distribution | Mint Pkg |
|---|---|---|
| 2004P, Lewis and Clark Bicentennial silver dollar, Uncirculated . . . . . . . . . . . . . . . . . . . . . . . . | 142,015 | $16 |
| 2004P, Lewis and Clark Bicentennial silver dollar, Proof. . . . . . . . . . . . . . . . . . . . . . . . . . . . . . . | (351,989) | 17 |
| Coin and Pouch set. Proof silver dollar and beaded pouch . . . . . . . . . . . . . . . . . . . . . . . . . . . . . . | | 18 |
| Coinage and Currency set. Uncirculated silver dollar, 2004D Sacagawea dollar, 2005P and 2005D nickels, Series of 1901 $10 Bison note replica, silver-plated Thomas Jefferson Peace Medal replica, three themed 37¢ postage stamps, and two booklets . . . . . . . . . . . . . . . . . . . . . . . . . . . . . . | | 20 |

## (2005) Chief Justice John Marshall

*See next page for chart.*

| | Distribution | Mint Pkg |
|---|---|---|
| 2005P, Chief Justice John Marshall silver dollar, Uncirculated . . . . . . . . . . . . . . . . . . . . . . . . | 67,096 | $16 |
| 2005P, Chief Justice John Marshall silver dollar, Proof. . . . . . . . . . . . . . . . . . . . . . . . . . . . | (196,753) | 16 |
| Coin and Chronicles set. Uncirculated silver dollar, booklet, and BEP intaglio portrait. . . . . . . . . . . . . . . | | 17 |
| American Legacy set. Proof Marine Corps and John Marshall dollars, 11-piece Proof set **(a)** . . . . . . . . . . | | 50 |

**a.** Same set as listed under Marine Corps 230th Anniversary.

### (2005) Marine Corps 230th Anniversary

| | Distribution | Mint Pkg |
|---|---|---|
| 2005P, Marine Corps 230th Anniversary silver dollar, Uncirculated . . . . . . . . . . . . . . . . . . . . . . | 49,671 | $30 |
| 2005P, Marine Corps 230th Anniversary silver dollar, Proof . . . . . . . . . . . . . . . . . . . . . . . . . . | (548,810) | 35 |
| Coin and Stamp set. Uncirculated silver dollar and themed 3¢ postage stamp . . . . . . . . . . . . . . . . . . | | 30 |
| American Legacy set. Proof Marine Corps and John Marshall silver dollars, 11-piece Proof set **(a)**. . . . . . . | | 50 |

**a.** Same set as listed under Chief Justice James Marshall.

### (2006) Benjamin Franklin Tercentenary

| | Distribution | Mint Pkg |
|---|---|---|
| 2006P, Benjamin Franklin "Scientist" silver dollar, Uncirculated. . . . . . . . . . . . . . . . . . . . . . . . | 58,000 | $16 |
| 2006P, Benjamin Franklin "Scientist" silver dollar, Proof . . . . . . . . . . . . . . . . . . . . . . . . . . . | (142,000) | 19 |

| | Distribution | Mint Pkg |
|---|---|---|
| 2006P, Benjamin Franklin "Founding Father" silver dollar, Uncirculated . . . . . . . . . . . . . . . . . . 58,000 | | $18 |
| 2006P, Benjamin Franklin "Founding Father" silver dollar, Proof. . . . . . . . . . . . . . . . . . . . . . (142,000) | | 20 |
| Coin and Chronicles set. Uncirculated "Scientist" silver dollar, four themed 39¢ postage stamps, *Poor Richard's Almanack* replica, and intaglio print . . . . . . . . . . . . . . . . . . . . . . . . . . . | | 17 |
| American Legacy set. Proof "Founding Father" silver dollar; Proof San Francisco Old Mint silver dollar; and Proof cent, nickel, dime, quarter, half dollar, and Sacagawea dollar **(a)**. . . . . . . . | | 45 |

a. Same set as listed under San Francisco Old Mint Centennial.

| | Distribution | Mint Pkg |
|---|---|---|
| 2006S, San Francisco Old Mint Centennial silver dollar, Uncirculated . . . . . . . . . . . . . . . . . . . . 67,100 | | $25 |
| 2006S, San Francisco Old Mint Centennial silver dollar, Proof . . . . . . . . . . . . . . . . . . . . . . . (160,870) | | 26 |
| 2006S, San Francisco Old Mint Centennial gold $5, Uncirculated . . . . . . . . . . . . . . . . . . . . . 17,500 | | 450 |
| 2006S, San Francisco Old Mint Centennial gold $5, Proof . . . . . . . . . . . . . . . . . . . . . . . . . . (44,174) | | 450 |
| American Legacy set. Proof San Francisco Old Mint silver dollar; Proof "Founding Father" silver dollar; and Proof cent, nickel, dime, quarter, half dollar, and Sacagawea dollar **(a)**. . . . . . . . | | 45 |

| | Distribution | Mint Pkg |
|---|---|---|
| 2007P, Jamestown 400th Anniversary silver dollar, Uncirculated . . . . . . . . . . . . . . . . . . . . . . . 81,034 | | 16 |
| 2007P, Jamestown 400th Anniversary silver dollar, Proof. . . . . . . . . . . . . . . . . . . . . . . . . . . (260,363) | | 20 |
| 2007W, Jamestown 400th Anniversary gold $5, Uncirculated . . . . . . . . . . . . . . . . . . . . . . . . 18,623 | | 450 |
| 2007W, Jamestown 400th Anniversary gold $5, Proof. . . . . . . . . . . . . . . . . . . . . . . . . . . . . (47,123) | | 450 |
| American Legacy set. Proof Jamestown silver dollar; Proof Little Rock Central High School Desegregation silver dollar; and 14-piece Proof Set **(b)**. . . . . . . . . . . . . . . . . . . . . . . . . . . | | 42 |

| | Distribution | Mint Pkg |
|---|---|---|
| 2007P, Little Rock Central High School Desegregation silver dollar, Uncirculated . . . . . . . . . . . 124,678 | | 16 |
| 2007P, Little Rock Central High School Desegregation silver dollar, Proof . . . . . . . . . . . . . . . . (66,093) | | 16 |
| Coin and Medal set. Uncirculated silver dollar, bronze medal. . . . . . . . . . . . . . . . . . . . . . . . . . . . | | 17 |
| American Legacy set. Proof Little Rock Central High School Desegregation silver dollar; Proof Jamestown silver dollar; and 14-piece Proof Set **(c)** . . . . . . . . . . . . . . . . . . . . . . . . . . . . | | 42 |

| | Distribution | Mint Pkg |
|---|---|---|
| 2008S, Bald Eagle Recovery and National Emblem clad half dollar, Uncirculated. . . . . . . . . . . 120,180 | | 10 |
| 2008S, Bald Eagle Recovery and National Emblem clad half dollar, Proof . . . . . . . . . . . . . . (220,577) | | 12 |
| 2008P, Bald Eagle Recovery and National Emblem silver dollar, Uncirculated. . . . . . . . . . . . . 119,204 | | 17 |
| 2008P, Bald Eagle Recovery and National Emblem silver dollar, Proof . . . . . . . . . . . . . . . . . (294,601) | | 16 |
| 2008W, Bald Eagle Recovery and National Emblem gold $5, Uncirculated. . . . . . . . . . . . . . . . 15,009 | | 450 |
| 2008W, Bald Eagle Recovery and National Emblem gold $5, Proof. . . . . . . . . . . . . . . . . . . . . (59,269) | | 450 |
| 3-coin set. Proof clad half dollar, silver dollar, and gold $5. . . . . . . . . . . . . . . . . . . . . . . . . . . . . | | 478 |
| Coin and Medal set. Uncirculated silver dollar and bronze Bald Eagle medal . . . . . . . . . . . . . . . . . | | 17 |
| Young Collector set. Uncirculated clad half dollar. . . . . . . . . . . . . . . . . . . . . . . . . . . . . . . . . . . . | | 10 |
| American Legacy set. Proof Bald Eagle silver dollar and 14-piece Proof Set . . . . . . . . . . . . . . . . . . | | 45 |

| | Distribution | Mint Pkg |
|---|---|---|
| 2009P, Louis Braille Bicentennial silver dollar, Uncirculated . . . . . . . . . . . . . . . . . . . . . . . . . . . 82,639 | | 16 |
| 2009P, Louis Braille Bicentennial silver dollar, Proof. . . . . . . . . . . . . . . . . . . . . . . . . . . . . . (135,235) | | 16 |
| Education set. Uncirculated silver dollar in tri-fold package. . . . . . . . . . . . . . . . . . . . . . . . . . . . . | | 17 |

| | Distribution | Mint Pkg |
|---|---|---|
| 2009P, Abraham Lincoln Bicentennial silver dollar, Uncirculated . . . . . . . . . . . . . . . . . . . . . . . 125,000 | | 21 |
| 2009P, Abraham Lincoln Bicentennial silver dollar, Proof . . . . . . . . . . . . . . . . . . . . . . . . . . . (325,000) | | 24 |
| Coin and Chronicles set. Proof silver dollar and the four Proof 2009S Lincoln Bicentennial cents . . . . . . | | 28 |

| | Distribution | Mint Pkg |
|---|---|---|
| 2010W, American Veterans Disabled for Life silver dollar, Uncirculated . . . . . . . . . . . . . . . . . . 78,301 | | 21 |
| 2010W, American Veterans Disabled for Life silver dollar, Proof. . . . . . . . . . . . . . . . . . . . . . (202,770) | | 16 |

| | Distribution | Mint Pkg |
|---|---|---|
| 2010P, Boy Scouts of America Centennial silver dollar, Uncirculated . . . . . . . . . . . . . . . . . . . . 105,020 | | 24 |
| 2010P, Boy Scouts of America Centennial silver dollar, Proof. . . . . . . . . . . . . . . . . . . . . . . . . (244,963) | | 21 |

**a.** Same set as listed under Benjamin Franklin Tercentenary. **b.** Same set as listed under Little Rock Central High School Desegregation. **c.** Same set as listed under Jamestown 400th Anniversary.

*Chart continued on next page.*

| | Distribution | Mint Pkg |
|---|---|---|
| 2011S, Medal of Honor silver dollar, Uncirculated | 44,752 | $28 |
| 2011P, Medal of Honor silver dollar, Proof | (112,833) | 28 |
| 2011P, Medal of Honor gold $5, Uncirculated | 8,233 | 450 |
| 2011W, Medal of Honor gold $5, Proof | (17,999) | 450 |
| 2011D, U.S. Army clad half dollar, Uncirculated | 39,442 | 18 |
| 2011S, U.S. Army clad half dollar, Proof | (68,332) | 40 |
| 2011S, U.S. Army silver dollar, Uncirculated | 43,512 | 28 |
| 2011P, U.S. Army silver dollar, Proof | (119,829) | 27 |
| 2011P, U.S. Army gold $5, Uncirculated | 8,052 | 450 |
| 2011W, U.S. Army gold $5, Proof | (17,148) | 450 |
| 2012W, Infantry Soldier silver dollar, Uncirculated | 44,348 | 26 |
| 2012W, Infantry Soldier silver dollar, Proof | (161,151) | 31 |
| 2012P, Star-Spangled Banner silver dollar, Uncirculated | 41,686 | 27 |
| 2012P, Star-Spangled Banner silver dollar, Proof | (169,065) | 28 |
| 2012W, Star-Spangled Banner gold $5, Uncirculated | 7,027 | 450 |
| 2012W, Star-Spangled Banner gold $5, Proof | (18,313) | 450 |
| 2-coin set. Proof silver dollar and gold $5 | | 478 |
| 2013W, Girl Scouts of the U.S.A. Centennial silver dollar, Uncirculated | 37,462 | 24 |
| 2013W, Girl Scouts of the U.S.A. Centennial silver dollar, Proof | (86,355) | 27 |
| Young Collectors set. Uncirculated silver dollar | | 24 |
| 2013D, 5-Star Generals clad half dollar, Uncirculated | 38,095 | 12 |
| 2013S, 5-Star Generals clad half dollar, Proof | (47,326) | 24 |
| 2013W, 5-Star Generals silver dollar, Uncirculated | 34,638 | 36 |
| 2013P, 5-Star Generals silver dollar, Proof | (69,283) | 40 |
| 2013P, 5-Star Generals gold $5, Uncirculated | 5,667 | 450 |
| 2013W, 5-Star Generals gold $5, Proof | (15,844) | 450 |
| 3-coin set. Proof clad half dollar, silver dollar, and gold $5 | | 515 |
| Profile Collection. Unc. half dollar and silver dollar, bronze MacArthur Congressional Gold Medal replica | | 50 |
| 2014D, National Baseball Hall of Fame clad half dollar, Uncirculated (d) | 142,405 | 16 |
| 2014S, National Baseball Hall of Fame clad half dollar, Proof (d) | (249,049) | 22 |
| 2014P, National Baseball Hall of Fame silver dollar, Uncirculated (d) | 131,910 | 32 |
| 2014P, National Baseball Hall of Fame silver dollar, Proof (d) | (267,847) | 30 |
| 2014W, National Baseball Hall of Fame gold $5, Uncirculated (d) | 17,674 | 450 |
| 2014W, National Baseball Hall of Fame gold $5, Proof (d) | (32,428) | 450 |
| Young Collectors set. Uncirculated clad half dollar (d) | | 32 |
| 2014P, Civil Rights Act of 1964 silver dollar, Uncirculated | 24,720 | 35 |
| 2014P, Civil Rights Act of 1964 silver dollar, Proof | (61,992) | 40 |
| 2015D, U.S. Marshals Service 225th Anniversary clad half dollar, Uncirculated | 30,231 | 13 |
| 2015S, U.S. Marshals Service 225th Anniversary clad half dollar, Proof | (76,549) | 15 |
| 2015P, U.S. Marshals Service 225th Anniversary silver dollar, Uncirculated | 38,149 | 450 |
| 2015P, U.S. Marshals Service 225th Anniversary silver dollar, Proof | (124,329) | 34 |
| 2015W, U.S. Marshals Service 225th Anniversary gold $5, Uncirculated | 6,743 | 450 |
| 2015W, U.S. Marshals Service 225th Anniversary gold $5, Proof | (24,959) | 450 |
| 3-coin set. Proof clad half dollar, silver dollar, and gold $5 | | 575 |

d. The obverse of each denomination is concave; the reverse is convex.

| | Distribution | Mint Pkg |
|---|---|---|
| 2015P, March of Dimes 75th Anniversary silver dollar, Uncirculated. | 24,742 | $32 |
| 2015W, March of Dimes 75th Anniversary silver dollar, Proof. | (32,030) | 26 |
| Special Silver set. Proof silver dollar, silver Proof and Reverse Proof dimes | | 30 |
| 2016P, Mark Twain silver dollar, Uncirculated. | 26,291 | 26 |
| 2016P, Mark Twain silver dollar, Proof | (78,549) | 26 |
| 2016W, Mark Twain gold $5, Uncirculated | 5,701 | 450 |
| 2016W, Mark Twain gold $5, Proof | (13,271) | 460 |
| 2016D, National Park Service 100th Anniversary clad half dollar, Uncirculated | 21,335 | 18 |
| 2016S, National Park Service 100th Anniversary clad half dollar, Proof | (54,962) | 18 |
| 2016P, National Park Service 100th Anniversary silver dollar, Uncirculated | 21,003 | 26 |
| 2016P, National Park Service 100th Anniversary silver dollar, Proof. | (77,367) | 28 |
| 2016W, National Park Service 100th Anniversary gold $5, Uncirculated. | 5,201 | 450 |
| 2016W, National Park Service 100th Anniversary gold $5, Proof | (19,510) | 460 |
| 3-coin set. Proof clad half dollar, silver dollar, and gold $5. | | 500 |
| 2017P, Lions Club International Century of Service silver dollar, Uncirculated. | 17,247 | 35 |
| 2017P, Lions Club International Century of Service silver dollar, Proof | (68,519) | 32 |
| 2017S, Boys Town Centennial clad half dollar, Uncirculated | 15,525 | 20 |
| 2017D, Boys Town Centennial clad half dollar, Proof. | (23,164) | 22 |
| 2017P, Boys Town Centennial silver dollar, Uncirculated | 12,234 | 35 |
| 2017P, Boys Town Centennial silver dollar, Proof. | (31,610) | 38 |
| 2017W, Boys Town Centennial gold $5, Uncirculated. | 2,947 | 450 |
| 2017W, Boys Town Centennial gold $5, Proof | (7,347) | 450 |
| 3-coin set. Proof clad half dollar, silver dollar, and gold $5. | | 500 |
| 2018P, World War I Centennial silver silver dollar, Uncirculated | 22,336 | 35 |
| 2018P, World War I Centennial silver silver dollar, Proof. | (127,837) | 40 |
| Air Service Medal set. Proof silver dollar and silver Air Service medal | | 80 |
| Army Medal set. Proof silver dollar and silver Army medal. | | 80 |
| Coast Guard Medal set. Proof silver dollar and silver Coast Guard medal. | | 80 |
| Marine Corps Medal set. Proof silver dollar and silver Marine Corps medal | | 80 |
| Navy Medal set. Proof silver dollar and silver Navy medal | | 80 |
| 2018D, Breast Cancer Awareness clad half dollar, Uncirculated. | 11,301 | 15 |
| 2018S, Breast Cancer Awareness clad half dollar, Proof | (22,392) | 18 |
| 2018P, Breast Cancer Awareness silver dollar, Uncirculated. | 12,526 | 35 |
| 2018P, Breast Cancer Awareness silver dollar, Proof | (34,542) | 40 |
| 2018W, Breast Cancer Awareness gold $5, Uncirculated (e) | 4,477 | 450 |
| 2018W, Breast Cancer Awareness gold $5, Proof (e). | (10,386) | 450 |
| Coin and Stamp set. Proof clad half dollar and themed First Class postage stamp. | | 80 |
| 2019D, Apollo 11 50th Anniversary clad half dollar, Uncirculated (d) | 41,738 | 15 |
| 2019S, Apollo 11 50th Anniversary clad half dollar, Proof (d). | (181,811) | 18 |
| 2019P, Apollo 11 50th Anniversary silver dollar, Uncirculated (d,f) | 59,697 | 35 |
| 2019P, Apollo 11 50th Anniversary silver dollar, Proof (d,f) | (223,737) | 35 |
| 2019P, Apollo 11 50th Anniversary 5-oz. silver dollar, Proof (d,f,g) | (68,259) | 160 |
| 2019W, Apollo 11 50th Anniversary gold $5, Uncirculated (d) | 12,035 | 450 |
| 2019W, Apollo 11 50th Anniversary gold $5, Proof (d). | (34,037) | 450 |
| Half dollar set. Uncirculated and Proof clad half dollars (d) | | 40 |

d. The obverse of each denomination is concave; the reverse is convex. e. Produced in "rose pink" gold, composed of .850 gold, .148 copper, and .002 zinc. f. In 2019, the fineness of U.S. Mint silver coins increased from .900 to .999. g. Identical in design to the regular-issue dollar coin, but enlarged to 3 inches in diameter.

*Chart continued on next page.*    

| | Distribution | Mint Pkg |
|---|---|---|
| 2019D, American Legion 100th Anniversary clad half dollar, Uncirculated . . . . . . . . . . . . . . . . . | *11,425* | $15 |
| 2019S, American Legion 100th Anniversary clad half dollar, Proof. . . . . . . . . . . . . . . . . . . . . . | *(27,300)* | 18 |
| 2019P, American Legion 100th Anniversary silver dollar, Uncirculated **(f)** . . . . . . . . . . . . . . . . | *13,788* | 35 |
| 2019P, American Legion 100th Anniversary silver dollar, Proof **(f)** . . . . . . . . . . . . . . . . . . . . . | *(63,144)* | 35 |
| 2019W, American Legion 100th Anniversary gold $5, Uncirculated . . . . . . . . . . . . . . . . . . . . . . | *3,090* | 450 |
| 2019W, American Legion 100th Anniversary gold $5, Proof. . . . . . . . . . . . . . . . . . . . . . . . . . . | *(10,920)* | 450 |
| 3-coin set. Proof clad half dollar, silver dollar **(d)**, and gold $5. . . . . . . . . . . . . . . . . . . . . . | | 500 |
| Silver Dollar and Medal set. Proof silver dollar **(d)** and silver American Veterans medal. . . . . . . . . . . . . | | |
| 2020D, Naismith Mem. Basketball Hall of Fame 60th Anniv. clad half dollar, Uncirculated **(d)** . . . | 13,635 | 15 |
| 2020S, Naismith Mem. Basketball Hall of Fame 60th Anniv. clad half dollar, Proof **(d)**. . . . . . . | (26,572) | 18 |
| 2020S, Naismith Mem. Basketball Hall of Fame 60th Anniv. clad half dollar, Proof, Colorized **(d)**. . . . . . . . . . . . . . . . . . . . . . . . . . . . . . . . . . . . . . | (32,581) | 75 |
| 2020P, Naismith Mem. Basketball Hall of Fame 60th Anniv. silver dollar, Uncirculated **(d,f)** . . . . | 21,317 | 35 |
| 2020P, Naismith Mem. Basketball Hall of Fame 60th Anniv. silver dollar, Proof **(d,f)** . . . . . . . . | (68,756) | 35 |
| 2020P, Naismith Mem. Basketball Hall of Fame 60th Anniv. silver dollar, Proof, Colorized **(d,f)** . | (25,719) | 100 |
| 2020W, Naismith Mem. Basketball Hall of Fame 60th Anniv. gold $5, Uncirculated **(d)** . . . . . . . . | 3,261 | 450 |
| 2020W, Naismith Mem. Basketball Hall of Fame 60th Anniv. gold $5, Proof **(d)**. . . . . . . . . . . . | (8,070) | 450 |
| Kids set. Enhanced Uncirculated clad half dollar **(d)** . . . . . . . . . . . . . . . . . . . . . . . . . . . | | 45 |
| 2020P, Women's Suffrage Centennial silver dollar, Uncirculated **(f)** . . . . . . . . . . . . . . . . . . . . | 12,601 | 22 |
| 2020P, Women's Suffrage Centennial silver dollar, Proof **(f)**. . . . . . . . . . . . . . . . . . . . . . . . . | *(43,446)* | 22 |
| Coin and Medal set. Proof silver dollar **(f)** and silver medal. . . . . . . . . . . . . . . . . . . . . . . . | | 40 |
| 2021P, Christa McAuliffe silver dollar, Uncirculated **(f)**. . . . . . . . . . . . . . . . . . . . . . . . . . . | *15,505* | |
| 2021P, Christa McAuliffe silver dollar, Proof **(f)** . . . . . . . . . . . . . . . . . . . . . . . . . . . . . . | *(54,214)* | |
| 2021D, National Law Enforcement Memorial and Museum clad half dollar, Uncirculated. . . . . . . . | *9,972* | 20 |
| 2021S, National Law Enforcement Memorial and Museum clad half dollar, Proof . . . . . . . . . . . | *(27,387)* | 20 |
| 2021P, National Law Enforcement Memorial and Museum silver dollar, Uncirculated **(f)** . . . . . . . | *9,294* | 27 |
| 2021P, National Law Enforcement Memorial and Museum silver dollar, Proof **(f)**. . . . . . . . . . . | *(33,967)* | 27 |
| 2021W, National Law Enforcement Memorial and Museum gold $5, Uncirculated . . . . . . . . . . . . | *1,878* | 450 |
| 2021W, National Law Enforcement Memorial and Museum gold $5, Proof. . . . . . . . . . . . . . . . | *(5,799)* | 450 |
| 3-coin set. Proof clad half dollar, silver dollar **(c)**, and gold $5. . . . . . . . . . . . . . . . . . . . . . | | 550 |
| 2022D, National Purple Heart Hall of Honor clad half dollar, Uncirculated. . . . . . . . . . . . . . . . . | | |
| 2022S, National Purple Heart Hall of Honor clad half dollar, Proof . . . . . . . . . . . . . . . . . . . . . | | |
| 2022W, National Purple Heart Hall of Honor silver dollar, Uncirculated. . . . . . . . . . . . . . . . . . . | | |
| 2022W, National Purple Heart Hall of Honor silver dollar, Proof . . . . . . . . . . . . . . . . . . . . . . | | |
| 2022W, National Purple Heart Hall of Honor silver dollar, Proof, colorized. . . . . . . . . . . . . . . . . | | |
| 2022W, National Purple Heart Hall of Honor gold $5, Uncirculated. . . . . . . . . . . . . . . . . . . . . | | |
| 2022W, National Purple Heart Hall of Honor gold $5, Proof . . . . . . . . . . . . . . . . . . . . . . . . | | |
| 3-coin set. Proof clad half dollar, silver dollar **(f)**, and gold $5. . . . . . . . . . . . . . . . . . . . . . | | |
| 2022D, Negro Leagues Baseball clad half dollar, Uncirculated. . . . . . . . . . . . . . . . . . . . . . . . | | |
| 2022S, Negro Leagues Baseball clad half dollar, Proof. . . . . . . . . . . . . . . . . . . . . . . . . . . . | | |
| 2022W, Negro Leagues Baseball silver dollar, Uncirculated . . . . . . . . . . . . . . . . . . . . . . . . . | | |
| 2022P, Negro Leagues Baseball silver dollar, Proof . . . . . . . . . . . . . . . . . . . . . . . . . . . . . | | |
| 2022P, Negro Leagues Baseball silver dollar, Proof, with privy mark . . . . . . . . . . . . . . . . . . . | | |
| 2022W, Negro Leagues Baseball gold $5, Uncirculated . . . . . . . . . . . . . . . . . . . . . . . . . . . | | |
| 2022W, Negro Leagues Baseball gold $5, Proof. . . . . . . . . . . . . . . . . . . . . . . . . . . . . . . . | | |
| 3-coin set. Proof clad half dollar, silver dollar **(f)**, and gold $5. . . . . . . . . . . . . . . . . . . . . . | | |
| Coin and medal set. Proof silver dollar and Jackie Robinson Proof silver medal . . . . . . . . . . . . . . . . . . | | |

**d.** The obverse of each denomination is concave; the reverse is convex. **f.** In 2019, the fineness of U.S. Mint silver coins increased from .900 to .999.

# PROOF COINS AND SETS

Proof coins can usually be distinguished by their sharpness of detail, high wire edge, and extremely brilliant, mirrorlike surface. Proofs are sold by the Mint at a premium.

Proof coins were not struck during 1943–1949 or 1965–1967. Sets from 1936 through 1972 include the cent, nickel, dime, quarter, and half dollar; from 1973 through 1981 the dollar was also included. From 1999 on, Proof sets have included the year's multiple quarter dollars, and since 2000 they have included the Mint's golden dollar coins. *Values shown are for original unblemished sets.*

Figures in parentheses represent the total number of full sets minted.

| | Mintage | Issue Price | Current Value | | Mintage | Issue Price | Current Value |
|---|---|---|---|---|---|---|---|
| 1936 . . . . . . . . . . . . . . . . . (3,837) | | $1.89 | $3,000 | 1981S, Type 1 . . . . . . . .(4,063,083) | | $11.00 | $4.00 |
| 1937 . . . . . . . . . . . . . . . . . (5,542) | | 1.89 | 1,800 | 1981S, Type 2 . . . . . . . . . . . . . . . * | | 11.00 | 150.00 |
| 1938 . . . . . . . . . . . . . . . . . (8,045) | | 1.89 | 750 | 1982S . . . . . . . . . . . . . .(3,857,479) | | 11.00 | 4.00 |
| 1939 . . . . . . . . . . . . . . . . . (8,795) | | 1.89 | 750 | 1983S . . . . . . . . . . . . . .(3,138,765) | | 11.00 | 5.00 |
| 1940 . . . . . . . . . . . . . . . . (11,246) | | 1.89 | 650 | 1983S, Prestige set | | | |
| 1941 . . . . . . . . . . . . . . . . (15,287) | | 1.89 | 625 | (Olympic dollar) . . . . . . (140,361) | | 59.00 | 25.00 |
| 1942, Both nickels . . . . . . (21,120) | | 1.89 | 650 | 1984S . . . . . . . . . . . . . .(2,748,430) | | 11.00 | 4.50 |
| 1942, One nickel . . . . . . . . . . . . . * | | 1.89 | 600 | 1984S, Prestige set | | | |
| 1950 . . . . . . . . . . . . . . . . (51,386) | | 2.10 | 500 | (Olympic dollar) . . . . . . (316,680) | | 59.00 | 18.00 |
| 1951 . . . . . . . . . . . . . . . . (57,500) | | 2.10 | 450 | 1985S . . . . . . . . . . . . . .(3,362,821) | | 11.00 | 4.50 |
| 1952 . . . . . . . . . . . . . . . . .(81,980) | | 2.10 | 200 | 1986S . . . . . . . . . . . . . .(2,411,180) | | 11.00 | 4.50 |
| 1953 . . . . . . . . . . . . . . . . (128,800) | | 2.10 | 150 | 1986S, Prestige set (Statue | | | |
| 1954 . . . . . . . . . . . . . . . . (233,300) | | 2.10 | 80 | of Liberty half, dollar) . . (599,317) | | 48.50 | 18.00 |
| 1955, Box pack . . . . . . . . . (378,200) | | 2.10 | 75 | 1987S . . . . . . . . . . . . . .(3,792,233) | | 11.00 | 3.75 |
| 1955, Flat pack . . . . . . . . . . . . . . . * | | 2.10 | 75 | 1987S, Prestige set | | | |
| 1956 . . . . . . . . . . . . . . . . (669,384) | | 2.10 | 45 | (Constitution dollar) . . . . (435,495) | | 45.00 | 20.00 |
| 1957 . . . . . . . . . . . . . . . .(1,247,952) | | 2.10 | 24 | 1988S . . . . . . . . . . . . . .(3,031,287) | | 11.00 | 3.75 |
| 1958 . . . . . . . . . . . . . . . . (875,652) | | 2.10 | 25 | 1988S, Prestige set | | | |
| 1959 . . . . . . . . . . . . . . . .(1,149,291) | | 2.10 | 20 | (Olympic dollar) . . . . . . (231,661) | | 45.00 | 18.00 |
| 1960, With LgDt cent . . .(1,691,602) | | 2.10 | 20 | 1989S . . . . . . . . . . . . . .(3,009,107) | | 11.00 | 3.50 |
| 1960, With SmDt cent. . . . . . . . . . * | | 2.10 | 22 | 1989S, Prestige set | | | |
| 1961 . . . . . . . . . . . . . . . .(3,028,244) | | 2.10 | 20 | (Congressional half, | | | |
| 1962 . . . . . . . . . . . . . . . .(3,218,019) | | 2.10 | 20 | dollar) . . . . . . . . . . . . . (211,807) | | 45.00 | 17.00 |
| 1963 . . . . . . . . . . . . . . . .(3,075,645) | | 2.10 | 20 | 1990S . . . . . . . . . . . . . .(2,793,433) | | 11.00 | 4.00 |
| 1964 . . . . . . . . . . . . . . . .(3,950,762) | | 2.10 | 20 | 1990S, With No S cent . . . . . (3,555) | | 11.00 | 3,500.00 |
| 1968S . . . . . . . . . . . . . .(3,041,506) | | 5.00 | 5 | 1990S, Prestige set | | | |
| 1969S . . . . . . . . . . . . . .(2,934,631) | | 5.00 | 5 | (Eisenhower dollar) . . . . (506,126) | | 45.00 | 3,500.00 |
| 1970S . . . . . . . . . . . . . .(2,632,810) | | 5.00 | 7 | 1990S, Prestige Set, | | | |
| 1970S, With SmDt cent. . . . . . . . * | | 5.00 | 50 | With No S cent . . . . . . . . . . . . . * | | 45.00 | 18.00 |
| 1971S . . . . . . . . . . . . . .(3,220,733) | | 5.00 | 3 | 1991S . . . . . . . . . . . . . .(2,610,833) | | 11.00 | 4.00 |
| 1972S . . . . . . . . . . . . . .(3,260,996) | | 5.00 | 3 | 1991S, Prestige set (Mt. | | | |
| 1973S . . . . . . . . . . . . . .(2,760,339) | | 7.00 | 7 | Rushmore half, dollar). . (256,954) | | 59.00 | 25.00 |
| 1974S . . . . . . . . . . . . . .(2,612,568) | | 7.00 | 7 | 1992S . . . . . . . . . . . . . .(2,675,618) | | 11.00 | 4.00 |
| 1975S, With 1976 quarter, | | | | 1992S, Prestige set | | | |
| half, and dollar . . . . . .(2,845,450) | | 7.00 | 7 | (Olympic half, dollar) . . . (183,293) | | 56.00 | 22.00 |
| 1976S . . . . . . . . . . . . . .(4,149,730) | | 7.00 | 7 | 1992S, Silver . . . . . . . . .(1,009,586) | | 21.00 | 12.00 |
| 1976S, 3-piece set . . . . .(3,998,621) | | 15.00 | 14 | 1992S, Silver Premier set . (308,055) | | 37.00 | 12.00 |
| 1977S . . . . . . . . . . . . . .(3,251,152) | | 9.00 | 7 | 1993S . . . . . . . . . . . . . .(2,409,394) | | 12.50 | 4.00 |
| 1978S . . . . . . . . . . . . . .(3,127,781) | | 9.00 | 6 | 1993S, Prestige set (Bill | | | |
| 1979S, Type 1 . . . . . . . .(3,677,175) | | 9.00 | 7 | of Rights half, dollar). . . (224,045) | | 57.00 | 28.00 |
| 1979S, Type 2 . . . . . . . . . . . . . . . * | | 9.00 | 30 | 1993S, Silver . . . . . . . . . . (570,213) | | 21.00 | 14.00 |
| 1980S . . . . . . . . . . . . . .(3,554,806) | | 10.00 | 4 | 1993S, Silver Premier set . (191,140) | | 37.50 | 14.00 |

* Included in number above.

*Chart continued on next page.*

| | Mintage | Issue Price | Current Value | | Mintage | Issue Price | Current Value |
|---|---|---|---|---|---|---|---|
| 1994S | (2,308,701) | $12.50 | $4.00 | 2007S, 5-pc qtr set | (672,662) | $13.95 | $4.00 |
| 1994S, Prestige set (World | | | | 2007S, 4-pc Pres set | (1,285,972) | 14.95 | 4.25 |
| Cup half, dollar) | (175,893) | 57.00 | 23.00 | 2007S, Silver 14-pc set | (875,050) | 44.95 | 27.00 |
| 1994S, Silver | (636,009) | 21.00 | 14.00 | 2007S, Silver 5-pc qtr set. | (672,662) | 25.95 | 18.00 |
| 1994S, Silver Premier set | (149,320) | 37.50 | 14.00 | 2008S, 14-pc set | (1,382,017) | 26.95 | 20.00 |
| 1995S | (2,010,384) | 12.50 | 6.00 | 2008S, 5-pc qtr set | (672,438) | 13.95 | 8.00 |
| 1995S, Prestige set (Civil | | | | 2008S, 4-pc Pres set | (836,730) | 14.95 | 6.00 |
| War half, dollar) | (107,112) | 57.00 | 45.00 | 2008S, Silver 14-pc set | (763,887) | 44.95 | 27.00 |
| 1995S, Silver | (549,878) | 21.00 | 25.00 | 2008S, Silver 5-pc qtr set. | (429,021) | 25.95 | 18.00 |
| 1995S, Silver Premier set | (130,107) | 37.50 | 25.00 | 2009S, 18-pc set | (1,477,967) | 29.95 | 19.00 |
| 1996S | (1,695,244) | 12.50 | 6.00 | 2009S, 6-pc qtr set | (635,423) | 14.95 | 4.00 |
| 1996S, Prestige set | | | | 2009S, 4-pc Pres set | (627,925) | 14.95 | 5.00 |
| (Olympic half, dollar) | (55,000) | 57.00 | 125.00 | 2009S, Silver 18-pc set | (694,406) | 52.95 | 30.00 |
| 1996S, Silver | (623,655) | 21.00 | 15.00 | 2009S, Silver 6-pc qtr set. | (299,164) | 29.95 | 21.00 |
| 1996S, Silver Premier set | (151,366) | 37.50 | 15.00 | 2009S, 4-pc Lincoln | | | |
| 1997S | (1,975,000) | 12.50 | 6.00 | Bicentennial set | (200,000) | 7.95 | 5.00 |
| 1997S, Prestige set | | | | 2010S, 14-pc set | (1,103,950) | 31.95 | 22.00 |
| (Botanic dollar) | (80,000) | 48.00 | 30.00 | 2010S, 5-pc qtr set | (276,335) | 14.95 | 7.00 |
| 1997S, Silver | (605,473) | 21.00 | 17.00 | 2010S, 4-pc Pres set | (535,463) | 15.95 | 7.00 |
| 1997S, Silver Premier set | (136,205) | 37.50 | 17.00 | 2010S, Silver 14-pc set | (585,414) | 56.95 | 28.00 |
| 1998S | (2,086,507) | 12.50 | 6.50 | 2010S, Silver 5-pc qtr set. | (274,003) | 32.95 | 18.00 |
| 1998S, Silver | (638,134) | 21.00 | 14.00 | 2011S, 14-pc set | (1,098,835) | 31.95 | 20.00 |
| 1998S, Silver Premier set | (240,658) | 37.50 | 14.00 | 2011S, 5-pc qtr set | (152,302) | 14.95 | 8.00 |
| 1999S, 9-pc set | (2,543,401) | 19.95 | 6.50 | 2011S, 4-pc Pres set | (299,853) | 19.95 | 17.00 |
| 1999S, 5-pc qtr set | (1,169,958) | 13.95 | 2.50 | 2011S, Silver 14-pc set | (574,175) | 67.95 | 33.00 |
| 1999S, Silver 9-pc set | (804,565) | 31.95 | 50.00 | 2011S, Silver 5-pc qtr set. | (147,901) | 39.95 | 20.00 |
| 2000S, 10-pc set | (3,082,572) | 19.95 | 5.00 | 2012S, 14-pc set | (794,002) | 31.95 | 55.00 |
| 2000S, 5-pc qtr set | (937,600) | 13.95 | 3.00 | 2012S, 5-pc qtr set | (148,498) | 14.95 | 8.00 |
| 2000S, Silver 10-pc set | (965,421) | 31.95 | 25.00 | 2012S, 4-pc Pres set | (249,298) | 18.95 | 30.00 |
| 2001S, 10-pc set | (2,294,909) | 19.95 | 6.50 | 2012S, Silver 14-pc set | (395,443) | 67.95 | 100.00 |
| 2001S, 5-pc qtr set | (799,231) | 13.95 | 3.00 | 2012S, Silver 8-pc | | | |
| 2001S, Silver 10-pc set | (889,697) | 31.95 | 25.00 | Limited Edition set | (50,169) | 149.95 | 140.00 |
| 2002S, 10-pc set | (2,319,766) | 19.95 | 5.00 | 2012S, Silver 5-pc qtr set. | (162,448) | 41.95 | 20.00 |
| 2002S, 5-pc qtr set | (764,479) | 13.95 | 3.50 | 2013S, 14-pc set | (802,460) | 31.95 | 24.00 |
| 2002S, Silver 10-pc set | (892,229) | 31.95 | 25.00 | 2013S, 5-pc qtr set | (128,377) | 14.95 | 7.00 |
| 2003S, 10-pc set | (2,172,684) | 19.95 | 5.00 | 2013S, 4-pc Pres set | (266,618) | 18.95 | 7.00 |
| 2003S, 5-pc qtr set | (1,235,832) | 13.95 | 2.00 | 2013S, Silver 14-pc set | (419,720) | 67.95 | 35.00 |
| 2003S, Silver 10-pc set | (1,125,755) | 31.95 | 25.00 | 2013S, Silver 8-pc | | | |
| 2004S, 11-pc set | (1,789,488) | 22.95 | 7.00 | Limited Edition set | (47,971) | 139.95 | 65.00 |
| 2004S, 5-pc qtr set | (951,196) | 15.95 | 3.00 | 2013S, Silver 5-pc qtr set. | (138,451) | 41.95 | 20.00 |
| 2004S, Silver 11-pc set | (1,175,934) | 37.95 | 25.00 | 2014S, 14-pc set | (714,661) | 31.95 | 24.00 |
| 2004S, Silver 5-pc qtr set. | (593,852) | 23.95 | 18.00 | 2014S, 5-pc qtr set | (115,179) | 14.95 | 9.00 |
| 2005S, 11-pc set | (2,275,000) | 22.95 | 5.00 | 2014S, 4-pc Pres set | (229,415) | 18.95 | 8.00 |
| 2005S, 5-pc qtr set | (987,960) | 15.95 | 2.00 | 2014S, Silver 14-pc set | (429,493) | 67.95 | 34.00 |
| 2005S, Silver 11-pc set | (1,069,679) | 37.95 | 25.00 | 2014S, Silver 8-pc | | | |
| 2005S, Silver 5-pc qtr set. | (608,970) | 23.95 | 18.00 | Limited Edition set | (42,614) | 139.95 | 76.00 |
| 2006S, 10-pc set | (2,000,428) | 22.95 | 5.00 | 2014S, Silver 5-pc qtr set. | (119,251) | 41.95 | 20.00 |
| 2006S, 5-pc qtr set | (882,000) | 15.95 | 2.00 | 2015S, 14-pc set | (662,854) | 32.95 | 25.00 |
| 2006S, Silver 10-pc set | (1,054,008) | 37.95 | 25.00 | 2015S, 5-pc qtr set | (99,466) | 14.95 | 7.00 |
| 2006S, Silver 5-pc qtr set. | (531,000) | 23.95 | 18.00 | 2015S, 4-pc Pres set | (222,068) | 18.95 | 8.00 |
| 2007S, 14-pc set | (1,702,116) | 26.95 | 10.00 | 2015S, Silver 14-pc set | (387,310) | 53.95 | 32.00 |

| Year | Mintage | Issue Price | Current Value |
|---|---|---|---|
| 2015S, Silver 5-pc qtr set. *(103,311)* | | $31.95 | $20 |
| 2016S, 13-pc set . . . . . . . (575,183) | | 31.95 | 35 |
| 2016S, 5-pc qtr set. . . . . . *(91,674)* | | 14.95 | 7 |
| 2016S, 3-pc Pres set . . . . *(231,549)* | | 17.95 | 8 |
| 2016S, Silver 13-pc set . . (356,683) | | 52.95 | 40 |
| 2016S, Silver 8-pc Limited Edition set, with 2016W American Silver Eagle. . . (49,647) | | 139.95 | 20 |
| | | | 80 |
| 2016S, Silver 5-pc qtr set. . (95,709) | | 31.95 | 19 |
| 2017S, 10-pc set . . . . . . . *(568,678)* | | 31.95 | 28 |
| 2017S, 5-pc qtr set. . . . . . *(88,909)* | | 14.95 | 10 |
| 2017S, Silver 10-pc set . . *(358,085)* | | 52.95 | 40 |
| 2017S, Silver 5-pc qtr set. *(89,632)* | | 31.95 | 20 |
| 2017S, Silver 8-pc Limited Edition set . . . . . (48,901) | | 139.95 | 125 |
| 2018S, 10-pc set . . . . . . . (517,053) | | 27.95 | 25 |
| 2018S, 5-pc qtr set. . . . . . (86,694) | | 15.95 | 12 |
| 2018S, Silver 10-pc set . . (332,268) | | 49.95 | 40 |
| 2018S, Silver 5-pc qtr set. . (79,300) | | 33.95 | 26 |
| 2018S, 50th Anniv silver 10-pc RevPf set . . . . . . (199,116) | | 54.95 | 52 |
| 2018S, Silver 8-pc Limited Edition set . . . . . (49,480) | | 144.95 | 150 |
| 2019S, 10-piece set, plus 2019W Proof cent. . . . . *(600,423)* | | 27.95 | 20 |
| 2019S, 5-piece qtr set. . . . *(78,777)* | | 15.95 | 12 |
| 2019S, Silver 10-pc set, Plus 2019W RevPf cent. . . . *(412,508)* | | 54.95 | 40 |
| 2019S, 4-piece American Innovation dollar set . . *(137,696)* | | 20.95 | |
| 2019S, Silv 5-pc qtr set. . . *(78,585)* | | 36.95 | 32 |
| 2019S, Silver 8-piece Limited Edition set. . . . . *(48,417)* | | 149.95 | 150 |

| Year | Mintage | Issue Price | Current Value |
|---|---|---|---|
| 2020S, 10-piece set, Plus 2020W Proof nickel. . . *(465,080)* | | $32.00 | $32 |
| 2020S, 5-piece quarter set *(64,242)* | | 18.50 | 20 |
| 2020S, 4-piece American Innovation dollar set . . *(101,593)* | | 24.00 | |
| 2020S, Silver 10-piece set, Plus 2020W Reverse Proof nickel. . . . . . . . *(313,184)* | | 105.00 | |
| 2020S, Siiv 5-piece qtr set *(64,012)* | | 60.00 | 45 |
| 2020S, Silver 8-piece Limited Edition set. . . . . *(49,995)* | | 201.00 | |
| 2020S, Silver 8-piece Limited Edition set. . . . . . . . . . . | | 150.00 | |
| 2021S, 7-piece set . . . . . . . . . . . . . | | 32.00 | |
| 2021S, 4-piece American Innovation dollar set . . . . . . . . . | | 24.00 | |
| 2021S, 4-piece American Innovation dollar RevPf set . . . . . | | 28.00 | |
| 2021S, Silver 7-piece set . . . . . . . . | | 105.00 | |
| 2021S, Silver 6-piece Limited Edition set. . . . . . . . . . . | | 235.00 | |
| 2022S, 10-piece set . . . . . . . . . . . . | | | |
| 2022S, 5-piece quarter set . . . . . . . | | 21.00 | |
| 2022S, 4-piece American Innovation dollar set . . . . . . . . . | | | |
| 2022S, 4-piece American Innovation dollar RevPf set . . . . . | | | |
| 2022S, Silver 10-piece set . . . . . . . | | | |
| 2022S, Silver 5-piece quarter set . . | | 73.00 | |
| 2022S, Silver 8-piece Limited Edition set. . . . . . . . . . . | | | |

## UNCIRCULATED MINT SETS

Official Mint Sets are specially packaged by the government for sale to collectors. They contain Uncirculated specimens of each year's coins for every denomination issued from each mint. Sets from 1947 through 1958 contain two examples of each regular-issue coin. No official sets were produced in 1950, 1982, or 1983. Privately assembled sets are valued according to individual coin prices. Only official sets are included in the following list. Unlike the Proof sets, these are normal coins intended for circulation and are not minted with any special consideration for quality. From 1942 to 1946, groups of two coins from each mint were sold in a cloth shipping bag with only minimal protection. Very few of those mailing packages were saved by collectors.

| | Mintage | Issue Price | Current Value |
|---|---|---|---|
| 1947 P-D-S . . . . . . . . . . . . . .5,000 | | $4.87 | $1,050 |
| 1948 P-D-S . . . . . . . . . . . . . .6,000 | | 4.92 | 750 |
| 1949 P-D-S . . . . . . . . . . . . . .5,000 | | 5.45 | 850 |
| 1951 P-D-S . . . . . . . . . . . . . .8,654 | | 6.75 | 700 |
| 1952 P-D-S . . . . . . . . . . . . .11,499 | | 6.14 | 650 |

| | Mintage | Issue Price | Current Value |
|---|---|---|---|
| 1953 P-D-S . . . . . . . . . . . . . .15,538 | | $6.14 | $525 |
| 1954 P-D-S . . . . . . . . . . . . . .25,599 | | 6.19 | 290 |
| 1955 P-D-S . . . . . . . . . . . . . .49,656 | | 5.45 | 225 |
| 1956 P-D . . . . . . . . . . . . . . .45,475 | | 3.34 | 225 |
| 1957 P-D . . . . . . . . . . . . . . .34,324 | | 4.40 | 225 |

*Chart continued on next page.*

| | Mintage | Issue Price | Current Value |
|---|---|---|---|
| 1958 P-D | 50,314 | $4.43 | $140.00 |
| 1959 P-D | 187,000 | 2.40 | 35.00 |
| 1960 P-D | 260,485 | 2.40 | 30.00 |
| 1961 P-D | 223,704 | 2.40 | 30.00 |
| 1962 P-D | 385,285 | 2.40 | 30.00 |
| 1963 P-D | 606,612 | 2.40 | 30.00 |
| 1964 P-D | 1,008,108 | 2.40 | 28.00 |
| 1965* | 2,360,000 | 4.00 | 9.00 |
| 1966* | 2,261,583 | 4.00 | 7.00 |
| 1967* | 1,863,344 | 4.00 | 8.00 |
| 1968 P-D-S | 2,105,128 | 2.50 | 4.00 |
| 1969 P-D-S | 1,817,392 | 2.50 | 4.00 |
| 1970 P-D-S | 2,038,134 | 2.50 | 10.00 |
| 1971 P-D-S | 2,193,396 | 3.50 | 3.00 |
| 1972 P-D-S | 2,750,000 | 3.50 | 2.75 |
| 1973 P-D-S | 1,767,691 | 6.00 | 9.00 |
| 1974 P-D-S | 1,975,981 | 6.00 | 8.00 |
| 1975 P-D | 1,921,488 | 6.00 | 8.00 |
| 1776–1976, 3-piece set. | 4,908,319 | 9.00 | 12.00 |
| 1976 P-D | 1,892,513 | 6.00 | 8.00 |
| 1977 P-D | 2,006,869 | 7.00 | 8.00 |
| 1978 P-D | 2,162,609 | 7.00 | 8.00 |
| 1979 P-D | 2,526,000 | 8.00 | 5.00 |
| 1980 P-D-S | 2,815,066 | 9.00 | 5.00 |
| 1981 P-D-S | 2,908,145 | 11.00 | 5.50 |
| 1984 P-D | 1,832,857 | 7.00 | 2.50 |
| 1985 P-D | 1,710,571 | 7.00 | 2.50 |
| 1986 P-D | 1,153,536 | 7.00 | 5.00 |
| 1987 P-D | 2,890,758 | 7.00 | 3.25 |
| 1988 P-D | 1,646,204 | 7.00 | 3.00 |
| 1989 P-D | 1,987,915 | 7.00 | 2.50 |
| 1990 P-D | 1,809,184 | 7.00 | 2.50 |
| 1991 P-D | 1,352,101 | 7.00 | 2.50 |
| 1992 P-D | 1,500,143 | 7.00 | 3.00 |
| 1993 P-D | 1,297,431 | 8.00 | 3.00 |

| | Mintage | Issue Price | Current Value |
|---|---|---|---|
| 1994 P-D | 1,234,813 | $8.00 | $2.50 |
| 1995 P-D | 1,038,787 | 8.00 | 3.00 |
| 1996 P-D, Plus | | | |
| 1996W dime | 1,457,949 | 8.00 | 10.00 |
| 1997 P-D | 950,473 | 8.00 | 4.00 |
| 1998 P-D | 1,187,325 | 8.00 | 3.00 |
| 1999 P-D (18 pieces) | 1,243,867 | 14.95 | 5.00 |
| 2000 P-D (20 pieces) | 1,490,160 | 14.95 | 8.00 |
| 2001 P-D (20 pieces) | 1,116,915 | 14.95 | 8.00 |
| 2002 P-D (20 pieces) | 1,139,388 | 14.95 | 8.00 |
| 2003 P-D (20 pieces) | 1,001,532 | 14.95 | 8.00 |
| 2004 P-D (22 pieces) | 842,507 | 16.95 | 8.00 |
| 2005 P-D (22 pieces) | 1,160,000 | 16.95 | 8.00 |
| 2006 P-D (20 pieces) | 847,361 | 16.95 | 8.00 |
| 2007 P-D (28 pieces) | 895,628 | 22.95 | 15.00 |
| 2008 P-D (28 pieces) | 745,464 | 22.95 | 18.00 |
| 2009 P-D (36 pieces) | 774,844 | 27.95 | 16.00 |
| 2010 P-D (28 pieces) | 583,912 | 31.95 | 16.00 |
| 2011 P-D (28 pieces) | 533,529 | 31.95 | 16.00 |
| 2012 P-D (28 pieces) | 392,224 | 27.95 | 40.00 |
| 2013 P-D (28 pieces) | 376,844 | 27.95 | 20.00 |
| 2014 P-D (28 pieces) | 345,813 | 27.95 | 20.00 |
| 2015 P-D (28 pieces) | 314,029 | 28.95 | 18.00 |
| 2016 P-D (28 pieces) | 296,582 | 28.95 | 24.00 |
| 2017 P-D (28 pieces) | 286,813 | 26.95 | 18.00 |
| 2017S, 225th Anniversary Enhanced Uncirculated Set (10 pieces) | 210,419 | 29.95 | 30.00 |
| 2018 P-D (20 pieces) | 257,531 | 20.95 | 22.00 |
| 2019 P-D (20 pieces), Plus 2019W cent | 346,117 | 21.95 | 18.00 |
| 2020 P-D (20 pieces) (a) | 211,787 | 25.65 | 20.00 |
| 2021 P-D (14 pieces) | | | |
| 2022 P-D (20 pieces) | | | |

*Note: Sets issued from 2005 to 2010 have a special Satin Finish that is somewhat different from the finish on Uncirculated coins made for general circulation. * Special Mint Set. a. An Uncirculated nickel from the West Point Mint was intended to be a premium for the 2020 Mint Set, but was canceled due to COVID-19.*

## Other Collectible Sets

| | Mint Pkg |
|---|---|
| **(2000) Millennium Coin and Currency Set** | |
| 3-piece set. Uncirculated Sacagawea dollar, Uncirculated American Silver Eagle bullion coin, and $1 Federal Reserve Note | $40 |
| **(2003) Legacies of Freedom™** | |
| Uncirculated American Silver Eagle bullion coin and Uncirculated 2002 £2 Silver Britannia coin | 45 |
| **(2004) Westward Journey Nickel Series™** | |
| Proof Sacagawea dollar, two 2004 Proof nickels, and silver-plated Peace Medal replica | 30 |
| **(2005) Westward Journey Nickel Series™** | |
| Proof Sacagawea dollar, two 2005 Proof nickels, and silver-plated Peace Medal replica | 30 |
| **(2009) Abraham Lincoln Coin and Chronicles** | |
| Proof Abraham Lincoln commemorative silver dollar, four copper Proof Lincoln cents, reproduction portrait of Abraham Lincoln, and replica of handwritten Gettysburg Address | 28 |

| | Mint Pkg |
|---|---|

**(2013) Theodore Roosevelt Coin and Chronicles**
Uncirculated Presidential dollar, silver Presidential medal, National Wildlife Refuge System
Centennial bronze medal, and Roosevelt print............................................... $90

**(2014) Franklin D. Roosevelt Coin and Chronicles**
Proof dime and Presidential dollar, bronze Presidential medal, silver Presidential medal,
four themed postage stamps (1¢, 2¢, 3¢, 5¢), and companion booklet...................... 40

**(2014) American $1 Coin and Currency Set**
2014D Native American – Native Hospitality Enhanced Uncirculated dollar and
$1 Federal Reserve Note.................................................................. 35

**(2015) Harry S. Truman Coin and Chronicles**
Reverse Proof Presidential dollar, silver Presidential medal, 1973 Truman 8¢ postage stamp,
and information booklet.................................................................. 150

**(2015) Dwight D. Eisenhower Coin and Chronicles**
Reverse Proof Presidential dollar, silver Presidential medal, 1969 Eisenhower 6¢ postage stamp,
and information booklet.................................................................. 105

**(2015) John F. Kennedy Coin and Chronicles**
Reverse Proof Presidential dollar, silver Presidential medal, 1964 Kennedy 5¢ postage stamp,
and information booklet.................................................................. 40

**(2015) Lyndon B. Johnson Coin and Chronicles**
Reverse Proof Presidential dollar, silver Presidential medal, 1973 Johnson 8¢ postage stamp,
and information booklet.................................................................. 40

**(2015) American $1 Coin and Currency Set**
2015W Native American – Mohawk Ironworkers Enhanced Uncirculated dollar and
$1 Federal Reserve Note.................................................................. 50

**(2016) Ronald Reagan Coin and Chronicles**
Reverse Proof Presidential dollar, Proof American Silver Eagle, bronze Ronald and Nancy Reagan
medal, engraved Ronald Reagan Presidential portrait, and information booklet................. 55

**(2016) American $1 Coin and Currency Set**
2016S Native American – Code Talkers Enhanced Uncirculated dollar and $1 Federal Reserve Note ... 50

**(2019) American $1 Coin and Currency Set**
2019W Native American – American Indians in Space Enhanced Uncirculated dollar and
$1 Federal Reserve Note..................................................................

**(2019) Youth Coin and Currency Set**
Five Proof America the Beautiful quarters and $2 Federal Reserve Note .......................

**(2020) George Herbert Walker Bush Coin and Chronicles**
Reverse Proof Presidential dollar, silver Presidential medal, 2019 George H.W. Bush "forever"
postage stamp, Barbara Bush bronze medal, and information booklet .......................

## AMERICA THE BEAUTIFUL™ SILVER BULLION COINS

Weight and purity
incused on edge
*Actual size 3 inches.*

| | Mintage | MS | SP | | Mintage | MS | SP |
|---|---|---|---|---|---|---|---|
| 25¢ 2010(P), Hot Springs (AR) . . .33,000 | | $165 | | 25¢ 2013P, Perry's Victory (OH) . .(17,707) | | | $180 |
| 25¢ 2010P, Hot Springs (AR). . . . .(26,788) | | | $180 | 25¢ 2013(P), Great Basin (NV) . . . .30,000 | | $165 | |
| 25¢ 2010(P), Yellowstone (WY) . . .33,000 | | 165 | | 25¢ 2013P, Great Basin (NV). . . . .(17,792) | | | 180 |
| 25¢ 2010P, Yellowstone (WY) . . .(26,711) | | | 180 | 25¢ 2013(P), Ft McHenry (MD) . . . .30,000 | | 165 | |
| 25¢ 2010(P), Yosemite (CA). . . . . .33,000 | | 165 | | 25¢ 2013P, Ft McHenry (MD) . . . .(19,802) | | | 180 |
| 25¢ 2010P, Yosemite (CA) . . . . . .(26,716) | | | 180 | 25¢ 2013(P), Mt Rush (SD) . . . . . . .35,000 | | 165 | |
| 25¢ 2010(P), Grand Canyon (AZ). . .33,000 | | 165 | | 25¢ 2013P, Mt Rush (SD) . . . . . . .(23,547) | | | 180 |
| 25¢ 2010P, Grand Canyon (AZ) . . .(25,967) | | | 180 | 25¢ 2014(P), Smky Mtns (TN). . . . .33,000 | | 165 | |
| 25¢ 2010(P), Mount Hood (OR) . . . .33,000 | | 165 | | 25¢ 2014P, Smky Mtns (TN) . . . . .(24,710) | | | 180 |
| 25¢ 2010P, Mount Hood (OR) . . . .(26,637) | | | 165 | 25¢ 2014(P), Shenand (VA) . . . . . .25,000 | | 165 | |
| 25¢ 2011(P), Gettysburg (PA) . . . .126,700 | | 165 | | 25¢ 2014P, Shenand (VA) . . . . . .(28,451) | | | 180 |
| 25¢ 2011P, Gettysburg (PA). . . . . (24,625) | | | 180 | 25¢ 2014(P), Arches (UT) . . . . . . . .22,000 | | 165 | |
| 25¢ 2011(P), Glacier (MT) . . . . . . .126,700 | | 165 | | 25¢ 2014P, Arches (UT). . . . . . . . .(28,424) | | | 180 |
| 25¢ 2011P, Glacier (MT) . . . . . . . .(20,856) | | | 180 | 25¢ 2014(P), Sand Dunes (CO) . . . .22,000 | | 165 | |
| 25¢ 2011(P), Olympic (WA) . . . . . .104,900 | | 165 | | 25¢ 2014P, Sand Dunes (CO) . . . .(24,103) | | | 180 |
| 25¢ 2011(P), Olympic (WA) . . . . . .(18,398) | | | 180 | 25¢ 2014(P), Everglades (FL) . . . . .34,000 | | 165 | |
| 25¢ 2011P, Vicksburg (MS). . . . . .58,100 | | 165 | | 25¢ 2014P, Everglades (FL). . . . . .(19,772) | | | 180 |
| 25¢ 2011P, Vicksburg (MS). . . . . .(18,594) | | | 180 | 25¢ 2015(P), Homestead (NE). . . . .35,000 | | 165 | |
| 25¢ 2011(P), Chickasaw (OK) . . . . .48,700 | | 165 | | 25¢ 2015(P), Homestead (NE) . . . . .(21,286) | | | 180 |
| 25¢ 2011P, Chickasaw (OK) . . . . .(16,827) | | | 180 | 25¢ 2015(P), Kisatchie (LA). . . . . . .42,000 | | 165 | |
| 25¢ 2012(P), El Yunque (PR). . . . . .24,000 | | 165 | | 25¢ 2015(P), Kisatchie (LA). . . . . . .(19,449) | | | 180 |
| 25¢ 2012(P), El Yunque (PR). . . . . .(17,314) | | | 200 | 25¢ 2015(P), Blue Ridge (NC) . . . . .45,000 | | 165 | |
| 25¢ 2012(P), Chaco (NM) . . . . . . .24,400 | | 165 | | 25¢ 2015(P), Blue Ridge (NC) . . . . .(17,461) | | | 180 |
| 25¢ 2012P, Chaco (NM) . . . . . . . .(15,776) | | | 180 | 25¢ 2015(P), Bombay Hk (DE). . . . .45,000 | | 165 | |
| 25¢ 2012(P), Acadia (ME). . . . . . . .25,400 | | 180 | | 25¢ 2015(P), Bombay Hk (DE). . . . .(17,309) | | | 180 |
| 25¢ 2012P, Acadia (ME). . . . . . . .(14,978) | | | 375 | 25¢ 2015(P), Saratoga (NY). . . . . . .45,000 | | 165 | |
| 25¢ 2012(P), Hawai'i | | | | 25¢ 2015P, Saratoga (NY) . . . . . . .(17,563) | | | 180 |
|     Volcanoes (HI). . . . . . . . . . . . . .20,000 | | 200 | | 25¢ 2016(P), Shawnee (IL) . . . . . . 105,000 | | 165 | |
| 25¢ 2012P, Hawai'i | | | | 25¢ 2016P, Shawnee (IL) . . . . . . .(18,781) | | | 180 |
|     Volcanoes (HI). . . . . . . . . . . . .(14,863) | | | 500 | 25¢ 2016(P), Cumberland (KY) . . . 75,000 | | 165 | |
| 25¢ 2012(P), Denali (AK). . . . . . . .20,000 | | 165 | | 25¢ 2016P, Cumberland (KY) . . . (18,713) | | | 180 |
| 25¢ 2012P, Denali (AK). . . . . . . .(15,225) | | | 250 | 25¢ 2016(P), Harpers Ferry (WV). . 75,000 | | 165 | |
| 25¢ 2013(P), White | | | | 25¢ 2016P, Harpers Ferry (WV) . . (18,896) | | | 180 |
|     Mountain (NH). . . . . . . . . . . . . .35,000 | | 165 | | 25¢ 2016(P), T. Roosevelt (ND) . . 40,000 | | 165 | |
| 25¢ 2013P, White | | | | 25¢ 2016P, T. Roosevelt (ND) . . . (18,917) | | | 180 |
|     Mountain (NH). . . . . . . . . . . .(20,530) | | | 165 | 25¢ 2016(P), Fort Moultrie (SC). . . 35,000 | | 165 | |
| 25¢ 2013(P), Perry's Victory (OH) 30,000 | | 165 | | 25¢ 2016P, Fort Moultrie (SC) . . . (17,882) | | | 180 |

*Note:* The U.S. Mint produces the America the Beautiful™ 5-oz. silver coins in bullion and numismatic versions. The bullion version, which lacks the P mintmark, has a brilliant Uncirculated finish and is sold only through dealers. The numismatic version, with the P mintmark, has a matte or burnished finish (although it is not marketed by the Mint as "Burnished"). These coins, designated Specimens (SP) by grading services, are sold directly to the public.

| | Mintage | MS | SP |
|---|---|---|---|
| 25¢ 2017(P), Effigy (IA) . . . . . . . | 35,000 | $165 | |
| 25¢ 2017P, Effigy (IA) . . . . . . . | (17,251) | | $180 |
| 25¢ 2017(P), Douglass (DC) . . . . | 20,000 | 165 | |
| 25¢ 2017(P), Douglass (DC). . . . . | (17,678) | | 180 |
| 25¢ 2017(P), Ozark (MO). . . . . . | 20,000 | 165 | |
| 25¢ 2017(P), Ozark (MO). . . . . . | (17,694) | | 180 |
| 25¢ 2017(P), Ellis Island (NJ) . . . | 40,000 | 165 | |
| 25¢ 2017(P), Ellis Island (NJ). . . | (17,670) | | 180 |
| 25¢ 2017(P), G.R. Clark (IN) . . . . | 35,000 | 165 | |
| 25¢ 2017(P), G.R. Clark (IN). . . . . | (14,731) | | 180 |
| 25¢ 2018(P), Pictured Rocks (MI). | 30,000 | 165 | |
| 25¢ 2018P, Pictured Rocks (MI) | (17,773) | | 180 |
| 25¢ 2018(P), Apostle (WI) . . . . . . | 30,000 | 165 | |
| 25¢ 2018(P), Apostle (WI) . . . . . . | (16,802) | | 180 |
| 25¢ 2018(P), Voyageurs (MN) . . . | 30,000 | 165 | |
| 25¢ 2018(P), Voyageurs (MN) . . . | (16,839) | | 180 |
| 25¢ 2018(P), Cumberland (GA) . . | 52,500 | 165 | |
| 25¢ 2018(P), Cumberland (GA) . . | (16,376) | | 180 |
| 25¢ 2018(P), Block Island (RI). . . | 80,000 | 165 | |
| 25¢ 2018P, Block Island (RI). . . | (15,912) | | 180 |
| 25¢ 2019(P), Lowell (MA) . . . . . . | 80,000 | 170 | |
| 25¢ 2019P, Lowell (MA) . . . . . . | (16,644) | | 185 |

| | Mintage | MS | SP |
|---|---|---|---|
| 25¢ 2019(P), Am. Mem. (NMI) . . | 80,000 | $170 | |
| 25¢ 2019P, Am. Mem. (NMI) . . | (16,287) | | $185 |
| 25¢ 2019(P), War in the Pacific (Guam). . . . . . . . | 72,500 | 170 | |
| 25¢ 2019P, War in the Pacific (Guam). . . . . . . . | (16,277) | | 185 |
| 25¢ 2019(P), Church (ID). . . . . . | 25,000 | 170 | |
| 25¢ 2019P, Church (ID). . . . . . | (16,310) | | 185 |
| 25¢ 2019(P), San Antonio (TX). . | 55,200 | 170 | |
| 25¢ 2019P, San Antonio (TX). . | (16,211) | | 185 |
| 25¢ 2020P, Am. Samoa (AS) . . . | 45,000 | 175 | |
| 25¢ 2020(P), Am. Samoa (AS) . . | (15,781) | | 195 |
| 25¢ 2020P, Weir Farm (CT) . . . . | 45,000 | 175 | |
| 25¢ 2020P, Weir Farm (CT) . . . | (15,326) | | 195 |
| 25¢ 2020P, Salt Riv. Bay (USVI) . . . | 45,000 | 175 | |
| 25¢ 2020(P), Salt Riv. Bay (USVI) | (13,566) | | 195 |
| 25¢ 2020P, Marsh (VT) . . . . . . . | 45,000 | 175 | |
| 25¢ 2020P, Marsh (VT) . . . . . | (13,545) | | 195 |
| 25¢ 2020P, Tallgrass (KS) . . . . . | 45,000 | 175 | |
| 25¢ 2020(P), Tallgrass (KS) . . . | (13,613) | | 195 |
| 25¢ 2021P, Tuskegee (AL). . . . . . . . . . | | 175 | |
| 25¢ 2021(P), Tuskegee (AL). . . . . . . . . | | | 195 |

*Note:* The U.S. Mint produced the America the Beautiful™ 5-oz. silver coins in bullion and numismatic versions. The bullion version, which lacks the P mintmark, has a brilliant Uncirculated finish and was sold only through dealers. The numismatic version, with the P mintmark, has a matte or burnished finish (although it was not marketed by the Mint as "Burnished"). These coins, designated Specimens (SP) by grading services, were sold directly to the public.

## $1 AMERICAN SILVER EAGLE COINS

Values below are based on spot silver value of $27 per ounce.

**Reverse, 1986–2021.**

**Reverse, 2021 to date.**

*See next page for chart.*

| | Mintage | Unc. | PF |
|---|---|---|---|
| $1 1986 | 5,393,005 | $38 | |
| $1 1986S | (1,446,778) | | $70 |
| $1 1987 | 11,442,335 | 30 | |
| $1 1987S | (904,732) | | 70 |
| $1 1988 | 5,004,646 | 30 | |
| $1 1988S | (557,370) | | 70 |
| $1 1989 | 5,203,327 | 30 | |
| $1 1989S | (617,694) | | 70 |
| $1 1990 | 5,840,110 | 30 | |
| $1 1990S | (695,510) | | 70 |
| $1 1991 | 7,191,066 | 30 | |
| $1 1991S | (511,925) | | 70 |
| $1 1992 | 5,540,068 | 30 | |
| $1 1992S | (498,654) | | 70 |
| $1 1993 | 6,763,762 | 30 | |
| $1 1993P | (405,913) | | 75 |
| $1 1994 | 4,227,319 | 32 | |
| $1 1994P | (372,168) | | 110 |
| $1 1995 | 4,672,051 | 31 | |
| $1 1995P | (438,511) | | 75 |
| $1 1995W | (30,125) | | 3,100 |
| $1 1996 | 3,603,386 | 32 | |
| $1 1996P | (500,000) | | 70 |
| $1 1997 | 4,295,004 | 31 | |
| $1 1997P | (435,368) | | 70 |
| $1 1998 | 4,847,549 | 30 | |
| $1 1998P | (450,000) | | 70 |
| $1 1999 | 7,408,640 | 30 | |
| $1 1999P | (549,769) | | 70 |
| $1 2000(W) | 9,239,132 | 30 | |
| $1 2000P | (600,000) | | 70 |
| $1 2001(W) | 9,001,711 | 29 | |
| $1 2001W | (746,398) | | 70 |
| $1 2002(W) | 10,539,026 | 29 | |
| $1 2002W | (647,32) | | 70 |
| $1 2003(W) | 8,495,008 | 29 | |
| $1 2003W | (747,831) | | 70 |
| $1 2004(W) | 8,882,754 | 29 | |
| $1 2004W | (801,602) | | 70 |
| $1 2005(W) | 8,891,025 | 29 | |
| $1 2005W | (816,663) | | 70 |
| $1 2006(W) | 10,676,522 | 29 | |
| $1 2006W, Burnished | 468,020 | 45 | |
| $1 2006W | (1,092,477) | | 70 |
| $1 2006P, Reverse Proof | (248,875) | | 90 |
| $1 2007(W) | 9,028,036 | 29 | |
| $1 2007W, Burnished | 621,333 | 40 | |
| $1 2007W | (821,759) | | 70 |
| $1 2008(W) | 20,583,000 | 29 | |
| $1 2009(W) (a) | 30,459,000 | $29 | |
| $1 2010(W) | 34,764,500 | 29 | |
| $1 2010W | (849,861) | | $70 |
| $1 2011(W)(S) | 40,020,000 | 29 | |
| $1 2011W, Burnished | 409,927 | 40 | |
| $1 2011S, Burnished | 99,882 | 150 | |
| $1 2011W | (947,355) | | 70 |
| $1 2011P, Reverse Proof | (99,882) | | 200 |
| $1 2012(W)(S) | 33,121,500 | 29 | |
| $1 2012W, Burnished | 226,120 | 40 | |
| $1 2012W | (869,386) | | 70 |
| $1 2012S | (285,184) | | 75 |
| $1 2012S, Reverse Proof | (224,981) | | 70 |
| $1 2013(W)(S) | 42,675,000 | 29 | |
| $1 2013W, Burnished | 222,091 | 40 | |
| $1 2013W, Enh. Unc. | 235,689 | 110 | |
| $1 2013W | (934,812) | | 70 |
| $1 2013W, Reverse Proof | (235,689) | | 90 |
| $1 2014(W)(P)(S) | 44,006,000 | 29 | |
| $1 2014W, Burnished | 253,169 | 40 | |
| $1 2014W | (944,770) | | 70 |
| $1 2015(W)(S) | 47,000,000 | 29 | |
| $1 2015W, Burnished | 201,188 | 40 | |
| $1 2015W | (707,518) | | 70 |
| $1 2016(W)(S) | 37,701,500 | 29 | |
| $1 2016W, Burnished | 216,501 | 40 | |
| $1 2016W | (651,453) | | 70 |
| $1 2017(W)(S) | 18,065,500 | 29 | |
| $1 2017W, Burnished | 176,739 | 40 | |
| $1 2017W | (440,586) | | 70 |
| $1 2017S | (123,799) | | 70 |
| $1 2018(W)(S) | 15,700,000 | 29 | |
| $1 2018W, Burnished | 138,947 | 40 | |
| $1 2018W | (411,513) | | 70 |
| $1 2018S | (246,485) | | 70 |
| $1 2019(W) | 14,863,500 | 29 | |
| $1 2019W, Burnished | 141,030 | 40 | |
| $1 2019W | (436,724) | | 70 |
| $1 2019W, Enh. RevPf | (99,675) | | 110 |
| $1 2019S | (200,696) | | 70 |
| $1 2019S, Enh. RevPf | (29,909) | | 900 |
| $1 2020(W)(S) | 30,089,500 | 29 | |
| $1 2020W, Burnished | 154,863 | 40 | |
| $1 2020W, 75th Anniversary of the End of WWII (with privy mark) | (75,000) | | 300 |
| $1 2020W | (405,553) | | 70 |
| $1 2020S | (258,855) | | 70 |
| $1 2021(W), Heraldic Eagle | | 29 | |

Note: "Burnished" refers to special American Eagle Uncirculated coins in silver, gold, and platinum sold directly by the U.S. Mint. Similar in appearance to ordinary Uncirculated American Eagle bullion coins, these coins can be distinguished by the presence of a mintmark and the use of burnished coin blanks. (Proof coins also have a mintmark but have highly reflective, mirrorlike surfaces.) **a.** No Proof dollars were made in 2009. Beware of alterations made privately outside the Mint.

# SILVER BULLION

| | Mintage | Unc. | PF | | Mintage | Unc. | PF |
|---|---|---|---|---|---|---|---|
| $1 2021W, Heraldic Eagle | | | $70 | $1 2021S, Flying Eagle, RevPf. | | | $110 |
| $1 2021W, Heraldic Eagle, RevPf | | | 110 | $1 2022(W)(S) | | $29 | |
| $1 2021(W)(S), Flying Eagle | | $29 | | $1 2022W, Burnished | | 40 | |
| $1 2021W, Flying Eagle, Burnished | | 40 | | $1 2022W | | | 70 |
| $1 2021W, Flying Eagle | | | 75 | $1 2022S | | | 70 |
| $1 2021S, Flying Eagle | | | 75 | | | | |

*Note:* "Burnished" refers to special American Eagle Uncirculated coins in silver, gold, and platinum sold directly by the U.S. Mint. Similar in appearance to ordinary Uncirculated American Eagle bullion coins, these coins can be distinguished by the presence of a mintmark and the use of burnished coin blanks. (Proof coins also have a mintmark but have highly reflective, mirrorlike surfaces.)

## American Silver Eagle Sets

| | |
|---|---|
| 1997 Impressions of Liberty Set | $3,650 |
| 2006 20th Anniversary Silver Coin Set. Uncirculated, Proof, Reverse Proof | 180 |
| 2006 20th Anniversary 1-oz. Gold- and Silver-Dollar Set. Uncirculated | 2,050 |
| 2011 25th Anniversary Five-Coin Set. 2011W Unc., Pf; 2011P RevPf; 2011S Unc.; 2011 Bullion. | 500 |
| 2012 75th Anniversary of San Francisco Mint Two-Piece Set. S-Mint Pf and RevPf silver dollars | 140 |
| 2013 75th Anniversary of West Point Depository Two-Coin Set. W-Mint Enhanced Uncirculated and Reverse Proof silver dollars | 200 |
| 2019 Pride of Two Nations Limited Edition Two-Coin Set. W-Mint Enhanced Reverse Proof and Royal Canadian Mint Silver Maple Leaf modified Proof | 140 |
| 2021 Reverse Proof Two-Coin Set. W-Mint, Heraldic Eagle, and S-Mint, Flying Eagle, Reverse Proof silver dollars | 160 |

# AMERICAN GOLD EAGLE COINS

Bullion values are based on spot gold at $1,800 per ounce.

Reverse, 1986–2021.      Reverse, 2021 to date.

## $5 Tenth-Ounce Gold

| | Mintage | Unc. | PF | | Mintage | Unc. | PF |
|---|---|---|---|---|---|---|---|
| $5 MCMLXXXVI (1986) | 912,609 | $200 | | $5 2004W | (35,131) | | $220 |
| $5 MCMLXXXVII (1987) | 580,266 | 200 | | $5 2005 | 300,043 | $195 | |
| $5 MCMLXXXVIII (1988) | 159,500 | 220 | | $5 2005W | (49,265) | | 220 |
| $5 MCMLXXXVIII (1988)P | (143,881) | | $225 | $5 2006 | 285,006 | 195 | |
| $5 MCMLXXXIX (1989) | 264,790 | 210 | | $5 2006W, Burnished | 20,643 | 200 | |
| $5 MCMLXXXIX (1989)P | (84,647) | | 225 | $5 2006W | (47,277) | | 220 |
| $5 MCMXC (1990) | 210,210 | 210 | | $5 2007 | 190,010 | 195 | |
| $5 MCMXC (1990)P | (99,349) | | 225 | $5 2007W, Burnished | 22,501 | 200 | |
| $5 MCMXCI (1991) | 165,200 | 210 | | $5 2007W | (58,553) | | 220 |
| $5 MCMXCI (1991)P | (70,334) | | 225 | $5 2008 | 305,000 | 200 | |
| $5 1992 | 209,300 | 195 | | $5 2008W, Burnished | 12,657 | 250 | |
| $5 1992P | (64,874) | | 220 | $5 2008W | (28,116) | | 220 |
| $5 1993 | 210,709 | 195 | | $5 2009 | 270,000 | 200 | |
| $5 1993P | (58,649) | | 220 | $5 2010 | 435,000 | 200 | |
| $5 1994 | 206,380 | 195 | | $5 2010W | (54,285) | | 220 |
| $5 1994W | (62,849) | | 220 | $5 2011 | 350,000 | 200 | |
| $5 1995 | 223,025 | 195 | | $5 2011W | (42,697) | | 220 |
| $5 1995W | (62,667) | | 220 | $5 2012 | 290,000 | 200 | |
| $5 1996 | 401,964 | 195 | | $5 2012W | (20,637) | | 220 |
| $5 1996W | (57,047) | | 220 | $5 2013 | 555,000 | 200 | |
| $5 1997 | 528,266 | 195 | | $5 2013W | (21,738) | | 220 |
| $5 1997W | (34,977) | | 220 | $5 2014 | 545,000 | 200 | |
| $5 1998 | 1,344,520 | 195 | | $5 2014W | (22,725) | | 220 |
| $5 1998W | (39,395) | | 220 | $5 2015 | 980,000 | 200 | |
| $5 1999 | 2,750,338 | 195 | | $5 2015W | (26,769) | | 220 |
| $5 1999W | (48,428) | | 220 | $5 2016 | 925,000 | 200 | |
| $5 1999W, Unc. Made from unpolished Proof dies | 14,500 | 600 | | $5 2016W | (37,312) | | 220 |
| $5 2000 | 569,153 | 195 | | $5 2017 | 395,000 | 200 | |
| $5 2000W | (49,971) | | 220 | $5 2017W | (20,969) | | 220 |
| $5 2001 | 269,147 | 195 | | $5 2018 | 230,000 | 200 | |
| $5 2001W | (37,530) | | 220 | $5 2018W | (22,155) | | 220 |
| $5 2002 | 230,027 | 195 | | $5 2019 | 195,000 | 200 | |
| $5 2002W | (40,864) | | 220 | $5 2019W | (19,612) | | 220 |
| $5 2003 | 245,029 | 195 | | $5 2020 | 350,000 | 200 | |
| $5 2003W | (40,027) | | 220 | $5 2020W | (24,033) | | 220 |
| $5 2004 | 250,016 | 195 | | $5 2021, Family of Eagles | | 200 | |
| | | | | $5 2021W, Family of Eagles | | | 220 |

| | Mintage | Unc. | PF |
|---|---|---|---|
| $5 2021, Head of Eagle | | $200 | |
| $5 2021W, Head of Eagle | | | $220 |

| | Mintage | Unc. | PF |
|---|---|---|---|
| $5 2022 | | $200 | |
| $5 2022W | | | $220 |

## $10 Quarter-Ounce Gold

| | Mintage | Unc. | PF |
|---|---|---|---|
| $10 MCMLXXXVI (1986) | 726,031 | $500 | |
| $10 MCMLXXXVII (1987) | 269,255 | 550 | |
| $10 MCMLXXXVIII (1988) | 49,000 | 900 | |
| $10 MCMLXXXVIII (1988)P | (98,028) | | $530 |
| $10 MCMLXXXIX (1989) | 81,789 | 900 | |
| $10 MCMLXXXIX (1989)P | (54,170) | | 530 |
| $10 MCMXC (1990) | 41,000 | 950 | |
| $10 MCMXC (1990)P | (62,674) | | 530 |
| $10 MCMXCI (1991) | 36,100 | 950 | |
| $10 MCMXCI (1991)P | (50,839) | | 530 |
| $10 1992 | 59,546 | 800 | |
| $10 1992P | (46,269) | | 530 |
| $10 1993 | 71,864 | 800 | |
| $10 1993P | (46,464) | | 530 |
| $10 1994 | 72,650 | 800 | |
| $10 1994W | (48,172) | | 530 |
| $10 1995 | 83,752 | 800 | |
| $10 1995W | (47,526) | | 530 |
| $10 1996 | 60,318 | 800 | |
| $10 1996W | (38,219) | | 530 |
| $10 1997 | 108,805 | 465 | |
| $10 1997W | (29,805) | | 530 |
| $10 1998 | 309,829 | 465 | |
| $10 1998W | (29,503) | | 530 |
| $10 1999 | 564,232 | 465 | |
| $10 1999W | (34,417) | | 530 |
| $10 1999W, Unc. Made from unpolished Proof dies | *10,000* | 1,100 | |
| $10 2000 | 128,964 | 465 | |
| $10 2000W | (36,036) | | 530 |
| $10 2001 | 71,280 | 800 | |
| $10 2001W | (25,613) | | 530 |
| $10 2002 | 62,027 | 500 | |
| $10 2002W | (29,242) | | 530 |
| $10 2003 | 74,029 | 465 | |
| $10 2003W | (30,292) | | 530 |
| $10 2004 | 72,014 | 465 | |
| $10 2004W | (28,839) | | 530 |
| $10 2005 | 72,015 | 465 | |
| $10 2005W | (37,207) | | 530 |

| | Mintage | Unc. | PF |
|---|---|---|---|
| $10 2006 | 60,004 | $465 | |
| $10 2006W, Burnished | 15,188 | 500 | |
| $10 2006W | (36,127) | | $530 |
| $10 2007 | 34,004 | 500 | |
| $10 2007W, Burnished | 12,766 | 500 | |
| $10 2007W | (46,189) | | 530 |
| $10 2008 | 70,000 | 350 | |
| $10 2008W, Burnished | 8,883 | 1,000 | |
| $10 2008W | (18,877) | | 530 |
| $10 2009 | 110,000 | 465 | |
| $10 2010 | 86,000 | 465 | |
| $10 2010W | (44,057) | | 530 |
| $10 2011 | 80,000 | 465 | |
| $10 2011W | (28,782) | | 530 |
| $10 2012 | 90,000 | 465 | |
| $10 2012W | (13,926) | | 530 |
| $10 2013 | 114,500 | 465 | |
| $10 2013W | (12,782) | | 530 |
| $10 2014 | 90,000 | 465 | |
| $10 2014W | (14,790) | | 530 |
| $10 2015 | 158,000 | 465 | |
| $10 2015W | (15,775) | | 530 |
| $10 2016 | 152,000 | 465 | |
| $10 2016W | (22,828) | | 530 |
| $10 2017 | *64,000* | 465 | |
| $10 2017W | (14,513) | | 530 |
| $10 2018 | *62,000* | 465 | |
| $10 2018W | (12,769) | | 530 |
| $10 2019 | *38,000* | 465 | |
| $10 2019W | *(11,861)* | | 530 |
| $10 2020 | *106,000* | 465 | |
| $10 2020W | *(15,806)* | | 530 |
| $10 2021, Family of Eagles | | 465 | |
| $10 2021W, Family of Eagles | | | 530 |
| $10 2021, Head of Eagle | | 465 | |
| $10 2021W, Head of Eagle **(a)** | 7,924 | — | |
| $10 2021W, Head of Eagle | | | 530 |
| $10 2022 | | 465 | |
| $10 2022W | | | 530 |

**a.** The Mint reported that 7,924 bullion-strike pieces were made in error with an unfinished Proof obverse die bearing a W mintmark. To date, just over 60 have been found.

## $25 Half-Ounce Gold

| | Mintage | Unc. | PF |
|---|---|---|---|
| $25 MCMLXXXVI (1986) | 599,566 | $950 | |
| $25 MCMLXXXVII (1987) | 131,255 | 950 | |
| $25 MCMLXXXVII (1987)P | (143,398) | | $1,060 |

| | Mintage | Unc. | PF |
|---|---|---|---|
| $25 MCMLXXXVIII (1988) | 45,000 | $1,500 | |
| $25 MCMLXXXVIII (1988)P | (76,528) | | $1,035 |
| $25 MCMLXXXIX (1989) | 44,829 | 1,600 | |

*Chart continued on next page.*

| | Mintage | Unc. | PF |
|---|---|---|---|
| $25 MCMLXXXIX (1989)P. . | (44,798) | | $1,060 |
| $25 MCMXC (1990). . . . . . | 31,000 | $1,800 | |
| $25 MCMXC (1990)P. . . . . | (51,636) | | 1,060 |
| $25 MCMXCI (1991) . . . . . | 24,100 | 2,300 | |
| $25 MCMXCI (1991)P . . . . | (53,125) | | 1,060 |
| $25 1992 . . . . . . . . . . . . | 54,404 | 1,000 | |
| $25 1992P . . . . . . . . . . . | (40,976) | | 1,060 |
| $25 1993 . . . . . . . . . . . . | 73,324 | 1,000 | |
| $25 1993P . . . . . . . . . . . | (43,819) | | 1,060 |
| $25 1994 . . . . . . . . . . . . | 62,400 | 1,000 | |
| $25 1994W . . . . . . . . . . . | (44,584) | | 1,060 |
| $25 1995 . . . . . . . . . . . . | 53,474 | 1,250 | |
| $25 1995W . . . . . . . . . . . | (45,388) | | 1,060 |
| $25 1996 . . . . . . . . . . . . | 39,287 | 1,100 | |
| $25 1996W . . . . . . . . . . . | (35,058) | | 1,060 |
| $25 1997 . . . . . . . . . . . . | 79,605 | 1,000 | |
| $25 1997W . . . . . . . . . . . | (26,344) | | 1,060 |
| $25 1998 . . . . . . . . . . . . | 169,029 | 950 | |
| $25 1998W . . . . . . . . . . . | (25,374) | | 1,060 |
| $25 1999 . . . . . . . . . . . . | 263,013 | 950 | |
| $25 1999W . . . . . . . . . . . | (30,427) | | 1,060 |
| $25 2000 . . . . . . . . . . . . | 79,287 | 950 | |
| $25 2000W . . . . . . . . . . . | (32,028) | | 1,060 |
| $25 2001 . . . . . . . . . . . . | 48,047 | 950 | |
| $25 2001W . . . . . . . . . . . | (23,240) | | 1,060 |
| $25 2002 . . . . . . . . . . . . | 70,027 | 950 | |
| $25 2002W . . . . . . . . . . . | (29,242) | | 1,060 |
| $25 2003 . . . . . . . . . . . . | 79,029 | 920 | |
| $25 2003W . . . . . . . . . . . | (28,270) | | 1,060 |
| $25 2004 . . . . . . . . . . . . | 98,040 | 920 | |
| $25 2004W . . . . . . . . . . . | (27,330) | | 1,060 |
| $25 2005 . . . . . . . . . . . . | 80,023 | 920 | |
| $25 2005W . . . . . . . . . . . | (34,311) | | 1,060 |
| $25 2006 . . . . . . . . . . . . | 66,005 | 920 | |
| $25 2006W, Burnished . . . . | 15,164 | 1,000 | |
| $25 2006W . . . . . . . . . . . | (34,322) | | 1,060 |

| | Mintage | Unc. | PF |
|---|---|---|---|
| $25 2007 . . . . . . . . . . . . | 47,002 | $950 | |
| $25 2007W, Burnished . . . . | 11,455 | 1,000 | |
| $25 2007W . . . . . . . . . . . | (44,025) | | $1,060 |
| $25 2008 . . . . . . . . . . . . | 61,000 | 920 | |
| $25 2008W, Burnished . . . . | 15,682 | 1,000 | |
| $25 2008W . . . . . . . . . . . | (22,602) | | 1,060 |
| $25 2009 . . . . . . . . . . . . | 110,000 | 920 | |
| $25 2010 . . . . . . . . . . . . | 81,000 | 920 | |
| $25 2010W . . . . . . . . . . . | (44,527) | | 1,060 |
| $25 2011 . . . . . . . . . . . . | 70,000 | 920 | |
| $25 2011W . . . . . . . . . . . | (26,781) | | 1,060 |
| $25 2012 . . . . . . . . . . . . | 43,000 | 920 | |
| $25 2012W . . . . . . . . . . . | (12,919) | | 1,060 |
| $25 2013 . . . . . . . . . . . . | 57,000 | 920 | |
| $25 2013W . . . . . . . . . . . | (12,716) | | 1,060 |
| $25 2014 . . . . . . . . . . . . | 35,000 | 920 | |
| $25 2014W . . . . . . . . . . . | (14,693) | | 1,060 |
| $25 2015 . . . . . . . . . . . . | 78,000 | 920 | |
| $25 2015W . . . . . . . . . . . | (15,820) | | 1,060 |
| $25 2016 . . . . . . . . . . . . | 71,000 | 920 | |
| $25 2016W . . . . . . . . . . . | (22,001) | | 1,060 |
| $25 2017 . . . . . . . . . . . . | 37,000 | 920 | |
| $25 2017W . . . . . . . . . . . | (12,715) | | 1,060 |
| $25 2018 . . . . . . . . . . . . | 32,000 | 920 | |
| $25 2018W . . . . . . . . . . . | (9,961) | | 1,060 |
| $25 2019 . . . . . . . . . . . . | 30,000 | 920 | |
| $25 2019W . . . . . . . . . . . | (10,703) | | 1,060 |
| $25 2020 . . . . . . . . . . . . | 70,000 | 920 | |
| $25 2020W . . . . . . . . . . . | (14,020) | | 1,060 |
| $25 2021, Family of Eagles. . . . . . . | | 920 | |
| $25 2021W, Family of Eagles. . . . . . | | | 1,060 |
| $25 2021, Head of Eagle. . . . . . . . | | 920 | |
| $25 2021W, Head of Eagle . . . . . . . | | | 1,060 |
| $25 2022 . . . . . . . . . . . . . . . . . . | | 920 | |
| $25 2022W . . . . . . . . . . . . . . . . . | | | 1,060 |

## $50 One-Ounce Gold

| | Mintage | Unc. | PF |
|---|---|---|---|
| $50 MCMLXXXVI (1986). . . | 1,362,650 | $1,870 | |
| $50 MCMLXXXVI (1986)W | (446,290) | | $2,100 |
| $50 MCMLXXXVII (1987) . . | 1,045,500 | 1,870 | |
| $50 MCMLXXXVII (1987)W | (147,498) | | 2,100 |
| $50 MCMLXXXVIII (1988). . . . | 465,000 | 1,870 | |
| $50 MCMLXXXVIII (1988)W | (87,133) | | 2,100 |
| $50 MCMLXXXIX (1989). . . . . | 415,790 | 1,870 | |
| $50 MCMLXXXIX (1989)W . . . | (54,570) | | 2,100 |
| $50 MCMXC (1990). . . . . . . . | 373,210 | 1,870 | |
| $50 MCMXC (1990)W . . . . . . | (62,401) | | 2,100 |
| $50 MCMXCI (1991) . . . . . . . | 243,100 | 1,870 | |
| $50 MCMXCI (1991)W . . . . . . | (50,411) | | 2,100 |
| $50 1992 . . . . . . . . . . . . . . . | 275,000 | 1,870 | |
| $50 1992W . . . . . . . . . . . . . . | (44,826) | | 2,100 |

| | Mintage | Unc. | PF |
|---|---|---|---|
| $50 1993 . . . . . . . . . . . . | 480,192 | $1,870 | |
| $50 1993W . . . . . . . . . . . | (34,369) | | $2,100 |
| $50 1994 . . . . . . . . . . . . | 221,633 | 1,870 | |
| $50 1994W . . . . . . . . . . . | (46,674) | | 2,100 |
| $50 1995 . . . . . . . . . . . . | 200,636 | 1,870 | |
| $50 1995W . . . . . . . . . . . | (46,368) | | 2,100 |
| $50 1996 . . . . . . . . . . . . | 189,148 | 1,870 | |
| $50 1996W . . . . . . . . . . . | (36,153) | | 2,100 |
| $50 1997 . . . . . . . . . . . . | 664,508 | 1,870 | |
| $50 1997W . . . . . . . . . . . | (32,999) | | 2,100 |
| $50 1998 . . . . . . . . . . . . | 1,468,530 | 1,870 | |
| $50 1998W . . . . . . . . . . . | (25,886) | | 2,100 |
| $50 1999 . . . . . . . . . . . . | 1,505,026 | 1,870 | |
| $50 1999W . . . . . . . . . . . | (31,427) | | 2,100 |

# GOLD BULLION

| | Mintage | Unc. | PF |
|---|---|---|---|
| $50 2000 . . . . . . . . . . . . 433,319 | | $1,870 | |
| $50 2000W . . . . . . . . . . . (33,007) | | | $2,100 |
| $50 2001 . . . . . . . . . . . . 143,605 | | 1,870 | |
| $50 2001W . . . . . . . . . . . (24,555) | | | 2,100 |
| $50 2002 . . . . . . . . . . . . 222,029 | | 1,870 | |
| $50 2002W . . . . . . . . . . . (27,499) | | | 2,100 |
| $50 2003 . . . . . . . . . . . . 416,032 | | 1,870 | |
| $50 2003W . . . . . . . . . . . (28,344) | | | 2,100 |
| $50 2004 . . . . . . . . . . . . 417,019 | | 1,870 | |
| $50 2004W . . . . . . . . . . . (28,215) | | | 2,100 |
| $50 2005 . . . . . . . . . . . . 356,555 | | 1,870 | |
| $50 2005W . . . . . . . . . . . (35,246) | | | 2,100 |
| $50 2006 . . . . . . . . . . . . 237,510 | | 1,870 | |
| $50 2006W, Burnished . . . . 45,053 | | 2,000 | |
| $50 2006W . . . . . . . . . . . (47,092) | | | 2,100 |
| $50 2006W, Reverse Proof. . (9,996) | | | 2,200 |
| $50 2007 . . . . . . . . . . . . 140,016 | | 1,870 | |
| $50 2007W, Burnished . . . . 18,066 | | 1,900 | |
| $50 2007W . . . . . . . . . . . (51,810) | | | 2,100 |
| $50 2008 . . . . . . . . . . . . 710,000 | | 1,870 | |
| $50 2008W, Burnished . . . . 11,908 | | 2,000 | |
| $50 2008W . . . . . . . . . . . (30,237) | | | 2,100 |
| $50 2009 . . . . . . . . . . .1,493,000 | | 1,870 | |
| $50 2010 . . . . . . . . . . .1,125,000 | | 1,870 | |
| $50 2010W . . . . . . . . . . . (59,480) | | | 2,100 |
| $50 2011 . . . . . . . . . . . . 857,000 | | 1,870 | |
| $50 2011W, Burnished . . . . . 8,729 | | 1,900 | |
| $50 2011W . . . . . . . . . . . (48,306) | | | 2,100 |
| $50 2012 . . . . . . . . . . . . 675,000 | | 1,870 | |
| $50 2012W, Burnished . . . . . 6,118 | | 1,900 | |
| $50 2012W . . . . . . . . . . . (23,630) | | | 2,100 |
| $50 2013 . . . . . . . . . . . . 758,500 | | 1,870 | |
| $50 2013W, Burnished . . . . . 7,293 | | 1,900 | |
| $50 2013W . . . . . . . . . . . (24,710) | | | $2,100 |
| $50 2014 . . . . . . . . . . . . 425,000 | | $1,870 | |
| $50 2014W, Burnished . . . . . 7,902 | | 1,900 | |
| $50 2014W . . . . . . . . . . . (28,703) | | | 2,100 |
| $50 2015 . . . . . . . . . . . . 594,000 | | 1,870 | |
| $50 2015W, Burnished . . . . . 6,533 | | 1,900 | |
| $50 2015W . . . . . . . . . . . (32,652) | | | 2,100 |
| $50 2016 . . . . . . . . . . . . 817,500 | | 1,870 | |
| $50 2016W, Burnished . . . . . 6,887 | | 1,900 | |
| $50 2016W . . . . . . . . . . . (40,044) | | | 2,100 |
| $50 2017. . . . . . . . . . . . . 228,500 | | 1,870 | |
| $50 2017W, Burnished . . . . . 5,800 | | 2,100 | |
| $50 2017W . . . . . . . . . . . (19,056) | | | 2,100 |
| $50 2018 . . . . . . . . . . . . 191,000 | | 1,870 | |
| $50 2018W, Burnished . . . . . 8,518 | | 1,900 | |
| $50 2018W . . . . . . . . . . . (15,564) | | | 2,100 |
| $50 2019 . . . . . . . . . . . . 108,000 | | 1,870 | |
| $50 2019W, Burnished . . . . . 6,365 | | 1,900 | |
| $50 2019W . . . . . . . . . . . (14,695) | | | 2,100 |
| $50 2020 . . . . . . . . . . . . 747,500 | | 1,870 | |
| $50 2020W, Burnished . . . . . 6,284 | | 2,200 | |
| $50 2020W . . . . . . . . . . . (17,358) | | | 2,200 |
| $50 2020W, 75th Anniversary of the End of WWII (with privy mark) . . . . . . . (1,939) | | | 10,000 |
| $50 2021, Family of Eagles . . . . . . . | | 1,870 | |
| $50 2021W, Family of Eagles . . . . . | | | 2,200 |
| $50 2021, Head of Eagle . . . . . . . . . | | 1,870 | |
| $50 2021W, Head of Eagle, Burnished . . . . . . . . . . . . . . . . . . | | 2,200 | |
| $50 2021W, Head of Eagle . . . . . . . | | | 2,200 |
| $50 2022 . . . . . . . . . . . . . . . . . . . | | 1,870 | |
| $50 2022W . . . . . . . . . . . . . . . . . . | | | 2,100 |

## Gold Bullion Sets

| | PF | | PF |
|---|---|---|---|
| 1987 Gold Set. $50, $25 . . . . . . . . . . . . . . . . | $3,200 | 1997 Impressions of Liberty Set. | |
| 1988 Gold Set. $50, $25, $10, $5 . . . . . . . . . . | 3,850 | $100 platinum, $50 gold, $1 silver . . . . . . . | $3,650 |
| 1989 Gold Set. $50, $25, $10, $5 . . . . . . . . . . | 3,850 | 1998 Gold Set. $50, $25, $10, $5 . . . . . . . . . . | 3,850 |
| 1990 Gold Set. $50, $25, $10, $5 . . . . . . . . . . | 3,850 | 1999 Gold Set. $50, $25, $10, $5 . . . . . . . . . . | 3,850 |
| 1991 Gold Set. $50, $25, $10, $5 . . . . . . . . . . | 3,850 | 2000 Gold Set. $50, $25, $10, $5 . . . . . . . . . . | 3,850 |
| 1992 Gold Set. $50, $25, $10, $5 . . . . . . . . . . | 3,850 | 2001 Gold Set. $50, $25, $10, $5 . . . . . . . . . . | 3,850 |
| 1993 Gold Set. $50, $25, $10, $5 . . . . . . . . . . | 3,850 | 2002 Gold Set. $50, $25, $10, $5 . . . . . . . . . . | 3,850 |
| 1993 Bicentennial Gold Set. $25, $10, $5, $1 silver eagle, and medal . . . . . . . . . . . . . | 1,900 | ·2003 Gold Set. $50, $25, $10, $5 . . . . . . . . . . | 3,850 |
| 1994 Gold Set. $50, $25, $10, $5 . . . . . . . . . . | 3,850 | 2004 Gold Set. $50, $25, $10, $5 . . . . . . . . . . | 3,850 |
| | | 2005 Gold Set. $50, $25, $10, $5 . . . . . . . . . . | 3,850 |
| 1995 Gold Set. $50, $25, $10, $5 . . . . . . . . . . | 3,850 | 2006 Gold Set. $50, $25, $10, $5 . . . . . . . . . . | 3,850 |
| 1995 Anniversary Gold Set. $50, $25, $10, $5, and $1 silver eagle . . . . . . . . . . . . . . . . | 6,500 | 2007 Gold Set. $50, $25, $10, $5 . . . . . . . . . . | 3,850 |
| | | 2008 Gold Set. $50, $25, $10, $5 . . . . . . . . . . | 3,850 |
| 1996 Gold Set. $50, $25, $10, $5 . . . . . . . . . . | 3,850 | 2010 Gold Set. $50, $25, $10, $5 (a) . . . . . . . | 3,850 |
| 1997 Gold Set. $50, $25, $10, $5 . . . . . . . . . . | 3,850 | 2011 Gold Set. $50, $25, $10, $5 . . . . . . . . . . | 3,850 |

a. The U.S. Mint did not issue a 2009 gold set.

*Chart continued on next page.*

| | PF |
|---|---|
| 2012 Gold Set. $50, $25, $10, $5.......... | $3,850 |
| 2013 Gold Set. $50, $25, $10, $5.......... | 3,850 |
| 2014 Gold Set. $50, $25, $10, $5.......... | 3,850 |
| 2015 Gold Set. $50, $25, $10, $5.......... | 3,850 |
| 2016 Gold Set. $50, $25, $10, $5.......... | 3,850 |
| 2017 Gold Set. $50, $25, $10, $5.......... | 3,850 |
| 2018 Gold Set. $50, $25, $10, $5.......... | 3,850 |

| | PF |
|---|---|
| 2019 Gold Set. $50, $25, $10, $5.......... | $3,850 |
| 2020 Gold Set. $50, $25, $10, $5.......... | 4,000 |
| 2021 Gold Set, Fam. Eagles. $50, $25, $10, $5 | 4,000 |
| 2021 Gold Set, Head Eagle. $50, $25, $10, $5 | 4,000 |
| 2021 $5 Gold Proof Two-Coin Set, Family of Eagles and Head of Eagle....... | 450 |
| 2022 Gold Set. $50, $25, $10, $5.......... | 4,000 |

## 2006 20th Anniversary Sets

| | |
|---|---|
| 2006W $50 Gold Set. Uncirculated, Proof, Reverse Proof ..................................... | $6,400 |
| 2006W 1-oz. Gold and Silver Coin Set. Burnished .............................................. | 2,050 |

## Gold Bullion Burnished Sets 2006–2008

| | Unc. |
|---|---|
| 2006W Burnished Gold Set. $50, $25, $10, $5 ............................................... | $3,700 |
| 2007W Burnished Gold Set. $50, $25, $10, $5 ............................................... | 3,600 |
| 2008W Burnished Gold Set. $50, $25, $10, $5 ............................................... | 4,250 |

# AMERICAN BUFFALO .9999 FINE GOLD BULLION COINS

| | Mintage | Unc. | PF |
|---|---|---|---|
| $5 2008W, Burnished ..... | 17,429 | $400 | |
| $5 2008W ............. | (18,884) | | $600 |
| $10 2008W, Burnished ..... | 9,949 | 800 | |
| $10 2008W ............. | (13,125) | | 900 |
| $25 2008W, Burnished .... | 16,908 | 1,000 | |
| $25 2008W ............. | (12,169) | | 1,400 |
| $50 2006 ............. | 337,012 | 1,850 | |
| $50 2006W ............. | (246,267) | | 1,950 |
| $50 2007 ............. | 136,503 | 1,850 | |
| $50 2007W ............. | (58,998) | | 1,950 |
| $50 2008 ............. | 189,500 | 1,850 | |
| $50 2008W, Burnished ..... | 9,074 | 2,000 | |
| $50 2008W ............. | (18,863) | | 2,600 |
| $50 2009 ............. | 200,000 | 1,850 | |
| $50 2009W ............. | (49,306) | | 1,950 |
| $50 2010 ............. | 209,000 | 1,850 | |
| $50 2010W ............. | (49,263) | | 1,950 |
| $50 2011 ............. | 250,000 | 1,850 | |
| $50 2011W ............. | (28,693) | | 1,975 |
| $50 2012 ............. | 100,000 | 1,850 | |
| $50 2012W ............. | (19,765) | | 1,975 |

| | Mintage | Unc. | PF |
|---|---|---|---|
| $50 2013 ............. | 198,500 | $1,850 | |
| $50 2013W ............. | (18,594) | | $1,975 |
| $50 2013W, Reverse Proof | (47,836) | | 2,000 |
| $50 2014 ............. | 180,500 | 1,850 | |
| $50 2014W ............. | (20,557) | | 1,975 |
| $50 2015 ............. | 223,500 | 1,850 | |
| $50 2015W ............. | (16,591) | | 1,975 |
| $50 2016 ............. | 211,000 | 1,850 | |
| $50 2016W ............. | (21,878) | | 1,975 |
| $50 2017 ............. | 99,500 | 1,850 | |
| $50 2017W ............. | (15,810) | | 1,975 |
| $50 2018 ............. | 121,500 | 1,850 | |
| $50 2018W ............. | (15,756) | | 2,025 |
| $50 2019 ............. | 61,500 | 1,850 | |
| $50 2019W ............. | (14,844) | | 2,025 |
| $50 2020 ............. | 242,000 | 1,850 | |
| $50 2020W ............. | (11,887) | | 3,000 |
| $50 2021 ..................... | | 1,850 | |
| $50 2021W ............. | | | 2,200 |
| $50 2022 ..................... | | 1,850 | |
| $50 2022W ............. | | | 2,025 |

## American Buffalo Gold Bullion Sets

| | Unc. | PF |
|---|---|---|
| 2008W Four-coin set. $50, $25, $10, $5. . . . . . . . . . . . . . . . . . . . . . . . . . . . . . . . . . . . . . . . . . . | | $5,500 |
| 2008W Four-coin set, Burnished. $50, $25, $10, $5. . . . . . . . . . . . . . . . . . . . . . . . . . . . . . | $4,200 | |
| 2008W Double Prosperity Set. Uncirculated $25 Buffalo and $25 American Gold Eagle coins . . | 2,000 | |

# FIRST SPOUSE $10 GOLD BULLION COINS
## Half-Ounce 24-Karat Gold

| Martha Washington | Abigail Adams | Jefferson's Liberty | Dolley Madison |
|---|---|---|---|

| | Mintage | Unc. | PF |
|---|---|---|---|
| $10 2007W, Martha Washington. . . . . . . . . . . . . . . . . . . . . . . . . . . . . (19,167) . . . . . . . 17,661 | | $920 | $930 |
| $10 2007W, Abigail Adams. . . . . . . . . . . . . . . . . . . . . . . . . . . . . . . . . . . (17,149) . . . . . . . 17,142 | | 920 | 930 |
| $10 2007W, Thomas Jefferson's Liberty. . . . . . . . . . . . . . . . . . . . . . (19,815) . . . . . . . 19,823 | | 920 | 930 |
| $10 2007W, Dolley Madison . . . . . . . . . . . . . . . . . . . . . . . . . . . . . . . . (17,943) . . . . . . . 12,340 | | 920 | 930 |
| $10 2008W, Elizabeth Monroe. . . . . . . . . . . . . . . . . . . . . . . . . . . . . . . (7,800) . . . . . . . . 4,462 | | 930 | 940 |
| $10 2008W, Louisa Adams . . . . . . . . . . . . . . . . . . . . . . . . . . . . . . . . . . (6,581) . . . . . . . . 3,885 | | 930 | 940 |
| $10 2008W, Andrew Jackson's Liberty. . . . . . . . . . . . . . . . . . . . . . . (7,684) . . . . . . . . 4,609 | | 930 | 940 |
| $10 2008W, Martin Van Buren's Liberty . . . . . . . . . . . . . . . . . . . . . (6,807) . . . . . . . . 3,826 | | 930 | 940 |
| $10 2009W, Anna Harrison . . . . . . . . . . . . . . . . . . . . . . . . . . . . . . . . . (6,251) . . . . . . . . 3,645 | | 930 | 940 |
| $10 2009W, Letitia Tyler . . . . . . . . . . . . . . . . . . . . . . . . . . . . . . . . . . . (5,296) . . . . . . . . 3,240 | | 930 | 940 |
| $10 2009W, Julia Tyler . . . . . . . . . . . . . . . . . . . . . . . . . . . . . . . . . . . . (4,844) . . . . . . . . 3,143 | | 930 | 950 |
| $10 2009W, Sarah Polk . . . . . . . . . . . . . . . . . . . . . . . . . . . . . . . . . . . . (5,151) . . . . . . . . 3,489 | | 930 | 950 |
| $10 2009W, Margaret Taylor . . . . . . . . . . . . . . . . . . . . . . . . . . . . . . . (4,936) . . . . . . . . 3,627 | | 930 | 940 |
| $10 2010W, Abigail Fillmore . . . . . . . . . . . . . . . . . . . . . . . . . . . . . . . (6,130) . . . . . . . . 3,482 | | 930 | 940 |
| $10 2010W, Jane Pierce . . . . . . . . . . . . . . . . . . . . . . . . . . . . . . . . . . . (4,775) . . . . . . . . 3,338 | | 930 | 940 |
| $10 2010W, James Buchanan's Liberty. . . . . . . . . . . . . . . . . . . . . . (7,110) . . . . . . . . 5,162 | | 930 | 940 |
| $10 2010W, Mary Lincoln . . . . . . . . . . . . . . . . . . . . . . . . . . . . . . . . . . (6,861) . . . . . . . . 3,695 | | 930 | 940 |
| $10 2011W, Eliza Johnson. . . . . . . . . . . . . . . . . . . . . . . . . . . . . . . . . . (3,887) . . . . . . . . 2,905 | | 930 | 940 |
| $10 2011W, Julia Grant. . . . . . . . . . . . . . . . . . . . . . . . . . . . . . . . . . . . (3,943) . . . . . . . . 2,892 | | 930 | 940 |
| $10 2011W, Lucy Hayes . . . . . . . . . . . . . . . . . . . . . . . . . . . . . . . . . . . (3,868) . . . . . . . . 2,196 | | 930 | 950 |
| $10 2011W, Lucretia Garfield . . . . . . . . . . . . . . . . . . . . . . . . . . . . . . (3,653) . . . . . . . . 2,168 | | 930 | 940 |
| $10 2012W, Alice Paul. . . . . . . . . . . . . . . . . . . . . . . . . . . . . . . . . . . . . (3,505) . . . . . . . . 2,798 | | 930 | 940 |
| $10 2012W, Frances Cleveland, Type 1 . . . . . . . . . . . . . . . . . . . . . . (3,158) . . . . . . . . 2,454 | | 930 | 940 |
| $10 2012W, Caroline Harrison. . . . . . . . . . . . . . . . . . . . . . . . . . . . . . (3,046) . . . . . . . . 2,436 | | 930 | 940 |
| $10 2012W, Frances Cleveland, Type 2 . . . . . . . . . . . . . . . . . . . . . . (3,104) . . . . . . . . 2,425 | | 930 | 940 |
| $10 2013W, Ida McKinley . . . . . . . . . . . . . . . . . . . . . . . . . . . . . . . . . (2,724) . . . . . . . . 2,008 | | 930 | 940 |
| $10 2013W, Edith Roosevelt . . . . . . . . . . . . . . . . . . . . . . . . . . . . . . . (2,840) . . . . . . . . 2,027 | | 950 | 950 |
| $10 2013W, Helen Taft. . . . . . . . . . . . . . . . . . . . . . . . . . . . . . . . . . . . (2,598) . . . . . . . . 1,993 | | 950 | 950 |
| $10 2013W, Ellen Wilson. . . . . . . . . . . . . . . . . . . . . . . . . . . . . . . . . . (2,511) . . . . . . . . 1,980 | | 950 | 950 |
| $10 2013W, Edith Wilson . . . . . . . . . . . . . . . . . . . . . . . . . . . . . . . . . (2,464) . . . . . . . . 1,974 | | 950 | 950 |
| $10 2014W, Florence Harding. . . . . . . . . . . . . . . . . . . . . . . . . . . . . . (2,372) . . . . . . . . 1,944 | | 950 | 950 |

*Chart continued on next page.*

| | Mintage | Unc. | PF |
|---|---|---|---|
| $10 2014W, Grace Coolidge | (2,315) | 1,949 | $950 | $950 |
| $10 2014W, Lou Hoover | (2,392) | 1,936 | 950 | 950 |
| $10 2014W, Eleanor Roosevelt | (2,377) | 1,886 | 950 | 950 |
| $10 2015W, Elizabeth Truman | (2,747) | 1,946 | 950 | 950 |
| $10 2015W, Mamie Eisenhower | (2,704) | 2,102 | 950 | 950 |
| $10 2015W, Jacqueline Kennedy | (11,222) | 6,439 | 950 | 950 |
| $10 2015W, Claudia Taylor "Lady Bird" Johnson | (2,611) | 1,927 | 950 | 950 |
| $10 2016W, Pat Nixon | (2,646) | 1,839 | 950 | 950 |
| $10 2016W, Betty Ford | (2,471) | 1,824 | 950 | 950 |
| $10 2016W, Nancy Reagan | (3,548) | 2,009 | 950 | 950 |
| $10 2020W, Barbara Bush | (2,896) | 1,817 | 950 | 950 |

## MMIX ULTRA HIGH RELIEF GOLD COIN (2009)

**MMIX Ultra High Relief Gold Coin**
*Photographed at an angle to
show the edge, lettered E PLURIBUS
UNUM, and the depth of relief.*

A modern version of the 1907 Ultra High Relief double eagle gold pattern was produced in 2009 at the Philadelphia Mint. It was made to demonstrate technical advances in minting techniques that make possible such a coin. The original design was never made for commercial use because it could not be made in sufficient quantities.

The design was by Augustus Saint-Gaudens. A version of it in much lower relief was used on double eagle coins minted from 1907 to 1933. To create the coin in ultra high relief, the 2009 version was made in a slightly smaller diameter, and composed of 24-karat gold, making it easier to strike and maintain the fidelity of the design. Through 21st-century technology the original Saint-Gaudens plasters were digitally mapped by the Mint and used in the die-making process. The date was changed to 2009, and four additional stars were added to represent the current 50 states. The inscription "In God We Trust" was not used on the 1907 version.

The MMIX Ultra High Relief gold coins are 4 mm thick and contain one ounce of .999 fine gold. All are Uncirculated (business strikes). All are made at the West Point Mint, and packaged by the Mint in a special mahogany box.

| | Mintage | SP |
|---|---|---|
| (2009) MMIX Ultra High Relief $20 Gold Coin | 114,427 | $2,100 |

## 400TH ANNIVERSARY OF
## THE MAYFLOWER GOLD COIN

In 2020 the United States Mint recognized the 400th anniversary of the Pilgrims' landing at Plymouth Rock aboard the *Mayflower*. Under authority granted by Congress to the secretary of the Treasury, the Mint issued two 1/4-ounce, ten-dollar gold coins from the West Point Mint, one in Proof and the other a Reverse Proof. Both have a reeded edge and a diameter of 22 mm, with a fineness of .9999. The Proof was sold individually, while the Reverse Proof was part of a two-coin set that also contained a gold £25 commemorative Proof coin from the British Royal Mint.

| | Mintage | Unc. |
|---|---|---|
| 2020W. | 4,743 | $450 |
| 2020W, Reverse Proof. | (4,881) | 480 |

## 75TH ANNIVERSARY OF THE
## END OF WORLD WAR II GOLD COIN

Under the Treasury secretary's authority to issue gold coins "from time to time" without specific commemorative legislation, in 2020 the Mint issued a .9999 fine gold twenty-five-dollar coin to mark the 75th anniversary of the end of World War II. Struck at the West Point Mint, the Proof coin weighs one-half ounce and measures 27 mm in diameter. Its edge is reeded. The Mint also issued a related one-ounce Proof silver medal, privy-marked West Point quarter dollars, and privy-marked gold and silver American Eagles in celebration of the anniversary.

| | Mintage | PF |
|---|---|---|
| 2020W. | 7,366 | $1,200 |

## AMERICAN LIBERTY
## HIGH RELIEF GOLD COINS

The first American Liberty High Relief .9999-fine gold coin, with a weight of one ounce and a face value of $100, was minted at West Point in 2015. The coin was not congressionally mandated, instead being created under authority granted to the Secretary of the Treasury by federal law. Its design was created in part to show "a 'modern' Liberty that reflects the nation's diversity."

The designs for the American Liberty High Relief gold coins are created to take full advantage of the same high-relief techniques used to create the MMIX Ultra High Relief gold coin. The series is slated to continue biennially, with a new design being issued every two years. In the years between gold issues, silver medals featuring the same designs will be issued.

2015-W

1792–2017-W

2018-W, $10

2019-W

2021-W

| | Mintage | Unc. | PF |
|---|---|---|---|
| $100 2015W, 1 oz. | 49,325 | $2,000 | |
| $100 1792–2017W, 1 oz. | (34,604) | | $2,100 |
| $10 2018W, 1/10 oz. | (45,598) | | 240 |
| $100 2019W, 1 oz., Enhanced Finish | 24,609 | 2,000 | |
| $100 2021W, 1 oz. | | | 2,100 |

## AMERICAN PLATINUM EAGLE COINS

The one-ounce American Eagle platinum coin is designated $100 and contains one ounce of pure platinum. Fractional denominations containing 1/2 ounce, 1/4 ounce, or 1/10 ounce are called $50, $25, and $10, respectively.

Bullion values are based on spot platinum at $1,050 per ounce.

Obverse for Bullion and Proof, All Years

Reverse for Bullion, All Years; for Proof in 1997

### $10 Tenth-Ounce Platinum

| | Mintage | Unc. | PF |
|---|---|---|---|
| $10 1997 | 70,250 | $120 | |
| $10 1997W | (36,993) | | $150 |
| $10 1998 | 39,525 | 120 | |
| $10 1998W | (19,847) | | 150 |
| $10 1999 | 55,955 | 120 | |
| $10 1999W | (19,133) | | 150 |
| $10 2000 | 34,027 | 120 | |
| $10 2000W | (15,651) | | 150 |
| $10 2001 | 52,017 | 120 | |
| $10 2001W | (12,174) | | 150 |
| $10 2002 | 23,005 | 120 | |
| $10 2002W | (12,365) | | 150 |
| $10 2003 | 22,007 | 120 | |
| $10 2003W | (9,534) | | 150 |

| | Mintage | Unc. | PF |
|---|---|---|---|
| $10 2004 | 15,010 | $120 | |
| $10 2004W | (7,161) | | $150 |
| $10 2005 | 14,013 | 120 | |
| $10 2005W | (8,104) | | 150 |
| $10 2006 | 11,001 | 120 | |
| $10 2006W, Burnished | 3,544 | 180 | |
| $10 2006W | (10,205) | | 150 |
| $10 2007 | 13,003 | 120 | |
| $10 2007W, Burnished | 5,556 | 150 | |
| $10 2007W | (8,176) | | 150 |
| $10 2008 | 17,000 | 120 | |
| $10 2008W, Burnished | 3,706 | 200 | |
| $10 2008W | (5,138) | | 175 |

### $25 Quarter-Ounce Platinum

| | Mintage | Unc. | PF |
|---|---|---|---|
| $25 1997 | 27,100 | $300 | |
| $25 1997W | (18,628) | | $350 |
| $25 1998 | 38,887 | 300 | |
| $25 1998W | (14,873) | | 350 |
| $25 1999 | 39,734 | 300 | |
| $25 1999W | (13,507) | | 350 |
| $25 2000 | 20,054 | 300 | |
| $25 2000W | (11,995) | | 350 |
| $25 2001 | 21,815 | 300 | |
| $25 2001W | (8,847) | | 350 |
| $25 2002 | 27,405 | 300 | |
| $25 2002W | (9,282) | | 350 |
| $25 2003 | 25,207 | 300 | |
| $25 2003W | (7,044) | | 350 |

| | Mintage | Unc. | PF |
|---|---|---|---|
| $25 2004 | 18,010 | $300 | |
| $25 2004W | (5,193) | | $350 |
| $25 2005 | 12,013 | 300 | |
| $25 2005W | (6,592) | | 350 |
| $25 2006 | 12,001 | 300 | |
| $25 2006W, Burnished | 2,676 | 350 | |
| $25 2006W | (7,813) | | 350 |
| $25 2007 | 8,402 | 300 | |
| $25 2007W, Burnished | 3,690 | 400 | |
| $25 2007W | (6,017) | | 350 |
| $25 2007W, Frosted FREEDOM | (21) | | — |
| $25 2008 | 22,800 | 300 | |
| $25 2008W, Burnished | 2,481 | 400 | |
| $25 2008W | (4,153) | | 370 |

### $50 Half-Ounce Platinum

| | Mintage | Unc. | PF |
|---|---|---|---|
| $50 1997 | 20,500 | $575 | |
| $50 1997W | (15,431) | | $700 |
| $50 1998 | 32,415 | 575 | |

| | Mintage | Unc. | PF |
|---|---|---|---|
| $50 1998W | (13,836) | | $700 |
| $50 1999 | 32,309 | $575 | |
| $50 1999W | (11,103) | | 700 |

*Chart continued on next page.*

| | Mintage | Unc. | PF |
|---|---|---|---|
| $50 2000 . . . . . . . . . . . . . | 18,892 | $575 | |
| $50 2000W . . . . . . . . . . . | (11,049) | | $700 |
| $50 2001 . . . . . . . . . . . . . | 12,815 | 575 | |
| $50 2001W . . . . . . . . . . . | (8,254) | | 700 |
| $50 2002 . . . . . . . . . . . . . | 24,005 | 575 | |
| $50 2002W . . . . . . . . . . . | (8,772) | | 700 |
| $50 2003 . . . . . . . . . . . . . | 17,409 | 575 | |
| $50 2003W . . . . . . . . . . . | (7,131) | | 700 |
| $50 2004 . . . . . . . . . . . . . | 13,236 | 575 | |
| $50 2004W . . . . . . . . . . . | (5,063) | | 750 |
| $50 2005 . . . . . . . . . . . . . | 9,013 | 575 | |
| $50 2005W . . . . . . . . . . . | (5,942) | | 700 |

| | Mintage | Unc. | PF |
|---|---|---|---|
| $50 2006 . . . . . . . . . . . . . | 9,602 | $575 | |
| $50 2006W, Burnished . . . . . | 2,577 | 650 | |
| $50 2006W . . . . . . . . . . . | (7,649) | | $700 |
| $50 2007 . . . . . . . . . . . . . | 7,001 | 575 | |
| $50 2007W, Burnished . . . . . | 3,635 | 600 | |
| $50 2007W . . . . . . . . . . . | (25,519) | | 700 |
| $50 2007W, RevPf . . . . . . . | (19,583) | | 800 |
| $50 2007W, Frosted FREEDOM . .(21) | | | — |
| $50 2008 . . . . . . . . . . . . . | 14,000 | 575 | |
| $50 2008W, Burnished . . . . . | 2,253 | 700 | |
| $50 2008W . . . . . . . . . . . | (4,020) | | 750 |

## $100 One-Ounce Platinum
### *Proof Platinum Reverse Designs*

1998: Eagle Over
New England.
"Vistas of Liberty" series.

1999: Eagle Above
Southeastern Wetlands.
"Vistas of Liberty" series.

2000: Eagle Above
America's Heartland.
"Vistas of Liberty" series.

2001: Eagle Above
America's Southwest.
"Vistas of Liberty" series.

2002: Eagle Fishing
in America's Northwest.
"Vistas of Liberty" series.

2003.

2004.

2005.

2006: Legislative Branch.
"Foundations of
Democracy" series.

2007: Executive Branch. "Foundations of Democracy" series.

2008: Judicial Branch. "Foundations of Democracy" series.

2009: To Form a More Perfect Union. "Preamble to the Constitution" series.

2010: To Establish Justice. "Preamble to the Constitution" series.

2011: To Insure Domestic Tranquility. "Preamble to the Constitution" series.

2012: To Provide for the Common Defence. "Preamble to the Constitution" series.

2013: To Promote the General Welfare. "Preamble to the Constitution" series.

2014: To Secure the Blessings of Liberty to Ourselves and Our Posterity. "Preamble to the Constitution" series.

2015: Liberty Nurtures Freedom. "Torches of Liberty" series.

2016: Portrait of Liberty. "Torches of Liberty" series.

Common Reverse. "Preamble to the Declaration of Independence" series.

2018. Life. "Preamble to the Declaration of Independence" series.

*Chart continued on next page.*

**2019. Liberty.**
**"Preamble to the Declaration**
**of Independence" series.**

**2020: Pursuit of Happiness.**
**"Preamble to the Declaration**
**of Independence" series.**

**2021: Freedom of Religion.**
**"First Amendment to the**
**U.S. Constitution" series.**

**2022: Freedom of Speech.**
**"First Amendment to the**
**U.S. Constitution" series.**

| | Mintage | Unc. | PF |
|---|---|---|---|
| $100 1997 . . . . . . . . . . . . | 56,000 | $1,100 | |
| $100 1997W . . . . . . . . . . | (20,851) | | $1,400 |
| $100 1998 . . . . . . . . . . . . | 133,002 | 1,100 | |
| $100 1998W . . . . . . . . . . | (14,912) | | 1,400 |
| $100 1999 . . . . . . . . . . . . | 56,707 | 1,100 | |
| $100 1999W . . . . . . . . . . | (12,363) | | 1,400 |
| $100 2000 . . . . . . . . . . . . | 10,003 | 1,100 | |
| $100 2000W . . . . . . . . . . | (12,453) | | 1,400 |
| $100 2001 . . . . . . . . . . . . | 14,070 | 1,100 | |
| $100 2001W . . . . . . . . . . | (8,969) | | 1,400 |
| $100 2002 . . . . . . . . . . . . | 11,502 | 1,100 | |
| $100 2002W . . . . . . . . . . | (9,834) | | 1,400 |
| $100 2003 . . . . . . . . . . . . | 8,007 | 1,100 | |
| $100 2003W . . . . . . . . . . | (8,246) | | 1,400 |
| $100 2004 . . . . . . . . . . . . | 7,009 | 1,100 | |
| $100 2004W . . . . . . . . . . | (6,007) | | 1,400 |
| $100 2005 . . . . . . . . . . . . | 6,310 | 1,100 | |
| $100 2005W . . . . . . . . . . | (6,602) | | 1,400 |
| $100 2006 . . . . . . . . . . . . | 6,000 | 1,100 | |
| $100 2006W, Burnished . . . . | 3,068 | 1,400 | |
| $100 2006W . . . . . . . . . . | (9,152) | | 1,400 |
| $100 2007 . . . . . . . . . . . . | 7,202 | 1,100 | |
| $100 2007W, Burnished . . . . | 4,177 | 1,300 | |
| $100 2007W . . . . . . . . . . | (8,363) | | 1,400 |
| $100 2007W, Frosted FREEDOM . . . . . . . . | (12) | | — |

| | Mintage | Unc. | PF |
|---|---|---|---|
| $100 2008 . . . . . . . . . . . . | 21,800 | $1,100 | |
| $100 2008W, Burnished . . . . | 2,876 | 1,400 | |
| $100 2008W . . . . . . . . . . | (4,769) | | $1,600 |
| $100 2009W . . . . . . . . . . | (7,945) | | 1,400 |
| $100 2010W . . . . . . . . . . | (14,790) | | 1,400 |
| $100 2011W . . . . . . . . . . | (14,835) | | 1,400 |
| $100 2012W . . . . . . . . . . | (9,081) | | 1,400 |
| $100 2013W . . . . . . . . . . | (5,763) | | 1,400 |
| $100 2014 . . . . . . . . . . . . | 16,900 | 1,100 | |
| $100 2014W . . . . . . . . . . | (4,596) | | 1,400 |
| $100 2015 . . . . . . . . . . . . | 20,000 | 1,100 | |
| $100 2015W . . . . . . . . . . | (3,881) | | 1,400 |
| $100 2016 . . . . . . . . . . . . | 20,000 | 1,100 | |
| $100 2016W . . . . . . . . . . | (9,151) | | 1,400 |
| $100 2017 . . . . . . . . . . . . | *20,000* | 1,100 | |
| $100 2017W . . . . . . . . . . | (8,890) | | 1,400 |
| $100 2018 . . . . . . . . . . . . | *30,000* | 1,100 | |
| $100 2018W . . . . . . . . . . | *(15,037)* | | 1,400 |
| $100 2019 . . . . . . . . . . . . | *40,000* | 1,100 | |
| $100 2019W . . . . . . . . . . | *(11,268)* | | 1,400 |
| $100 2020 . . . . . . . . . . . . | *56,500* | 1,100 | |
| $100 2020W . . . . . . . . . . | *(8,883)* | | 1,400 |
| $100 2021 . . . . . . . . . . . . | | 1,100 | |
| $100 2021W . . . . . . . . . . | | | 1,400 |
| $100 2022 . . . . . . . . . . . . | | 1,100 | |
| $100 2022W . . . . . . . . . . | | | 1,400 |

## Platinum Bullion Sets

| | Mintage | Unc. | PF | | Mintage | Unc. | PF |
|---|---|---|---|---|---|---|---|
| 1997 Plat. Set. $100, $50, $25, $10 . . . | | | $2,500 | 2006W Plat. Set. $100, $50, $25, $10. . | | | $2,500 |
| 1998 Plat. Set. $100, $50, $25, $10 . . . | | | 2,500 | 2006W Plat. Burnished Set. | | | |
| 1999 Plat. Set. $100, $50, $25, $10 . . . | | | 2,500 | $100, $50, $25, $10 . . . . . . . . . . . . | | $2,500 | |
| 2000 Plat. Set. $100, $50, $25, $10 . . . | | | 2,500 | 2007W Plat. Set. $100, $50, $25, $10. . | | | 2,500 |
| 2001 Plat. Set. $100, $50, $25, $10 . . . | | | 2,500 | 2007W Plat. Burnished Set. | | | |
| 2002 Plat. Set. $100, $50, $25, $10 . . . | | | 2,500 | $100, $50, $25, $10 . . . . . . . . . . . . | | 2,400 | |
| 2003 Plat. Set. $100, $50, $25, $10 . . . | | | 2,500 | 2008W Plat. Set. $100, $50, $25, $10. . | | | 2,500 |
| 2004W Plat. Set. $100, $50, $25, $10. . | | | 2,500 | 2008W Plat. Burnished Set. | | | |
| 2005W Plat. Set. $100, $50, $25, $10. . | | | 2,500 | $100, $50, $25, $10 . . . . . . . . . . . . | | 2,700 | |

Prices are for original Uncirculated or Proof pieces with box and papers.

## American Eagle 10th Anniversary Platinum Set

| | Unc. |
|---|---|
| Two-coin set containing one Proof platinum half-ounce and one Enhanced Reverse Proof half-ounce dated 2007W. Housed in hardwood box with mahogany finish . . . . . . . . . . . . . . . . . . . . . | $1,500 |

# AMERICAN PALLADIUM EAGLE COINS (2017 TO DATE)

*Designer Adolph A. Weinman; composition .9995 palladium; net weight 1 oz. pure palladium; diameter 32.7 mm; reeded edge; mints: Philadelphia, West Point.*

The $25 American Palladium Eagle features a high-relief obverse design derived from artist Adolph Weinman's Winged Liberty dime of 1916 to 1945. The reverse is a high-relief version of Weinman's 1907 American Institute of Architects gold medal reverse, showing an eagle grasping a branch.

Bullion-strike coins are minted in Philadelphia and distributed through the Mint's authorized purchasers. Proof, Reverse Proof, and Uncirculated numismatic versions struck at the West Point Mint are sold by the Mint directly to collectors.

As of this printing, the spot price of palladium is about $2,000 per ounce.

| | Mintage | Unc. | PF |
|---|---|---|---|
| $25 2017 . . . . . . . . . . . . . . . . . . . . . . . . . . . . . . . . . . . . . . . . . . . . . . . . . . . . | *15,000* | $2,400 | |
| $25 2018W . . . . . . . . . . . . . . . . . . . . . . . . . . . . . . . . . . . . . . . . (14,986) . . . . . . . . . . . . | | | $2,500 |
| $25 2019W, Reverse Proof . . . . . . . . . . . . . . . . . . . . . . . . . . . . . . . (18,662) . . . . . . . . . . . . | | | 2,500 |
| $25 2020W . . . . . . . . . . . . . . . . . . . . . . . . . . . . . . . . . . . . . . . . . . . . . . . . . . . . | *9,583* | 2,400 | |
| $25 2021 . . . . . . . . . . . . . . . . . . . . . . . . . . . . . . . . . . . . . . . . . . . . . . . . . . . . . | | 2,400 | |
| $25 2021W . . . . . . . . . . . . . . . . . . . . . . . . . . . . . . . . . . . . . . . . . . . . . . . . . . . . | | | 2,500 |
| $25 2022W . . . . . . . . . . . . . . . . . . . . . . . . . . . . . . . . . . . . . . . . . . . . . . . . . . . . | | | 2,500 |

Private coins were circulated in most instances because of a shortage of regular coinage. Some numismatists use the general term *private gold* to refer to coins struck outside of the United States Mint. In the sense that no state or territory had authority to coin money, *private gold* simply refers to those interesting necessity pieces of various shapes, denominations, and degrees of intrinsic worth which were circulated in isolated areas of our country by individuals, assayers, bankers, etc. Some numismatists use the words *territorial* and *state* to cover certain issues because they were coined and circulated in a territory or state. While the state of California properly sanctioned the ingots stamped by F.D. Kohler as state assayer, in no instance were any of the gold pieces struck by authority of any of the territorial governments.

The stamped ingots put out by Augustus Humbert, the United States assayer of gold, were not recognized at the United States Mint as an official issue of coins, but simply as ingots, though Humbert placed the value and fineness on the pieces as an official agent of the federal government.

## TEMPLETON REID
### Georgia Gold 1830

The first private gold coinage in the 19th century was struck by Templeton Reid, a jeweler and gunsmith, in Milledgeville, Georgia, in July 1830. To be closer to the mines, he moved to Gainesville, where most of his coins were made. Although weights were accurate, Reid's assays were not, and his coins were slightly short of claimed value. Accordingly, he was severely attacked in the newspapers and soon lost the public's confidence. His mint closed before the end of that October.

| | VG | VF |
|---|---|---|
| 1830, $2.50 | $50,000 | $100,000 |
| 1830, $5 | 150,000 | 250,000 |
| 1830, TEN DOLLARS | 250,000 | 500,000 |
| (No Date) TEN DOLLARS | 300,000 | 650,000 |

## California Gold 1849

1849 TEN DOLLAR CALIFORNIA GOLD *(unique, in Smithsonian collection)*. . . . . . . . . . . . . . . . . . . . . . . . .

# THE BECHTLERS
# RUTHERFORD COUNTY, NC, 1831–1852

Two skilled German metallurgists, Christopher Bechtler and his son August, and later Christopher Bechtler, Junior, a nephew of Christopher the elder, operated a private mint at Rutherfordton, North Carolina. Rutherford County, in which Rutherfordton is located, was a principal source of the nation's gold supply from 1790 to 1848.

## Christopher Bechtler

|  | VF | EF | AU | Unc. |
|---|---|---|---|---|
| ONE DOLLAR CAROLINA, 28.G, N Reversed . . . . . . . . . . . . . . . . . . . . . | $1,350 | $2,000 | $3,000 | $6,500 |
| ONE GOLD DOLLAR N. CAROLINA, 28.G, No Star . . . . . . . . . . . . . . . . | 2,500 | 3,500 | 5,000 | 12,000 |
| ONE GOLD DOLLAR N. CAROLINA, 30.G. . . . . . . . . . . . . . . . . . . . . . . . | 1,500 | 2,350 | 3,500 | 8,500 |
| 2.50 CAROLINA, 67.G., 21 CARATS . . . . . . . . . . . . . . . . . . . . . . . . . . . | 3,500 | 5,500 | 7,000 | 12,500 |
| 2.50 CAROLINA, 70.G, 20 CARATS. . . . . . . . . . . . . . . . . . . . . . . . . . . . | 3,500 | 6,000 | 7,500 | 13,500 |
| 2.50 GEORGIA, 64.G, 22 CARATS. . . . . . . . . . . . . . . . . . . . . . . . . . . . . | 4,000 | 6,500 | 9,000 | 15,000 |
| 2.50 NORTH CAROLINA, 75.G., 20 C., RUTHERFORD | | | | |
|     in a Circle. Border of Large Beads. . . . . . . . . . . . . . . . . . . . . . . . . | 12,000 | 15,000 | 25,000 | 50,000 |
| 2.50 NORTH CAROLINA, 20 C. Without 75.G. . . . . . . . . . . . . . . . . . . . | 12,000 | 15,000 | 25,000 | 50,000 |

*Entry continued on next page.*

Without 150.G.

| | VF | EF | AU | Unc. |
|---|---|---|---|---|
| 5 DOLLARS NORTH CAROLINA GOLD, 150.G., 20.CARATS . . . . . . . . . | $12,500 | $20,000 | $35,000 | $65,000 |
| Similar, Without 150.G. . . . . . . . . . . . . . . . . . . . . . . . . . . . . . . . . . . | | — | — | |
| 5 DOLLARS CAROLINA, RUTHERFORD, 140.G., 20 CARATS | | | | |
|   Plain Edge . . . . . . . . . . . . . . . . . . . . . . . . . . . . . . . . . . . . . . . . . | 4,000 | 5,500 | 7,500 | 12,500 |
|   Reeded Edge . . . . . . . . . . . . . . . . . . . . . . . . . . . . . . . . . . . . . . . | 10,000 | 17,500 | 22,500 | 35,000 |
| 5 DOLLARS CAROLINA GOLD, RUTHERF., 140.G., 20 CARATS, | | | | |
|   AUGUST 1, 1834 . . . . . . . . . . . . . . . . . . . . . . . . . . . . . . . . . . . | 6,500 | 9,500 | 17,500 | 35,000 |
|   Similar, but "20" Distant From CARATS. . . . . . . . . . . . . . . . . . | 3,500 | 6,500 | 7,500 | 15,000 |
| 5 DOLLARS CAROLINA GOLD, 134.G., 21 CARATS, With Star . . . . . . . . | 3,500 | 4,500 | 5,500 | 10,000 |
| 5 DOLLARS GEORGIA GOLD, RUTHERFORD, 128.G., 22 CARATS . . . . . . | 4,000 | 5,500 | 8,500 | 15,000 |
| 5 DOLLARS GEORGIA GOLD, RUTHERF, 128.G., 22 CARATS . . . . . . . . . | 4,000 | 5,500 | 8,500 | 15,000 |

## August Bechtler

| | VF | EF | AU | Unc. |
|---|---|---|---|---|
| 1 DOL:, CAROLINA GOLD, 27.G., 21.C. . . . . . . . . . . . . . . . . . . . . . . . . | $1,000 | $1,450 | $1,750 | $2,750 |
| 5 DOLLARS, CAROLINA GOLD, 134.G:, 21 CARATS . . . . . . . . . . . . . . . | 3,000 | 5,000 | 7,500 | 20,000 |

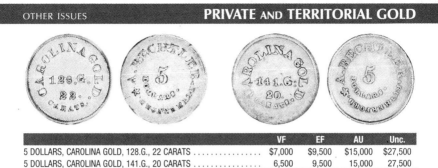

| | VF | EF | AU | Unc. |
|---|---|---|---|---|
| 5 DOLLARS, CAROLINA GOLD, 128.G., 22 CARATS ............... | $7,000 | $9,500 | $15,000 | $27,500 |
| 5 DOLLARS, CAROLINA GOLD, 141.G., 20 CARATS ............... | 6,500 | 9,500 | 15,000 | 27,500 |

## NORRIS, GREGG & NORRIS
## SAN FRANCISCO 1849

Numismatists consider these pieces the first of the California private gold coins. A newspaper account dated May 31, 1849, described a five-dollar gold coin struck at Benicia City, though with the imprint San Francisco, and the private stamp of Norris, Gregg & Norris.

| | F | VF | EF | AU | Unc. |
|---|---|---|---|---|---|
| 1849 Half Eagle, Plain Edge........................ | $3,500 | $4,500 | $7,500 | $10,000 | $20,000 |
| 1849 Half Eagle, Reeded Edge...................... | 3,500 | 4,500 | 7,500 | 10,000 | 20,000 |
| 1850 Half Eagle, With STOCKTON Beneath Date *(unique, in Smithsonian collection)* | | | | | |

## MOFFAT & CO.
## SAN FRANCISCO 1849–1853

The firm of Moffat & Co. was perhaps the most important of the California private coiners. The assay office they conducted was semi-official in character, and successors to this firm later sold its facilities to the Treasury Department, which used them to create the San Francisco Mint.

In June or July, 1849, Moffat & Co. began to issue small rectangular pieces of gold in values from $9.43 to $264. The $9.43, $14.25, and $16.00 varieties are the only known types. A similar ingot was made by the firm of Meyers & Company at this same time.

| | EF |
|---|---|
| $9.43 Moffat Ingot *(unique, in Smithsonian collection)*. . . . . . . . . . . . . . . . . . . . . . . . . . . . . . . . . . . . . . . | — |
| $14.25 Moffat Ingot *(unique, in Smithsonian collection)*. . . . . . . . . . . . . . . . . . . . . . . . . . . . . . . . . . . . . | — |
| $16.00 Moffat Ingot. . . . . . . . . . . . . . . . . . . . . . . . . . . . . . . . . . . . . . . . . . . . . . . . . . . . . . . . . . . . | $115,000 |
| $18.00 Meyers Ingot *(unique)* . . . . . . . . . . . . . . . . . . . . . . . . . . . . . . . . . . . . . . . . . . . . . . . . . . . . . | — |

*Entry continued on next page.*         

The dies for the five-dollar and ten-dollar pieces were cut by Albrecht Küner. The words MOFFAT & CO. appear on Liberty's coronet instead of the word LIBERTY as in regular United States issues.

|  | F | VF | EF | AU | Unc. |
|---|---|---|---|---|---|
| 1849 FIVE DOL. *(all varieties)* | $1,250 | $2,000 | $2,500 | $3,500 | $9,000 |
| 1850 FIVE DOL. *(all varieties)* | 1,250 | 2,000 | 2,500 | 3,750 | 10,000 |
| 1849 TEN DOL. | 2,000 | 3,000 | 5,000 | 10,000 | 22,500 |
| 1849 TEN D. | 2,250 | 3,500 | 6,000 | 11,000 | 25,000 |

# UNITED STATES ASSAY OFFICE
## Augustus Humbert
### United States Assayer of Gold, 1851

When Augustus Humbert was appointed United States assayer, he placed his name and the government imprint on the ingots of gold issued by Moffat & Co. The assay office, a provisional government mint, was a temporary expedient to accommodate the Californians until the establishment of a permanent branch mint. The fifty-dollar gold piece was accepted as legal tender on a par with standard U.S. gold coins.

### *Lettered Edge Varieties*

|  | F | VF | EF | AU | Unc. |
|---|---|---|---|---|---|
| 1851 50 D C 880 THOUS., No 50 on Reverse. Sunk in Edge: |  |  |  |  |  |
| AUGUSTUS HUMBERT UNITED STATES ASSAYER OF GOLD |  |  |  |  |  |
| CALIFORNIA 1851 | $14,500 | $22,000 | $37,500 | $60,000 | $125,000 |

**50 on Reverse**

|  | F | VF | EF | AU | Unc. |
|---|---|---|---|---|---|
| 1851 50 D C 880 THOUS, Similar to Last Variety, but | | | | | |
| 50 on Reverse.............................. | $15,000 | $25,000 | $40,000 | $70,000 | $135,000 |
| 1851 50 D C, 887 THOUS., With 50 on Reverse ......... | 14,500 | 22,500 | 37,500 | 60,000 | 115,000 |

### *Reeded Edge Varieties*

|  | F | VF | EF | AU | Unc. |
|---|---|---|---|---|---|
| 1851 FIFTY DOLLS, 880 THOUS., "Target" Reverse....... | $12,500 | $15,000 | $25,000 | $30,000 | $65,000 |
| 1851 FIFTY DOLLS, 887 THOUS., "Target" Reverse....... | 12,500 | 15,000 | 25,000 | 30,000 | 65,000 |
| 1852 FIFTY DOLLS, 887 THOUS., "Target" Reverse....... | 12,500 | 15,000 | 25,000 | 32,500 | 67,500 |

Moffat & Co. proceeded in January 1852 to issue a new ten-dollar piece bearing the stamp MOFFAT & CO.

|  | F | VF | EF | AU | Unc. |
|---|---|---|---|---|---|
| 1852 TEN D. MOFFAT & CO........................ | $2,500 | $4,500 | $8,500 | $22,500 | $42,500 |

*Entry continued on next page.*                                            **263**

|  | F | VF | EF | AU | Unc. |
|---|---|---|---|---|---|
| 1852 TEN DOLS. 1852, 2 Over 1 .................... | $2,000 | $3,500 | $5,000 | $9,500 | $17,500 |
| 1852 TEN DOLS. ............................... | 2,000 | 2,500 | 4,500 | 8,500 | 15,000 |

|  | F | VF | EF | AU | Unc. |
|---|---|---|---|---|---|
| 1852 TWENTY DOLS., 1852, 2 Over 1 ................ | $5,000 | $7,500 | $12,500 | $25,000 | $65,000 |

## United States Assay Office of Gold – 1852

The firm of Moffat & Co. was reorganized by Curtis, Perry, and Ward, who assumed
the government contract to conduct the United States Assay Office of Gold.

|  | F | VF | EF | AU | Unc. |
|---|---|---|---|---|---|
| 1852 FIFTY DOLLS., 887 THOUS. .................... | $12,500 | $15,000 | $20,000 | $25,000 | $50,000 |
| 1852 FIFTY DOLLS., 900 THOUS. .................... | 12,500 | 16,000 | 22,500 | 27,500 | 55,000 |

|  | F | VF | EF | AU | Unc. |
|---|---|---|---|---|---|
| 1852 TEN DOLS., 884 THOUS. | $1,500 | $2,000 | $3,000 | $4,500 | $10,000 |
| 1853 TEN D., 884 THOUS. | 4,000 | 8,500 | 15,000 | 20,000 | 40,000 |
| 1853 TEN D., 900 THOUS. | 2,500 | 3,500 | 4,500 | 7,500 | 12,500 |
| 1853 TWENTY D., 884 THOUS. | 4,500 | 6,500 | 11,500 | 16,500 | 30,000 |
| 1853 TWENTY D., 900 THOUS. | 1,500 | 2,000 | 3,000 | 4,500 | 8,500 |

## Moffat & Company Gold

The last Moffat issue was an 1853 twenty-dollar piece that is very similar to the U.S. double eagle of that period. It was struck after the retirement of John L. Moffat from Moffat & Company.

|  | F | VF | EF | AU | Unc. |
|---|---|---|---|---|---|
| 1853, TWENTY D. | $2,750 | $4,000 | $6,500 | $11,000 | $22,500 |

# CINCINNATI MINING & TRADING CO. (1849)

The origin and location of this company are unknown. It might have been organized in Ohio, and conducted business in California.

|  | EF | Unc. |
|---|---|---|
| 1849 FIVE DOLLARS | — | — |
| 1849 TEN DOLLARS. | $650,000 | — |

## MASSACHUSETTS AND CALIFORNIA COMPANY

This company was believed to have been organized in Northampton, Massachusetts, in May 1849. Pieces with 5D are not genuine.

| | F | VF | EF |
|---|---|---|---|
| 1849 FIVE D. | $75,000 | $105,000 | $185,000 |

## MINERS' BANK
## SAN FRANCISCO 1849

The institution of Wright & Co., exchange brokers located in Portsmouth Square, San Francisco, was known as the Miners' Bank.

A ten-dollar piece was issued in the autumn of 1849, but the coins were not readily accepted because they were worth less than face value.

| | VF | EF | AU | Unc. |
|---|---|---|---|---|
| (1849) TEN D. | $11,000 | $18,500 | $27,500 | $55,000 |

## J.S. ORMSBY
## SACRAMENTO 1849

The initials J.S.O., which appear on certain issues of California privately coined gold pieces, represent the firm of J.S. Ormsby & Co. The firm struck both five- and ten-dollar denominations, all undated.

| | VF |
|---|---|
| (1849) 5 DOLLS *(unique)* | — |
| (1849) 10 DOLLS *(4 known)* | $300,000 |

## PACIFIC COMPANY, SAN FRANCISCO 1849

The origin of the Pacific Company is uncertain. All data regarding the firm are based on conjecture.

Edgar H. Adams wrote that he believed that the coins bearing the stamp of the Pacific Company were produced by the coining firm of Broderick and Kohler. The coins were probably hand struck with the aid of a sledgehammer.

| | EF |
|---|---|
| 1849, 1 DOLLAR *(2 known)* | — |
| 1849, 5 DOLLARS *(4 known)* | $250,000 |
| 1849, 10 DOLLARS *(4 known)* | 350,000 |

## F.D. KOHLER
## CALIFORNIA STATE ASSAYER 1850

The State Assay Office was authorized on April 12, 1850. That year, Governor Peter Burnett appointed F.D. Kohler, who thereupon sold his assaying business to Baldwin & Co. Kohler served at both the San Francisco and Sacramento offices. The State Assay Offices were discontinued when the U.S. Assay Office was established, on February 1, 1851. Ingots ranged from $36.55 to $150.00.

| | EF |
|---|---|
| $36.55 Sacramento | — |
| $37.31 San Francisco | — |
| $40.07 San Francisco | — |
| $45.34 San Francisco | — |
| $50.00 San Francisco | — |
| $54.09 San Francisco | — |

## DUBOSQ & COMPANY
## SAN FRANCISCO 1850

Theodore Dubosq, a Philadelphia jeweler, took melting and coining machinery to San Francisco in 1849.

| | VF |
|---|---|
| 1850, FIVE D. | $175,000 |
| 1850, TEN D. | 175,000 |

## BALDWIN & CO.
## SAN FRANCISCO 1850

George C. Baldwin and Thomas S. Holman were in the jewelry business in San Francisco and were known as Baldwin & Co. They were the successors to F.D. Kohler & Co., taking over its machinery and other equipment in May 1850.

| | F | VF | EF | AU | Unc. |
|---|---|---|---|---|---|
| 1850, FIVE DOL. | $4,500 | $7,500 | $14,500 | $22,000 | $35,000 |
| 1850, TEN DOLLARS, Horseman Type | 25,000 | 50,000 | 75,000 | 100,000 | 165,000 |

| | F | VF | EF | AU | Unc. |
|---|---|---|---|---|---|
| 1851, TEN D. | $7,500 | $17,500 | $25,000 | $42,500 | $100,000 |

| | VF | EF | AU | Unc. |
|---|---|---|---|---|
| 1851 TWENTY D. | $150,000 | $350,000 | — | — |

## SHULTZ & COMPANY
## SAN FRANCISCO 1851

The firm, located in back of Baldwin's establishment, operated a brass foundry beginning in 1851. Judge G.W. Shultz and William T. Garratt were partners in the enterprise.

| | F | VF |
|---|---|---|
| 1851, FIVE D. | $20,000 | $35,000 |

## DUNBAR & COMPANY
## SAN FRANCISCO 1851

Edward E. Dunbar operated the California Bank in San Francisco. Dunbar later returned to New York City and organized the famous Continental Bank Note Co.

| | VF | EF |
|---|---|---|
| 1851, FIVE D. | $135,000 | $300,000 |

## WASS, MOLITOR & CO.
## SAN FRANCISCO 1852–1855

The gold-smelting and assaying plant of Wass, Molitor & Co. was operated by two Hungarian patriots, Count S.C. Wass and A.P. Molitor. They maintained an excellent laboratory and complete apparatus for analysis and coinage of gold.

|  | F | VF | EF | AU | Unc. |
|---|---|---|---|---|---|
| 1852, FIVE DOLLARS............................. | $2,500 | $5,000 | $12,500 | $20,000 | $35,000 |

Large Head Small Head

|  | F | VF | EF | AU | Unc. |
|---|---|---|---|---|---|
| 1852, TEN D., Large Head......................... | $1,750 | $2,500 | $3,500 | $7,500 | $17,500 |
| 1852, TEN D., Small Head......................... | 4,000 | 5,000 | 12,500 | 17,500 | 40,000 |
| 1855, TEN D.................................... | 6,500 | 8,000 | 12,500 | 15,000 | 30,000 |

Large Head Small Head

|  | F | VF | EF | AU | Unc. |
|---|---|---|---|---|---|
| 1855, TWENTY DOL., Large Head ................:......... | — | — | $300,000 | — | — |
| 1855, TWENTY DOL., Small Head .................... | $7,500 | $17,500 | 22,500 | $35,000 | $75,000 |

| | F | VF | EF | AU | Unc. |
|---|---|---|---|---|---|
| 1855, 50 DOLLARS . . . . . . . . . . . . . . . . . . . . . . . . . . . . . | $20,000 | $35,000 | $45,000 | $65,000 | $115,000 |

## KELLOGG & CO.
## SAN FRANCISCO 1854–1855

When the U.S. Assay Office ceased operations, a period ensued during which no private firm was striking gold. The new San Francisco branch mint did not produce coins for some months after Curtis & Perry took the government contract. The lack of coin was again keenly felt by businessmen, who petitioned Kellogg & Richter to "supply the vacuum" by issuing private coin. Their plea was soon answered, for on February 9, 1854, Kellogg & Co. placed their first twenty-dollar piece in circulation.

| | F | VF | EF | AU | Unc. | PF |
|---|---|---|---|---|---|---|
| 1854, TWENTY D. . . . . . . . . . . . . . . . . . . . . . . | $2,000 | $3,000 | $4,000 | $6,000 | $13,500 | |
| 1855, TWENTY D. . . . . . . . . . . . . . . . . . . . . . . | 2,000 | 3,000 | 4,000 | 6,000 | 15,000 | |
| 1855, FIFTY DOLLS . . . . . . . . . . . . . . . . . . . . . | | | | | | $500,000 |

## OREGON EXCHANGE COMPANY
## OREGON CITY 1849
### The Beaver Coins of Oregon

On February 16, 1849, the territorial legislature passed an act providing for a mint and specified five- and ten-dollar gold coins without alloy. Oregon City, the largest city in the territory with a population of about 1,000, was designated as the location for the mint. However, Oregon was then brought into the United States as a territory. When the new governor arrived on March 2, he declared the coinage act unconstitutional. Still, a local company coined these private pieces.

|  | F | VF | EF | AU | Unc. |
|---|---|---|---|---|---|
| 1849 5 D. | $20,000 | $30,000 | $45,000 | $85,000 | — |
| 1849 TEN.D. | 45,000 | 85,000 | 150,000 | 250,000 | — |

## MORMON GOLD PIECES
## SALT LAKE CITY, UTAH, 1849–1860

Brigham Young was the instigator of the coinage system and personally supervised the mint, which was housed in a little adobe building in Salt Lake City. The mint was inaugurated late in 1848 as a public convenience.

|  | F | VF | EF | AU | Unc. |
|---|---|---|---|---|---|
| 1849, TWO.AND.HALF.DO. | $7,500 | $12,500 | $20,000 | $35,000 | $55,000 |
| 1849, FIVE.DOLLARS | 6,500 | 12,500 | 17,500 | 25,000 | 50,000 |

|  | F | VF | EF |
|---|---|---|---|
| 1849, TEN.DOLLARS | $150,000 | $250,000 | $350,000 |
| 1849, TWENTY.DOLLARS | 75,000 | 125,000 | 175,000 |

| | F | VF | EF | AU | Unc. |
|---|---|---|---|---|---|
| 1850, FIVE DOLLARS ........................... | $6,000 | $12,500 | $17,500 | $27,500 | $55,000 |
| 1860, 5.D. ..................................... | 12,000 | 18,500 | 25,000 | 40,000 | 65,000 |

## COLORADO GOLD PIECES
### Clark, Gruber & Co.
### Denver 1860–1861

Clark, Gruber & Co. was a well-known private minting firm in Denver, Colorado, in the early 1860s.

| | F | VF | EF | AU | Unc. |
|---|---|---|---|---|---|
| 1860, 2 1/2 D ................................. | $1,200 | $1,500 | $2,200 | $3,500 | $8,500 |
| 1860, FIVE D ................................... | 1,250 | 2,000 | 3,000 | 4,000 | 10,000 |

| | F | VF | EF | AU | Unc. |
|---|---|---|---|---|---|
| 1860, TEN D ................................... | $5,500 | $9,000 | $13,500 | $20,000 | $35,000 |
| 1860, TWENTY D. ................................ | 35,000 | 85,000 | 150,000 | 250,000 | 500,000 |

| | F | VF | EF | AU | Unc. |
|---|---|---|---|---|---|
| 1861, 2 1/2 D. ................................. | $1,200 | $1,850 | $2,500 | $4,500 | $8,500 |
| 1861, FIVE D. .................................. | 1,500 | 2,250 | 3,000 | 5,500 | 20,000 |
| 1861, TEN D. ................................... | 2,500 | 3,250 | 4,000 | 6,000 | 21,500 |

*Entry continued on next page.*        273

| | F | VF | EF | AU |
|---|---|---|---|---|
| 1861, TWENTY D. | $25,000 | $45,000 | $75,000 | $100,000 |

## John Parsons & Company
### Tarryall Mines – Colorado, 1861

Very little is known regarding the mint of John Parsons and Co., although it is reasonably certain that it operated in the South Park section of Park County, Colorado, near the original town of Tarryall, in the summer of 1861.

| | VF |
|---|---|
| (1861) Undated 2 1/2 D. | $175,000 |
| (1861) Undated FIVE D. | 250,000 |

## J.J. Conway & Co.
### Georgia Gulch, Colorado, 1861

Records show that the Conway mint operated for a short while in 1861. As in all gold mining areas, the value of gold dust caused disagreement among the merchants and the miners. The firm of J.J. Conway & Co. solved this difficulty by bringing out its gold pieces in August 1861.

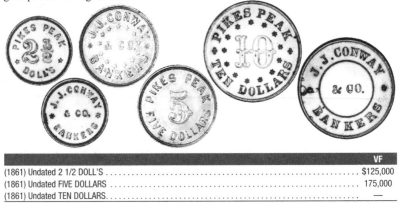

| | VF |
|---|---|
| (1861) Undated 2 1/2 DOLL'S | $125,000 |
| (1861) Undated FIVE DOLLARS | 175,000 |
| (1861) Undated TEN DOLLARS. | — |

## CALIFORNIA SMALL-DENOMINATION GOLD

There was a scarcity of small coins during the California Gold Rush and, starting in 1852, quarter, half, and dollar pieces were privately minted from native gold to alleviate the shortage. The need and acceptability of these pieces declined after 1856 and they then became popular as souvenirs. Authentic pieces all have CENTS, DOLLAR, or an abbreviation thereof on the reverse. The tokens are much less valuable. Modern restrikes and replicas (often having a bear in the design) have no numismatic value.

The values in the following charts are only for coins made before 1883 with the denomination on the reverse expressed as CENTS, DOL., DOLL., or DOLLAR.

### Quarter Dollar – Octagonal

|  | EF-40 | AU-50 | MS-60 |
|---|---|---|---|
| Liberty Head | $75 | $100 | $200 |
| Indian Head | 90 | 125 | 200 |
| Washington Head | 350 | 700 | 1,100 |

### Quarter Dollar – Round

|  | EF-40 | AU-50 | MS-60 |
|---|---|---|---|
| Liberty Head | $75 | $100 | $200 |
| Indian Head | 80 | 125 | 250 |
| Washington Head | 350 | 550 | 1,000 |

### Half Dollar – Octagonal

|  | EF-40 | AU-50 | MS-60 |
|---|---|---|---|
| Liberty Head | $75 | $100 | $200 |
| Liberty Head / Eagle | 500 | 700 | 1,250 |
| Indian Head | 100 | 125 | 300 |

### Half Dollar – Round

|  | EF-40 | AU-50 | MS-60 |
|---|---|---|---|
| Liberty Head | $85 | $135 | $250 |
| Indian Head | 75 | 110 | 200 |

### Dollar – Octagonal

|  | EF-40 | AU-50 | MS-60 |
|---|---|---|---|
| Liberty Head | $200 | $300 | $750 |
| Liberty Head / Eagle | 800 | 1,650 | 2,500 |
| Indian Head | 250 | 400 | 800 |

### Dollar – Round

|  | EF-40 | AU-50 | MS-60 |
|---|---|---|---|
| Liberty Head | $1,000 | $1,450 | $2,250 |
| Indian Head | 1,000 | 1,500 | 2,500 |

## HARD TIMES TOKENS (1832–1844)

During the financial crises of 1832 to 1844 many government coins were hoarded, and privately made tokens were used out of necessity. The so-called Hard Times tokens of this period were slightly smaller and lighter than normal large cents. They were made of copper or brass and are of two general groups: political tokens whose theme centered on President Andrew Jackson's fight against the Bank of the United States, and tradesmen's cards, issued by merchants. Many different designs and varieties exist.

| | VF | EF |
|---|---|---|
| Hard Times Tokens, 1832–1844, most common pieces | $15 | $25 |

## CIVIL WAR TOKENS (1860s)

Civil War tokens are generally divided into two groups: tradesmen's tokens, and anonymously issued pieces with political or patriotic themes. They came into existence only because of the scarcity of government coins and disappeared as soon as the bronze coins of 1864 met the public demand for small copper change.

These tokens vary greatly in composition and design. A number were more or less faithful imitations of the copper-nickel cent. A few of this type have the word NOT in very small letters above the words ONE CENT.

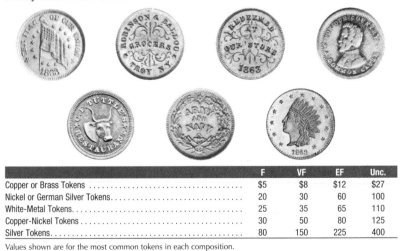

| | F | VF | EF | Unc. |
|---|---|---|---|---|
| Copper or Brass Tokens | $5 | $8 | $12 | $27 |
| Nickel or German Silver Tokens | 20 | 30 | 60 | 100 |
| White-Metal Tokens | 25 | 35 | 65 | 110 |
| Copper-Nickel Tokens | 30 | 50 | 80 | 125 |
| Silver Tokens | 80 | 150 | 225 | 400 |

Values shown are for the most common tokens in each composition.

In April 1899 control of the Philippine Islands was officially transferred from Spain to the United States, as a condition of the treaty ending the Spanish-American War. In July 1901 a civilian government (led by American judge William Howard Taft) replaced the islands' military administration; one of its first tasks was to sponsor a new territorial coinage that was compatible with the old Spanish issues, but also legally exchangeable for American money at the rate of two Philippine pesos to the U.S. dollar. The resulting coins—which bear the legend UNITED STATES OF AMERICA but are otherwise quite different in design from regular U.S. coins—today can be found in many collections, having been brought to the States as souvenirs by service members after World War II or otherwise saved.

The coins, introduced in 1903, also bear the Spanish names for the islands: FILIPINAS. Following Spanish custom, the dollar-sized peso was equivalent to 100 centavos. Silver fractions were minted in denominations of fifty, twenty, and ten centavos, and minor coins (in copper-nickel and bronze) included the five-cent piece, the centavo, and the half centavo.

Dies for the coins were made at the Philadelphia Mint. From 1903 to 1908 the coins were struck at the Philadelphia Mint (with no mintmark) and the San Francisco Mint (with an S mintmark). From 1909 through 1919, they were struck only at San Francisco. In the first part of 1920, one-centavo coins were struck in San Francisco; later in the year, a new mint facility was opened in Manila, and from that point into the early 1940s Philippine coins of one, five, ten, twenty, and fifty centavos were struck there. The coins produced at the Manila Mint in 1920, 1921, and 1922 bore no mintmark. No Philippine coins were struck in 1923 or 1924. The Manila Mint re-opened in 1925; from then through 1941 its coinage featured an M mintmark.

Rising silver prices forced a reduction in the fineness and weight for each silver denomination beginning in 1907, and subsequent issues are smaller in diameter. The smaller size of the new silver issues led to confusion between the silver twenty-centavo piece and the copper-nickel five-centavo piece, resulting in a mismatching of dies for these two denominations in 1918 and again in 1928. A solution was found by reducing the diameter of the five-centavo piece beginning in 1930.

Japanese military forces advanced on the Philippines in 1942, prompting the civil government to remove much of the Philippine treasury's bullion to the United States. Nearly 16 million pesos' worth of silver remained, mostly in the form of one-peso pieces of 1907 through 1912. These coins were hastily crated and dumped into Manila's Caballo Bay to prevent their capture by Japan, then at war with the United States. The Japanese occupied the Philippines and did manage to recover some of the sunken coins (probably fewer than a half million). After the war, over the course of several years, more than 10 million of the submerged silver pesos were retrieved under the direction of the U.S. Treasury and, later, the Central Bank of the Philippines. Most of them show evidence of prolonged salt-water immersion, with dark corrosion that resists cleaning. This damage to so many coins has added to the scarcity of high-grade pre-war silver pesos.

Later during World War II, in 1944 and 1945, the U.S. Mint struck coins for the Philippines at its Philadelphia, Denver, and San Francisco mints.

The Philippines became an independent republic after the war, on July 4, 1946. Today the coins of 1903 to 1945, including a set of commemoratives issued in 1936, remain as interesting mementoes of a colorful chapter in U.S. history and numismatics.

The following are general descriptions of Philippine issues by type. For detailed date-by-date charts with mintages and retail values, see the *Guide Book of United States Coins, Deluxe Edition.*

# BRONZE COINAGE UNDER U.S. SOVEREIGNTY (1903–1936)

**Half Centavo**                                    **One Centavo**

The bronze half centavo was struck from 1903 through 1908 (except for 1907), with some dates struck in Proof format only. Dealer buy prices for the most common pieces are $2.25 in EF to $40 in MS-63; for the most common Proofs, $125 to $150, depending on quality. The rarest Proof is the 1905, generally worth $125 to $800.

The bronze centavo was struck from 1903 through 1936. Dealers buy the most common pieces for $1.25 in VF to $35 in MS-63. The 1918-S, Large S, variety is the rarity of the series, valued from $125 (VF) to $1,500 (MS-63). Proofs were struck several years in the early 1900s; the most common Proofs bring buy prices of $60 to $95.

# COPPER-NICKEL COINAGE UNDER U.S. SOVEREIGNTY
## (1903–1935)

**Large-Size Five Centavos**          **Reduced-Size Five Centavos**
**(1903–1928)**                       **(1930–1935)**

Copper-nickel five-centavo coins were struck by the millions in various years from 1903 through 1935. The most common dates are bought by dealers for $1.25 to $3.50 in VF, and for $25 to $250 in MS-63. The rare dates are the 1916-S ($85 to $1,300) and the 1918-S mule with the small-date reverse of the 20-centavo die ($500 to $8,000). Proofs were struck in some years of the early 1900s; the most common Proofs are bought by dealers for $65 to $140, depending on their state of preservation.

# SILVER COINAGE UNDER U.S. SOVEREIGNTY (1903–1935)

**Basic Design for Ten-, Twenty-, and**
**Fifty-Centavo and 1 Peso Pieces**
*(Large-size fifty centavos shown.)*

Silver ten-centavo coins were struck by the millions in various years from 1903 through 1935. The most common dates are bought by dealers for their silver bullion value in VF, and for $45 to $60 in MS-63. The rarest dates are the 1903-S ($20 to $1,500) and the 1909-S ($20 to $1,000). Proofs were struck in some years of the early 1900s; the most common Proofs are bought by dealers for $75 to $125, depending on their state of preservation.

Silver twenty-centavo coins were struck in quantity in various years from 1903 through 1929. The most common dates are bought by dealers for their silver bullion value in VF, and for $85 to $250 in MS-63. There are several rarer dates in the series; the 1903-S, 1915-S, and the 1928-M mule (with a reverse of the 1903–1928 five centavo die) are bought for about $15 (VF) to $2,000 (MS-63). Proofs were struck in some years of the early 1900s; the most common Proofs are bought by dealers for $100 to $175, depending on their state of preservation.

Silver fifty-centavo coins were struck in quantity in various years from 1903 through 1921. The most common dates are bought by dealers for their silver bullion value in VF, and for $120 to $190 or more in MS-63. The rarest collectible date in the series, the 1905-S, is bought for $20 in VF but up to $4,500 in MS-63. Proofs were struck in some years of the early 1900s; the most common Proofs are bought by dealers for $120 to $175, depending on their state of preservation.

Silver pesos were struck in quantity in various years from 1903 through 1912. The most common dates are bought by dealers for $10 in VF, and for $325 to $350 in MS-63. There are several rarities in the series; the rarest, the 1906-S, is bought for $2,000 in VF and $35,000 in MS-63. Proofs were struck in some years of the early 1900s; the most common Proofs are bought by dealers for $300 to $550, depending on their state of preservation.

## COINAGE UNDER THE COMMONWEALTH (1937–1945)

**Basic Reverse Design for Commonwealth Coinage**
*(1936 peso shown.)*

By 1935 the momentum for Philippine independence justified the creation of a Philippine Commonwealth, with full independence planned by 1946. Circulating coins struck for the commonwealth (1937–1945) featured the same basic obverse designs as those struck under U.S. sovereignty (1903–1936), and shared a common reverse design of an eagle-surmounted shield (the coat of arms of the commonwealth). All are fairly common, with mintages ranging from the millions to tens of millions, and dealer buy prices ranging from $0.25 to $3 in VF.

A set of three 1936-dated commemorative silver coins was issued to mark the beginning of the commonwealth. The fifty-centavo coin and one of the pesos feature busts of Philippine president Manuel L. Quezon and of outgoing U.S. governor-general Frank Murphy. The other peso has busts of Quezon and U.S. president Franklin D. Roosevelt. The fifty-centavo coin has a buy price of about $130 in MS-63, and the pesos of about $240 each.

These charts show the bullion values of silver and gold U.S. coins. These are intrinsic values and do not reflect any numismatic premium a coin might have. The weight listed under each denomination is its actual silver weight (ASW) or actual gold weight (AGW).

In recent years, the bullion price of silver has fluctuated considerably. You can use the following chart to determine the approximate bullion value of many 19th- and 20th-century silver coins at various price levels—or you can calculate the approximate value by multiplying the current spot price of silver by the ASW for each coin, as indicated. Dealers generally purchase common silver coins at around 15% below bullion value, and sell them at around 15% above bullion value.

Nearly all U.S. gold coins have an additional premium value beyond their bullion content, and thus are not subject to minor bullion-price variations. The premium amount is not necessarily tied to the bullion price of gold, but is usually determined by supply and demand levels in the numismatic marketplace. Because these factors can vary significantly, there is no reliable formula for calculating "percentage below and above bullion" prices that would remain accurate over time. The gold chart below lists bullion values based on AGW only; consult a coin dealer to ascertain current buy and sell prices.

## Bullion Values of Silver Coins

| Silver Price Per Ounce | Wartime Nickel .05626 oz. | Dime .07234 oz. | Quarter .18084 oz. | Half Dollar .36169 oz. | Silver Clad Half Dollar .14792 oz. | Silver Dollar .77344 oz. |
|---|---|---|---|---|---|---|
| $15.00 | $0.84 | $1.09 | $2.71 | $5.43 | $2.22 | $11.60 |
| 16.00 | 0.90 | 1.16 | 2.89 | 5.79 | 2.37 | 12.38 |
| 17.00 | 0.96 | 1.23 | 3.07 | 6.15 | 2.51 | 13.15 |
| 18.00 | 1.01 | 1.30 | 3.26 | 6.51 | 2.66 | 13.92 |
| 19.00 | 1.07 | 1.37 | 3.44 | 6.87 | 2.81 | 14.70 |
| 20.00 | 1.13 | 1.45 | 3.62 | 7.23 | 2.96 | 15.47 |
| 21.00 | 1.18 | 1.52 | 3.80 | 7.60 | 3.11 | 16.24 |
| 22.00 | 1.24 | 1.59 | 3.98 | 7.96 | 3.25 | 17.02 |
| 23.00 | 1.29 | 1.66 | 4.16 | 8.32 | 3.40 | 17.79 |
| 24.00 | 1.35 | 1.74 | 4.34 | 8.68 | 3.55 | 18.56 |
| 25.00 | 1.41 | 1.81 | 4.52 | 9.04 | 3.70 | 19.34 |
| 26.00 | 1.46 | 1.88 | 4.70 | 9.40 | 3.85 | 20.11 |
| 27.00 | 1.52 | 1.95 | 4.88 | 9.77 | 3.99 | 20.88 |
| 28.00 | 1.58 | 2.03 | 5.06 | 10.13 | 4.14 | 21.66 |
| 29.00 | 1.63 | 2.10 | 5.24 | 10.49 | 4.29 | 22.43 |
| 30.00 | 1.69 | 2.17 | 5.43 | 10.85 | 4.44 | 23.20 |
| 31.00 | 1.74 | 2.24 | 5.61 | 11.21 | 4.59 | 23.98 |
| 32.00 | 1.80 | 2.31 | 5.79 | 11.57 | 4.73 | 24.75 |
| 33.00 | 1.86 | 2.39 | 5.97 | 11.94 | 4.88 | 25.52 |
| 34.00 | 1.91 | 2.46 | 6.15 | 12.30 | 5.03 | 26.30 |
| 35.00 | 1.97 | 2.53 | 6.33 | 12.66 | 5.18 | 27.07 |
| 36.00 | 2.03 | 2.60 | 6.51 | 13.02 | 5.33 | 27.84 |
| 37.00 | 2.08 | 2.68 | 6.69 | 13.38 | 5.47 | 28.62 |
| 38.00 | 2.14 | 2.75 | 6.87 | 13.74 | 5.62 | 29.39 |
| 39.00 | 2.19 | 2.82 | 7.05 | 14.11 | 5.77 | 30.16 |
| 40.00 | 2.25 | 2.89 | 7.23 | 14.47 | 5.92 | 30.94 |
| 41.00 | 2.31 | 2.97 | 7.41 | 14.83 | 6.06 | 31.71 |
| 42.00 | 2.36 | 3.04 | 7.60 | 15.19 | 6.21 | 32.48 |
| 43.00 | 2.42 | 3.11 | 7.78 | 15.55 | 6.36 | 33.26 |
| 44.00 | 2.48 | 3.18 | 7.96 | 15.91 | 6.51 | 34.03 |

*Note:* The U.S. bullion coins first issued in 1986 are unlike the older regular issues. They contain the following amounts of pure metal: silver $1, 1 oz.; gold $50, 1 oz.; gold $25, 1/2 oz.; gold $10, 1/4 oz.; gold $5, 1/10 oz.

| Silver Price Per Ounce | Wartime Nickel .05626 oz. | Dime .07234 oz. | Quarter .18084 oz. | Half Dollar .36169 oz. | Silver Clad Half Dollar .14792 oz. | Silver Dollar .77344 oz. |
|---|---|---|---|---|---|---|
| $45.00 | $2.53 | $3.26 | $8.14 | $16.28 | $6.66 | $34.80 |
| 46.00 | 2.59 | 3.33 | 8.32 | 16.64 | 6.80 | 35.58 |
| 47.00 | 2.64 | 3.40 | 8.50 | 17.00 | 6.95 | 36.35 |
| 48.00 | 2.70 | 3.47 | 8.68 | 17.36 | 7.10 | 37.13 |
| 49.00 | 2.76 | 3.54 | 8.86 | 17.72 | 7.25 | 37.90 |
| 50.00 | 2.81 | 3.62 | 9.04 | 18.08 | 7.40 | 38.67 |

Note: The U.S. bullion coins first issued in 1986 are unlike the older regular issues. They contain the following amounts of pure metal: silver $1, 1 oz.; gold $50, 1 oz.; gold $25, 1/2 oz.; gold $10, 1/4 oz.; gold $5, 1/10 oz.

## Bullion Values of Gold Coins

| Gold Price Per Ounce | $5.00 Liberty Head 1839–1908 Indian Head 1908–1929 .24187 oz. | $10.00 Liberty Head 1838–1907 Indian Head 1907–1933 .48375 oz. | $20.00 1849–1933 .96750 oz. |
|---|---|---|---|
| $1,525.00 | $368.85 | $737.72 | $1,475.44 |
| 1,550.00 | 374.90 | 749.81 | 1,499.63 |
| 1,575.00 | 380.95 | 761.91 | 1,523.81 |
| 1,600.00 | 386.99 | 774.00 | 1,548.00 |
| 1,625.00 | 393.04 | 786.09 | 1,572.19 |
| 1,650.00 | 399.09 | 798.19 | 1,596.38 |
| 1,675.00 | 405.13 | 810.28 | 1,620.56 |
| 1,700.00 | 411.18 | 822.38 | 1,644.75 |
| 1,725.00 | 417.23 | 834.47 | 1,668.94 |
| 1,750.00 | 423.27 | 846.56 | 1,693.13 |
| 1,775.00 | 429.32 | 858.66 | 1,717.31 |
| 1,800.00 | 435.37 | 870.75 | 1,741.50 |
| 1,825.00 | 441.41 | 882.84 | 1,765.69 |
| 1,850.00 | 447.46 | 894.94 | 1,789.88 |
| 1,875.00 | 453.51 | 907.03 | 1,814.06 |
| 1,900.00 | 459.55 | 919.13 | 1,838.25 |
| 1,925.00 | 465.60 | 931.22 | 1,862.44 |
| 1,950.00 | 471.65 | 943.31 | 1,886.63 |
| 1,975.00 | 477.69 | 955.41 | 1,910.81 |
| 2,000.00 | 483.74 | 967.50 | 1,935.00 |
| 2,025.00 | 489.79 | 979.59 | 1,959.19 |
| 2,050.00 | 495.83 | 991.69 | 1,983.38 |
| 2,075.00 | 501.88 | 1,003.78 | 2,007.56 |
| 2,100.00 | 507.93 | 1,015.88 | 2,031.75 |
| 2,125.00 | 513.97 | 1,027.97 | 2,055.94 |
| 2,150.00 | 520.02 | 1,040.06 | 2,080.13 |
| 2,175.00 | 526.07 | 1,052.16 | 2,104.31 |
| 2,200.00 | 532.11 | 1,064.25 | 2,128.50 |
| 2,225.00 | 538.16 | 1,076.34 | 2,152.69 |
| 2,250.00 | 544.21 | 1,088.44 | 2,176.88 |
| 2,275.00 | 550.25 | 1,100.53 | 2,201.06 |
| 2,300.00 | 556.30 | 1,112.63 | 2,225.25 |
| 2,325.00 | 562.35 | 1,124.72 | 2,249.44 |
| 2,350.00 | 568.39 | 1,136.81 | 2,273.63 |
| 2,375.00 | 574.44 | 1,148.91 | 2,297.81 |
| 2,400.00 | 580.49 | 1,161.00 | 2,322.00 |

Note: The U.S. bullion coins first issued in 1986 are unlike the older regular issues. They contain the following amounts of pure metal: silver $1, 1 oz.; gold $50, 1 oz.; gold $25, 1/2 oz.; gold $10, 1/4 oz.; gold $5, 1/10 oz.

The precursor to the best-selling *Guide Book of United States Coins* (the "Red Book") was *The Handbook of United States Coins With Premium List,* popularly known as the "Blue Book" because of its cover color. The mastermind behind the Blue Book was R.S. Yeoman, who had been hired by Western Publishing Company as a commercial artist in 1932. He distributed Western's Whitman line of "penny boards" to coin collectors, promoting them through department stores, along with children's books and games. He eventually arranged for Whitman to expand the line of penny boards into other denominations, giving them the reputation of a more serious numismatic endeavor rather than a "game" of filling holes with missing coins. He also developed these flat boards into a line of popular folders.

Soon Yeoman realized that coin collectors needed other resources and supplies for their hobby, and he began to compile coin mintage data and market values. This research grew into the Blue Book: now collectors had a coin-by-coin, grade-by-grade guide to the prices dealers would pay, on average, for U.S. coins. The first and second editions were both published in 1942, indicating the strong demand for this kind of hobby-related information.

In the first edition of the Red Book, published four years later, Whitman Publishing would describe the Blue Book as "a low-priced standard reference book of United States coins and kindred issues" for which there had been "a long-felt need among American collectors."

The Blue Book has been published annually (except in 1944 and 1950) since its debut. Past editions offer valuable information about the hobby of yesteryear as well as developments in numismatic research and the marketplace. Old Blue Books are collectible, but they are not yet as avidly sought as the Red Book, and most editions after the 12th can be found for a few dollars in VF or better condition. Major variants were produced for the third, fourth, and ninth editions, including perhaps the only "overdate" books in American numismatic publishing. Either to conserve the previous years' covers or to correct an error in binding, the cloth on some third-edition covers was overstamped "Fourth Edition," and a number of eighth-edition covers were overstamped "Ninth Edition." The third edition was produced in several shades of blue ranging from light to dark. Some copies of the fourth edition were also produced in black cloth—the only time the Blue Book was bound in other than blue.

### Valuation Guide for Select Past Editions of the Blue Book

| Edition | Title-Page | Copyright | VF | EF | Edition | Title-Page | Copyright | VF | EF |
|---|---|---|---|---|---|---|---|---|---|
| 1st | 1942 | 1942 | $50 | $100 | 7th | 1949 | 1948 | $10 | $15 |
| 2nd | 1943 | 1942 | 20 | 50 | 8th | 1950 | 1949 | 7 | 12 |
| 3rd | 1944 | 1943 | 20 | 35 | 9th | 1952 | 1951 | 4 | 7 |
| 4th | None | 1945 | 20 | 30 | 10th | 1953 | 1952 | 3 | 6 |
| 5th | None | 1946 | 12 | 15 | 11th | 1954 | 1953 | 2 | 4 |
| 6th | 1948 | 1947 | 10 | 15 | 12th | 1955 | 1954 | 2 | 4 |

* During its early years of production, the Blue Book's date presentation was not standardized. Full information is given here to aid in precise identification of early editions.

Combined with dealer's buying prices, auction data can help advanced collectors understand the modern market for high-end rarities.

It is important to understand that the following prices include a buyer's premium (a surcharge which the buyer pays the auction house over the final "hammer price," or winning bid; contemporary auction houses charge around 17.5%) and the seller's commission (a small percentage of the hammer price which the individual selling the coin pays to the auction house; this fee can sometimes be negotiated to less than 5%).

| Rank | Price | Coin | Grade | Firm | Date |
|---|---|---|---|---|---|
| 1 | $18,872,250 | $20, 1933 **(A)** | MS-65 | Sotheby's | Jun-21 |
| 2 | 10,016,875 | Silver $, 1794 | PCGS SP-66 | Stack's Bowers | Jan-13 |
| 3 | 9,360,000 | Pre-Fed, 1787 Brasher EB on Wing **(B)** | NGC MS-65★ | Heritage | Jan-21 |
| 4 | 8,400,000 | $5, 1822 | PCGS AU-50 | Stack's Bowers | Mar-21 |
| 5 | 7,680,000 | Silver $, 1804 Class I **(C)** | PCGS PF-68 | Stack's Bowers | Aug-21 |
| 6 | 7,590,020 | $20, 1933 **(A)** | Gem BU | Soth/Stack's | Jul-02 |
| 7 | 7,200,000 | $20, 1861 Paquet Reverse | PCGS MS-67 | Heritage | Aug-21 |
| 8 | 6,600,000 | Silver $, 1794 **(CC)** | PCGS MS-66+ | Heirtage | Aug-21 |
| 9 | 5,280,000 | $10, 1804 Plain 4 BD-2 | PCGS 65+ DC | Heritage | Jan-21 |
| 10 | 4,993,750 | Silver $, 1794 **(CC)** | PCGS MS-66+ | SBG/Sotheby's | Sep-15 |
| 11 | 4,582,500 | Pre-Fed, 1787 Brasher EB on Wing | NGC MS-63 | Hertage | Jan-14 |
| 12 | 4,560,000 | 5¢, 1913 Liberty Head **(D)** | PCGS PF-66 | Stack's Bowers | Aug-18 |
| 13 | 4,140,000 | Silver $, 1804 Class I **(C)** | PCGS PF-68 | B&M | Aug-99 |
| 14 | 3,960,000 | Trade $, 1885 | NGC PF-66 | Heritage | Jan-19 |
| 15 | 3,877,500 | Silver $, 1804 Class I **(E)** | PCGS PF-62 | Heritage | Aug-13 |
| 16 | 3,737,500 | 5¢, 1913 Liberty Head **(F)** | NGC PF-64 | Heritage | Jan-10 |
| 17 | 3,737,500 | Silver $, 1804 Class I **(E)** | NGC PF-62 | Heritage | Apr-08 |
| 18 | 3,600,000 | $20, MCMVII Ultra HR LE **(G)** | NGC PF-68 | Heritage | Feb-21 |
| 19 | 3,360,000 | $10, 1795 9 Leaves BD-3 **(DD)** | PCGS MS-63+ | Heritage | Jan-22 |
| 20 | 3,360,000 | Silver $, 1804 Class I **(H)** | PCGS PF-65 | Stack's Bowers | Dec-20 |
| 21 | 3,290,000 | Silver $, 1804 Class I | PCGS PF-65 | SBG/Sotheby's | Mar-17 |
| 22 | 3,290,000 | 5¢, 1913 Liberty Head **(F)** | NGC PF-64 | Heritage | Jan-14 |
| 23 | 3,172,500 | 5¢, 1913 Liberty Head | PCGS PF-63 | Heritage | Apr-13 |
| 24 | 2,990,000 | $20, MCMVII Ultra HR LE **(I)** | PCGS PF-69 | Heritage | Nov-05 |
| 25 | 2,990,000 | Pre-Fed, 1787 Brasher EB on Breast | NGC EF-45 | Heritage | Jan-05 |

## KEY

**Price:** The sale price of the coin, including the appropriate buyer's fee.

**Coin:** The denomination/classification, date, and description of the coin, along with pertinent catalog or reference numbers. Abbreviations include: dbln = doubloon; HR = High Relief; J = Judd; LE = Lettered Edge; Pattern = a pattern, experimental, or trial piece; Prefed = pre-federal issue; S = Sheldon. Letters in parentheses, **(A), (B),** and **(C)**, denote instances in which multiple sales of the same coin rank within the Top 25.

**Grade:** The grade of the coin, plus the name of the grading firm (if independently graded). NGC = Numismatic Guaranty Corporation of America; PCGS = Professional Coin Grading Service.

**Firm:** The auction firm (or firms) that sold the coin. B&M = Bowers & Merena; Soth = Sotheby's; Stack's Bowers or Stack's Bwrs = Stack's Bowers Galleries (the name under which Stack's and B&M merged in 2010; also encompasses the merger of Stack's and American Numismatic Rarities in 2006).

**Date:** The month and year of the auction.

*Auction records compiled and edited by P. Scott Rubin.*

# GLOSSARY

Over the years coin collectors and dealers have developed a special jargon to describe coins. Here are some terms frequently used within the hobby.

*altered date*—A false date on a coin; a date fraudulently changed to make a coin appear to be one of a rarer or more valuable issue.

*bag mark*—A surface mark, usually a small nick, acquired by a coin through contact with others in a mint bag.

*blank*—The formed piece of metal on which a coin design will be stamped.

*bullion*—Uncoined silver, gold, or platinum in the form of bars, ingots, or plate.

*certified coin*—A coin that has been graded, authenticated, and encapsulated in plastic by an independent third-party (neither buyer nor seller) grading service.

*circulation strike*—A coin intended for eventual use in commerce, as opposed to a Proof coin.

*clad coinage*—U.S. dimes, quarters, half dollars, and some dollars made since 1965. Each coin has a center core of pure copper and a layer of copper-nickel or silver on both sides.

*die*—A piece of metal engraved with a negative-image design and used for stamping coins.

*die variety*—Any minor alteration in the basic design of a coin type.

*dipped coin*—A coin that has been chemically cleaned to remove oxidation or foreign matter from its surfaces.

*doubled die*—A die that has been given two misaligned impressions from a hub (positive-image punch); also, a coin made from such a die.

*encapsulated coin*—A coin that has been authenticated, graded, and sealed in plastic by a professional third-party grading service.

*error coin*—A mismade coin not intended for circulation.

*field*—The background portion of a coin's surface not used for a design or legends.

*fineness*—The purity of gold, silver, or other precious metal, expressed in terms of one thousand parts. A coin of 90% pure silver is described as being .900 fine.

*gem*—A coin of exceptionally high quality, typically considered MS-65 or PF-65 or better.

*intrinsic value*—The bullion or "melt" value of the actual silver or gold in a precious-metal coin.

*junk silver*—Common-date silver coins in circulated grades, worth only their bullion value.

*key coin*—One of the scarcer or more valuable coins in a series.

*legend*—A principal inscription on a coin (e.g., E PLURIBUS UNUM).

*luster*—The brilliant or "frosty" surface quality of an Uncirculated coin.

*mintmark*—A small letter or other mark on a coin, indicating the mint at which it was made.

*Mint set*—A set of Uncirculated coins, packaged and sold by the U.S. Mint, containing one of each of the coins made for circulation at each of the mints in a particular year.

*Mint State*—The grade of a circulation-strike coin that has never been used in commerce, and has retained its original surface and luster; also called Uncirculated.

*obverse*—The front or face ("heads") side of a coin.

*planchet*—The blank piece of metal on which a coin design is stamped.

*Proof*—A coin struck for collectors by the Mint using specially polished dies and planchets.

*Proof set*—A set of each of the Proof coins made during a given year, packaged by the Mint and sold to collectors.

*raw coin*—A coin that has not been encapsulated by an independent third-party grading service.

*reeded edge*—The edge of a coin with grooved lines that run vertically around its perimeter, as seen on modern U.S. silver and clad coins.

*reverse*—The back or "tails" side of a coin.

*rim*—The raised outer portion of a coin that protects the design from wear.

*slab*—A hard plastic case containing a coin that has been graded and encapsulated by a professional grading service.

*spot price*—The daily quoted market value of a precious metal in bullion form.

*third-party grading service*—A professional firm that authenticates and grades a coin, encapsulating it in a protective hard plastic case; called *third-party* because it is neither the buyer nor the seller of the coin.

*token*—A privately issued piece, similar to a coin but not official legal tender, typically with an exchange value for goods or services.

*type*—A series of coins defined by a shared distinguishing design, composition, denomination, and other elements. For example, Barber dimes or Morgan dollars.

*type set*—A collection consisting of one representative coin of each type, of a particular series or period.

*Uncirculated coin*—A circulation-strike coin that has never been used in commerce, and has retained its original surface and luster; also called Mint State.

*variety*—A coin with a die characteristic that sets it apart from the normal issues of its type.

## Colonial Issues

Bowers, Q. David. *Whitman Encyclopedia of Colonial and Early American Coins*. (2nd ed.). Pelham, AL, 2020.

## Cents

Bowers, Q. David. *A Guide Book of Half Cents and Large Cents*. Atlanta, GA, 2015.

Bowers, Q. David. *A Guide Book of Lincoln Cents* (3rd ed.). Pelham, AL, 2018.

Snow, Richard. *A Guide Book of Flying Eagle and Indian Head Cents* (3rd ed.). Atlanta, GA, 2016.

## Nickels and Dimes

Bowers, Q. David. *A Guide Book of Barber Silver Coins*. Atlanta, GA, 2015.

Bowers, Q. David. *A Guide Book of Buffalo and Jefferson Nickels* (2nd ed.). Pelham, AL, 2017.

Bowers, Q. David. *A Guide Book of Mercury Dimes, Standing Liberty Quarters, and Liberty Walking Half Dollars*. Atlanta, GA, 2015.

Bowers, Q. David. *A Guide Book of Shield and Liberty Head Nickels*. Atlanta, GA, 2006.

## Quarter Dollars and Half Dollars

Bowers, Q. David. *A Guide Book of Barber Silver Coins*. Atlanta, GA, 2015.

Bowers, Q. David. *A Guide Book of Mercury Dimes, Standing Liberty Quarters, and Liberty Walking Half Dollars*. Atlanta, GA, 2015.

Bowers, Q. David. *A Guide Book of Washington and State Quarters* (2nd ed.). Pelham, AL, 2017.

Tomaska, Rick. *A Guide Book of Franklin and Kennedy Half Dollars* (3rd ed.). Pelham, AL, 2018.

## Silver Dollars

Bowers, Q. David. *A Guide Book of Morgan Silver Dollars* (6th ed.). Pelham, AL, 2020.

Burdette, Roger W. *A Guide Book of Peace Dollars* (4th ed.). Pelham, AL, 2020.

Newman, Eric P., and Kenneth E. Bressett. *The Fantastic 1804 Dollar, Tribute Edition*. Atlanta, GA, 2009.

Standish, Michael "Miles," and John B. Love. *Morgan Dollar: America's Love Affair With a Legendary Coin*. Atlanta, GA, 2014.

## Gold Coins

Bowers, Q. David. *A Guide Book of Double Eagle Gold Coins*. Atlanta, GA, 2004.

Bowers, Q. David. *A Guide Book of Gold Dollars* (2nd ed.). Atlanta, GA, 2011.

Fivaz, Bill. *United States Gold Counterfeit Detection Guide*. Atlanta, GA, 2005.

Garrett, Jeff, and Ron Guth. *Encyclopedia of U.S. Gold Coins, 1795–1933* (2nd ed.). Atlanta, GA, 2008.

## Commemoratives

Bowers, Q. David. *A Guide Book of United States Commemorative Coins* (2nd ed.). Pelham, AL, 2016.

## Proof and Mint Sets

Lange, David W. *A Guide Book of Modern United States Proof Coin Sets* (2nd ed.). Atlanta, GA, 2010.

## Bullion Coins

Mercanti, John M., with Michael Standish. *American Silver Eagles: A Guide to the U.S. Bullion Coin Program* (3rd ed.). Pelham, AL, 2018.

Moy, Edmund C. *American Gold and Platinum Eagles: A Guide to the U.S. Bullion Coin Programs*. Atlanta, GA, 2013.

Tucker, Dennis. *American Gold and Silver: U.S. Mint Collector and Investor Coins and Medals, Bicentennial to Date*. Atlanta, GA, 2016.

## Tokens and Medals

Bowers, Q. David. *A Guide Book of Civil War Tokens* (3rd ed.). Pelham, AL, 2018.

Bowers, Q. David. *A Guide Book of Hard Times Tokens*. Atlanta, GA, 2015.

Jaeger, Katherine, and Q. David Bowers. *100 Greatest American Medals and Tokens*. Atlanta, GA, 2007.

Jaeger, Katherine. *A Guide Book of United States Tokens and Medals*. Atlanta, GA, 2008.

Tucker, Dennis. *American Gold and Silver: U.S. Mint Collector and Investor Coins and Medals, Bicentennial to Date*. Atlanta, GA, 2016.

## U.S./Philippine Coins

Allen, Lyman L. *U.S. Philippine Coins*. Oakland Park, FL, 1998.

Shafer, Neil. *United States Territorial Coinage for the Philippine Islands*. Racine, WI, 1961.

## Type Coins

Bowers, Q. David. *A Guide Book of United States Type Coins* (3rd ed.). Pelham, AL, 2019.

Guth, Ron, and Jeff Garrett. *United States Coinage: A Study by Type*. Atlanta, GA, 2005.

Garrett, Jeff, with Ron Guth. *100 Greatest U.S. Coins* (5th ed.), Pelham, AL, 2019.

Schechter, Scott, and Jeff Garrett. *100 Greatest U.S. Modern Coins* (3rd ed.), Atlanta, GA, 2014.

## Die Varieties

Fivaz, Bill, and J.T. Stanton. *The Cherrypickers' Guide to Rare Die Varieties (various editions and volumes)*. Atlanta, GA, and Pelham, AL.

# AMERICAN WOMEN QUARTERS, 2022–2025

A new coinage series from the United States Mint—the American Women Quarters™ Program—celebrates the accomplishments of prominent women and their contributions to the development and history of our nation.

Each year from 2022 to 2025, the program features five new reverse designs honoring the likes of author, memoirist, and performer Maya Angelou; scientist and astronaut Dr. Sally Ride; Native American chief Wilma Mankiller; activist and political leader Adelina "Nina" Otero-Warren; and film, stage, and television actress Anna May Wong.

The coins have another connection to a famous American woman: On their obverse, they feature a portrait of George Washington originally designed for the quarter dollar of 1932 (but not used in circulation until now), by renowned artist Laura Gardin Fraser.

The American Women quarters are produced for circulation at the Philadelphia and Denver Mints. The San Francisco Mint makes special Proof versions for collectors, in copper-nickel and in silver. For collectors, San Francisco also makes the coins in an Uncirculated finish (in copper-nickel); the San Francisco coins are sold directly to collectors by the United States Mint (www.usmint.gov).

For the circulating coins, a P mintmark (for Philadelphia coins) or a D mintmark (for Denver) is under the date on the obverse. San Francisco's S mintmark is in the same position.

Philadelphia mintmark.

Denver mintmark.

San Francisco mintmark.

The Circulating Collectible Coin Redesign Act of 2020 launched the American Women quarters. The program is significant for many reasons. With its 2022 honorees it introduces numerous "firsts" to American coinage. Dr. Sally Ride was the first American woman in space. Wilma Mankiller was the first female principal chief of the Cherokee Nation. Anna May Wong was the first Chinese American film star in Hollywood. Before Nina Otero-Warren, no Hispanic woman had run for Congress, and she was the first female superintendent of public schools in Santa Fe. Maya Angelou's "On the Pulse of Morning" marked the first time an African American woman wrote and presented a poem at a presidential inauguration.

The return of Laura Gardin Fraser's George Washington portrait to American coinage is also noteworthy. The artist originally submitted it as a candidate for the new Washington quarter of 1932. It was recommended by the U.S. Commission of Fine Arts, but ultimately Treasury Secretary Andrew Mellon preferred, and chose, John Flanagan's portrait of the president. It would be several generations before Fraser's design was used on a coin—the $5 gold piece of 1999 that marked the bicentennial

Laura Gardin Fraser with sculptures
in the House Chamber, U.S. Capitol.

of Washington's death. Now, ninety years after "what might have been," Fraser's artistry takes its place on its intended denomination, the quarter dollar.

The design selection involves input and recommendations from the public, consultation with the U.S. Commission of Fine Arts, and review by the Citizens Coinage Advisory Committee. In addition, the Treasury secretary consults with the Smithsonian Institution American Women's History Initiative (National Women's History Museum) and the Bipartisan Women's Caucus.

The Circulating Collectible Coin Redesign Act of 2020 is one of the most significant pieces of coinage legislation in United States history. It gives generations of Americans many historically and culturally important coins to collect directly from our pocket change.

Fraser's 1932 George Washington portrait on a 1999 gold commemorative.

A preliminary design rendering of Fraser's work as it might look on the American Women quarters. (The mintmark was moved before coin production started.)

Freshly minted 2022 American Women quarters.

**The American Women quarters were launched in 2022 with these five prominent leaders in the arts, sciences, civil rights, and politics.**

**Maya Angelou** (1928–2014) rose to international acclaim after her groundbreaking autobiography *I Know Why the Caged Bird Sings* was published in 1969. As a writer, her work spanned poetry, fiction, nonfiction, and journalism, including many best-selling books. Beyond the written word, her career included dance, musical composition, and theatrical performance. Throughout her many fields of creativity Angelou was an activist for social progress. In 1992 she was the second poet in history (after Robert Frost) to write and present a poem at a presidential inauguration. In 2010 she was awarded the Presidential Medal of Freedom for her contributions to American culture. When she passed away, Wake Forest University, where she had been professor of American studies since 1982, described her: "Dr. Angelou was a national treasure whose life and teachings inspired millions around the world."

**Dr. Sally Ride** (1951–2012) was an astronaut and educator. When she was finishing her PhD in physics at Stanford University in 1977, Ride saw an article in the student newspaper: NASA was looking for astronaut candidates. It was the first time women could apply. In 1983 she was aboard the space shuttle *Challenger* as both the first American woman to fly in space, and also the youngest American, at age 32, to do so. Her barrier-breaking flight made her a hero to generations of young women. Dr. Ride worked to motivate students—especially girls and minorities—to study science, technology, engineering, and math. She earned many awards including the NASA Space Flight Medal (twice), induction into the Aviation Hall of Fame and the Astronaut Hall of Fame, and, posthumously, the Presidential Medal of Freedom.

**Wilma Mankiller** (1945–2010) was the first female principal chief of the Cherokee Nation, and the first woman elected as chief of a major American Indian tribe. She spent her life fighting for social justice. In 1969 Native American protests and the takeover of the federal penitentiary on Alcatraz Island awakened her sense of social activism. The women's movement further inspired her to restore pride in Native heritage and to use tribal sovereignty and treaty rights to benefit the Cherokee community. In 1985 Mankiller was chosen to serve as the Cherokee Nation's principal chief. Its population more than doubled during her ten years of leadership, and education, employment, healthcare, and housing services were improved. Chief Mankiller was inducted into the National Women's Hall of Fame in 1993. In 1998 she was awarded the Presidential Medal of Freedom.

**Adelina "Nina" Otero-Warren** (1881–1965) was the first female superintendent of public schools in Santa Fe, New Mexico, and the first Hispanic woman to run for a U.S. Congress seat. She used her influence to educate Hispanic Americans in the women's suffrage movement in both Spanish and English. She was active in the Republican Party and spearheaded her state's lobbying for the 19th Amendment, which granted women the right to vote. Appointed Santa Fe's superintendent of public schools in 1917, Otero-Warren won reelection and vigorously held the role until 1929, using it as a springboard to promote adult education, establish and improve schools, and raise teacher salaries.

Proud of her Spanish heritage, she encouraged bicultural education and arts. She held important positions in state and federal public health and education through the 1930s and 1940s.

**Anna May Wong** (1905–1961), born Wong Liu-tsong, grew up in Los Angeles's Chinatown when the American film industry was moving from the East Coast to California. At the age of nine she decided to become a movie star and later created the name "Anna May Wong." Her first role was as an extra in 1919's *The Red Lantern*. In 1921 she dropped out of high school to become a full-time actress. In 1922 she landed her first leading role, in *The Toll of the Sea*, one of the earliest movies filmed in Technicolor, and in 1924 she appeared in Douglas Fairbanks's *The Thief of Bagdad*. She became internationally famous and a fashion icon as a chic "flapper." Wong acted on stage and in films in Europe. She strived for positive depictions of Asians in American movies.

## GRADING: A CRUCIAL FACTOR IN COIN VALUES

If you can properly grade your coins, you can estimate their value.

A coin's *grade* is a way of classifying its physical condition—how much wear it has received. Such wear might come from being transported in a bag from the coinage press to a storage vault, or from being circulated hand to hand in everyday business transactions.

When you examine your coins for circulation wear, look for slight changes in color, surface texture, and sharpness of fine details. Signs of handling and abrasion are first seen on the highest parts of a coin's design. They become rounded or flattened, with fine details merging together in small spots. More and more circulation wears away the coin's mint luster (its brilliant shiny surface), starting on the highest areas, then the flat fields, and finally the recessed areas. The high details of the design continue to merge together, the coin's rim smooths away, and finally the entire surface flattens.

A coin's grade is perhaps the single most important factor that affects its relative value. Supply (rarity) and demand are important, too, of course. But those factors being equal, an attractive, higher-grade coin of a particular type and date/mintmark will be worth more than a lower-grade example. Look at the 1901 Morgan silver dollar as an example. In Very Fine condition, a dealer might pay $35 for the coin. In About Uncirculated, its wholesale value jumps to $300. And in MS-63, you can expect to receive $7,000 or more.

| MS-65 (Mint State) | VF-20 (Very Fine) | G-4 (Good) |

These Mercury dimes grade MS-65 (Mint State), VF-20 (Very Fine),
and G-4 (Good). Note their differences in luster, the details in
Miss Liberty's portrait, and the sharpness of the lettering and dates.

### Grading Case Studies

The following descriptions and enlarged photographs show you examples of grades for popular and commonly seen coin types. Each is illustrated in several grades. Understanding the level of wear in your coins will help you evaluate the offers you get from coin dealers when the time comes to sell.

## Grading Wheat Reverse Lincoln Cents

**MS-63 (Choice Uncirculated)**—Blemishes or contact marks are visible but mint luster is attractive.

**MS-60 (Uncirculated)**—Noticeable blemishes or contact marks are present; luster may be dull, and color may be uneven.

**AU-50 (About Uncirculated)**—Traces of wear are visible on high points: cheek and jaw (obverse) and wheat stalks (reverse).

**EF-40 (Extremely Fine)**—High points of wheat stalks are worn but lines are clearly defined.

**VF-20 (Very Fine)**—Ear and bow tie are worn but bold. Wheat stalks are worn flat with few details remaining.

**F-12 (Fine)**—Ear and bow tie are visible. Top wheat lines are worn but separated.

**VG-8 (Very Good)**—Features are visible but worn smooth. About half the lines at the top of the wheat are merged.

**G-4 (Good)**—Facial features are just discernible. Legend and date are weak but visible.

MS-65 (Mint State)

VF-20 (Very Fine)

G-4 (Good)

## Grading Buffalo or Indian Head Nickels

**MS-63 (Choice Uncirculated)**—No trace of wear. Light blemishes.

**MS-60 (Uncirculated)**—No trace of wear. May have several blemishes.

**AU-50 (About Uncirculated)**—Traces of light wear are visible only on the high points of the design. Half of the original mint luster is present.

**EF-40 (Extremely Fine)**—The horn is lightly worn. Slight wear is seen on the Indian's hair ribbon.

**VF-20 (Very Fine)**—Much of the horn is visible. The Indian's cheekbone is worn.

**F-12 (Fine)**—The horn and tail are smooth but partially visible. The obverse rim is intact.

**VG-8 (Very Good)**—The horn is worn nearly flat.

**G-4 (Good)**—The legends and date are readable. The bison's horn does not show.

MS-65 (Mint State)

VF-20 (Very Fine)

G-4 (Good)

## Grading Mercury Dimes

**MS-63 (Choice Uncirculated)**—No wear. Attractive mint luster.

**MS-60 (Uncirculated)**—No trace of wear. Light blemishes.

**AU-50 (About Uncirculated)**—There are slight traces of wear. Most mint luster is present.

**EF-40 (Extremely Fine)**—Only slight wear is seen on the diagonal bands. The braids and hair before the ear are clearly visible.

**VF-20 (Very Fine)**—The diagonal bands are definitely visible.

**F-12 (Fine)**—All the sticks in the fasces are defined. The diagonal bands are worn nearly flat.

**VG-8 (Very Good)**—Half of the sticks in the fasces are discernible.

**G-4 (Good)**—The letters and date are clear. The lines and bands in the fasces are obliterated.

MS-65 (Mint State)

VF-20 (Very Fine)

G-4 (Good)

## Grading Barber Quarters

**MS-63 (Choice Uncirculated)**—Attractive mint luster is present, as are contact marks or minor blemishes. Denticles on rim are very sharp.

**MS-60 (Uncirculated)**—Blemishes are more obvious; surface may be dull, spotted, or heavily toned.

**AU-50 (About Uncirculated)**—Traces of wear are seen on high points: cheek, leaf tips, and hair over forehead (obverse); and head, neck, tail, and wing tips (reverse).

**EF-40 (Extremely Fine)**—Light wear extends to cap. LIBERTY is sharp and band edges are clear.

**VF-20 (Very Fine)**—Shield is worn, but most details are visible. Denticles are worn but separated.

**F-12 (Fine)**—Letters in LIBERTY are weak but visible. Horizontal shield lines are merged; vertical lines are separated.

**VG-8 (Very Good)**—A few letters in LIBERTY are clear; eagle's eye is just visible. Denticles are rounded, and some merge.

**G-4 (Good)**—LIBERTY and most denticles are worn away. Eagle is flat but completely outlined.

MS-65 (Mint State)

VF-20 (Very Fine)

G-4 (Good)

## Grading Standing Liberty Quarters

**MS-63 (Choice Uncirculated)**—Mint luster is attractive, but contact marks or minor blemishes are evident.

**MS-60 (Uncirculated)**—Surface may be dull, spotted, or heavily toned. Head details may be incomplete.

**AU-50 (About Uncirculated)**—Traces of wear show on high points: head, breast, and shield (obverse), and wing feathers, eagle's breast, and tail feathers (reverse).

**EF-40 (Extremely Fine)**—Wear extends to center of right leg; at least half of the gown over the thigh is visible.

**VF-20 (Very Fine)**—Wear shows on foot. Beads on edge of shield are clear but very weak next to the breast.

**F-12 (Fine)**—Drapery is nearly smooth across the body, but shows at the sides. About half of wing feathers remain distinct.

**VG-8 (Very Good)**—Bottom right obverse star is worn flat. Only a third of wing feathers are distinct.

**G-4 (Good)**—Legend and date are weak but visible. Eagle is nearly flat but completely outlined.

MS-65 (Mint State)

VF-20 (Very Fine)

G-4 (Good)

## Grading Liberty Seated Half Dollars

**MS-63 (Choice Uncirculated)**—Contact marks or blemishes detract from lustrous surface.

**MS-60 (Uncirculated)**—More marks are seen than on MS-63. Surface may be dull, spotted, or heavily toned.

**AU-50 (About Uncirculated)**—Traces of wear show on high points; foot is separated from sandal.

**EF-40 (Extremely Fine)**—LIBERTY on obverse shield is complete and scroll edges are raised. Eagle's neck feathers and talons are distinct.

**VF-20 (Very Fine)**—Horizontal shield lines are weak at center but letters in LIBERTY are visible.

**F-12 (Fine)**—All shield lines and letters in LIBERTY are weak but visible. Talons are worn flat but still separated.

**VG-8 (Very Good)**—Obverse shield is three-quarters outlined and some letters in LIBERTY are clear. Foot merges with sandal. Eagle and leaves show only a bold outline.

**G-4 (Good)**—Overall design is reduced to outlines and obverse shield is worn off. For coins after 1865, the motto is partially visible.

MS-65 (Mint State)

VF-20 (Very Fine)

G-4 (Good)

## Grading Liberty Walking Half Dollars

**MS-63 (Choice Uncirculated)**—No wear. Some distracting contact marks or blemishes in prime focal areas. Impaired luster possible.

**MS-60 (Uncirculated)**—No trace of wear. Light blemishes.

**AU-50 (About Uncirculated)**—There is slight trace of wear on Liberty's head, knee, and breasts, and on the eagle's claws and head.

**EF-40 (Extremely Fine)**—All skirt lines are bold.

**VF-20 (Very Fine)**—Skirt lines are sharp, including in the leg area. There is only a little wear on the breast and right arm.

**F-12 (Fine)**—All skirt lines are evident, but worn in spots. The details of the sandal below the motto remain clear.

**VG-8 (Very Good)**—The motto is distinct. About half of Liberty's skirt lines at the left are clear.

**G-4 (Good)**—The rims are defined. The motto IN GOD WE TRUST is legible.

MS-65 (Mint State)

VF-20 (Very Fine)

G-4 (Good)

## Grading Morgan Dollars

**MS-65 (Gem Uncirculated)**—Only light, scattered contact marks that are not distracting. Strong luster, good eye appeal.

**MS-64 (Uncirculated)**—A few scattered contact marks. Good eye appeal and attractive luster.

**MS-63 (Choice Uncirculated)**—No trace of wear; full mint luster; few noticeable surface marks.

**MS-60 (Uncirculated)**—No trace of wear. Full mint luster is present, but may be noticeably marred by scuff marks or bag abrasions.

**AU-50 (About Uncirculated)**—Slight trace of wear on the bust shoulder and the hair to the left of the forehead, as well as on the eagle's breast and top edges of the wings.

**EF-40 (Extremely Fine)**—All hair lines are strong, and the ear is bold. The eagle's feathers are all plain, but with slight wear on the breast and wing tips.

**VF-20 (Very Fine)**—Two thirds of the hair lines from the top of Liberty's forehead to the ear are visible. The ear is well defined. The feathers on the eagle's breast are worn.

**MS-65 (Mint State)**

**AU-50 (About Uncirculated)**

**VF-20 (Very Fine)**

## Grading Peace Dollars

**MS-65 (Gem Uncirculated)**—Only light, scattered contact marks that are not distracting. Strong luster, good eye appeal.

**MS-64 (Uncirculated)**—A few scattered contact marks. Good eye appeal and attractive luster.

**MS-63 (Choice Uncirculated)**—Some distracting contact marks or blemishes in prime focal areas. Impaired luster is possible.

**MS-60 (Uncirculated)**—No trace of wear. Full mint luster, but possibly marred by stains, surface marks, or bag abrasions.

**AU-50 (About Uncirculated)**—Slight trace of wear. Most of mint luster is present, although marred by contact marks.

**EF-40 (Extremely Fine)**—Hair lines over the brow and ear are strong, though slightly worn. Outside wing feathers at right and those at top are visible but faint.

**VF-20 (Very Fine)**—Hair over the eye is well worn. Some strands over the ear are well defined. Some eagle feathers on the top and outside edge of the right wing are visible.

MS-65 (Mint State)

AU-50 (About Uncirculated)

VF-20 (Very Fine)